FRONTIER EXPANSION IN AMAZONIA

edited by Marianne Schmink
and Charles H. Wood

foreword by Charles Wagley

Frontier Expansion in Amazonia

Frontier Expansion in Amazonia

Edited by
Marianne Schmink and Charles H. Wood

Foreword by Charles Wagley

Sponsored by the Amazon Research and Training Program,
Center for Latin American Studies,
University of Florida

UNIVERSITY PRESSES OF FLORIDA
University of Florida Press
Gainesville

UNIVERSITY PRESSES OF FLORIDA is the central agency for scholarly publishing of the State of Florida's university system, producing books selected for publication by the faculty editorial committees of Florida's nine public universities: Florida A&M University (Tallahassee), Florida Atlantic University (Boca Raton), Florida International University (Miami), Florida State University (Tallahassee), University of Central Florida (Orlando), University of Florida (Gainesville), University of North Florida (Jacksonville), University of South Florida (Tampa), University of West Florida (Pensacola).

ORDERS for books published by all member presses of University Presses of Florida should be addressed to University Presses of Florida, 15 NW 15th Street, Gainesville, FL 32603

Library of Congress Cataloging in Publication Data
Main entry under title:

Frontier expansion in Amazonia.

   Selected papers presented at the 31st Latin American Conference, held Feb. 8–11, 1982, at the University of Florida.
   Includes index.
   1. Land settlement—Amazon River Region—Congresses.
2. Indians of South America—Amazon River Region—Government relations—Congresses. 3. Agricultural ecology—Amazon River Region—Congresses. 4. Investments—Amazon River Region—Congresses. I. Schmink, Marianne.
II. Wood, Charles H., 1945– . III. Latin American Conference (31st: 1982: University of Florida)
HD469.A43F76 1984   330.981'1'008998   84–25707
ISBN 0–8130–0785–2

Contents

PART 3 Ecology and Development Potential

PART 4 State and Private Capital

Foreword

Charles Wagley

IT HAS BEEN ten years since the first conference on the Amazon region was held at the University of Florida. This earlier conference, which resulted in the publication of *Man in the Amazon* (Center for Latin American Studies, University of Florida Press, 1974), was stimulated by the renewed interest of Brazil in the development of the huge portion of that nation which is part of Amazonia. In 1973 the construction of the Transamazon Highway and the linked road systems that were to break the isolation of the region from the rest of the nation was well underway.

Most of the papers in *Man in the Amazon* are concerned with the background of the region, its environment, and the situation of the indigenous people and their history; or they are focused upon such applied problems as soils, agriculture, health, and education. In 1982, the second conference on the Amazon was held at the University of Florida, entitled Frontier Expansion in Amazonia. This conference focused upon policies, both explicit and implicit, of the various Amazon countries in regard to the development of their Amazon territories. Such policies are especially crucial today since it seems inevitable that this last great frontier of the world will be occupied and "developed" in one way or another in the next generation. How will occupation proceed, what form of development will take place, and whose benefit will development serve? The answers to these questions depend to a large extent on the governments' policies. The extent of the penetration of central governments into Amazon occupation and future development ac-

tivities is indicated by the proliferation of agencies known generally by their acronyms, agencies such as INCRA (Brazil), INCORA
(Colombia), CENCIRA (Peru), INCRAE, and INC (Bolivia), to name
only those involved with land reform and colonization. The papers
in this volume are concerned with empirical and objective facts of
Amazon society and the policy problems that must be confronted.

It must be said at once that Latin American nations are actively pushing the occupation and development of their Amazon
territories. In Brazil, the occupation of Amazonia has become almost a patriotic endeavor, generating such slogans as "New Lands
for New People" and "Land Without People for People Without
Land." In Peru, the press, radio, and television are filled with "news
of colonists, or the vicissitudes of petroleum exploration" in the
Amazon lowlands, and the Amazon is looked upon as a possible
solution to food shortages, overpopulation, and crowded conditions in the Andean highlands (cf. Aramburú in this volume). And
in Ecuador, where a national motto states that "Ecuador is an Amazonian nation," its Amazon territory is described as "the creation
of live frontiers" (cf. Uquillas, in this volume).

One reason for this surge of interest in Amazonia by concerned South American nations is obviously geopolitical. All Amazon nations hover nervously over their relatively "empty" Amazon territories. They fear expansion by their neighbors and even
imperialistic designs by more distant powers. Bolivia lost territory
to Brazil at the turn of the century. Ecuador has already lost Amazon territory to Colombia, Brazil, and Peru. And Brazil, with the
largest Amazon territory and a history of encroachments on the
territories of its neighbors, has worried for over a century about
the *cobiça* ("covetousness") of other nations of its Amazon territory. In fear of encroachment, it established "federal territories"
for better control over such strategic frontier areas as Amapá, Rio
Branco, Acre, and Rondônia. Today most of the Brazilian Amazon
is considered "a region of national security" and the Security Council takes an active role in policies concerning the region.

Perhaps a more important reason for the resurgence of interest
in the Amazon is not directly geopolitical but economic: the search
for fresh sources of raw materials. In recent years, previously unknown natural resources have been found. In Peru and Ecuador,
petroleum in modest but commercially leasable amounts has been
discovered. Throughout the Brazilian Amazon, fresh deposits of
minerals have come to light, especially after the RADAM satellite

mapping of the region. In one limited area known as the Serra dos Carajás between the Tocantins-Araguaia and the Xingu rivers, one of the world's richest deposits of iron ore has been located. Nearby there is also tin, bauxite, manganese, copper, and gold. The Great Carajás project designed to extract these riches calls for an enormous hydroelectric plant at Tucuruí, now in the last stages of development. An 800-kilometer railroad is being laid from the mines to an Atlantic port near São Luis in Maranhão state. This gigantic project calls for the building of roads, air strips, and camps for workers; and for improved communications throughout the region.

Once in production, this mining operation will transform the whole lower Amazon region. The small town of Marabá on the Transamazon Highway through which the new railroad will pass has already tripled in population, growing from a modest 15,000 to 45,000 people. It is estimated that by the year 2000 Marabá will be a city of two hundred thousand. Along the railroad, middle-sized cities of fifty to a hundred thousand are expected to take form. Belém, with over a million people, and São Luis, now about five hundred thousand, are expected to double in population in the next two decades.

Throughout Amazonia new highways have opened up vast regions for colonists. Government sponsored colonization and resettlement projects have been undertaken in all Amazon countries. The Brazilian colonization program along the Transamazon Highway and the program in Rondônia (Brazil) are discussed in this volume by Emilio Moran. But more numerous than colonists on government sponsored projects are the voluntary migrants. In the Andean countries such people come down from the crowded highlands to seek land along the new roads. In Brazil they move spontaneously from the arid Northeast, from the mountains of Minas Gerais, and from the more densely inhabited South to settle on unoccupied land. In Brazil alone between 550,000 and 847,000 people are estimated to have entered Amazonia between 1970 and 1980 (cf. Wood and Wilson in this volume).

This is not an overwhelming rush of people into the Amazon region, especially as compared to the rural-urban movement in the same countries. Yet it is sufficient to create serious social, even political, problems. Most of these people are small peasant farmers. Unless they are fortunate enough to secure a plot from a government sponsored program, they settle on unoccupied land as *posseiros* or squatters. Land titles are confused, and in time a "legal" owner turns up to claim the land. Without funds, the squatters are defenseless in courts and are evicted. Most often the peasant squatter simply moves farther along the frontier to clear a new plot or hires on as a laborer for the large landowners. Even land recipients of planned colonization programs are often forced to sell out to large landowners after several seasons of declining fertility and poor yields. As the process continues in the Amazon frontier, the distribution of land comes to resemble the *latifundio-minifundio* pattern in the long-settled regions of South America.

In recent years, government policy in most Amazon countries has seemed to favor large-scale agribusiness in one form or another. The rationale seems to be that large capital investment is necessary for Amazon development, especially to produce export credit. Tax incentives and government land at low price have attracted many national and multinational corporations to acquire huge tracts of Amazon land. A well-known example is the gigantic tree farm established on the Jari River in Brazil, which was recently sold to a consortium of Brazilian companies. Until recently, however, most of these large capitalistic endeavors with enormous tracts of land have been aimed at cattle raising (cf. Hecht in this volume). Cattle raising has not been especially successful, and converting forest to pasture has been blamed for serious deterioration of the soils, concentration of land, and marginalization of small landholders. It is suspected that some large corporations are holding land merely to speculate on the increase in land values.

The future trend in Amazon development is now at stake. Planned colonization schemes have proven to be very expensive and not generally successful. Spontaneous migration has been disorderly and has produced land conflicts. It would be difficult at this time to point to any agribusiness that is both profitable and adaptable to the Amazon ecology. Can it be that the Amazon region will again be a "counterfeit paradise" and that this spurt of activity in the 1970s will prove to be another boom to be followed by a bust? Is the Amazon destined to remain an area of only an extractive economy furnishing certain raw materials such as rubber and now minerals? Will the population remain sparse and eke out an existence by shifting agriculture? I think that this is not the case; but the present situation indicates that governmental plans and policies for Amazon development need rethinking. Planning for Amazonia calls for research in the applied sciences such as soils and agriculture and in the sciences of society.

The words that I wrote thirty years ago seem more apt today than ever before:

> The "conquest" of the Amazon Valley, when it does take place . . . will call for the adaptation of standard techniques and of technological equipment to new conditions. Nutrition, agronomy, modern engineering, and other applied sciences have developed for the most part during the last century in countries which have a temperate climate. Our most advanced technology is, therefore, aimed at controlling and exploiting the temperate zone. When civilized man has lived in the tropics he has tried to do so as if he were still in the temperate zone. . . . A whole new field of applied science must be developed for tropical conditions." (*Amazon Town: A Study of Man in the Tropics*, New York: 1st ed., 1953)

In the same book I also wrote, "A new technology will not be enough. Human factors will have to be considered in the 'Conquest of the Amazon'." This calls for a better understanding of Amazon history, of the new society which is taking form under the conditions of the late twentieth century. We must understand the social and economic effects of technological innovations. Only in recent years have the social and economic problems of Amazonia been seriously studied. In the nineteenth century, a group of pioneer naturalists such as Henry Walter Bates, Alfred Russell Wallace, Spix and Martins, Francisco de Castelnau, and Luis Agassiz, to name a few, opened up the study of the Amazon environment. In the nineteenth and twentieth centuries, anthropologists such as Karl Von Den Steinen, Kock Grunberg, Curt Nimuendaju, and others more recently have provided a picture of the indigenous peoples of the region. But as late as 1973, when the first University of Florida conference on man in the Amazon was held, only a handful of studies could be found concerned with contemporary Amazon society. Now a whole new generation of social scientists has appeared—historians, economists, geographers, social anthropologists, and sociologists. Some of these Amazonists are authors of papers in this volume. In the files of the Amazon Research and Training Program there are the names of over six hundred scholars of various disciplines who have carried out research in the Amazon in recent years. It can almost be said that scientists and scholars have "rediscovered" the Amazon region in the last ten years and are now creating a tropical zone science. This volume emphasizes the social sciences and the human factors involved in development. Only by following the objective lessons of this growing body of scientific and scholarly knowledge, such as that which is incorporated in this book, can the Amazon nations of South America develop a rational, fruitful, and equitable policy for this last frontier.

Preface

THIS VOLUME is part of a series of publications sponsored by the Amazon Research and Training Program (ARTP) at the Center for Latin American Studies, University of Florida, Gainesville. The ARTP began in September of 1980 with the financial support of the Andrew W. Mellon Foundation and the University of Florida. Building on the university's long history of research and training experience in the region, the program focuses on issues related to the socioeconomic impact of Amazon development. Its aim is to consolidate and further the achievements in Amazon research at the Center for Latin American Studies by creating an ongoing program that will provide a resource for scholars and policymakers throughout the world.

The program's general goals are to expand and focus existing knowledge on problems of contemporary Amazon development; to provide an institutional framework that will stimulate interdisciplinary training and research initiatives; to improve the opportunities for interchange and communication between the University of Florida and other institutions in the United States and Latin America; and to develop documentation and dissemination mechanisms that will make research results more widely available to scholars and to policymakers concerned with lowland areas of Latin America. ARTP activities include an annual graduate seminar, seed money research grants for ARTP faculty and students, a program of visiting scholars, and a series of publications (Amazon

Research Newsletter, Roster of Amazon Researchers, and Amazon Research Monographs).

Activities related to Amazon research at the University of Florida did not begin with the ARTP. Anthropologist Charles Wagley has spent many years studying the region. Since coming to the University of Florida as Graduate Research Professor in 1971, he has trained numerous students through the Tropical South America Program. In 1973 he organized the Twenty-third Annual Latin American Conference at the University of Florida, entitled "Man in the Amazon." That meeting focused on the Brazilian Amazon region, and it attracted nearly two hundred participants. From it was published a book by the same title, edited by Charles Wagley.

As a follow-up to the 1973 meeting, the ARTP hosted the Thirty-first Annual Latin American Conference entitled "Frontier Expansion in Amazonia," held February 8–11, 1982. The conference provided an international scholarly forum in which to present and discuss current research findings related to socioeconomic aspects of land use and development in the various nations that make up Amazonia. Members of the ARTP Executive Committee (Terry L. McCoy, Marianne Schmink, Nigel Smith, Charles Wagley, and Charles H. Wood) were responsible for planning the meeting. ARTP Executive Director Marianne Schmink served as conference coordinator. Financial support for the conference was provided by the Andrew W. Mellon Foundation, the Inter-American Foundation, the University of Florida Office of Academic Affairs, and the U.S. Department of Education.

Participants were invited, not as representatives of any group or institution, but on the basis of their direct research experience relevant to the themes of the meeting. Twenty-eight formal papers were presented during seven conference sessions, which were organized to permit comparative national perspectives on a variety of topics. The conference program included forty-eight persons from eight countries as paper presenters, discussants, or moderators. The meeting was open to the public and was attended by nearly two hundred persons. Simultaneous translation in English, Portuguese, and Spanish was provided throughout the meeting.

Conference activities included two exhibits held in the Grinter Galleries (University of Florida): "Philosophical Voyage: Naturalist Alexandre Rodrigues Ferreira in the Amazon, 1783–1792" and "Aesthetic Resurgence in Amazonian Ecuador." The latter exhibit, organized by Dorothea S. Whitten and Norman E. Whitten, Jr., featured wooden sculptures by the Puyo Runa group of the Canelos Quechua in Amazonian Ecuador. The university's Map Library exhibited "Amazonia in Maps: Yesterday and Today," and the Latin American Collection of the University Libraries exhibited recent materials on the Amazon. The success of the conference was made possible by the hard work of the staff and students of the Center for Latin American Studies, unfortunately too many to name here.

The conference forum provided the opportunity for discussion among scholars of different nationalities and disciplines. Authors were requested not to focus on narrow empirical results or case study materials but to address broad issues related to specified themes. This approach was designed to facilitate comparative discussion and to stimulate cross-disciplinary insights.

Similar goals guided the preparation of this volume. Although there is a wealth of written material on the Amazon region, including much that is recent and accessible, most of it consists of excellent but narrowly focused case studies. Published works that take a cross-national perspective are relatively few. Our objective in compiling the present volume was thus to draw on selected papers prepared for the conference, especially those by authors less well-known to the English-speaking scholarly community, in order to maximize a cross-national perspective on a limited number of themes central to the process of socioeconomic development in the region. The foreword by Charles Wagley and the editors' introductions to the four sections of the book place the collected papers in the context of the issues and debates in the field of Amazon studies.

Subsequent to their selection, nearly half of the papers were translated into English from Portuguese or Spanish. Many were revised in order to better suit the overall structure of the collection, and all were edited. We are grateful to the authors for their cooperation and enthusiasm throughout this sometimes tedious process. Translations were carried out by John Wilson, Diane Rocheleau, Kathleen Ruppert, and the editors themselves. Abby Walters cheerfully and competently carried out the seemingly endless secretarial tasks, and provided moral support and editorial suggestions throughout the preparation of the manuscript. ARTP funds from the Andrew W. Mellon Foundation were used for the production of the

book and for faculty and student time that went into its preparation. Domenick Dellino provided technological assistance in coax-
ing different computer systems to communicate with one another.
The staff of University Presses of Florida deserves our thanks for
its attention to the details of publishing this volume.

Indians and Indian Policy

PART 1

THE EXPANSION OF DEMOGRAPHIC and economic frontiers into Amazonia is often seen as the movement of people and of new activities into unoccupied, empty spaces. In fact, these regions are rarely as clear of human inhabitants as is generally supposed. Rather, the existence of occupants who predate the expanding national frontier is frequently ignored. Because of their unique system of resource management and low population density, indigenous Amazonian peoples are seldom viewed as effective and productive occupants of the territories they inhabit. Furthermore, the cultural and linguistic distinctiveness of forest peoples often disqualifies them from the rights accorded "legitimate" citizens of the national society, including the right to occupy land. The apparent invisibility of native groups and their ambiguous role in the nation's life make them vulnerable. As powerful social and economic groups move into the Amazon region, indigenous peoples face increasing threats to their cultural and social integrity. In some cases their very physical survival is at stake.

The papers in part I of this book address the history and current situation of Indians in several Amazonian countries and the Indian policies of those countries. Although the authors have direct experience in both research and action projects with particular native groups in the countries in question, here they present not case studies but overviews of the situation in the country with which they are familiar. The concluding essay by David Maybury-Lewis was originally presented as part of a round table summing up on the topic of Indians and Indian policies in Amazonia. In reviewing the findings of the country-specific papers, he delineated a general pattern by which Indian groups are overpowered by more dominant social forces whose objective is the exploitation of resources under the control of the Indians. The economic basis of this exploitative relationship has been masked, and continues to be, by an accompanying ideological system that defines the Indian as an inferior being who must be Christianized, civilized, or otherwise brought into the mainstream of national society—where incorporation will take place at its lowest rung.

3

Both missionizing and economic agents during the colonial and immediate postcolonial periods brought with them European diseases that decimated many existing native populations. Since colonial institutions of labor control, such as the *encomienda,* were less effective among the dispersed indigenous groups in the South American lowlands, their impact was generally later and less than in the neighboring highlands. Yet Amazonian Indians nevertheless felt the devastating impact of introduced diseases. They suffered the disruption of their cultural and economic traditions first as a result of missionaries, later and more directly through the demand for their labor, particularly during the rubber boom. The brutality of the use of indigenous labor during this period in Amazonia was curtailed only by the short duration of the boom itself. Once the demand for natural latex fell off, lowland Indians could not be easily transferred to economic activities located elsewhere. As a result, lowland peoples were less subject to direct exploitation as laborers than were highland peoples. Many of the latter may have sought refuge in the less accessible jungle regions.

The relative safety of lowland areas has gradually been eroded with the movement of national demographic and economic frontiers. This push to develop the Amazon region by increasing its population and economic production has proceeded at different paces in the various Amazonian countries over the past few decades. As Maybury-Lewis notes, if the first conquest annihilated the coastal Indians of the Americas, the second conquest is now taking place in the interior, motivated by the drive to develop new resources. With the emphasis on development and colonization of the Amazon region, most massively in Brazil, more recently in Peru, and selectively in the other Amazonian countries, the object of exploitation is not Indian labor but Indian land. Land rights have therefore become the centerpiece of the struggle by lowland native peoples to survive.

Each of the papers focusing on a specific country traces these general historical patterns and outlines the ideological concepts that have served to justify the treatment of indigenous peoples. The historic conception of Indians as inferior beings in need of conversion to dominant cultural values and economic practices has provided the rationale for the destruction of their unique cultural traditions. In his comments during the conference round table, Norman E. Whitten, Jr. noted that national ideological systems justify racial segregation and exploitation by means of a model based on sets of asymmetrical paired oppositions: Christian/heathen; civilized/savage; educated/ignorant; city/jungle; development/resistance; progressive/backward; hierarchical/egalitarian; national/indigenous (or black). It is on the basis of these constructs that policies are conceived and carried out in ways that threaten the interests of indigenous peoples.

A focus on formal Indian policy is only one aspect of the task of analyzing the situation of native peoples in Amazonia. The papers also trace the more general impact of economic trends and policies, including those that encourage colonization of the region (see part 2). Such a comprehensive approach to the analysis of the frontier in Amazonia, which places contemporary events in the context of the broad structural transformations underway in the various countries, is a common theme throughout the volume. The conceptual basis for a perspective that investigates the reciprocal interrelationships between economic, political, and ideological factors is more fully developed in part 4.

Striking historical similarities are revealed in the papers that follow. In his study of Ecuador, William Vickers argues that the official neglect of formal Indian policy in that country has functioned to support exploitative patterns of interaction between Indians and non-Indians. Similar historical patterns are found by Anthony Stocks and James Jones in their studies of Peru and Bolivia. Stocks demonstrates that formal and informal Indian policies have consistently served to support the conquest of Indian labor and land. Given the importance of international agencies in support of development programs in Bolivia's Amazon region, Jones calls on these institutions, as well as on the national government, to enact policies to protect the rights of native peoples.

In Brazil, Peru, and more recently Venezuela and Ecuador, policy initiatives have emerged that purport to defend the rights of Indians. The papers by Stocks and Vickers argue that such policies tend to be short lived given the strength of opposing forces whose primary interest is in gaining access to the resources that native groups control. Official Indian policy in Brazil has been cited as a humane and advanced model for other countries. Yet Ramos outlines how internal corruption, lack of autonomy, and vulnerability to outside pressures have impeded the effective protection of Indian rights by the institutions established for this purpose. In recent years, growing pressures for economic expansion in the Amazon region have led to attempts from both within and outside official agencies to undermine the provisions of the Indian statute.

Furthermore, even well-intentioned Indian protection policies are often based on an inadequate understanding of indigenous economic and cultural systems. Land grants to indigenous groups tend to follow models of peasant agriculture based on small individual plots, ignoring indigenous patterns of communal ownership and greatly underestimating the territory needed to support complex native systems of forest management. While more enlightened policies may help to expand the political options open to native groups and their supporters, such policies may also serve to legitimize exploitative practices and to undermine the emergence of genuine indigenous-rights movements. The paper by Nelly Arvelo-Jimenez emphasizes the manner in which dominant beliefs regarding native peoples have been used to justify actions by the Venezuelan state that have led to the fragmentation of Indian land. She concludes that no official policy can truly represent the interests of indigenous peoples. These groups, in her view, must carry out their own struggle for survival as culturally distinct segments of the Venezuelan nation-state.

While overall prospects for Amazonian indigenous peoples remain relatively bleak, their demise should not be presumed inevitable. Certain forms of basic material support, including protection from disease and guarantees to an adequate land base, will go a long way toward improving their chances for survival. Growing political pressure for these guarantees is cited as the most optimistic element of the situation of native groups in most Amazonian countries. This enhanced political strength is based on a growing awareness of and support for indigenous causes at both national and international levels and, above all, on the promising growth of political organizations composed of native groups themselves.

Anthropologists and other scientists are also reevaluating their role vis-à-vis the indigenous groups that are their objects of study. During the conference round table, Darcy Ribeiro described the emergence in Brazil of a new ethnology that is loyal not to objectives of the dominant society but to the Indians themselves. Many Brazilian anthropologists have concluded that they can no longer study Indian art or language without addressing the imminent threats these societies face. The potential scientific contribution to the cause of Amazonian Indians is twofold. On the one hand, scientists involved in research among native groups are increasingly taking an activist stance on such practical and political issues as land demarcation. Second, scientists concerned with the fate of indigenous peoples have the responsibility of turning their analytical tools on the dominant institutions and ideologies. Maybury-Lewis thus advocates the demystification of the development concept. Similarly, Whitten points out that such ideas should be regarded as folk models that serve to justify racial segregation and exploitation. This more critical stance on the question of development requires the understanding of the process affecting not only indigenous peoples but also other subordinate groups including peasants and the urban poor. This theme is taken up again later in this volume.

Finally, anthropologists in particular can play an important role in increasing the recognition of the valuable knowledge embodied in native traditions. Whitten's comments emphasized that, far from being marginal groups, Amazonian peoples have their own paradigms that are central to a positive, syncretic, culture-building system in Amazonia. Our conference round table participants emphasized the remarkable durability and adaptability of Indian traditions and cultural identity, even in the face of massive, often long-standing assaults by dominant social forces. The repeated failures of development projects in the region, which contrast with the highly stable and successful ecological systems developed over centuries by indigenous peoples, testify to the fact that valuable lessons have yet to be taken seriously in development planning. The legitimation of indigenous cultural and economic systems and the recognition of their positive contribution to panhuman society will help to establish the respect and tolerance needed to achieve a more just interethnic social system.

Indian Policy in Amazonian Ecuador

William T. Vickers

E CUADOR, THOUGH one of the smallest of the Amazonian
nations, has a rich inventory of native cultures and has
been involved in some of the momentous events of Amazonian
history from the voyage of Francisco Orellana in 1543 to recent oil
discoveries and conflicts with Peru. Estimates indicate that today
there are from 36,000 to 51,000 indigenous people in the Oriente
(Ecuador's term for its Amazon region). Two large sociolinguistic
groupings, the jungle Quechua (25,000–35,000) and the Jivaroan

NOTE: During the period from 1972 to 1980 I made four field trips to Amazonian Ecuador. I would like to thank and acknowledge the sources of my
support for these various periods of research: National Defense Education
Act Title IV (1972), Henry L. and Grace Doherty Foundation (1973–74),
National Institute of Mental Health (grant no. 1 Fol MH 58552-01; 1974–
75), the Latin America and Caribbean Center and the College of Arts and
Sciences of Florida International University (1979–80), the Florida International University Foundation, Inc. (1979), and Cultural Survival, Inc.
(1980). The host country affiliations for my research have been with the
Instituto Nacional de Antropología e Historia of Ecuador (1972, 1973–75,
1979) and the Instituto Nacional de Colonización de la Región Amazónica Ecuatoriana (1980). Those who have been generous with their
ideas and practical assistance include William E. Carter, Charles Wagley,
Hernán Crespo Toral, Norman E. Whitten, Jr., Vivian Nolan, Theodore
Macdonald, Jr., Julio Enrique Vela, Jorge Uquillas R., Mark B. Rosenberg,
Anthony P. Maingot, James A. Mau, Michelle Lamarre, Orville and Mary
Johnson, William Eddy, and all of the Siona, Secoya, and Cofán people I
have known.

peoples (10,000–15,000), form the bulk of this population, whereas the remaining groups of Cofán (297), Waorani (500), Siona and Secoya (347), and Záparo (7) survive only in small numbers (Vickers 1980, Whitten 1981a). The 1974 national census indicated a population of 173,500 for the entire Oriente, or 2.7 percent of the national population (Vreugdenhil 1978).

Today the native peoples of eastern Ecuador, like other Amazonian Indians, are involved in a difficult struggle to defend their land and resources against a rapidly expanding economic and social frontier, which threatens to overwhelm them. The principal aim of this paper is to describe and analyze the history and current status of the Indians of Ecuador's Amazon region from the perspective of national politics and policies. As a case study in formal Indian "policy," Ecuador presents an interesting problem because it has never had comprehensive, integrated programs articulated specifically for Amazonian Indians. There has been no Ecuadoran figure like Brazil's Candido Mariano da Silva Rondon, and the government has never created a bureaucratic equivalent of Brazil's Fundação Nacional do Índio (FUNAI). But it would be an error to assume that the lack of an integrated political policy for Amazonian Indians means that there is no policy at all. Internal policy ultimately refers to the nature of the relations, and even the absence of relations, among the political, social, and economic components of the nation. In this sense Ecuador has always had a de facto Indian policy and always will (insofar as native peoples survive).

Historically, the inattention of Ecuadoran governments to formal Indian policy actually constituted a de facto policy of neglect, which supported the traditional and exploitative economic and social patterns of interaction between non-Indians and Indians. This policy was and is rooted in the colonial past, when the unequal status of the Indian was codified and institutionalized. The perceptions of most Ecuadorans of European or even mestizo descent concerning *indios* continue to be negative ones (cf. Stutzman 1981, Whitten 1981b). Amazonian Indians are typically stereotyped as *aucas* or *salvajes* who are uncivilized and dangerous (cf. Salomon 1981). Such attitudes are centuries old in Ecuador and continue to influence interethnic relations and the decision making of many bureaucrats in significant ways.

Traditionally the articulation of Ecuadoran governments with Amazonian peoples has occurred through the sporadic passage of laws concerning land tenure and labor relations, and through the irregular contacts native peoples have had with petty officeholders, with government officials in specific ministries, or with proxy organizations that operate under government fiat (e.g., missionaries). A major consequence of this pattern has been that the presentation of Indian grievances has proceeded on an ad hoc basis, which has produced inadequate and inconsistent responses from a succession of governments. *Peregrinaje,* or the practice of sending countless delegations of Indian representatives to Quito or lesser seats of government, has proven to be a bankrupt process.

The essential aspect of Ecuador's latent Indian policy over the years has been the promotion of ethnic assimilation and an emphasis on national integration and development. Despite past trends and present realities, some important political events in Ecuador in recent years have been positive in that they offer new structures within which native peoples may strive for the recognition of their lands and civil rights, and which may *potentially* ameliorate some of the negative consequences of the expanding frontier. The most significant such development is the formation of political and cultural organizations of indigenous peoples, of which the Shuar Federation (founded in 1964) is the most widely known example (Salazar 1977, 1981; Taylor 1981). In recent years the number of such organizations has multiplied dramatically, and these may ultimately coalesce into a pan-Indian movement with real political influence. In this regard native peoples are attempting to fill the void left by the government's unwillingness or inability to provide mechanisms for indigenous political self-expression.

Another important political development was the victory of President Jaime Roldós and Vice-President Osvaldo Hurtado in the 1978 elections. Although Roldós subsequently perished in a tragic plane crash in 1981, he articulated a strong human rights and pro-indigenous philosophy during his campaign and brief tenure as president (cf. Whitten 1981c). Without a doubt, the rhetoric of Roldós raised the expectations of the indigenous peoples of Ecuador and provided an atmosphere of support for the minority of government officials who were actively concerned about the well-being of such peoples. Hurtado, as Roldós's successor, likewise seems receptive to the cause of native peoples although at least one analysis indicates that his intellectual commitment in the past has been more toward *indomestizaje,* or the assimilation of native peoples into a mestizoized and nationalized cultural type (Whitten 1981c).

One factor must temper any optimism concerning these developments: both Roldós and Hurtado have met with strong political infighting in attempting to implement their policies, which conservative factions view as threatening to their interests and to the stability of the business economy. Another very real problem is that policies formulated in Quito often carry little force on the Amazon frontier, where Indian territories face ever-escalating invasions from colonists, lumbermen, oil companies, agribusiness concerns, land speculators, and the military.

History of Ecuador's Indian policy

As indicated previously, Ecuador has not had a coordinated policy for Amazonian Indians; instead it has tended to manifest de facto and somewhat amorphous policies that emphasize national identification, integration, and development.

The European exploration of the Amazon from the west began with the incredible expedition of Gonzalo Pizarro, which departed from Quito in late February 1541. After an arduous ten-month period of exploring what is today the Ecuadoran Oriente, Pizarro's lieutenant Francisco Orellana began a voyage down the Napo to the Amazon and ultimately to the Atlantic Ocean. The first Spanish settlements in the Oriente were at Baeza, Achidona, and Ávila, where they exploited Indian labor for the growing of cotton under the *encomienda* system (Phelan 1967:24). An Indian revolt in 1579 reduced the Spanish presence to the limited area around Baeza, but the Spanish ultimately broke the rebellion and by 1625 had five settlements in what then was referred to as the Province of Quijos (Phelan 1967:27). By the early seventeenth century the Spanish began pacification of the upper Marañón, which they referred to as the Province of Mainas. Franciscan and Jesuit missionaries were also present during this early period of the subjugation of the Oriente. In 1635 a revolt by Indians led to the deaths of thirty-four Spaniards, but twelve families managed to save themselves at the provincial capital of San Francisco de Borja. In the latter part of the seventeenth century and in the eighteenth century, the Jesuits were the major external presence in Mainas; they established numerous missions or *reducciones* of Indians, but these were buffeted by recurring epidemics, uprisings, and Portuguese intrusions (Phelan 1967:31–38, Vickers 1981a).

In the central Oriente the Dominicans established their mission of Canelos in the sixteenth century, were supplanted there by the Franciscans in 1803, but returned to the region in the late nineteenth century (Whitten 1976:10). This area, currently the home of the lowland Quechua peoples, was profoundly influenced by contact with the Spanish and figured prominently in highland-lowland trading networks. In the south the famous Jívaro uprising of 1599 and subsequent hostilities limited Spanish penetration to the area of Macas in the Upano Valley, and it was not until the mid-nineteenth century that peaceful trade relations were established (Harner 1972:16–29).

During the colonial era official policy toward Indians emanated from the Royal Council of the Indies in Spain and was mediated by the Audiencia of Quito. Indians were categorized as free vassals of the Crown with legally defined rights (inferior to those of Spaniards and Creoles but superior to those of blacks) and obligations (tribute or taxes paid in goods or labor). They were entitled to live in native communities under native *caciques* in accordance with the encomienda system (Haring 1963). As in other audiencias, the encomienda system was corrupted and evolved into a debt-peonage system in which much of the native labor force, particularly in the highlands, was exploited on haciendas and in *obrajes* ("textile workshops"). The hacienda system made a somewhat limited penetration into the Oriente, but native labor was also sought for the panning of gold and the collection of forest products. Overall, however, the Amazonian Indians were able to retain a greater degree of autonomy because of the geographical barrier of the Cordillera Oriental de los Andes and because of the resistance offered by a number of the native groups. During this period the Jesuits, Franciscans, and other missionary orders acted as proxies in carrying European influences to them, although missionary policies did not always coincide with peninsular and Creole desires.

Ecuador's independence from Spain essentially meant that the *criollo* elite was able to extricate itself from Spanish governance and could assume greater autonomy in its oppressive exploitation of the Indians. The nineteenth century, therefore, represented a period of intensification of the hacienda system. As Osvaldo Hurtado, a political scientist and president of Ecuador, has written:

The new republican order served only to negate some of the indigenous protective dispositions of previous colonial legislation, despite the fact that the Laws of the Indies were still theoretically in force (a penal code was not issued until 1837, and a civil code would not be forthcoming until 1861). On the other hand, some former laws of a more avaricious and repressive nature were maintained and in a few cases became even more rigid under the new legal codes. Quite rightly the Quiteños referred graphically and ironically to independence as the last day of despotism and the first day of the same. (Hurtado 1980:62)

Most of the official statements of policy toward Indians in the twentieth century have come in the form of laws that have attempted to ameliorate some of the more abusive aspects of the hacienda system and land tenure structure. In 1918 a law was passed abolishing the right of *hacendados* to have their *conciertos* (peons whose labor was contractually bound to the estate) jailed for nonpayment of debts (Hurtado 1980:49). The Ley de Comunas Campesinos of 1937 and the Ley de Cooperativas of 1938 allowed indigenous communities to form agricultural production cooperatives and provincial federations (Tobar 1979:19). The Ley Especial de Oriente of 1955 abolished arbitrary work obligations on haciendas in Amazonian Ecuador and stipulated that such haciendas should have facilities for treating the health problems of workers (Oberem 1980:120). In response to U.S. President John F. Kennedy's Alliance for Progress initiative, Ecuador instituted the 1964 Ley de Reforma Agraria y Colonización, which abolished traditional forms of debt peonage and established the Instituto Ecuatoriano de Reforma Agraria y Colonización (IERAC). Although this law proposed that land should be allocated to *campesinos,* it also emphasized the existence of *tierras baldías* ("uncultivated lands") in the Oriente which could absorb the land-hungry. In fact these vacant lands were inhabited by lowland Indian peoples.

Overall, the nineteenth century and the early twentieth century can be characterized as a period of growing white economic penetration into the Oriente. As a result, Indians became increasingly bound up in an extractive trading economy in which gold and forest products were exchanged for salt and cheap manufactured goods, and the hacienda mode of agricultural production was extended into some lowland areas (particularly in the central Oriente). In addition to this increasing economic and territorial penetration, native peoples continued to experience deadly epidemics of European-introduced diseases.

A new form of penetration of the Oriente in the modern era began with the construction of highways from the Andean highlands into the lowlands. The first such highway received major impetus from the petroleum exploration activities of the Royal Dutch Shell Company in the 1930s and 1940s; and by 1947 Puyo had been linked with Ambato (Hegen 1966:123). The most momentous event of this period was the 1941 invasion by Peru, which resulted in the loss of approximately one-third of Ecuador's national territory along the common Amazonian border. The erosion of Quito's initially extensive Amazonian claims had begun in the late colonial period and continued into the national period. The 1941 humiliation only exacerbated Ecuador's frustration with this process and has heightened the national determination to keep the issue of the lost areas alive. Ecuador rejects the provisions of the 1942 Protocol of Rio de Janeiro arbitration, claiming that its representatives were subjected to unfair coercion by the United States, which was anxious to end the dispute due to the expanding war in Europe. The skirmishing in the Cordillera del Condor region in 1981 was the most recent outbreak of armed hostilities in this long-standing conflict. The geopolitical aspects of the conflict with Peru have had a significant effect on Ecuadoran policies for the Oriente, and the native peoples residing in the contested areas have been profoundly affected by the militarization of the frontier and official attempts to curtail travel across the jungle border.

By 1970 new roads linked Cuenca with Macas in the southern Oriente and Quito with Lago Agrio and Coca in the northern Oriente. The construction of the Quito-Coca route was associated with the construction of a 318-mile trans-Andean pipeline by a Texaco-Gulf consortium following the discovery of significant oil deposits in the Aguarico River basin in 1968. These new roads have brought a flood of spontaneous colonization, agribusiness activity, and land speculation to the Oriente. Oil development and road construction have continued apace, and today the Amazon region of Ecuador is experiencing a rapid socioeconomic transformation as it is increasingly overrun by the expanding frontier of the national society.

The colonization and integration mentality underlying Indian policy during this period was articulated by President Guillermo Rodriguez Lara in 1972. On September 25 of that year, the president flew to Puyo in the central Oriente and made a lengthy speech stressing such development objectives as the construction of roads, the provision of public services, and the acceleration of colonization and cash crop production (Whitten 1976:265–66). When a bishop raised the issue that fifty thousand Indians lived in the affected areas, Rodriguez Lara did not address himself to economic, political, or legal matters, but maintained that all Ecuadorans were part Indian. "There is no more Indian problem," he insisted. "We all become white men when we accept the goals of the national culture" (Whitten 1976:268). Shortly thereafter an executive decree established a new "law of national culture," and throughout 1972 and 1973 the military government gave considerable publicity to its goal of using military institutions to create a "national culture."

After nine years of military rule, Ecuador began a "return to democracy" in 1978. This involved a contentious and sometimes violent electoral campaign in which the ticket of Jaime Roldós Aguilar and Osvaldo Hurtado won out and was finally installed in office on August 10, 1979. Roldós began his presidential term of office with an inaugural speech, delivered partly in Quechua, that promised a new sensitivity to the concerns of the indigenous peoples of Ecuador, including those of the Oriente, whose groups he mentioned by name (Whitten 1981c:777). Roldós's views on cultural policy, in recognizing the value of Ecuador's diverse cultural roots and accepting ethnic pluralism, represented a turning away from previous arguments that favored a uniform national culture based on indomestizaje.

The Plan Nacional de Desarrollo del Gobierno Democrático articulated the position of the Roldós government "with respect to native peoples" (Ecuador 1980:9–14). The document recognized that Ecuador is a multicultural nation and proposed policies designed to make culture a factor of national integration without ignoring ethnic pluralism. It set out objectives and strategies to reinforce the awareness of national unity while studying and protecting the cultures of the Quechua, the black, the Shuar, and others. To this end the document proposed several instruments: a new Law of Culture; the contracting of the technical services of the national universities and institutes of anthropology for research on native cultural forms; and the creation of a Department of Research and Dissemination of National Cultural Identities. The goal of the latter would be to propose specific programs of cultural development for indigenous communities and to articulate these with the work of regional institutions.

Roldós's first year in office, however, was marked by difficult opposition within the legislative branch (led by the populist Assad

Bucaram) and from the business community at large, which was wary of Roldós's social and economic policies. Roldós's liberal rhetoric raised expectations among the indigenous peoples but was not immediately translatable into effective programs of action. Indeed, many government ministries and agencies were nearly paralyzed during 1979–80 because the legislative infighting caused lengthy delays in the approval of their budgets.

In January 1981 border skirmishes broke out between Ecuador and Peru in the contested Cordillera del Condor, and national attention shifted to the events of the conflict. Roldós was highly visible as the leader of the nation during this period and made visits to the southern region of the country to consult with field commanders. A plane crash took Roldós's life on May 24, 1981.

One of President Roldós's last official acts was the May 22, 1981, decree to expel the Summer Institute of Linguistics (SIL) from Ecuador. (The Ministerio de Educación y Cultura's contract with SIL stipulated that either party could terminate the agreement by giving one year's notice; therefore the actual withdrawal of SIL was set for 1982.) The government stated that it had given profound consideration to the SIL issue and had concluded that the termination of its contract was "in the highest interests of national sovereignty and the preservation of the aboriginal groups" (*El Comercio*, May 23, 1981:A1).

The decree also specified that the Institute's programs in linguistic and anthropological research, health care, and bilingual education would be transferred to the Ministerio de Educación y Cultura and the Ministerio de Salud Pública or be contracted to national universities and institutes. The research and educational priorities for these programs are to be studied by the Concejo Nacional de Ciencia y Tecnología (CONACYD) and the Concejo Nacional de Desarrollo (CONADE). Furthermore, the Instituto Ecuatoriano de Crédito Educativo y Becas should provide financial assistance for the training of native teachers, the Ministerio de Bienestar Social should assist in developing native community organization (to guarantee the preservation of these ethnic minorities), and the Servicio Ecuatoriano de Capacitación Profesional should develop technical programs for the well-being of ethnic communities (without altering the traditional customs of the aboriginal groups). The decree also called for the establishment of a corps of native language translators to serve government agencies and for the Secretaria de Desarrollo Rural to collaborate with regional development agencies in the planning of integrated rural development projects (*El Comercio*, May 23, 1981:A2).

Osvaldo Hurtado succeeded to the presidency in a period of political uncertainty created by the accidental death of Jaime Roldós. In part this was because Ecuador's powerful conservatives perceived Hurtado to be even farther to the political left than Roldós had been. Hurtado had been a founder of Ecuador's Christian Democrat party, but had joined Roldós's Concentration of Popular Forces party during the 1978 elections. Following this successful campaign, he left Roldós's party to join a branch of the Christian Democrats known as the Popular Democracy party, which held only six of the sixty-nine seats in Congress. With the death of Roldós, Hurtado faced the necessity of building a strong political base and erasing the military establishment's distrust of his socialist leanings (*Miami Herald*, June 1, 1981:13A).

Hurtado was to find it difficult to establish a solid base of political support. In January 1982 the Ecuadoran news magazine *Vistazo* published an interview with Hurtado that included remarks concerning Roldós's term in office. Although the general thrust of the remarks was positive, Hurtado stated that Roldós, "found it difficult to choose between the good of the state and the affection of a few friends" (*El Miami Herald*, January 27, 1982:4). This upset Vice-President León Roldós, brother of the deceased Jaime Roldós, who announced that his People, Change, and Democracy party (PCD) was joining Hurtado's political opposition.

In the wake of these events, two ministers belonging to Roldós's party resigned from Hurtado's cabinet. On January 27 Hurtado replaced his minister of defense, the chief of the combined military command, and the general commander of the army. Vice-President León Roldós then joined some high-ranking military officers in charging that Hurtado was planning to accept the terms of the Protocol of Rio de Janeiro, thus relinquishing Ecuador's claims to the lands it lost to Peru in 1941. Meanwhile, Hurtado was forming a new majority coalition between his Popular Democracy party and the populist Concentration of Popular Forces (*Miami Herald*, January 30, 1982:18A). These continuing trends of official infighting in Ecuador reinforce the impression that the social agendas of the administrations of both President Jaime Roldós and subsequently of President Osvaldo Hurtado were forced to take a back seat to their struggles for political survival.

Prior to assuming the vice-presidency in Roldós's government, Hurtado made a telling analysis of the governing process in Ecuador:

> Like many other political concepts, planning has not found in Ecuador a propitious environment for effective operation . . . politicians lack economic training, parties lack technical expertise, and both are reticent to accept the counsel of technocrats; [plans] are put into operation for presidential campaigns only [and the politicians] . . . scorn . . . long-range programs; . . . the electoral movement tends to attract individuals of varied ideological inclinations; the president is deprived of a homogeneous team of expert advisors capable of carrying out a coherent . . . program; with the chief of state transformed into a dispenser of favors who is concerned with reelection, what interests him principally is gratifying his . . . clientele and adopting measures that will have an immediate impact on the masses rather than solving fundamental problems and adopting long-range projections; the . . . congress is incapable of approving a budget to respond to the priorities established . . . , exaggerated administrative centralism stunts . . . action, . . . thwarting the coordinating of public agencies; chronic political instability . . . has resulted in a constant procession of presidents and ministers and repeated definitions of programs and objectives. (Hurtado 1980:284–85; originally published in 1977.)

This blunt assessment by Hurtado the political scientist seems to apply well enough to the administration of Hurtado the president. It also throws light on how the Ecuadoran political process impedes the establishment of effective policies, including those dealing with indigenous peoples.

Government ministries and agencies as mediators of Indian policy

While the government of Jaime Roldós represented a shift from emphasis on a national culture based on Hispanic and indomestizaje forms to a recognition of the reality of ethnic pluralism, it did not create a general bureau for dealing with Indian affairs. Rather Roldós's plan, as expressed in both the Plan Nacional de Desarrollo and the decree terminating the contract of the Summer Institute of Lingustics, was to press his policies predominantly through existing agencies of the government. Government-Indian relations have been and continue to be articulated through a wide variety of ministries, institutes, and other official entities.

Even during periods when there was no formally stated Indian policy per se, there were always de facto policies comprised of the diverse and often conflicting actions taken by government agencies and officials. In effect, each minister, official, *teniente politico*, or army officer has been free to express his own policy toward Indians based on his own attitudes, prejudices, and perceptions about how things ought to be. Since most government officials have tended to view themselves as educated and Indians as stereotypically ignorant, it also follows that their ideas and plans are superior to anything that the Indians might come up with. This attitude has also been communicated to Indians; Siona people I know often refer to whites and mestizos as *racionales*.

Ministerio de Educación y Cultura

The Ministry of Education and Culture has had a profound effect on the Amazonian Indians of Ecuador because schooling is the primary vehicle for disseminating concepts of nationhood, citizenship, and progress. In some of the more accessible areas of the Oriente, the ministry has established *escuelas fiscales*, which are similar to state-supported schools in other regions of the country. For lack of infrastructure and resources, however, it was unable to operate schools for many native communities. To fill this gap, the Ministry of Education contracted with missionary organizations such as the Summer Institute of Linguistics and the Salesian Order of the Catholic Church to establish Indian schools. This arrangement has had tradeoffs for both parties. On the one hand, the government extended its hegemony into areas where it formerly lacked the energy to penetrate. On the other, the missionaries achieved official sanction for their activities within the native communities. The ideologies of Ecuadoran nationality and Christianity were both brought to the natives. These ideologies share a central precept; they tell the Indian that it is necessary to find a better life by eschewing old traditions and by seeking progress and true religion.

The SIL schools are bilingual, but they stress Spanish after the second year of instruction. The curriculum is regulated by the

Ministry of Education and Culture and emphasizes Ecuadoran history, basic literacy, and mathematical skills. Students begin each school day by singing the national anthem, and the national shield hangs in the classroom. These bilingual schools employ native teachers who have been trained by ministry instructors during annual courses held at the SIL base camp at Limoncocha. Teacher candidates are selected by SIL's missionary-linguists on the basis of aptitude and receptiveness to the SIL program and frequently replace headmen and shamans as the de facto leaders of native communities (Vickers 1981a, 1981b). Their high income relative to other Indians, based on salaries paid by the Ministry of Education and Culture, and their ability to serve as cultural brokers contribute to their status. In essence, education has reoriented many Indians to the national culture and has done much to modify traditional structures of authority and worldview.

Still, it would be an error to claim that education routinely negates native culture. The Shuar Federation has established mass instruction in the native language via its *escuelas radiofónicas* (radio schools), and it publishes large numbers of treatises on ethnography as part of its *Mundo Shuar* series (Salazar 1981:599–601). The SIL has prepared native language school texts and, to a lesser extent, accounts of indigenous life. Native teachers have demonstrated considerable freedom of thought and some eventually question the external assumptions presented to them. Shuar leaders, in particular, have become highly visible advocates of native rights and culture. Roldós's termination of the SIL contract indicates that these questions are also being considered in high places.

Ministerio de Agricultura y Ganadería (MAG)

The Ministry of Agriculture and Ranching is a large and complex bureau composed of various institutes and offices. The activities of many of these agencies affect Indians directly or indirectly. In general, it is accurate to say that the ministry has represented powerful land interests and has favored the expansion and development of Ecuador's agricultural base. Several of the significant agencies of MAG are discussed below.

1. Instituto Ecuatoriano de Reforma Agraria y Colonización (IERAC). One of the most important entities within MAG is the Ecuadoran Institute of Agrarian Reform and Colonization. The con-

cept of agrarian reform has never been popular with Ecuador's ruling elites because they are the beneficiaries of a socioeconomic structure based on the institution of the hacienda (cf. Hurtado 1980:45–64). Nevertheless, the administration of U.S. President John F. Kennedy brought pressure for agrarian reform under the Alliance for Progress development plan, and Ecuador responded with the Ley de Reforma Agraria y Colonización in 1964.

Instead of shaking up the overall agrarian structure, the newly created IERAC divided up a number of estates in the sierra that had been owned by the state and by the Catholic Church and emphasized colonization in the lowlands as the best way to relieve demographic pressures in the Andean areas. In effect, this safety valve strategy sidestepped the real issue of inequitable land distribution in the highlands. Within the Oriente, IERAC has preoccupied itself with the problems of directed, semidirected, and spontaneous colonization. In 1980, IERAC's director, Dr. Ricardo Moreno, stated that the colonization of the Amazonian region of Ecuador was one of the agency's first priorities and that between 1964 and 1979, 1.5 million hectares benefiting 34,464 colonist families had been adjudicated in the Oriente (IERAC 1980:6).

In 1974 I visited IERAC's central office in Quito to discuss the land needs of the Siona-Secoya Indians; one high official told me, "The Indians have plenty of land in the jungle; we don't even have enough surveying teams to deal with the colonists along the roads." Indeed, IERAC has seemed to be overwhelmed in its attempts to deal with the multiple demands of colonists to survey land, settle conflicting claims, and provide services to the centers of government-sponsored settlement. While the colonists complain of poor service, the Indians have been all but ignored. Whitten characterizes IERAC as "a dynamic national bureaucracy aimed at opening new land claims for people self-identifying as non-Indian" (1976:276).

This is not to say that IERAC *never* adjudicates land for Amazonian Indians. During 1978–79, for example, it gave titles to the Cofán communities of Dovino and Dureno, and the Siona-Secoya communities of San Pablo and Cuyabeno (3863, 9571, 7043, and 744 hectares respectively). The problem, however, is that such allocations are not based on studies of native land-use patterns and do not take into account requirements for such activities as hunting, fishing, and the collecting of wild plant foods and craft materi-

als, all of which are fundamental to the native adaptation. Instead
IERAC assumes that the land requirements of indigenous peoples
are little different from those of the colonists (the communal
grants to the Siona-Secoya and Cofán average about a hundred hectares per household—i.e., they are larger than the fifty-hectare
grants made to colonists, but not significantly so).

2. Instituto Nacional de Colonización de la Región Amazónica Ecuatoriana (INCRAE). The title of the National Institute of
Colonization of the Amazon Region of Ecuador (INCRAE) seems re-
dundant with IERAC, but it was created during a later period as
part of the 1977 Ley de Colonización de la Región Amazónica
Ecuatoriana. Promulgated by Ecuador's military government on
December 28, 1977, the decree (No. 2092) outlines the conditions
for encouraging colonization of the four provinces of Ecuador's
Amazon region. People from the more populated areas of the sierra
and the coast should be favored for displacement in order to develop the culture and productivity of the Amazon region. This
colonization effort should be carried out through a careful coordination of public and private initiatives, while respecting the rights
of natives of the region (Registro Civil, January 12, 1978:2).

These manifest statements indicate the government's concern with Amazonian development, population redistribution, integrated planning, and human rights. Another key concern related
to the promulgation of this law, although not mentioned in the
preamble, was the government's preoccupation with the strategic
aspects of the Oriente. That is, the military government wanted to
establish a more potent Ecuadoran presence on the jungle frontiers
with Peru and Colombia. The historic erosion of Ecuador's Amazonian claims and the newly discovered oil reserves in the Oriente
doubtless contributed to this concern. For example, Article Six of
the new law stated that national security and territorial integrity
would be given priority in colonization; Article Eight stipulated
that colonization was principally for Ecuadoran citizens, and in no
case could individuals of other nationalities colonize areas within
fifty kilometers of a border. Article 28 provided for military assistance in the development of infrastructure in the colonization
zones; Article 29 included ex-conscripts as one of the primary
groups from which colonists would be selected; Article 30 stated
that the armed forces would participate in the selection of colonists; and Article 31 required that the colonist cooperatives be di-

rected by the armed forces for a period of not less than eighteen months. Finally the ministers of defense and foreign relations would sit on the ten-member executive board of INCRAE. The first two directors of the Institute were also military men.

Although INCRAE has obvious security functions, it is not simply a front for the armed forces. It was intended as, and attempts to be, a regional planning institute. The law creating INCRAE made specific references to indigenous and environmental concerns and to integrated planning (Articles 5 and 23; *Registro Civil*, January 12, 1978:3-4). INCRAE was inaugurated on February 9, 1978, but did not really begin operations until May of that year, when it received its budget (INCRAE n.d.:13). During the initial period following the foundation of the Institute, its personnel had a sense of high mission and lofty expectations concerning the tasks at hand. Among the staff were professional anthropologists, sociologists, and other specialists who were genuinely concerned about indigenous and environmental issues in the Amazon. In November 1978 INCRAE sponsored a two-week conference on management of ecological systems and alternative modes of agricultural, forestry, and pasture production. Another conference on the sociocultural problems of Ecuador's Amazonian region was held in March 1979 and was attended by Siona, Secoya, Cofán, lowland Quechua, and Shuar representatives. The publications and documents produced by INCRAE during this period indicated a sensitivity and strong concern for the plight of indigenous peoples (INCRAE n.d., *El Agropecuario* 1979, Uquillas 1979).

Despite these optimistic trends, INCRAE has faced serious problems. Initially, at least, relations between INCRAE and the more established IERAC were marked by misgivings and competitive tendencies. When INCRAE attempted to exercise its legal mandate to regulate development, it ran into hostile opposition from powerful economic and political interests. And, ironically, Jaime Roldós's assumption of the presidency in 1979 led to a turnover in INCRAE's personnel as some of the Institute's most qualified staff were replaced by political appointees. The legislative stalemate following Roldós's election also tied up the approval of INCRAE's budget and prevented it from delivering on many of its promises to colonist and indigenous communities. By 1980 the effectiveness and morale of the Institute had been considerably reduced.

3. Centro de Reconversión Económica del Azuay, Cañar, y

Morona Santiago (CREA). The CREA is a regional agency of colonization that focuses on the southern Oriente. Ernesto Salazar describes its activities:

> The official involvement of the Ecuadoran government in
> the colonization of the southern lowlands started in the
> early 1960s through the establishment of . . . CREA . . . a
> highland institution with its central office in Cuenca.
> CREA is at present managing three projects of semidi-
> rected colonization in Shuar territory, resettling hundreds
> of highland families in the lowlands.
> It is apparent that the ever-increasing advance of the
> colonization frontier has become a serious threat to the
> interests of the Shuar population. Furthermore, the inva-
> sion of Indian lands, coupled with CREA's open bias toward
> the colonists is gradually reducing their vital space. . . .
> Indeed CREA's reports hardly mention the Shuar, gen-
> erally using low population figures to justify the no-man's-
> land status of Shuar territory. (Salazar 1981:593, 607)

4. Dirección General de Desarollo Forestal (DGDF). The Office
of Forestry Development is housed within MAG and is charged
with establishing the lines and methods of forestry development
and conservation, national parks, and conservation and management of flora and fauna (INCRAE 1980:4). Ecuador has passed a variety of laws establishing national parks and ecological reserves,
protecting endangered species, and regulating the trade and expor-
tation of animals and animal products (Ministerio de Agricultura y
Ganadería 1977). The DGDF has also made extensive studies of the
Oriente in assessing potential sites for national parks, ecological
reserves, and sanctuaries (Vreugdenhil 1978). Examples of Amazonian areas that have already been legally designated as protected
zones include the Yasuní National Park, the Cuyabeno Wildlife
Reserve, and the Cayambe-Coca Ecological Reserve.
While the designation of protected natural areas is a laudable
effort, they present some very real difficulties for Amazonian Indians. For example, the Yasuní National Park is located within the
traditional territory of the Waorani Indians, and the Cayambe-
Coca and Cuyabeno reserves are located in areas inhabited by the
Cofán and Siona-Secoya, respectively. The legal status and rights

of the Indians residing within the designated parks and reserves are open to question. Park guards, for example, have threatened the Cofán community of Sinangoë with expulsion from the Cayambe-Coca Reserve. Some high-ranking DGDF officials also feel that Indian hunting and fishing should be severely restricted in the reserves. The Siona-Secoya living within the Cuyabeno Reserve have been allowed to remain there, but those on the adjacent Aguarico River are denied entrance to the reserve (which is superimposed on one of their traditional hunting and fishing grounds) by the military.

5. La Comisión Interinstitucional del Ministerio de Agricultura y Ganadería. On August 20, 1980, the then Minister of Agriculture Dr. Antonio Andrade Fajardo issued an accord, which formally established an interinstitutional commission of MAG bureaus and other entities to analyze and propose suggestions for actions to "assure the cultural values . . . of native populations, especially in areas where their subsistence and property are threatened so that their incorporation into the . . . state will be effective, respected, and progressive" (Ministerio de Agricultura y Ganadería 1980:2). The commission was to include the general coordinator of MAG, the directors (or their representatives) of IERAC, INCRAE, DGDF, and Desarrollo Campesino, and an attorney from the Dirección de Asuntos Jurídicos (MAG).

The creation of this interinstitutional commission was based on the recognition of the need for coordinating the native affairs aspects of MAG's diverse agencies. Cultural Survival, Inc. of Cambridge, Massachussetts, played a vital role in supporting the formation of the commission (cf. *Cultural Survival Newsletter* 1980 (10):11). Its first major activity was an Indian lands demarcation project, which studied the territorial needs of the Cofán, Siona, Secoya, and Waorani Indians. The groundwork for the project began with meetings in 1979, and during June–September 1980 extensive research was carried out in the designated tribal areas by representatives of INCRAE, IERAC, DGDF, consulting anthropologists, and other natural and social scientists. The concept behind this first effort was that it would serve as a pilot project in developing methods of land needs assessment that could subsequently be applied in other areas of the Oriente. Unlike the traditional IERAC procedure of allocating land according to an arithmetical standard of hectares per household, the research conducted by the interinsti-

/

tutional commission attempted to determine land requirements for hunting and fishing territories as well as for anticipated growth in the native populations.

After completing their initial field research, commission members and native representatives met in Quito in September 1980 to formulate a preliminary report concerning the three cultural groups. At the present time the interinstitutional commission still exists, although the degree to which its recommendations have been implemented is unknown to me at the present time. The actual surveying and titling of land remains the responsibility of IERAC.

Las Fuerzas Armadas Ecuatorianas (FAE)

Ecuador has a considerable military presence in the Oriente, and this leads to frequent military-Indian contacts. Although I am not aware of a formal military policy for Indians, it is clear that this interaction often has negative consequences for native individuals and communities. For example, Indian cultural areas do not coincide with Ecuador's international frontiers with Colombia and Peru. Indians who wish to cross these frontiers to visit kin, hunt, fish, or trade are usually prevented from doing so, particularly on the Peruvian frontier. The military on the Aguarico River even perceive the Secoya as Peruvian spies because their traditional homeland on the Santa María River (a northern tributary of the Napo) is now de facto Peruvian territory, although claimed by Ecuador. Consequently, the Secoyas are harassed and denied hunting and fishing rights on the Cuyabeno and lower Aguarico which are near the present border. The Siona and Secoya have also experienced rape, forced labor to clear military trails through the forest, and forced conscription at the hands of Ecuadoran soldiers.

In general, the Indians of the Aguarico perceive the soldiers as abusive and they fear them. In August 1980 I discussed these issues with the commander of the Colonización Agrícola Militar Ecuatoriana (CAME) 3 army base at Lago Agrio but found him noncommittal: "There must be a reason for [the soldiers' behavior] . . . the Indians don't want to assist the soldiers . . . and the Peruvians know about our positions." The major went on to express the perceived notion that the Secoyas could be spies and said that he could not allow them access to areas near the border unless ordered to do so by a higher command. (These problems were addressed in a report, Vickers 1980, prepared for the Interinstitutional Commission of MAG.)

Registro Civil

Ecuadoran law presumes that all citizens have access to offices of the Civil Register and therefore have birth certificates or subsequent documentation of birthplace and date. Documentation of birth is necessary in order to get a *cédula* ("national identification card") and a *tarjeta militar* ("military registration"). Many of the Indians of the Oriente lack these documents, and this becomes a serious problem as the development frontier expands into native territories. When Indians travel outside their immediate communities, they are frequently harassed for not having documents by a variety of petty officials, police, and soldiers, and may be turned back from road checkpoints, kicked off buses, and threatened with jail or military conscription for not complying with Ecuadoran laws.

Although the government has given lip service to the concept of sending registration teams to native and other remote communities to assist in the legally required documentation, many areas have been ignored or poorly served (cf. Salazar 1981:607). Indians who wish to pursue the documentation process on their own are faced with the prospect of multiple trips to established Registro Civil offices, with concurrent losses of time and money. And even with such efforts they frequently do not receive the required cédulas due to their lack of familiarity with the application process or to bureaucratic inattention.

Other official entities and events

The preceding discussion has outlined some of the more important government entities whose activities affect the Indians of the Oriente, but it is by no means exhaustive. For example, native communities that wish to organize themselves formally into *comunas* do so under the Ministerio de Previsión Social (Ministry of Social Security; cf. Whitten 1976:13, 246). The Ministerio de Salud (Ministry of Health) sometimes carries out inoculation programs among Indian populations, and malaria control units spray houses with DDT twice a year (with many natives complaining of negative health effects for both humans and domesticated animals). Ecuador is also a signatory to the Tratado de Cooperación Amazónica, or Amazon Pact, which was signed in 1978 and ratified in 1980. The goals of this accord are to "seek technical, scientific and economic solutions to developing the Amazon while preserving its environment" (*The Miami Herald*, October 26, 1980:6E). During July 27–30, 1981 the government of Ecuador and the Instituto Indigenista Interamericano sponsored the first Amazon Conference on Indigenous Affairs for the member nations of the Pact (Ecuador, Brazil, Bolivia, Colombia, Guayana, Peru, Venezuela, and Surinam). In general, the papers and workshops at this meeting addressed concerns for indigenous land and civil rights, cultural values, education, health care, and environmental protection. Missionary and other foreign influences were broadly criticized by the participants, who included government representatives, native people, social scientists, and other observers.

The native response

This paper has attempted to throw some light on Ecuador's multi-faceted and disjointed Indian policies rather than detailing the specific situations of localized native groups. However, the growing tendency of native peoples to organize themselves in order to defend their rights and resources, and to make themselves heard is also of crucial importance. In many ways this is the most exciting and potentially significant development for native peoples in the Oriente in recent years. The best known example of Indian organization in Ecuador is the Shuar Federation, which was mentioned earlier. Although the Salesian Order figured significantly in the initial development of the Federation (Salazar 1981), it has by now become an articulate, sophisticated, highly visible, and authentic Indian movement. It maintains a permanent office in Quito to represent the interests of its members, and Shuar delegates regularly attend international conferences on indigenous rights. As discussed previously, the Federation is very active in using radio and print media for education and communication.

The Shuar Federation example has served as something of a model for other indigenous groups of the Oriente and the list of organizations seems to expand continually. Some of the better known ones include the Federación de Organizaciones Indígenas del Napo (FOIN), Federación de Organizaciones Indígenas de Pastaza (FOIP), and the Asociación Independiente del Pueblo Shuar del Ecuador (AIPSE). Even the relatively small population of the Secoya now have an organization entitled Organización de Indígenas Se-

coyas del Ecuador (OISE). Of course, it is more likely that the larger
cultural groups such as the Quechua and Shuar will develop more
political influence via the federation model because they have the
critical mass that the Cofán, Siona, Secoya, and Waorani lack. Unless the various native organizations can generate a genuine pan-
Indian movement, the smaller ethnic groups are likely to be dependent on whatever safeguards the government can provide.

Conclusion

In this paper I have argued that Ecuador has never really formulated an integrated policy for its Amazonian natives. Instead, its de
facto policies toward these peoples have long been shaped by ster-
eotypical perceptions of non-Indian cultural supremacy and Indian inferiority and by the economic exploitation of native peoples
and lands. Even though some influential Ecuadorans have begun to
develop an increasing appreciation for native cultures in recent
years, the government has failed to develop truly effective mechanisms for guaranteeing Indian land and civil rights. The data presented in this paper indicate that more enlightened *statements*
and *plans* are now coming from a variety of government bureaus,
but that these are still expressed in an essentially ad hoc and abstract manner and are hampered by the contentious nature of the
Ecuadoran political process. One can only hope that the glimmer-
ings of official sensitivity will continue to grow and will ultimately lead to more concrete and integrated results. The indigenous Indian movements that are forming offer an additional ray of
optimism. But the development of the Oriente is occurring at a
dramatic pace and is driven by powerful economic and demographic
forces, which threaten to overwhelm both the native peoples and
their tropical forest environment.

References Cited

El Agropecuario
     1979   El INCRAE y las Culturas Nativas. November 15, 1979:6.
El Comercio
     1981   Instituto Lingüístico Deberá Abandonar el Ecuador. May 23,
               1981:A1–A2. Quito.
Cultural Survival Newsletter
     1980   Ecuador: Land Demarcation 4(4):10–11.

Ecuador, Gobierno de
  1980   *Plan Nacional de Desarrollo del Gobierno Democrático 1980–84,* Part II: Vol. 4: *Políticas y Programas Sectorales: Desarrollo Social: Cultura y Educación.* Vol. 2. Quito.
Haring, C.H.
  1963   *The Spanish Empire in America.* New York: Harcourt, Brace, and World, Inc.
Harner, Michael J.
  1972   *The Jívaro: People of the Sacred Waterfalls.* Garden City, N.Y.: Doubleday/Natural History Press.
Hegen, Edmund Eduard
  1966   *Highways into the Upper Amazon Basin: Pioneer Lands in Southern Colombia, Ecuador, and Northern Peru.* Gainesville: University of Florida Center for Latin American Studies, Latin American Monograph No. 2 (2d ser.).
Hurtado, Osvaldo
  1980   *Political Power in Ecuador.* Nick D. Mills Jr., trans. Albuquerque: University of New Mexico Press.
Instituto Ecuatoriano de Reforma Agraria y Colonización (IERAC)
  1980   IERAC Trabaja por el Oriente. *El Campesino,* April 1980:6.
Instituto Nacional de Colonización de la Región Amazónica Ecuatoriana
  n.d.   INCRAE. Quito.
El Miami Herald
  1982   Hurtado Pone Fin a Polémica con el Vice-Presidente Roldós. January 27, 1982:4.
Miami Herald
  1980   Eight Amazon Nations Vow to Change Forest into Resources "Treasure House." October 26, 1980:6E.
  1981   New Leader of Ecuador Faces Trouble. June 1, 1981:13A.
  1982   Ecuador Regime Splits, Regroups. January 30, 1982:18A.
Ministerio de Agricultura y Ganadería
  1977   *Recopilación de Leyes de Parques Nacionales, Reservas, y Conservación de Flora y Fauna Silvestres del Ecuador 1926–1977.* Quito: Dirección General de Desarrollo Forestal, Departamento de Administración de Áreas y Vida Silvestres.
Oberem, Udo
  1980   *Los Quijos: Historia de la Transculturación de un Grupo Indígena en el Oriente Ecuatoriano.* Otavalo, Ecuador: Instituto Otavaleño de Antropología.
Phelan, John L.
  1967   *The Kingdom of Quito in the Seventeenth Century: Bureaucratic Politics in the Spanish Empire.* Madison: University of Wisconsin Press.

Registro Civil
    1978   Ley de Colonización de la Región Amazónica Ecuatoriana.
            January 12, 1978:2–6. (Quito).
Salazar, Ernesto
    1977   An Indian Federation in Lowland Ecuador. Copenhagen: In-
            ternational Work Group for Indigenous Affairs Document No.
            28.
    1981   The Federación Shuar and the Colonization Frontier. In *Cul-
            tural Transformations and Ethnicity in Modern Ecuador*.
            Norman E. Whitten, Jr., ed. Pp. 589–613. Urbana: University
            of Illinois Press.
Salomon, Frank
    1981   Killing the Yumbo: A Ritual Drama of Northern Quito. In
            Cultural Transformations and Ethnicity in Modern Ecuador.
            Norman E. Whitten, Jr., ed. Pp. 162–208. Urbana: University
            of Illinois Press.
Taylor, Anne-Christine
    1981   God-Wealth: The Achuar and the Missions. In *Cultural
            Transformations and Ethnicity in Modern Ecuador*. Nor-
            man E. Whitten, Jr., ed. Pp. 647–76. Urbana: University of Il-
            linois Press.
Tobar, Nestor
    1979   Las Organizaciones Campesinas y su Funcionalidad. In *La
            Problemática Socio-cultural de la Amazónia Ecuatoriana*.
            Jorge Uquillas R., ed. Pp. 19–28. Instituto Nacional de Colo-
            nización de la Región Amazónica Ecuatoriana Publicación
            No. 9. Quito: Ministerio de Agricultura y Ganadería.
Uquillas R., Jorge, ed.
    1979   *La Problemática Socio-cultural de la Amazónia Ecuatori-
            ana*. Instituto Nacional de Colonización de la Región Ama-
            zónica Ecuatoriana Publicación No. 9. Quito: Ministerio de
            Agricultura y Ganadería.
Vickers, William T.
    1980   Informe Preliminar Acerca de las Culturas Siona, Secoya y
            Cofán para la Comisión Interinstitucional de INCRAE, IERAC, y
            Dirección de Desarrollo Forestal. Proyecto Delimitación de
            Territorios Nativos. September 8, 1980. Typewritten Report.
    1981a   The Jesuits and the SIL: External Policies for Ecuador's Tuca-
            noans through Three Centuries. In *Is God an American? An
            Anthropological Perspective on the Missionary Work of the
            Summer Institute of Linguistics*. Soren Hvalkof and Peter
            Aaby, eds. Pp. 51–61. Copenhagen: International Work Group
            for Indigenous Affairs/Survival International.
    1981b   Ideation as Adaptation: Traditional Belief and Modern Inter-

vention in Siona-Secoya Religion. In *Cultural Transformations and Ethnicity in Modern Ecuador.* Norman E. Whitten, Jr., ed. Pp. 705–30. Urbana: University of Illinois Press.

Vreugdenhil, Daniel
  1978   Inventario de las Areas Silvestres de la Cuenca Amazónica Ecuatoriana. Segunda Impresión. Quito: Dirección General de Desarrollo Forestal and Ministerio de Agricultura y Ganadería.

Whitten, Norman E., Jr.
  1976   *Sacha Runa: Ethnicity and Adaptation of Ecuadorian Jungle Quichua.* Urbana: University of Illinois Press.
  1981a   Amazonia Today at the Base of the Andes: An Ethnic Interface in Ecological, Social, and Ideological Perspectives. In *Cultural Transformations and Ethnicity in Modern Ecuador.* Norman E. Whitten, Jr., ed. Pp. 1–41. Urbana: University of Illinois Press.
  1981b   Introduction (with the assistance of Kathleen Fine). In *Cultural Transformations and Ethnicity in Modern Ecuador.* Norman E. Whitten, Jr., ed. Urbana: University of Illinois Press.
  1981c   Afterward. In *Cultural Transformations and Ethnicity in Modern Ecuador.* Norman E. Whitten, Jr., ed. Pp. 776–97. Urbana: University of Illinois Press.

Indian Policy in Eastern Peru

Anthony Stocks

INDIAN POLICY refers to both the goals and practices of interest groups toward Indians. Interest groups refer to all organizations that behave purposefully toward Indians, including Indian groups themselves. I do not, by this definition, limit policy to official government laws, pronouncements, or programs. When policy is "official," I shall refer to it as formal policy. But every group that has dealt closely with Indians in Peru over the past 350 years has had policy, whether covert or overt. As often as not, the national government has either been unaware of specific practices, unofficially in favor of them, or powerless to change them even if it wished to do so.

This definition of policy includes both cognitive and behavioral aspects. Goals of policy may be either conscious or unconscious, at varying levels of specificity. At the broadest level, we can isolate three qualitatively different kinds of policy that have

NOTE: Research into recent developments in Peru upon which much of this paper is based was supported by the Faculty Research Committee at Idaho State University, which allowed funds for research in Peru during the summer of 1981. The historical research was supported by the Social Science Research Council, Fulbright-Hays, National Science Foundation, the Tropical South American Research Program of the University of Florida, and the *Centro Amazónico de Antropología y Aplicación Práctica*. I would especially like to thank Charles Wagley for encouraging this research, Alejandro Camino for his support, and Carlos Mora, Jaime Regan, and Margarita Benavides for their willingness to be interviewed during the summer of 1981.

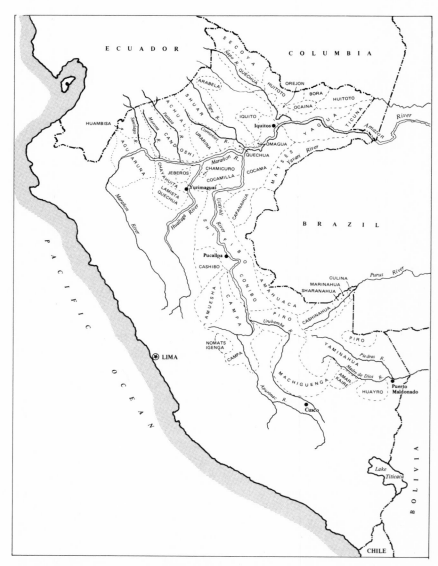

Fig. 1. Major tropical forest ethnic groups in Peru (cf. table 1).

TABLE 1. Major tropical forest ethnic groups in Peru

Group	Population	Group	Population
Achual	3,000	Jeberos	3,500
Aguaruna	25,000	Machiguenga	12,000
Amahuaca	2,000	Marinahua	50
Amarkaire	800	Matsés	1,000
Amuesha	500	Nomatsigenga	6,000
Arabela	180	Ocaina	200
Bora	800	Omagua	600
Campa	28,000	Orejon	600
Candoshi	4,000	Piro	3,500
Capanahua	800	Quechua-Lamas	22,000
Cashibo	2,000	Quechua-Napo	12,000
Cashinahua	600	Quechua-Tigre	1,200
Chamicuro	80	Secoya	700
Chayahuita	7,000	Sharanahua	300
Cocama-Cocamilla	21,000	Shipibo	9,000
Conibo	6,000	Shuar	800
Culina	800	Ticuna	5,000
Huambisa	5,000	Urarina	1,500
Huayro	900	Yagua	2,700
Huitoto	600	Yamihahua	2,000
Iquito	250		

SOURCE: Based mainly on the estimates of Uriarte 1976.

NOTE: Not shown on the accompanying map are small (alleged) populations of Andoa, Arasaeri, Pukirieri, Capishto, Chaninahua, Iñapari, Isconahua, Kisambaeri, Mastanahua, Sapiteri, Toyoeri, Wachipaeri, and Remo.

been actively pursued toward Indians during the past four centuries and a fourth which has been only occasionally pursued. The first kind of policy might be referred to as "civilization" policy. This goal emphasizes the transformation of the cultural values of the Indians toward those of Western culture, viewed ethnocentrically as "civilized." All civilization policy carries with it certain not-necessarily-desired consequences such as getting Indians to work and to settle in sedentary life-styles, but these are not always primary goals. Civilization policy has been most characteristic of religious missionary groups throughout the history of contact, although modern times have seen other kinds of missionaries than the religious.

The second kind of policy derives from the "conquest" mentality, and we may term it conquest policy. Associated concepts are economic development and progress. In this constellation of concepts, the products of the land and water are the object of desire, and Indian policy, such as it is, is devoted toward mobilizing and controlling Indian labor. Civilization policy can be, and has been, a means to that end. At times conquest policy has dictated that the land itself is of value, particularly in the Andean foothills. To the degree that the labor of Indians on their own former holdings is significant, conquest policy is applied. If the labor of Indians is not needed, another kind of policy is brought into play (see below). Conquest policy has been the rationale behind the most pervasive and characteristic institutions that have linked Indians to whites and mestizos over time. Conquest policy has been carried out by commercial interests, military forces, political leaders, church officials, and even the Indians themselves at times.

The third kind of policy might be termed "advocacy" policy. Its thrust is to protect Indian rights, cultural values, or lands. Such policy can either be paternally isolationist (Indian parks and reserves), rare in Peru, or it can be integrative, dedicated toward guiding and aiding Indians to take their place in a modern world (see Varese 1972 for an eloquent defense of the latter possibility).

A fourth kind of policy is that of extermination or removal, but this has rarely been a goal in Peru though it has been in other countries in South America. Until recently very little of anything, including land, has been valuable in eastern Peru without Indian labor. Military reprisals for Indian resistance to other policies, primarily civilization and conquest, have normally been the channel for this sort of policy; but from time to time, colonists and commercial interests have been known to pursue extermination policy in order to free lands for occupation or exploitation, usually by capital-intensive rather than labor-intensive methods.

Peru has never developed an institutional complex such as the SPI and later FUNAI in Brazil, agencies which deal, in however flawed a manner, specifically with Indian policy and/or welfare. Developments such as the first Native Community Law in 1974, which attempted to deal rationally with the problem of integrating forest Indians into the national structure, are altogether unprecedented in the country's history of relations with tropical forest Indians. Indeed, if anything has saved these groups it is the impersonal factors of topography and geopolitics. Peru presently has a population of tropical forest Indians that is estimated at nearly 220,000 (Uriarte 1976, Varese 1972; see figure 1 for a general guide to tribal locations and table 1 for their populations as of 1971), two-and-a-half times the native Indian population of all of Brazil. This may be explained in two ways. The Spanish crown, through the Jesuit missionary establishment and the use of troops, was able to impose a shifting political boundary between what is now Brazil and Peru by the early eighteenth century, thereby minimizing the effects of slave expeditions emanating from Brazil. Secondly, the coastal and Andean rulers of Peru have always been prevented, by the difficulties of access to the eastern frontier, from effecively dominating the region until the present, except along major rivers. These accidents of history and geography allowed Peru to become a refuge for immigrating Indians in the sixteenth and seventeenth centuries (Bollaert 1861, Fritz 1922, Vasquez 1881), and protected and preserved many aspects of Indian culture up to the present. Even today, communication with, and transportation to, the Peruvian tropical forest region is somewhat difficult. Outside the influence zones of cities such as Iquitos, Yurimaguas and Pucallpa, messages can still take weeks to travel a hundred miles, and travel is often slow and hazardous.

The structure of this paper is historical and chronological since it purports to treat Indian policy in the past and the present. Much of the story, as I tell it, is from the perspective of the Indians themselves, but I shall at times provide other descriptions and analyses of policy. My sense of historical periods is informed by a desire to isolate periods significant to Indian peoples. In this intent I differ from other students of eastern Peruvian history (San Roman 1975, Werlich 1968). Successively, I will discuss the period of the Jesuit missions of Mainas, the period of slavery under military rule in the post-Jesuit era, the period of independence through the rubber boom, the rubber boom itself, the postboom depression, and the period of military rule that ended in 1980. Special emphasis is given to the period since 1974 when Peru, for the first time in history, actually began to effectively apply a coherent formal advocacy policy with respect to the tropical forest peoples. A final section will discuss the recent movement toward native solidarity and self-determination.

My purpose in creating historical periods is to characterize the relationships that linked Indians to the dominant economic systems at various times in the past, in accordance with my con-

ceptual scheme of kinds of policy. Some kinds of relations between Indians and white-mestizos—patron-client relations and
debt peonage—have endured over centuries until the present;
nevertheless, each period may be said to have certain practices
that, under my definition, amount to Indian policy. In the absence
of focused, formal, and directed governmental Indian policy, it is
precisely these practices that are the most significant to Indian
peoples.

I have found it useful to distinguish between the *montaña*,
the eastern Andean foothills above 500 meters in elevation, and
the *selva*, the tropical lowlands. The two regions have had very
different histories, although much has been written about the
montaña and little about the selva. I have also distinguished between the mostly riverine Christianized and acculturated Indians,
now called *cholos* by their lowland countrymen, and the less acculturated and generally non-Christian Indians. The two categories have had quite different relations with European culture over
the course of history, and some policies, especially conquest policy, have been applied in the extreme to the cholo populations.

The mission period (1638–1768)

The period of Jesuit occupation of the missions of Mainas and the
Paraguayan missions constitutes the first period, after the initial
forays of explorers, in which formal policy was specifically directed toward Indians in the tropical lowlands. This period is often
pictured as a more or less halcyon age in which Indians were merely
instructed in Christian traditions, within the complex mission institutions. It is true that the Jesuits in the Mainas missions tended
to protect Indians at times from the terrible effects of slavers coming from Brazil, but to see the Jesuits only in this light is to seriously distort the meaning of their presence. The period was characterized by coherent policies toward Indians, both by those who
wished to exploit them through the mechanism of *encomienda* (a
form of conquest policy) and by the Jesuits, who wished to reduce
them in two senses. The Indians were to be "reduced" to the faith
by bringing them back to Christianity, following medieval religious theory, and they were to be reduced geographically to population concentrations that could be efficiently managed.

The Indians of the selva, unlike the montaña Indians, largely
escaped the effects of encomienda and later *repartimiento* during
the Jesuit period. The Mainas Indians (a specific ethnic group) on

the Marañón River were carried off to work in encomienda for the landowners of the new town of Borja (Jimenez de Espada 1889–92:154, Chantre y Herrera, 1901:32–46), but they soon rebelled in 1635, putting an end to the encomienda system in the selva. By 1638, the Jesuits had been called in to pacify the savages.

The Jesuit enterprise included the lower Marañón River, the lower Huallaga River, and the upper Amazon River including all the rivers flowing into the Marañón from the north. The enormous Ucayali River region and the drainage of the Madre de Dios River remained hinterlands during most of this period except for scattered and somewhat irregular Franciscan activity in parts of the Ucayali region. The Franciscans, perhaps because of their harsh regimen for the missions, seem to have had a genius for causing Indian uprisings. At least four times as many Franciscans as Jesuit fathers were killed in the selva and montaña (Izaguirre 1923–29, vols. 1 and 2). The Franciscan missions on the Ucayali, Pisqui, Archani, and Aguaytia rivers had about two thousand Indians by 1766 but were totally destroyed in that year by an uprising and were not reoccupied for a quarter of a century (Izaguirre 1923–29, vol. 2:2234–65). Likewise, the Franciscan mission of La Merced in the central montaña became the object of a rebellion that began in 1737 and resulted in the loss of the entire central montaña by the Franciscans for nearly 100 years (see Metraux 1942 for a report on this revolt).

The Jesuits were successful initially because they possessed steel tools, which totally altered the relations of Indians with their forest environment. Indians of the time would do anything for steel axes and machetes, even move into mission surroundings to listen to the bearded fathers. Those who did not voluntarily move to mission sites, insofar as they could be located, were rounded up by armed soldiers accompanied by priests in expeditions called *en-tradas*. When the Indians discovered, as soon happened, that more than their souls were at stake—the Jesuits wished to radically transform their subsistence habits, their moral precepts, and their social organization in ways unacceptable to the Indians—they fled in large numbers, beginning a series of rebellions that were suppressed only by military force. The Jesuits were never opposed to the use of force in the task of Christianizing Indians, but they were cautious in its use in the early years until they had firmly consolidated their position.

Once the Indian rebellions in the Mainas area were crushed by

1680, the Indians could be forced into full compliance with Jesuit policy. Indians served as largely unpaid laborers in the construction and maintenance of the missions. They were used as guides and canoemen by the few Spanish soldiers in the region. The formal policy, according to one priest, was "to make of brutes, men, and of men, Christians" (Figueroa 1904:180). The work regime was viewed as a necessary part of making men from brutes. Indians worked the land under mission supervision and raised money by transporting mission products to the few available markets. They also were "loaned" to the few trading entrepreneurs who plied the upper Amazon River at this early time, and they served as a Jesuit militia to make up for the lack of Spanish troops.

To sum up this initial contact experience under Jesuit civilization policy, the Indians were dominated by a religious-military complex that resembled a form of slavery, although probably not as harsh a form as existed on the Brazilian plantations. When paid at all, they received very little. They died in large numbers from the effects of imported diseases (see Stocks 1981 for a summary of these effects on one tribal population). For those who would consider the term slavery misapplied to the Jesuit missions, one might alternatively consider that the exchange of iron tools for work and attention to the missionaries constituted an asymmetrical system of reciprocity which foreshadowed the more severe debt peonage and patron-client relations the Indians were to have later with white and mestizo populations.

A final effect of the mission period should be mentioned: that of separating the Indian world into two classes, Christians and non-Christians. This separation has had profound effects in terms of Indian policy in subsequent times. Christianized and acculturated Indians, now called *civilizados* or cholos, constitute a great forgotten class in eastern Peru as far as formal government policy is concerned. Such formal policy is directed toward the more colorful Indians and neglects the cholos.

Post-Jesuit military rule (1768–1824)

Formal government policy toward Indians in the years following the expulsion of the Jesuits in 1768 was directed toward maintaining populations in concentrations sufficient to be an economic resource for the support of the growing white-mestizo sector. Many Indians, particularly those north of the Marañón River, dispersed. The remaining Indians of the former Mainas missions were held, when possible, as a captive population under direct military control in the form of Spanish governors over troops posted in many of the old missions. Religious control was so weakened by the withdrawal of the Jesuits that it was never fully regained. Some of the Indians of the Ucayali River returned to the tutelage of the few Franciscan missions of the region in 1790, but under policies which formally resembled the Jesuit "reduction" policy. The Franciscans were also given the Mainas missions in 1790, but they never fully reconsolidated the old Jesuit network (Compte 1885).

The immediate power of disposition with respect to Indians passed from the religious establishment to the military and civilian sectors. Debt peonage began to replace the missions, encomienda, and *mita* as the major forms of relating Indians to the dominant sectors. Military troops, under Francisco Requena's command, dominated the northern part of the selva and established a base in Teffé (now part of Brazil) to protect the frontier. The cholos of the lower Marañón and Huallaga rivers were pressed into service to supply the troops. Requena's policies toward Indians favored whipping and prison for miscreants who would not work, the establishment of Spanish language instruction in the few schools in existence, and the abolition of many Indian customs and practices among groups over which the Spanish had control (Izaguirre 1923–29, vol. 7:237–38; vol. 8:16–38). His policies therefore were a curious mixture of conquest and the Jesuit practice of making men out of brutes.

In this period, conquest policy was for the first time associated with the initial development of the tropical lowlands. Henceforth, missionaries were taken seriously only if they could specify what economic advantage to the crown, and later to the nation, lay in a proposed move (Werlich 1968). In the eastern Andean valleys of the montaña, many groups of Indians simply ceased to exist as haciendas and colonists overran their lands. Cash cropping in these valleys rapidly created peasants out of surviving tribal peoples. The overall effect on the Indians was to widen the gap between the Indians who had managed to regain or maintain their tribal autonomy by living in isolated regions and those Indians who could not escape the impact of these changes.

Policy, such as it was, favored the colonization of the lands at whatever cost to the Indians. The colony was having difficulty feeding itself and the long period of rebellion in this area and the decay of the Mainas missions in post-Jesuit times had made such

policies necessary in the eyes of the viceroy (Werlich 1968:273).
Scattered Indian rebellions, in the southern lowlands particularly,
continued throughout this period, especially in the latter part of
the eighteenth century.

The Republic to the rubber boom (1824–85)

When the nation of Peru was born in 1824 after the last battle of
independence, lowland and highland Indians became the focus of a
series of laws designed to prevent abuses of Indian labor. Indians
were freed from labor "contributions," made citizens of the state,
and given "the lands they presently occupy." Forced labor was legally abolished (see the various volumes of Larrabure y Correa
1905–09 for legal texts). If any of these high-minded formal policies in the shape of laws, decrees, and resolutions were actually
implemented in the selva, there exists little documentation of the
fact. Actually, independence had the effect of relieving the Indians
from the oppression of military forces and allowing them to disperse. A thirty-year political and economic vacuum ensued as the
monopoly over Indian labor held by Spanish governors was broken. The vacuum was filled by the merchants, gold seekers, colonists (in the montaña), and eventually lowland hacienda owners in
the selva after the introduction of steamships in mid-century. The
selva Indians north of the Marañón River rebelled, took over their
territory, and were not again pacified until the end of the century.
The southern Indians in Madre de Dios also rebelled. The Indians
between the Ucayali River and the Brazilian frontier, who only
minimally had felt the conquest and mission and postmission policies, were left alone; only one Franciscan missionary remained on
the Ucayali River.

Effective conquest policy toward the Christian cholos and
other riverine populations in the nineteenth century took the form
of contests between institutions competing for their labor, their
lands, or both. The primary sectors in this competition were political authorities, merchants and extractive entrepreneurs, the
priests, and, after 1853, the lowland haciendas. Development was
almost strictly confined to the main Amazon, Huallaga, and upper
Marañón rivers. The political authorities, who almost without exception were commercially involved, had the advantage initially
in linking Indians to themselves through politically enforced debt
peonage, forced labor, and tribute demands (the *remesa*). Herndon
(1853) describes many of these practices. Ordinary merchants uti-

lized wage-labor, while priests were able to make their somewhat minor demands through moral persuasion because of their importance in ritual in the emerging native/Catholic syncretized religion. The hacienda owners, however, emerged as the temporary winners after the middle of the century, possibly because of the diversity of their economic strategies, or because of the extent of their land base on which Indians could be isolated from potential official protection. Indians who were in the orbit of the selva haciendas were allowed to carry on subsistence activities but they were also required to carry out both agricultural and extractive activities for the hacienda patron in exchange for their enforced "purchases" at the hacienda store at prices set by the *patron*. Indians alive today on the Huallaga River still bitterly define slavery as the "inability to purchase from whom one chooses" (Stocks 1981).

Competition for Indian labor resulted in many of the national and state laws mentioned earlier in this section. Despite these laws, authorities usually collaborated with commercial interests since profits also accrued to them in kickbacks: to some degree, the two sectors must be seen as one. The Catholic Church, however, was gradually marginalized and denied rights over Indian labor with the rationale that priests were supposed to be salaried by the state (Lagunas Parish Archives, papers of Zacarías Peña).

In order to summarize Indian policy during this period, one would wish to distinguish between formal policy (laws and resolutions) and actual behaviors as documented. Differences also exist between the Indians in remote areas of the selva, who had successfully separated themselves from policy and its effects, and the Christian Indians, who were unfortunate enough to live on or near rivers that were avenues of nascent development. Despite the existence of protective laws, effective policy for these survivors of the mission and postmission period amounted to an official green light in using their labor for capital formation and then selling them the goods purchased with their labor at prices designed to maintain them in the workforce. Patron-client and debt-peonage relations characterized the times. The real estate of the selva had also become the object of competition. Finally, Indian peasant food-producing systems were systematically depressed by excessive demands on Indian labor to the point that by 1870 the lowland selva of eastern Peru, with some of the finest alluvial soils in the Amazon Basin, had become a food importing region (Larrabure y Cor-

rea 1905–09:16, 129–30). The conquest policy had created un-
breakable and ever-ramifying dependencies between the Christian
natives and the white-mestizos.

The rubber boom (1885–1915)

One might, with some justification, consider the rubber boom era
simply as an extension of the general fervor of the nineteenth century for extracting forest products. However, in terms of the development of Indian policy, it must be singled out for special treatment, both for the total relaxation of controls on the uses of Indian
labor and the abandonment of any pretense of defending or protecting Indians, and for the consequent devastating effects the period had on the Indians of eastern Peru.[1]

The invention of the pneumatic tire transformed lowland Peruvian society as thoroughly as it did the societies that actually
used the device, but in a more temporary and much less pleasant
way. Demand for natural latex (rubber) impelled a nearly complete
collusion of commercial and government sectors, which had always overlapped considerably even in the best of times. Indians
were left defenseless against forced temporary takeovers of their
lands while the boom lasted. The Jesuit/military custom of the
entrada, in which soldiers and priests would enter Indian territory
on *tierra firme* and bring back groups to the rivers to work in the
missions, was revived under the name of the *correría* (roundup).
Villages of Indians were, under one pretext or another, conquered
by police and rubber gatherers and put to work. Entire provinces
were depopulated by 50 percent or more all over the lowlands as
the network of rubber contractors removed populations for work.
This effect was not restricted to the Putumayo River, the site
of the major publicized scandals. One governor in Alto Amazonas
province, for example, reported on the "continuous and inhumane
persecution that the rubber exploiters visit on the residents, to
the extreme that the few who are left are forced to abandon the
villages, separating themselves great distances in order not to be
found" (Archives of the Yurimaguas Sub-Prefecture 1903, author's
translation). Farabee (1922) reported Indians working latex everywhere he traveled in Peru even slightly after the boom.

The demographic effects of such policies, official or not, were
disastrous. Whole ethnolinguistic groups were eliminated entirely
by forced labor and starvation as their native agricultural systems
were suppressed. Casement (Singleton-Gates and Girodias 1959)

estimated that the Putumayo region alone lost 40,000 Huitotos and Boras. Not one square foot of the Peruvian lowlands was left unscathed, and Indians today who have remained in remote regions are, almost without exception, refugees of one sort or another. Neither the Christians nor non-Christians were spared, although the acculturated Christian Indians were probably more disease resistant than their less-acculturated counterparts.

Huge tracts of the forest were given to private companies in "concession" by the national government beginning in 1891, a practice that has been recently revived in Peru. These land grants were given without any apparent regard for the Indians who might have occupied them. On the contrary, concessions given to the companies, typified by that to the Peruvian Corporation in the central montaña, specifically required that the area be "colonized" (presumably by non-Indians) within nine years on pain of losing the land. The Indians, Campa in this case, became virtually company property. Formal development policy was increasingly subject to economic forces on a national and world scale and consequently became more removed from the Indians. The Indians were, in fact, considered to be an obstacle to progress, as is made clear by Raimondi (1874). However, it should be emphasized that because rubber gathering was labor intensive, the labor of the Indians was still of local concern at least. In later times, with capital-intensive economic exploitation, the Indians would often simply be in the way, their labor value discounted.

The scandal of the treatment of Indians during this time provoked a wave of reaction in Lima and, indeed, in the world. Inquiries and trials were held in Iquitos (Valcarcel 1915), and a few lower-level personnel in the chain of dependant contractors, which linked the concessionaires to the Indians, were convicted of abuses. But by this time, the price of rubber had fallen and the lowland region entered a long period of depression.

Depression to the 1968 military coup (1915–68)

The collapse of the rubber market in 1912 was brought about both by factors external to Peru, the introduction of rubber plantations in Southeast Asia with stolen plants, and by internal factors, the greed and rapacity of the Amazon collectors themselves. They had operated a system of short-term profits with so little regard for the welfare of either their Indian workers or the rubber trees themselves that production was already dropping off by 1907, well before the bottom dropped out of the market in 1912 (U.S. Congress 1912). The effect of this collapse was different for various groups. The remote groups north of the Marañón River, east of the Ucayali River, in the Gran Pajonal region of the central selva, and in the state of Madre de Dios saw a relaxation of the pressures on them, and many groups settled into a way of life that involved only sporadic trading contacts with the outside. Policy toward these Indians was incoherent and local, ranging from violence to attempts to reincorporate them into a debt-peonage structure. Some, particularly those east and south of the Ucayali and north of the Marañón River, were left in comparative peace for the next sixty years, so long as they provided hides, poultry, labor, meat, and other products for the local traders and officials and did not do anything so foolish as to attack colonists or mistreat missionaries.

The riverine acculturated and Christianized groups, now called cholos, and the natives of the central montaña on the Andean frontier were not so fortunate. The Campa of the Perene River began to be overrun by Andean colonists intent upon reestablishing the hegemony of white-mestizo society in the region. The price of coffee boomed in 1930 (although it had been raised commercially since the mid-nineteenth century), accelerating this trend, since the montaña lands were the best Peruvian lands for raising the crop. The lowland selva groups began to be overrun by the riffraff of the rubber industry, those formerly standing in the chain of debt and dependency between Indian workers and the absentee corporate owners (who took their profits and ran). Left jobless and largely penniless after the collapse of the rubber market, those unfortunate souls became the first large group since the nineteenth-century hacienda owners that actually homesteaded lowland rural lands. Their small holdings, *fundos*, sprang up everywhere, limited in size only by the number of Indians they could induce to work for them for minimal wages. Since good farming land in the floodplain tends to be associated with natural levees on the riverbank, and since the rivers are the highways of the selva, these colonists occupied much formerly Indian land (San Roman 1975:176ff.). In addition, new and oppressive decrees were promulgated to keep the Indians from dispersing. Their rubber patrons and the politicians with whom they were allied were reluctant to give up a labor source so easily. Among the official policies emanating from Iquitos at this time we find obligatory military service, forced road and trail work, total curtailment of Indian travel except with written permision of the patrón, and the granting of police status to patrones so that they could arrest Indians (Lagunas Municipal Archives 1913).

As the white-mestizos colonized the riverbanks in the post-rubber era, they began to create a rural society. Schools were built. Towns were formed around them. In many rural Indian villages, Catholic missionaries began to open schools, which actively suppressed Indian customs and language. The missionary zeal to bring orthodox truth, beauty, and rationality to the backsliding pupils of the Jesuits and Franciscans of another era was a major factor in cultural suppression.

In the 1940s, the national government in Lima extended a road from the eastern Andean valley town of Huanuco out to the central Ucayali River, thus ending the relative isolation of this region. Numbers of Panoan-speaking Indians were brought into immediate and close contact with white-mestizo culture in its urban form as the city of Pucallpa exploded into being. The Indians became the object of the first intensive attempt by Protestants to convert Peruvian selva Indians. The flood of missionaries was prominently represented by the Wycliff Bible Translators (Summer Institute of Linguistics), who established their home base near Pucallpa and gradually extended a net of missionaries to the most remote groups in Peru. At the same time, large-scale, capital-intensive, industrial colonization schemes such as Tourneauvista became part of the scene.

The Indians were increasingly caught up in this web of colonization and conquest policy. The granting of citizenship, supposedly in force over a hundred years before by the new Peruvian nation, had never been applied. Only Indian males who had done military service had documents and could legally travel, vote, or hold land. Probably 90 percent or more of the total Indian population, including both Christians and non-Christians, had no legal status whatsoever.

In the late 1930s and 1940s, both rubber and *barbasco* (fish poison) prices boomed again, causing a rush to capture riverine groups to clear plantations and collect rubber, just as in the prior rubber boom.[2] Again, as in the past, there was a closing of ranks between the patrones and the politicians. Debts incurred in white-mestizo stores were rigorously collected by dispatching the police to Indian villages and rounding up the males for work under threat of shooting (Cocamilla oral history). Indian villages often became occupied by white-mestizo patrones. The nineteenth-century hacienda pattern was temporarily revived. The unhappy state of affairs came to an abrupt end when the bottom fell out of the barbasco market in 1953. The patrones retired to the provincial cities if they were lucky, or resumed their status as poor rural whites if they were not.

Policy toward the less compliant and more remote Indians of the selva was clearly shown in the postwar colonization era when the Matsés Indians east of the lower Ucayali River began to be invaded by colonists out of Requena in the mid-1960s. The Matsés attempted to defend their territory and attacked settlers. They were immediately attacked by a punitive expedition of the Peruvian army aided by able-bodied vigilantes from Requena. Jet aircraft, helicopters, machine guns, and other modern weaponry, obtained mainly from the United States, were used against them. They were routed from their villages; the survivors hid in the forest for seven years, afraid to make a village, before they were induced into further contact by Protestant missionaries from the Wycliffe Bible Translators in the early 1970s (Romanoff 1976).

The policy of conquest made explicit by the government of Fernando Belaunde Terry (Belaunde Terry 1965) was a policy that had, in the past, largely ignored the presence of Indians except as a potential labor force. In 1957, the policy was tempered by the passage of a supreme decree (D.S. 03) that allowed for reserves to be created for Indians. This advocacy policy action was sparked by the pressure colonists were putting on the Indians of the central montaña, especially the Campa and Amuesha. Their lands were being taken at will by colonist groups. There was nothing unusual in this—it had been going on for well over a hundred years with official government sanction—but there was a new factor present: international observers and a worldwide network of communication. D.S. 03 allowed ten hectares of land for each Indian over five years of age. The decree failed to consider population growth, Indian land-use patterns, or, in fact, any rational land-use policy; however, it did result in the creation of various reserves for the Campa. As far as I know, it was never applied in any other region of the montaña or selva. Even such reserves as were created were soon to be contested (Chirif 1975).

The revolutionary years (1968–80)

In 1968, Indian policy for eastern Peru's Indian populations began to be transformed when the Velasco military regime took power in a coup. This coup was only one of many in Peru's history, but it was particularly significant to lowland Indians in that the military government was interested in socialist solutions to Peru's problems, and in that the condition of lowland peoples became a matter of national concern. Pro-Indian policies had not generally been applied to the eastern lowlands groups, except in a haphazard and idealistic way (i.e., without effective infrastructure). The government created a job for a young anthropologist, Stefano Varese, who began writing a national-level policy toward lowland Indians, taking into account the problems of D.S. 03, the "reserve" law. Varese's idea was to create officially recognized "native communities," which would have the legal status of corporate persons. Land of various kinds, according to the local ecosystem, would be held in common within such a structure, and the law would take into account various Indian settlement patterns (see Varese 1972 for an analysis of his intent, and Uriarte 1974 for an analysis of the expected effects). Such native communities were to have special access to credit and were to reimburse private landholders for land expropriated for the community. Clearly this solution was an attempt to compromise between the government's hardcore "conquest" plans for the lowlands and the legitimate needs of the Indians, for lands not demarcated as native community lands were then officially vacant and could be developed with no fear of exciting international controversies about the displacement of Indians.

After the law (D.L. 20653, Ley de Comunidades Nativas y de Desarrollo Agrario de las Regiones de Selva y Ceja de Selva) was published in 1974, teams of idealistic young government employees under Varese's successors, Alberto Chirif and Carlos Mora, created a national network of support under SINAMOS, the organizational and promotional arm of Velasco's military government. Native communities, under the Office of Support for Native Communities, were politicized and organized to receive land titles. The attention of the government employees was first directed mainly to the Indians closest to the colonist frontier in the montaña, the Campa, Aguaruna, Machiguenga, Amuesha, and others. Eventually (as of 1981), 341 native communities were established, involving 11,327 families, and 1,390,818 hectares of

TABLE 2. Lands titled to native communities as of 1981

DEPARTMENT Province	Number of communities	Number of families	Total area awarded (in hectares)	Projected usage (area in hectares)			Average cropping land per family (in hectares)
				Cattle grazing	Timber cutting	Cropping	
AMAZONAS:							
Bagua	77	3,563	354,742	74,583	218,070	62,089	17.4
LORETO:							
Coronel Portillo	63	2,036	123,047	22,149	86,133	14,765	7.3
Maynas	59	1,795	230,210	43,935	118,386	67,889	37.8
Alto Amazonas	35	877	292,518	62,370	131,134	99,014	112.9
Ucayali	19	540	55,695	10,025	38,987	6,683	12.4
CUSCO:							
Paucartambo and La Convención	4	280	14,682	3,801	9,043	1,838	6.6
JUNÍN:							
Satipo	24	599	31,086	4,187	14,708	12,191	20.4
Tarma	14	279	8,386	1,299	5,367	1,720	6.2
MADRE DE DIOS:							
Manu and Alto Madre de Dios	9	157	147,166	26,490	103,016	17,660	112.5
SAN MARTÍN:							
Rioja, Moyobamba	8	171	56,765	10,217	39,736	6,812	39.8
PASCO:							
Oxapampa	29	1,030	76,521	12,410	41,880	22,231	21.6
National totals:	341	11,327	1,390,818	271,466	806,460	312,892	27.6

SOURCE: Peruvian Ministry of Agriculture.

NOTE: Ministry figures for the areas titled to native communities have been rounded to the nearest hectare. Figures for the average cropping land per family have been recalculated since the ministry's averages appear to have been published incorrectly.

land were reserved for land titles in seven departments of Peru that have selvatic lands. Table 2 shows the Peruvian Agricultural Ministry's breakdown of the total.

Policy was thus directed toward cultural preservation and the establishment of corporate land bases for lowland Indians for the first time in Peru's history. Unfortunately, the Christianized cholo sector was not a focus of this organizational effort, although the cholos had historically suffered the most severe losses of any of the survivors of the original conquest. Government planners and functionaries generally tend to lump together poor white-mestizo peasants and Indian peasants in their plans for development. Such peasants were to organize into *communidades campesinas* under a separate law. This effort never was effective in the selva, and the cholo sector was largely ignored. But the forms of social life, the values, the organization of work, and the land-tenure system were different for Indian cholo peasants than for their white-mestizo counterparts, even within a common framework of rural poverty. Moreover, Indian peasants were despised and discriminated against by white-mestizos, and they in turn held low opinions of the white-mestizos (Stocks 1981).

Varese's idealism with regard to Indians was always at cross-purposes with long-term historical trends in Indian policy, which emphasized conquest of the forest lands and their economic development. The Native Community Law was modified in 1976 to allow much larger tracts of private property to be held in the selva than had originally been allowed. Law 22175, which replaced 20653, opened the way for large-scale capitalist exploitation of the national forests without state participation. Under a later decree (D.S. 002/79AA), priority was given to projects that would offer wage-labor employment or maximize the exploitation of diverse tree species (Ballon Aguirre 1980). The period of oil exploration, which began virtually as the Native Community Law was put into effect, showed clearly this dysfunction between the idealistic advocacy policy and the conquest policy. Large concessions, on the model of the 1891 rubber concessions, were given to oil companies to explore enormous tracts of the lowlands. The natives were considered not to have subsurface rights of any kind. Nearly every Indian group in eastern Peru was affected as gangs of brush cutters cut survey lines through their lands all over the forest. Many individuals in isolated groups were brought into the wage-labor workforce temporarily, and many were induced to migrate in search of more work when the majority of the companies left beginning in 1975. Pressure on other Indians along the montaña continued through this period also, not from oil exploration, but from colonists in groups that were sometimes private and unofficial and sometimes government sponsored.

During the first few years of the "revolution" the Indians retained more than nominal government support. This situation began to change when, in 1975, two years after the first native community law was passed, the government began to respond to pressures from capitalist interests. Velasco turned over the government to another general, Morales Bermudez, and the regime drifted back to the right. SINAMOS was soon in grave trouble, accused of being full of communists, and the Office of Support for Native Communities became defunct. Indian policy is now handled by the Ministry of Agriculture. In Loreto, the offices in ORDELORETO, a new development-minded combined ministry, included only one anthropologist with a B.A. Indian policy was submerged in development policy and special permission must now be sought by anyone wishing to study or aid native communities.

By 1978, no more land titles were signed, essentially because the native communities had rights to forest exploitation guaranteed by D.L. 22175 and companies in the central selva and montaña considered such rights to be a threat to them (Ballon Aguirre 1980). Since 1978, it is reported that over a thousand Indian petitions and title applications have accumulated in Lima for signatures, which have not been forthcoming. In the opinion of some (see Basurto and Trapnell 1980), the problem has revolved around the lands of the Campa and Amuesha, which are hotly contested by lumber companies, colonists, and Indians. Previously titled Indian lands are now being withdrawn, and sources speculate that the government actually intends to remove Indians in this region to other "nonoccupied" lands for consolidation, an action that would allow colonists and companies to take over the most fertile lands in the region. Meanwhile, lands that were surveyed as long as two years ago among groups remote from the colonists' pressures of the central montaña await titles from a government bureaucracy, which seems to be resistant.[3]

A severe blow was dealt to the Indians with the passage of Legislative Decree No. 2 by the new Belaunde government. This law (Ley de Promoción y Desarrollo Agrario) amplified further the amount of land large companies could be granted in the lowlands and guaranteed that, in cases of extensions of over fifty thousand hectares, the state would be a shareholder. The most sombre effects of the new law result from changes in D.L. 22175, in which land adjudications in large quantities no longer require a special declaration of "national priority" to be accomplished. Furthermore, small- and medium-sized agriculturalists who work for the companies and reside within the concessions (i.e., Indian and white-mestizo rural peasants) can be awarded small plots within the concession. In other words, the hacienda system is rearing its head again, this time with large corporations as the owners and legal *minifundismo* for the worker population, be they Indians or poor white-mestizos, thus guaranteeing a supply of cheap labor for the projects (Ballon Aguirre 1980). Already as much as 90 percent of the national forests in some areas has been given over through such concessions. In effect, the smoothness of the transfer of power from the military to the civilian government gives credence to the assertion that the government had been drifting toward a reinstatement of capitalist "solutions" for five years prior to the change. Ominously enough, and also supporting this view, the 1979 constitution, which evolved as the nation was preparing to return to civilian rule, now allows under Article 163 the sale of native community lands by a two-thirds majority vote of the community. It also allows for the expropriation of such lands by the government for purposes defined to be in the "public interest."

The latest blow to Indian rights comes again in the Campa area, this time in the valleys of the Pichis and Palcazu rivers where the Peruvian government, in association with USAID, plans to settle colonists and companies in an area already densely populated with Indians and poor but independent colonists (see *Amazonía Indígena* 1:3 (April 1981), for an analysis of the effects of this plan). This project is being carried out, apparently, as much for its symbolic value as for economic reasons, since at least one major tropical soils and agronomic research station in Peru has privately informed the government that the project is not economically feasible (Bandy, personal communication). It is also currently rumored in Lima that the government plans to put a carpet of colonists on the Ecuadoran frontier in the Sierra del Condor to consolidate the border. This is perplexing since almost all of the arable land in the

region is held by Aguaruna or Huambisa Indians who are, theoretically at least, citizens of the state (Rivera Chavez 1982).

To sum up this eventful and disappointing period, I perceive a
direct clash between the idealism of the early Velasco regime's
policy and the long-term conquest and development policy that
has characterized the national government since before independence. The relative political and economic weight of the opposing
sides is clearly shown by the brief duration of effective progress toward creating a land base and a potentially attractive economic future for lowland Indians. The situation today pits both the Indians
and poor colonists against the large companies in a contest for the
resources and lands of the forest. If Indians do not destroy the forest, it will be done for them. Indian lands enjoyed a brief period of
protection, but the pressure to consolidate scattered Indian populations and to free more land for colonization and exploitation in
the central montaña is enormous and will increase. Likewise, the
colonization of the northern montaña, lands of the Huambisa and
Aguaruna, will increasingly put pressure on the Indians of the region. It is also of some interest that while surveying of lands goes
on in a dilatory fashion under D.L. 22175, the communities being
called native communities with which I am familiar are actually
communities of colonists rather than of Indians.

Attempts at Indian solidarity: the shape of the future

Pressure on Indians from oil and timber interests and from colonists, particularly in the montaña, has provoked a response both
among Indians and among groups that wish to support them.
Communities threatened with loss of lands have filed literally
thousands of *denuncios* and petitions. Emerging from the dust of
the struggle are federations of communities and tribal organizations in many parts of the selva and montaña. Indians have been
aided, indeed politicized and organized as well as supported, in
their struggle by a heterogeneous group of national and international organizations that have taken up the reins where the "revolutionary" government left off with the fall of Velasco. Prominent
among these organizations are the following:

1. Centro de Investigación y Promoción Amazónica (CIPA).
The principal figures in this group are Carlos Mora and Alberto
Chirif, both ex-government employees who followed Stefano Va-

Examined to Shrsen 30th

rese in the Office of Support for Native Communities. This private group, financed by English, Dutch, and Swiss sources, has been extremely effective in mobilizing both montaña and selva groups, in providing forums for information interchange and consciousness-raising among tribal groups, and in publishing literature about Indian problems in eastern Peru.

2. Centro Amazónico de Antropología y Aplicación Práctica (CAAAP). This organization has a base both in Iquitos and in Lima. Financed by Catholic groups in Europe and Canada, the CAAAP has research, publication, and action arms. Today the CAAAP has a number of projects in the selva and montaña, including the construction of "native houses" in large urban areas to house Indians who wish to market products or deal with the government. CAAAP acts as intermediary in Iquitos and in Lima between the government and Indians with problems. The action section supports projects ranging from helping Quechua fisherman to buy nets to general community development. They do not limit their help to Indians, however, but also include projects among poor settlers of any ethnic group. CAAAP has several bilingual projects underway, and the publication division in Lima has been extremely active in publishing work on Peru's native populations. The CAAAP is the source of the academic journal *Amazonía Peruana*.

3. Summer Institute of Linguistics (SIL). While primarily devoted to missionary work and biblical translation, this missionary organization conducts a number of community-action programs and especially programs in bilingual education. They are one of the groups, along with SIM (Swiss Indian Mission) and SEM (South American Evangelical Mission) to support SEPAS (*Servicio Evangélico Peruano de Acción Social*), a group involved in Christian community action mainly on the Ucayali River.

4. Solidaridad con los Grupos Nativos (COPAL). This new organization is based in Lima and publishes *Amazonía Indígena*, a bulletin that presents analytical articles on the situation of Indians in the tropical forest regions of Peru. It is headed by Margarita Benavides, a young activist, and coordinates the activities of support groups.

5. Comisión pro Defensa de Tierras Nativas. This organization is a recent coalition of CIPA, CAAAP, COPAL, the Comité Nacional de Derechos Humanos, and the University of San Marcos group, Seminario de Estudios Antropológicos de la Selva. The

group meets weekly in Lima and tries to coordinate the activities of members and of native groups. They accompany natives to government offices, sign petitions, and publish a bulletin of their activities.

The varied results of all these organizational activities can be understood in terms of the varied character and historical experience of the Indian groups themselves. Groups along the montaña colonization frontier have had a long history of defending themselves against land invasions. Such groups, having experienced a demographic frontier, are quite easily aroused and organized. Once organized and supported, they manage their own affairs with little but financial and advisory help. Thus, the most effective native organizations in Peru are those of the Aguaruna and Campa. Other more remote selva groups such as the Candoshi, with whom I am personally familiar, have experienced a sporadic economic frontier, and are much less acculturated to white-mestizo patterns. It is difficult to observe in such groups a feeling for pan-Indian problems or even much feeling for the unity of the ethnic group. Their loyalties tend to be to the local kin group, and they see outside organizers as useful insofar as they can be manipulated to obtain such amenities as boat motors and chainsaws. Their market connections are still mainly through patrones. Such groups will probably need to experience extensive colonization and the necessity to defend their actual lands in order to become coherent political voices. Riverine cholo groups such as the Cocamilla, atomized and fragmented by historical demands for labor and threatened with imminent loss of their lands, wish to have rights to exploit their forest resources themselves. Such groups tend to respond positively to offers of support. Both the Shipibo and the Cocamilla have operating federations of native communities at present, and both are trying to break the chain of dependencies that link them to markets in order to obtain more direct market relations. Their major problems are in the fragmentation process itself, in the time and distance between communities, and in the problems all groups with egalitarian political organization suffer when trying to organize hierarchically. The fragmentation process has created an extreme range of acculturation within communities, such that many individuals see their main chance as disaffiliating themselves from the ethnic community.

Ubiquitous within all groups, remote or not, is a tendency for community leaders to become patrones to their own people. The famous SIL creation, Tariri, is such a patron, but it would be a very great mistake to assume that only Protestant groups have created such figures among native groups. The effects of intervention in all groups are increased solidarity and political sophistication at the expense of increased social differentiation internally. Culture brokers rise in status by controlling the source of external funds and of external political power for groups. This price may be un-avoidable as long as Peru's Indian societies need help from out-siders. This need cannot be projected to have an end in the fore-seeable future as Indians in various stages of political development are faced with an increasingly rapacious array of economic devel-opment forces and are without effective advocacy within their own government.

Summary and conclusions

This paper has traced the course of three hundred fifty years of In-dian policy in the Peruvian Amazon region, distinguishing be-tween montaña and selva Indians and for the latter group, between Christians and non-Christians. Four distinct policy themes have been applied to Peru's Indians by various groups at various times in history: civilization, conquest, advocacy, and (rarely) extermi-nation policy. Historically, several policy trends can be distin-guished. During the Jesuit mission period, the selva Indians were the object of civilization policy designed both to pacify them and to bring them into the Christian fold. Missionary activity took on renewed importance in Indian policy beginning in the post—rubber era. The most pervasive policy theme in Peru's history, often combined with civilization policy, is the conquest theme. This policy has been directed toward mobilizing and controlling Indian labor and/or land. The products of the land and waters are the real object, and Indians become the means of creating value. Montaña Indians found that both their labor and their lands were objects of conquest policy as mita and encomienda were applied to them early on. It is notable that economic and political interests have always coalesced in the application of conquest policy, while religious interests have gradually been marginalized. The con-quest mentality and its accompanying development viewpoint have provided the most pervasive paradigm for Indian and white-mestizo relations.

Advocacy policy, that directed toward the protection of Indian rights, cultural values, or lands, has not generally been pursued in

Peru by any group except the Indians themselves until fairly recently. Unfortunately formal government advocacy policy, as represented by the Native Community Laws of 1974 and 1976, was of
brief duration. Such policy is now pursued by persons mainly outside the government although often with the permission of, or
contracted by, the government.

Current government policy toward tropical forest Indians is
aggressively conquest oriented. With new capital-intensive means
of exploiting the forest resources, the labor of the Indians has become less important, and current policies seem to view Indians as
obstacles in the way of development and "progress," continuing a
trend that began over a hundred years ago. The prognosis for Peru's
Indians is for a long and difficult struggle with most of their support coming from outside organizations rather than from within
the government. However, it should be emphasized in closing that
the native peoples of eastern Peru are a political force increasingly
to be reckoned with by the government, business corporations,
and colonists. Whatever the future holds for them, they will not
simply be trampled without an outcry. They are now, and will continue to be, a party in negotiations about the future of the region.

Notes

1. Eyewitness accounts are to be found in Roger Casement's (1912)
report to the British government; in his diaries (Singleton-Gates and Girodias 1959); in the Congressional report, Slavery in Peru (1913), and in
many newspapers of the time in Peru.

2. Barbasco was used as a source for rotenone, a chemical used in
insecticides. The chemical was artificially synthesized in 1953, which
caused a drop in the market value of barbasco.

3. This situation of frozen land title applications may be relaxing
somewhat. A letter from Arturo Tapayuri Murayari, the president of the
Federación Nativa Cocamilla, reports that the community of Achual Ti-
pishca had actually received its land title in August of 1982. He expected
titles for several other villages of the federation to follow.

References Cited

Amazonía Indígena
1981   1(3) (April): entire issue
Ballon Aguirre, Francisco
1980   *La Nueva Conquista de la Amazonía. Promoción Agraria para Quien?: Análisis de la Ley de Promoción y Desarrollo Agrario.* José Manuel Mejía, ed. Lima: Tiempo Presente.
Basurto, Rosario and Lucy Trapnell
1980   Proceso Colonizador y Desintegración del Territorio Étnico Campa: Los Valles de Satipo y Perene. *Amazonía Indígena* 1(1):8–14.
Belaunde Terry, Fernando
1965   *Peru's Own Conquest.* Lima: American Studies Press.
Bollaert, William (translator)
1861   *The Expedition of Pedro de Ursua and Lope de Aguirre in Search of El Dorado and Omagua in 1559–61.* Translated from Fray Pedro Simon's *Sixth Historical Notice of the Conquest of Tierre Firme.* London: Hakluyt Society.
Casement, Roger
1912   The Putumayo Indians. *The Contemporary Review* 102:317–28.
Chantre y Herrera, P. José
1901   *Historia de las Misiones de la Compañia de Jesús en el Marañón Español 1637–1767.* Madrid: Imprenta de A. Avrial.
Chirif, Alberto
1975   Ocupación Territorial de la Amazonía y Marginación de la Población Nativa. *América Indígena* 35(2):265–95.
Compte, Francisco Maria O.F.M.
1885   *Varones Ilustres de la Orden Seráfica en el Ecuador, desde la Fundación de Quito hasta Nuestros Dias.* 2d ed., Vol. 2. Quito: Imprenta del Clero.
Farabee, W.C.
1922   *Indian Tribes of Eastern Peru.* Papers of the Peabody Museum of Archaeology and Ethnology, vol. 10. Harvard University.
Figueroa, Francisco de
1904   *Relación de las Misiones de la Compañia de Jesús en el País de los Maynas.* (Colleción de Libros y Documentos Referentes a la Historia de América, vol. 1). Madrid.
Fritz, Samuel
1922   *Journal of the Travels and Labours of Father Samuel Fritz in the River of the Amazons Between 1686 and 1723.*

(Trans. from the Evora ms. and edited by the Rev. George
Edmundson.) London: The Hakluyt Society, 2d ser., no. 51.

Herndon, William Lewis, and L. Gibbon

1853   *Exploration of the Valley of the Amazon Made under the
Direction of the Navy Department.* Part I. Lt. Herndon.
Washington: Robert Armstrong, Public Printer.

Izaguirre, P. Fr. Bernadino

1923–29   *Historia de las Misiones Franciscanas y Narración de los
Progresos de la Geografía en el Oriente del Perú: Relatos
Originales y Producciones en Lenguas Indígenas de Varias
Misioneros.* Lima: Talleres Tipográficos de la Penitenciaría.

Jimenez de Espada, Marcos, ed.

1889–92   *Noticias Auténticas del Famoso Río Marañón y Misión
Apostólica de la Compañia de Jesús de la Prov. de Quito
en los Dilatados Bosques de Dicho Río: Enscribiales por
los Años de 1738 un Misionero de la Misma Compañia y
las Publica Ahora por la Primera Vez Marcos Jimenez de
la Espada.* Vols. 26–30. Madrid: Boletín de la Sociedad
Geográfico.

Lagunas Municipal Archives

1913   Documents from the Archive of the Consejo Municipal
in Lagunas. Province of Alto Amazonas: Department of
Loreto.

Larrabure y Correa, Carlos

1905–09   *Colección de Leyes, Decretos, Resoluciones e Otros Documentos Oficiales Referentes al Departamento de Loreto.*
Lima: Imprenta de La Opinión Nacional.

Métraux, Alfred

1942   A Quechua Messiah in Eastern Peru. *American Anthropologist* 44:722–25.

Raimondi, Antonio

1874–79   *El Perú.* 4 vols. Lima: Imprenta del Estado (vols. 1–3); Librería e Imprenta Gil, 1902 (vol. 4).

Rivera Chavez, Lelis

1982   Alto Marañón: Viejo Mito en Nueva Versión. *Amazonía
Indígena,* 2(4) (Jan. 82):12–21. Lima: COPAL.

Romanoff, Steven

1976   Informe Sobre el Uso de la Tierra por los Matsés en la Selva
Baja Peruana. *Amazonía Peruana* 1:97–130.

San Roman, Jesus

1975   *Perfiles Históricos de la Amazonía Peruana.* Lima: Edi-
ciones Paulinas, Publicaciones C.E.T.A.

Singleton-Gates, Peter, and Maurice Girodias
    1959   *The Black Diaries of Roger Casement.* New York: Grove Press.
Stocks, Anthony
    1981   *Los Nativos Invisibles: Notas Sobre la Historia y Realidad Actual de los Cocamilla del Río Huallaga, Perú.* Lima: CAAP.
United States Congress
    1913   *Slavery in Peru.* 63d Congress, 3d Session. House Document No. 1366.
Uriarte, Luis
    1974   *En Torno a la Ley de Selva.* Lima: CEAS.
    1976   Poblaciones Nativas de la Amazonía Peruana. *Amazonía Peruana* 1:9–58.
Valcarcel, Carlos A.
    1915   *El Proceso del Putumayo.* Lima: Imprenta Comercial, Horacio La Rosa y Cia.
Varese, Stefano
    1972   *The Forest Indians in the Present Political Situation of Peru.* IWGIA Document 8. Copenhagen: International Work Group for Indigenous Affairs.
Vasquez, Francisco
    1881   *Relación de Todo lo que Sucedió en la Jornada de Omagua y Dorado Hecha por el Gobernador Pedro de Orsua.* Feliciano Ramirez de Arellano, ed. Publicaciones de la Sociedad de Bibliofilos Españoles, vol. 20. Madrid: Imprenta de Miguel Ginesta.
Werlich, David
    1968   The Conquest and Settlement of the Peruvian Montaña. Ph.D. dissertation, University of Minnesota.
Yurimaguas Sub-Prefecture Archives
    1903   Documents from the Archive of the Sub-Prefecture of the Province of Alto Amazonas, Department of Loreto.

Native Peoples of Lowland Bolivia

James C. Jones

B Y CONTRAST with Brazil, little has been written on Amazonian Indians of Bolivia. The eastern lowlands of Bolivia remain ethnically, physiographically, and historically one of the least-known regions of Amazonia. The aims of this article are accordingly broad. The Bolivian Amazon is first delineated demographically, geographically, and in terms of ethnic and class attitudes that predominate there and that distinguish it from the western uplands of the country. Second, a historical overview is provided in order to suggest the interplay of formative socioeconomic forces. Also discussed is the position of the lowland Indian within the national jural and political framework during different historical periods. The agrarian reform of 1953 and its impact on the lowlands are singled out for special treatment. Policies aimed at lowland tribal Indians are analyzed in a separate section. The article concludes with comments on power and policy as they affect the native of the Oriente.

Lowland peoples of Bolivia

Bolivia is perhaps more aptly described as an Amazonian rather than an Andean country, for the eastern lowlands, or the *Oriente,* comprise just over 70 percent of the national territory. All of the departments of Santa Cruz, Beni, and Pando fall within the lowlands, as do portions of the departments of La Paz, Cochabamba, Chuquisaca, and Tarija. The populations of Santa Cruz, Beni, and Pando, totaling 911,566 inhabitants (per 1976 census), account for

19.4 percent of the national population. As over the rest of Amazonia, population densities are low: Beni, for example, both the second least populated and the second least densely populated department of the Republic, supported 0.79 inhabitants per square kilometer in 1976 (Bolivia 1978:9). The lowlands are further characterized by an unusual diversity of ethnic and linguistic groups, as noted by the first Europeans who entered the region in the late sixteenth century.

More than the Andes divide east and west in Bolivia. The two areas differ profoundly both historically and culturally, and strong regionalist attitudes condition relations between highlanders and lowlanders. The highlander, who refers loosely to the lowlander as *camba*, has traditionally viewed most of the Oriente as a wild frontier, a land where uncivilized Indians stalk jaguar-infested selvas, and where caymans and serpents everywhere bask ominously in the humid heat. It is to Beni, for example, that highland miscreants have often fled or been consigned for penance, and to Beni that vanquished and ousted politicians have gone to live as domestic exiles and thus escape otherwise certain reprisals. *Kolla* is the term used by the lowlander for the highlander. While kolla can apply to any highlander, it seems to apply especially to individuals of marked native Andean physical features. The local stereotype of the kolla denigrates him as sullen, withdrawn, squat, darkskinned, more than slightly bovine, lacking in the social graces, and having an offensive body odor. Shortly after the author's arrival in a small Beni town, a young woman of the Hispanic (white) sector told him that he was fortunate to be studying our Indians instead of the kollas, for the former were tall, white, robust, and receptive, while the latter were squat, dark, and withdrawn.

The explanation for such attitudes rests in part on postColumbian historical relations between the highland and lowland regions of the country. The Oriente has rarely figured more than marginally and fleetingly in the mainstream of national history—indeed, the mainstream itself has been largely defined by the highlanders. Held to be a backwater by governments notoriously highland in composition and character, until recently the Oriente has been neglected in terms of the distribution of national power and resources.

Ethnic and class divisions abound within the Oriente, where they are reflected by an array of terms cum stereotypes. Feelings of racial purity and superiority vis-à-vis the peasant sector run high among individuals of the economic and power elite in towns across the region, who think of themselves as *blancos* ("whites"), as distinguished from cambas. In contrast to highland usage, the epithet camba is used over much of the Oriente by such elites to refer, often pejoratively, to an individual of the peasant sector, either mestizo or Indian, though the term seems to refer with special poignance to the Indian peasant.[1] Camba might translate into English as rube, rustic, or hick. Ranchers and planters of the region are forever maligning the proverbial *camba flojo* ("lazy camba").

Different from the camba, or peasant, is the *bárbaro* ("barbarian"), or unacculturated tribal Indian. According to a stereotype shared by both peasant and elite, the bárbaro, or *salvaje* ("savage"), is wild, nomadic, without religion, and often treacherous. In sum, he is wholly without, if not a threat to, the defining attributes of *civilización*, a state of society so dear to elites of the region.

Local native groups have also stereotyped the Hispanic elite. Peasant Indians of the Beni pampas, for example, whose ancestors were settled in Jesuit mission towns for a century during colonial times, refer to Hispanics as *caraiyana* (singular *carai*), a Tupí term they gloss into Spanish as *gente blanca* ("white people"). Such elites are not only seen as intruders, but are viewed as immoral, as irreligious and irreverent, as lacking in respect for the saints, and as having a corruptive influence on the community. They may be further described as *mesquino* ("stingy"), a most degrading term.

By population numbers, Bolivia is an overwhelmingly Indian country. On the eve of the Revolution of 1952, *campesinos* ("peasants") accounted for at least three-fourths of the national population. Fewer than one-third of them knew Spanish (Heath, Erasmus, and Buechler 1969:51). From the viewpoint of national policy and those who make it, the Indian in Bolivia is the native dweller of the highlands and the valleys, not the native of the Oriente. This viewpoint squares with the far greater native population size and density in the western uplands and with the historical ignorance and neglect of the eastern lowlands by national governments, invariably of highland cast. At the national level, then, the native of the Oriente has played only a marginal role in matters of policy.

Demographic estimates and counts of native peoples of the lowlands vary widely. The national census of 1950 reports the sylvatic population of the Republic to include more than fifty-four tribes and 87,000 inhabitants. Heinz Kelm, a German ethnologist writing nearly twenty years later, argues that the 1950 figure is too high and estimates the population at 77,099 (Kelm 1971:218). The Summer Institute of Linguistics (SIL) put the indigenous population in 1972 at between 68,850 and 70,350 (Riester 1976:34). The German anthropologist Jurgen Riester, whose systematic field researches of recent years are among the best to date for the Oriente, rejects all previous figures as too low (Riester 1976:31–37, 61–63). According to Riester, forty-one tribes, with a total estimated population of between 119,968 and 131,303, are found in the lowlands today. By whatever set of figures, it is certain that the native population of the lowlands forms an appreciable fraction of the total population there. The author estimates that the indigenous population of Beni, for example, accounts for between 24 and 28 percent of the official population (1976 census) of 167,969 (Jones 1980:41).[2]

Ignoring other social divisions as well as numerous gradations and nuances, the three-tiered scheme of blanco, camba, and bárbaro serves to broadly classify the human element of the Oriente. From a policy standpoint, two distinct categories of Indians are recognized, at least implicitly, by non-Indian politicians and policymakers of both the Oriente and the uplands. First, there is the peasant Indian, who forms part of the larger camba group in the Oriente. While often retaining native language and custom, the peasant Indian lives within the framework of regional and national institutions and to some degree shares in regional and national cultures. To the extent that national policy and legislation targeted at the Indian impact the Oriente at all, it is the peasant Indian who is affected.[3] Second, there is the unacculturated tribal Indian, the bárbaro, who remains, by contrast, at the margin of regional and national institutions. National laws and policies aimed specifically at the tribal Indian are few and their impact virtually nil.

The contemporary dynamics among these groups can better be understood as the result of economic and political changes through the history of the Oriente. Reports by the first Europeans who entered this remote lowland vastness of marked physiographic diversity during the late sixteenth and early seventeenth centuries suggest a level of native sociocultural complexity that ranged from small nomadic groups to tropical-forest chiefdoms (Steward and Faron 1959:252–57). Any generalizing treatment of post-European historical forces at work on these early native societies is rendered difficult by differing historical currents at play over the different subregions. Except for the rubber boom, with its voracious demand for cheap native labor, and the Chaco War (1932–35), with its sundering of the old order and consequent clamors for change that abetted the radical structural reforms of the 1950s, panregional formative historical forces are decidedly absent. It is thus convenient to speak of four subregions when discussing history in the Oriente: a central subregion, focusing on the city of Santa Cruz; the floodplains to the north and east of Santa Cruz; the forested northwestern subregion, composed of northern Beni and Pando; and the southern desert subregion, or Gran Chaco.[4]

Jesuit and early Republican periods

History in the Oriente has since conquest times turned fundamentally on the central subregion, especially on the city of Santa Cruz, which was founded in 1561 from Paraguay and served the Europeans as a pied-à-terre in the quest for metallic wealth reputed to lie on the plains to the north. Nearby Chiriguano, Itatín, and Guarayo Indians provided the new settlement with slaves and guides in the exploration of the northern lands (i.e., Moxos and Chiquitos). When the search for wealth soon proved unavailing, the encomienda system was instituted with only modest results. Indian populations were small and dispersed, so that control required a degree of intimacy between Spaniard and Indian unknown to the more densely settled highland areas. Substantial mestization thus occurred early in the new colony. A peculiar creole variety of Hispanic culture seems to have crystallized in colonial Santa Cruz during those years and to have diffused northward into Beni and Pando during the nineteenth century with migrating *Cruzeños*.

Santa Cruz remained an outpost of the Province of Charcas (Alto Peru) during the colonial period and supplied the highland centers of Potosí and Sucre with sugar, cotton, rice, and fruits in exchange for European goods from Spain. The commercial tie extended well into the Republican period, thereby contributing importantly to national self-sufficiency, and was severed only during the latter 1800s when the completion of rail lines between the highlands and the outside shifted trade patterns. The region subsequently entered upon a period of decline and further retreat into isolation.

History took a different course on the floodplains to the north and east of Santa Cruz, where European settlements did not take hold during the colonial period owing to the asperities of terrain and climate and to attacks by hostile Indians. There, the conquest was spiritual and was reserved for the Jesuits. In lands immediately to the north and east of Santa Cruz was Chiquitos, a mission enterprise dependent on the Jesuit Province of Paraguay. The mission of Chiquitos (1692–1767) included ten towns, or *reducciones*, located in what are today the departmental (Santa Cruz) provinces of Velasco, Nuflo de Chavez, Chiquitos, and Sandoval (Riester 1967:54–55). Farther north and to the west, on either bank of the Mamoré, lay the missions of Moxos, dependent on the Jesuit Province of Peru with seat in Lima. The Moxos mission (1667–1767), which ultimately encompassed an area corresponding roughly to what is today the Beni Department, included twenty-five towns, a few of them only short-lived (Vargas Ugarte 1964:102, 112–14).

Sequestered from the influence of Spanish secular society, the Jesuits wrought profound transformations in native society and culture. Iberian political forms (e.g., the *cabildo*) were instituted to govern the towns, and native charges were given intense religious instruction through catechisms tailored to aboriginal languages and cultures (Marban 1894). Arts, crafts, and music flourished in the towns: Moxos textiles were famous in Europe. The Jesuits also introduced European epidemic diseases, especially smallpox and measles, which periodically decimated native populations. The missions were further plagued by incursions of both Mamelucos from São Paulo and slave-raiding expeditions from Santa Cruz.

The Jesuit era is important to an understanding of contemporary Beni and northern Santa Cruz, for a large fraction of lowland natives there today are descendants of mission Indians and remain settled in the areas of former mission towns. In their organizational forms and their culture, which exhibit a high degree of syncretism, they bear the indelible stamp of the period of Jesuit tutelage. The post-Jesuit history of these mission areas, down to the present day, has witnessed heroic efforts on the part of these native peoples to accommodate to the shifting tides of capitalism and an ever more secular world.

Those efforts began immediately with the expulsion of the Jesuits from Spanish dominions in 1767, an ominous event that signaled the beginning of more than two centuries of rapine and decay in the mission towns of Moxos and Chiquitos. After a lengthy session of scrimmaging between church and state, control in the towns was apportioned between civil administrators and poorly trained secular clerics hailing mainly from Santa Cruz. Administrator, cleric, and trader, the latter beginning to enter the mission domains freely, all cast a venal eye on the resources and docile native labor of the Jesuit legacy. Mission cattle herds, which with time came to roam the pampas semiferal for want of care, were plundered for their hides, and nineteenth-century revolutionary armies periodically swept through the area in search of wild horses and to sack the silver artifacts of the churches.

Explicit policies concerned with Indian welfare began to emerge in the nineteenth century following Bolivia's establishment as an independent Republic. Under the government of Bolivar, a law in 1826 banned unremunerated personal service and declared the Indian a citizen with equal rights. But because executive organs at the time held that the Indian had not yet come of age, the law was never implemented (Kelm 1971:222). There was considerable attention given during the early years of the Republic, as there had been since the expulsion of the Jesuits, to the administration of the former mission towns of the Oriente, especially those of Moxos and Chiquitos (see Jones 1980:85–116).

In the ambience of economic liberal thought under the presidency of José Ballivián, the Beni Department was created in 1842 as part of an attempt to integrate the Oriente with the rest of the country, mainly through commerce. After observing that the laws and constitutional guarantees enjoyed by Bolivians elsewhere were not enjoyed by the natives of Moxos, Ballivián decreed that "the inhabitants of Moxos . . . be elevated to the status of Bolivian citizens, able to enjoy the rights of equality, liberty, and property that the laws guarantee to all Bolivians" (Burton Rodriguez, 1978:33; author's translation). The president declared further, however, that "it is a duty of the government to seek increases in the public wealth, an objective that cannot be achieved without (private) property, commerce, and other kinds of industry" (Burton Rodriguez 1978:33; author's translation). House sites as well as agricultural and pastoral lands were to be distributed among the native residents, and, importantly, the towns were opened for settlement by non-Indians, who were to be assigned properties

(Jones 1980:100–101). The historical record is vague regarding the actual disposition of the liberal reforms, but the communal integrity of the once Jesuit towns was definitely under assault by new concepts of free trade, free labor, and individual private property. The stage was set for the rubber boom.

The rubber boom

Whites entered the mission areas in ever greater numbers throughout the nineteenth century to trade in hides, cacao, and textiles and in response to flurries of demand for forest products such as vanilla, bees wax, and Peruvian bark (*cinchona*). But all such activities paled by comparison with the rubber boom, which dominated economic life throughout the Oriente during the latter quarter of the century.

This extractive enterprise, with its insatiable demand for native labor, marked an era the grimness of which for native peoples is matched only by the European conquest itself. Native populations resident in the extraction zones of the forest of northern Beni and Pando, a subregion theretofore essentially undisturbed by Europeans, were effectively liquidated by the frenzy. From other subregions of the Oriente, especially from the mission areas to the south, natives were transported, often en masse, to work as boatmen, gatherers, and menials in forests along the lower reaches of the Beni, Mamoré, and Iténez rivers. Labor was universally secured through debt peonage, an arrangement not uncommon today in parts of the Oriente. Disease, inanition, and exposure took a frightful toll.

The demand for cheap labor left some of the mission towns of Beni virtually deserted, and by the late 1880s there were violent clashes between Indians and whites (Jones 1980:108–116). Dispatched to the Beni as prefect by the national government to put a halt to the chaos there, José María Urdininea analyzed the situation and wrote at about 1887:

> These Indians are not able to be citizens because they are incapable of governing themselves; they have the character of children and need the tutelage and protection of the missionary, who is to them both father and defender of their rights. In a word, to revive the Beni it is necessary to protect the Indian, to subject him to the old regime ob-

served by the Jesuits that produced such brilliant results.
The same cause will produce the same results. (Quoted in
Rene-Moreno 1974:80; author's translation.)

This attitude is quite common today in the Oriente. Legislation
emerged in 1896, the Leyes de enganche ("Enlistment Laws"), to
correct the worst abuses of the system of debt peonage in the rubber fields (Fifer 1970:140), but real relief came only with the collapse of the market. By 1912, when the demand for Amazonian
rubber had dropped precipitously, calm was returning to the
forests of northern Bolivia and men searched for more equable
pursuits.

More recent actions taken by the national government on behalf of the Indians include a requirement in 1929 that landowners
with more than twenty-five *colonos* ("tenants") erect primary
schools on their properties. A few were erected on the larger Beni
sugar estates. A decree in 1937 made August 2 the Dia del Indio
("Indian Day"), a national holiday (Kelm 1971:223).

The Chaco War (1932–35) between Bolivia and Paraguay, a
conflict that produced great carnage on both sides, was a prelude
to the signal reforms of the 1950s and a national interest in the
Oriente. The war, which Bolivia lost, not only disrupted work regimes on lowland ranches and estates but also engendered national self-doubts and profound misgivings about the socioeconomic ordering of Bolivian society. The disquiet was vented in
the Revolution of 1952 and its concomitant reforms in land tenure
and labor relations.

The Revolution of 1952 and its aftermath

The Revolution of 1952 ushered in a profound transformation of
Bolivian society. The chief instrument of that transformation was
the Agrarian Reform of 1953, which has been augmented by subsequent legislation. The new government sought to integrate the
rural Indian masses of the country and thereby set Bolivia on the
road to modernization. Among the fundamental objectives of the
agrarian reform were: the abolition of latifundia; the commercialization of agriculture; and, importantly, the integration of the
Oriente with the rest of the country (Heath, Erasmus, and Buechler
1969:332).

The last thirty years have witnessed the first sustained expansion of a European frontier in the eastern lowlands, mainly in the

Santa Cruz subregion and to a lesser extent in the mission areas. The forests of northern Beni and Pando, today supporting only a dispersed population engaged in subsistence agriculture and the small-scale extraction of forest products such as latex and Brazil nuts (*castaña*) for export to Brazil, are no longer a locus of frontier expansion. European penetration into the Gran Chaco, fourth of the subregions, has always been limited; thus could Olen Leonard describe the area in the early 1950s as having a sparse population consisting mainly of nomadic Indians (Leonard 1952:26). Found there today are a few scattered oil-extracting installations and some exploitation of manganese deposits. Development schemes of the 1950s envisioned the Oriente, with its sparse population and its extensive unoccupied lands, as a site for large-scale agricultural enterprises that would feed the country, for the resettlement of Indians from the densely populated uplands, and for the establishment of foreign colonists with a knowledge of agriculture.

Lowland Bolivia, especially the Santa Cruz area, assumed critical importance in national planning and development under the Movimiento Nacionalista Revolucionario (MNR), the party that made the revolution. The first MNR plan for national development sought to develop agriculture and petroleum in the region of Santa Cruz, thus making the country less dependent on mining and effecting import substitution and thus self-sufficiency in the agricultural sector. The plan was largely successful by 1962, with dramatic increases in the lowland production of rice and sugar (Zondag 1966:219). Technical assistance from the United States played a crucial role in the development of Santa Cruz during the early postrevolutionary years in road construction, land clearing, and agricultural credit. Colonization of the Oriente also loomed important in postrevolutionary development plans, with continuing efforts made to alleviate upland population pressures through the resettlement of highland Indians in the lowlands, particularly around Santa Cruz, where the government has also promoted colonization by Italians, Japanese, Okinawans, and Mennonites.

The framers of the basic agrarian reform decree, the Decreto Supremo No. 03464 (Aug. 2, 1953), concerned to reform the systems of land tenure, land use, and agricultural labor relations of the densely settled highland and valley areas of the country, were oblivious to such systems in the lowlands. For the Oriente there existed no agronomic data, no classification of soils, no cadastral surveys, and no substantive knowledge of agricultural systems

(Heath, Erasmus, and Buechler 1969:30–31, 350–51). Efforts to apply reform legislation to the Oriente, therefore, have often been clumsy.

As elsewhere, the reform brought changes to the lowlands in land tenure and labor relations. Few lands of the Oriente were titled prior to 1953, but were instead, at least from a national jural viewpoint, *baldíos* ("vacant lands") used by ranchers, estate operators, and peasants at the sufferance of the state. At the regional level, ownership of such lands was validated through possession or use. Ranchers and estate operators, sensing the insecurity of tenure without title, obtained titles to their properties from the newly created National Agrarian Reform Service (SNRA). The lowland peasant, however, did not.

Workers on the estates of the Oriente in prereform times, often bound by debt peonage, were commonly permitted a house site and sufficient forest for making domestic gardens. The reform granted to colonos of latifundios (the image is from the uplands) the estate lands on which they lived and which they worked for domestic consumption. Some lowland estate proprietors in the area of Santa Cruz became reluctant to let workers make domestic gardens on their properties for fear that they would initiate claims to such lands through local agrarian reform authorities (Heath, Erasmus, and Buechler 1969:333–34).

In Beni, the region best known to the author (see Jones 1980), peasants with any type of guarantee to land today are few indeed. There, agrarian reform has operated in the face of rapid commercialization of beef cattle, which in turn has precipitated a land rush and rampant land speculation. This unique region of Amazonia, mainly savanna with gallery forest along the numerous rivers and sporadic islands of forest amid the pampas, is part of an inland basin of poor drainage that is beset annually by chronic flooding. When the savannas flood between January and March, cattle, now dense over the area, must take refuge and feed on forested high ground, where gardens are made. Many peasants lose an entire year's plantings to the depredations of roving, hungry cattle, especially zebus and mestizo breeds now common in the area. Garden sites free of the cattle menace are thus much sought by peasants today, but they are increasingly difficult to find. As a further constraint on the subsistence cultivator, many white landowners and ranchers of the area are loathe to allow the felling of trees on their properties. This attitude is due not only to the potential value of some of the timbers, should it one day become economic to extract them, but also to a fear that the value of their land investment will be reduced in the future. The nearby availability of wild food game is also an important criterion determining settlement and garden site. The widespread use of firearms among the peasantry in recent years, coupled with the commercialization of hides and pelts, including the hide of the peccary, an important food animal, has rendered many areas virtually devoid of game.

All of the above factors tend to disperse the peasants of Moxos from the mission towns on which their societies and cultures have turned since Jesuit times. Dispersion, however, has its limits. Peasants are dependent on white ranchers for at least seasonal work and sometimes for sale of their modest agricultural surpluses, and on merchants, often itinerant, who provide them with necessities. Such opposing forces generate considerable stress among regional peasants, who now exhibit high geographical mobility as they move about in quest of improved fortunes. The post-1950 reforms have failed the Beni peasant; favored instead have been the powerful cattle interests.[5]

A principal aim of the agrarian reform was the development of the Indian Community. One of the three classes of peasant community under the reform, the Indian Community is held to exist by virtue of titles issued by either the Colonial or Republican governments or by virtue of traditional occupation (Art. 123; Villarroel and Barrios 1969:40). While little has been done anywhere under this piece of legislation, the Indian Community is not even recognized for the Oriente (Heath, Erasmus and Buechler 1979:338). The one-time mission towns of Moxos and Chiquitos, most of which have been bicultural communities (i.e., having both white and Indian sectors, each with its sociocultural forms) since at least 1920, still constitute an important communal form for a significant fraction of the native population of the lowlands. There is, however, no provision for the uniqueness of such communities under the reforms.

Another fundamental objective of the initial reform decree of 1953 and subsequent legislation was the abolishment of the centuries-old *sistema de colonato* ("labor system") of the latifundia and of all unremunerated personal service. The agricultural worker was to be protected by national labor laws; wages and salaries stipulated by contract would govern all agricultural labor, and a minimum wage was instituted by region (Villarroel and Barrios 1969:44, 172–75). Labor systems in the Oriente had always been different from those in the uplands. For example, it could be argued that wages had traditionally been paid in the Oriente, since debt peonage was cast in terms of a nominal cash wage. Implementation of the new labor legislation in the lowlands led to the cancellation of worker debts, thereby dissolving the bonds of debt peonage and thus dealing a severe blow to the traditional scheme of labor procurement.

Jurgen Riester notes that some owners of agricultural (mainly sugar) estates in the Chiquitos area of Santa Cruz Department, rather than comply with the new legislation and minimum wage, abandoned their enterprises and turned to cattle ranching with its modest labor requirements (Riester 1971:209).[6] Clark observed that many ranchers in the cattle regions of the Oriente in the early 1970s were reluctant to enter into written contract agreements with workers for periods in excess of three months, in order to avoid legally prescribed social benefits should the workers be fired or choose to leave (Clark 1974:24–25). Further, legislation prescribing medical and other worker benefits had not been implemented in these regions. The same holds for the cattle regions of Beni today: during nearly two years of field work in the area, the author encountered not a single written labor contract nor any intervention by a work inspector, the official charged with monitoring labor conditions in the countryside.

The reforms of recent years notwithstanding, the tendency toward debt peonage as a form of labor procurement remains strong in the lowlands. Although abuses are today perhaps less rampant than they were forty years ago and the duration of bondage not so long, it is basically through a nominal salary, often paid in goods and against which a worker can draw, that labor is attracted and kept. The scheme is widespread in the cattle regions of Beni, where, in the community studied by the author, local ranchers provided officers of the Mounted Police with foodstuffs and other favors. The latter reciprocated by pursuing debt shirkers and generally biasing law enforcement to suit the ranchers. Fines, often levied capriciously by the police against Indian peasants, were commonly paid with the proceeds of labor rendered to local ranchers.

Today Santa Cruz remains a key area in the development of lowland Bolivia. In recent years it has been a base for families in-

volved in the illegal production of cocaine for export, a highly lucrative traffic that has flooded the area with coca dollars and created a thriving black market in consumer goods.

In the former mission areas, especially in the Beni with its extensive natural grasslands, post-1950 development efforts have
centered on the production of beef cattle, a Jesuit legacy in the region. For the past thirty years, cattle have been slaughtered at air-
strip abattoirs and the fresh beef flown immediately to highland
cities and mining centers, thereby satisfying the upland demand
for beef. Ranching in these remote parts has been highly lucrative
for many, so that the region has witnessed a scramble for lands
over the past twenty years. But the vast majority of the population,
native peasant descendants of former mission Indians, own no
cattle and have been pushed from pillar to post by the powerful
ranching sector that has been effectively favored by agrarian and
other reforms of the Revolution of 1952. From the 1950s to the
present, the socioeconomic scenario of the region has essentially
been one of land rush, land conflicts, land reform, and rampant
graft, land speculation, cattle rustling, and violence (see Jones
1980).

The commercialization of the skins and pelts of fauna has also
been consequential over much of the lowlands. The hide of the
large cayman acquired commercial value in the mid-1940s, followed by the pelts of the *londra* ("river otter") and of the felines,
notably the jaguar. The hide of the peccary, an animal important in
the peasant diet, accounts for a large fraction of the traffic today.
The generalization of firearms in the region over the past thirty
years has increased the efficiency of this exploitation, the results
of which are alarming. The large cayman is now an endangered
species; the felines, in particular the jaguar, are rare; and, according to peasants in parts of Beni, the river otter is already extinct
there.

Tribal Indian politics

Reform legislation has dealt only cursorily with the isolated tribal
Indians and has had little direct impact on them. As Kelm correctly observes, there is no state institution to effectively protect
this group (Kelm 1971:224). The original reform decree of 1953
treats only of *reducciones selvicolas* ("sylvatic settlements") under the rubric "peasant organizations." It defines such groups as

those "in a savage state and with a primitive organization" and places them under protection of the state (Art. 129; Villarroel and Barrios 1969:41, author's translation). Further, rural schools and authorized private institutions (to be at all times under strict control of the state) charged with incorporation of such groups shall have sufficient lands to settle the Indians and "convert them to independent agriculturalists" (Art. 130). And lastly, institutions working to incorporate the tribal Indian must encourage "cooperative work systems" (Art. 41).

The case of tribal Indians was again addressed more than ten years after the initial reform decree in the context of legislation governing colonization in the Oriente. In Decree Law No. 07765 of July 31, 1966, one objective of colonization was to protect "marginal ethnic groups" existing in colonization zones, as well as to "respect their traditional areas of dispersion" (Art. 2; Villarroel and Barrios 1969:198, author's translation). A series of articles follows the decree (see Villarroel and Barrios 1969:216). "Marginal ethnic groups" are defined to be "tribes or social aggregates in a nomadic or seminomadic state that have their traditional areas of dispersion in the sylvatic regions of the Republic" (Art. 91; author's translation). The Institute of Colonization and Development of Rural Communities, operating under the Ministry of Agriculture, is charged with the protection of such groups in colonization zones (Art. 92). The Institute must respect "in the strictest manner" the collective and individual areas of exploitation of marginal groups when assigning lands to colonists (Art. 93). The Institute will further provide facilities to organizations charged with promoting the "development" and national "integration" of such groups (Art. 94). Finally, the labors of organizations referred to in the preceding article must be "gradual" and must not violate the "traditional organization," the "customs," or the "forms of collective expression" of marginal groups (Art. 95).

Such legislation has had little impact on the lowland tribal Indian, who, like his peasant brother, has in the main responded in catch-as-catch-can fashion to an advancing white frontier. Virtually the only institutions that have focused on the tribal Indian have been ecclesiastical ones, both Catholic and Protestant. The Catholic Church, which has a numerous following and marked influence among the native Jesuitized peasantries of the former mission areas, is a far-flung organization of clergy and lay people reduced to working with few resources in a harsh hinterland. Despite the sometimes heroic efforts of individual clergy and lay people to alleviate the painful plight of native peoples of the region, the Catholic Church *as organization* too often bends to the pressures of socially and economically dominant groups of the region (Riester 1976:347). Protestants, or *evangelistas,* endowed with resources from Europe and North America, have been widely engaged in mission work among peasant and tribal natives all over the Oriente in recent years. While recognizing their laudable endeavors in the areas of health care and education, one must note that the overwhelming thrust of these religious enterprises is evangelical in character, with all other activities subordinate to that end. At odds with the government's professed aim of national integration, such proselytism often occasions intraethnic conflict (as among some of the Jesuitized groups) as well as interethnic barriers to communication. Evangelical groups of the region, too often acting with a zeal that blinds, simply fail to grasp the nature, the dimensions, and the ramifications of the dilemma now confronting the lowland native.

Power and policy

The welfare of native peoples of the Oriente has always been a function of the demand for labor and land by the economically and socially dominant white sector, which views the Indian as an inferior and irrational being. Rancher, estate proprietor, collector, and merchant all comprise the cutting edge of an advancing frontier, each accumulating wealth at the expense of the native lowlander. Indian legislation and policies have generally done little to correct this state of affairs—indeed, on occasion have even furthered it.

The Agrarian Reform and related development policies of the past thirty years have in effect been largely indifferent to lowland native interests. An economist with the Food and Agricultural Organization (FAO), citing the potential for modern farming in the Oriente, wrote in 1954 that the rigid social structure of the Indian of the plateau tends to conflict with the concept of modern farming, whereas in the east the nomadic Indian has no established pattern of land use which would act as a deterrent (Flores 1954:124). Hence the argument: investment in the Oriente should concentrate on the development of large-scale efficient agricultural enterprises, which would reduce a serious national food deficit as well as create conditions that would stimulate colonization from the uplands. A new era of recklessness vis-à-vis lowland native welfare thus began.

Problems besetting agrarian reform in the Oriente have been numerous. As already noted, the reforms were not designed with the eastern lowlands in mind. Inadequate financing, personnel poorly trained and poorly paid, and rampant graft have further plagued reform efforts. In the Beni, where reform has had to accommodate a land rush, cattle lands have been surveyed for titling using only the compass of a light airplane. Graft among reform officials, especially surveyors, has been notorious.

More generally, extreme political instability and scarce resources have always limited the reach of the national government into the remote vastness of the Oriente. Further, even that modest reach has been checked and challenged throughout the Republican era by a white elite there. During the early 1970s, with the accession to national power of military officers either from the lowlands or with interests there, that elite emerged to challenge upland power centers at the national level. Referred to by the Chilean magazine APSI as a real and aggressive capitalist class based on agriculture and cattle raising, this elite, centered in Santa Cruz, was a source of instability in the military government (see Denuncia 1981:3–4).

An economist summed up in the following way his findings from a study of land tenure and labor relations twenty years after the onset of the agrarian reform in the lowland cattle regions:

> The implications of the development policy currently followed in the lowland cattle-raising regions are too important to be ignored. This importance derives from the fact that a more effective application of Bolivia's current agrarian legislation, in combination with a policy of protecting the customary rights of Indian tribes, could go a long way toward solving the problems currently encountered in the regions. In the absence of a public will to shoulder this responsibility, international agencies should review their loan policies more carefully in order to try to foresee the effects of their programs on the local tenure structure in recipient countries. (Clark 1974:37–38)

Whatever the outcome of the current struggle for power in Bolivia, the future for native peoples of the lowlands is not a bright one. Simply put, there is no organized body in the country with sufficient power to counter special interests of the region and thus guarantee native welfare. It must be observed, however, that much of the change in the Oriente over the past thirty years could not have occurred without massive infusions of aid from the United States and international lending agencies. It can only be hoped that governments and agencies working in Bolivia and other countries will in the future express a more effective concern for the welfare of indigenous peoples.

Notes

1. *Camba* is a term of Tupí origin, meaning "friend," while *kolla* (pronounced koh'-ya) is a Quechua term designating that part of the once-Inca realm corresponding to highland Bolivia. There is much confusion among non-Bolivians over the connotation of the term "camba," confusion which seems in part due to varying local usage over the Oriente. Jurgen Riester, an anthropologist who has done extensive fieldwork among native descendants of the Jesuit missions of Chiquitos, Department of Santa Cruz, notes that the numerically inferior white elite of those towns readily use the term to refer to themselves (Riester 1971:210). This difference merely points to the difficulties attendant on generalization in a multiethnic region where communities are extremely isolated from one another and often contrast sharply in terms of historical experience. Usage of the term in this article corresponds to that in towns of the once Jesuit mission province of Moxos, Beni Department, a usage which, as Riester observes, is common in the city of Santa Cruz. Perhaps this is not surprising since the elites of the community studied by the author are in the main descendants of Cruzeños who settled there following the rapid demise of the rubber economy in lands to the north about seventy years ago.
2. Using the Latin American cultural classificatory scheme of Wagley and Harris (1968:81–117), the indigenous population is composed of Tribal Indians (1.8–2.2 percent of Beni population) and Indian Peasants (23–25.4 percent of Beni population). The latter are almost entirely pampean (savanna) Indians whose ancestors inhabited the mission towns during the period of Jesuit occupation.
3. As part of the reforms brought by the Revolution of 1952, the term

indio ("Indian") is banned from official usage. The term *campesino* ("peasant") is preferred, though *indígena* ("indigene") is sometimes used—e.g., *comunidad indígena* ("indigenous community")—in order to stress the Indian quality.

4. The historico-geographical framework proposed by Heath (1966) is here loosely adopted.

5. For a detailed description and analysis of socioeconomic change in Beni, especially since 1950 and with a focus on one of the former Jesuit mission towns, San Ignacio de Moxos, see Jones (1980).

6. Other factors also bear on this switch. As part of the economic development plan of the MNR government for the Oriente, a region with extensive unused land (much of it savanna) and sparse population, land extensive (i.e., large-scale commercial agriculture) and/or capital intensive (with capital supplied from abroad, especially from Point Four monies from the United States) projects were favored by developers (Flores 1954:123–24). Accordingly, the production of sugar was rationalized through capital investment in large refineries near Santa Cruz. Parallel in time was the commercialization of beef cattle, abundant in both Moxos and Chiquitos, in response to rising beef prices in highland cities and to the availability of cheap surplus airplanes (from the war) to airlift beef to the highlands.

References Cited

Bolivia
  1978   *Estadísticas Regionales. Beni-Bolivia.* La Paz: Instituto
              Nacional de Estadística.
Burton Rodriguez, Guillermo
  1978   *Departamento del Beni: Su Creación.* Trinidad: Universidad Boliviana José Ballivián.
Clark, Ronald James
  1974   Land-Holding Structure and Land Conflicts in Bolivia's
              Lowland Cattle Regions. *Inter-American Economic Affairs* 28(2):15–38.
Denuncia
  1981   What Are the Roots of Instability? *Newsletter* 22 (July
              1), Comité Nacional de Defensa de la Democracía en
              Bolivia (CONADE). Washington, D.C.
Fifer, J. Valerie
  1970   The Empire Builders: A History of the Bolivian Rubber
              Boom and the Rise of the House of Suarez. *Journal of
              Latin American Studies* 2(20):113–46.

Flores, Edmundo
1954   Land Reform in Bolivia. *Land Economics* 30(2):112–24.
Heath, Dwight B.
1966   Ethnohistory of the Eastern Lowlands of Bolivia. *América Indígena* 26(2):143–51.
Heath, Dwight B., Charles Erasmus, and Hans Buechler
1969   *Land Reform and Social Revolution in Bolivia.* New York: Praeger.
Jones, James C.
1980   Conflict between Whites and Indians on the Llanos de Moxos, Beni Department: A Case Study in Development from the Cattle Regions of the Bolivian Oriente. Ph.D. dissertation, University of Florida. Gainesville, Florida.
Kelm, Heinz
1971   La Situación Actual de las Poblaciones Indígenas en el Oriente Boliviano. In *La Situación del Indígena en América del Sur.* Pp. 217–35. Montevideo: Tierra Nueva.
Leonard, Olen E.
1952   *Bolivia: Land, People, and Institutions.* Washington, D.C.: The Scarecrow Press.
Marban, Pedro
1894 (1701) *Arte de la Lengua Moxa, Con Su Vocabulario y Cathecismo.* Leipzig: Julio Platzmann.
René-Moreno, Gabriel
1974   *Catálogo del Archivo de Mojos y Chiquitos.* La Paz: Librería Editorial Juventud.
Riester, Jorge (Jurgen)
1967   Exploraciones en el Llano del Oriente de Bolivia. *Revista de la Universidad Autónoma "Gabriel René-Moreno"* 14(27, 28):53–62.
1971   Camba y Paico: La Integración de los Indígenas del Oriente Boliviano. In *La Situación del Indígena en América del Sur.* Montevideo: Tierra Nueva.
1976   *En Busca de la Loma Santa.* La Paz and Cochabamba: Editorial Los Amigos del Libro.
Steward, Julian and Louis Faron
1959   *Native Peoples of South America.* New York: McGraw-Hill.
Vargas Ugarte, Ruben
1964   *Historia de la Compañia de Jesús en el Peru.* Vol. 3. Burgos, Spain: Aldecoa.

Villarroel, Buenaventura, and Guillermo Barrios Ávila
    1969   *Legislación Agraria y Jurisprudencia.* La Paz.
Wagley, Charles, and Marvin Harris
    1968   A Typology of Latin American Subcultures. In *The Latin American Tradition.* Charles Wagley, ed. Pp. 81–117. New York and London: Columbia University Press.
Zondag, Cornelius H.
    1966   *The Bolivian Economy, 1952–1965: The Revolution and Its Aftermath.* New York: Praeger.

Frontier Expansion and Indian Peoples in the Brazilian Amazon

Alcida R. Ramos

SINCE THE discovery of Brazil, contact between Indians and whites has been a repeated history of Indian decimation, flight, and withdrawal, until now when there is no refuge left. Hemming (1978) has written in great detail of the destruction and displacement of Indian groups from 1500 to the 1760s. Darcy Ribeiro (1970) provides a vivid account of the losses suffered by indigenous peoples in their tragic contact with whites into the twentieth century. From an estimated population of two to five million in the 1500s, the number of Indians in Brazil dropped to around 150,000 in the 1950s.

In this century alone, at least eighty-seven Indian groups have become extinct or nearly so. In 1900 about 46 percent of the estimated total Indian population was isolated from white contact. Sixty years later, only half that percentage was still living in isolation (Ribeiro 1970:237). Today there are at most three or four uncontacted groups. These data convey some idea of the intensity and speed of encroachment on Indian populations. The total number of Indians in Brazil is now estimated to be just under 190,000, or less than 0.2 percent of the country's population (*Por-*

NOTE: Credit is due to Lux Vidal, who presented an overview at the conference of the situation of the Brazilian Amazon Indians and who provided background materials to assist the author in preparing this paper.

83

antim, April 1982:3–13). Their total territory has been reduced to less than 6 percent of the country's area.

From the sixteenth century to the present, Indian decimation and displacement in Brazil have resulted from continued attempts to attain economic development at the expense of the country's Indian inhabitants. Beginning on the coast during the sixteenth century, many Indians were enslaved, to work first in the extraction of *pau-brasil* and later on the sugar plantations of the Northeast. Much Indian territory was expropriated. Crowded into missionary "reductions," thousands of Indians died of imported Old World diseases. Most of the early aboriginal inhabitants of the Northeast have disappeared, and the remaining groups are a small remnant of their original populations (Ribeiro 1970:57, Carvalho 1982).

Cattle ranching has threatened Indian life in the Northeast and other regions. In the South, land-hungry cattle ranchers occupied enormous tracts of land and organized expeditions to kill off entire Indian communities. The remnants of the Kaingang and Guarani populations are practically the only survivors of that era. Other groups such as the Oti-Shavante and the Carijó disappeared altogether (Ribeiro 1970, Moura Pires 1975). Later, colonizing Europeans and coffee planters continued the massacres and usurpation of lands of surviving Indian groups in the South. In summary, the opening up of new frontiers has historically resulted in the decimation and, in many cases, the total extinction of Indian groups. Western diseases, slavery, and punitive expeditions have been the three main instruments which have wiped out Indian populations in Brazil (Ramos 1980a:222).

Economic activities and their attendant missionization are not new in Amazonia. The region has witnessed several surges in the extraction of products, including sarsaparilla, various essences, resins, rubber, guaraná, pepper, jute, and, more recently, cocoa. Since the sixteenth century these activities were carried out often at the cost of Indian lives and welfare, taking the heaviest toll on those groups who lived along the main rivers. By the end of the eighteenth century, such groups as the Omagua and the Tapajós were extinct, after having been culturally deprived by the force of missionary action (Meggers 1971). The rubber industry was responsible for much enslaving, uprooting, unrest, and death among Indian populations forcibly engaged in latex extraction.

Indians became a demographic minority not only in Brazil but also in Canada and in the United States. In these North American countries, Indian groups were relegated to land areas of negligible size compared to the territories they originally occupied. The struggle to maintain even those small holdings continues, not only in Brazil but also in most New World countries. While disease has been a major cause of decimation (Jennings 1975, Ribeiro 1970), economic forces and official policies and legislation vis-à-vis indigenous people have also played a part.

A massive intensification of economic activities has occurred in recent decades in Amazonia, with disastrous effects for the region's indigenous populations. In response to the threats posed by these numerous development projects, a pan-Indian movement began to emerge in Brazil in the 1970s. In the remainder of this paper, I will explore recent economic changes in Amazonia, evolving official policies vis-à-vis Indians in Brazil, and the responses of indigenous groups to these threats.

The Amazonian frontier

The current intensified assault on Amazonia had its origin several decades ago. During and after World War II, the so-called *Marcha para o Oeste* called for the occupation of the hinterlands west of the coastal states and Minas Gerais. Ideological justifications stressed national sovereignty and the need for Brazilians to occupy these "empty spaces." The states of Goiás and Mato Grosso were the main targets of the Marcha, and Indian groups living in these areas were directly affected by the expansion of the national society. Led by the Villas Boas brothers and others, the Roncador-Xingu expedition in the late 1940s resulted in the creation of the Xingu Park, in which congregated more than a dozen Indian groups. During this period, peoples such as the Bororo and Tapirapé went through an acute phase of depopulation. The Sherente were plagued by conflicts with invading cattle ranchers. The Shavante were pacified in the 1940s. Of the three known Shavante divisions, only the Akwê survive; the Oti are extinct, and the Ofaié have been reduced to less than thirty people living in very precarious conditions (*Porantim* No. 38, April 1982:12).

In the 1950s the construction of highways linked to the new capital of Brasília provoked another crisis for a number of small Indian groups. These Indian peoples underwent a sudden transition from isolation from *civilizados* to a dependence on the products of the national society: medicines, steel tools, clothing, salt, sugar, transistors, batteries, matches, alcohol. Prostitution, begging, and general social chaos replaced traditional ways of life.

The Carajá are a pathetic example of social and physical deterioration due to disruptive contact with the national society. A previously proud and self-sustaining group, the Carajá were overtaken by an incipient tourist industry in their homeland, the Island of Bananal, which suffered from relative proximity to the new capital installed at Brasília. Their habitat along the Araguaia River became a paradise for sportsmen and was eventually occupied by scores of Brazilian settlers. The Carajá are now notorious for their drunkenness, dirtiness, and defeatism. Even their crafts, once highly regarded for their aesthetic expression, are no longer of artistic value.

The military coup of 1964 did little to slow the demise of Indian populations. Instead, the locus of frontier expansion and investment shifted from the Center-West to Amazonia proper. The road construction program that began during President Médici's National Integration Plan (PIN) was followed by President Geisel's Polamazonia program of mineral research and extraction, and the massive establishment of agribusiness and construction of hydroelectric dams. The same priorities have been followed by the current Figueiredo administration. The impact of road construction and of the implementation of large-scale development projects has been documented for numerous cases in the Amazon region.

Highways constructed under the PIN infringed on the territory of no less than ninety-six Indian groups (56 percent of the total number in Amazonia). Another sixty-five Indian groups are located within a hundred kilometers of one or another highway (Goodland and Irwin 1975:74). Road construction has had disastrous effects on formerly isolated Indian communities that were exposed to workers carrying measles, malaria, influenza, and other respiratory diseases. The Parakaná lost 45 percent of their population within a year of exposure to workers on the Transamazon highway (Bourne 1978:233). With the construction of the Cuiabá-Santarém road (BR-165), the Krenakarore were reduced from more than 350 to only 79 people in less than twenty months (Heelas 1978:25–27). In the northern territory of Roraima, the Perimetral Norte highway severely disrupted the Yanomami. The first villages reached by the road lost 22 percent of their occupants from contagious diseases. In 1978, as a further consequence of the opening of the road, 50 percent of the population of four Yanomami villages on the upper Catrimani River died in a measles epidemic (Ramos 1979).

National and multinational firms, responding to government incentives for agribusiness in the Amazon region, also threaten native communities. In the mid-1970s it was reported that these Indians would suffer the direct consequences of deforestation and occupation of their lands: nine Apalaí villages and several Kayapó groups in the state of Pará; the Tembé/Urubu Kaapor Indian reserves in Maranhão; the northern groups of the Xingu Park, several Shavante reserves, the Tapirapé Indians and the Araguaia Indian Park in Mato Grosso (*Opinião*, April 18, 1975; Davis 1977). Agribusiness projects have also affected the Yanomami. Those who live on the Mucajaí River are being deprived of nearly half of the area designated for them by the government because it is being taken over by a large agricultural scheme in Roraima (Taylor 1979). Those who live on the Ajarani and Apiaú rivers have already lost most of their land to colonization projects and sawmills.

Among the largest colonization enterprises in Amazonia is the Polonoroeste Project in the states of Mato Grosso and Rondônia. One of its main purposes is to rationalize the settlement process in the area in question, which experienced a population increase on the order of 11 percent per year between 1970 and 1980. By 1985 it is expected to have over 2 million people. For the future settlement of 30,000 families in the area, the Brazilian government will invest approximately $1.4 billion (35 percent of which is a loan from the World Bank) to construct and pave a vast road network, and to demarcate 3 million hectares of rural properties (*Jornal de Brasília*, May 28, 1981). The project also provides for extraction of minerals and forest products as well as for agribusiness operations.

There are about thirty Indian groups in the area with a total of around 8,000 people living in fifty-eight villages. While different groups vary in their degree of contact with the national society, the land rights of all groups are equally threatened (CEDI 1982). The Nambiquara have been particularly disrupted by the occupation of the Guaporé Valley. With the opening of the Cuiabá–Porto Velho road (the BR-364) in the early 1960s, the invasion of Nambiquara lands was quick and devastating. From 1968 to 1979 no less than twenty-two firms established agribusiness enterprises in the valley. From an estimated population of 20,000 at the beginning of this century, the Nambiquara were reduced to 650 in 1980, 250 of them in the valley (Carelli and Severiano n.d.). An alternative route to the BR-364 under construction in 1983 passed through the homelands of four groups that have not been given reserves, and within a short distance of three established reserves that are entirely too small. Scarcely ten years after coming into permanent contact with Western society, Guaporé Nambiquara will find themselves living in a neon jungle (Price 1981:26). The damage from this new road can already be seen in the economic deprivation, health problems, and social disorganization of these Indians (*Porantim*, March 1982:4).

The mining operations programmed during the Geisel administration have also had disruptive effects on Indian groups. Those perhaps worst hit so far have been the Indians of the Aripuanã area in Rondônia and Mato Grosso, where large deposits of cassiterite and other minerals have been found. The Cinta Larga, Suruí, Arara, and other groups of the region have had the size of their territories drastically reduced, and their populations have declined considerably. The presence of minerals in their lands has subjected the Cinta Larga to air bombings, food poisoning, and other acts of violence by adventurers in search of riches. These events were much publicized in 1963. And, again, Western diseases have contributed heavily to the near extinction of this group.

The Yanomami of the Surucucu mountains in the Federal District of Roraima, which borders Venezuela, live in an area where radioactive minerals and cassiterite have been detected. In 1975–76 a group of 500 placer miners (*garimpeiros*) found their way into the area to extract cassiterite under the complacent eyes of high officials of the National Indian Foundation (FUNAI). Surface mining is illegal on Indian lands, but it was only after serious incidents occurred between Indians and miners that the latter were removed by order of the minister of the interior. Later reports mentioned the first cases of tuberculosis and venereal diseases among the Indians in Surucucu. Since then, several invasions by garimpeiros in search of gold have been reported in the press. Surucucu lands continue to be a target for future extraction, and Roraima politicians have invested much time, energy, and money campaigning for the reopening of the Surucucu *garimpo*. A massive campaign in defense of the Yanomami launched in 1979 (CCPY 1979) seems to have had some effect in curbing these attempts and was even successful in getting the federal government to interdict an area of over 7 million hectares as Yanomami territory. The slow pace of the decision to delimit and demarcate this area suggests that the interdiction may have been a move to gain time against the tide of public protests from within Brazil and from abroad. Both government and opposition party politicians in Roraima included in their campaign for the 1982 elections the promise to stop FUNAI's protective actions in the area and to open up Indian lands for white occupation.

The most recent threat to Indians in Amazonia is posed by the enormous Carajás Project in Pará and Maranhão. The project will directly affect nine Indian groups in Pará, Maranhão, and Northern Goiás, a total of 4,360 Indians living in 42 villages. With a total cost of $62 billion, this initiative is comprised of numerous subprojects that involve a mineral-metallurgical scheme and agricultural, cattle-ranching, and reforestation projects. Related infrastructural investments include the Tucuruí dam, construction of the railroad from Carajás (in southern Pará) to Itaqui (on the Atlantic coast), and a network of 2,000 kilometers of river routes on the Araguaia and Tocantins. Six great industrial poles are being prepared in Pará and Maranhão (Porantim, No. 43, September 1982:8–10).

The initial phase of the project began in 1973 with the construction of the Tucuruí dam. Although the Carajás project has been under way for at least ten years, authorities have failed to provide the necessary protective measures for Indian peoples. The dam's power line was installed through the Mãe Maria reserve of the Gaviões Indians who had to fight for compensation for the 800 Brazil nut trees and other valuable woods cut down in its path. The territory occupied by the Parakaná, whose vulnerability to Western diseases has already cost them nearly half their number, will be flooded by the reservoir created by the dam. Since their "pacification," the Parakaná have suffered malaria and influenza epidemics. From FUNAI employees they have contracted syphilis and have been pressured to give up their way of life: they were forbidden to bury their dead in the traditional way, and even to make family fires indoors. In June of 1981, they were no longer able to endure the effects of the rapid deforestation carried out by CAPEMI, the company clearing the area for the future lake. Twice previously removed by FUNAI, the Parakaná have taken charge of their own transfer (CEDI 1982:43). The land set aside for them, however, has not been protected by FUNAI and is being rapidly invaded by squatters.

The Carajás-Itaqui railroad is being constructed along the southern border of the Pindaré Indian reserve where 3,000 Guajá and Guajajara live. The Guajá, one of the few remaining groups of hunters and gatherers in South America, have already suffered invasions of their lands by peasants, ranchers, and speculators and face the threat of extinction (CEDI 1982:32). The Gaviões of Mãe María will be even closer to the railroad and will have to confront noise, dust, water pollution, the work of maintenance teams, and the constant presence of the train. It is predicted that twelve trains with 160 cargo wagons will make the round trip from Carajás to Itaqui daily for the next eighty years (CEDI 1982:43).

Many other cases could be cited of Indian peoples who have been victimized by the expansion of Brazilian national society into Amazonia. Their presence belies the centuries-old rhetoric calling for the occupation of the nation's *espaços vazios* ("empty spaces"). The persistence of Indian populations, despite severe threats to their existence, poses a continuing dilemma for those seeking to promote frontier activities. Official Indian policies have addressed this question over the past seventy years.

Official Indian policy

Before 1910 there was no overall federal policy regarding Indian populations in Brazil. Land donations, expropriations, evictions, and deals of various kinds related to Indians were in the hands of the colonial officials and later of the provincial and state authorities. The creation of the SPI (Indian Protection Service) in 1910 marked the new era of state responsibility for the Indians. Since then the Brazilian state has assumed the role of intermediary between the rights of the Indian peoples and the interests of the national (and sometimes foreign) society.

Since the creation of the SPI, official efforts have been directed toward bringing hostile or isolated Indians into contact with national society under the supervision of the protectionist agency. It was the SPI's founder, Marshall Candido Mariano da Silva Rondon, who established the practice known as pacification, more recently relabeled attraction. Pacification or attraction teams approach Indians who either have no contact or are hostile to whites and lure them into accepting the presence of invaders. Steel tools, beads, cooking pots, combs, and other trinkets are used in the process. It sometimes takes many years before an Indian group finally gives in and lets itself be persuaded to accept the outsiders in a friendly way. But by that time the Indians have become accustomed to the free gifts provided. The all-too-common begging that follows pacification may result from this phase of courting (a term used by the *sertanistas*). Attraction teams produce what must seem to an Indian an inexhaustible supply of trade goods. The shock of realizing that they have to pay dearly for these goods comes too late to most Indians. Successful pacification is but the first step to forcing the Indians into an irreversible condition of dependence on the national society, one from which they are unlikely ever to escape.

With the creation of the Indian Protection Service, Brazilian Indians came to be legally considered minors under the wardship of the state. The civil code is explicit in declaring the Indians, along with individuals under eighteen years of age, to be relatively incapable. Indians could not be considered normal citizens due to their ethnic specificities and their unfamiliarity with the ways of the national society. In order to provide legally for the special status of the Indians vis-à-vis Brazilian citizens, the government adopted this solution of guardianship, which had been practiced in the New World since the eighteenth century (Bennett 1978:7). Although their condition as wards of the state leaves the Indians highly vulnerable to paternalistic attitudes and actions, it is nevertheless one way to guarantee their protection against exploitation.

The humanitarian and conscientious attitude that apparently guided the pioneer pacification teams has steadily deteriorated. In recent years there have been cases of Indians catching venereal diseases, tuberculosis, influenza, measles, and other illnesses from members of attraction teams. Increasing corruption and complicity with outside interests eventually led to the collapse of the SPI. In 1967 an investigative committee documented the corruption and criminal activities of many SPI employees. The lengthy report (5,115 pages) concluded that the SPI was no longer able to defend Indian rights. In 1968 a new agency replaced the SPI, the National Indian Foundation (FUNAI).

FUNAI not only inherited the basic problem that crippled its predecessor; it also generated problems of its own. Being a division of the Ministry of the Interior, FUNAI does not possess sufficient political and financial autonomy to assist the Indians when such aid runs contrary to interests of the government or of the private sector. Moreover, even within its narrow margin for operation as genuine protector and guardian of Indian interests, FUNAI is often ineffective. Unwarranted decisions taken by incompetent bureau-

crats at all levels of its rigid hierarchy, and corruption by some of
its officials, have led to some lamentable performances by FUNAI.

For two or three years after it was created, FUNAI was administered by people who, if not stern defenders of Indian rights, at
least could not be considered enemies of the Indians. But from
1970 on, with few exceptions, FUNAI's presidents and high officials
have taken actions that have definitely harmed Indian interests.
General Bandeira de Mello, whose term coincided with Médici's
highway program in Amazonia, is notorious for having issued a
number of negative certificates to cattle ranchers in the Guaporé
Valley. These certificates, the issuing of which is FUNAI's exclusive
responsibility, affirm that since no Indians live in the area in question, the land is available for occupation. In fact, it is well known
that the Guaporé Valley has been the homeland of many Nambiquara communities as well as those of other groups. Yet Bandeira
de Mello defended the routing of highways through Indian areas as
a means of bringing progress to the Indians.

In 1974 the presidency of FUNAI passed from General Bandeira
de Mello to General Ismarth de Araújo Oliveira, a change that
meant a three-year period of relative respite for the Indians. But
before the end of Araújo's term, the Indians faced one of the greatest threats to their ethnic and territorial integrity, the attempt to
emancipate them by presidential decree. This attempt will be explored in greater detail.

General Ismarth's presidency was followed by a short-lived
hopeful period under Adhemar Ribeiro da Silva (former director of
the National Highway Department) who, to everyone's surprise,
showed himself inclined to defend the Indian cause. He resigned
after seven months. His successor, Colonel João Nobre da Veiga,
made Bandeira de Mello seem a mild figure by comparison. He issued outright anti-Indian statements, and his allegiance to economic groups interested in Indian resources was unconcealed.
There were mass firings of competent anthropologists who had
been hired during the terms of his two predecessors. Incompetent
and ultrarightist military advisors were installed. Indian areas
were closed to researchers, journalists, and other concerned people.
All these actions contributed to a period of terror for Indians and
for whites involved in Indian problems. The infamous criteria of
Indianness, which will be discussed, were prepared during Nobre
da Veiga's term of office.[1]

In 1981 Nobre da Veiga was replaced by Colonel Paulo Moreira Leal. As a member of the National Security Council, Leal had appeared to understand and sympathize with Indian problems. But within a year of his installation in office, Leal showed signs of moving in the opposite direction. Some positive results were achieved, such as the demarcation of the Tapirapé tribal territory. But Leal was under tremendous presssure from interest groups, especially in the turmoil of the preelection period.

The most outstanding victims of this pressure were the Hāhā-hāe Pataxó in the state of Bahia. Powerful entrepreneurs had been leasing Pataxó lands since the 1920s, which had caused the Indians to be evicted from their own communities. In April of 1982, backed by FUNAI and the Federal Police, they returned to their homeland after having been dispersed in Bahia and Minas Gerais. There was quick, strong reaction from the cattle ranchers and cocoa growers in the area, with the undivided support of the governor, Antônio Carlos Magalhães of Bahia state. In the interest of the incumbent PDS party, facing an electoral challenge, together they pressured the president of FUNAI to move the Indians to another place. Colonel Leal gave in and illegally proceeded to transfer fifty Pataxó families, promising them that they could return to their land in a few months (after the election on November 15, 1982).

Brazilian Indian policy has become more closely linked with questions of landownership and as such has become part of the national security issue. Land problems are now handled by the newly created Ministério Extraordinário para Assuntos Fundiários (Extraordinary Ministry for Land Issues) under the responsibility of General Danillo Venturini, secretary of the National Security Council.[2]

The Indian Statute

In 1973, Law 6,001, the Indian Statute, was passed in Congress. Although not a single Indian was consulted about this legislation, the statute (and articles 4 and 198 of the 1967 Constitution) provides for the protection of Indian rights to land, to natural resources, to community life, and to their own culture and traditions. Some of its provisions, however, permit a margin for the government to remove Indians from their lands legally whenever national interests are at stake. Article 20 says that Indian groups can be removed to another area as an exceptional measure and by decree of the president of the Republic. Furthermore, according to Brazilian law, subsoil resources belong to the Union and not to those who own or occupy the land. This provision makes mining on Indian lands perfectly legal if done by means other than surface collecting. With these provisions in hand, the state has the necessary legal tools to remove Indian populations by simply declaring an Indian area to be a National Security Area. Nevertheless, as it stands, the Indian Statute still guarantees many Indian rights, for example, the Indian populations' exclusive usufruct of the land they occupy (ownership rights belong to the Union) and to all its natural resources (excluding the subsoil).

Since the late 1970s, there have been several attempts by FUNAI, the Ministry of the Interior, and some politicians to find a way around the Indian Statute. The first attempt was the emancipation decree. In 1978, Minister of the Interior Rangel Reis prepared the draft of a decree that would have made it possible to impose emancipation on Indian groups and individuals. Willingly or not, the president of FUNAI, General Ismarth Araújo, had to go along with his superior. As a result of the tremendous rash of protests within Brazil and from abroad against this initiative, the emancipation decree was shelved. Three years later, however, FUNAI was said to be consulting the attorney general's office with a preliminary proprosal to alter the Indian Statute in its chapters relating to this question (CEDI 1982:81), something that FUNAI has denied. Since the shelving of the emancipation decree, reliable news from FUNAI has been scarce, largely consisting of leaked information.

The emancipation decree can be seen as an attempt on the part of the authorities to liberate Indian lands by terminating the wardship of the Indians. With emancipation, ownership of the land would be transferred from the Union to the Indians themselves in the form of individual titles. Because such measures have historical precedents elsewhere in the New World, we may surmise their probable outcome. The Indians would soon be relieved of their newly acquired property by the pressures put upon them by non-Indians. For example, the Dawes Act, passed by the U.S. Congress during the last century, called for "the individual allotment of Indian lands as a first step toward the adoption of the 'habits of civilized life' by the Indians of the United States. When the Dawes Act was passed in 1887, U.S. Indians owned approximately 140 million acres of land. Over the next forty-five years, more than 90 million acres passed from Indian to white hands" (Davis 1978:1, see also Eggan 1978). Similarly, in the 1960s Canadian Indians were threatened by two attempts to force their emancipation from special constitutional status and to rule that their territories would no longer be federal lands. But in this case, both attempts failed, and the Indians not only were able to maintain their reserves but also have been moving steadily toward self-determination (Sanders, 1978).

By declaring the Indians emancipated, the Brazilian government would become the accomplice of those whose economic interests result in the exploitation of Indian populations. The minister's rhetoric was reminiscent of the North American rationale for the Dawes Act: the intention of the government, the minister once said, was in the long run to allow the Indians to become politicians, generals, and even presidents of the Republic (*Jornal de Brasília*, October 19, 1978; *Time*, November 13, 1978). But the history of Indian-white contact and the present trend of Brazilian economy and politics suggest that the emancipation decree would have put the Indians in an impossible situation, unable to continue with their traditional ways of life yet ill-equipped to cope with white society. Predictably the emancipation plan was received with a blast of criticism from those who argue that development should not be achieved at the expense of the Indians.

Turning Indians suddenly into ordinary Brazilian citizens would have other consequences besides the loss of official protection of their lands. It would also mean a threat to their freedom to act according to their own traditions. Common practices such as polygamy, infanticide, nudity, the use of hallucinogens, some mortuary rites, and certain modes of social control would automatically fall under the sanctions contained in the national civil and penal codes and no doubt would be instantly outlawed from the moment an Indian individual or community became emancipated. The repercussions of such prohibitions would naturally be numerous and are not too difficult to imagine. Social disruption would quickly follow the initial phase of psychological disorientation and shock. The performance of the Salesian missionaries in the upper Rio Negro area, for instance, amply demonstrates the effects of cultural deprivation imposed upon Indian groups. Fifty years of missionizing produced a population of demoralized, nearly cultureless, socially incongruous individuals, because of the constant pressure by nuns and priests to change and civilize Indian practices (Reichel-Dolmatoff 1972; see also the Upper Rio Negro case as presented to the Fourth Russell Tribunal in Rotterdam, 1980). In another example, a Guajajara Indian of Maranhão was arrested and tortured by the military police for the crime of belonging to a culture which makes ritual use of marijuana (CIMI 1978a).

Another attempt to weaken Indian protection policies was the so-called criteria for Indianness, a creation of Colonel Zanoni Hausen, a FUNAI advisor left over from Nobre da Veiga's era. In January 1981, Zanoni created a committee of three FUNAI employees to devise a list of more than sixty items which were meant to be indices of Indianness or of integration, among them whether the Indian is a bearer of a "primitive mentality," of a "mongolic birthmark," of relative lack of body hair; whether he shows "social marginalization"; whether his character identity is latent; and many other such senseless propositions. Zanoni also proposed the "blood criteria," which consisted of taking blood samples from Indians to check for the presence of elements such as the Diego Factor said to be most frequent among American Indians. The idea behind this exercise was to place Indian individuals and populations on a scale of zero to 100; those who showed less than 50 percent of the traits were considered non-Indians, therefore falling outside the sphere of FUNAI's protection. In response, outraged Indians, missionaries, anthropologists, lawyers, and journalists bombarded FUNAI in the press, in public gatherings, and in professional meetings with accusations of racism. The criteria were apparently dropped, but not before their application to some Indians in the Northeast and to the Guarani of Ocoí, who lived in the area to be flooded by the Itaipu dam. The remarkable thing about these criteria was their unabashed illegality. The Indian Law defines as Indian anyone of pre-Columbian origin who considers himself to be Indian and who is considered by others as such, regardless of specific physical traits, psychological disposition, or degree of contact. The Indian Statute also provides for the emancipation of Indians, when they are well versed in the national way of life and *at their own request*.

Besides these attempts from within FUNAI to find loopholes in the Indian Statute or to modify it outright, there have been occasional suggestions from individuals outside the organization to change the Indian Law. A case in point was Roraima Representative Hélio Campos, who makes no secret of his interest in the minerals buried in Yanomami territory. In the name of national security, Campos proposed that all Indians be removed from the 150-

kilometer strip along the country's borders and sent to its interior. He cited the example of the United States Indian Removal, a historical event known as the Trail of Tears, which resulted in the death of four thousand Cherokee during their removal west of the Mississippi. His proposal would mean the displacement of nearly half of the Indian population in Brazil, who would be thrown into areas already riddled with land conflicts. Campos's main argument was that the Indians, being ignorant, are easy prey to foreign mineral smugglers who pose as missionaries, so the matter became one of national security. Because it was blatantly unconstitutional, the project was rejected after having been denounced in the press.

The purpose of these legal gambits—emancipation, criteria of Indianness, displacement of Indian populations—is integration of the Indians, that is, the elimination of their cultural specificities. The emancipation of Indian groups from the condition of wards of the state is not a new idea; it dates back at least to the creation of the SPI. Marshall Rondon was convinced that Indians would be happier if civilized. His philosophy, borrowed from Comte's positivism, maintained, contrary to the notions of the time, that the Indians were not inherently backward and incapable of improving their lot. Rather, they had the potential to develop their society and therefore assure their own advancement if given the chance of becoming acquainted with the dominant culture. Rondon's expectation was that as soon as the Indians experienced the ways of the civilized, they would willingly imitate them, giving up their traditional way of life. With this premise to guide his actions, Rondon set up the structure of the SPI. Under the guidance of its employees, the Indians would learn the way to become assimilated into white society. Great emphasis was given to the need for a slow, gradual process of integration, as a way of avoiding disruption of lives and cultures, thus preserving the Indians for their later enjoyment of civilization. Since then the matter of integration has been present in all legislation that concerns Indians, culminating with the Indian Statute.

Indian response

In the early 1970s, under the sponsorship of the Indigenist Missionary Council (CIMI), a progressive branch of the Catholic Church, Indian leaders from various parts of the country began to get together to exchange experiences. By providing transportation and accommodations, CIMI gave the necessary spark for the beginnings of a pan-Indian movement in Brazil.

The increasing awareness on the part of the Indians of their rights and how to fight for them was given a strong boost in 1978 by the government's attempt to emancipate the Indians. In a statement addressed to the president of the Republic, leaders from thirteen different Indian groups took a firm position against the emancipation decree. Their awareness of its implications is clear in their statement:

> Just as public opinion has condemned this emancipation so we also, in the name of the Brazilian Indian Community, repudiate this emancipation. Let it be removed from your office and let our claims be taken into consideration. . . . Let it be recognized that the Indian is the legitimate heir and owner of his land and let the reserves be recognized as the collective property of the Indian communities . . . If pretty words solved our problems, today we would not be in this situation which is so different from that guaranteed by the Indian Statute. The emancipation desired by the Minister will only bring detribalization to the Indian communities, and therefore the collective and individual destruction of their members (CIMI 1978b:22–24).

In 1980 a group of Indians assembled in Campo Grande, Mato Grosso do Sul, created the first Brazilian Indian organization, UNI or UNIND (União das Nacões Indígenas). This was during Colonel Nobre da Veiga's term as president of FUNAI. Repression against the Indians took various forms. One was the withdrawal of scholarships from young Indians studying in Brasília and the express order that they return to their original areas. Some went back; some did not. International events such as the Russell Tribunal and the Merida and Puyo meetings of the Interamerican Indigenist Institute no doubt contributed to curbing further repressive actions, although the distaste of the authorities for the existence of UNI was hardly concealed. There was, in fact, an attempt by General Golbery do Couto e Silva to introduce a provision in the Indian Statute that would outlaw UNI, with the justification that Indians

under the wardship of the state cannot create an autonomous organization (*Porantim*, May 1981:4). This attempt has apparently
been abandoned; but the authorities, including the various presidents of FUNAI, were unanimous in rejecting the concept of "Indian nations," viewed as a threat to national security. Brazil, they
say, is a Union which admits of no nations in its midst.

To assist the Indians in their new organizational needs, and to
keep open the channels for denunciation of breach of their rights
and for claims for just treatment, a number of white support groups
were formed in the late 1970s. Most states have at least one of
these groups, which are represented in Brasília by a central executive secretariat. They have provided legal advice, have amassed
funds for nationwide Indian meetings, and have published material on Indian problems.

Why did Brazilian Indians take so long to organize themselves?
There are several reasons. The gigantic size of the country and the
difficulties of transportation and communication between remote
areas impede mobilization. Indian peoples are dispersed throughout nearly all states and territories. They are also fragmented into
a myriad of small societies with different languages, customs, and
degrees of contact with whites. Last, but not least, organization
has been impeded by the nature of official actions regarding the
wardship of Indian peoples. In total command of the affairs of Indian villages, the government, first through the SPI and later
through FUNAI, has been an inadequate guardian both by omission
and by its harmful actions. Lack of access to education as well as
economic, administrative, and political obstacles to intercommu-
nication are the norm. Keeping the Indians ignorant is one way of
retaining control over them (Ramos 1982).

The Indians are now beginning to organize themselves after
decades of neglect and misinformation. At last they are beginning
to play an active role in their own history. The pattern of the Brazilian Indian movement is the reverse of other associations in
South America. In Ecuador, for instance, organization has grown
from the base upwards. The fact that in Brazil the Indian movement has only been able to emerge from the top results from the
deprivations mentioned, which were imposed on the Indian populations of the country by the authoritarian nature of official policy
and practice. The most active leaders of the movement are young
Indians who have managed to overcome these deprivations.

Conclusion

It is neither a new nor a surprising revelation that frontier expansion is accomplished to the detriment of Indian populations. The process of extermination of Indian lives and of illegal expropriation of their lands has as long a history as Brazil itself. There has been a remarkable continuity of this trend throughout the centuries. If anything is new about these past decades, it is the scope, the speed, and virulence of the impact that national society is having on practically all Indian peoples in the country. While in the past a group under pressure would last some centuries before its final collapse, nowadays a few months of contact are sufficient to bring an Indian group to the brink of extinction. This is true in spite of the fact that for more than seventy years the Indians have been under official protection.

In terms of legislation, Brazil's provisions for its Indian populations have been considered by outside critics to be humane and advanced. The 39th International Labor Conference of 1956, for example, approved the Indian policy of Brazil and recommended that other countries adopt it (Ribeiro 1970:141). But is legislation alone enough to protect the Indians? More than half a century of experience shows that it is not. Indeed there are many cases where the Indians needed to be protected from their assigned protectors.[3] Such are the contradictions of the wardship system as it is put into actual practice.

It is common to hear people express the opinion that the Indians are doomed, that the inexorable march of progress leaves no room for atavisms such as Indian cultures. Will they survive? If we take the position that Indians are only those who live in the jungle, hunt with bow and arrow, go naked, and know nothing of white society, then the answer is no. Chances are that these characteristics will not survive in the present conditions of wholesale Western expansionism.

The creation of the criteria of Indianness was a manipulation of such a definition of the Indian. Yet ethnicity cannot be measured by culture traits alone, much less by blood types. Ethnicity involves a sentiment of belonging, an esprit de corps; it is an assertion of a *we* which is different from others. In this sense the Indians are here to stay. Their overall population is growing. They are Indians in the process of profound transformations in their way of life, in their world view, but nevertheless they are Indians. The nationwide meeting attended by 200 Indian leaders in June 1982 in Brasília was a living demonstration of this resilience. Using Portuguese as their lingua franca, these people spoke and listened, made decisions and plans, and insisted on their autonomy as a political body vis-à-vis all whites, including those who assisted them.

The Indian movement is aware that Indian policy is still firmly in the hands of the state, and its members have to come to terms with this reality. They need and use the support of civil society, but it is with the government that they must interact and negotiate their claims. It is thus impossible to understand Indian policy and the Indian movement without reference to the state, the same state that promotes the expansion of the internal frontiers.

Notes

1. During Nobre da Veiga's term news began to circulate about a FUNAI plan to transfer many of the agency's responsibilities either to the states or to FUNAI's regional delegacies. The consequences of this measure are potentially disastrous, as local governments are notoriously antagonistic to Indians. For example, in the early 1960s, while Leonel Brizola was the governor of Rio Grande do Sul, four Kaingang-Guarani reserves were extinguished in the name of a pseudo-agrarian reform. Decentralization would also mean the diffusion of responsibility and accountability of the federal government with regard to the making and implementation of official Indian policy.

2. Rumors have it that FUNAI will be moved from the Ministry of the Interior to the newly created Land Ministry. About the social and political implications of this militarily occupied ministry, see Martins (this volume, and 1984).

3. By way of illustration we might mention a few cases. For decades the Gaviões in the state of Pará had been exploited by FUNAI as the exclusive buyer of their Brazil nut production. FUNAI paid the Indians about 20 percent of the market price. In 1975, aided by an anthropologist, the Gaviões broke their dependence on FUNAI agents and began to market their own products at a profit.

Having been invited by the organizers of the 1980 Fourth Russell Tribunal, Mário Juruna, a Shavante leader, was denied permission to leave the country with the allegation that he was not emancipated. The Supreme Court ruled in Juruna's favor, against FUNAI, and he was able to go to Rotterdam and chair part of the meetings.

The Xokleng Indians in the state of Santa Catarina have requested a

lawyer to assist them in suing FUNAI for damages from the construction
of a dam and the felling of trees in their territory. FUNAI was forced to put
a stop to the cutting and selling of the timber.

The case of the removal of the Pataxó is being taken to court by a
number of Indian support groups on grounds of illegality, according to the
provisions of the Indian Statute, on the part of FUNAI's president.

References Cited

Bennett, Gordon
   1978   *Aboriginal Rights in International Law.* London: Royal An-
             thropological Institute of Great Britain and Ireland/Survival
             International, Occasional Paper No. 37.
Bourne, Richard
   1978   *Assault on the Amazon.* London: Victor Gollancz.
Carelli, Vincent and Milton Severiano
   n.d.   *Mão Branca Contra O Povo Cinza.* São Paulo: Brazil De-
             bates.
Carvalho, Maria Rosário G. de
   1982   Indian Ethnic Identity in the Northeast of Brazil. Paper pre-
             sented at the symposium "Territoriality, Indian Policy, and
             Ethnic Identity," 82nd Annual Meeting of the American An-
             thropological Association, Washington, D.C.
Centro Ecumênico de Documentação e Informação (CEDI)
   1982   *Povos Indígenas no Brasil/1981.* Aconteceu. São Paulo: CEDI.
Comissão pela Criação do Parque Yanomami (CCPY)
   1979   Yanomami Indian Park: Proposal and Justification. In *The
             Yanomami in Brazil 1979.* Copenhagen: ARC/IWGIA/SI Docu-
             ment 37, pp. 99–170.
Conselho Indigenista Missionário (CIMI)
   1978a   Boletim No. 50, October.
   1978b   Boletim No. 52, December.
Davis, Shelton
   1977   *Victims of the Miracle.* New York: Cambridge University
             Press.
   1978   Emancipation: A Dawes Act for Brazilian Indians. Anthro-
             pology Resource Center Newsletter 2(4):1.
Eggan, Fred
   1978   Beyond the Bicentennial: The Future of the American Indian
             in the Perspective of the Past. *Journal of Anthropological Re-
             search* 34(2):161–80.

Goodland, Robert, J.A. and H.S. Irwin
1975 *Amazon Jungle: Green Hell to Red Desert?* Amsterdam: Elsevier.
Heelas, Richard
1978 An Historical Outline of the Panara (Kreen-Akarore) Tribe of Central Brazil. *Survival International Review* 3, 2(22):25–27.
Hemming, John
1978 *Red Gold.* London: Macmillan.
Jennings, Francis
1975 *The Invasion of America.* New York: W.W. Norton and Company.
Jornal de Brasília
1978 October 19.
1981 May 28.
Martins, José de Souza
1984 *A Militarização da Questão Agrária no Brasil.* Petrópolis: Vozes.
Meggers, Betty
1971 *Amazonia: Man and Culture in a Counterfeit Paradise.* Chicago: Aldine.
Melatti, Julio C.
1970 *Índios do Brasil.* Brasília: Coordenada Editora de Brasília, 1st ed.
Moura Pires, Maria Lígia
1975 Guarani e Kaingang no Paraná. M.A. thesis, Universidade de Brasília.
Opinião
1975 April 18.
1981 May
1982 March
1982 April
1982 September
Porantim
1982 March, April, September
Price, David
1981 The Nambiquara. In *In the Path of the Polonoroeste: Endangered Peoples of Western Brazil.* Occasional Paper 6. Cambridge, MA: Cultural Survival Inc., pp. 23–27.
Ramos, Alcida R.
1979 Yanoama Indians in Northern Brazil Threatened by Highway. In *The Yanoama in Brazil 1979.* Copenhagen: ARC/IWGIA/SI Document 37, pp. 1–41.
1980a Development, Integration and the Ethnic Integrity of Brazilian Indians. In *Land, People and Planning in Contempo-*

rary *Amazonia.* F. Barbira-Scazzocchio, ed. Pp. 222–29. Cambridge: Centre of Latin American Studies, University of Cambridge.

1980b *Hierarquia e Simbiose. Relações Intertribais no Brasil.* São Paulo: Hucitec.

1982 O Brasil No Movimento Indígena Latino-americano. Paper read at the Conference A Nova Consciência Indígena during the Semana do Índio, Museu Paraense Emílio Goeldi, Belém, Pará, April 19.

Reichel-Dolmatoff, Gerardo

1972 El Misionero ante las Culturas Indígenas. *América Indígena* 32(4):1138–49.

Ribeiro, Darcy

1970 *Os Índios e a Civilização.* Rio: Civilização Brasileira.

Sanders, Douglas

1978 The Unique Constitutional Position of the Indian. IwGIA *Newsletter* 19. Copenhagen: IWGIA.

Taylor, Kenneth I.

1979 Development Against the Yanoama: The Case of Mining and Agriculture. In *The Yanoama in Brazil 1979.* Copenhagen: ARC/IWGIA/SI Document 37:43–98.

Time

1978 November 13.

The Politics of Cultural Survival in Venezuela: Beyond *Indigenismo*

Nelly Arvelo-Jiménez

T HE ANALYSIS of the current situation of the Indian peoples in Venezuela south of the Orinoco[1] brings into sharp relief the politics of indigenismo, a system of policies pertaining to indigenous peoples in which the relation between the state and Indian peoples is defined. Indigenismo, previously used by European colonial societies to explain and justify their political actions in America, was adopted by Latin American nation-states to justify their own relations with the Indians. In the colonial and neo-colonial periods, indigenismo provided the ideology that "legalized" or "normalized" the condition of domination that was introduced in order to impose a Latin or European way of life. Nevertheless, the successive generations of indigenistas have failed to produce the definitive moral excuse, in terms of the dominant society itself, that would allow for continuous and open repression as the normal method for imposing total homogeneity on the culturally and historically distinct Indian peoples.[2]

This paper outlines the evolution of different forms of indigenismo in Venezuela and of the development of legal mechanisms whose implementation has resulted in the fragmentation, disintegration, or total expropriation of the Indian territories in Venezuela. This process is important because the territorial base plays a crucial role in retaining the cultural integrity and uniqueness of a people, while the loss of land brings with it the disintegration of social and political structures. In addition, extensive literature on the topic demonstrates how the destruction of the territorial base has been widely used, throughout the last five centuries, as a mechanism to undermine the sovereignty of the Indian peoples and to reduce them to a mere sector of national society, the most impoverished one.

Indigenismo in Venezuela

On obtaining independence from Spain, Venezuela eliminated the special status that the Indian communities had held under earlier protective legislation. In its place, from 1821 onward, arose continuous efforts to destroy the communal land tenure that the Crown had recognized and legitimized with colonial titles. Between 1821 and 1936, various laws were passed that broke up the land base of Indian nations and permitted the state to appropriate the lands through the judicial ploy of baldíos ("undeveloped lands") (1821, 1836, 1838, 1885, 1904, and 1936).[3]

Subject to these laws and their implementation, the Indian nations in non-Amazonian Venezuela have dispersed. The populations that demonstrated a consciousness of cultural distinctiveness or that adhered to collective ownership of the land disappeared.[4]

The process of disintegration of Indian territories spared only the frontier areas, perceived at that time as remote, inhospitable, and lacking in resources. The law explicitly excluded Guajira and Amazonia. It is in this frontier zone that the Indian peoples have, up to the present, maintained a large part of their ancestral lands. It is here that they have been able to maintain their cultural uniqueness. This situation is changing, however, following the institution of a series of measures since 1922 that have transferred to the frontier zone a policy that breaks up tribal territories, settles Indian populations into sedentary communities, and breaks down cultural autonomy and economic self-sufficiency, eventually leading to the dissolution of the Indian nations.

Missionary indigenismo.—Over the past fifty years, this indigenista policy has been implemented by a series of church and state institutions, which are outlined below. The establishment of missionary centers in frontier tribal territories that had never been conquered militarily nor directly and permanently occupied represented the beginning of the last stage of conquest and colonization of the Indian people, who had managed to avoid domination by the majority society between 1821 and 1922. As such, it is feasible to interpret the settlement by Catholic missionaries, with authority delegated by the state, as a direct occupation that reinforces the legal expropriation of tribal territories. In fact, one of the measures of national political integration implemented by military dictator Juan V. Gomez was the assignment of the frontier areas to the Catholic missions through an agreement with the Holy See. They were to control the areas and to dedicate themselves to the "reduction and attraction to national citizenry of the tribes and Indian groups which still exist in different regions of the Republic." On three occasions (1922, 1937, and 1944), the state signed contracts with specific religious orders pertaining to the management of the Indian territories. During this period, 1922–48, which could be called the period of missionary indigenismo, the integrationist policy was indistinguishable from the social doctrine of the Catholic Church.

Due primarily to the method used to impose change, the education of children and young people in internment centers, there evolved among native peoples a rejection of self, of their own heritage.[5] Even more significant to the understanding of the poverty engendered by this type of indigenismo is the rejection or abandonment of traditional subsistence activities. This rejection stems, in part, from the fact that the educational system does not prepare young people for these activities; rather it instills aspirations and creates needs that the traditional system cannot satisfy. Thus education is related to the drastic changes in land use, in settlement patterns, and in the perception of resources within the immediate environment. A small percentage of the missionary school graduates are absorbed by the mission center, settling on individual plots around the center itself. This group devotes itself primarily to activities that are economically useless for the self-development of the population. The rest of the young people migrate toward the cities and are employed as unskilled labor in industry or in the service sector in the cities of the Guayana region.[6]

> With the installation of the missionary comes poverty for some and affluence for others; these irregularities are reflected in the spatial changes that begin to appear in the territorial space which has always been the Indian's domain. The Church and its possessions occupy the central, largest, and best part of the community (space for the church, priest's residence, schools, infirmary, mission

fields and pastures, etc.), and the Indians' affected communities begin to retreat, to be divided into separate
streets, houses, and family gardens, having less all the
time. Thus, the traditional leaders (village chief, shamans,
historians, and wise men) have no influence. It is not to
them that one turns for counsel, but to the missionary.
The visitors (government employees, the military, the national guard, scientists, etc.) all go to the missionary's
house. This has subordinated Indian culture, relegating it
to a secondary level, and it has facilitated the occupation
and subdivision of the tribal territory. (Jiménez 1981)

The mission functions according to a model of clustered population, arguing that that is the only way to deliver services. However, this alteration of the traditional settlement pattern has economic and ecological consequences, which have been extensively
analyzed in the literature concerning development potential in
Amazonia (Seijas and Arvelo-Jiménez 1978:253–71, Descola 1981,
Goodland 1980:1–20, Barbira-Scazzocchio 1980:iii–xvi, Sioli
1980:257–68, Smith 1981:12–13). My own interpretation is that
nucleation is a mechanism leading to the fragmentation and reduction of tribal territory.

The evaluation by the missionaries of the work carried out in
the vicarate of Caroní indirectly supports the above interpretation.
The missionaries affirm that they were the only builders of the cities and towns that today constitute the visible signs of the presence of the state in the frontier zone (Armellada 1980a, 1980b).
However, despite the towns created and the demographic growth
experienced by the Pemon, the concentration of population in
mission towns does not have the effects that the missionaries
claim. Rather, they have not enlarged the occupation of frontier
territory. On the contrary, many areas have been depopulated due
in part to the nucleation and in part to the phenomenon of migration previously mentioned.

An area of particular interest and the current focus of attention is the Yanomama Territory in the Upper Orinoco. There the
work of the Indian mission has caused spatial, economic, and ecological changes as already mentioned in the case of the State of
Bolivar. The uniqueness of the Yanomama and their isolation until
a few decades ago from direct and continuous contact with non-

indigenous peoples make this Indian nation a special case. Since the missionaries opened the way for civilization and Christianity, the Yanomama have been converted into an object of exploitation for tourism, the film industry, and medical experimentation. They have become raw material for testing of anthropological theories and for ill-conceived agricultural programs (Fuentes 1981). They have been forced to accept changes introduced by paramedical personnel assigned to the area by health officials (Colchester 1981, Fuentes 1981). The impact of these combined forces of change on the Yanomama population is such that, in less than a decade, the situation has gone from serious to critical, from a biological as well as a cultural perspective. The population has stopped growing (Lizot 1976) and has been placed in an extremely vulnerable position. In spite of widespread documentation of this fact, the authorities and other co-authors of this dramatic change have admitted neither their responsibility nor the corresponding obligation to resolve the situation (Lizot 1976, 1977; Colchester 1981; Semba 1981).

Missionary indigenismo has continued up to the present, with some formal stylistic changes produced as an adaptive reaction to the creation of the Indian Commission in 1948 (and a series of Indian offices that proliferated in the 1970s), and to reform movements within the Catholic Church itself. Today there is a coexistence between religious orders that adhere to the spirit and the letter of the Mission Law of 1915 and those that adhere to more modernized and sophisticated forms of evangelism (for example, a conversion process that first promotes autochthonous cultural symbols of the peoples in order to render conversion more significant and effective).

State indigenismo.—Inspired by the principles that emerged from the first Interamerican Indianist meeting held in Pátzcuaro, the pioneers of modern indigenismo took advantage of the moment in which Venezuela was trying to break the political monopoly held by the military in order to establish a democratic regime. They pressed for the foundation of a technical consultancy on Indian affairs. In 1948 the Comisión Indigenista Nacional (National Indian Commission) was created, under the Ministry of the Interior,[7] but without ideological and administrative autonomy and subordinate to previous contracts between the state and the Catholic Church. Its mandate was to study the demographic and social

conditions of the Indians and to inform the Ministry about "that
which is necessary and expedient for the protection of the Indians
and their lands" (*Boletín Indigenista Venezolano* 1–11, 1953–67).

During 1948 a new military dictatorship brought to a close
the brief period of democratic liberalization, and dictator Pérez
Giménez subsequently allowed the Catholic missionaries to maintain total control of the fate of the Indians for another decade. The
activity of the Indian Commission was restricted to work outside
of the mission territories, for which reason the Indian Office concentrated its efforts on the revalidation of the colonial titles of the
Kari'ña nation. This was a measure of urgent necessity for the survival of these people, subjected to the explorations for and subsequent exploitation of oil resources in the eastern part of the country (Schwerin 1978:9).

During this same period Executive Decree No. 250, still in
effect in 1983, was passed to regulate expeditions to the Indian
areas. More recently, under the democratic governments since
1958, the decree has been reinterpreted and applied in different
ways, almost exclusively enforced against anthropologists. It has
never served to avert land grabbing and speculation in the tribal
territories by nonindigenous peoples, or the exploitation of Indian
labor.

In 1959 the Indian Commission, made up of representatives of
the ministries that had a direct or indirect interest in indigenismo,
took a supervisory role over the Central Office of Indian Affairs
(OCAI), a newly created agency with certain executive functions.
OCAI was assigned to coordinate the work of the Venezuelan agencies that participated in Indian assistance and to formulate Indian
policy "according to scientific standards and methodology" (*Boletín Indigenista Venezolano*, 1964–65:134).

For eleven years, the work of OCAI was limited to the founding of centers for pilot projects in tribal territories[8] consisting of
growth poles, which had some degree of success in concentrating
the Indian population. In many areas this has constituted the preliminary stage for the establishment of jurisdiction over the Indian peoples, which is carried out by creating positions for paramedical personnel, commissioners, etc. Meanwhile, the policy
already initiated by missionary indigenismo, that of direct occupation of tribal lands, continued.

In 1960 the Agrarian Reform Law was passed, guaranteeing for
Indian populations that maintain a communal or extended family

status "the right to utilize the lands, forests, and waters they occupy, or that form part of the areas that they habitually inhabit, without prejudice to their incorporation into national life according to this or other laws" (Ley de Reforma Agraria, 1960, Article 2, Section d). Despite this legislation, during the 1960s OCAI did not realize a single one of the tasks it was mandated to accomplish. The virtual anarchy of indigenista activities was recognized and regretted repeatedly by the technical secretary of OCAI in his annual reports. In the latter he accused the missionaries and the governors of acting on their own and of bypassing OCAI. Thus he complained that half of his scarce resources were transferred by law to the Catholic missions, although he did not explain that the instruction that had reached some communities stayed in the hands of the missionaries throughout this period (Iribertegui 1980). OCAI did not succeed in creating an Indian policy independent of the Church, nor did it use the Agrarian Reform Law. The latter omission had critical consequences, since during this period the invasion and appropriation of land increased south of the Orinoco and in some other areas, such as the State of Apure. The land problem reached such a level of open conflict that in 1968 there was a massacre of Guajibo (Jiwi) Indians in the Venezuelan-Colombian borderlands.

During the 1970s, international economic interest in the zone south of the Orinoco and the geopolitical strategies of neighboring pan-Amazon countries provoked a response from Venezuelan military and economic sectors. This aggravated the land-grabbing in Indian territories and intensified criticism of the state for its failure to clearly define indigenismo (see Barandiaran and Coppens 1971 and the numerous news articles written by members of the Venezuelan Society of Applied Anthropology, [SOVAAP]). Unfortunately, the criticism was not, in most cases, inspired by a real concern to defend the integrity of Indian cultures and the tribal territories. Rather, for some it represented a mechanism to establish a political space for themselves within the official indigenismo dominated almost exclusively by missionaries. For still others indigenismo was a stepping stone toward the regional level, where political and economic decisions were made about the South, including the Cedeño district of the State of Bolivar and the Amazon Federal Territory.

Between 1958 and 1981, the state has slowly broadened its programs of direct involvement with the Indian communities, as it has implemented the Agrarian Reform Law, the Integrated Security and Defense Law, and the National Plan for Conservation, Protection, and Improvement of the Environment. As such the government has progressively regained control over the frontier region and over the Indian population, formerly ceded to the missionaries by the Mission Law. During this process of recovery of the frontier areas, decisions have been made that introduce drastic changes in the ownership, use, and control of tribal territories without giving the thousands of inhabitants a chance to express their opinion on the matter.

New indigenismo.—In 1970 the Christian Democratic government began the implementation of its program with respect to frontier matters. An area called marginal/frontier was demarcated in which the Venezuelan state should establish a presence, and the Southern Conquest was thereby launched. Technicians (the "new indigenistas") were assembled rapidly in the government offices charged with agrarian reform in the south. From this nucleus emerged an explicit and integrated Indian policy from 1971 to 1978. This policy was itself superimposed on the openly anti-Indian trend also present in public administration, known as "developmentalism." Based upon the Agrarian Reform Law and the First Declaration of Barbados, and cognizant both of the international interest in Amazonia and of national geopolitical objectives, this nucleus forged a policy that lent legitimacy to the conquest of the marginal/frontier lands. While seeming to reject the concept of conquest, this group astutely created an Indian leadership, which gives an aura of legitimacy to its Indian strategies before the public.

The new indigenismo is based upon three basic strategies: collective grants of land to the Indians, the creation of regional Indian federations, and the foundation of community production units called "enterprises." Its consolidation required overcoming the challenges created by firm and continuous criticism from diverse sectors.

The developmentalist sector presented Indians as obstacles to development of the southern region and as problems for national security. These views were used to justify the colonization of the marginal/frontier area by criollo contingents.[9] The prodevelopment group argued that criollo colonization had the double advantage of involving groups with an established national identity that were capable of practicing efficient modern agriculture. The notion that the frontier region was "totally abandoned" by national society was not diminished by the change in government between 1974 and 1979. Instead it was rescued by the Frontier Group, a private association consisting of civilians and military members, which has pressured continually for the approval of a civilian-military colonization of the frontier spaces that they insist on calling "empty spaces."

A small sector of the university community accuses the new indigenistas of having misinterpreted their writings and of having converted their ideas and objectives—self-government, self-determination, and liberation struggle—into hollow, manipulated concepts. In retrospect, the new indigenistas have been strengthened by this polemic with new arguments that are easily converted into political slogans to disguise, refine, and deepen the growing process of neocolonization. Expropriating the concepts of liberation indigenismo and aborting the Indian movement, which has been reduced to nominal federationism, the new indigenistas have proven that, contrary to what some thought in the 1960s, the nature of indigenismo is political and not technical.

Public verbal criticism has been voiced by an Indian minority, which sees in the new indigenismo the most refined program of domination of all the programs designed up until the present. There is also an intangible resistance by the Indian majority, which demonstrates indifference to development programs in which their communities have been involved without having been previously consulted.

Each of the strategies introduced by the new indigenismo helped to consolidate its policy as the dominant trend by 1978. The new indigenismo has won various political victories and from these the majority criollo society has gained certain advantages. It avoided physical violence and placated the violent Indian protest that arose due to the monopolization of land that occurred throughout the 1960s. It fought against spontaneous and official colonization in the marginal, or frontier, area. In place of colonization, it pressed for recognition of part of the ancestral Indian lands as belonging to their original occupants. It directed the spontaneous mobilization of the Indians and slowed colonization through the founding of the so-called Indian Federations, which became the peaceful mechanism of the Indians' political struggle. Since

the creation of the federations, other forms of struggle have been
repressed by the establishment of federation leaders as the "legitimate" opposition.

Of great economic and political significance is the founding of
community and intercommunity production units or Indian enterprises. From the political point of view, these promote the rise of a
resident leadership within the communities themselves; the executive boards of the enterprises, with a totally new exogenous
power, enter into conflict with the traditional leadership composed of elders and wise men. From the economic point of view,
although the structure of these production units assigns to the executive board the tasks of centralizing, supervising, and taking responsibility for the enterprise, in practice the economic decisions
are made outside. Credit, crops, and technology to be used are all
introduced as a package whose design responds to the needs of the
majority society, to the point that they are expressed in the official
Regional Agricultural Plan. As a political strategy the executive
boards reinforce the leadership that the new indigenismo created
in the first stage (1972–73), centered around the Indian Federations. The economic strategy breaks down the self-sufficiency
of the communities, making them dependent on credit and on a
technology not managed by them (mechanical deforestation, fertilizers, insecticides, fungicides, etc.) and links them irreversibly
to a production process that they do not control.

The new indigenismo presents other disadvantages for indigenous populations. In the Agrarian Reform Law the Indian and the
peasant are treated alike since only a single sector is recognized as
beneficiary: the dispossessed rural population. This entails political and economic disadvantages for the Indians. Their settlement
pattern, land use, and perception and exploitation of resources, to
mention only a few of the aspects most closely related to the land
question and consequently to the size of the land grant, are qualitatively different from those of the peasant sector. Indian populations employ an integrated management of space according to
their own technological, economic, and religious patterns. This
integrated use under traditional conditions has contributed substantially to securing their near absolute economic self-sufficiency
and cultural autonomy. The most obvious effect in the communities that have been titled is the fragmentation of tribal lands, in
some cases reducing them to a minimal holding, a condition that,
as we have noted, produces a disintegration of social and cultural

structure. This process converts the Indian peoples into a subordinate sector of the majority criollo society.

In utilizing the law without questioning the assimilation of
the Indian into the peasant sector, the new indigenista nucleus,
which justifies this as a political strategy to incorporate the Peasant Federation into the Indian struggle, in practice helps to assure
the assimilation implicit in the law. This wedding to the peasantry
does not even represent a contact or an alliance with the peasant
sector. It is rather the contact of one Indian leadership group managed by Indians with the peasant leadership that is itself alienated
from its base and that acts to legitimize State agrarian policies that
do not really work in the campesino's favor, but rather in favor of
the powerful agricultural-industrial sector (Guerere 1977). The
peasant leadership at the national as well as the regional level has
felt both justified and motivated to participate in indigenismo. It
has tried to absorb the claims and demands of the Indian struggle
as an appendage of the peasant struggle and has attempted to represent the Indians, eliminating their own voice from this political
space.

The production units of the Indian enterprises constitute yet
another reinforcement to this Indian/peasant metamorphosis. The
first agrarian organizations founded among the Warao Indians of
the Orinoco delta in 1972 and 1973 were named Peasant/Indian
Enterprises. The structure of these, as of all the others founded
since 1975, had to be adapted to the format of the peasant enterprises previously defined in Articles 105 and 107 of the Agrarian
Reform Law. Of the eighty enterprises founded and set in motion
by the new indigenismo, only *one* has attained and sustained a
substantial level of production. Convincing explanations for this
failure have yet to be presented, particularly in view of the large
investment of technical and financial resources in the enterprises.

Several questions remain to be addressed by promoters of the
enterprises: How do they plan to resolve the conflict that has been
shown to exist between this introduced structure and the traditional organization of work? (Arvelo-Jiménez 1980:215–20, Morales and Arvelo-Jiménez 1981). How will they manage the social
stratification that must arise in these communities of closely related people if the enterprises are to attain sustained production
for the market? What real possibilities for success do these small
production units have within a monopolistic economy such as
that of Venezuela? In the absence of solutions to these problems,

the impact of the enterprises is to break the traditional economy and its relative self-sufficiency and to initiate an external dependency.

In creating an Indian leadership at the local (enterprise), regional (federation), and national (confederation) levels to utilize on a permanent basis, with the double objective of repressing any protest and of legitimizing official Indian policy, the new indigenismo created a domination-legitimization model that has been rapidly adopted by various government agencies. This leadership placed itself like a straitjacket on the Indian population. In addition to the leadership already mentioned, other elites have been formed by the governing body (Regional Indian Council and commissioners), by the Ministry of Education (teachers and promoters), and by the Ministry of Health and Social Welfare (nurses and auxiliary personnel). All of these constitute the Voice of the Indians, which facilitates and legitimizes the penetration of the state into the ancestral territories (collective grants, creation of parks and forest reserves); in the traditional economy (enterprises, cooperatives, and application of conservation laws); in the education of the youth (Intercultural Bilingual Education); in health services (paramedics; eradication of malaria and onchocerciosis); and religion and traditional values (Christian missionaries of various sects, Indian pastors, and the agents of educational extension services, such as paratechnical agricultural agents).

Prospects

We have analyzed the consecutive stages through which the Venezuelan state, supported by laws and decrees, has compromised and limited the sovereignty of the Indian peoples. Physical domination has been achieved through three means. Fragmentation and stratification of the tribal territories has progressively reduced them to splintered land grants; zoning has become so advanced that certain areas are declared free zones and the government has taken direct custody over others, such as the frontier security zones, national parks, and forest reserves. The militarization of certain areas keeps some Indian communities in a virtual state of siege. The enterprises, cooperatives, and other development programs effectively control other groups. Cultural domination has been exercised through Christianization, education controlled by the missionaries, and intercultural bilingual education. Political domination has been exercised through the Indian federations and the nominal

Indian elites, which assure the completion of the process with a minimum of physical violence.

Foremost among the plethora of organizations that now share the task of colonizing the marginal frontier region, the missionary sector reiterates its intent and capability to remain in indigenismo. Their critique contrasts the patient, continuous, and direct participation in the Indian areas characteristic of missionary indigenismo with the desk-top indigenismo and shock visits of the new indigenistas and other technicians. The missionary sector recalls the important work of safeguarding and caring for the frontier zones, work already accomplished by them through the foundation of towns and the introduction of national symbols into the frontier schools that have been and still are under their control. Today, in the face of Presidential Decree No. 283 of 1979, which declares intercultural bilingual education to be obligatory, the missionary sector claims to have founded the first bilingual programs. Playing up to the Fronteras pressure group, the missionary sector stresses its greater competence and predisposition to act as guardian of the democratic system in the frontier zone, in contrast to military and political personnel. Evidence that this self-professed political role of the missionaries is accepted in military and political circles was contained in the unofficial statements made by various politicians and the military during the 1980 investigation ordered by Congress into the activities of the New Tribes Mission. At that time it was admitted that despite the regrettable and proven ethnocidal work of this fundamentalist group, the government considered it important to defend the role played by missionaries in the politico-strategic space, since it feared that it might otherwise be filled by enemies of the democratic system.

Other official actions provide additional clues as to future policy directions. In December of 1978 various national parks were created, most of which are located in the Amazon Territory. In September of 1981 the magazine *Indian Voice* published the "Mineralogical Map of Venezuela" together with the current governor's plans for Venezuelan Amazonas. The National Conservation Plan of the Environmental Ministry, in referring to lands for agriculture proposed the following: "as for the zone to the south of the Orinoco . . . there exists, essentially, a national consensus considering a large part of this region as a hydrologic reserve for *energy* production and other *future* development required by succeeding gen-

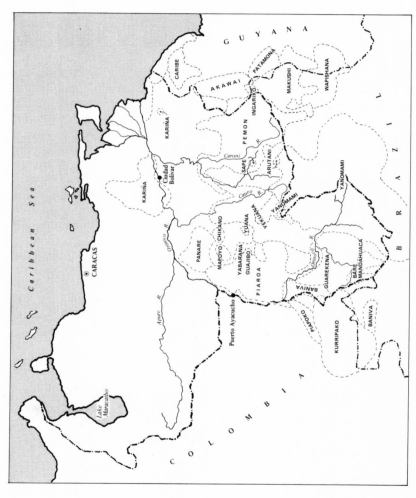

Fig. 1. Indian ancestral territories in southern Venezuela.

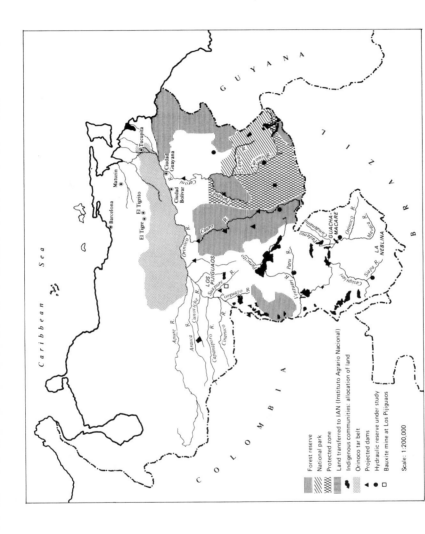

Fig. 2. Planning for development: regional zonation in southern Venezuela.

erations, when a more adequate technology will exist for management of the humid tropics" (MARN n.d.:176, emphasis added).

These recently created national parks in Amazonia are located coincidentally with sizable mineral deposits. The governor's declaration to the effect that the Amazon Federal Territory "will be the nuclear center of Venezuela," and his project to create two new administrative departments, the Ventuari Department and the Upper Orinoco Department, take on more meaning when the position of the future departments is linked to the location of the mineral deposits and of the parks (see Figures 1 and 2). These initiatives contrast with the conservationist policy for Venezuelan Amazonas during the presidency of C.A. Pérez (1974–79), which held back the conquest of the South.

From the point of view of short-term, strictly domestic needs in Venezuela, it seems that the intention is to focus on exploitation of the Orinoco Bituminous Belt and later, perhaps close to the year 2000, to shift to exploitation of the mineral resources in the Amazon Federal Territory. Nonetheless, powerful pressure groups have not relented in their push to *immediately* break the tenuous barriers that still maintain the Amazon Territory as a zone partially closed to a full assault on its resources. Although the Venezuelan state may decide to continue with the aforementioned policy over the next ten to fifteen years, external factors such as the geopolitical strategies of neighboring states and the interests of international groups, with their ramifications at the national level, may force a growing escalation of the military presence in the frontier area. Conditions are ripe for launching an assault to fully disintegrate the Indian nations situated south of the Orinoco.

Militarization could further exacerbate the existing situation. I believe that if it occurs, not only would the majority of Indians that now resist quietly react, but there would be a more important reaction by the militant Indian leadership that has been created in the last ten years. This group is still not completely corrupted nor totally alienated from the values and feelings of the peoples to which it belongs.

Another possibility is that the dividends from oil exploitation in the Orinoco Belt will not be as substantial as those which the governors have managed during the 1970s. This would bring about a global readjustment that would be felt more acutely in the Amazon Territory because it is considered a marginal zone. This hypothetical economic readjustment would seriously cripple the officially sponsored Indian leadership, which under such conditions would find itself unemployed. This in turn could spawn a positive reaction on the part of this Indian elite, which wields power insofar as it acts as an instrument of repression against Indian protest.

The role the created leadership finally decides to play is important because a unified struggle can still change the balance of power. In this political game the Indian peoples can acquire their own voice, through which they could establish a basis for negotiation with the Venezuelan state. A reversal by this leadership is not a utopian proposition: an example lies with the bilingual teachers and professionals in Mexico, who realized the instrumental role they had been assigned by the state in the destruction of their cultures. Cases of Indian leaders in Venezuela who abandoned the life of false status and privileges in the capital of the Amazon Territory and returned to work in their communities have already occurred in the Amazon during the last four years. They are still isolated cases, however.

A reversal by the official leadership would create the conditions for a change in the balance of power, given that a strong resistance already exists. This resistance has been beaten down, corralled, and silenced, but is nevertheless strong. The large number of leaders that the indigenista agencies have had to fabricate provides a measure of the intensity of rejection demonstrated by the Indian population toward the strategies of domination introduced in the last decade.

In the sixteenth and seventeenth centuries, policies that presumed the inevitability of slavery were designed to regulate and humanize that institution. Indian policies have played a similar role in undermining challenges to the domination by the state of native peoples. Political space for negotiation will have to be won in spite of an indigenismo that has had five centuries of experience in producing reformist formulae.

Notes

1. We refer especially to the populations located south of the Orinoco in a zone that spans the State of Bolivar and the Amazon Federal Territory although it does not correspond to what Venezuela includes within its

Amazonia. This southern zone is taken as a unit of analysis for this work because the Indian peoples located there have developed common cultural adaptive strategies to the tropical rainforest.

2. Present-day governmental technicians charged with justifying the imposition of the industrial way of life include anthropologists, planners, agronomists, sociologists, geographers, and historians. Their predecessors were Vitoria, Dominic Soto, de las Casas, Alaya, Dudley Field, John Westlake, Oppenheim, Lawrence—theologians, philosophers, and internationalists who, during the sixteenth, seventeenth, nineteenth, and twentieth centuries, produced and debated excuses for colonial domination.

3. The Law of Wastelands and Commons of August 21, 1936, which regulates the use of and movement through lands "without recognized owners," addresses the case of lands that had belonged to extinct Indian communities; but it does not consider the territories of existing communities. This omission leaves a legal vacuum, which probably by default places these lands in the category of wastelands. As our discussion of the Agrarian Reform Law implies, this only partially resolves the problem.

4. An exception is the Kari'ña enclave in the northeastern part of the country. This entire process of legalized theft of Indian lands during the twentieth century warrants intensive archival research not yet undertaken. Therefore, it is possible to point out only in very general terms the consequences of said laws for the Indian populations.

5. Capuchin missionary Julio Lavandero (1981) provides a detailed description of this phenomenon but without discussing its causes.

6. A published literature describes how, in Venezuela and other countries where various Christian sects compete for conversion of the Indian, division over religious differences deepens the schisms in the traditional society, opening new lines of intraethnic disputes and producing confusion, disorientation, and divisiveness in the social organization of Indian peoples (see, for example, Grunberg 1972, Grupo de Barbados 1979, Hvalkof and Aaby 1981). Skirmishes between Christian sects have so much affected the Yanomama that they were denounced in an open letter by Jacques Lizot and Napoleon Chagnon to the First Venezuelan Congress of Sociologists and Anthropologists, 1969. In this letter they called for the intervention of the Venezuelan authorities to halt the struggle between Christian sects and to work for the well-being and survival of the Indians. Although I have no knowledge of migration (only of relocation and changes in the settlement pattern) of the Yanomama caused by these sectarian divisions, their effects in other indigenous cultures seem to provoke migration and abandonment of tribal territories, as among the Curripaco of Guainia—Río Negro (Hill and Arvelo-Jiménez 1981). Religious differences, a factor also in intertribal dissension, contribute their share to the factionalism that blocks the development of a strong Indian movement, which would work concertedly for decolonization.

7. This ministry is responsible for the political security of the country.
8. These pilot centers were: Riecito in the State of Apure; Yaguasiru-Japreria in the State of Zulia; Ratón in the Amazon Federal Territory; El Casabe in the State of Bolivar; and Curiapo in the Delta Amarcuro Federal Territory, representing, like mission centers, sites of direct occupation of tribal territories by the Venezuelan State.
9. "Criollo" is a concept originally used to refer to the descendants of Spanish colonists born in America. In Venezuelan Spanish today, the term refers to all non-Indian peoples born in Venezuela, including the mixed descendants of Africans, Indians, and Europeans and to their cultures.

References Cited

Armellada, F. de
  1980a   Ley de Minorías Étnicas. *Venezuela Misionera* 490: 187−88.
  1980b   Extra-Territorialidad de las Misiones? *Venezuela Misionera* 487:88−89.
Arvelo-Jiménez, N.
  1980   Development Programs among Indigenous Populations of Venezuela: Background, Consequences and a Critique. In *Land, People and Planning in Contemporary Amazonia*. F. Barbira-Scazzocchio, ed. Pp. 210−21. Cambridge: Centre of Latin American Studies, University of Cambridge.
Barandiaran, D. de
  1971   Los Valores Nacionales y el Indio. SIC 338:366−369.
Barandiaran, D. and W. Coppens
  1971   Ensayo de Formulación de una Doctrina Indigenista Venezolana. *América Indígena* 21.
Barbira-Scazzocchio, F.
  1980   From Native Forest to Private Property: The Development of Amazonia for Whom? In *Land, People and Planning in Contemporary Amazonia*. F. Barbira-Scazzocchio, ed. Pp. iii−xvi. Cambridge: Centre of Latin American Studies, University of Cambridge.
Boletín Indigenista Venezolano
  1953−1967   Volumes 1−11. Caracas: Ministerio de Justicia.
  1964/1965   *Informe Anual*. Caracas: Ministerio de Justicia.
Colchester, M.
  1981   Proposal for Yanomami Medical Aid and Research Pro-

gram to be Integrated into Royal Geographical Society
Expedition to the Sierra Neblina National Park, Venezuela. (manuscript)

Descola, P.
1981   Limitaciones Ecológicas y Sociales del Desarrollo de la
Amazonía: Un Estudio de Caso en la Amazonía Ecua-
toriana. Presented at the Primera Reunión Técnica sobre
Problemas de las Poblaciones Indígenas de la Región Amazónica. Puyo, Ecuador.

Fuentes, Emilio
1981   Situación Actual de los Yanomama. *In* The Yanomama
Biosphere Reserve. Proposal and Justification. M. Colchester, ed. (ms.)

Goodland, R.J.A.
1980   Environmental Ranking of Amazonian Development
Projects in Brazil. *In* Land, People and Planning in Contemporary Amazonia. F. Barbira-Scazzocchio, ed. Pp. 11–
20. Cambridge: Centre of Latin American Studies, University of Cambridge.

Grunberg, G., ed.
1972   *La Situación del Indígena en América del Sur.* Montevideo: Tierra Nueva.

Grupo de Barbados
1979   *Indianidad y Descolonización en América Latina. Documentos de la Segunda Reunión de Barbados.* Mexico:
Nueva Imagen.

Guerere, Alberto
1977   *Nuevo Rumbo a la Reforma Agraria.* Caracas: El Nacional, Caracas.

Hill, J. and N. Arvelo-Jiménez
1981   La Influencia de la Evangelización en la Organización Social de los Arawakos del Río Negro, Amazonas, Venezu-
ela. (manuscript).

Hvalkof, S. and P. Aaby, eds.
1981   *Is God an American? An Anthropological Perspective on
the Missionary Work of the Summer Institute of Linguistics.* Copenhagen: IWGIA/SI.

Iribertegui, R.
1980   Misiones Si, Misiones No . . . *Venezuela Misionera*
487:78–79.

Jimenez, Simeon
1981   Muerte Cultural con Anestesia. Cambridge. (manuscript)

Lavandero, J.
1981   La Educación Intercultural Bilingüe y la Oficialidad Re-

gional de las Lenguas Indígenas. *Venezuela Misionera*
498:409–14.
Ley Forestal de Suelos y Aguas
     1965   Caracas: Imprenta Nacional.
Ley Orgánica de Seguridad y Defensa
     1976   Caracas: Imprenta Nacional.
Ley de Protección a la Fauna Silvestre
     1970   Caracas: Imprenta Nacional.
Ley de Reforma Agraria
     1960   Caracas: Editorial de la Torre. Duodécima Edición.
Lizot, J.
     1976   The Yanomami in the Face of Ethnocide. Copenhagen:
                    IWGIA Document 22.
     1977   Population, Resources, and Warfare Among the Yano-
                    mami. *Man* 12 (3/4):497–517.
Ministerio del Ambiente y Recursos Naturales (MARN)
     n.d.   Documento Preliminar sobre la Elaboración del Plan Na-
                    cional de Conservación, Defensa y Mejoramiento del
                    Ambiente. Documento interno. (manuscript)
Morales, F. and Arvelo-Jiménez, N.
     1981   Hacia un Modelo de Estructura Social Caribe. *América
                    Indígena* 41:603–26.
Schwerin, Karl
     1978   Political Change, Economic Progress and Karinya Rela-
                    tions to the Land in Venezuela. Second Annual Confer-
                    ence on Latin America: People and the Land. Macomb,
                    Ill., Western Illinois University.
Seijas, H. and N. Arvelo-Jiménez
     1978   Factores Condicionantes de los Niveles de Salud en
                    Grupos Indígenas Venezolanos. Estudio Preliminar. In
                    Unidad y Variedad. Ensayos en Homenaje. J.M. Crux-
                    ent, E. Wagner, and A. Zucchi, eds. Caracas: IVIC/CEA
                    253–71.
Semba, Richard
     1981   Medical Care and the Survival of the Yanomamo of
                    Southern Venezuela. Stanford Medical Center. (manu-
                    script)
Sioli, H.
     1980   Forseeable Consequences of Actual Development
                    Schemes and Alternative Ideas. In *Land, People and
                    Planning in Contemporary Amazonià.* Francoise Barbira-
                    Scazzocchio, ed. Pp. 257–68. Cambridge: Centre of Latin
                    American Studies, University of Cambridge.

Smith, R.C.
   1981   Development Planning in Peru's Amazon-Palcazu. *Cultural Survival* 5(3):12−13.

Voz Indígena
   1981   Efectiva Participación Popular en Gobierno del T. F. Amazonas Implementa Actual Gobernador. 3(12):26−35.

Demystifying the Second Conquest

David Maybury-Lewis

THE PRECEDING chapters give details of what is happening in the Amazonian regions of various countries of South America. I shall therefore take one of the privileges of being an aging anthropologist and speak more generally. One may find a remarkable correspondence between the generalities I shall mention and the specifics of the foregoing chapters. That correspondence is not accidental, nor is it simply because I was asked to comment on the papers given, since the gist of my remarks was prepared before I had seen them. I find it both satisfying and unsurprising that the things I have to say underline what the papers talk about. Similarly, I was delighted, but not surprised, to note the macroscopic approach taken by their authors, who talk in broad terms about the history, law, politics, economics, and national and local ideologies of the countries to which they refer. This, I think, is the only way in which one can set about examining what is happening to the peoples of Amazonia—or, indeed, to minority peoples anywhere in the world today.

At the same time, it does make depressing reading. As I read these papers, I had to conquer a terrible feeling of déjà vu. I can almost predict what is coming next. In a sense one feels, "My God, I know it all," and the Indians are always going to get it in the neck in the end. Why should this be so? Are Indian societies really doomed in some sense? There is a powerful body of opinion around the world that thinks they are; it assumes that by some sort of neo-Darwinian process these societies are simply not going to make it in the modern world. We can shed tears about it if we wish, but there is no way to stop that process. There is also a powerful body of orthodox Marxist opinion in other parts of the world which holds that such societies are out of step historically and therefore that they had better get in step. But, getting in step, in this case, also means, in a sense, that their way of life is doomed. This is because getting in step means getting rid of their own Indian-ness, becoming like everybody else—catching up with the other people who presumably are in step with history.

I do not agree with either of these formulations. I do not think that these societies are doomed. I think that Indians, like all traditional societies, are suffering from something much simpler that the public at large does not like to confront. That is, they are suffering from the simple ability of stronger peoples, nations, institutions to overpower weaker ones. Furthermore, and this will be the central focus of my remarks, dominant groups are able to invent ideologies to justify that fact.

These ideologies have a remarkable persistence. You cannot find a better example of the sort of thinking that has permeated the relationships between the outsiders and Indians in the Americas than in the famous debates that took place between Las Casas and Sepulveda at the court of Spain in the seventeenth century. Las Casas held that the Indians had souls, which of course defined them as human in the contemporaneous Catholic sense, that they were Christian subjects, or could potentially be, of his majesty in Spain. And Sepulveda, his academic opponent, argued to the contrary that the Indians were beings beyond the pale. They were idolators who had to be Christianized. They were cannibals, and therefore not deserving of human compassion. Furthermore, they abused the weak in their societies, and therefore had to have good government brought to them by outsiders like the Spaniards (who presumably did not abuse the weak in their own society).

With the wisdom of hindsight, it is quite clear to us that these were all self-serving justifications. Not all Indians were cannibals. Even if they were, it is not obvious why the ritual eating of people should be any worse than flaying them alive, or enslaving them, or torturing them judicially, which were customary procedures among Europeans in the seventeenth century. Nor is it clear why it should justify any peculiarly draconian actions against them on the part of the Europeans. As for teaching them good government, if the weak needed protection against the strong anywhere, they needed it in Europe much more than they did in the interior of the Americas. It is clear too that the arguments were self-serving in another sense. Whenever Las Casas got the upper hand, he was overruled at the frontier. The planters were never willing to accept Las Casas's view, even when it was backed by the authority of the court. At one stage, as you remember, there was a revolt in the Andean countries against the authority of Spain precisely because the king tried to issue new laws protecting the Indians. However, when the Sepulveda faction got the upper hand, the planters on the frontier claimed that they now had legal opinion on their side. Power was the last answer, and the justifications for it were entirely self-serving.

These arguments have been updated into our own times. We no longer talk about Christianizing the Indians, but there are plenty of people who are still willing to talk about "civilizing" them. Indeed, many of the papers in this section have shown how the opposition between Indians and "civilized peoples" permeates the whole discourse and all the relationships with Indians in many parts of the Amazon—so much so that even the Indians themselves have picked up the terms and used them.

Later on in the nineteenth century, European imperialists spoke of their civilizing mission vis-à-vis the backward peoples of the world. This was justified in terms of bringing them a higher rationality: a move from their souls to their minds. The Europeans were the scientists, and presumably owed it to the natives to conquer them and bring them up to the scientific stage. Learned tomes were written about the prelogical thought and mentality of native societies. I hardly need to emphasize that there is no modern anthropologist who believes that sort of nonsense. Ever since the pioneering work of scholars like Evans-Pritchard on the logic of witchcraft or Lévi-Strauss on the savage mind, it has been clear to all of us that there really is no important difference between the capacities of various societies to think.

How then, do we justify the way that we treat smaller societies? Nowadays, it is usually done, unfortunately, in the name of development. It is therefore in the name of development that we are witnessing in Amazonia today nothing less than a second conquest. The first conquest virtually annihilated the coastal Indians, decimated and enslaved the highland Indians, and drove the remainder into the interior. It is in this interior—the last refuge of the Indian peoples—that the second conquest is now taking place.

It is powered by a worldwide quest for resources in which all the Amazonian nations find themselves engaged. The new conquest, unlike the first one, is not particularly interested in Indian labor. It is very interested in Indian land. The threat to the Indians is not this time one of slavery, but of expropriation of their lands and total destruction of their way of life, if not of their persons as well.

What is disquieting is that the oft-proferred justification for this is sometimes accepted by the public at large: that Indians stand in the way of development and that they must therefore give up being Indians and join the mainstream. Why? Because the mainstream, the country at large, needs resources, and we cannot have a small population of Indians sitting on valuable economic goods. It is presented as an argument favoring the greatest good for the greatest number. There is even a slight implication that small Indian societies, and indeed the people who speak for them, are being mildly selfish. Here they are, sitting on all these resources which the rest of us ought to have to fuel national development.

This argument depends on certain assumptions that are worth thinking about. It depends on the assumption that there is going to be equity at the end of the developmental process. It also depends on the assumption of the nonadaptability of the Indian societies we are dealing with. Even if you accept the assumptions of the argument, which I do not, it is a morally disturbing one. The idea that Indian societies must die, and often Indian individuals too, so that we, that is the developed world, may live, is not a pretty one to contemplate. In any case, the argument breaks down once one begins to examine the problem of equity. Brazil, for example, has a massive foreign debt, the world's largest. It needs the money; therefore, the argument runs, it must go into Indian lands and if necessary annihilate the Indians to get at the resources there.

But what sort of development are we talking about here? The Brazilian model, which was so highly touted in the sixties, is no longer regarded, I think, even in economic circles, as a miracle. It has delivered neither equity nor sustained growth. In fact it is close to being regarded as some sort of a Western disaster, something which may very well produce the crash of the 1980s if the Brazilians do not discover how to pay their debts or if the developed countries do not agree to roll them over. This, I suggest, is due not solely to the rising price of oil but to the strategies pursued in Brazil for the last fifteen years, which have paid insufficient attention to structural change and modernization in Brazilian society and which were enthusiastically supported by the world at large. I can remember talking many years ago to a distinguished economist about my misgivings regarding the Brazilian model. He said, "But you can't argue with those statistics." But you can, and that is exactly what I am doing.

This particular ideology of development is a poor justification for the dispossession of smallholders or the elimination of Indians. In this model, all that is foreseen for the Indians is that they should somehow be preserved or eliminated. These are the only alternatives considered. Adaptation is never considered as a serious option. When I say "preserved," I mean preserved as they have been in the National Park of the Xingu, in a showcase. Here you have the romantic Indians, kept going as an example to the outside world and to visiting tourists, Indians who are encouraged not to wear Western dress, not to get into the Western economy, but to behave in the way that we would like to picture Indians as behaving. The Indian lives here in a created illusion, pictured as a noble savage, but a savage nonetheless. It follows from that image, the Xingu image of the Indian, that there is no place immediately thought of for the Indians in the national society. They can be preserved as tourist attractions or they can vanish, legally and perhaps physically.

Yet, adaptation is a serious option, one which is taken by many Indian societies when they have the opportunity for it, one which is recognized in Brazilian law. Those interested in the legal aspects of the Brazilian Indian question might like to look at a publication of Cultural Survival called *Brazilian Indians and the Law* (Occasional Paper No. 5, 1981). In these proceedings of a conference sponsored by Cultural Survival in 1980, it is shown from the wording of the Brazilian Indian Statute itself that, although official government policy was to integrate Indians into Brazilian society, *integration did not mean assimilation*. On the contrary, integration was defined as a status that could be obtained by an Indian individual or an Indian group within an interethnic system. This sort of adaptation is only possible if the viability of a multiethnic society is recognized. Moreover, it is only possible if we recognize antiadaptive ideologies as self-serving; if we demystify them and encourage a new way of thinking in societies with Indian populations and a new way of thinking among the agencies that deal with those populations.

Is this utopian? I do not think so. People used to say a hundred years ago that it was utopian to think of abolishing slavery. After all, it was argued, people were naturally unequal; everybody knew that. It appeared quite impossible to do away with this institution that had been with us since the beginning of time. I sometimes think of those debates concerning slavery when I am especially depressed about what is now happening to the Indians. This can be changed, but only if multiethnic societies are considered as possible by the people who live in them, and as desirable options.

Why should they not be? Strange though it may seem, Indians are often considered to pose a threat to nation-building. Even when their numbers are small, they are thought to pose an ideological challenge. A threat to the nation, a challenge to its mainstream values—such matters provoke violent reactions, and not only in the Amazonian regions. Some of you may remember "Man, A Course of Study," a program developed by anthropologists for the education of school children in the United States. It provoked an outcry in Congress because they said anthropologists were subverting American ideology by teaching school children that other peoples' values were acceptable.

It is thus not the Amazonian countries alone that have these problems, but the Amazonian nations must rethink their own idea of themselves to make it possible for Indians, and other minority cultures, to become separate but equal. They will have to accept the idea of communal land tenure, for example, without insisting that this is communism. They must tolerate the idea of different customs without considering them as a bar to citizenship. Above all, they will have to accept and to deal with the Indian movements. They will have to revise their relationship with the Indians, who are no longer passive, but must be accepted as actors in the political process. Even social scientists and anthropologists interested in the problem have not yet quite got used to this.

I often speak to colleagues who say, "Well, there's a problem, you see, because when you deal with an Indian community nowadays, there's so much politicking going on, you don't know whether the leaders really represent the community. They can't agree among themselves about what they want." To this I can only reply that that is very much like the communities that we are used to dealing with in non-Indian society. We do not expect the communities we live in to be in total unanimity about everything. Why should we expect the same from Indian communities? It is once again a projection of an image of a sort of homogeneous, primitive, preindustrial society.

These comments imply that we will have to do a lot of rethinking. But it is possible, and it is our task to educate the public in general as well as learned opinion, so that it is no longer regarded as acceptable or natural, nor even as a sad necessity, to trample on Indian rights, or even on the rights of other non-Indian peoples. The two are closely interconnected. Hence, the tremendous importance of liberal legislation. It is tempting, as we look on in anguish at what is happening to the Indians, to sneer at the liberal legislation that is occasionally passed and say, "But it's not enforced at the frontier." History has shown that the frontier is always anti-Indian. We know that from the start. It is when the metropolis, too, is anti-Indian that the Indian societies suffer most. This was true in the Spanish Empire, and it was also true at the time of the worst excesses of the Serviço de Proteção aos Índios in Brazil, which took place at the height of repressive developmentalism in the national society at large.

It is only when the metropolis is liberal that it creates some sort of counterweight and exerts tension against the natural dynamic of the frontier. It is out of this tension that the Indians have a chance: no guarantee, but only a chance. And that is why the role of civil society, which was emphasized by so many of the papers in this section, is so important. That is why the Commissões Pro-Índio and the Indian organizations themselves are so critical. If a proper climate of opinion is created, then, and only then, can some sort of reasonable action follow.

Reasonable action *is* possible. The most remote tribal Indians are capable of adapting when they are no longer isolated, if they are given medical assistance, land guarantees, and educational help. These items are not too expensive to be included in development projects, and developmental strategies could very well be rethought to include them. Indeed, they are being so in some places. The World Bank has already shown the way by requiring such guarantees from the Brazilian government in their negotiations over a loan in the Northwest of Brazil. Similarly, in Peru USAID backed off its original ideas about what should be done in the Pichis Palcazu region. They are at least rethinking what is going to be done there in light of the response that they got from the Indians themselves and from the social scientists assisting them. In Ecuador, my colleague Ted McDonald is working with governmental organizations to demarcate Indian lands. Indian peoples throughout the Americas have shown the ability to participate in, and contribute to, their national societies. It does not matter whether they are Shuar in Ecuador, Cuna in Panama, or Shavante in Brazil, they are quite capable of contributing if they are only given a reasonable opportunity to do so.

That means that we have to come up with strategies of development that offer reasonable and equitable opportunities to participate to all members of the society, both Indians and non-Indians. I do not think we can separate the two. It is precisely the society that is willing to step on the smallholders that is equally willing to step on the Indians. Our task is to analyze this phenomenon and to expose the false justifications that are offered by people in power and by the general public for what is happening to the Indians. Then we must persuade both the world at large and the people who have some influence over the destiny of the Indians that there are alternatives, viable alternatives, and we must help them come up with these alternatives. It is our task, above all, to support the seekers of those alternatives, most importantly the Indian organizations themselves, but also the other organizations such as the Commissões Pro-Índio, which are supporting the Indian organizations. They need more than our hearts at this moment. They need, as well, the best that our minds can offer them.

Colonization and
Spontaneous Settlement

PART 2

SMALL-FARMER MIGRANTS in the Amazon region of five different countries are the subjects of the following papers. Their authors have conducted extensive field research in the Amazon region. Instead of presenting particular findings, however, in these papers they have viewed colonization and spontaneous settlement broadly. They examine the complexities of these population movements in the frontier setting and seek out the implications of recent research findings for the design and implementation of national policies for development in the region. The issues are fundamental and difficult ones, and the authors have used their own direct experience as well as their knowledge of the scientific literature as the points of departure for analysis.

The broad view of colonization and spontaneous migration in each case places events related to the Amazon region within their larger national context. It necessarily includes a historical perspective on the role of Amazonia in the different nation-states that make up the region, and it implies a concern with the structural causes and characteristics of migration and settlement there. These essays move beyond the superficial affirmation that migration results from road construction or from other government-sponsored programs to ask what factors lie behind these initiatives in the first place. They focus on the elements that propel spontaneous migration into the rugged Amazon environment even in the absence of overt governmental policies. In so doing, they also examine the assertion heard in all five countries (Bolivia, Brazil, Ecuador, Colombia, and Peru) that occupation of the relatively unpopulated Amazon region constitutes a politically acceptable solution to the problems of population overconcentration, insufficiency of domestic production of food, and social unrest that plague the Amazon nations.

Charles Wood and John Wilson, writing about Brazil, focus on the question of the extent to which the Amazon region can realistically absorb excess population from other regions of Brazil. Using data from Brazil's recent censuses, they find the size of the nation's surplus population to far surpass the population that the Amazon region is capable of absorbing. A similar finding emerges from the empirical work of Carlos Aramburú writing about Peru: despite massive migration into the Amazon region in recent decades, the population absorbed in Peru's *selva alta* still accounted for less than 10 percent of the country's overall growth in population. Donald Sawyer's essay on the expansion and contraction of Brazil's Amazon frontier similarly concludes that the region cannot hold the solutions to other regions' problems of insufficient food production and overpopulation. His findings are especially important since national policies for the Amazon region consistently claim these as objectives.

In discussions of the evolution of frontier settlements, the papers in this section also call attention to the complexities of frontier movement and consolidation. Most models of frontier expansion posit a succession of stages in a progressive forward movement. In the initial stage the frontier is isolated from the national system of production and distribution. Traditional extractive activities exist, but there is no market for land or for labor. Peasant migrants informally appropriate state property for the production of subsistence crops plus a small marketable surplus. Labor exchange, clientage, debt relations, and forced labor are common forms of labor control. In the subsequent stage (or stages, depending on the scheme adopted), agriculture is capitalized and the newly settled region is progressively linked to the national economy. Concurrently, there is heavy in-migration, an increase in the price of land, and the emergence of a wage labor market. Although the petty commodity sector persists and may even expand, capitalist social relations of production become dominant.

The reorganization of the structure of production and accumulation, which defines the stages of the moving frontier, does not occur without social conflict. In the later stages, antagonism is concretely expressed in the struggle for land, a form of class conflict especially salient on the frontier. Disputed claims are resolved through violence or through face-to-face negotiation between the various parties. In other instances the state is more directly involved via the intervention of bureaucratic or legal institutions (see Santos and Martins in part 4 of this volume).

Stage models of frontier settlement typically presume a unilinear transition from one form of production to another. Sawyer's analysis goes beyond this limiting assumption. The novelty of his approach is to conceptualize in a single framework both the ebb and flow of migration into the Brazilian Amazon. Sawyer's thesis for the Brazilian case is that the increasing concentration of capitalist markets in the most recent stage of that country's development has provoked an actual retraction in productive occupation of the frontier. As new land is increasingly held by speculators, neither peasants nor capitalist firms can put it to productive use. Aramburú finds in Peru a similar complexity in the simultaneous incorporation and degradation of frontier lands.

Aramburú, Sutti Ortiz, Allyn Stearman, and Jorge Uquillas respectively draw on material from Peru, Colombia, Bolivia, and Ecuador to outline the distinct phases of small-farmer settlement. Movement through these various phases entails considerable spatial dislocation within the settlement area itself. Their analyses illustrate the complex motives and strategies that lead small farmers to move from subsistence crops to the planting of pasture and the impediments to their success in either farming or ranching. In later stages of settlement, these authors find, as Sawyer does for Brazil, an increasing concentration of landownership and accelerated depletion of soils, on the one hand, and a growth of population concentration in small and middle-sized urban centers, on the other.

It is during the later phases of settlement that internal differentiation of the settler population becomes most evident and that small-farmer migrants are increasingly joined by frontier settlers from other social groups. Aramburú and Ortiz suggest that as urban centers grow, more prosperous migrants move into them, leaving their less successful neighbors in rural areas where soils are slowly being depleted. Stearman finds that, in Bolivia, the secondary regrowth or *barbecho* crisis forces farmers either to enter cattle ranching (if they have sufficient capital) or to abandon their plots and move on. Ortiz similarly finds availability of capital to be the limiting factor in the success of small-scale cattle ranching in Colombia. Aramburú suggests that in Peru later migrants move in to occupy plots already depleted and abandoned by their predecessors. It is the least powerful small-farmer migrants who are unable to hold their own as tenure becomes formalized and landownership more concentrated. At this stage, competition for land between different social groups may lead to out-migration or to serious social tensions, or both (as noted by Aramburú for Peru, Ortiz for Colombia, and Sawyer for Brazil). While their analyses differ somewhat, taken together these case studies underscore the importance of viewing frontier settlement as a process whose character evolves in sometimes contradictory ways, thus presenting a changing social and natural environment for migrants.

The diversity of characteristics of small-farmer migrants is recognized by many of the authors in this section. What these settlers have in common, as discussed by Aramburú and Sawyer, is a production system primarily based on family labor and direct control over the means of production. Unlike the classic conception of peasants, however, Amazon migrants are also linked to some degree to markets for commodities, capital, land, and labor. Despite the autonomy and resilience of the family-based farm, access to these resources can be crucial for survival in the frontier system. As Emilio Moran's paper points out, a colonist's future success in agricultural production is more adequately predicted on the basis of past success in manipulating these markets than on the characteristics (such as family size or region of origin) commonly used as criteria for colonist selection.

A more realistic assessment of the potential offered by the Amazon region and its settlers is needed. Given the large scale of the problems faced by Amazon settlers, governmental programs can be expected to provide little more than palliatives and these only to a limited number of farmers. Still, while the agricultural development of the region cannot be construed as a solution for serious structural problems outside its boundaries, the authors suggest practical ways in which the populations that do move into the region might be more adequately assisted in their efforts to survive and prosper. As pointed out by Uquillas, and as more fully addressed in parts 1 and 3 of this volume, policies dealing directly or indirectly with colonization must come to grips with the potential threat it poses to indigenous inhabitants and to the complex ecology of the region. Furthermore, for programs targeted at small-farmer colonization, the authors stress the importance of recognizing the heterogeneous nature of their social and economic existence. The papers by Aramburú, Ortiz, and Moran especially argue that a more accurate understanding of the characteristics and goals of small farmers would allow planners to design support systems to suit their particular needs. On the whole, there is agreement that governments should deemphasize ambitious and paternalistic approaches to small-farmer colonization and stress instead the importance of local input into program decisions and of support for spontaneous migrants. Drawing on his experience with the Transamazon colonization project in Brazil and on his analysis of the repeated errors in planning in this and other colonization programs, Moran proposes a planning model that would permit a more flexible and incremental, and therefore realistic and adaptable, approach.

If we stand back from the specifics of each analysis, the papers in this section help us to place the fate of the small-farmer migrant in perspective. They demonstrate that the behavior of settlers is conditioned by complex historical and structural factors, which have also led the governments of several Amazon nations, at different historical moments and to different degrees, to stimulate settlement of relatively remote jungle areas. Often seen as the solution to persistent national problems, the settlement programs designed to encourage these migrants have rarely addressed their needs and capabilities effectively. A more realistic assessment of their situation, and of what can and cannot be achieved through occupation of the Amazon, should inform practical recommendations to better serve the interests of pioneers who have already made the region their home.

The Magnitude of Migration to the Brazilian Frontier

Charles H. Wood and John Wilson

B RAZIL'S CURRENT initiative to populate its vast northern
territories is hardly a new concern. For geopolitical reasons the settlement of the country's hinterland has been considered a priority since the colonial period. But in recent years this
issue has taken on a new dimension, one more directly associated
with the country's contemporary patterns of population growth
and distribution. The unprecedented magnitude of rural-to-urban
migration and the problems associated with the rapid expansion of
metropolitan areas in central and southern Brazil are among the
demographic realities that have stimulated the formulation of major policy initiatives.

Kubitschek's decision in the late 1950s to move the nation's
capital thousands of kilometers westward from Rio de Janeiro to
Brasília and the completion in the 1960s of the highway linking
the newly constructed capital to the northern city of Belém were
among the earlier attempts to interiorize the population. In 1970
the Program for National Integration (PIN) was launched by President Médici with a similar purpose in mind. The cornerstones of
PIN, which included the Transamazon Highway and the creation
of colonization projects, were designed to relieve demographic
pressure in the densely populated Northeast and to shift the flow
of migrants away from the urban South to the relatively unoccupied regions of Amazonia. More recently, policies supporting

semidirected colonization have been concentrated in Rondônia (see Moran, this volume).

The policies noted above raise a number of questions that have received little systematic attention. In the wake of the dramatic expansion of the frontier in the 1970s, much of the research effort has justifiably centered on the social and economic changes *within* Amazonia. But, to the extent that the frontier itself is part of the overall demographic context of Brazil, such a focus is incomplete. It is apparent, for example, that an assessment of the role of colonization and spontaneous settlement, either as a solution to demographic pressure or as a means to redirect population movement, cannot be made in the absence of an analysis of the demographic characteristics of the country as a whole. It is to this task that the following analysis is directed.

If the opening of the Amazon frontier is to have an appreciable effect on rural-to-urban migration in Brazil, as the rationale for many policies would have it, it must absorb a significant proportion of the country's excess rural population. From this standpoint the first step in our analysis is to estimate the magnitude of Brazil's rural exodus during the 1960s and 1970s. These values, in turn, serve as reference points by which to evaluate recent trends in Amazonia. The analysis presented later shows that the volume of the urbanward flow is so large that it far exceeds the capacity of the frontier to absorb population. These findings are significant in that they provide quantitative estimates that serve to inform the current debate over the style of development appropriate to Amazonia and to the nation. The data unequivocally support the conclusion that the frontier cannot be viewed as a realistic solution to the problem of population pressure and to the longstanding structural factors (principally the concentration of land ownership) that characterize rural Brazil.

The rural exodus, 1960–70 and 1970–80

In the absence of direct information regarding geographical mobility in Brazil, estimates of net migration can be derived from a number of indirect techniques. A common approach is the residual method. In a closed population (no migration in or out) population growth is due solely to the rate of natural increase of the population (the excess of births over deaths). In an open population, subject to in- and out-migration, population growth is due to the combined effects of natural increase and net migration. These two components of population growth can be separated using a population projection. The age distribution of the population (at time 1), together with estimates of the level of fertility (total fertility rate, age specific fertility rates) and mortality (a life table), provide the basis for projecting the size of a population forward. The projected size of population at time 2 is the expected number of inhabitants due to natural increase alone. The projected population minus the actual number of persons enumerated at time 2 provides an estimate of net migration. Hence, the magnitude of net migration is computed as the residual between the total change in population during an intercensal period and the change that is due to natural increase.

Estimates of the volume of net rural to urban migration in Brazil are given in Table 1. The total rural population in 1960 was 38,767,000 (row 1). Estimates of rural fertility and mortality for the decade were used to project the population forward ten years.[1] On the basis of these vital rates, the expected number of rural inhabitants in 1970 was 54,844,000 (row 2). This value is consider-

TABLE 1. Estimates of net rural-to-urban migration, Brazil, 1960–70 and 1970–80

Row number		Numbers in thousands	Rate
	1960–70		
1	Rural population in 1960	38,767	
2	Projected rural population in 1970	54,844	
3	Actual population in 1970	41,054	
4	Net migrants (row 3 minus row 2)	−13,790	
5	Net migration rate[a]		−35.6
	1970–80		
6	Rural population in 1970	41,054	
7	Projected population in 1980	55,944	
8	Actual population in 1980	38,616	
9	Net migrants (row 8 minus row 7)	−17,328	
10	Net migration rate[b]		−42.2

SOURCE: Fundação IBGE, Demographic Census for 1960 and 1970; advanced tabulations for 1980.

a. Rate = (net migrants 1960–70)/(rural population 1960) × 100.
b. Rate = (net migrants 1970–80)/(rural population 1970) × 100.

ably above the actual number of people recorded in the countryside by the 1970 census (41,054,000) (row 6). The actual 1970
population minus the projected number in 1970 is an estimate of
net rural-to-urban movement (row 4). Between 1960 and 1970,
rural Brazil experienced a net loss of approximately 13,790,000
people. If we assume that the rate of out-migration was constant
over the period, these estimates imply an annual departure of well
over 1.3 million persons.

Turning to the preliminary results of the 1980 census, it is apparent that the rural area of Brazil is increasingly *less* capable of
maintaining population. For the first time in the history of the
country, census data indicate an absolute decline in the number of
persons enumerated in the countryside. Whereas the rural population was 41,054,000 in 1970, ten years later it had fallen to
38,620,000 (row 8), an annual change of −6.1 per thousand. A decline in the total number of rural dwellers implies that the magnitude of the rural exodus was so large during the 1970s that it
drained off from the countryside all of the demographic growth
that was due to natural increase plus additional population.

Estimates for 1970−80 indicate a net loss of 17,328,000 over
the decade (row 9). Compared to the 1960s (row 4), the absolute
number of net out-migrants rose 3.5 million during the 1970s.
This is reflected in a change in the rate of net migration (per 100
inhabitants), which increased from −35.6 in 1960−70 to −42.2 in
1970−80.

The frontier in national perspective

Given the vast expanse of available land in Amazonia, the ambitious development projects adopted in the 1970s appeared to
present a plausible solution to the problems of population pressure
and rural out-migration in the northeastern region and in other
densely settled areas of Brazil. Moreover, these initiatives were politically appealing for many reasons, not the least of which was
that they appeared to come to grips with the problem of rural development without facing the risks involved in altering the land
tenure system through agrarian reform. But can the opening of the
Amazon be considered a solution to these issues? A preliminary
answer to this question can be formulated by placing the colonization projects and the spontaneous occupation of the northern region into a broader demographic perspective. More specifically, the

empirical results presented in the previous section provide reference points for a more detailed investigation of the implications of
recent trends in the Amazon frontier.

Official colonization projects

In 1970 the newly installed president, General Médici, announced
the National Integration Plan (PIN), a decision that was to alter the
character of state involvement in the planning and execution of
development projects in the Amazon. PIN called for the construction of the Transamazon and the Cuiabá-Santarém highways and
declared a commitment to finance and administer (through the
National Institute of Colonization and Agrarian Reform [INCRA])
the colonization of lands made accessible by the new roads. The
goal of the colonization project was to settle 100,000 families between 1971 and 1974. However, by 1977 INCRA had succeeded in
distributing lots to only 7,839 families in Marabá, Altamira, and
Itaituba, the three colonization projects along the Transamazon. If
we include all federal colonization projects in the northern region
(mostly in Rondônia), the figure reaches 24,242 families (Arruda
1978, cited by Sawyer in this volume).

The reasons underlying the problems INCRA encountered in
its settlement effort and the sociopolitical factors that contributed
in the mid-1970s to a shift in development priorities away from
small-farmer schemes are critical issues that we will leave aside.
Instead, let us take at face value the original goal of the colonization projects carried out under the aegis of PIN. The target of settling 100,000 families by 1974 was, no doubt, more in the nature
of political rhetoric than a carefully formulated estimate of an at-
tainable objective. Yet, even if INCRA had fully succeeded in this
attempt, it is our conclusion that the colonization project would
have made little difference, at least in terms of the program's stated
objectives.

This can be demonstrated by turning to the findings presented
in the previous section. Consider, for example, the volume of net
rural-to-urban migration in 1960–70 and 1970–80. As noted in
Table 1, the total number of net migrants was 13,790,000 in the
1960s and approximately 17,328,000 in the following decade. To
convert these figures into a more meaningful statistic, we can divide them by the average household size in rural Brazil (5.2), thus
yielding a rough estimate of the number of households involved in
this migration flow (2,651,923 in 1960–70; 3,332,230 in 1970–

80). Using these figures as a base, we can say that, if PIN had been executed as planned, the program would have absorbed 3.8 percent of the rural to urban flow in the 1960s and 3.0 percent of the movement in the 1970s.

If we use as the basis of comparison the *actual* number of families settled through 1977, the findings are even more extreme. The 7,839 households established in the first seven years of PIN represent only 0.2 percent of the rural exodus between 1970 and 1980. Similarly, the 24,242 families, which represent the total number settled in the entire northern region, are less than one percent (0.7) of the net rural exodus during the decade of the 1970s.

Total net migration to Amazonia

The colonization projects are only one aspect of the potential for labor absorption on the Amazon frontier. In addition to the families who directly participated in the government-sponsored programs, many more migrated to the North in search of land. Because the demand for lots in the official projects far exceeded the supply, migrant families often cleared whatever land was accessible and unoccupied. In many instances these lots were simultaneously (or subsequently) claimed by ranchers and other powerful interest groups, a situation that largely accounts for the intense land conflicts on the frontier (see Schmink 1982). Since the colonization projects were relatively small by comparison, it is generally understood that the volume of this unplanned settlement process during the 1970s accounted for the bulk of the migration flow to Amazonia.

The number of in-migrants who established lots beyond the boundaries of the official colonization areas or who moved to urban settings in the region was impossible to approximate prior to the 1980 census. The publication of these data, however, permit rough estimates of the magnitude of the total net migration that took place in the recent period. The method adopted follows the same principle as that used previously. In this case, the vital rates (fertility and morality) that correspond to each state or territory are used to project its population ten years forward. Using the logic of the residual approach, the difference between the projected value and the actual population enumerated at the end of the decade is attributed to net population movement.[2]

Table 2 presents the results of the analysis for the states and territories that comprise Amazonia and the Central West. Goiás

TABLE 2. Net migration in Amazonia and Central West, 1970–80

REGION: State or territory[a]	Population 1970 (1)	Population, 1980		Net migrants	
		Projected (2)	Actual[b] (3)	(3) − (2) (4)	Rate[c] (5)
AMAZONIA:					
Acre, Amapá, Roraima, Rondônia	481,607	693,312	1,049,202	+355,890	+203.5
Amazonas	955,253	1,399,715	1,432,066	+ 32,351	+ 3.4
Pará	2,167,018	3,033,674	3,411,868	+378,194	+ 17.5
All Amazonia	3,603,878	5,126,701	5,893,136	+766,435	+ 21.3
CENTRAL-WEST					
Mato Grosso[d]	1,597,090	2,093,566	2,511,994	+418,428	+ 26.2
Goiás	2,938,677	4,000,620	3,865,482	−135,138	− 4.6
All Central-West	4,535,767	6,094,186	6,377,476	+283,290	+ 6.2
All Amazonia and Central-West	8,139,645	11,220,887	12,270,612	+1,049,725	+ 12.9

SOURCE: Fundação IBGE, Demographic Census for 1970; advanced tabulations for 1980.

a. The advanced tabulations of the 1980 census permit fertility and mortality estimates only for the combined areas of Acre, Amapá, Roraima, and Rondônia. For the purposes of this analysis, they are therefore treated as a single population.

b. From advanced tabulations of the 1980 census, subject to revision.

c. Net migration rate = [(net migrants, 1970–80)/(total population, 1970)] × 100.

d. Includes Mato Grosso and Mato Grosso do Sul.

experienced a net loss of about 135,138 people (col. 4). This net out-migration is a reversal in direction of the population movement recorded in the 1960s, when Goiás was an area of intense occupation. The shift from net in- to net out-migration reflects the northward and westward trajectory of the moving frontier during the 1960s and 1970s.

In 1970–80 Mato Grosso gained population through migration (+418,428), as did Amazonia. Between 1970 and 1980 the population of Pará increased by 378,194 as a result of population movement. The highest rate of in-migration (+203.5) occurred in Acre, Amapá, Roraima, and Rondônia (net in-migration of 355,890). The aggregation of these areas in the advanced tabulations of the 1980 census obscures substantial variation among the various territories. Although difficult to quantify precisely, it is clear that the bulk of the in-migration flow was directed toward Rondônia, an area of frontier expansion in the 1970s.

An estimate of the total number of net migrants to Amazonia is shown in Table 2. Using the residual method, the data indicate a net increase of 766,435 people as a result of migration. This implies a total of about 147,000 households (assuming an average household size of 5.2). The relatively small size of these values is to be noted. The decade of the 1970s was, after all, a period of intense activity in the region. The highway construction projects, the colonization schemes, and the spontaneous migration into the region were among the most salient factors that altered the demographic profile of the area. But despite these events, Amazonia apparently absorbed only a relatively limited number of people. This can be seen by turning, again, to the figures presented in the earlier section. Using the estimates in Table 1 as a reference point, we can say that the total in-migration into Amazonia over the entire decade represents a value that is only about half of the volume of rural to urban migration in Brazil in a single year (1.7 million). Similarly, the estimated influx of population in Amazonia in the 1970s (766,435) is a figure that is less than 5 percent of Brazil's total rural exodus during the ten-year period (17.3 million). Even if the reference point is more broadly defined to include both Amazonia and the Central West, the conclusion remains the same. The total number of in-migrants for the two regions combined (1,049,725) is substantially lower than the yearly number of people who exited the rural area in the 1970s and represents only 6 percent of the total rural exodus in Brazil during the decade.

TABLE 3. Rates of increase for rural and urban areas in Amazonia
and Central-West, 1970–80

REGION: State or territory	Annual percentage increase, 1970–80		Percentage urban		Change in percentage urban
	Rural (1)	Urban (2)	1970 (3)	1980 (4)	(4) − (3) (5)
AMAZONIA:					
Rondônia	17.6	14.6	53.6	47.3	− 6.3
Acre	0.8	8.3	27.6	43.8	16.2
Amazonas	0.4	7.8	42.5	60.0	17.5
Roraima	2.6	10.8	42.8	48.9	6.1
Pará	4.3	5.0	47.2	48.9	1.7
Amapá	3.3	5.2	54.6	59.2	4.6
CENTRAL-WEST:					
Mato Grosso	2.8	10.9	38.8	57.5	18.7
Mato Grosso do Sul	− 1.9	7.3	45.3	67.1	21.8
Goiás	− 1.5	6.9	42.1	62.2	20.1

SOURCE: Fundação IBGE, Demographic Census for 1970; advanced
tabulations for 1980.

It is important to note that the expansion of the frontier into
the Center West and Amazonia does not imply, as one might expect, an increasingly rural population. To the contrary, with the
exception of Rondônia, estimates of the rate of population growth
from 1970 to 1980 are consistently higher in urban than in rural
areas, as shown in Table 3. This is especially true in the Central
West. In Mato Grosso, Mato Grosso do Sul, and Goiás, the urban
percentage rose between 18 and 22 points. A similar increase took
place in Acre and Amazonas and, to a lesser degree, in Roraima,
Pará, and Amapá. Changes in the spatial distribution of the population in frontier areas thus appear to reproduce the highly urban
character of the population found in the rest of Brazil.

Conclusion

Taken together, the analysis of the colonization projects and the
estimates of the overall rate of in-migration to the frontier area
suggest the same conclusion. Although these events have profoundly affected the socioeconomic, ecological, and demographic

character of Amazonia, the number of persons absorbed by the frontier is minimal relative to the magnitude of population growth and the size of the rural-to-urban migration stream.

The implications of these results are far reaching. Political discourse as well as popular perceptions of the frontier invoke the notion of the hinterland as a solution to population pressure in the already-settled rural areas. Associated with this assumption is the idea that urban underemployment and unemployment, exacerbated by the cityward flow of migrants from the countryside, can be effectively resolved by redirecting migration streams to newly opened territories.

The apparent plausibility of this solution is undoubtedly one reason why such conceptualizations of the frontier regularly make their appearance in the planning documents of virtually every Amazonian country that has taken initiatives to populate its lowland areas. But the persistence of this common theme can also be traced to the ideological role that it plays in the formulation and the execution of development policy. To envision the frontier as a collecting basin for surplus population effectively shifts the object of intervention away from the structural factors that cause this surplus to begin with. Key among these factors are the extreme concentration of land ownership (see Guimarães 1977, Graziano da Silva 1978, Hoffman 1979, 1975) and the mechanization of agricultural production (see Lopes 1977).

From this standpoint, frontier schemes that profess to resolve the problem of population pressure can be viewed as concrete manifestations of the overall ideological framework that orients public policy. While this conceptualization of the frontier may well serve those interest groups with a stake in the status quo, the empirical analysis presented here leaves little doubt that, in the absence of fundamental reform, Amazonia's capacity to absorb surplus labor is little more than false rhetoric.

Notes

1. Input data for the projection include: rural age distribution, by sex, 1960, from the 1960 census; total fertility rate and age specific fertility rates for rural Brazil, 1960–70; rural life expectancy, by sex, 1960–70 (Carvalho 1977); South model life table.

2. Fertility declined sharply in Brazil in the 1970s (Carvalho 1980). Since the rate of net migration is a residual between the actual and the projected population, lower fertility (by reducing the size of the projected population) results in a higher rate of in-migration. The fall in mortality has the opposite effect. Changes in vital rates during the 1970s are taken into account in this analysis.

References Cited

Arruda, H.P.
1978   *Colonização Oficial e Dirigida*. Brasília: INCRA.
Carvalho, J.A.
1977   *Relatório de Pesquisa: Fecundidade e Mortalidade no Brasil—1960/1970*. Belo Horizonte, Brazil: CEDEPLAR.
1980   Evolução Demográfica Recente no Brasil. *Pesquisa e Planejamento Econômico* 10(2):527–54.
Graziano da Silva, J.F. (coordinator)
1978   *Estrutura Agrária e Produção de Subsistência na Agricultura Brasileira*. São Paulo: Hucitec.
Guimarães, A.P.
1977   *Quatro Séculos de Latifúndio*. Rio: Paz e Terra.
Hoffmann, R.
1979   A Concentração da Posse da Terra no Brasil. *Encontros com a Civilização Brasileira* 7:207–21.
Hoffman, R. and J.F. Graziano da Silva
1975   A Estrutura Agrária Brasileira. In *Tecnologia e Desenvolvimento Agrícola*. C.B. Contador, ed. Pp. 233–65. Rio: IPEA/INPES, Monograph No. 17.
Lopes, Juaréz R.B.
1977   Empresas e Pequenos Produtores no Desenvolvimento do Capitalismo Agrário em São Paulo (1940–1970). *Estudos CEBRAP* 22 (Oct.–Dec.):41–110.
Prado Junior, Caio
1978   *História Econômica do Brasil*. São Paulo: Brasiliense (21st edition).
Schmink, Marianne
1982   Land Conflicts in Amazonia. *American Ethnologist* 9:341–57.

Expansion of the Agrarian and Demographic Frontier in the Peruvian Selva

Carlos E. Aramburú

A MAZONIA is now in vogue. It is a rare day when the press, radio, and television do not offer some news of a new highway project, the departure of new colonists, or the vicissitudes of petroleum exploration in this region. Amazonia has been recently discovered by the inhabitants of the coastal cities and by their governors in turn. To what do we owe this growing interest in the jungle? Is it truly the Promised Land and the solution to the grave problems of overpopulation, food shortage, and unequal distribution that plague the Peruvian population? What is the potential for success of an official policy intent on the introduction of the "spirit of capitalism" and big business, and which marginalizes the peasant-colonist and the native in its development plans? These are a few of the many questions surrounding Amazonia that we propose to consider in this brief essay.

In an effort to construct a historical synthesis, the phenomena that first come clearly to our attention are the qualitative and quantitative changes in the region over the past thirty to forty years. Although the earliest intrusions of foreign populations into Amazonia date from pre-Hispanic times (Camino 1976), and although missionaries and Spanish military had penetrated deep into the Amazon Valley (Rumrrill 1974), the massive Andean exodus to the selva alta is a recent phenomenon. Until the middle of this century, the expansion of the economic frontier during the cycles of quinine, *barbasco*, rubber, timber, and animal hide extraction did not lead to the expansion of the demographic frontier. Extractive activities reordered and on occasion decimated the regional native populations without provoking a massive influx of migrants (Varese 1974).

National transformations, which began during the third decade of this century, are, we believe, the changes that pushed the Andean population into the selva alta. First we may attribute the rapid process of population growth in Peru since the 1940s to a sharp decline in mortality and a fertility rate that has remained high until very recently. Parallel to this process we find, since the end of the past century, an expansion of *haciendas* and a concentration of land ownership in the Peruvian Andes. Both processes contributed to the impoverishment of the peasant population, causing the rural exodus that acquired, during the 1960s, the characteristics of a flood. Migration is not due to factors of expulsion alone. The diffusion of education and the rapid acculturation of the Andean population, as well as the expansion of penetration highways from the coast to the jungle, are factors of attraction that condition the attitude of and the means by which the Andean peasant becomes a migrant.

Until the 1950s, development in the Amazon occupied a secondary place in the political panorama. The problems of urban saturation, food deficits for an urban population that was doubling every fourteen years, and conservative interests opposed to profound agrarian reform led to the adoption of the colonizing of Amazonia as a solution to these difficulties and as a substitute for change in the structure of landholdings.

Two political events were of great importance to the future of the Peruvian selva. One was the Treaty of Amazonic Cooperation signed by eight countries having Amazonian territories (Bolivia, Brazil, Colombia, Ecuador, Guyana, Peru, Surinam, and Venezuela). This international mechanism began operation with a first technical meeting in Lima in August of 1981. It would be premature to draw any conclusions concerning the impact of this treaty, due to the habitually slow implementation of such international agreements. Scientific investigation and development, one of five areas given priority, is being implemented through bilateral accords.

The second political event relevant to Amazonia is the re-initiation, since the return to power in July of 1980 of President

Fig. 1. Peru: departments and natural regions.

Fernando Belaunde Terry, of programs for road building and for the expansion of the agrarian frontier. This event has revived the debate over the potential for Amazonia in national development. Not only have plans for the development of roads and infrastructure been revived, so also has the thesis that the Peruvian selva is the principal agrarian and demographic frontier—supposedly "empty" and "unpopulated"—for the reorientation of surplus rural and urban population.

These plans have the support of important financial sources (above all, USAID and the World Bank) for the development or reactivation of colonization projects in the selva alta (such as Palcazu-Pichis in the Department of Pasco in the central selva, and Alto and Medio Huallaga in the Departments of Huanuco and San Martín Selva). The significant financial assistance of the United States government can be explained by the pressure of the U.S. Congress for the eradication of coca cultivation. The Peruvian government has mounted campaigns of eradication and police control, which appear to have had greater psychological than direct impact on the decrease of illegal coca cultivation.

The factors mentioned above have stimulated the process of spontaneous colonization of the Peruvian selva during the last few decades. In the remainder of this paper, the demographic, economic, and sociocultural characteristics of the population taking part in this colonization are reviewed. The historical dynamics of occupation of the Amazon region are analyzed, with special emphasis on the movement of Andean migrants into the selva alta. Against this background, a theoretical interpretation is offered of the prevailing form of socioeconomic reproduction in these areas of colonization and of the nature of its articulation with the national society and economy. The concluding section synthesizes the practical policy implications derived from these findings.

Population process and expansion of the demographic frontier

As we have noted, even well into the twentieth century, the economic cycles of the Peruvian Amazon did not result in the expansion of the demographic frontier. It was not until the 1940s and 1950s that the regional population began to grow rapidly. Between 1940 and 1981 the population of the selva grew from little more than 400,000 inhabitants to over 1,800,000 (see Table 1). In relative terms, the Amazonian population increased from 6.7 percent

TABLE 1. Peru's population size and growth, by natural regions, 1940–81

Natural region	1940		1961		1972		1981		Annual growth rate		
	Population	%	Population	%	Population	%	Population	%	1940–61	1961–72	1972–81
Coast	1,759,573	28.3	3,859,443	39.0	6,242,993	46.1	8,512,944	50.0	3.8	4.5	3.5
[Lima]	[645,172]	[10.4]	[1,845,910]	[18.7]	[3,302,523]	[24.4]	[4,600,891]	[27.0]	[5.1]	[5.5]	[3.7]
Sierra	4,033,952	65.0	5,182,093	52.3	5,953,293	44.0	6,704,390	39.4	1.2	1.2	1.3
Selva	414,452	6.7	865,210	8.7	1,341,922	9.9	1,813,887	10.6	3.6	4.1	3.4
All Peru	6,207,977	100.0	9,906,746	100.0	13,538,208	100.0	17,031,221	100.0	2.2	2.9	2.6

SOURCE: Instituto Nacional de Estadística. *Perú: Algunas Características de la Población* (Resultados Provisionales del Censo del 12 de Julio de 1981). Boletín Especial—No. 6. Lima, October 1981:28, table 8.

of the total population to 10.6 percent at the end of this period. The absolute increase over these forty years was almost 1,400,000 inhabitants—or 4.4 times the size of the original population. We should recall that during this same period the Peruvian population went through a demographic transition, which began with a brisk decline in mortality (mainly between 1940 and 1960) and later showed a slight decline in fertility (after 1970). This has meant rapid population growth over the past forty years, peaking between 1961 and 1972, when the annual growth rate climbed to 2.9 percent.

Analyzing the rates of population increase over large natural regions, we can show that during the last three intercensal periods the growth rate of the Amazonian population has exceeded the growth rate of the total population. The difference between the growth rates of the Amazonian and national populations was greatest in the period 1940–61. During this period the Amazonian population showed a growth rate 64 percent higher than that of the nation as a whole. The difference fell to 41 percent during the period 1961–72, and to 31 percent in the period 1972–81. This would indicate that, although the Amazonian population has grown more rapidly than the total population since 1940, the difference appears to be diminishing. This is attributed to a decline in the annual growth rate of the regional population, which was 3.6 percent in the period 1940–61, rose to 4.1 percent between 1961 and 1972, and later declined to 3.4 percent in the last decade. The period 1960–70 marks the culmination of the penetration process into Amazonia and the period of its greatest vegetative growth.

It is likewise interesting to note from the figures in Table 1 that the demographic growth of the selva is only slightly inferior to that of the coastal region. Both zones have been receiving population from the sierra (the mountain region), which has been expelling population since 1940. In the past decade we see a decline in the population growth rates nationally and by region—with the exception of the sierra, which has shown a slow but constant growth. Lacking data on the evolution of vital rates during the last period and on the rate of census omission, it is difficult to estimate the weight of these factors in the decline of the demographic growth rate observed in the last intercensal period. In any case, it should be noted that the population count in July of 1981 (17,031,221 inhabitants) is much inferior to the projections based on the 1972 census, which had estimated for 1981 a population between 17.8 and 18.3 million (The Futures Group 1981).

The growth of the population and its regional distribution have responded to great regional differences in economic and demographic conditions. Table 2 presents a few indicators of population in the three large regions of Peru. In relation to indicators of mortality, we observe that the selva shows a level falling between that of the most developed region, the coast, and that of the most deprived, the sierra. With respect to the birth rate, however, the selva has the highest of all three. The crude birth rate is almost forty-five births per thousand inhabitants, the total fertility rate is 7.3 children per woman, and the proportion less than fifteen years of age is 48.6 percent of the regional population. Altogether this seems to indicate that the Amazonic population still remains in the early stages of the demographic transition—i.e., it has had a recent decline in mortality and has high levels of fertility due to early and universal marriage and to uncontrolled reproduction.

With regard to the spatial distribution of the Amazonian pop-

TABLE 2. Demographic and socioeconomic indicators,
by natural regions

Indicator	Costa	Sierra	Selva	All Peru
1. Crude mortality rate, 1970–75	8.9	17.1	13.3	13.0
2. Infant mortality rate, 1970–75	62.9	156.2	127.7	113.7
3. Life expectancy, 1970–75	62.0	50.2	53.8	55.2
4. Crude birth rate, 1975	31.0	44.6	44.9	38.2
5. Total fertility rate, 1975	4.2	7.0	7.3	5.6
6. Percent population under 15 years old, 1980	40.5	44.6	48.6	42.8
7. Inhabitants per sq km, 1981	53.0	17.3	2.5	13.3
8. Percent EAP in agriculture, 1981	16.8	63.9	59.6	38.4
9. Percent illiteracy (in population over 15 years old), 1972	13.5	44.3	24.8	27.6

SOURCES: INE, 1981:6, table 2, and III:15. Lima, June 1981.

ulation, one frequently encounters the opinion that the region is unpopulated. The figures in Table 2 (row 7) appear to confirm this since the population density in 1981 was only 2.5/km². This is seven times less than the sierra and twenty-one times less than the coastal region. Nevertheless, if we consider the population distribution within Amazonia, we find a high concentration in areas that are favored ecologically, economically, and socially, such as the banks of large rivers. In effect, 87 percent of the regional population lives on the margins of the great rivers, such as the Amazon, the Ucayali, and the Huallaga (CENCIRA 1974). Along these narrow riverine strips—the "varzea" (Meggers 1971)—the soils are more fertile and permit more intensive annual agriculture, especially on the *barriales,* or submersed islets. Also, fish are abundant and more accessible, and communication is easier since the rivers are the roadways of Amazonia. The riverine concentration of the Amazonian population reflects as much an ancestral adaptive pattern as it does the appearance of a new urban network that, as we shall see farther on, has shown a very dynamic growth in the past few years.

According to national census figures, the selva is embracing a growing proportion of the total population of Amazonia. Growth has been more pronounced in the selva alta (or Ceja de Selva) compared to the selva baja (or Amazonian plain). The Ceja de Selva increased its share of the Amazon population from 38.4 percent in 1940 to 58 percent in 1981. The population of the selva alta grew at an annual rate of 4.1 percent in the period 1940–61, increasing to 5 percent in the period 1961–72 and falling again to 4.2 percent in the period 1972–81. These rates of demographic increase are higher than the national average for this period and higher than the rates for the coastal region (see Table 1).

We have defined the selva alta as those provinces of the Andean eastern slopes whose capitals lie between 2,000 and 500 meters above sea level. This definition may seem arbitrary in strictly ecological terms, but our criteria have singled out those zones subject to the process of colonization that receive *Andean* immigrants. This dynamic of colonization from the Andes has been penetrating ever more deeply into Amazonia, most significantly in the valleys where the process first began. While the selva alta is receiving the larger part of spontaneous colonization, in many regions the Andean colonist is already reaching the Amazon plain. The rapid expansion of the demographic frontier in the selva alta may be explained primarily by the immigration of an Andean population, as we shall demonstrate below. The selva baja, on the contrary, shows much lower rates of demographic increase over the same period: 2.8 percent per year between 1940–61, 3.0 percent between 1961–72, and 2.5 percent between 1972–81. These growth rates may be attributed almost entirely to natural increase (births minus deaths) since they are quite similar to the average rates of increase for the total national population.

A gross estimate of migration in the selva alta for each year during the periods being considered may be obtained by subtracting the rate of natural increase observed for the selva baja from the overall rate of growth for the selva alta, then estimating the difference as a proportion of the total growth rate (selva alta) registered in the Census. It is assumed that (a) the selva baja sustained no growth due to migration and (b) the rates of natural increase observed for the selva baja are similar to those of the selva alta. Following this procedure we have estimated net migration, as a component of the total population growth of the selva alta, to be on the order of 32 percent between 1940 and 1961, 40 percent between 1961 and 1972, and 40.5 percent between 1972 and 1981. From these figures it becomes clear that migration is of growing importance in the expansion of the demographic frontier in the selva alta.

Colonization of the selva alta

From the available evidence it may be concluded that colonization in the Peruvian selva alta reached its peak during the 1960s. This period witnessed a massive mobilization of Andean peasants, who penetrated the eleven discrete river basins or valleys where colonization has occurred. Population movements from the Andes were motivated and consolidated during this decade by the important development of penetration roads into the selva alta. Likewise, these settlements were linked to the expansion of commercial crops such as coffee, rice, fruits, coca, and tea. These crops expanded the economic frontier and connected these zones to national and international markets. The selva alta therefore reveals a greater demographic and economic dynamism than the selva baja in recent years. There are, however, important variations internal to each subregion.

The question arises whether colonization of the selva alta constitutes an alternative for the resettlement of Andean migrants

TABLE 3. Population distribution and growth, subregions of the selva alta[a]

DEPARTMENT and province	Total population, 1981	Distribution in percent						Annual Growth Rate			
		1961		1972		1981		Urban		Rural	
		Urban	Rural	Urban	Rural	Urban	Rural	1961–72	1972–81	1961–72	1972–81
AMAZONAS											
Bagua	143,547	21.3	78.7	22.2	77.8	22.2	77.8	9.7	4.8	3.2	4.9
Bongará	14,235	71.3	28.7	63.4	36.6	59.2	40.8	2.9	2.7	6.4	4.7
CAJAMARCA											
Jaén	125,719	20.2	79.8	25.0	75.0	28.9	71.1	7.7	4.9	5.0	3.1
San Ignacio	84,502	9.9	90.1	10.1	89.9	11.4	88.6	8.6	5.6	8.4	4.1
CUZCO											
La Convención	106,967	17.0	83.0	16.8	83.2	20.2	79.8	2.7	4.8	2.9	2.2
HUÁNUCO											
Pachitea	42,980	10.8	89.2	11.9	88.1	10.2	89.8	2.6	4.5	1.6	3.6
Leoncio Prado	81,241	24.3	75.7	33.8	66.2	40.7	59.3	11.1	6.4	6.5	3.0
JUNÍN											
Satipo	64,595	20.3	79.7	21.1	78.9	23.5	76.5	9.6	7.4	9.1	5.7
Chanchamayo	98,508	17.8	82.2	22.8	77.2	22.9	77.1	7.9	6.6	4.8	7.1
MADRE DE DIOS											
Tambopata	24,873	39.7	60.3	37.9	62.1	50.7	49.3	4.3	9.4	5.0	3.2
PASCO											
Oxapampa	49,857	18.3	81.7	16.8	83.2	17.7	82.3	3.8	3.1	4.1	2.4
SAN MARTÍN											
Moyobamba	36,281	84.0	16.0	79.7	20.3	66.1	33.9	2.0	4.2	4.7	12.5
Mariscal Cáceres	54,231	53.6	46.4	42.9	57.1	41.3	58.7	3.2	4.0	7.4	4.7
Rioja	37,935	89.8	10.2	78.3	21.7	55.8	44.2	2.9	11.0	11.7	24.6
San Martín	95,265	68.0	32.0	69.6	30.4	71.6	28.4	3.6	3.5	2.9	2.4
All selva alta	1,059,686	30.7	69.3	30.1	69.9	32.1	67.9	4.9	4.8	5.1	3.9
All Peru	17,031,221	47.4	52.6	59.5	40.5	65.1	34.9	5.1	3.6	0.5	0.9

SOURCE: Elaborated from INE, 1981, table 3.

a. Selva alta provinces include those with all or most of their districts on the eastern slopes of the Andes between 500 and 2,000 meters above sea level.

or, in different terms, whether the selva alta has been capable of absorbing a significant part of the nation's demographic increase. While the population of the selva alta, as a percentage of the total population, has grown over the last forty years (from 6.7 percent of the total population increase between 1940 and 1961, to 8.6 percent between 1961 and 1972, and to 9.6 percent between 1972 and 1981), it nevertheless accounts for less than 10 percent of population growth even in the last decade. As for the importance of colonization in the selva alta as an alternative for the Andean migrant, our calculations show that less than one of five persons leaving the sierra during the last intercensal period chose the selva alta as their destination. The remaining four preferred the coastal region.

It is evident that the colonization process does not constitute an alternative to urbanward migration in the coastal region; furthermore, the selva alta itself is undergoing a process of urbanization (see Table 3). While the population of the selva alta remains predominantly rural (68 percent in 1981), the rate of growth of the urban population (4.8 percent) surpassed that of the rural population (3.9 percent) in the past decade. During the previous decade (1960–70) the rural population grew at an annual rate of 5.1 percent as compared to 4.9 percent for the urban population. The accelerated pace of urbanization in the selva alta, with rates exceeding the national mean, reflects the depletion of the agricultural frontier in the oldest areas of settlement (see Table 3). The trend toward urbanization reveals a demographic process of internal redistribution and the development of service activities, commerce, and small-scale manufacturing. It may be hypothesized that the urbanization process in the colonization zones is due to an internal migratory flow, whereby wealthier colonists relocate to the region's towns and cities to engage in service activities, commerce, and small-scale manufacturing. On the other hand, the rural zones continue to be populated by recent migrants from the Andes of a lower socioeconomic level (Recharte 1981) in a pattern that might be called "relay migration" (migración de relevo). Evidence from a good number of case studies reveals that migratory patterns and currents in the selva alta colonization zones are multiple and complex. They depend, among other factors, on the age of the penetration process.

Stages in the migratory process

Unfortunately we lack aggregate data on the magnitude and characteristics of migratory flows to the selva alta. The evidence presented below and the hypotheses inferred from it are based on our own study of a few colonization cases (Aramburú 1980, ORDEPUNO 1980, FDN 1981). Hence, their validity is somewhat limited. As we have suggested in an earlier work (Aramburú 1981b), three stages may be distinguished in spontaneous migration to the selva alta.

Stage one.—The initial penetration process is dominated by a "pendular" type of migration by Andean peasants, who clear and exploit a parcel in the colonization zone while maintaining lands in their place of origin. The family group controls resources located in different ecological zones, reproducing the ancestral pan-Andean pattern of simultaneous control of ecological niches (pisos) (Murra 1975). The Andean migrant often arrives first as hired labor for a hacienda or lumber mill and later becomes independent, according to studies of the Alto Huallaga (Cencira 1974, Bedoya 1981), Chanchamayo (Recharte 1981), and La Convención (Fioravanti 1974). During this first phase, stays in the colonization zone are brief (2–3 months) and coincide with the months of planting and harvest. Only household heads and their eldest sons of working age participate in this pendular migration. The wife and younger children remain in charge of land and animals in the place of origin. Timing of migration depends on the compatibility of the Andean agricultural calendar with the crops planted in the colonization zone.

Stage two.—As the migration process intensifies, pressure on the better lands increases as a function of their fertility and/or location. This obliges the colonist to settle in a more stable form, implying a change of residence for the family. Consequently, the sex ratio of the local population tends to decline during this phase. A good portion of the colonists continue to have access to lands in the town or community of origin through kin relations with members of the extended family. This diminishes the risk of being left with no alternatives should the colonization attempt prove a failure. The area planted and the cultivation of permanent commercial crops both expand as initial colonists are definitively settled. This generates a growing demand for seasonal labor, which gives rise to new pendular flows—in this case of a young labor force arriving to offer its labor power. This demand for hired labor beyond

the family is highly seasonal and is determined by the harvest periods of permanent crops (since the stable labor force consists of
the family members of the colonist). A relation of complementarity emerges between migratory flow and types of relations of
production in the family enterprise: those based on the self-
exploitation of the nuclear family labor force and those based on
wage relations for seasonal migrants, who submit to a process of
semiproletarianization.

Stage three.—Once the agricultural frontier is occupied and
the best parcels are consolidated, a process of internal urbanization is generated by the movement of the economically more successful colonists to the towns within the region. This internal flux
also implies the transfer of investments to nonagricultural activities such as commercial stores, workshops, and restaurants. This
stage usually coincides with the ecological deterioration of soils
under intensive agricultural use. The latter leads to the sale or outright abandonment of many parcels, especially those located on
slopes. Although the influx of new Andean migrants tends to diminish, it does not disappear completely. The new migrants settle
on depleted and eroded soils, which limits the viability of their agricultural activities.

A migratory current away from the colonization zone also
appears during this stage. It is composed of the dependents of
wealthier colonists who leave to attend school and of impoverished colonists who leave the region in search of new opportunities for work. During this phase many colonization zones in the
selva alta lose population. The great distance to market, insufficient local demand, high costs of nonagricultural inputs, and a
lack of local energy sources all limit opportunities for local development of manufacturing and service activities. Since the growth
of the labor force exceeds opportunities for employment, emigration increases in volume and intensity.

The critical factors that explain the change in migration tendencies appear to be as much the rapid saturation of the agrarian
frontier under existing technological conditions as the ecological
deterioration resulting from increased demographic pressure and
greater consumption expectations of the colonists. The intensification of land use is not accompanied by technological innovation to recuperate the fertility of the soil. Although this is a
complex issue, it casts some doubt on the well-known thesis of
Boserup (1965) concerning demographic growth as the impetus for

technological innovation that permits an intensification of resource exploitation. In the light of available evidence from colonization zones of the humid tropics, it is possible to contend that a rapid increase in demographic pressure without adaptive technological change leads to the depredation of natural resources and a decline in the rate of immigration.

Land resources: access and use

It is now commonplace to emphasize the poverty of soils in the forests of the humid tropics, as well as their fragility, diversity, maturity, and high acidity (Meggers 1971). In the high forest, the zonal soils (latisols and oxisols) are of medium to low fertility on the valley slopes of the eastern Andean river basin (Ponce del Prado 1981). Their principal limitations are the broken topography and steep gradient, which lead to rapid erosion and leaching when these lands are deforested and utilized for annual crops. Consequently, they are generally used for permanent crops such as coffee, tea, coca, citrus fruits, and avocado. The main limiting factor on the expansion of the first three crops is temperature, which varies in these regions as a function of altitude. Therefore, these commercial crops are concentrated on the high part of the river basins, above 1000 meters, and are frequently exploited under commercial forms of production. The spontaneous settlement of migrants on the sloping soils results in their rapid destruction as they are utilized intensively for annual crops (maize, manioc, yucca), which provide little ground cover. As a result, one frequently finds that the soils on slopes in the colonization zones are very eroded and almost devoid of agricultural plantings. Such is the case in the high parts of valleys like Alto Huallaga, Chanchamayo, and Tambopata. In the first of these zones a strategy of replacement has led to the planting of coca—largely destined to illegal commerce—on the soils of the slopes (FDN 1981). In Chanchamayo, however, where ecological conditions are not favorable to coca, the poorest hillside soils are destined to the cultivation of fruit trees and pineapples (Recharte 1981). Lastly, in other colonization zones such as Tambopata, these soils are practically abandoned, being used only for extensive grazing (ORDEPUNO 1980). Later migrants and those with the least economic resources tend to settle in these areas during the third stage described above, establishing a pattern we have called relay migration.

The second important soil type in the high forest is the azonal soil, made up of edaphic formations of alluvial origin. These are young, fertile soils and are appropriate for intensive use without fertilization. They are found on the valley floors of the high forest, offer a more level topography and good drainage, and are for the most part not subject to flooding. They have been utilized for the intensive cultivation of annual crops such as rice, maize, soy beans, peanuts, manioc, sorghum, and tobacco (Ponce del Prado 1981). These soils are the first to be occupied by colonists, as much for their greater natural fertility as for their frequently favorable location near communication routes—rivers and highways. Although it is difficult to generalize, our study of Alto Huallaga (CENCIRA 1973) indicated that colonists from the selva or from the coastal region preferred to settle on these level lands, whereas colonists from the sierra preferred the ecologically poor hillside lands. It is difficult to determine whether this pattern of differential settlement responds to sociocultural factors or to the antiquity of the migratory flow. The degradation process is less pronounced on these soils, and it is here that we find the emergence of the most economically viable farms—a group that represents the beginnings of a regional agrarian petty bourgeoisie. In the oldest colonization zones new crops such as cacao, tobacco, soy beans, and improved pastures are frequently introduced. This change in cultivation patterns responds not only to ecological considerations of soil conservation but also to price incentives linked to the expansion of national and international markets. The azonal soils are of economic importance in the colonization zones of Huallaga, Perené, Chanchamayo, Satipo, Apurimac, and Marañón.

Figures differ among the various sources (see, for example, CENCIRA 1974 and Ponce del Prado 1981), yet we may estimate that, of the total land area of the Peruvian Amazon (76–78 million hectares), 2.7 percent of the soils are azonal (apt for intensive use), 6 percent are intrazonal (transitional), and the remainder, 91.3 percent are zonal (severely limited for agricultural use) (Malleux 1978). The available agrarian frontier is estimated at 3.5 million hectares, which exceeds the total area under agricultural use in the country (2.4 million hectares). Varese (1974) has calculated the theoretical support capacity of the Amazon region based on prevailing technological conditions and using the area suggested by the Ministry of Agriculture for family farms according to soil type. As can be seen in Table 4, he finds the region's total support capacity to be about 460,000 families, or 2.5 to 2.6 million inhabitants. Although

TABLE 4. Peruvian Amazon: Soil quality and
agricultural support capacity

Type of soil (1)	Potential use (2)	Total area		Required hectares per family[a] (5)	Support capacity (no. of families) (3) ÷ (5) (6)
		hectares (3)	% (4)		
I	Intensive agriculture	2,292,000	3.0	20	114,600
II	Permanent crops	9,932,000	13.0	40	248,300
III	Pasture	19,100,000	25.0	200	95,500
IV–V	Forest without agricultural value	44,916,000	59.0	—	—
		76,240,000	100.0		458,400[b]

SOURCE: Varese 1974:22.

a. Considering the technology in use and two minimum salaries per family (agrarian reform model).

b. 2,600,000 inhabitants.

this theoretical estimate is significantly higher than the 1.2 million persons who currently depend on agricultural activities in Amazonia, we should remember that the area presently in use does not amount to half a million hectares. The incorporation of 3.5 million hectares of new lands would require almost two centuries at the present rate of frontier expansion.

In general, as the figures in Table 5 show, the spatial advance of the agrarian frontier is summarily slow, in spite of the fact that one-third of the total of new lands incorporated annually in Peru is in the selva. Occupation of new lands is realized above all by spontaneous migrants in the selva alta, who are responsible for 65 percent to 75 percent of lands cleared in the Amazon forest each year. The direct role of the state does not appear to be significant in the selva or in the sierra (where both cultivated area and rural population have stagnated). Consequently, it is probable that the opening of new lands on the initiative of the peasantry has brought about an ecological deterioration and the loss of farm land. These are thus contradictory and parallel processes of incorporation and loss

TABLE 5. Expansion of the agrarian frontier by regions and colonizing agent

Period and region	Public		Private		Total	
	hectares/yr	%	hectares/yr	%	hectares/yr	Percent of na-tional total
1951–64						
Selva	5,275	26.6	14,540	73.4	19,815	38.7
Sierra	3,084	29.0	7,540	71.0	10,633	20.8
Costa	12,464	60.0	8,310	40.0	20,774	40.5
Peru	20,823	40.7	30,390	59.3	51,222	100.0
1965–80						
Selva	5,275	33.5	10,478	66.5	15,762	29.0
Sierra	5,500	37.6	9,113	62.4	14,613	26.9
Costa	16,349	68.3	7,563	31.3	23,912	44.1
Peru	27,124	49.9	27,154	51.1	54,287	100.0

SOURCE: CENCIRA 1974:36, table 5.

of agricultural land. The end result, positive or negative, is difficult to estimate—especially in the case of the high forest, due to the rapid pace of the colonization process. Some studies (Malleux 1975, Dourojeanni 1981) estimate that 4.5 million hectares of high forest have been deforested and degraded as a result of spontaneous migration and colonization. In any case, the estimates and plans of agrarian frontier expansion in the humid tropical forests should consider not only the lands gained but also those abandoned and degenerated in terms of productive capacity through the act of colonization. The process of soil degradation cannot, however, be attributed entirely or exclusively to spontaneous colonization. Diverse studies have shown the devastating effects of mechanized land clearing carried out by private firms and cooperatives with state support (CENCIRA 1973, Ministerio de Agricultura 1976, Bedoya 1981).

To conclude, we may point out that the ratio of land use per capita in the Peruvian Amazon appears to have stagnated in the last decade (see Table 6). In 1980 the estimated area under agricultural production was 0.295 hectares per inhabitant. The national mean was 0.18 hectares per inhabitant. The selva represents 17.7 percent of the total cultivated area in the country. The most obvious difference between the region's agriculture and the rest of the country is the minor role of perennial food crops (35 percent of total area cultivated compared to 60 percent at the national level) and the predominance of permanent commercial crops, coffee being the most important. Nevertheless, the tendency appears to

TABLE 6. Land use in the selva region
(in hectares per capita)

	1951–55	1960–64	1970	1975	1980
Total area cultivated	0.238	0.346	0.306	0.302	0.295
Perennial crops	0.104	0.112	0.116	0.121	0.125
Food[a]	0.088	0.098	0.107	0.112	0.118
Industrial[b]	0.015	0.013	0.010	0.008	0.007
Permanent crops[c]	0.013	0.234	0.190	0.181	0.170

SOURCE: CENCIRA 1974:44.

a. Predominantly rice, yucca, and maize.
b. Predominantly tobacco, soybeans, and sorghum.
c. Predominantly coffee, cacao, tea, and bananas and other fruits.

reverse in recent years (see Table 6). Perennial food crops are expanding more rapidly, and perennial industrial and permanent crops are declining in relation to area cultivated per inhabitant.

Expansion of the peasant economy

Having presented in broad strokes the tendencies and characteristics of demographic and agricultural frontier expansion in the colonization zones of the selva alta, we must now consider, on a more concrete level, the predominant type of economic enterprise in these zones. First we shall present a few working hypotheses about the predominant modes of production, which later will be illustrated briefly by evidence collected in case studies in the northern and southern selva of Peru.

Through the colonization process, spontaneous migrants reproduce their existence as peasants by taking control of a parcel and exploiting it primarily with family labor (Aramburú 1979). While spontaneous colonization usually assumes the reproduction of noncapitalist modes of production, this does not mean that they are reproduced in isolation from the market. On the contrary, the colonist's production unit reinforces ties with the market since a significant proportion of total production is destined for the marketplace. For Andean migrants, commercialization of production is much greater than would have been possible in their Andean economy. Ties with the labor market are also reinforced even though, as we have noted, this is seasonal labor and functions as a complement to the family labor force.

Another general hypothesis is that the spontaneous colonization process in the selva alta contributes to the process of capitalist accumulation. This occurs (1) through the expansion of the agrarian frontier and (2) through the insertion into the national and international markets of a set of agricultural products, the prices for which do not cover their real costs of production (Aramburú 1979). As has been noted, the first of these is primarily carried out through the efforts of the family enterprise, which assumes the costs of expanding and preparing new areas (felling trees, clearing, burning, cleaning, etc.). Few capitalist enterprises have been successful in pioneering the colonization of the humid tropics. The high costs of labor, technology, and inputs and the sharp fluctuations in prices for the commercial products they have developed have made investments both risky and expensive. (Le Torneau on the Pachitea River, SALPAL in the Alto Huallaga, and large forestry projects such as Jari in the Brazilian Amazon are a few examples). The family enterprise, however, has abundant labor of its own, which represents a fixed cost equivalent to its consumption. Family labor can be utilized intensively even though its marginal productivity is not equal to the capitalist wage. Likewise, the family enterprise utilizes its own low-cost and easily replaced technology, which even appears to be better than mechanized clearing for the conservation of soil fertility. Lastly, the crops of colonists tend to be more diversified, part for household consumption and part for sale. They are therefore less vulnerable to price fluctuation in the marketplace. This would all suggest that peasant enterprises enjoy certain advantages compared to large private or state (including cooperative) enterprises in the initial process of colonization.

We shall illustrate the above propositions with results obtained from recent fieldwork in Alto Huallaga of the north-central selva (FDN 1981) and in the Tambopata and Inambari valleys of the southern selva (Aramburú and Ponce 1981). These case studies represent two different colonization processes. The first (Alto Huallaga), though it was initiated spontaneously by Andean migrants from the sierras of Huanuco, since 1966 had received heavy investments and service programs directed by the state. Tambopata and Inambari, however, are the result of spontaneous peasant settlement originating in the altiplano of Puno and have not received significant assistance from state-directed programs.

Independent family agriculture or ranching is the predominant occupation among the rural population of both zones (97 percent of household heads in Alto Huallaga and 94 percent in Tambopata). We also found a high rate of labor participation by other family members: 54 percent in the Alto Huallaga and 51 percent in Tambopata. Among working family members over the age of six, 96 percent in Alto Huallaga and 87.5 percent in Tambopata labored as nonremunerated family workers within the family enterprise. This finding is reinforced by the fact that 94 percent of the family heads in Alto Huallaga and 80 percent in Tambopata stated that they received nonremunerated assistance from family members. Of the family members who contribute their labor, the majority are members of the nuclear family; wives and older sons represent the stable labor force that the colonists depend on throughout the year. This is characteristic of the peasant economy and reveals the reproduction, in the colonization process, of the noncapitalist elements of a population that belongs primarily to an Andean cultural tradition.

Nevertheless, as we have indicated above, there exists an important market for wage labor linked to the intermittent cycles of commercial crops such as coffee, coca, cacao, and tea. Among the colonists of Alto Huallaga, 75 percent of family heads contracted wage labor during the year but only 19 percent hired permanent labor. In Tambopata 49 percent hired seasonal labor and only 4 percent hired permanent workers. The evident difference is due to the greater size of parcels and of the scale of commercial production in the more developed Alto Huallaga. Obviously, family cash income is significantly different between zones: in Alto Huallaga it ranged from 70–75,000 soles per month in March 1981 (about $150), whereas in Tambopata family income was only 25,000 soles per month (about $50). The relatively high income of colonists in Alto Huallaga may be explained primarily by the illegal cultivation of coca. It is surprising to find that the predominant type of productive relations among the colonists is largely independent of the degree of capitalist development in the region. Family scale agricultural production remains the predominant form.

The colonists are basically peasants and therefore orient their economic decisions within the logic and rationality of the domestic economy (Chayanov 1974). Production is characterized by the intensive use of family labor, high rates of participation in economic activities, use of simple technology of low cost and replacement, diversification of crops, and an orientation to the satisfaction of basic family needs. The differences from the classical model of peasant economy consist in the greater articulation of the colonist with the market for products and labor. Consequently, prices exercise a decisive influence on production, which explains, among other things, the rapid diffusion of more profitable crops such as coca, cacao, and coffee. This means also that certain colonists achieve significant levels of capital accumulation even though a good part of these earnings is channeled into nonagricultural investments, given the low profit margins for most agricultural activities in the selva alta. This pattern, found frequently in the more developed colonization zones, reveals a peasantry in transition and the formation of an agrarian petty bourgeoisie.

The reasons for the economic success of some colonists are still unclear and require studies of greater depth. One aspect mentioned above that requires further investigation is the estimate of the real costs of family-scale production based on an imputed value of harvest labor at local wage levels. After deducting this and other monetary costs of production from the value of the surplus harvest (at local prices), it would be possible to estimate real profits and wages. Our research among peasants of the mountains and the coast indicates that a significant proportion of these families have little or no real earnings and that self-attributed salaries are below the level paid in the local market (Aramburú and Ponce 1981).

In the case of Tambopata a calculation was made based on the total family income that would be obtained if all working members earned at least the minimum wage. It was found that 56 percent of the families earned less than this amount—which lends plausibility to our supposition. If this finding were generally true, it would confirm the hypotheses of self-exploitation on the part of the peasant economy and of its contribution to the process of capital accumulation (Bartra 1979, Bengoa 1979). Consequently, it is necessary to locate the colonization process as part of the dynamic of reproduction of noncapitalist forms of production and their transformation into entrepreneurial forms, elucidating the factors that accelerate or retard this process and its variability among regions and social groups.

Summary

The expansion of the agricultural and demographic frontier in the Peruvian selva alta is primarily due to the spontaneous migration of Andean peasants, who reproduce the social and economic conditions of their domestic economy in the new region (Schuurman 1980). This process forms a social, economic, and cultural space through colonization that clearly differentiates the selva alta from the Selva Baja in the Peruvian Amazon and generally distinguishes the case of the Andean countries with zones in the selva alta from countries of the Amazon plain such as Brazil.

The colonization process and "Andeanization" of the high forest has increased rapidly since the 1950s as the result of the growing demographic pressure on Andean agriculture, the expansion of roads, and the diffusion of a conservative political thesis that offers colonization as a substitute for agrarian reform. During the 1960s the process reached its culmination with the colonization of eleven important river basins on the eastern slopes of the Andes. During the past decade, the penetration and settlement process has proceeded more slowly, reflecting the progressive saturation of the land as well as the decline in the national rate of demographic increase. Altogether, the colonization zones of the selva alta, in spite of their rapid population growth, do not play an important role in the absorption of population. Less than 10 percent of national demographic growth has been absorbed by these regions and less than 20 percent of Andean emigrants have chosen to move to the selva alta over the past forty years.

The older colonization zones reveal changes in migratory patterns and population redistribution. We have suggested that there are three stages in the penetration process. In the initial phase, pendular migration from the forest parcel to the Andean parcel predominates. During the second, older migrants establish themselves permanently and pendular migrations emerge in response to seasonal labor markets. In the third stage, emigration begins due to soil depletion, stagnation of the agrarian frontier, and lack of educational and investment opportunities for wealthier colonists. Population growth declines although poor Andean peasants continue to arrive in the form of relay migrants. It is also during this third phase that we see an internal urbanization process and a redistribution of the local population. More successful colonists and more acculturated migrants with greater resources settle in the urban centers, while the new Andean migrants settle in the agricultural zones that are depleted and have low use potential. The processes described reveal serious limitations of the capacity of these regions to continue absorbing additional population. Between 1970 and 1980, eleven of the fifteen provinces in the selva alta subject to colonization showed a decrease in the rate of population growth over the previous decade.

The limits to continued expansion of the demographic frontier in the selva alta stem as much from the low fertility of most soils as from their inappropriate use. As demographic and economic pressure on the land increase, the mean size of parcels tends to diminish. Fallowed areas tend to be reduced, and crop patterns show an increase in the cultivation of permanent crops of greater commercial value. This change toward the intensification of land use occurs without technological innovations to protect or recuperate soil fertility. The consequences are contradictory: the agrarian frontier expands in terms of land taken from the forest, yet land is lost through deforestation and erosion.

The viability of Amazonia as a privileged region for the expansion of the agricultural frontier and as food producer for the rest of the country appears to be limited in the medium term. The major problem is not the absolute scarcity of fertile land. We have noted the existence of some 3.5 million hectares of land suitable for intensive use, an area almost 1.5 times larger than that already in use in the country today. Fewer than 0.5 million hectares are in production in the Peruvian Amazon, and the rate of expansion of the agrarian frontier is only between 16,000 and 20,000 hectares per year. Furthermore, this expansion is concentrated in the selva alta, where topography leaves the land more susceptible to erosion. Demographic pressures are increasing in the most fragile ecological zones. Given the persistence of slash and burn agriculture, carrying capacity under continuous use is very low. In the last few decades the *availability* of agricultural land in use per capita appears to have stagnated and even diminished slightly.

Finally, we have posed the question of the persistence and reproduction of the peasant or family economy in the colonization zones. This point is not only of academic interest; it also has significant practical relevance in the definition of the type of development policy that the state can implement in these zones. Several authors wielding technical arguments defend the total planning of the colonization process, arguing that unplanned or spontaneous settlement should be entirely avoided (Ponce del Prado 1981:58). State participation in planning settlement would involve detailed study of area resources, selection and qualification of future colonists, assignment of parcels and tenure regulation, industrial development policy, commercialization, and the organization of multifamily enterprises (Malleux 1975).

Our principal objection to this kind of planning is that under present conditions it cannot be realized. It would be impossible to detain and control spontaneous migration while soil surveys are carried out. Even if such studies did exist, the control of settlement would require an extremely high investment of human and financial resources per family settled. Furthermore, certain measures taken by directed colonization projects have failed (granting of land titles and regularization of tenure; mechanized clearing and the introduction of mechanical technology; promotion of exotic commercial monoculture or activities of long-term maturation such as ranching; introduction of credit and new inputs; and the promotion of multifamily, collective property settlements). In some cases they failed because they were inconsistent with the rationality of a peasant economy, in others because of the large investments required, and in still others because they were not compatible with current prices and with cultural characteristics of the population (Schuurman 1980, Aramburú 1981a).

We believe a more viable alternative to be a policy that is extensive and comprehensive, yet selective (i.e., limited to certain critical aspects), and geared to reinforce the family enterprise, which is predominant in these regions. Accordingly, the specific characteristics of a peasant economy should be taken into account, such as risk aversion, subsistence needs of the family, crop diversification and the capacity to utilize family labor intensively. The state would participate by concentrating its efforts on research and extension work in agricultural activities and on the promotion of both food and commercial crops. Likewise, the control of settlements would be limited to the hillside zones, to the study of soils in unoccupied zones, and to reforestation of depleted zones. Programs for technological innovation would require not only research efforts but also an active extension service, including participation by the producers themselves. In addition, a policy of subsidized pricing would be indispensable to stimulate the adoption of new crops and inputs. Lastly, such a policy would promote service cooperatives for the commercialization of crops and inputs, since these appear more appropriate to the cultural traditions of the colonists.

In the long run, the most fruitful state investment would be agricultural and socioeconomic research concerning the humid tropics and their populations. In spite of recent advances, Amazonia still remains an immense and unknown frontier.

References Cited

Aramburú, Carlos Eduardo
    1979 *Las Migraciones a las Zonas de Colonización en la Selva Peruana: Perspectivas y Avances.* Lima: INANDEP.
    1981a Problemas del Desarrollo Rural y la Colonización en la Amazonía Peruana. *Debates en Antropología* 6(September). Lima: Univ. Católica. pp. 41–70.
    1981b *Migración Interna en el Perú: Perspectivas Teóricas y Metodológicas.* Lima: INANDEP.

Aramburú, Carlos E. and Ana Ponce
    1981   *Organización Socio-Económica de la Familia Campesina y Migración en Tres Regiones del Perú.* Lima: INANDEP.
Bartra, Roger
    1979   La Teoría del Valor y la Economía Campesina. In *Economía Campesina.* Orlando Plazo, ed. Pp. 289–308. Lima: DESCO.
Bedoya, Eduardo
    1981   *La Destrucción del Equilibrio Ecológico en las Cooperativas del Alto Huallaga.* Lima: CIPA, Serie Documento 1.
Bengoa, Jose
    1979   Economía Campesina y Acumulación Capitalista en Plaza. In *Economía Campesina.* Orlando Plazo, ed. Pp. 243–88. Lima: DESCO.
Boletín Amidep
    1981   III:15, June 1981. Lima.
Boserup, Esther
    1965   *The Conditions of Agricultural Growth: The Economics of Agrarian Change Under Population Pressure.* Chicago: Aldine.
Camino, Alejandro
    1976   Raids and Trade Between Lowland Tribes and Quechua People in the Urubamba Region. Ms.
Centro Nacional De Capacitación e Investigación Para la Reforma Agraria (CENCIRA).
    1973   *Diagnóstico Socio Económico de la Colonización Tingo María —Tocache —Campanilla.* Lima: Dir. de Investigación.
    1974   *Lineamientos Generales para una Política de Colonización en la Selva.* Lima: Dir. de Investigación.
Chayanov, Alexander
    1974   *La Organización de la Unidad Económica Campesina.* Mexico: Nueva Visión.
Dourojeanni, Marc J.
    1981   Impacto Ambiental de las Carreterras en los Bosques Tropicales. Paper presented at Seminar on Proyectos de Investigación Ecológia para el Manejo de los Recursos Naturales Renovables del Bosque Tropical Húmedo. Iquitos, Peru, October 12–18.
Fioravanti, Eduardo
    1974   *Latifundio y Sindicalismo Agrario en el Perú: El Caso de los Valles de la Convención y Lares (1958–1964).* Lima: I.E.P.
Fundación Para el Desarrollo Nacional.
    1981   *Estudio Sobre el Proyecto de Desarrollo Rural Integral del Alto Huallaga.* Lima: Convenio USAID, Ministerio de Agricultura FDN.
Instituto Nacional de Estadística.
    1981   *Perú: Algunas Características de la Población (Resultados Provisionales del Censo del 12 de Julio de 1981).* Lima: Boletín Especial No. 6.

Malleux, J.
1975   *Mapa Forestal del Perú.* Lima: Univ. Nacional Agraria.
1978   La Ecología y los Recursos Naturales. Paper presented at the conference on Amazonía: Conquista del Presente. Lima, Octubre 6–9.

Meggers, Betty
1971   *Amazonia: Man and Land in a Counterfeit Paradise.* Chicago: Aldine-Athenton.

Ministerio de Agricultura
1976   *Características de los Suelos de la Colonización Tingo Maria—Tocache—Campanilla.* Parte II. Avcavacu, Peru: Ministerio de Agricultura.

Murra, John
1975   *Formaciones Económicas y Políticas del Mundo Andino.* Lima: I.E.P.

ORDEPUNO
1980   *Migración y Colonización en Puno.* Puno, Peru: Convenio UNEPA-ORDEPUNO.

Ponce del Prado, Carlos
1981   Los Recursos Naturales Renovables de la Amazonía y su Uso: Situación Actual y Perspectivas. Paper presented at DESCO seminar on Situación Actual y Perspectivas del Problema Agrónomo en el Perú. Lima, December 9–11.

Recharte, Jorge
1981   Los Límites Socioecológicos del Crecimiento Agrícola en la Ceja de Selva. Tesis Licenciatura Antropología, Univ. Católica, Lima.

Rumrrill, Roger
1974   La Selva; Mas de 100 Anos de Soledad. *Revista Participación* 5:3–12. Lima: SINAMOS.

Schuurman, Frans
1980   Colonization Policy and Peasant Economy in the Amazon Basin. In *Land, People and Planning in Contemporary Amazonia.* F. Barbira-Scazzocchio, ed. Cambridge: Centre of Latin American Studies, University of Cambridge.

Varese, Stefano
1974   La Selva, Viejas Fronteras, Nuevas Alternativas. *Revista Participación* 5:13–25. Lima: SINAMOS.

Frontier Expansion and Retraction in Brazil

Donald R. Sawyer

THE AMAZON Basin, most of which lies within Brazil, is one of the last large areas of the world currently undergoing frontier settlement. Understanding the Brazilian case can contribute to the proper evaluation of future prospects for population redistribution worldwide and for tapping the natural resources of areas only partially incorporated into the world economy. This is not to say that the Amazon can offer solutions to population or resource problems of the rest of the world. At least at this point in history, the capacity of the region to absorb population and investments productively is quite limited.

This paper is based on a series of investigations carried out individually or in teams that included members of the Center for Development and Regional Planning of the Federal University of Minas Gerais since 1968. The paper is an attempt to make sense of numerous observations and analyses, which cannot all be presented here. It thus constitutes an essay rather than a research paper.

NOTE: A previous version of this paper was presented in Informal Session I.2 at the XIX General Conference of the International Union for the Scientific Study of Population, Manila, Philippines, December 9–16, 1981. The main sources of support for the different research projects on which it draws were Harvard University, the National Science Foundation, the Ford Foundation, Superintendency for Development of the Amazon (SUDAM), Ministry of Agriculture, FINEP, and the International Development Research Centre. None of these institutions bears any responsibility for the views expressed here.

Frontiers in Brazil are usually perceived and analyzed in terms of economic expansion, occupation of new lands, absorption of migrants, and other "flows." Along with such forward movement, apparently contrary "ebb" processes are now beginning to appear in the Brazilian Amazon. These, associated with economic stagnation, cuts in public and private investments, out-migration, and rural exodus, have been generally neglected or treated as separate phenomena. The purpose of this paper is to place these two types of movement, ebb and flow, into a single analytic framework of the spatial tendencies of capitalist production in Brazil.

In studies to date, much has been written, on the one hand, about "expansion of capitalism and penetration of capitalism in the countryside" (for example, see Cardoso and Müller 1977). On the other hand, there are well-known tendencies, especially in less-developed capitalist economies like Brazil's, for economic activities and population to become increasingly concentrated, especially in metropolitan areas (Singer 1972). In the literature on spatial dimensions of development, agriculture in Brazil is normally treated differently from industry, since increase in agricultural output has been achieved primarily through incorporation of new lands, i.e., through horizontal instead of vertical expansion (Singer, 1981). Such isolated or dichotomous analyses must be overcome. From this standpoint, the observed expansion and retraction of the frontier should be conceptualized as different spatial manifestations of a single process of development.

A common tendency in the literature on Brazil is to distinguish between the demographic and the economic frontiers (Waibel 1979). This analysis does not follow that precedent. On the one hand, demographic occupation is impossible without some form of economic activity. To ignore the latter, or to treat it separately, thus runs counter to one of the main goals of this paper: to point out the role of recent market networks in stimulating frontier migration. On the other hand, some economic activities involve little or no absorption of labor, a phenomenon of special relevance in the most recent phase of Amazonian development. The purpose of this analysis can be described as an attempt to conceptually join, rather than to isolate, the demographic and economic processes that characterize the dynamics of frontier expansion in Brazil.

It may be useful to draw a distinction (which is linguistically easier in Portuguese than in English) between *conditions* that are favorable or unfavorable to the expansion of certain types of activity,

frontier
vs
front

and the actual *activities* themselves. In the following discussion, we shall use the term "frontier" to refer to general conditions, and the term "front," in contradistinction, to refer to actual activities. The frontier is thus a more general and abstract space, which may be favorable or unfavorable to different activities according to their specific characteristics and their interrelationships. The various fronts can be differentiated by their specific forms of economic organization: commodity peasant fronts, capitalist ranching fronts, placer-mining fronts, and others noted below.

The paper is divided into sections on the growth of surplus population in Brazil, migration to the Great Frontier in the postwar period, more recent capitalist expansion in this area and, finally, present conflicts and possible future trends. Our main concern is with economic and demographic aspects, but ecological factors are also included in the analysis because of the special characteristics of the Amazon's physical environment. Attention is focused on frontiers in contemporary Brazil, with no attempt to generalize to other societies or to other historical periods. Whatever relevance the analysis may have to countries beyond Brazil would be due to similarities in their market structures, the principal force which, according to our analysis, has determined expansion and retraction of frontiers in Brazil. The analysis is thus framed in such a way that parallels and contrasts with other historical situations may be drawn.

Growth of surplus population in Brazil

Brazil's history is, to a large extent, the history of frontier expansion and retraction. Production of sugar, precious minerals, coffee, rubber, and other tropical exports all took place on what could be considered expanding frontiers. A fundamental characteristic of the diverse primary activities on which this expansion was based is that their spatial location depends to a large extent on the distribution of resources, wherever they have been placed by nature. This means that primary activities must spread out over available territory in search of new sources of natural wealth, fertile soil, or open space. This tendency to spread is especially true for extractive as distinct from agricultural activities. In both cases, the tendency to diffusion contrasts sharply with the spatial concentration of urban-industrial development, increasingly dominant in twentieth-century Brazil. Even when spatially dispersed, as in the case of precious minerals and rubber, the frontiers of the primary-export period were central to the process of accumulation in Brazil.

With the exception of rubber, early frontiers relied heavily on imported labor. Planters and miners left aside the domestic population, which continued to grow in size as previous frontiers stagnated and as natural population increase occurred. They first preferred African slaves, and later European immigrants, over native Brazilians, of increasingly mixed descent. The latter groups eked out a subsistence in the interstices or on the fringes of the economies based on sugar, mining, coffee, or incipient industry, or were left behind when the centers of growth moved elsewhere. From the point of view of the dominant form of economic organization, they can be considered surplus population.

After 1930, during the import substitution phase of Brazilian development, internal migration replaced international migration as the principal source of labor for the expansion of new economic activities. In contrast to the earlier agroextractive frontiers, these activities assumed an increasingly urban-industrial character. The new dynamic poles of the economy, especially in industry and urban services, began to use labor drawn from reserves within the country. This substitution of imported labor by mobilization of the growing surplus population within Brazil is a process that can be called "nationalization of the labor force."

The growth of surplus population was increasingly propelled by capitalist development itself. The substitution of machines for labor through technical change is a process that requires no further comment. Equally important, in terms of labor absorption, is the fact that technical change almost always involves new sources of energy, which are often imported or which require little labor to produce. Petroleum, much of which was imported, and electricity, generated from petroleum or from hydroelectric potential, replaced human and animal power, firewood, charcoal, vegetable and animal oils, and other traditional energy sources. Through competition with these and other goods and services produced by peasants, artisans, and household members, as well as through expropriation of the means of production, especially land, capitalist development destroyed or disorganized forms of production based primarily on human labor. Thus technical change and the expansion of capitalist relations of production, even though they absorbed some labor in new activities, contributed to the growth of surplus population in Brazil.

Economic stagnation, which at first sight appears to be the opposite of development, has also been pointed out as a structural cause of population pressure leading to migration (Singer 1972). Where so-called factors of stagnation predominate, population growth outstrips gains in agricultural yields in the subsistence economy. Access to more land is restricted, either because it is totally occupied or because of the monopolization of space by latifundia. It should be remembered, nevertheless, that such stagnation occurred in Brazil where a higher level of development had been reached previously, as in the sugar areas of the Northeast or the rubber areas of Amazonia. Stagnation did not occur because dynamic activities never appeared or because they were totally abandoned, but because they moved elsewhere: to the West Indies and São Paulo state in the case of sugar; to Asia and petrochemical plants, in the case of rubber. In the final analysis, stagnation of the productive forces in certain regions of Brazil corresponds to their further development in other regions. The retraction of frontiers of the primary-export period is an integral part of the same process of development that generated them. The dichotomy between stagnation and change is superficial; the problem is basically one of location in space of diverse manifestations of a single underlying process.

It should also be mentioned, although space does not permit adequate exploration of the mechanisms and their results, that development stimulated the rate of natural increase (births minus deaths) of the population. Mortality probably decreased because of the transition from slave to free labor. It certainly declined as a result of technological progress in medicine and public health, as in other parts of the world. It is also probable that fertility increased as free labor replaced slavery and as the large family became a viable and functional institution for all sectors of the population, not just the dominant classes. Thus, high rates of natural increase in recent decades can also be considered to be part of capitalist development, rather than given, "exogenous," or simply "traditional."

A more complete analysis would need to take into account such factors as expansion of wage labor, relationships between formal and informal sectors of the economy, economic cycles, regional differences, and the recent downward trend in fertility. Nevertheless, it may not be too great a simplification to say that capitalist development in Brazil involves, on the whole, less growth in the demand for labor than in the size of the population. Consequently, there was an expanding surplus population, which could not be absorbed in capitalist relations of production. Such a surplus is a structural characteristic of urban-industrial development in Brazil and constitutes the background against which frontier settlement can and should be analyzed.

Migration to the Great Frontier since 1940

After World War II, when the above-mentioned economic and demographic changes of the import substitution phase were well advanced, part of the growing surplus population began to penetrate the fringes of Brazil's West and Amazon regions, areas inhabited by a sparse population of Indians and descendants of settlers who had arrived during the mining or rubber booms. For our purposes, this vast territory, including the state of Maranhão, will be called the Great Frontier. We shall now examine the most important migratory flows to the Great Frontier, the economic and political forces that generated these flows, and aspects of economic and social organization on the frontier before the more recent advance of large capitalist enterprises.

The principal tendency of spatial distribution of Brazil's population in recent decades has been rapid urban growth. The level of urbanization rose from 31.2 percent in 1940 to 67.8 percent in 1980, with increasing concentration in metropolitan areas. Nonetheless, migration in the opposite direction has also been significant. As can be seen in Table 1, while the population of the eight largest capital cities increased from 11.0 percent to 18.1 percent of the total for Brazil between 1940 and 1980, the Great Frontier increased its share from 9.6 percent to 14.7 percent.

Within the Great Frontier, the areas that received most migrants were along its southern and eastern periphery. The greatest volume of migrants left the Northeast of Brazil, penetrating the pre-Amazonian area of western Maranhão in the 1940s and 1950s and subsequently entering northern Goiás and eastern Pará. Migrants from the states of Bahia and Minas Gerais joined Northeasterners in a second stream settling parts of central Goiás and Northern Mato Grosso. The construction of Brasília in the late 1950s attracted migrants from all over Brazil, especially public servants from the Center-South and unskilled labor from the Northeast. It also stimulated settlement of southern Goiás, although this process was already well underway, with migration primarily from Minas Gerais, before the construction of Brasília. The third

TABLE 1. Distribution of Brazil's population (in percentages)

Type of area	1872	1920	1940	1980
Large capital cities[a]	6.6	8.7	11.0	18.1
Coastal areas except for large capital cities[b]	84.3	81.3	79.4	67.2
Great Frontier[c]	9.2	10.0	9.6	14.7
All Brazil	100.1	100.0	100.0	100.0

SOURCE: Calculated from data in *Sinopse Preliminar do Censo Demográfico*, 1980:4–7.

a. Fortaleza, Recife, Salvador, Belo Horizonte, Rio de Janeiro, São Paulo, Curitiba, and Porto Alegre.
b. All of Brazil except Great Frontier.
c. North and West regions and the State of Maranhão.

main stream of migration to the Great Frontier had its origins in the South, populating the present states of Mato Grosso do Sul and Mato Grosso and the territory of Rondônia. These migrants came primarily from Rio Grande do Sul and Paraná. Some of the migrants who left Paraná in recent years had arrived there from Minas Gerais and São Paulo two or three decades before during expansion of the coffee frontier westward from São Paulo.

Economic and political factors

Even though numerous government policies and programs were supposed to promote frontier settlement, the relations of cause and effect between policies and actual settlement are not clear. Policies were discontinuous and programs generally modest, under both authoritarian and democratic regimes, while migration was massive and continuous throughout the period in question. Adequate analysis of the role of the state in frontier settlement requires attention to the way in which policies not directly aimed at settlement, but at other goals such as land tenure, national security, taxation, export promotion, and credit, may hinder settlement. Thus, in order to place political factors in proper perspective, it is important to look first at the economic factors with the greatest influence on the rhythm, intensity, and spatial distribution of settlement in the Great Frontier. The most important factors were markets, transportation, and land.

Markets—The unification and spatial extension of markets was a fundamental characteristic of the Brazilian economy during the historical phases known as import substitution and associated-dependent development. By the end of the 1950s, the production of intermediate and consumer durable goods (metals, petrochemicals, automobiles, household appliances, etc.) created pressures toward unification of the different regional markets, which had been adequate for the initial development of "traditional" textile, food, and beverage industries. Such unification resulted in a new and broader consumer market more appropriate to the scale of modern, oligopolistic industries. Industrial production, in combination with the expansion of services and rapid urban growth, deepened the social division of labor and multiplied the demand for raw materials and foodstuffs. In other words, there emerged an internal market for agricultural and extractive products, which previously had been produced within Brazil's farms and ranches in nearly autarkic fashion. In addition to consumer and product markets, markets for labor and land also grew during import substitution.

These changes in the economy of the Center-South transformed all of its elements, including labor power, into commodities. In other words, the country moved increasingly toward a fully capitalist economy. What is important to recognize, in the case of the frontier, is that different markets develop with different rhythms and in different spaces. In the 1940s, 1950s, and 1960s, markets for consumer goods and for primary products stretched far into the interior, while land and labor markets remained within a shorter radius. Thus, the space covered by circulation of commodities for capitalist production, commodities bought or sold by petty producers, was larger than the space devoted to capitalist production as such. For the period in question, the difference between the two spaces can be considered as the frontier.

Seen from this angle, frontier settlement in the postwar period was not simply demographic occupation, nor was it organized as a subsistence economy in which participation in the market was merely coincidental. Expansion of markets was essential in its origins and in its functioning. Terms such as "demographic frontier" and "subsistence economy" easily lend themselves to ideological use, either in populist critiques of capitalism or in the technocratic bias against small-scale producers considered backward and unproductive. In reality, at least since World War II, the reproduction of Brazil's rural population requires significant participation in the market. Its needs have been historically redefined to include goods such as manufactured textiles and shoes, aluminum pots and pans, soap, kerosene, alcoholic beverages, and modern medicines. To acquire them, it is necessary to have monetary income, if not through wage labor, then through the sale of agricultural products. Because of this, settlement on the Great Frontier was only important in areas where migrants encountered the necessary conditions for participation in consumer and product markets. Petty commodity production was predominant, capitalist production being limited to isolated points or spread thinly over large areas, especially ranches.

Transportation.— A system of transportation connecting the frontier to urban and industrial centers is a precondition for participation in product or consumer markets. In recent decades, such connections were established by the construction of a vast new network of roads. Trucking largely replaced the use of rivers, which do not connect the frontier to industrial centers in the south. The most important new road was the Belém-Brasília, which provided an important link between Belém and São Paulo. The Brasília-Acre road, also initiated in the 1950s, formed a western axis. These were true penetration roads, which exercised the above-mentioned connecting function and stimulated the economic and demographic occupation of vast areas. A network of secondary or feeder roads served the same purpose on a local level. The grandiose road-building projects of the 1970s—the Transamazon, Cuiabá-Santarém, Northern Perimeter Highway, Porto Velho-Manaus and Manaus-Caracaraí—did not perform these functions in the same way and did not stimulate much settlement. The general conclusion that can be drawn from the study of different roadbuilding experiences is that what counts most with regard to effects on settlement is the ease of movement of commodities to and from urban-industrial centers. Commodities move back and forth constantly, while migrants move only once.

It is also worth pointing out that roads through frontier areas are built for a variety of purposes, not always directly related to the effects they may have along their routes. The Belém-Brasília and the Brasília-Acre roads were built primarily to provide interregional links. Settlement along them seems to have been an unintended consequence more than a planned objective. The Transamazon, which was planned and made public months before President

Médici's well-publicized visit to the drought-stricken Northeast and announcement of the National Integration Program, was essentially a military project, which the government tried to justify (as well as mystify) in social terms, appending showcase colonization projects. The sort of roads that actually prompt most settlement are secondary or feeder roads built in response to political bargaining for already-settled populations, rather than as the result of state planning and policies.

Land.—The role of land distribution to settlers in highly visible colonization projects, like the role of spectacular roads, has often been overestimated and misunderstood. By 1978, only 24,242 families had been settled in federal colonization projects in the North region. Within the National Integration Program, which had the announced goal of transferrring 100,000 families in four years, only 7,839 families were settled along the Transamazon (Arruda 1978:25). These numbers should be compared with the more than 2,500,000 families that were added to the population of the Great Frontier between 1950 and 1980, of which more than 600,000 can be considered to be direct or indirect results of migration if natural increase is assumed to be 3.5 percent a year (total population from demographic censuses; number of families calculated assuming five persons per family).

How could so many people be absorbed in so many different areas? A first answer would be that state and local governments also distributed land, not in colonization projects as they are commonly thought of but in areas undergoing spontaneous settlement. For example, between 1940 and 1978, the state of Pará distributed 20,516 final deeds and a greater number of provisional deeds or other temporary documents (Sawyer 1979a:791). In Pará and elsewhere, the role of government action was almost always to legitimize de facto situations, as a response to settlement processes already under way.

Still, most rural settlement occurred outside colonization areas, on private or public lands. In English the process bears the pejorative name of "squatting," i.e., occupation without legal title. Rather than a result of state action, it would be more accurate to consider such occupation as being due to official inaction. On the whole, the state favored large landowners against squatters, through its land policies, its condoning of hired gunmen, and judicial action and eviction by police forces.

The general conclusion that can be reached with regard to access to land on the Great Frontier is that even though the state distributed a limited number of small lots, the political balance was undoubtedly in favor of large properties and against the mass of settlers. Official colonization should be viewed more as a conquest of the settlers than as a response to incentives offered by the state or as a necessity of capitalist expansion.

Another factor, which would deserve more attention if space permitted, is the role of traditional systems of trade and lending through middlemen who also exercised considerable social and political influence over their clients. Recognition of the importance of this form of patronage would also attenuate the weight commonly given to the state as the mastermind and prime mover behind frontier migration.

More detailed argumentation is not possible here. The main results suggested by the analysis carried out so far are: (1) the underlying economic factors of both a "push" and "pull" nature are more important than explicit settlement policies; (2) the policies most relevant to frontier migration are those that have other objectives and act upon economic factors; (3) the net effect of government policies on frontier migration is probably negative; and (4) the few outrightly favorable policies that appeared were official responses to already existing situations rather than a primary cause of settlement.

In sum, it does not seem appropriate to view frontier settlement as the result of some preconceived plan or even an implicit process to mobilize labor power for future capitalist activities. Brazil's surplus population needed few if any special incentives to migrate to the Great Frontier. Most settlement can be considered "spontaneous," if we use this term to refer to lack of correspondence with the most relevant government policies, rather than to the motives and will of the individual migrant.

Peasant fronts and alternative social space

In several essential respects, settlement of the Great Frontier after World War II was different from frontier expansion in the primary-export period. In both spatial and economic terms, contemporary frontier expansion occurred on the periphery rather than at the center of recent development. It resulted in a combination of surplus population from coastal areas with surplus land in the interior. This land and this population were not necessary for urban-industrial development, which was incapable, for the time being, of directly dominating all of the potential productive forces in Brazil.

In spite of recent attempts to interpret frontier settlement in terms of mobility of labor power, it seems more appropriate to recall that such settlement actually ran contrary to the general tendency toward proletarianization. In many cases, migrant families even gained access to means of production, especially land. It would seem more appropriate to say that they moved and settled simply as population, not as labor power. Frontier settlement was, of course, linked to the process of capitalist development in Brazil. But it did not constitute, at least for the time being, capitalist development in the sense of spreading relations of production based on wage labor. In some cases, wage labor did catch up with migrants to the frontier, but there is reason to believe, as will be argued below, that the gap may now be widening rather than narrowing.

The paradigm of economic organization on the Great Frontier in the postwar decades was the family unit of production combining family labor with productive forces found in nature, especially land. When the family has possession of the means of production directly involved in the appropriation of nature and retains part of the product for its own consumption, while another part is appropriated by third parties as surplus, it can be included in the category of "peasants." This is an analytic category that is useful for interpreting processes such as recent frontier settlement; it does not necessarily correspond to the common or conventional use of the term. Particularly, it is not limited to "subsistence" production, but also includes petty commodity production, as long as labor and means of production come from within the family unit rather than being purchased on the market (Sawyer 1979b:chap. 2).

Accordingly, settlement on the Great Frontier can be characterized in terms of peasant fronts, including squatters, colonists, smallholders, sharecroppers, and other small farmers. Other Amazonian peasantries, which were already present, include mestizos involved in small-scale extraction and subsistence agriculture ("caboclos"), autonomous rubber tappers, and detribalized Indians. It is important to recognize the diversity of these peasantries and their varying relationships with land, markets, and surrounding society. Although quantification is difficult, available data indicate that these small-scale, relatively independent producers make up the greater part of the rural population on the frontier and that they are responsible for most of the food crops (Ministério de Agri-cultura/CEDEPLAR-UFMG 1979).

Although heterogeneous in other ways, the different peasan-tries are all precapitalist, in the sense that they do not involve wage labor nor generate surplus value. Beneficial as they may be, in some ways, to accumulation of capital, they remain locked in a contradiction that, sooner or later, will become manifest. Instead of being destroyed in the course of history, peasantries on the whole actually grew in Brazil, in both numerical and spatial terms. This fact presents a particular challenge for explanations of the frontier, which must account at the same time for expansion of capitalism and of precapitalist forms.

In addition to this economic contradiction, peasant fronts also involve political resistance to domination and exploitation. This dimension does not appear in analysis of secondary data but in in-terviews and observation in the field. Many migrants say that they want to get away from various forms of servitude and that they have had enough of working for others. They want to work on their own account, to be their own bosses, to plant their own land. Thus, frontier migration represents an alternative to exploitation and proletarianization. It is a special form of class struggle, not be-tween classes as such, but among groups that want to avoid be-coming a class, at least a working class, as long as they can.

We can thus see that the frontier is an alternative space in both economic and sociopolitical terms, a kind of refuge for those who flee from the advance of big capital. In some respects it is also a demographic alternative for those segments of the population who seek to continue having large families, a possibility that was extended to the population as a whole during the transition from slavery to free labor but that is now becoming a liability in the more developed areas. Fertility rates in frontier areas in the post-war period were high and increasing, while in the more developed areas they are at intermediate levels and have been decreasing, es-pecially since the mid-sixties (Sawyer 1981; Carvalho, Paiva, and Sawyer 1981).

Of course, the frontier is far from being a peasant paradise. Many and diverse pressures, both from within and from without the region, make reproduction and even survival of the various peasantries increasingly difficult. Some of the most important pressures will be discussed in the following section.

Speculative fronts on the Great Frontier

Even though market conditions on the Great Frontier favored both peasant and capitalist forms of occupation, Brazil's surplus population generally arrived there first, before capital. During the import substitution phase, almost all available capital was concentrated in urban-industrial development. The continued surplus of noncapitalist agricultural and extractive products permitted available financial resources to be applied to infrastructure, industrial plants, and modern services, while the hinterland was articulated with the core through circulation. It was neither necessary nor feasible, economically or politically, to transform agricultural production, which continued to expand output by incorporating new lands rather than by modernizing production techniques.

In the phase of associated-dependent development, however, relations between the urban-industrial core and the Great Frontier changed. After the mid-sixties, there was enough capital accumulated to be applied outside the core, especially during the economic "miracle" of 1968–1972, when growth rates averaged 10 percent per year. Agriculture began to absorb industrialized inputs and equipment (tractors, fertilizers, insecticides, and feed) and to produce raw materials and food that were in turn industrialized (processed fruits and vegetables, oil, fruit juice, and animal feed). It became possible to initiate a process of direct subordination of production on the Great Frontier.

The first move of capitalist enterprise was to acquire land. The land market expanded so that its limits reached and surpassed the previously mentioned limits of the markets for agricultural products and for consumer goods. Capitalist relations of production, on the other hand, remained within a smaller radius, with some exceptions. Acquisition of vast areas of land by large corporations was facilitated by government policies of withdrawal of support for rubber production, by public land sales, auctions and grants, by outright financial incentives, and by general government support of big business. But what most interested the new investors was the rapid increase in the value of land because of new roads, highly optimistic predictions regarding possibilities for ranching, and discovery of mineral and timber resources. This was especially important in an inflationary economy where real estate has long been a convenient hedge.

It would be inappropriate to characterize capitalist penetration of the Great Frontier in terms of "capitalist fronts," to the extent that this term refers to the organization of production. A better term may be "speculative fronts." These fronts include, in addition to pure speculation, related elements such as easy access to subsidized credit, outlets for profits that could not all be remitted abroad, portfolio diversification of oligopolistic firms, some experiments with new agricultural or ranching technology, and even a measure of production that requires little investment and maintenance, especially in ranching. Nevertheless, for the most part, land is neither a subject nor an instrument of labor, for appropriation of nature or as a site for combining purchased inputs. Labor is practically absent. Land is primarily a store of value, a source of future ground-rent.

In sum, capital's entry into the Great Frontier was not yet capitalist in the sense of transforming production through introduction of wage labor and technical progress. Although development generated in urban-industrial areas had become strong enough to take control of surplus land all over Brazil, it was still too weak to combine this land with the population upon it in capitalist relations of production.

Present conflict and possible future trends

The conflict that has become a characteristic of the Great Frontier in recent years—eviction of squatters; murders of hired gunmen, ranch managers, and rural union leaders; accusations of infiltration in the Catholic Church—can be understood as a symptom of the shock between peasant fronts and speculative fronts. Instead of following behind peasant occupation, land markets have now jumped ahead, far ahead. Practically all of the land in the Great Frontier already has owners, not in the formal sense (indeed, legal title is often questionable or nonexistent), but in the concrete sense of keeping squatters away. It is true that formal ownership of vast unoccupied areas has existed in Brazil since colonial times, when royal land grants were made. But owners were not always interested in defending their supposed rights to property, nor were they always able to do so. Today, even on untitled or public lands, it is difficult for migrants to find a spot where they can peacefully settle. There is no more land without end, free and available to whomever has the courage and determination to penetrate the forest and establish homesteads.

Thus, instead of providing ever greater opportunities for

appropriation of land by peasants, the frontier now involves decreasing opportunities or outright expropriation. The expulsion of settlers already on the land is almost always violent, particularly as settlers become conscious of the fact that there is no land available further inland or upriver, and that they can find strength in unity.

The closing off of access to land also leads to accumulation of new migrants in small- and medium-sized urban centers. The results of expulsion from the countryside and concentration of the population in cities and towns can be observed in data from the 1980 census. Average annual growth rates of rural and urban population between 1970 and 1980 were calculated and mapped for all of Brazil's 361 microregions. While data permitting estimates of fertility and mortality on the basis of the 1980 census are not yet available, differences in growth rates among microregions are so dramatic that the overall pattern of migration can readily be discerned. While natural increase for Brazil as a whole between 1970 and 1980 was about 2.5 percent (assuming that net international migration was negligible), natural increase for the Great Frontier would be higher, particularly in areas of rapid in-migration. Carvalho and Moreira (1976) calculated that the rate of natural increase for the North region between 1960 and 1970 was 3.6 percent per year. While fertility in Brazil as a whole declined in the seventies, it is not clear from available data that this occurred in frontier areas. In previous decades, fertility rates in the frontier areas apparently increased. Cross-sectional estimates at the microregional level for 1970 show a strong correlation between in-migration and high fertility rates (Sawyer 1981; Carvalho, et al. 1981). Thus, the figure of 3.5 percent is arbitrary but probably suitable as a point of reference for the rough comparisons to be made here.

The most noteworthy facts with regard to rates of growth of the rural population on the Great Frontier between 1970 and 1980 pertain to three distinct belts or zones (see Figure 1):

Zone 1: In practically all of Mato Grosso do Sul and Goiás, growth rates were well below 3.5 percent per year, or even negative. Such widespread out-migration from rural areas that in the fifties and sixties had been dynamic frontier areas with very high growth rates constitutes a dramatic turnaround in migration patterns.

Zone 2: The belt extending from Rondônia through Mato

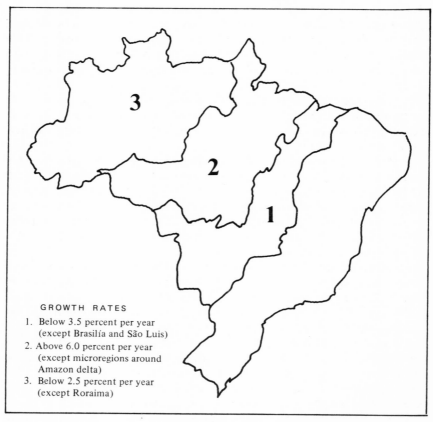

GROWTH RATES
1. Below 3.5 percent per year
   (except Brasilía and São Luis)
2. Above 6.0 percent per year
   (except microregions around
   Amazon delta)
3. Below 2.5 percent per year
   (except Roraima)

Fig. 1. Growth rates of rural population on Great Frontier, 1970–80.

Grosso and into eastern Pará, except for the area of the Amazon estuary, had growth rates above 6 percent per year. In some microregions, annual rates were as high as 12 percent. This belt across the middle of the Great Frontier was the only extensive area in Brazil that did not conform to the overall tendency of rural outmigration, which in the 1970s, for the first time, resulted in an absolute decrease in the size of the rural population. There was estimated net rural-urban migration of between 13.3 and 14.6 million during the decade (Wood and Wilson in this volume). Of course, the rates of growth in frontier areas are high because of small initial base population, and so-called microregions in the Amazon region are in fact immense, so that large areas on the map give an impression of large numbers. If we assume that natural increase in this belt was 3.5 percent per year, net in-migration would only be about half a million.

Zone 3: In the states of Amazonas and Acre, growth rates were clearly below rates of natural increase. This tendency toward rural out-migration on the other side of the belt of rapid settlement, where the natural rubber economy was in decline, was already underway in the sixties, for reasons that have been touched upon.

With regard to urban population, growth rates were above 3.5 percent in all of the three above-mentioned belts or zones, in many cases above 10 percent per year. This growth suggests that there was rural-urban migration within the first and third belts and migration from other areas to cities and towns of the second belt, perhaps combined with local rural-urban movement.

These data show that, in spite of its name, the Great Frontier is now undergoing a process of rural outmigration in most of its area. This requires that we stop and think about the meaning of the "frontier" in Brazil today. The historical and structural interpretation of the spatial distribution of the country's economic activities and population sketched out in previous sections of this paper, with emphasis on the relationships between expansion and retraction, may provide some insights with regard to this apparently curious reversal of previous trends.

First, however, some comments should be made on interpretations that view population decline in frontier areas in terms of continuous forward movement. Geographers write of the "hollow" frontier, thinking of exhaustion of soil fertility and the onward movement of most intense pioneer activity, which leaves behind relatively empty areas (James 1942). Second, and sometimes in association with this view, other authors describe the reproduction on the frontier of agrarian structures typical of older areas, leading to concentration of landholdings, which may in turn push new settlers onward to new frontiers farther inland. Finally, specific crops or activities such as soybeans or ranching can provoke the same sort of displacement of settlers.

These interpretations have some validity, but they do not seem to be sufficient. Analysis of frontier areas in Brazil today would seem to require consideration not only of processes of expansion but also of retraction (Martine 1981). Greater attention should be

paid to the centripetal forces that seem to have intensified in recent years and that may counterbalance the timid or grandiose
efforts to organize capitalist production in the Amazon region.
The main novelty of this approach would be to connect frontier
retraction with the expansion of capitalism, to link the ebb and
flow. The following analysis focuses on three interrelated factors:
transport costs, industrialization of agriculture, and ecological
conditions in Amazonia.

Rapid increase in transport costs because of growing distance
between the moving peasant and capitalist fronts and fixed market
centers, as well as higher petroleum prices after 1974, affected the
spatial configuration of markets for primary products and for consumer goods. The "radius" of these markets, in which the effects
of transport costs are proportional to distance, stopped growing, or
even shrank. Thus, the frontier in the sense we have suggested, a
space with conditions that favor commodity production, either became smaller or at least did not continue to expand as expected,
even when the new roads were opened.

Rising transport costs are especially important for capitalist
production, which requires, in addition to getting goods to market, a series of modern inputs: seeds, insecticides, herbicides,
fungicides, fertilizers, machinery, spare parts, fuel, veterinary products, and feed. The obstacles to the free flow of such commodities
dealt capitalist agriculture in frontier areas a double blow.

In addition to commodities, capitalist agriculture also depends on various services such as financing, extension, maintenance of equipment, and communication with the Center-South.
Furthermore, it requires personal services considered essential by
the agricultural bourgeoisie or "middle-class," especially schools,
hospitals, and cultural resources. These various production and
personal services do not circulate but have to be located near the
production sites. They are not effectively installed in isolated
areas as long as demand is weak, and the lack of them discourages
expansion of capitalist production.

The recent weakening of expansion is more than a downward
swing in a series of cycles. Rather, it is related to a structural tendency of capitalist production in agriculture. Capitalist agriculture is fundamentally different from peasant agriculture, including
peasant commodity production, in that it becomes increasingly
similar to industrial production. Land becomes more an instrument of labor than a subject of labor. It comes to be used simply as

physical space in which a series of inputs and services acquired on the market are combined, as in a factory. As inputs and services increase, the space needed for the same amount of output decreases, i.e., yields per hectare increase. Capitalist agriculture begins to be distributed in space in accordance with external economies of the type that affect location of industry. A tendency to concentrate replaces the tendency to spread; expansion becomes "vertical" instead of "horizontal." This can be seen in the case of sugar cane in São Paulo state, irrigated rice in Rio Grande do Sul, and chicken farms near metropolitan areas, to cite a few examples.

In addition to these spatial obstacles, captalist agriculture must also contend with ecological problems presented by the Amazon rainforest. The technology developed in temperate zones for homogeneous cultivation of large areas has been found to be vulnerable to rapid exhaustion of tropical soils and to numerous diseases, pests, and weeds, unless fertilizers and other chemical products are massively applied. Partial technification increases economic and environmental risks, without providing control of the various causes of failure. Therefore, "transitional" agriculture, in the middle range of technification, is highly risky in the humid tropics. The safer alternatives are to imitate traditional systems of polyculture, with low levels of investment, or to go to the other extreme, with complete technification. In the latter alternative, each input in the "package" guarantees returns to the others and minimizes the risks of total loss when nature strikes back. The first alternative is usually dismissed as "backward" and "irrational" without study or evaluation of possible adaptations. The second is restricted to very small areas in Amazonia where all of the necessary physical and institutional support can be provided. The middle level of technification, due to poor planning or inadequate conditions, has proved disastrous, or at least disappointing, in rubber plantations, tree farming, and cattle ranching. The exuberant flora and fauna of Amazonia have turned out to be stubborn enemies of "modern" agriculture. Capitalist producers are rediscovering the advantages of more developed areas and of the savannas of central Brazil.

For all of these reasons, which place restrictions on the frontier as a potential space for agriculture, speculative fronts in the Amazon region have not turned into productive capitalist fronts. Instead of opening the way for capitalist production, the speculative fronts have been left stranded. The tide has turned.

The most unfortunate consequence of this situation, from the collective point of view, is that the speculative fronts, in addition to not producing, do not let anyone else produce. This is due primarily to their monopoly of land, which can no longer be used by petty commodity producers. Land is no longer a surplus factor, but neither is it a factor of production. At the same time, large expanses of idle land make it less feasible to build infrastructure and organize services that would benefit both the petty producers and the capitalists, providing conditions for expansion of agricultural production. The paradox of this situation is that the expansion of capitalism ended up generating its opposite: retraction, involution, stagnation of the economy on its periphery. Occupation of empty spaces is confused with emptying out of occupied spaces. This is not due to the sort of stagnation in which land will not support additional occupation. To the contrary, land in much of Amazonia remains practically untouched. As in the historical cases mentioned previously, development of productive forces takes place in other areas. Stagnation on the frontier is not a step backward, except on a local level, but is part of the forward movement of capitalist development as a whole.

Such redefinition of the economic space of the frontier also involves disintegration of the social space that provided alternatives for the population that could not or did not want to be absorbed by the archaic structures of the countryside or by capitalist relations of production elsewhere in Brasil. The basic precondition for putting the frontier alternative into practice has been, and still is, access to land. Today, however, this possibility is only open to limited numbers, like the small landholders who have the means to pay for plots offered in private colonization projects. Monetarization of subsistence activities and proletarianization reduce the space for nonwage forms of production in the cities as well, even in metropolitan areas.

It is in this context of reduction of an alternative economic and social space that we can think of the so-called closing of the frontier. It is totally different from the closing that occurred in the United States at the end of the nineteenth century, when the dividing line between occupied and unoccupied areas of the West dissolved. Nor is it a case of physical exhaustion of soil or natural resources, of the capacity to absorb more population, either as surplus or as labor power. In spite of its economic causes, the closing is juridical and political, at the level of the superstructure. It may therefore be reversible.

In the short and medium run, political considerations of what to do with Brazil's growing surplus population may be important. There are no juridical or political means available to keep part of this population from turning to the frontier, especially as opportunities are also closed off in the cities. The frontier has no gate that can be locked, nor can barbed wire hold back people who are desperate and determined.

Policies favoring a certain reopening of the frontier may become more likely to the extent that political pressures, including those of an electoral nature, build up, while speculative fronts are not turned to production. This would provide an economic basis for political initiatives that might seem, on the basis of prevailing interpretations of capitalist expansion on the frontier, to go entirely against the current. Signs of such opening include the creation of executive land agencies with special powers to distribute land in the Araguaia-Tocantins (GETAT) and Baixo Amazonas (GEBAM), as well as the new law giving squatters rights to the land they occupy after only five years, instead of ten (Perpétuo 1981). These measures would, of course, protect large landholdings, but they begin to require that the land be put to social use and that its monopolization not present political risks to the continuity of the system as a whole.

In the longer run, there are possibilities for new frontier expansion on a more solid basis. Industry shows some signs of decreasing concentration. The demand for food and raw materials continues to grow and to spread. Ground rents in the Center-South rise to constantly higher levels. There are external diseconomies such as pollution, congestion, environmental degradation, and increased risks of pests in agriculture. The gravitational model, according to which economic activity and population become increasingly concentrated, also has its limits.

Final considerations

At the end of such a tentative and exploratory essay, it may seem pretentious to reach conclusions of any kind. Nonetheless, still in the spirit of an essay and on the basis of other research not included here, the following points can be presented in summary form:

1. The Amazon frontier should not be seen as a solution for national or international problems of either an economic or demographic nature.

2. It would be more realistic and socially more just to take migration to the Great Frontier as given, seeking to reorient it and consolidate settlement in areas already partially occupied.

3. Given the idle capacity of land and labor in the region, as well as considerable potential for production, strengthening of peasant commodity production would bring benefits to the frontier population and to Brazilian society as a whole.

4. Capitalist agriculture should only be stimulated in the few small areas and for the few crops in which it has real chances of success, in order to avoid waste of public resources and widespread damage to the environment.

5. Political instruments to achieve points 3 and 4 should take into account the indirect effects of the various policies that influence economic and demographic trends in the region, with possibly unexpected results.

6. There is a shortage of adequate knowledge of natural resources on the frontier and of the means of exploiting them that would be most appropriate in economic, social, and environmental terms.

This essay will have served its purpose if it helps to raise hypotheses on interrelationships between demographic, ecological, economic, and political aspects of settlement in Brazil and other countries that still have frontiers.

References Cited

Arruda, H.P.
   1978   *Colonização Oficial e Dirigida.* Brasília: INCRA.
Cardoso, F.H. and G. Müller
   1977   *Amazônia: Expansão do Capitalismo.* São Paulo: Brasiliense.
Carvalho, J.A.M. and M.M. Moreira
   1976   *Migrações Internas na Região Norte.* Belém: SUDAM/ CEDEPLAR.
Carvalho, J.A.M., P.T.A. Paiva, and D.R. Sawyer
   1981   The recent sharp drop in fertility in Brazil: Economic boom, social inequality and baby bust. Mexico City: Population

Council, Latin America and Caribbean Office. Working Paper
No. 8.

James, P.
1942   *Latin America.* New York: Odyssey.
Martine, G.
1981   Expansão e Retração do Emprego na Fronteira Agrícola. Paper
presented in the Seminário Regional sobre Expansão da Fronteira Agrícola e Meio Ambiente na América Latina, CEPAL,
Brasília, November 10–13.
Ministério de Agricultura/CEDEPLAR-UFMG
1979   *Ocupação Agrícola da Amazônia: Primeiros Estudos para a
Fixação de Diretrizes.* Belo Horizonte and Brasília.
Perpétuo, F.A.
1981   GETAT: Consideração Política da Questão da Terra. Paper presented in the Seminário Regional sobre Expansão da Fronteira Agrícola e Meio Ambiente na América Latina, CEPAL,
Brasília, November 10–13.
Sawyer, D.R.
1979a   Colonização na Amazônia: Migração de Nordestinos para uma
Frente Agrícola no Pará. *Revista Económica do Nordeste:*
10:3 (July/September):773–812.
1979b   Peasants and Capitalism on an Amazon Frontier. Ph.D. dissertation, Harvard University.
1981   Fecundidade e Mortalidade na Amazônia: Nota Sobre as Es-
timativas e Interpretações. In *Anais Segundo Encontro Nacional Estudos Populacionais.* Pp. 113–83. São Paulo: ABEP.
Singer, P.
1972   Migraciones Internas: Consideraciones Teóricas Sobre su Estudio. In H. Muñoz et al., eds., *Migración y Desarrollo: Consideraciones Teóricas,* pp. 45–67. Buenos Aires: CLACSO.
1981   Crescimento Econômico e Distribuição Espacial da Popu-
lação. Paper presented in the Simpósio sobre a Questão Mi-
gratória no Brasil, CNPQ, Brasília.
Waibel, L.
1979   As Zonas Pioneiras do Brasil. In *Capítulos de Geografia
Tropical e do Brasil,* 2d ed. Pp. 279–312. Rio de Janeiro: IBGE.

Colonization in the Colombian Amazon

Sutti Ortiz

F RONTIER expansion in Colombia has been slow but persistent throughout its history. Population pressure has
pushed the boundaries of all settlements outwards until each center no longer existed as an isolated enclave. But migrants have also
colonized far-off niches, claiming them as food resources for urban
settlers or as resources of exportable crops or raw materials. Frontiers moved in response to population pressure, to shortage of
land, and to opportunities believed to exist in particular regions.
Some of the suspected opportunities proved unrealistic, leaving
impoverished or dying frontier enclaves. In many cases, however,
products found a ready export market or a large urban demand,
thus assuring the enlargement of the enclave and its eventual inte-

NOTE: I would like to thank the staff members of the IBRD for their cooperation with information about the Caquetá area and colonization
projects. Klaas Haasjes was, among many others, particularly generous
with his time and helpful in his guidance. The information on Guaviare
was gathered when I was acting as a consultant for the IBRD. The opinions expressed here are the sole responsibility of the author and do not
reflect necessarily the opinion or official position of any individual or institution. While I was in Guaviare, Oscar Cordon helped me to understand local farming possibilities. I thank the personnel of INCORA in
Bogotá and Guaviare for their generous sharing of information and experience. Many individuals have contributed data, references, and arguments.
I owe a special thanks to L. Jarvis, Michael Taussig, Kathy Durham, and
Theodore Scudder.

gration into the national and international community. Silver, gold, rubber, cattle, and coffee are the classic and dramatic examples for Colombia, but the demand for pork and more mundane food staples also proved a powerful incentive for the poorer *colonos.*

Some migrants intentionally settled in upper and lower Amazonia areas as early as the nineteenth century. They went there in search of fortune, laborers, land, or trading opportunities. Some stayed, creating enclaves that served as nuclei of colonization for latecomers. Others either succumbed to fevers, or left with the money they made from trade and rubber exploitation. A sensible but speculative assumption is that others left empty handed. As in the rest of Colombia, the activities of these early migrants sketched the scenario for later colonization movements that have so far claimed only the upper reaches of the Amazon affluents in Colombia.

The steady expansion of the frontier into Amazonia did not start until the turn of the century. It was then that Capuchin missionaries and peasants from Nariño moved down into the Sibundoy valley of the Putumayo. It was also about the same time that a smaller number of settlers moved into Caquetá, though this area did not become flooded with colonos until much later (1950–70). The Guaviare early settlers, in contrast, remained in isolation until much later. The territory that separated them from their connecting link to the highlands, the Llanos de Meta, had first to be occupied. The frontier moved east and south first through the Llanos, reaching the Guaviare only ten years ago.

Readers familiar with the economic history of Colombia will note that entrepreneurs, peasants, and *hacendados* were busily exploring and exploiting the sparsely inhabited ecological niches within the highland area, about the same time that population movements were beginning to push out the Indians of Amazonia. Antioqueños moving south were converting river valleys into cattle *haciendas* and transforming the slopes of Caldas and Quindío into small and large coffee plantations at the same time as Nariñenses were settling into the Sibundoy valley. A bit later, entrepreneurs transformed the Cauca valley into a major sugar-producing zone. During the first half of the twentieth century, peasants and wealthier farmers were cutting through the forested slopes of eastern Cauca to plant pasture, coffee, and potatoes. Presently only Amazonia and the eastern llanos remain as the major frontier areas.

Hence a meaningful review of the colonization of Amazonia must see it as not unlike other migratory movements and must consider both the politico-economic realities of Colombia and the ecological characteristics of Amazonia, for which the works of Rice (1910, 1914), Christ and Guhl (1957), and Hegen (1966) are especially helpful. A comparative historical approach helps to refute the thesis that road construction has been the guiding force of colonization. Roads, of course, do serve as spearheads for migratory movements, but Amazonia is likely to have been settled whether roads were there or not. McGreevy's thesis that coffee expansion followed railroad construction has proved incorrect (Palacios 1980). A similar conclusion can be reached if we examine closely the colonization of Putumayo and Guaviare. In the former area migration and road building went hand in hand; in the latter there was road and water transport much before the inflow of migrants. Roads have an impact and may enhance the migratory flow, but they do not necessarily cause migration. To discourage road building may discourage some types of colonization, rather than block colonization.

If one looks at all frontier movements and migration into far-off enclaves in Colombia during the late nineteenth and twentieth centuries, it also becomes clear that colonizers are not an homogenous group of people. Some are peasants poor in land, cash, and other opportunities. Others are entrepreneurs with limited resources, or traders from small towns, who find it profitable to shift back and forth between agriculture and trading activities. Wealthy merchants or landowners, as well as capitalists, have sometimes found it profitable to invest and even settle in frontier areas, usually when other investments seem dubious, when speculative prospects are appealing, or when land acquisition in frontier areas is the only way to recoup losses. Amazonia, as well as other earlier frontier areas of Colombia, has become dotted with large plantations, cattle ranches, unexploited haciendas, and small colono farms. It will thus be helpful to the reader to focus on migration into Amazonia within the context of the events that have shaped certain forms of colonization and development in Colombia as a whole. With this background, the remainder of this essay will examine in detail the post-1950 influx of population and the process of settlement in the area. Policy implications of this analysis are discussed in the concluding section.

History of colonization in Amazonia

Already in the seventeenth century Amazonia felt the intrusion of outsiders: *encomenderos* crossed the area demanding tribute labor and missionaries settled within it. But only the latter made an impact by organizing settlements, which much later were to serve as focal centers for migratory movements. The most active mission centers were in Putumayo, where the Capuchins were given free reign to pursue their "civilizing" activities. Eventually they acquired land, organized road construction using Indian labor, and developed new towns. By 1913 they had amassed an estate of 2,000 hectares, which was exploited with forty-one peons and five permanent employees. Three hundred head of cattle pastured in their land, which also was used to produce grain and staples. Capuchins also established a number of small enterprises—liquor production, marble quarries and saw mills—and encouraged settlers to come into the area. Rural small holders displaced by the War of a Thousand Days responded to missionary incentives, some of them purchasing land which the mission had acquired from the Indians (Bonilla 1972). Closeness to highland markets of Nariño favored the earlier frontier development in Putumayo, which would have been more impressive if the Colombian economy had been stronger and political stability greater. This was not the case for Caquetá and Guaviare, where missionaries were less aggressive and settlements more isolated.

At the time when settlers were moving into Putumayo and entrepreneurs were entering the more remote areas in search of rubber, Colombia was going through serious political and economic upheavals. The War of a Thousand Days (1899–1902) devastated many rural areas. Not surprisingly in Nariño, one of the areas more directly affected by the war, rural dwellers looked for peace in the eastern slope of the Andes.

Trade was disrupted not just by rural violence but also by national policy that made paper money the compulsory medium of exchange in international trade. Shortage of money hindered transactions and discouraged production for the internal market. The only Colombians not touched by this economic policy were producers who sold in the export market, as they could exchange their goods for gold or foreign currency. Rubber extraction therefore became very enticing, for the product attracted foreign buyers. Rubber extracting entrepreneurs, furthermore, did not suffer from the shortage and high cost of labor that large coffee haciendas had to face during and after the war. Rubber was collected by Indians who were enslaved and tortured to increase their productivity.

By the beginning of this century, the only entrepreneurs profiting from the exploitation of resources in Amazonia were the rubber traders. They penetrated far down Putumayo, Caquetá, and Vaupés wherever they found valuable rubber trees. Their use of Indian labor led to the decimation and scattering of the native population. The Indians of Putumayo encountered land pressure on the western side due to missionization and on the eastern end from the activities of rubber collectors. They found little protection from missions in this area (Bonilla 1972, Wesche 1967, Steward 1948).

The only town that can trace its origin to the rubber period is Florencia, which was founded in 1902 and was intended as a supply and collection center for the hinterland. The regional and hinterland centers could have developed further if settlers had been encouraged to come, and independent small entrepreneurs allowed. But the rubber trade was soon to be monopolized by the Peruvian Amazon Company, known locally as Casa Araña, which had a policy to discourage and actually push out colonos and independent entrepreneurs (Roberts 1975:71, Bonilla 1972). The company was registered in London and had the rights to extract and export rubber in Colombia, Ecuador, and eventually Peru. Most of the trade routes went out of Colombia via Amazonia so that not even the neighboring highland centers profited from the venture. By the time the trade began to subside in 1905, the only mark it left was one of decimation; by 1920 the rubber boom had ended.

The turn of the century was a period neither for internal commercial expansion nor for the intensification of large-scale agriculture and cattle ranching. There was a shortage of capital and labor and a shrinking internal market for meat and staples. Only foreign plantations that did not depend on national capital flourished; small peasant producers who grew coffee for export managed to survive. But many large cattle ranchers and coffee planters went bankrupt. This was not the time to intensify large-scale agriculture or to displace tenants and squatters. Frontier expansion had a limited appeal; Antioquia, Caldas, and Quindío provided enough scope for the activities of those who either did not depend on capital, like the peasant producer, or had sufficient capital.

The end of the war did not ease the plight of producers and

consumers in Colombia. Inflation continued, money was still in shortage, and national coffers were empty. Growing external and internal debts paralyzed government action. This state of affairs indirectly affected the future development of Amazonia. The government's solution to its fiscal problems was to issue bonds that could be redeemed with public land. The holder of the bond could either sell or redeem it. If he chose the second option, he had to pay for the cost of survey, demarcation, and titling. Given the state of the economy, many chose to hold the bonds and await an improvement in the market for land. The fate of large extensions of land in the llanos and Amazonia as well as other parts of Colombia was set at this early date.

The bonds may have passed through many hands and were often not redeemed until much later, but when they were exchanged for a land title it was for extensions ranging from 1,000 to 14,000 hectares. Even though in many cases the actual holdings were subsequently subdivided, the possession of large tracts was an opportunity only open to investors who did not reside in Amazonia. It was probably these events that gave birth to the large estates that appeared in Llanos and Caquetá, attracting the attention of landless peasants searching for land or work or both. Road construction had little to do with these earlier speculative investments. The first large landholdings were owned by wealthy urban traders and industrialists who had access to capital and could convert the holdings into cattle ranches. The advantage of such an investment was that it did not require much labor and could be used to produce hides for export.

The public bonds policy was probably responsible for the emergence of a number of estates in Caquetá that were later to be consolidated by the Lara family into one large *latifundio*. In other words, by the 1930s missionaries and government had through their efforts and policies assured the private ownership of large tracts of valuable land in Amazonia. These large private properties were ready to be exploited with immigrant laborers whenever a propitious circumstance presented itself. But that moment would have to await economic recovery from the depression and the resolution of border litigations with Peru.

The depression of the thirties affected Colombia very seriously. All sectors suffered, and production could not easily expand; in fact, Colombia had to rely on food imports. Unemployed urban settlers had once again to move out into the countryside and search for areas where subsistence production was at least possible. Although Putumayo lowlands had an appeal for settlers of Nariño, Caquetá and Guaviare were too far away for impoverished families. Furthermore, it was just as possible, though more uncertain, to squat on unused land nearer their urban location. These movements caused considerable social unrest, and politicians began to look toward Amazonia as a solution for the ever-growing political problems of the highlands.

Migration to Amazonia became a popular theme among politicians for a number of other reasons. The supposedly fertile areas of Amazonia could be made to produce food cheaply for the internal markets, thus avoiding the import of staples. New settlers could ensure national territorial rights as tension was building up with Peru. These thoughts inspired some visionary politicians and newspaper editors into organizing foolhardy settlement projects.

The war with Peru introduced a new dimension. Troop movements required roads and food provision. Traders and peasants were encouraged to move and found this new opportunity enticing; they began to settle not in the foothills but in the lowland reaches of Amazonia. Thus colonization enclaves were formed that later served as nuclei for frontier expansion.

With this renewed attention to the lowlands area, the Capuchin missionaries were finally able to obtain subsidies to continue the road all the way to Puerto Asís, and Florencia residents profited from a road connection to highland Huila. Amazonia ceased to be totally isolated; most major settlements now had a connection to a major marketing center. The other impact of the war was the growth of at least some small agricultural centers for the provisioning of troops. Although these centers disappeared with the end of the war, new ones grew as conscripts were encouraged to remain in the area. The large haciendas could now count on a labor resource, albeit small, but sufficient to initiate expansion. The opening of new urban markets and the collapse of highland beef industry in Colombia served as further incentives.

It was about this time, 1939, that the above-mentioned Lara family, a merchant-industrialist family from the highlands, began to purchase land in Caquetá. The original hacienda of 1,800 hectares soon expanded with the labor of resident colonos and ex-soldiers. The Laras began to purchase other haciendas and eventually to absorb the improved land of indebted colonos. By 1960 they had amassed 35,000 hectares and had built a port and an airport. They became the major employer of migrant laborers, offering them medical services, selling them their supplies, and marketing their crops.

The next chapter in the history of Colombia had a deep effect on the development of Amazonia. The *Violencia* left many peasants in Antioquia and Huila homeless and landless. When calm finally was established in rural areas during the 1950s, peasants began to search for new areas of settlement either as farmers or rural wage laborers. Caquetá was one such area. Government policies definitely encouraged and fostered such moves, but it is most likely that they would nevertheless have occurred spontaneously in response to the need for workers and availability of jobs in Caquetá towns and cattle ranches. The process of settlement in the lowlands and policy questions related to colonization will be considered in detail in the remainder of this essay.

As Amazonia has now developed its own set of larger towns with internal food demands and the potential for development of processing and craft industries, it is most likely that the influx of population will continue. But the population coming into the area will now be more diversified and the possibility that other opportunities will be exploited is more likely. The question that planners should retain in mind is whether to ensure an even distribution of income through the retention of peasant production or to transform this sector into a more productive and powerful group, able to ensure the income and welfare of its members. Another equally important question, which at the moment is hardly ever voiced by planners, is how the growth of regional centers will affect secondary migratory waves and the mode of integration of urban and rural sectors into national policy and economics.

Government colonization projects

During the late 1950s and 1960s, government and private individuals devised some elaborate colonization programs for Caquetá and Guaviare, the two major Amazonian centers that remained underpopulated. Within Caquetá new roads were built and the Agrarian Bank attempted to settle 1,040 families in 1961. However, bad planning and poor selection of colonos led to disastrous results; only 570 of the original colono families chose to stay. A more curious but equally disastrous plan was devised for Guaviare. In 1968, a journalist from Bogotá, with support of the Air Force, advertised for prospective colonos. Half of the prospective settlers would stay in urban areas and subsidize a partner, who would clear two parcels of land, one for himself and one for his supporter in Bogotá. Settlers were allowed to claim fifty to sixty hectares in a specified area of Guaviare. Lack of support, isolation, and malaria forced many of the survivors to return to the highlands.

The failure of these colonization projects did not discourage further spontaneous migrations, particularly where some form of supplemental wage employment was available. Putumayo offered the added attraction of temporary labor in the Texaco fields or as food suppliers to their workers; Caquetá offered the possibility of work in the established haciendas. In these two regions, about 30 percent of colonos depended on wage labor. Colonos began to come at a fast rate; during some years Caquetá had to cope with an influx of 4,000 migrants (Table 1). The growth rate in all colonization areas is highest during the initial period (8.5 percent) slowing down as the area reaches saturation.

While the first colonos settled along roads or on the fertile flood plains of rivers, later comers were willing either to clear the less fertile lands disregarded by others or to clear areas between river drainages in order to have easy access to markets and already established medical and educational services. Thus, in Putumayo most of the population is nowadays concentrated on the higher ill-drained but fertile valleys and along the river basins as far down as Puerto Asis and Leguizamo—that is, between existing townships. In Caquetá, most colonos have stayed in the area around Florencia and the roads that skirt the foothills, where most of the older haciendas are also located. In Guaviare settlers prefer to find a farm near the single road that connects the area with its urban center linking it to Villavicencio and Bogotá as well. While some colonos are willing to face isolation in order to gain access to more fertile soil, most of them settle in the periphery only when available land is not suitable for agriculture.

Frontier expansion in areas of colonization is not simply due to the new influx of colonos but also to population movements within established areas. Migrants who fail to raise enough revenue to cover subsistence expenses sell already cleared land in order to pay off debts. Other colonos, who had hoped to pasture cattle in their new grassland but were not able to obtain credit to purchase animals, likewise are willing to sell their farms and use the returns to clear virgin forest and acquire some animals.

TABLE 1. Population growth in three Amazonian areas

Year	Putumayo	Caquetá	Rural Guaviare
1951	28,099[a]	40,950[b]	—
1964	56,284[a]	103,718	—
1971	—	—	664[c]
1972	—	168,000	—
1973	—	—	3,839[d]
1978	—	—	18,000[c]

a. Data derived from Wesche 1967 : 9.
b. Data derived from DANE population census, 1965. DANE publications do not always cite the same figure, and they provide no explanation for disparities. For 1951 there is another estimate of 46,000. Inclusion of Indians or certain territories may explain the disparity.
c. Data collected by the Malaria Service, probably the most accurate information for the rural hinterland.
d. INCORA, 1977; these data are not as reliable as those for 1978. Data for the urban center of San José were obtained for 1978, but they ranged from 4,000 to about 8,000.

Wealthier settlers and local hacendados have profited from this venture and thus managed to accumulate pasture land without having to invest any labor or much capital.

This pattern of land concentration is most clearly illustrated in Caquetá from Marsch's (1980) survey of 8,840 farms (see Table 2) and Roberts's (1975) study in a hinterland area. Roberts's survey is much smaller and limited to a more distant area of colonization where there were also some earlier settlers. By 1975, 5 percent of the farmers he studied had not yet managed to acquire land; 85 percent controlled only 45 percent of claimed land, while 10 percent of farmers controlled 45 percent of the land. Roberts's survey points to incipient maldistribution which may be corrected only slightly in later years when more recent arrivals can expand their farms. In both surveys a small proportion of farmers control about half of the land in use whereas most farmers do not manage to get above fifty hectares of land, the minimum size for self-sustaining growth. Land shortage is not the issue. Shortage of labor and capital is what keeps farms from expanding. The same pattern is visible in Putumayo, though less dramatically so, as farms here are not as extensive as in other areas of Amazonia (Table 3).

Guaviare, on the other hand, is still in the first colonization

TABLE 2. Land distribution in Caquetá

Size of properties (in hectares)	Percentage of properties	Percentage of land area
Over 500	1.2	36.1
200–500	5.7	16.0
100–200	13.5	18.0
50–100	16.7	16.7
0–50	53.9	12.5

SOURCE: Marsch 1980.

NOTE: These figures are based on a survey of 8,840 farms. Which areas of Caquetá were sampled and their representativeness are not indicated.

TABLE 3. Land distribution in Putumayo, Sibundoy and Mocoa valleys

Size of properties (in hectares)	Number of properties	Percentage of properties	Total area (in hectares)	Percentage of land area
Over 100	23	1.2	4,622	18.7
20–100	278	14.2	11,129	44.7
3–20	996	47.5	7,927	31.8
0–3	714	37.1	1,292	4.8

SOURCE: Wesche, 1967: 166–67.

stages so it does not yet show a clear pattern of land concentration. There are a few large farms, but so far only 28 percent of cleared land is controlled by 13 percent of colonos, and some of the large farms are only about 160 hectares, or sixty hectares more than the minimum viable size.

These internally induced expansionist movements as well as the inflow of new migrants into Amazonia have threatened Indian populations within the area. For Caquetá alone it has been estimated that about 2,500 Indians were displaced during the 1950s and 1960s and another 1,475 have been affected by colonos moving further down river in recent years. A more forceful policy of protection of Indian land is necessary if we are to protect the source of their subsistence and the viability of their settlements. Not all Indians have been displaced; some have stayed in the area and have chosen to adapt to changing circumstances by working for wages or producing staples for local rural towns. By so doing they lend themselves to exploitative relations that could be avoided if marketing services and financial aid were made more readily available to them.

To assist colonists, the Instituto Colombiano de Reforma Agraria (INCORA) has become active in Caquetá and Guaviare in demarcating boundaries and helping farmers gain title to their properties. In 1963 with the support of AID, the range of operations was further expanded within Caquetá: old roads were improved; new roads, hospitals, and schools were built; cooperatives were organized, and larger number of colonos were able to profit from supervised credit. In the mid-1960s, as funds dried up, the World Bank extended a loan for the 1971–76 period which was refinanced for the period from 1975–80. With added funds and experience INCORA once again expanded the range of its activities, as can be seen from Table 4.

Although no official colonization project has been carried out in Guaviare, nor any international funding been received, INCORA has been active there since 1970 offering supervised loans, helping with titling, and extending technical information. By 1978 INCORA had extended credit to 303 families or 11.3 percent of the colono population to clear land, purchase cattle, and improve farm facilities. It has also managed to survey property and extend adjudication contracts—that eventually become legal land titles after due process—to 209 families. The Agrarian Bank has an office in San José but serves only very few colonos with short term small loans to purchase a cow or help clear a field. It does not help poorer colonos with long range investments. Other Colombian organizations have had personnel with technical expertise to help in some specific projects. SENA (Servicio Nacional de Aprendizaje) not only can connect a group of interested peasants with appropriate agencies but has some technicians in the area.

The loans extended have been to clear pasture land, plant crops, improve farm and farm equipment, purchase cattle, or fatten cattle. Interest rates vary with year and purpose of loan but have ranged between 8 and 12 percent. The Caja Agraria also offers credit to farmers; but the terms are not so advantageous, and the conditions are such that it cannot to any considerable extent help

TABLE 4. Families receiving benefits from INCORA activities in Caquetá

Year	Land titles (number)	(%)	Loans (number)	(%)	Roads (kilometers)	(%)
1971	8,934	—	5,845	—	346	—
1978	10,274	51	7,264	36	481	16

SOURCE: Compiled from Marsch 1980.

the poorer colono and recent arrivals. INCORA has attempted to attend the small colono population; however, it does require that applicants be married, have references, and have a title of adjudication to a farm with twenty to thirty hectares of pasture land. Just as important has been the financial support given to Coöpeagro in Caquetá to subsidize purchase of cattle for fattening, to maintain a farm supplies store, and to serve as a marketing cooperative. INCORA has also negotiated with Fondo Ganadero to aid farmers in the utilization of pasture through joint ventures on cattle purchases for fattening.

The question is thus not whether INCORA and World Bank projects are responsible for the colonization, since the migratory movement had a momentum of its own already by 1964, but what impact such limited projects can have in an area being colonized by large numbers of poor peasants and rural laborers and already being exploited by large cattle ranches. The inequities of the colonization process are too entrenched to be eradicated by some limited projects. More pervasive government policies are required to ensure the survival of immigrants as colonos or as appropriately remunerated wage laborers. At the moment Caquetá and Putumayo face serious labor upheavals and guerilla movements.[1]

What these so-called rural projects have not taken into account are: the transformation of areas of colonization into heterogeneous regions with growing urban centers demanding food from the hinterland; a self-sufficient agricultural sector that has geared production to export of cattle—Caquetá contributes 1.8 percent of national beef production—to the rest of Colombia; a virgin hinterland with an Indian population that must be protected. Although the projects have not accommodated these changes, entrepreneurs have taken advantage of some newly created opportunities. In a town near Florencia there is a yucca flour mill that, if it manages to expand, would make yucca production a viable crop for small farmers. In the hinterland, some colonos are exploiting timber resources, but the potential of the lumber industry for the region has not been evaluated. Nevertheless, the projects have made an impact: they have at least allowed for the survival of a peasant sector, the creation of an infrastructure of services needed by all, and serious evaluation of an ecologically viable exploitation of the area (experiments with rubber, palm oil, cacao, etc.).

Strategies of colonists

The settlers of Amazonia are a very heterogeneous group: missionaries, entrepreneurs, land speculators, traders, hacenderos, wage laborers, and peasants. I will discuss here the last two groups and their attempts to establish themselves as farmers. It should be kept in mind that the chances of success for the poorer colono do not depend just on ecological constraints, but also on the availability of wage labor as an alternative source of income, of outlets for crops, loans for investment, and capital to start a farm. Each area of Amazonia has attracted different colonos and offered different opportunities. In recent years wage labor opportunities eased the plight of new settlers in Caquetá and Putumayo; low interest rate loans have also reached a larger number of colonos in these areas than in Guaviare. Putumayo is closest to urban markets and thus can offer more varied opportunities, but in Caquetá, Florencia is large enough to be a demand center. Many of the settlers in Caquetá came by themselves; hence, without the labor support of families, they were forced to become wage laborers or to attach themselves to other households. In Guaviare most colonos came as young families that could count on the labor of growing children for several years to come.

The process of settling in is slow and uncertain. If the families come with meager resources, they will probably settle near a fellow countryman or kinsman, build a makeshift house, and clear a few hectares of land. In exchange for some labor they may either receive wages or support until they harvest their first food crop.

If the land first cleared can sustain crops and is near water and if the virgin area available is large enough for the growth of a family, the colono family will stay in the neighborhood of their kinsmen or fellow countrymen. Families prefer to be close to amenities, roads, schools, and medical services. At the same time they hope to claim about a hundred hectares of land in Guaviare (Ortiz

1980) or fifty hectares per adult person in Caquetá (Roberts 1975). It takes from one to three years for colonos to find what they hope will be their permanent farm in the area. Population shifts within colonization areas affect the integration of neighborhoods and the ability of each to organize cooperative marketing and transport activities that would benefit poor colonos.

Once adequate land is found or purchased, the colono marks boundaries with stakes or clears a path all around the property. Although in Guaviare colonos did respect each other's markings, these boundaries cannot be enforced until a proper title or a contract of adjudication is obtained. Such contracts can be obtained through INCORA but the colono can only petition for one-third as much land as he has cleared.[2] The most practical strategy is to invest labor initially in clearing and planting, some fields in subsistence crops and the rest in pasture, which requires less labor. Colonos expect to clear about ten hectares the first year and five hectares annually after that.[3] Without added help, in five to seven years they are ready to request an adjudication contract of fifty hectares and in thirteen years they can add another fifty hectares. But because of time spent searching for property, need to work for others to buy food, and shortage of labor, most colonos in Guaviare had managed to clear at best twenty hectares by the end of their third year in the region. By the end of five years at most they managed to clear thirty hectares, only 11 percent managing more than that. After seven years, 27 percent have cleared forty hectares and 27 percent have cleared more than that. How much each manages to clear depends on health as well as ability and size of family. Guaviare and Caquetá are malaria areas and much of the population is affected.

As land is cleared, colonos plant a half to one and a half hectares in subsistence crops and about four hectares in maize or rice or both. Some of the maize and rice is consumed, but the major part of it is sold to raise cash to cover other household needs. Although in most of Amazonia yields are low and the fallow periods required are long (which discourages cash cropping as a major means of subsistence), there are some clear exceptions to this rule. On some river banks, it is useful to plant rice, and in some areas sugar cane gives reasonable to good yields. In Guaviare, where only 7 to 8 percent of recent settlers earn beyond the most basic family needs, four hectares of maize did not produce enough to cover the household's food and basic cash needs (cash revenue was about \$Col. 8,800, while minimal cash needed was \$Col. 50,000—60,000). But in Caquetá there were more fertile soils and a larger variety of easily marketable crops: plantains and pineapples were profitable, and yucca could be sold for processing as flour in some areas of Caquetá. Consequently many colonos planted larger extensions with food crops than in Guaviare.[4] In Putumayo likewise there were areas of more intensive use of land for agriculture. The labor required for cash cropping is intensive, and it would be hard for a new colono to be able to expand his field while clearing two-thirds of the land he hopes to claim. Poorer colonos can pursue cash cropping only after they are well established. The common strategy in Guaviare is for the new colono to convert the maize-rice field into pasture and to plant the rest of cleared land with grass.

It may very well be that pasture depletes the soil, having disastrous ecological effects on the region, which will affect future prospects for small farmers. But before passing final judgment, a greater understanding is needed of the soils and ecological conditions in Caquetá, where cattle ranching has been carried out for about twenty years. As outlined above, there are practical reasons why colonos are using the present strategy of conversion to pasture instead of to permanent crops. Many of them have experimented on a small scale with cacao and with coffee, crops they were familiar with, and all have fields of manioc and buy pigs as soon as they are able to. Pasture conversion is seen as the major revenue raising activity, as the first step in development of a cattle farm with a potential for expansion. Pasture conversion plays the same role that coffee played at the turn of the century in highland areas. But the old coffee varieties did not require deforestation nor fertilizers and the market for coffee showed more promise at the turn of the century. Finally, cattle ranching is not a strategy unique to Amazonia. It has been tried in Cauca and is a popular option at present.

The question remains as to how successful colonists are in their choice of strategies. When we look at figures for the recently colonized areas we note that the success is related to availability of capital. During the first year a colono hopes to clear ten hectares and to use half of it for pasture. The second year he hopes to clear five hectares and plant pasture in the field that had been previously planted with maize or rice; in this way he continues the expansion of pasture land. In effect, colonists nearly reach this goal, often taking seven years to clear up to forty hectares, of which thirty are likely to be in pasture.[5]

Theoretically, once pastureland is available animals can be acquired. There are several procedures open to colonos who want to pasture animals: to request a loan from Caja Agraria for a milking cow to feed the family, to purchase with own savings, to agree to a share contract with a cattle rancher, to rent pasture, or to apply to INCORA. Although often two people per family work as domestics or as agricultural laborers, only a few of the families have an annual total income greater than what is required to cover most basic needs and the average demand for drugs. Only those who have escaped malaria, who have sons or daughters old enough to contribute to the family income, or who came with capital, are able to acquire animals from savings. Not surprisingly few manage to start a herd during the first few years.[6] Loans or capital are thus required. Most banks, however, could not service the colono since his financial requirements are rather particular. It has been estimated that the typical colono can sustain a 16 percent interest loan for a period of twelve years but only with a four-year grace period. With such a loan farmers with about twenty hectares in pasture (40–50 percent of farmers) could acquire the minimal size herd that five years later would bring some revenue. In twelve years the loan could be repaid and the income would be sufficient to generate savings yet would not require more than sixty-six hectares in pasture.

Cattle ranching is thus not feasible unless colonos have capital or access to credit with the above specified conditions. Why then do they prefer the strategy? The reason is that as INCORA operates in all colonization areas there is an expectation that it will be possible to obtain loans from the agency. Furthermore, there are the other above-mentioned options if no access to credit is possible: to rent pasture land or to agree to a share contract. There is no information on renting or share contracts for Guaviare, but it is clear that in Caquetá it was a frequently used alternative. In the area studied by Roberts, 42 percent of families that had not yet started a herd had opted for a share contract arrangement. The most frequently available share contracts are agreements with wealthier colonos, but they are not very advantageous as there are few safeguards against exploitation.[7] More profitable are contracts with Fondo Ganadero, a semiofficial government agency that purchases cattle and places the animals in colonos' pastures. The colono cares for the animal and receives 65 percent of the profits accrued, of which 5 percent of the total profit must be reinvested in the fund. The Fondo Ganadero, however, does not serve the poorer colono who does not yet have cattle on his land; it specializes in middle-income farmers. The third option open to farmers without capital is to rent the pasture to others; rates of return to the farmer have not been specified.

The last option left to a poorer colono is to sell improved farms, when the prices of land in their neighborhood increase, and with the capital acquired to start a new farm and buy cattle. Such assets management is typical of a later stage in the colonization process and is responsible for frontier movement. Caquetá has already entered that stage, but we do not yet know whether colonos have correctly timed the sale of their farms to realize a surplus for investment in cattle ranching. There is no information on the market for land nor on whether colonos are being pushed to sell instead of being free to determine the timing of the sale.

In summary, colonos in Amazonia are able to acquire land; but without access to capital, they cannot transform the virgin forest into the desired cattle ranch.[8] Nor have they desirable alternatives, given the present state of the market for agricultural products and the limited opportunities locally available. By renting their pastureland and working for wages, they are able to survive. But, without help from development agencies, it is unlikely that they will ever move beyond the stage of poor colonos.

Discussion

Amazonia has been colonized by poor peasants, wage laborers, entrepreneurs, industrialists, hacendados, and speculators as well as traders and technical experts. Since the turn of the century small and not-so-small communities have begun to claim the forest and Indian lands. The growth of population in the area has not been at a constant rate; it accelerated during the 1960s and has been increasing since. Furthermore, the growth rate has not been homogeneous across the region: small towns, military bases, oil companies, roads, and rivers have directed migrants to particular spots. As these centers of attraction grow, secondary migratory waves spread out along new roads or river basins.

Entrepreneurs, industrialists, and hacendados probably came to diversify their investment or because of expectations of high return to investments. At the other end of the scale, peasant farmers and wage laborers came looking for available land that they could either claim with their labor or buy at very reasonable prices; in some cases they came for jobs.[9]

For the immigrants and investors (industrialists, hacendados) who came to Amazonia with capital during the thirties and forties, cattle ranching seemed the most attractive activity. It required little labor, was therefore possible in sparsely populated areas, and, since cattle could walk, required no transport to markets. Furthermore, the market for meat was expanding in Colombia, and the possibility to export to Venezuela and Peru was an added incentive. In more recent years, in an attempt to recoup from the slump in food production caused by the Violencia, the government encouraged colonization and investment in the agricultural sector. Financial resources were made available to these early settlers through the Caja Agraria. The government concern for peasants, as reflected in the early colonization schemes, was not motivated by an interest in peasant agriculture but by a concern to resolve rural violence and political unrest. Ranchers, for their part, welcomed the influx of potential laborers and colonos, who might clear the forest for them.

The poorer colono who migrated to these areas had no choice but to replicate the strategy of larger investors. Local demand for food products was initially limited. Peasant production can never generate new trading networks in areas of colonization. The colonizers have to sell their products to the haciendas or ranchers who will transport them to larger centers,[10] or they have to sell to the middlemen who handle the marketing of what is produced in ranches and large haciendas or to middlemen who are looking for lowland products to satisfy specific demands at their regional market. Costs of transport are too high for peasants to travel in search of buyers for a few specialized products.

The belief held by some planners that extension of trunk roads and building of bridges will profit the small colono because it will increase his marketing opportunities and reduce his marketing costs is not always warranted. It is true that middlemen with larger trucks will come directly into the area, but such middlemen specialize in certain products and will not necessarily cater to colonos who want to diversify their farming activities. Furthermore, as it was clearly illustrated in Guaviare, the colono is not always able to sell directly to the trucker, who often is the highest bidder. Truckers have to maximize the use of their vehicle and can only afford to buy from peasants who are at their customary place of loading when they arrive. In Colombia, market days are not coordinated in such a way as to institutionally facilitate the flow of goods from producer to middlemen. In areas of colonization, lack of coordination is extreme, and the peasant has to first sell to a local middleman who will transport and store the product until buyers from higher order bulking centers arrive.[11] A reorganization of regional transport and regional marketing must then go hand in hand with road building if the colono is to profit from the latter.

Marketing reforms through the organization of cooperatives may sometimes be effective. For the areas of colonization reviewed here, it is difficult to estimate the success of the cooperative movement encouraged by INCORA. Coopeagro received subsidies from the government to allow its members to open a store and market their grain and cattle. Project reports hint at the many organizational difficulties and tensions about the time when Coopeagro had to begin to rely on its own financial resources. It is successful in the sense that it has survived, that it manages a successful cattle buying and selling operation for its members, and that by 1973 it had assets amounting to fourteen million pesos, half of which were in the cattle portfolio. But it is not clear how Coopeagro selects its members; at any rate it has only 3,000 members out of a colono population of 20,000. Nor is it clear that Coopeagro can easily explore intraregional marketing opportunities.

Marketing reform through government price support agencies (IDEMA) has not been successful. In the first place, as Thirsk (1981) has pointed out, price support policies that help larger farmers are subsidized by all concerned. In the second place IDEMA only purchases 25 percent of the harvest and clearly favors large growers or regionally important middlemen rather than farmers. In Guaviare there was a considerable uproar at the unwillingness of IDEMA to ensure equal access to all farmers.

Transport cooperatives with links to middlemen at bulking centers may be a possible solution to ensure that, during the early period of colonization, farmers will realize maximum return on their maize and rice harvest in order to ensure their welfare and subsidize long-range strategies. Proposed marketing reforms should consider the adaptability of the suggested channels for the distribution of food staples—with the added problem of frequent price fluctuations—when regional growth opens new market opportunities to colonos.

It is only in later stages, when areas of colonization develop their own internal markets for specific agricultural products and when entrepreneurs begin to develop processing industries, that the number of options to colonos increases.[12] Ironically, as regional urban centers develop, new immigrants have to settle further away from them because virgin land is no longer available for newcomers and land prices near roads and towns increase beyond their reach. Furthermore, the older colono who had once settled near Florencia, Puerto Asis, or San José de Guaviare but who never managed to establish a cattle farm may become so indebted to traders and ranchers that he will be forced to sell when land prices go up and to move again to the hinterland before availing himself of the opportunity to produce for local urban demand. Roberts records the fear of forced relocation that was expressed by some Guaviare colonos. It is in order to avoid recurrent isolation and high transport costs that trunk road improvement should always be accompanied by improvement and subsequent expansion of feeder road systems. The Caquetá projects have contributed to an improvement of regional road systems, but a proper balance has not yet been achieved.

Caquetá has now entered this second stage with a large city where about 30 percent of the population resides. Florencia, with over 30,000 inhabitants, approximates what Pasto was to Putumayo during the early stages of colonization of that region. In fact, Florencia with its slaughter house has now replaced Garzon in commercial importance; cattle and agricultural products are now transported directly to various major markets in other regions. The once dependent marketing center has thus become a high-ranking marketing center supplied by large ranchers and a colono population of small farmers. Now should be the time to reexamine the demand potential of the city (staples and food processing industries) and determine to what extent it can be met by regional peasant production. A new farm investment program that does not rely so heavily on cattle may now be appropriate. Care should be taken to ensure that a change in investment strategy will not depress incomes and welfare within the peasant colono sector. Putumayo has not entered this second stage of development. Furthermore, it is integrated into the national economy through Nariño, a department that has lost much of its initial commercial and economic importance.

The major problem for colonos in Amazonia has been to acquire cattle. A cattle farm with eighteen to twenty-five animals should allow meat production for urban markets, thus ensuring the welfare of colonos. Furthermore, as the population increases in the area the colono could exploit his cattle for milk and hides, options feasible now only in Caquetá and Putumayo. The plight of colonos during their initial period has been made clear in the preceding section. Without INCORA's help, few of them have been able to acquire cattle. This situation favors cattle ranchers: they can expand their herds at a very reasonable cost using colonos' grassland. This could be a suitable regional strategy ensuring maximum utilization of resources if it did not have some serious drawbacks.

First, cattle ranchers are prominent and influential and therefore able to set contractual terms that favor them over colonos. Second, as many ranchers have other interests in the same region or in other parts of the country, they are not particularly concerned with the long-range protection of a particular area in pasture land. They can favor some colonos according to the state of the pasture and select others once pastures are depleted. This may lead to an overutilization of pastureland and progressive improvishment of the colono population. Without protection from usurious contractual arrangements, the poorer colonos will suffer most. A social infrastructure that could ensure the effective sanctioning of contracts would be most important. It should be kept in mind that colonization areas never started as democratic regional systems; rather, they grew up as unstable neighborhoods around elite settlers who had political power or economic resources.

Supervised loans will ensure that there is no total polarization of economic groups—those with pasture only and those with pasture and cattle. INCORA has so far been the only agency that could serve the promising group of colonos at low interest rates while assuming the considerable overhead of supervision and infrastructure. But it has been able to support only a small proportion of farmers (7 percent in Guaviare, 20 percent in Caquetá), not enough to have an impact on income distribution and power. I have calculated for Guaviare that INCORA should reach about 30 percent of the colono population to ensure the stability of this population and the flow of benefits to newcomers. The proportion will vary from area to area depending on existing income and power distribution as well as on alternative sources of capital available to small colonos.

Only in one of the three Amazonia areas of colonization have any concerted efforts been made to help small colonos. In Caquetá, INCORA, with World Bank support, has surveyed land, extended titles, granted loans for farm improvements and cattle purchases, contributed to road building, health clinics, and school building projects, and been instrumental in supporting the organization of a farmers' cooperative movement and the involvement of Fondo Ganadero in joint investments with smaller colonos. There is no question that it has helped many farmers and made a long-range contribution in infrastructure.

With the benefit of that experience, it is now time to consider the impact that an agency, which has ambivalent support from its own national government, can have in an area where cattle ranches were already established and where an elite already controlled the flow of resources and marketing arrangements. The flow of resources to INCORA has not always been as smooth as expected, and the agency was able only slowly to increase the number of beneficiaries it supported. Only in later years was it able to reach about 20 percent of colono population; in the beginning, as in Guaviare, it could offer services only to a limited group of small colonos. Consequently, colonization projects have not succeeded in ensuring a proper balance of economic power and political leverage for the smaller colono.

Some critics have charged that projects that encourage cattle ranching are not beneficial to the small colono and contribute to the degradation of the environment. It has been suggested that in areas of Amazonia that are being spontaneously settled, permanent crop agriculture should be encouraged. This suggestion may now apply to Caquetá, as INCORA has been experimenting, on a share basis with a number of colonos, with the exploitation of various permanent crops. But it was not a suitable strategy at first when investment was risky, return delayed, and marketing organization nonexistent for the produce in question. It could have been done earlier only if technical knowledge for the area had been available and if the agency had received adequate financial support.

Whatever the advice given to the development agency for initial stages of colonization, the government should support projects without the usual delays and stop-and-go processes that seem to characterize them. In developing road systems and infrastructure, agencies should be mindful of eventual requirements when investment strategies change with the rise of regional urban centers. For

some regions of Amazonia, the ecological viability of certain lending policies should be examined now that opportunities have diversified. A serious evaluation of present trends in income and
power distribution in the area, as well as a strong commitment to
improving these, are required in order to avoid the repetition of social upheavals that occurred in the older highland areas of colonization during the 1920s and 1930s and again in the next two decades; rural violence is in fact now gaining momentum in Caquetá.

Notes

1. *El Espectador*, October 24, 1981. The organizations with local
representation are ANUE, Organización de Usuários, Sindicato de Trabajadores de Doncellos, Trabajadores de Paujil, Trabajadores Agrícolas del
Cauca. For some time there have been some serious confrontations with
guerilla groups like FARC and M-19, both of which seem to have a presence in the area.

2. According to the Law 97 of 1946, title to public land can be
granted for a hundred hectares under the conditions that two-thirds of the
land be exploited. Exceptions to the extension are made for certain areas
of the country as well as for regions with natural pasture that cannot be
improved or regions far from centers of economic activities. The Law 135
of 1961 allows for an extension of 450 hectares. INCORA's rule of thumb is
to grant titles for about a hundred hectares per family unless more is under use at the time the petition is made.

3. See INCORA 1977 for the background study for the Retorno area.

4. Marsch's (1980) survey of INCORA credit applicants reveals that
nearly 40 percent of their income came from agriculture (p. 277); the figure was lower, however, for those who had received credit: only 16 percent of their income came from the sale of agricultural products. The survey may just reflect the characteristics of the surveyed area and location
of colonos who have contact with INCORA, but it does at least show a diversification of activities. Roberts's (1975) data, though limited, confirm
my supposition. In his area, which received a group of colonos during the
first stages of colonization but has been settled mostly in recent time, 8.5
percent of colonos had a minimal subsistence plot of five hectares, 59.8
percent had up to ten hectares in subsistence and cash cropping, 16 percent had a considerable extension in cash cropping (up to twenty hectares), 16 percent had from twenty to seventy hectares in cash cropping,
and one had a hundred hectares in cash crops.

5. In Guaviare, according to INCORA's 1977 survey, half of the total
population of colonos have managed to plant pastures. According to a

Colombo Dutch Survey in three neighborhoods, 45 percent had ten to twenty hectares in pasture and 44 percent had more than twenty hectares. In Caquetá, Roberts's survey (1975) shows that, regardless of when they came, 86.3 percent of colonos had some pasture, 41 percent had ten to twenty hectares, and 44 percent had more than twenty hectares. Most farmers (33 percent) managed to plant between ten and thirty hectares.

    6. In Guaviare only 49.5 percent had acquired cattle without IN-CORA's help and only 5 percent had managed to accumulate a herd of twenty-five head, which is considered the basic number to generate family welfare and a surplus for reinvestment. In Caquetá, Roberts (1975) indicates that 50 percent of the colonos who had pasture had managed to acquire at least one animal and 32 percent had acquired more than 25 animals. It is hard to determine from his tables the proportion of colonos who managed a viable herd beyond the 32 percent who had more than twenty-five head.

    7. Wealthy colonos may undervalue the animals at the end of contract, or they may terminate the contract before animals have gained sufficient weight, thus making it unprofitable for the owner of the pasture.

    8. A survey by the author of thirty-five farmers with sufficient and well-established credit, who had applied for but not yet received loans from INCORA in Caquetá, indicated that 63.5 percent of the cattle pasturing in colonos' fields were owned by other colonos, 20 percent were owned by Fondo Ganadero, 2.4 percent were purchased with Caja Agraria credit, and 13 percent were owned by the colono himself.

    9. During the early 1960s, wages in Caquetá were twice the wage of an agricultural laborer in Cauca and about half as high as those of workers in Huila and Valle. But by 1976 the only agricultural workers who would profit from migrating to Caquetá were those from Cauca and some areas further north.

    10. Palacios 1980. Historically, this was a frequent option throughout Colombia. In fact, coffee produced by peasants was at first marketed through larger plantations.

    11. In Guaviare some farmgate prices did not cover cost of production if labor is calculated as a cash cost. Production was warranted only because it served for subsistence and due to the hope of selling at San José prices. It is the middleman who buys from colonos near Calamar and resells in San José who realizes a profit of $600 per ton if he is a small operator and has to resell it there to local middlemen, or $2,500 if he has the capital and storage facilities to wait for the boatmen or is able to sell it to IDEMA (this agency is known to buy first from the large producers and important middlemen and then, if facilities permit, to purchase from others). Transport bottlenecks and organizational arrangements of marketing cut profits realized by farmers. At the moment the colono who lives far from San José has to sell at from one-third to one-half of the price his

product brings in San José. The middlemen are unemployed young men, San José traders or bus drivers, or wealthier colonos who own jeeps. 12. Instituto Geográfico Agustin Codazzi n.d., INCORA 1977, Marsch 1980, Roberts 1975. Putumayo colonos derived their income from growing maize, plantain, bananas, rice, and sugarcane, from exploiting timber resources, and raising hogs. The major source of income (40 to 73 percent) was derived from cattle and dairy products. In Caquetá, income was derived from maize, rice, rubber, cacao, pineapples, manioc, lumber, and cattle. In Guaviare the only available alternatives were cattle, maize, and rice.

References Cited

Bonilla, Victor Daniel
    1972   *Servants of the Gods or Master of Men*. London: Penguin.
Crist, Raymond E., and Ernesto Guhl
    1957   *Pioneer Settlements in Eastern Colombia*. Smithsonian Report for 1956. Pp. 391–414. Washington, D.C.: Smithsonian Inst.
DANE
    1965   *Anuário General de Estadística*. Bogotá.
El Espectador
    1981   Caquetá Nuevo Departamento. Bogotá. December 2.
Guhl, Ernesto
    1975   *Colombia, Bosquejo de su Geografía Tropical*, vol. 2. Bogotá: Instituto Colombiano de Cultura.
Hegen, Edmund Edward
    1966   *Highways into the Upper Amazon Basin*. Gainesville: Center for Latin American Studies, University of Florida.
INCORA
    1977   *Proyecto de Colonización en el Retorno-Vaupés. Diagnóstico de la Situación actual*. Vol. 1. Bogotá: Ministério de Agricultura.
Instituto Geográfico Agustin Codazzi
    n.d.   *Problemas de la Colonización en el Putumayo*. Bogotá.
Marsch, Robin
    1980   Colonization and Integrated Rural Development. The Case of Caquetá. Master's thesis, University of California, Los Angeles.
Ortiz, Sutti
    1980   The Transformation of Guaviare in Colombia. In *Land, People, and Planning in Contemporary Amazonia*. F. Barbira-

Scazzocchio, ed. Centre for Latin American Studies, University of Cambridge.

Palacios, Marco
1980   *Coffee in Colombia 1850–1970*. Cambridge: Cambridge University Press.

Rice, Hamilton
1910   The River Vaupes. *Geographical Journal* 35:682–700.
1914   Further Explorations in the North-West Amazon. *Geographical Journal* 44:139–65.

Roberts, Ralph Leon
1975   Migration and Colonization in Colombian Amazonia: Agrarian Reform or Neo-Latifundismo. Ph.D. thesis, Syracuse University.

Steward, Julian.
1948   The Witotoan Tribes, and Western Tucanoan Tribes. In *Handbook of South American Indians*. Steward, ed. Washington, D.C.: Smithsonian Institution.

Thirsk, Wayne R.
1980   Income Distribution Consequences of Agricultural Price Supports in Colombia. In *Economic Policy and Income Distribution in Colombia*. A. Berry and R. Soligo, eds. Boulder: Westview Press.

Wesche, Rolfe Jürgen
1967   The Settler Wedge of the Upper Putumayo River. Ph.D. dissertation, University of Florida.

Colonization in Santa Cruz, Bolivia: A Comparative Study of the Yapacaní and San Julián Projects

Allyn MacLean Stearman

B OLIVIA is often described as an Andean state, but like many South American nations whose history has unfolded primarily in the highlands, it also encompasses a vast lowland region to the east. This segment of the Amazon basin in Bolivia is known as the Oriente and represents almost two-thirds of the nation's territory.

The largest political division in the Oriente is Santa Cruz, also the largest of Bolivia's nine departments (see Figure 1). The inhabitants of this region are largely mestizo people, their Spanish antecedents having exterminated or intermarried with the indigenous population in the latter part of the sixteenth century. The Spanish expeditions to Santa Cruz did not originate in the highlands, however, but were explorations westward from Argentina and Paraguay. Thus the inhabitants of Santa Cruz trace their origins and their loyalties not to distant cities in the Andes but to the centers of Patagonia. They call themselves "Cambas," from the Guaraní word meaning "friend," and find little in common with highland people, whom they term "Kollas," a Quechua word designating the residents of the Bolivian region of the Inca Empire.

Geographic and cultural isolation characterized the Santa Cruz region until 1954, when an all-weather road to the lowlands was

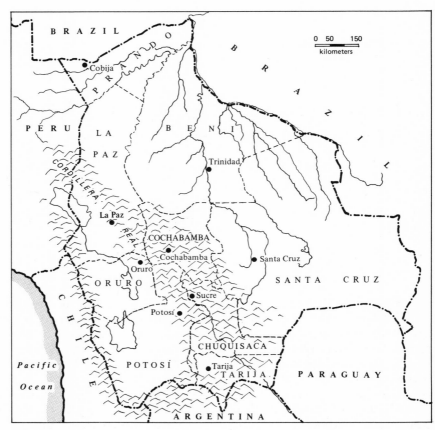

Fig. 1. Bolivia.

opened. The construction of this road was the result of efforts by the newly formed revolutionary government of Victor Paz Estenssoro, head of the Movimiento Nacional Revolutionario (MNR) party. The Social Revolution of 1952 led by Paz and the MNR brought radical changes to the old social order. Land was expropriated from the *patrones* and given to the peasants, the mines were nationalized, and debt peonage was abolished. There were also plans to begin to exploit the mineral, timber, and land resources of the Oriente. The road to the lowlands not only would open this territory for use but also would serve to link Santa Cruz with the rest of the nation and thus bring about a greater sense of national integration. Much of this integration, it was felt, could be achieved by encouraging highland people to take up farming in the lowlands. Thus, the colonization of new lands would serve three purposes—to expand Bolivia's agricultural production, to alleviate population pressures in the highlands, and to dilute the isolationist tendencies of the Cambas of Santa Cruz.

In the thirty years since the Social Reform, these three manifest goals of the 1952 revolutionary government have slowly moved toward realization. Ironically however, colonization was not to be the primary impetus in the development of Santa Cruz. Other factors such as the discovery of oil, the growth of commercial agriculture, increased industrialization, economic opportunities in service sectors, and, in recent years, the cocaine trade have all contributed to the growing importance of the department in the national scene. Nonetheless, for many years the colonization effort was a major fact in the development plan for Bolivia, involving considerable expenditures in monetary and human resources. Was it successful?—a heatedly debated question frequently posed. A major obstacle in trying to formulate an adequate response is that of defining what is meant by success. One should have to answer in the negative if cost effectiveness were consistently applied. It is also true that most settlement projects have failed to establish stable populations, another criterion frequently used. On the other hand, colonization has played an important role in the overall development process of the lowlands, albeit often at the expense of the colonist.

Because all projects to settle new lands in Bolivia offer such complexities in approach and outcome, this debate over success or failure will likely continue for some time. While to resolve the question of success may not be possible at present, a long-term analysis of the events and factors influencing the evolution of an agricultural colony provide some useful insights into the problem. In Santa Cruz, two colonization projects are of particular interest because of the degree of planning, financial support, and technical assistance available to each. The first, the Yapacaní colony, was established in the early 1960s and is now an independent farming area. The second, San Julián, is a much newer colony and currently is undergoing settlement. The Yapacaní and San Julián colonies offer differing approaches to the problem of new lands settlement. As will be shown, planners of the San Julián colony are attempting to avoid the pitfalls of earlier settlement initiatives with varying degrees of success. Before examining these two case studies, however, it is first necessary to place them in historical context with similar projects in Santa Cruz.

An overview of colonization in Santa Cruz

Four agricultural colonies were begun in Santa Cruz between 1954 and 1956. The first, Aroma, located fifteen kilometers northeast of Montero, was initiated by two individuals and later taken over by the Corporación Boliviana de Fomento (CBF). This agency superseded the military's Colonial Division, previously charged with the lowland resettlement operation. Although the administration of colonial affairs was transferred to civil authority, the military continued to provide manpower and equipment for land clearing efforts. Then too, many of the officials appointed by CBF to perform administrative roles in the colonies were military or ex-military personnel.

Aroma colonists were required to volunteer three two-month terms of labor in land clearing, house construction, and road building in order to qualify for twenty-five hectares of land. CBF provided them with food and tools during this initial settlement period. Later, technical and medical assistance were made available. By the end of the decade, two hundred families had been settled in Aroma. Still, the attrition rate was high, and according to one source, "approximately 60 percent of these colonists returned to their places of origin" (Ferragut 1961:130). But those who vacated their land were replaced by others, and today Aroma continues as a small agricultural community of about two hundred forty families (Crist and Nissley 1973:137). All assistance has been withdrawn from the colony, which is inhabited largely by highland *campesinos* working their land not as colonists but as individual, self-reliant farmers.

The colonies of Cuatro Ojitos and Huaytú were begun by the military in 1955 and 1956 respectively, soon after the establishment of Aroma. These settlements were ambitious projects initiated by sending in four army batallions to build roads and bridges, erect houses and schools, clear farmland, and drill wells for drinking water. The highland soldiers who accomplished the task of clearing were to be the recipients of the tracts of land opened for settlement. Civilian highlanders working in lowland canefields were also given an opportunity to claim a parcel in the new colonies. CBF replaced the army in 1958, but military advisors and nine hundred soldiers continued to execute the program. Attrition again was high, and only 10 percent of the conscripts actually settled on parcels. Over half of the colonists were civilians, primarily ex-harvesters of sugarcane. Both colonies are now under civil authority with a total of six hundred families in Cuatro Ojitos and one hundred seventy families in Huaytú (Crist and Nissley 1973:138).

In 1958 the Bolivian army began widening the trail from the Yapacaní River to Puerto Grether on the Río Ichilo with the intent of establishing another colony. This location had been an early settlement site for lowland agriculturalists, but the distance to market coupled with the difficulty of crossing the unpredictable and flood-prone Yapacaní River had left the area virtually uninhabited. A few Cambas continued to live in the main settlement three kilometers from the river, most earning their livelihood by hunting animals for pelts and by fishing.

Highlanders at first were slow to arrive in the Yapacaní colony. Many quickly became discouraged and returned to their places of origin or sought farmland in less remote areas. As with other colonies at the time, CBF administered settlement procedures in the Yapacaní. Technical assistance and small loans were available to the colonists, but without market access they faced only continual indebtedness and incredible hardships.

During the initial years of government efforts at resettlement, foreign groups as well as Bolivian highlanders were encouraged to colonize the lowlands. In 1954, fifty Volga-German Mennonites arrived in Santa Cruz. They were followed in 1958 by another fifty Dutch-German Mennonite families and, in 1964, an additional fifty-four families from this same European religious group settled in the department. The Mennonites were guaranteed religious freedom, exemption from military service, the right to establish their own schools, and duty-free access for farm equipment. In the late 1950s more than three thousand Old Colony Mennonites arrived from a parent colony in Mexico (Lanning 1971). These settlers located in the arid zone to the south of Santa Cruz where, in spite of environmental difficulties, they established productive farm units. All of the Mennonite colonies have resisted any form of assimilation into lowland Bolivian society. Marriage outside of the religious sect is prohibited, and only the males are taught Spanish for marketing purposes.

In addition to the Mennonite settlers, the Bolivian Oriente

has been the recipient of several hundred Japanese and Okinawan migrant families. On August 2, 1956, an agreement that provided 35,000 hectares of land for Japanese colonization was signed between the governments of Japan and Bolivia (Thompson 1968:201). By June 1965, the new San Juan colony comprised some 262 households and 1,546 individuals. In spite of its somewhat better location on the near side of the river directly opposite the Yapacaní colony, the San Juan settlement suffered many of the same problems as the fledgling CBF project. During the initial years of Japanese colonization in San Juan, much of the rice produced remained in homes and storehouses, unable to be shipped to market. The road out from the colony was unimproved and virtually impassable when wet. Once the main road to Montero was reached, another five or six hours' travel was necessary to arrive at lowland markets. In spite of tremendous obstacles, the colonists persisted in their efforts to wrest a living from the wilderness and in recent years most have prospered. The improvement of the colonial feeder road combined with the paving of the Montero-Yapacaní highway have given the Japanese of San Juan expectations of further success. Most farms are now mechanized, rural electrification reached the area in 1979, and large marketing cooperatives have been formed.

Another agreement among the Bolivian, Okinawan, and U.S. governments opened land east of Montero for Okinawan settlements. Three colonies have been founded by the island agriculturalists, and, with the paving of the road that extends through Okinawan lands from Montero, the colonies have attained permanence. The Okinawans are engaged primarily in rice, cane, and cotton production. In the late 1970s they began experimenting with tropical wheat, which continues to show promise. Unlike the Mennonites, the Japanese and Okinawans have intermarried with Cambas as well as with highlanders residing in the lowlands. Spanish is taught in their schools, and children are enculturated as Bolivians, in addition to learning Japanese or Okinawan values.

By the beginning of the 1960s, efforts by the Bolivian government to establish viable agricultural colonies of highlanders began to falter. In most instances, colonies had been opened for settlement before adequate market routes were made available, leaving the settler cut off not only from the marketplace but also from medical, educational, and social support. The colonies became known as options only for the desperate and destitute and were avoided by scores of prospective migrants searching for land. Colonists frequently used the settlements as temporary stopping places until they could acquire farmland with better market access.

The early 1960s also witnessed the failure of other projects initiated by the revolutionary government. In many cases, railroad construction was halted only a few kilometers from the starting point; hydroelectric dams were erected where water supplies were inadequate for operation; agricultural extension stations were built and abandoned because of lack of funding. Much of the fault lay with the poor coordination among the various government agencies and the absence of a directive office in charge of long-range national planning. As a result of these deficiencies, the Junta Nacional de Planeamiento was formed in 1962 with technical advisors supplied by the United Nations. Once again, problems arose from a lack of articulation with other governmental bureaucracies, and a subsequent reorganization of the junta occurred. The agency was taken from direct control by the president and placed under the direction of the Ministerio de Planeamiento y Coordinación, the Consejo Nacional de Economía y Desarrollo Social, and the regional planning offices (Zondag 1968:263). The old junta became the Servicio de Planeamiento.

One of the principal tasks of the new service was to implement the recently enacted ten-year plan for economic development, the Plan Nacional de Desarrollo Económico y Social, covering the period 1962–71. The plan dealt with all sectors of the economy including the major problem areas, mining and agriculture. In order to increase agricultural production and at the same time provide an outlet for growing labor pressures in the mines, the economic development program called for additional efforts to colonize the lowlands. An ambitious settlement program was devised, which would be centered in three lowland regions: the Alto Beni east of La Paz, the Chapare east of Cochabamba, and the Yapacaní northwest of Santa Cruz.

Loans were obtained from the Inter-American Development Bank (IDB) and from other nations, primarily the United States, to finance road building, land clearing, and resettlement of highland miners and campesinos. The colonization program proposed to resettle 8,000–10,000 families over a ten-year period at an initial cost of US $6,500,000 (IDB 1970). The Corporación Boliviana de Fomento was to administer the project (INC 1970:8). By 1969, settlement expenditures had reached 9.1 million dollars but only

4,984 families had been relocated (IDB 1970). In the meantime, CBF had been superseded by the newly organized Instituto Nacional de Colonización, brought into existence by supreme decree on June 28, 1965 (INC 1970:9). As a result, all colonization activities would be centralized under one agency whose only task involved the opening and settlement of new lands.

The three colonies were plagued from the outset by problems of unstable administration, graft, improper allocation of food-stuffs, and excessive paternalism. During one year, the attrition rate for the Yapacaní colony reached 90 percent (IDB-Bolivia 1971). The ten-year plan ended in 1971, at which time the lowland colonies lost financial support from the government. In the three areas combined, 5,055 families had been settled as of 1970 (Galleguillos 1970:3). Abandonment rates for the 1962–71 period averaged from over 50 percent for the Alto Beni project to 33 percent for the Yapacaní (Galleguillos 1970:4–6). Still, the figures for abandonment can be somewhat misleading. They represent a turnover in population, not vacant land. At present, colonies are filled to capacity. In other words, what is lacking is not settlers to occupy land, but rather a stable population of colonists who have remained on their parcels since arrival.

Since 1971 the Instituto Nacional de Colonización has continued to supply administrative assistance to colonial centers, but there have been no repetitions of the financially ambitious settlement projects characterizing the 1960s. Colonization at present is spontaneous, or semidirected, whereby INC supplies primarily secondary or tertiary roads, some technical assistance, water, and schools in some localities.

In 1975 the United States and West German governments financed the construction of two graveled roads west of the Río Grande in the post-1969 flood victim resettlement location of Chané-Piray and through the old San Julián colony. In addition, USAID provided INC with US $200,000 to fund the relocation of four thousand highlanders over a five-year period in San Julián. This latter settlement program officially commenced in 1976 although nine colony zones, or *nucleos,* had already been established. In contrast to projects of the past, San Julián has received relatively little monetary support, and the majority of the colonists are ex-harvesters with prior lowland experience rather than highlanders brought directly from the interior.

In the Santa Cruz region, INC-sponsored colonization is occurring only in the Chané-Piray and San Julián sectors. The remaining colonies, including the Yapacaní, have all become agricultural communities under civil authority and local control. As new lands are opened in the future, the INC will attempt to provide infrastructure and initial technical assistance in concert with international agencies involved in resettlement programs. Even so, the primary emphasis today is on the provision of land and market access. Paternalism has been replaced by individual colonist initiative. Perspective settlers no longer are dragged out of the highlands and thrust unprepared into the wilderness. The present-day colonist tends to be an agriculturalist, an ex-harvester and an individual who is eager to obtain a parcel of Cruceñan farmland.

The rapid expansion of the lowland economy, better market roads, and increasing numbers of people in search of farm property have given value to much of the hinterlands of the northern Santa Cruz region. No longer are the colonies viewed as a type of purgatory, but rather as areas of extremely desirable agricultural land. Unlike the early days of colonial planning and the almost Shanghai tactics employed to obtain settlers, the active colonies now have people waiting in line to receive property. Land cooperatives have become popular as alternative means to acquiring the always sought-after virgin forest by direct solicitation to the government. The great numbers of highlanders in the Santa Cruz region who are seeking arable land in the vicinity of market routes have brought about the introduction of "sooning" to the lowlands. As quickly as word or rumor spreads that a road is to be opened, cooperatives jump the land before actual allocation is made. The battle then begins to legalize their claims, but most cooperatives are able to rally their membership into paying additional quotas to provide for the necessary bureaucratic adjustments.

With this overview of the colonization process in Santa Cruz completed, we will move to an in-depth analysis of the two case studies, the Yapacaní and San Julián colonies. The first, the Yapacaní, has the longest and most costly history of settlement. The second, the more recently settled San Julián colony, exemplifies current trends in colonization as well as characteristics of the settlers presently attracted to life in the colonies.

The Yapacaní colony

In 1963 the gravel-surfaced highway north from Montero branched in two directions near the Guabira sugar refinery, the western road leading to the Yapacaní River, where it terminated (see Figure 2). At the river's edge, a few pilings could be seen, remnants of unsuc-

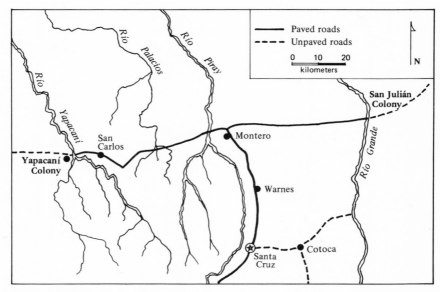

Fig. 2. Northern Santa Cruz area.

cessful efforts to span the waterway. On the far side lay the Yapacaní colony, consisting of ten-, twenty-, and fifty-hectare parcels
strung out along a sixty-two kilometer stretch of road cleared by
the Bolivian army (Figure 3). At several intervals along the trail,
side paths, or *fajas*, had been opened into the jungle and additional
parcels surveyed for settlement.

The main camp, Villa Germán Busch, was located three kilometers in from the river. In order for colonists or administrative
personnel to reach the colonial headquarters at Villa Busch, the
Yapacaní River had to be crossed first. Individuals rode in canoes
and paid the boatman from US $.10 to $.50, depending on the condition of the river. Motor vehicles had to be loaded on large wooden
pontoon barges, which were powered by outboard motors fixed to
the fore and aft hulls. If the Yapacaní was running full and swift,
a three- to four-day waiting period was necessary before the river
could be crossed. Travelers marooned at the river's edge would
have to camp out or seek lodging at the few fishermen's shacks
along the banks.

Once the river had been traversed, the next phase of the jour-
ney to Villa Busch or points beyond was the three-kilometer stretch

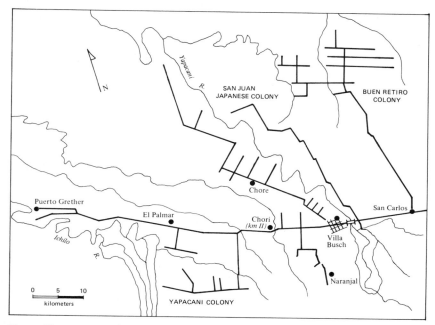

Fig. 3. Yapacaní settlement area.

of trail from the western shore of the Yapacaní into the encampment. For those on foot, it was a tedious struggle through bog and thicket, but pedestrian travel was the surest means of getting there. Vehicles not only had to grind their way through seemingly endless traps of quagmire, but also were required to navigate across two or three slippery logs placed as bridges over the frequent creeks and streams along the track.

During these years, Villa Busch offered little more than the large mud-and-wattle, tin-roofed structure that housed the Corporación Boliviana de Fomento personnel who administered the colony, a few CBF outbuildings, a thatched and bamboo barracks for the soldiers stationed in the colony, and several huts inhabited by Camba fishermen and hunters. At night, a small generator gave light to the main administration building. A radio shack manned by a young Cruceñan was often the colony's sole link with the outside world.

The first CBF colonists were brought into the lowlands on

trucks. Many of them were ex-miners whom the government was seeking to relocate, and most came without their families. The majority became discouraged and returned to the interior within months or even days of their arrival. In the meantime, however, radio broadcasts and word of mouth spread the news of the new agricultural colonies to the east. A great many promises were made, and prospective colonists soon began to trickle into Villa Busch in search of land. These later settlers came on their own initiative, were frequently accompanied by their wives, children, and other relatives, and were for the most part agriculturalists. The Corporación gave them tools, seed, and foodstuffs on a long-term arrangement and then sent them off down the road to find a parcel. The army had constructed a few houses in the colony, but most colonists arrived to no more than wilderness right to the edge of the road. For weeks they would have to live in a palm lean-to until a better dwelling could be built.

The principal crop of the Yapacaní was, and continues to be, dry rice. Early harvests in the colony simply remained there or were laboriously hauled out, bag by bag, on the backs of men, women, children and horses. Abandonment of parcels continued to plague colonization officials, and the settlers began using the colony only for the purpose of earning enough to acquire land closer to lowland markets.

In 1966 construction financed by USAID began on the Yapacaní bridge. The span was part of a package project that included paving the two branch roads from Montero and providing a gravel road twenty-two kilometers into the Yapacaní colony. As work began, interest in the Yapacaní settlement grew. It was evident that a great deal of land in the colony would soon have all-weather market access. Parcel value increased, and even sites previously ignored because of extreme isolation were now being claimed by highland migrants. Although no titles to property had been given in the Yapacaní, buying and selling of farm plots was increasing steadily. Technically, all that was sold were the improvements to the property. But new arrivals understood, as did the resident colonists, that the former were buying not only a house, kitchen, pig pen, or whatever, but also the land they stood on. When a price had been agreed upon, the buyer and seller would present themselves to the CBF and, later, to the INC office in Villa Busch to arrange for a transfer of settlement rights and obligations. In essence, the buyer received nothing more than the knowledge that his name now replaced that of the previous colonist beside the parcel number in a ledger. Any outstanding debts to the colonization program incurred by the seller were transferred to the new resident. Since little effort was made to collect these debts, however, this too became simply a matter of shuffling papers.

The paved highway to the limit of the Yapacaní River was opened early in 1968, but several floods interrupted the completion of the bridge. The primary road nevertheless meant an increase in the number of vehicles in the area, subsequent competition for cargoes, and lower transport fees. Although development in the colony was still hindered by the lack of a bridge and poor internal transit networks, truckers were now paying the cost of crossing the river by barge and braving the terrible roads in their search for cargoes of rice and hardwoods. Villa Busch began to grow rapidly. A small outdoor market opened in the field set aside for a town plaza where colonists could buy goods shipped from Montero and Santa Cruz. The urban lots that had been plotted years earlier were finally finding buyers.

When I returned to the Yapacaní area in 1975 after an absence of almost seven years, I found that the colony had undergone an amazing metamorphosis—a comment on the impact of direct market access. Villa Busch had become a bustling frontier town of more than 1,000 inhabitants (Solari 1975). The old Camba huts had been replaced by highlander-owned structures of brick and cement. An office of the civil police authority, DIC (Departmento de Investigación Criminal), had superseded the military post for maintaining order and settling disputes. A potable water system, evening-hour electricity, a twelve-bed hospital run by the Methodists, and a savings and loan cooperative had also appeared. Most notable, however, was the huge covered market, which had grown up in an area across the road from its original site.

Buying and selling activity in the colony had long outgrown the projected plaza zone, which was now just that, the town square. A large section of Villa Busch was allocated for the new market, jointly funded by Obras Públicas and by INC, and brick and tin-roofed stalls were constructed on the site. The market itself was almost invisible from the road since colonists and vendors had erected wooden kiosks on any available space in the area. On weekends, itinerant sellers from Montero and other towns, along with residents from all over the colony, made their way into Villa Busch to participate in the marketing festivities. *Chicherías* had also sprung up on the outskirts of the community, attesting to the economic prosperity of the Yapacaní.

The schools situated at seven- and ten-kilometer intervals along the main colony road had become focal points for community development, and the road itself had been graded and surfaced with rock. But perhaps most importantly, the Yapacaní bridge now spanned the river. An expanse of brilliant white concrete eight hundred meters long linked the colony to the rest of Santa Cruz, Bolivia, and the world. A trip to the departmental capital could be made in three hours instead of three days or more.

With the opening of the Yapacaní bridge and graveled road twenty-two kilometers into the colony, this section of the Yapacaní colony had become largely a continuation of the farming and marketing complex of the northern Santa Cruz region. Most of the land has been deforested and has passed through the progression of rice, maize, bananas, and manioc to pasture. Those colonists who have financially weathered land fertility depletion over the years, and have converted much of their land to pasture, are now involved in dairying. A truck from Santa Cruz makes the trip daily to the Yapacaní to collect for the PIL (Productores Integrados de Leche) pasteurization plant near Warnes. Even so, according to an extension agent working in the colony, most settlers are working land much farther out, since dairy operations remain small and do not supply adequate incomes alone. This same source commented that there are approximately thirty-five cooperatives between Villa Busch and kilometer 27 and that most were formed to acquire wilderness. It has also been noted that many of these co-ops are funded by outside sources, which have an interest in acquiring large tracts of land for speculation.

As word circulates that the road from the Yapacaní ultimately will be linked with the Chapare highway, forming part of the multination Carretera Marginal de la Selva, colonists are rushing out to claim land. While some of these are new arrivals, most are old Yapacaní colonists, who are members of land cooperatives. By paying a fee averaging about 3,000 pesos ($ US 136) a man can join a co-op and hope for a piece of land. There are no guarantees, however, and the money is never returned. The fact that some may get land and others not has caused disgruntlement and divisiveness in many of these co-ops. But the hunger for virgin forest is so great among colonists that most who are able to raise the initial fee are willing to take the risk of losing it all. Once a participant in such a co-op, the prospective settler will be solicited monthly for additional funds to pay for surveying, the purchase of chain saws, rental of vehicles to carry men in and out, money for various officials and food and other supplies. In the beginning, the co-op members would wait until a certain parcel of land was designated for colonization. Now, with the high degree of competition for forest, co-ops are jumping land, claiming tracts, and then paying bribes to hold onto it. Since titles are never part of the process, money is passed around with nothing legally binding in return, jeopardizing no one but the recipient of the property. In the long run, he too will pass the land to someone else for a fee and move on. Even in the older part of the colony, the process of conferring land titles moves slowly. As of 1978, fourteen years after the initiation of the project, no one had received a clear title to his parcel.

The Yapacaní is now under public authority and Villa Busch operates as an independent community. The town continues to expand as new neighborhoods spring up on the outskirts of what once were the operational headquarters of the colony. In 1979, the northern rural electrification project reached Villa Busch, supplying the town with power twenty-four hours a day. The market area has grown also, and prices frequently are competitive with those in the large Santa Cruz markets. Many vendors explained that they received their produce such as potatoes and onions directly from Cochabamba, not through middlemen in Santa Cruz. Easy access to the colony has also made it a spot for urban people to spend Sundays. Cars loaded with middle-class Cambas and Kollas make weekend excursions to the Yapacaní River. Here they enjoy fish dinners served in thatched restaurants located along the river's edge, they swim and boat and then travel the three kilometers to Villa Busch to drink beer and visit the market. On one Sunday in 1978 when I visited the colony, three young men were waterskiing back and forth under the Yapacaní bridge, a sight I had difficulty reconciling with memories of the early 1960s.

Cambas also have begun to move into Villa Busch in greater numbers. In 1975, a census conducted by a Salesian priest listed 1,151 inhabitants in the community, representing four countries outside of Bolivia and all of the nation's departments except the Pando and Santa Cruz (Solari 1975). The total absence of Cambas in Villa Busch at this time is questionable, for I know of a few families who moved into the area prior to the census. Still, Villa Busch and, to a large extent, the colony as a whole traditionally have been Kolla strongholds. Many highlanders have expressed their feelings that, although Cambas have been given land in the Yapacaní, the area was opened primarily for the benefit of highland peoples. In 1980, however, I was surprised to find a new and predominantly Camba neighborhood to the south of Villa Busch. Interviews with several of the residents indicated that the increasingly urban aspects of the town had attracted these lowlanders. While a few were renting farm parcels out in the colony from highlanders, most were engaged in day labor or the running of small neighborhood kiosks, typical income-producing activities among rural Cambas.

The San Julián colony

The eastern branch of the Montero highway leads to the Río Grande, or at least to within nine kilometers of the river's western shore. On the other side, the San Julián colony begins, stretching in a northerly direction seventy-two kilometers along a graveled road (Figure 4). The colony ends at the San Julián River, but the road continues into eastern Santa Cruz and to the villages of San Ramón, Santa Rosa de la Mina, and San Javier. All of these are Camba communities founded by the Franciscans as *reducciones* for Guarayó Indians of the area.

San Julián, like the Yapacaní to the west, has a sporadic history of settlement. An initial zone near the Río Grande was inaugurated about 1968. Fifty-hectare plots were laid out at 150-meter intervals along the unimproved road for a distance of forty kilometers. Prior to this period, however, lowlanders from San Javier and even the more remote village of San Ignacio had settled on parts of the proposed colonial territory. Squatters' rights prevailed and the colony had to be planned around the squatters. Later, when San Julián was opened for official colonization, a few highlanders responded to the offer of free farmland, but the majority of residents continued to be Cambas from nearby villages. The Instituto Nacional de Colonización, operating from an encampment at kilometer 40, supplied land parcel surveys and wells with hand pumps every four kilometers, but little more. Soon it was evident that the colony was not progressing as planned and funding was withdrawn.

The agricultural boom of the 1970s awakened new interest in San Julián. Financing for settlement of the area beyond kilometer 40 was obtained from USAID (US $200,000) along with a West

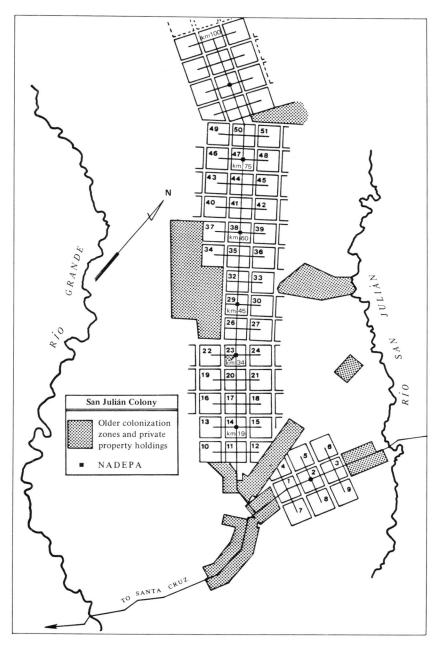

Fig. 4. San Julián colony.

German loan, which included technical assistance for the construction of a secondary road from the Río San Julián to the Río
Grande—the length of the zone set aside for colonial development. By 1976, the road had been completed.

Unlike the first forty kilometers of the old section of the
colony, which was laid out on a linear plan, the next segment of
San Julián, opened in 1972, was divided into nine *nucleos* with
forty pie-shaped parcels radiating out from each settlement nucleo. The nine nucleos occupied an area 144 kilometers square,
with nucleos 1, 2, and 3 located along the main road at kilometers
52, 57, and 62, respectively. Nucleos 4, 5, and 6 along with 7, 8,
and 9 were lateral to the roadside settlement, forming a compact
colonization block. All nine nucleos had wells with hand pumps.

At the time of my first visit to the colony in June 1975, the
slack season between crops, very few colonists were actually in
residence. Only nucleos 1, 2, 7, and 8 were open for settlement,
and 7 and 8 were virtually empty. Nucleo 1 was composed of highlanders, many related to one another and all ex-harvesters. Even
then there was an indication that this nucleo would eclipse the
others by its prime location and attention to commerce rather
than farming.

Nucleo 2 was a settlement of mixed inhabitants, but the majority were Cambas of Guarayó Indian origin. In the interest of
peace, the INC was submitting to pressure to segregate the colony
into Camba and Kolla residential zones, and two Camba families
previously living in nucleo 1 had been requested to change their
location to nucleo 2. Part of the pressure on these lowlanders to
move to another nucleo was exerted by the highland colonists in
nucleo 1, who wanted the property for family members planning
to move to the colony.

Nucleo 7 was settled by a group of migrants from the Potosí
area, but none were present. Other colonists stated that a few
of the Potosinos had returned to the interior to visit relatives but
that most had gone into Montero to work in the cane and cotton
harvests.

The final area, nucleo 8, was granted to a group of Bolivians
who had been living illegally in Chile and were expelled *en masse*.
The Bolivian government was faced with the problem of relocating
these repatriots, and apparently found San Julián an available solution. There were only five of the original forty families in residence at the time of the 1975 study, many having found a means of

returning to Chile. Thus nucleos 1 and 2, situated on the main road, were the only areas within the new San Julián colony that contained their full complement of colonists. From the nucleated section to the San Julián River, or some twelve kilometers, there were a few Guarayó families squatting on the government land.

In many respects, the San Julián colony resembled the Yapacaní of former years. The Río Grande had to be crossed on a barge or in a canoe; like the Yapacaní River, it was prone to flash flooding. In addition, the improved road through the colony was only partially completed, and transport costs were prohibitive. Other than by walking, the colonists' sole way in and out of San Julián was on logging trucks that were at work in the forests beyond the colony. The new secondary road has lowered the cost of transport from U.S. $1.00 to U.S. $.90 per hundred pounds but the colonists must await the completion of a bridge spanning the Río Grande before any significant drop in cartage fees will occur. The Río Grande bridge is still a long time from becoming a reality.

Unlike the Yapacaní, however, San Julián's first nine nucleos will not solve the majority of their problems by building roads and bridges. The area is too arid for profitable rice production and as yet the colonist has no viable substitute (Cochrane 1973:261; 358).[1] Much of the older section of the colony (kilometers 1 to 40) already has been consolidated into large cattle ranches, and it appears that ranching will become the economic base for most of the nine- nucleo area.

A revisit to nucleo 8 in 1978 with a USAID evaluation team revealed that the settlers were not progressing. Only three of the original Chilean migrants remained, and the other 37 parcels had been claimed by highlanders from Cochabamba and Potosí (many of the Potosinos were relatives of colonists in nucleo 7). We met in the center of the nucleo with about twenty-five men and women, all very vocal since, despite our best efforts to dissuade them, they felt we could change the course of their lives. Several attempts at planting rice, the crop with the highest market value, had failed from lack of rain. Maize grew well, the colonists explained, but the price at 50 pesos (U.S. $2.35) per *quintal* (hundred pounds) minus the 20 pesos (U.S. $.90) for transport left little profit after production expenses. The settlers were also angry that the Banco Agrícola Boliviano (BAB) had not extended them any credit in spite of numerous costly expeditions to the office in Montero. Most admitted that they were barely subsisting on their farms and had to spend long periods in the Montero area working as day laborers to supplement their incomes. They also expressed some concern that the original nine nucleos had all but been abandoned by the INC now that the new area of colonization had been opened along the Brecha Casarabe, a road cut perpendicular to the improved San Julián road at kilometer 44.

In September 1974, INC signed a loan agreement with the U.S. Agency for International Development in the amount of $8.36 million to develop an area to be known again as the San Julián colonization project. Realizing that the area extending beyond the original nine nucleo settlements would continue to present climatic problems, the INC cut a new trail north into wetter territory. Along this trail, called the Brecha Casarabe, a new zone would be established. Initially, it would extend eighty kilometers into the wilderness and consist of thirty-nine nucleos.The loan provided $5.16 million for roads, $298,000 for construction of an agricultural service center and health post, $38,000 for credit, $325,000 for wells, $1.08 million for technical assistance, research, and project administration, and $1.124 million for food provided by the World Food Program (Nelson 1978:2). The total cost of the project, including roads, to settle 4,680 families was estimated at $1,790 per family, substantially less than any previous effort.[2] The San Julián project also differed significantly from other Bolivian colonization projects in that colonists would undergo a training period to prepare them for the rigors of the lowland life-style. Participation in this four-month orientation program was mandatory for the acquisition of any land parcel in the colony.

In another departure from tradition, the INC contracted the orientation program to an interdenominational church organization known as the United Church Committee (CIU). This group, consisting primarily of Catholic, Methodist, and Mennonite members, came into existence in 1967 to assist with the feeding, housing, and eventual resettlement of that year's flood victims in the northern Santa Cruz region. Many of these people were resettled in a wilderness area to be known as the Chané-Piraí colony, across the river from San Julián. The CIU experimented at the time with an orientation program designed to alleviate some of the human suffering associated with relocation. In addition to providing a low-cost training and transition period for the flood victims, the orientation program also attempted to avoid the paternalistic stance so prejudicial to planned settlement in the past.

While the San Julián project along the Brecha was in the planning stages, CIU presented the Instituto Nacional de Colonización with an updated version of its flood victim program. The plan was accepted, a contract was drawn up, and an American CIU missionary with twenty years of experience in Santa Cruz was named settlement advisor. A multinational group consisting of CIU members, CIU personnel, and other Bolivian development workers formed the core of the orientation staff. Although this group technically operated within the bureaucratic confines of the INC, its multinational composition created a certain autonomy. This autonomy, no doubt, contributed to the flexibility of decision making, good rapport among the members, and thus to the successes enjoyed by the project.

The orientation program as implemented by the United Church Committee gives San Julián part of its unique place in settlement history and practice. The goals of the program were three: to help colonists adapt to a new environment, to promote community solidarity, and to stimulate the socioeconomic integration of colonists (CIU-INC 1975). In order to meet these objectives, CIU exposed each colonist to an intensive four-month-long program.

The colonists from the highlands arrived in groups formed either as the result of government-sponsored propaganda campaigns there or through the INC branch office in the nearest urban center, Montero. When they reached San Julián, they were met by the social promoter (*promoter social*), a trained community development worker and CIU staff member who had been assigned to that group and would remain with it throughout the course of the program. Two 10-by-16 meter *galpones*, or tin-roofed sheds, were already on site and had been prepared as sleeping quarters for the colonists. A 4-by-3 meter palm-thatched outbuilding had also been constructed for use as a communal kitchen. In addition, the *parque*, or food storage area, had been placed in the center of the nucleo settlement. Here food provided by the World Food Program would be stored and dispensed to colonists. The parque also served as the residence and base of operations for the social promoter. Finally, the initial settlement infrastructure was completed with a deep well, a hand pump, and two latrines.

During the first week of orientation, the promoter took the initiative. Cooking duties were set up on a rotational basis, and the two-hectare machine-cleared area in the center of the settle-

ment was cleaned of weeds. In most instances, colonists immediately set up goal posts in this field for evening and weekend soc-
cer games, frequently their only recreation and entertainment
during these early years. The community garden was prepared,
and other basic settling-in activities took place. After about a week,
the nucleo elected its first leader for a term of one month. Thus,
by the end of the orientation process, the group had experienced
an initial learning period of decision making with four different
leaders. At the end of the orientation program, a leader was elected
for one year, and five or six individuals were selected to serve on a
board known as the *mesa directiva.* The function of the mesa was
to deal with other nucleos, the INC, or with the United Church.
Interestingly, leaders most often selected were not the individuals
who may have held positions of power and authority in the highlands. The colonists appeared to recognize that here in a new environment other kinds of skills might be necessary. Hence, leaders
tended to be younger men who had demonstrated both ability and
interest in coping with colonial life.

Three major projects were completed before the orientation
period ended and settlement certificates were issued (no actual
land titles had been conferred at the time of the study). The nine
hectares of urban area, or *radio urbano* was cleared in addition to
the initial two hectares cleared by the INC machinery. This space
would be used for dwellings, kitchens, latrines, and family gardens. Each colonist built a palm-thatched house with a latrine.
Forty hectares of farmland were cleared. Land clearing was done
cooperatively, although each community decided whether this
was to be completed by small work groups or collectively as a unit.
The actual fifty-hectare parcels were not surveyed until the latter
part of the program, so that no individual knew exactly whose
land was being cleared during the collective effort. For six weeks
during this land-clearing phase, an *orientador* was made available
to each nucleo. This person most frequently was a lowlander or at
least a highlander with extensive lowland farming experience. The
orientador gave assistance in house-building, methods of thatch-
ing, techniques of slash-and-burn horticulture, and proper use and
care of tools.

Throughout the orientation period, floating CIU staff visited
each nucleo on a two-day basis every other week. This staff included a *mejoradora del hogar*, who assisted with organization of
the communal kitchen, gave instructions in use of PMA foods, and

taught general nutrition and hygiene; a nurse-paramedic, who took care of health problems, made referrals to the doctor based at the INC center located at Km. 42 on the main road, and trained two community members from each nucleo in basic first aid procedures; a cooperative specialist, who gave instruction in consumer cooperatives and their management. During the orientation period an actual consumer co-op was set up and colonists received experience in this type of activity. At the end of the orientation, the co-op was disbanded, to be reformed if initiated by the colonists themselves. Reinstitution of co-ops was only partially successful, however, due both to colonist apathy and to a reluctance on the part of the more entrepreneurial types to create an institution that would compete with their own business interests.

Each colonist received seeds for the first year, along with various perennial plants. Three types of rice seed were distributed: Carolina, a dry, long-grain rice, which matures in ninety days, and Bluebonnett and Dorado, shorter grained, stickier varieties of rice. The latter two have a somewhat better market since they are frequently selected by the mills due to lower breakage rates and lowland dietary preferences. In addition to rice, two types of maize seed, soybeans, common beans, peanuts, eating and cooking bananas (guineos and plátanos), citrus, pineapple, papaya, mango, sweet potatoes, and garden seeds were provided to the colonists. Although several of the perennial varieties would take years to reach maturity and bear fruit, the colonist did have an initial variety of crops to draw upon for an adequate and varied diet during the first year. By the second year, colonists were marketing some of these crops with varying degrees of success.

At the end of the four-month orientation period, a ceremony, or clausura, was held and each colonist received a settlement certificate. Although the certificate had no legal validity, it had the colonist's name and date of settlement inscribed on it. Thus, it theoretically could be used as a lever in the land titling process to pressure the government in meeting its two-year title delivery commitment. The clausura ceremony marked the end of the initial settlement phase and CIU withdrew from active participation, although PMA food would continue for another five months.

One excellent indicator of the promise demonstrated by the orientation program in dealing with problems of physical, social, and emotional adaptation to the colony was the remarkable reduction in settlement attrition rates. Although these data cover only the first year or two of settlement and are not long-term indicators, an abandonment rate of 20 percent (AID-PES 1978) is significant in comparison to the average of 42 percent for other colonies cited by the INC (1970). It also must be remembered that the highest rates of abandonment in previous Bolivian colonization efforts occurred during the first and second years of settlement.

To date, the majority of colonization projects, such as the Chapare, Yapacaní, Huaytú, Surutú and spontaneous sectors of Chané-Piraí have been settled in a linear fashion along penetration roads. While this pattern allows for regularly shaped parcels and fairly extensive frontages along the access road, colonists are spaced much like beads on a string. This lack of centralization has both immediate and long-range consequences. First, colonists are separated from one another, which creates a sense of social as well as spatial isolation. Traditional cooperative work groups such as the *minka* are difficult to initiate in colonies where spatial separation has contributed to the problem of settlers' disparate places of origin.[3] Second, a linear orientation makes it almost impossible to provide services such as health care, education, and technical assistance. It is difficult to disseminate information and to initiate group activities. Third, the linear plan retards the consolidation phase wherein communities form and secondary services are provided. In some of the older colonies, such as the Yapacaní, community formation has been retarded in several areas. Instead, people have sold their land or divided the family to move into urbanized zones whose distance from the farm parcel precluded simultaneous rural and urban lifestyles.

On the other hand, the nucleated settlement pattern as exemplified by the San Julián colony offers numerous advantages. The NADEPA (Nucleo Agrícola de Producción Asociada) concept consists of forming nucleos of forty families with fifty-hectare parcels each, into a nine-nucleo block. The central nucleo of the block is the NADEPA, where in addition to the lots supplied for the forty resident families, space is provided for an urban lot for each of the remaining 320 colonist families in the other eight nucleos. In this manner, the NADEPA system provides urban opportunity for each colonist at a maximum distance of ten kilometers from the farmstead.

The forty-family unit, although small for a community, allows for continued solidarity and optimum communication among its members. With the NADEPA concept, these small settlements are members of a large one, which can effectively and economically supply primary services that would be unfeasible at a lower level of organization.

Along the Brecha, the NADEPA system seems to be working successfully. By 1978, little more than two years after settlement, the NADEPA at nucleo 14 had small businesses along the main road, and there were two rice mills (*peladoras*) in competition with one another. Colonists interviewed appeared to understand that this nucleo would eventually become the service center for that sector. The other NADEPAS had been settled for only a few months, so it was too early to make any judgment with regard to the implementation of the system in these areas. It should also be noted that the development of the NADEPA at nucleo 14 was of a spontaneous nature. Although the settlement pattern had been predetermined, the colonists received no impetus either from CIU or INC staff to begin actual development of the center. When compared to other colonies, this natural evolution toward consolidation indicates the importance of the initial settlement pattern in the planning of agricultural colonies.

In March 1979, the major participants in the United Church Committee (CIU) involved with the San Julián project formed a new group called FIDES (Fundación Interamericana para el Desarrollo). The basic Methodist-Mennonite composition remained constant, with the general assembly composed of fourteen members, seven American missionaries and seven Bolivians trained by American missionaries. It would appear that the reasons for setting up this group were twofold. First, it was necessary to secularize the group, at least for appearances' sake, to make it more acceptable to international funding agencies such as AID; and second, by diversifying its membership the organization would have greater access to private funding.

The first project tackled by FIDES was to prepare a proposal for the consolidation of San Julián and its sister colony across the Río Grande, Chané-Piraí. In the past, colonization programs initiated by INC or its forerunners were concerned only with the pioneering phase. According to Michael Nelson's settlement paradigm of three phases (pioneering, consolidation, and growth), the first normally lasts from five to ten years (Nelson 1973). With the inclusion of an orientation program and well-trained and coordinated technical assistance, the San Julián colony was able to move through the pioneering stage in two to three years. The old CIU team, now FIDES, was interested not only in seeing the colony through those early settlement years but into the growth phase as well. In 1978, AID sent an international multidisciplinary team into San Julián to assess the prospects for funding a first-time consolidation project. Nelson and I were both members of this seven-person team consisting of an economist, ecologist, soils specialist, agricultural economist, management specialist, regional planner, and anthropologist. The team was favorably impressed with the

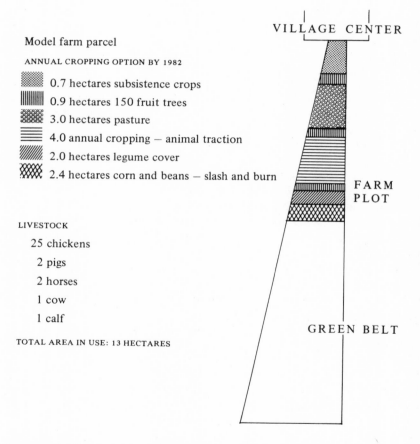

Model farm parcel

ANNUAL CROPPING OPTION BY 1982

     0.7 hectares subsistence crops

     0.9 hectares 150 fruit trees

     3.0 hectares pasture

     4.0 annual cropping — animal traction

     2.0 hectares legume cover

     2.4 hectares corn and beans — slash and burn

LIVESTOCK

     25 chickens

     2 pigs

     2 horses

     1 cow

     1 calf

TOTAL AREA IN USE: 13 HECTARES

VILLAGE CENTER

FARM PLOT

GREEN BELT

Fig. 5. Model farm parcel, annual cropping option in 1982.

progress of the colony and recommended that a consolidation program be undertaken. After a planning study was carried out in October 1979 by a private counseling firm, the FIDES proposal was completed and submitted to AID in La Paz.

FIDES was to receive for its consolidation program the largest cooperative agreement grant ever given to a private volunteer organization in Latin America: US $1,500,000 to be disbursed over a period of three years (Donna Chavez, personal communication, 1980). This grant would finance projects to establish various services within the colony, such as marketing systems, agricultural extension centers, schools, and health posts. A particularly interesting concept to be developed was the model farm, with either a cropping or cattle emphasis. Each parcel ideally would be subdivided in such a way as to provide both short- and long-range income possibilities in terms of livestock, perennial tree crops, and annual cash crops as well as a variety of subsistence crops to lessen cash dependence on food items (Figure 5). The FIDES planners' objective was to offer a diversified farm model that would stabilize the colony's population by avoiding monocropping practices of the past. Since the diversified farm plan had been only recently implented at the time of the 1978 study, it was not possible to determine the outcome.

Conclusions

Colonization in the Santa Cruz region of Bolivia has a long and checkered history. Planned projects have proved costly and overly paternalistic, often creating an ongoing dependency relationship between settlers and government agencies. For the most part, resettlement programs have failed in achieving their objectives both to move significant numbers of highlanders into the lowlands and to stabilize populations within colonization zones. Much of the population instability experienced by colonization projects can be attributed to shifting agricultural practices. The abundance of virgin land, which offers high yields when the forest cover is cut and burned, may frequently be the struggling colonist's only option. Once weeds and grass invade his cropland, the average settler has neither the expertise nor the capital to combat the problem and simply moves on. Increasingly, this second growth, or *barbecho*, is being acquired by those who have the capital for the necessary conversion to mechanization or the raising of livestock. In addition to obtaining land at bargain prices, the new owner has been spared the expense of initial clearing.

Thomas Royden and Boyd Wennergren, with the UTAH/USAID project in Bolivia, have stated:

> The settling and clearing of state land and the subsequent sale of the partially improved property is emerging as a way of life for spontaneous colonists, such as those who will have migrated successfully to new frontier areas twice in the last ten years. The colonist frequently has contributed to the development of someone else's production unit, while making limited progress towards improving his own economic and social status. While the commercial farmer expands his production, the colonist achieves little more than survival and a subsistence level of living. It should be noted, however, that such development patterns are not uncommon in opening and settling virgin land areas. The spontaneous and mobile colonizer performs the role of making the initial clearing and settlement of the new area. (Royden and Wennergren 1973:72)

For the majority of colonists, their future as small farmers is locked into shifting agriculture. Without capital to meet this "barbecho crisis," as economist Simon Maxwell terms it (Maxwell 1979), most settlers continue moving into the virgin forest.

The problems of distance and space have also consistently plagued efforts to develop new lands. Both the Yapacaní and San Julián cases clearly demonstrate the significant role that market access plays in the economic progress of the settlement. Although certainly not the sole determinant for success, market availability is crucial to the overall well-being of a colony. The use of space within the colony is another aspect that contributes to specific patterns of development. In the case of the Yapacaní, a linear settlement plan inhibited the formation of communities. In San Julián on the other hand, a new model was developed to help overcome spatial problems encountered in the past.

The selection and preparation of colonists has also shifted from simply bringing people directly from the highlands and turning them loose in the wilderness to offering land to already acclimated highlanders and then training them in lowland agriculture. In San Julián, these efforts appear to have had a positive impact on colonist attrition, at least in the early years. At the same time, the implementation of a diversified farming model may help stabilize a population accustomed to shifting agriculture. A reevaluation of the San Julián project at a later date will be necessary to determine if these innovations bring about the expected results.

Notes

(Portions of this paper will appear in the author's forthcoming book, *Camba and Kolla: Migration and Development in Santa Cruz, Bolivia,* University Presses of Florida, 1985.)

1. Mean annual precipitation for the Yapacaní is 1,500 mm, while that of the San Julián area along the road measures approximately 800 mm (Cochrane 1973:261; 358).

2. The Alto Beni, Chimoré, and Yapacaní averaged US $3,025 per colonist in settlement costs (Nelson 1978).

3. The *minka* is a short-term cooperative work group oriented primarily toward agricultural needs such as plowing, planting, and harvesting.

References Cited

Agency for International Development–Project Evaluation Summary (AID-PES)
  1978   Project Evaluation Summary. San Julián: La Paz.
Cochrane, Thomas T.
  1973   *El Potencial Agrícola del Uso de la Tierra en Bolivia. Un Mapa de Sistemas de Tierras.* La Paz: Misión Británica en Agricultura Tropical, Ministerio de Agricultura.
Crist, Raymond E. and Charles M. Nissly
  1973   *East from the Andes.* University of Florida Social Sciences Monograph Series No. 50. Gainesville: University of Florida Press.
Ferragut, Castro
  1961   *Principal Characteristics of the Agricultural Colonies of Bolivia and Suggestions for a Colonial Policy.* La Paz: FAO, United Nations.
Galleguillos, Adolfo
  1970   *Análisis y Resultados Obtenidos en la Promoción y Asentamiento de Colonos.* La Paz: INC.

Instituto Nacional de Colonización (INC)
    1970   *La Colonización en Bolivia*. La Paz: Departamento de Promoción de Migraciones y Servicios Sociales.
Interamerican Development Bank (IDB)
    1970   *Tenth Annual Report. 1969*. Washington, D.C.: IDB.
Interamerican Development Bank–Bolivia (IDB-Bolivia)
    1971   *Informe Final del Préstamo*. La Paz: IDB.
Lanning, James Walter
    1971   The Old Colony Mennonites of Bolivia: A Case Study. M.S. thesis, Texas A. and M. University.
Maxwell, Simon
    1979   *Colonos Marginalizados al Norte de Santa Cruz. Avenidas de Escape de la Crisis del Barbecho*. CIAT, Documento de Trabajo 4.
Nelson, Michael
    1973   The Impact of Access Roads on Spontaneous Colonization. USU Series 2373. Logan: Utah State University.
    1978   *Final Report. AID Evaluation of San Julián Colonization Project*. La Paz: AID.
Royden, Thomas and E. Boyd Wennergren
    1973   *The Impact of Access Roads on Spontaneous Colonization*. USU Series 23/73. Logan: Utah State University.
Solari, Tito (Fr.)
    1975   Census of San Carlos Parish and Environs. Unpublished.
Stearman, Allyn MacLean
    1973   Colonization in Eastern Bolivia: Problems and Prospects. *Human Organization* 41(4).
    1978   The Highland Migrant in Lowland Bolivia: Multiple Resource Migration and Horizontal Archipelago. *Human Organization* 37(2).
Thompson, Stephen
    1968   Religious Conversion and Religious Zeal in an Overseas Enclave: The Case of the Japanese in Bolivia. *Anthropological Quarterly* 41(4).
Zondag, Cornelius
    1968   *La Economía Boliviana: 1952–1965. La Revolución y Sus Consequencias*. Bolivia: Los Amigos del Libro.

Colonization and Spontaneous Settlement in the Ecuadoran Amazon

Jorge Uquillas

THE OCCUPATION of the Ecuadoran Amazon by outsiders throughout Ecuador's history has been a response to social and demographic factors and to policies that have created conditions favorable to human displacement from other regions of the country. Demographic growth, unequal resource distribution (primarily land), and scarce opportunities for employment have resulted since about 1950 in the intensification of efforts to occupy zones of low population density and ill-defined land ownership. The most attractive zones have been located in the Costa, especially the Nor-Occidente, which includes portions of the Provinces of Manabí, Pichincha, and Esmeraldas. Since 1970 especially, attractive zones have arisen also in Amazonia, among them the Nor-Oriente, which embraces the valleys of the Napo and Aguarico rivers.

Human displacement to Amazonia has for the most part accompanied the creation of spontaneous settlements. This phenomenon is apparently associated with the structural factors mentioned above (population growth and economic inequality). In contrast, a less extensive process of directed colonization is related to certain state policies applied at the national level. These policies are fundamentally concerned with national security (border defense, protection of petroleum areas), the reduction of demographic and social pressures in the sierra and costa, and the extension of the agricultural frontier (incorporation of new lands into production).

This paper will analyze the details and implications of Amazonian occupation, both through directed and semidirected colonization and through the formation of spontaneous settlements. The first section presents the historical pace of the region's population growth since the time when the indigenous peoples held total control of the forest, and since the first attempts by colonizers to form nuclei of concentrated population, up to the contemporary period in which stable settlements have been formed of natives and colonists. This will be followed by an analysis of the most recent statistics on migration to Amazonia, with special emphasis on the Nor-Oriente and the principal policies that have, in one way or another, determined the occupation process in the region. The paper continues with a case study, which focuses on both directed and spontaneous colonization in the petroleum zone of the Nor-Oriente. Directed colonization is defined as a populating process by groups from outside the region that includes prior planning and technical and economic assistance from a public entity. In contrast, occupation, or spontaneous colonization, refers to situations in which the state does not intervene directly and which occur as a consequence of initiatives taken by the colonists or migrants themselves. Finally, the consequences of the colonization process in general are analyzed and policy implications for the region are outlined.

The history of human settlements

Indigenous settlers.—The first groups to settle the Ecuadoran Amazon were those who are generically known as *indigenes* or natives. It is known that at least three distinct waves of human migrants entered the region. The first purportedly came from the Caribbean, crossing the valley of the Orinoco River and the Venezuelan and Colombian plains before entering the eastern forests of Ecuador. The second apparently ascended the Amazon River from Brazil and settled along its tributaries: the Aguarico, Napo, Pastaza, and Santiago rivers. A third wave, crossing the Andean cordillera heading east, included the Shuar, who possibly had some relations with the ancient Paltas and Malacatos of southern Ecuador.

Little is known of Amazonian Ecuador's ethnohistory. The earliest references to indigenous groups in the region are found in chronicles of sixteenth-century Spanish explorers and missionaries. From studies of these accounts (see Naranjo 1977), it has been deduced that the Ecuadoran Amazon of the sixteenth century was populated primarily by Shuar (Jívaros), who occupied the river basins of the Santiago and Morona in the south of the region, and by the Coronados, natives who shared some cultural identity with the Oas (or Oaquis), Roamaynas, and Záparos (or Zapas), groups occupying the river basins of the Napo, Pastaza, and Curaray in the central-north of the region.

In the seventeenth century, in addition to the Shuar, Muratos, and Andoas, who inhabited the central-south, were found the Gayes and Simigayes as well as the aforementioned Coronados and related groups, all living in a large portion of the central region. Also mentioned are the Aushiris or Avishiras and the Encabellados, who lived in the river basins of the Curaray and Aguarico-Putumayo, respectively.

In the eighteenth century, the basins of the Napo, Pastaza, and other intermediate rivers were occupied primarily by the Quijos, Záparos, and Canelos, the latter being the result of a fusion of representatives of Shuar, Záparo, and Quijos-Quechuas del Napo cultures (Naranjo 1977, IEAG, 1976:39). The river basins of the Santiago and Morona continued under the dominion of the Shuar and Achuar. The southern bank of the Napo and the river basin of the Curaray were settled by the Aushiris, and minor groups such as the Encabellados were located on the Aguarico and Putumayo.

It is significant to note that the Canelos, a Quechua-speaking ethnic group, was formed due to the interrelation of numerous groups disseminated through the center-east of Ecuador and even of indigenous elements from the sierra. Apparently this was a refuge zone to which populations of surrounding zones have migrated over the years (Naranjo 1977).

In the nineteenth and early twentieth centuries the native ethnic groups suffered slow transformations. The Shuar and Quechua consolidated their presence, while smaller groups survived in areas of the Selva Baja, and still others, such as the Záparos, entered into a period of clear decline, which would end in their disappearance as a cultural entity.

Frontier expansion.—The occupation of the Ecuadoran Amazon by extraregional human groups has fluctuated in the past but did not reach major proportions until around 1970. From the sixteenth to the end of the nineteenth century, the principal goals of occupation were conversion of the Indians to Catholicism and exploitation of the gold mines and famous cinnamon trees.

The missionaries who generally accompanied the Spanish explorers attempted to dominate and evangelize the numerous indigenous groups found in the region. Since the extreme dispersal of these groups was not convenient to the missionaries' interests, they induced the Indians to congregrate in nuclei. Among these were found the famous *reducciones* of the Jesuits and the mission posts of the Dominicans. By 1567, the latter had in their charge the province of Quijos, specifically the Reducción de Baeza, and in 1621 they founded the mission posts of Bobonaza and Canelos. In 1658 the Jesuits also arrived in Bobonaza, and in 1668 they founded San Javier de los Gayes. The presence of the Catholic missions was not continuous, as for example in the Canelos area where from 1567 to 1828 the Dominicans, Jesuits, and Franciscans alternated control (IEAG 1976:13–14). Furthermore, although the majority of the mission centers were later converted into stable communities or *villas*, some came to be abandoned or destroyed by indigenous rebellions; San Javier de los Gayes was abandoned; Tena and Archidona were destroyed by the Cacique Jumandi of the Coronados or Quijos in 1578; Logroño and Sevilla del Oro were razed in 1599 by the Shuar in 1599 led by the Cacique Quirrube. Finally, we should point out that many native groups rejected the advances of explorers and missionaries alike. Among these, the Shuar were never overcome by the Spanish (Gonzáles Suárez 1970, Harner 1973, Naranjo 1977, Munzel and Kroeger 1981).

In a broad sense the period between the sixteenth and late eighteenth century was characterized by territorial dominion by the natives and by attempts on the part of both missionaries and *encomenderos* to gather the Indians in mission posts, reducciones, or villas. There was a concomitant effort to populate the region with colonists:

> The initial attempt at colonization, realized after the discovery of gold in the Upano and Paute rivers during the sixteenth century, was ephemeral. Three centuries later there were more successful attempts which brought permanent colonists to the intermontane, subtropical valleys (Baeza, Macas). These true frontier colonies were inserted between the mountain walls of the Andes and the hostile tribes of the lowlands . . . connected to the highland cities by long and rugged mountain paths which practically limited agricultural production to goods which

could transport themselves on foot. Hence, pastoral agriculture for the production of meat became the only viable form of agricultural enterprise (Wright 1977:20).

In 1775, the Canelos zone reawakened the interest of the Spanish colonial administration, which sent explorers and missionaries with the triple mission of exploiting recently discovered gold, taking an inventory of cinnamon trees, and evangelizing the indigenous Achuales and Muratos. The activities of this important expedition, which lasted several years, allowed the appearance of the first white-mestizo villages of the zone (IEAG 1976:13–14).

Throughout the nineteenth century and until about 1970, there was a gradual increase in the penetration of nonnative elements, especially from the sierra. Diverse factors contributed to these migrations: the construction of access roads; the desire for lands for the production of sugar cane, *naranjilla,* tea, and cattle; rubber extraction; petroleum exploration and extraction; and the growing presence of the state military and administrative apparatus.

Important migratory currents from the sierra advanced on the Pastaza River basin and the Upano Valley from the nineteenth century on. Beginning with Baños, settlements such as Mera, Puyo, Canelos, and Montalvo formed and grew. Similarly, population increased along the Palora-Arapicos-Macas road. The population was predominantly from the provinces of Tunguragua and, less so, Chimborazo. Recent arrivals, generally peasants eager for land and a better life, dedicated themselves to subsistence agriculture. The most prosperous and ambitious took to more lucrative activities— growing sugar cane and cultivating pasture for cattle raising.

The attraction grew more powerful in the twentieth century. To missionary zeal, the search for gold, and a growing demand for agricultural land were added the worldwide demand for rubber (abundant in Amazonia), hydrocarbon exploration, and the growing presence of the state (in both military and bureaucratic personnel).

Exploitation of the natives and their dislocation from traditional areas of occupation threatened their survival more than ever before. The rubber boom at the end of the nineteenth and beginning of the twentieth century led to major abuses of the indigenous peoples. Entrepreneurs and adventurers frequently took the Indians from their villages and forced them to live in distant and inhospitable places and to extract the resins from the trees. For example, it is reported that more than two hundred families were taken as slaves from the Tena zone to the San Miguel River (MAG-ORSTOM 1978:16).

In the south of the region, in the province of Morona Santiago, colonization received a major impetus at the start of the twentieth century with the arrival of the Salesian missionaries and the new gold boom:

> The establishment of the Salesian missions gave rise to the movement of marginalized peasant groups from the province of Azuay to the mission centers which provided the peasants with lands to begin cultivation. Undoubtedly this was one of the first stimuli to colonization.
>
> In 1920, as a consequence of the resurgence of the mining industry, a numerous contingent of peasants from Azuay settled in Méndez, Limón, and Gualaquiza. The gold fever reached a climax between 1930 and 1941, during which time thousands of Azuayos searched for the precious metal. They settled from the limits of Zamora Chinchipe, at the summit of the point called Los Encuentros, to the confluence of the Paute and Upano rivers. Later, many returned to their regions of origin, yet others remained in the province as colonists. (JNP 1976:11–12)

The following decade, 1940–50, was most significant for the central zone of Amazonia. Petroleum exploration, mounted by the Leonard Corporation and Royal Dutch Shell, provoked a boom in activity and the migration of major population contingents—as much to engage in labor related to the exploration as to occupy land, exploit timber, and establish agricultural–cattle raising establishments. To facilitate the search for oil, encampments were set up in the forest, highways constructed (automobile transport was possible as far as Puyo), airstrips were built, and penetration advanced into forest areas of exclusive native dominion. This constituted a true colonizing offensive, which repelled the indigenous peoples who sought more secure habitats in the direction of the selva baja. Many of the natives were persecuted, dispossessed of their lands, and at times assassinated under the pretext of real or imagined resistance to petroleum exploration (see IEAG 1976). Over time, settlements were consolidated throughout the high forest

and intermontane valleys of Amazonia, the majority of them dedicated to farming and ranching.

The state, in turn, intensified its efforts to integrate the region
with the national economy and life, efforts which translated into
more highways, more schools, more military barracks, and more
missionaries. The scenario for a major invasion from the sierra
and costa was gradually forming. Perhaps the most important
factor facilitating the massive demographic shift was the construction of various access routes to Amazonia. By around 1970
there were four viable penetration highways: Quito-Baeza,
Ambato-Puyo-Tena, Cuenca-Limón-Méndez, and Loja-Zamora.

Demographic patterns and recent policies

Migration and settlement.—In a broad sense migration can be defined as the movement of people from one place to another, generally implying a change of residence. Nevertheless, to facilitate the
collection of data and its measurement we shall consider as migration proper only a change of residence to a different political administrative unit. In reference to the Ecuadoran Amazon, the term
colonization is generally used synonymously with immigration.
This is due to the fact that the region has maintained a low population density and to the erroneous assumption that the lands are
without owners and therefore "colonizable." Furthermore, all of
the nonnative inhabitants of Amazonia are freqently described as
colonists, making no distinction between recent arrivals and those
who are descendants of old migrants.

According to the 1974 National Census, Amazonia had, by
that date, received a net migration of 42,320 persons, representing
21 percent of the enumerated population. Net migration, or the
migratory balance at the provincial level, presented special characteristics in 1974. Zamora Chinchipe received an increase equal to
38.4 percent of its resident population while Napo received 25.4
percent, Morona Santiago 19.8 percent, and Pastaza 11.3 percent.

Although firm data are not yet available, it is presumed that
the migratory process has continued, although at a slower pace.
From 1974 to 1976, the population of Napo grew from 62,186 to
85,700. It is estimated that in 1981 the total should have reached
150,000 inhabitants. The majority of Amazonian immigrants registered in 1974 were from the sierra (88 percent). The Amazonian
province receiving the greatest proportion of coastal immigrants
was Napo, where they made up 21.5 percent of total immigrants.

The motives and causes behind the movement of these people to Amazonia are varied. The principal cause of migration to the region is the colonists' desire to possess relatively large parcels of land and to become farmers and ranchers. The principal forces of expulsion from other regions can be attributed to demographic pressure in the sierra and costa and maldistribution of resources, particularly land. As secondary causes we may cite expectations to exploit gold and timber resources, the possibilities of finding employment in the petroleum zones or on agricultural enterprises, and the desire to reunite with relatives or friends already settled in the region (see MAG-INIAP 1977, MAG-ORSTOM 1978, Vreugdenhil 1976).

With the exception of settlements formed after 1970 in the petroleum zone of the Nor-Oriente, the principal settlements of migrants or colonists have tended to arise in the intermontane valleys of the sub-Andean region. In contrast to the indigenous groups, who traditionally have lived in small dispersed settlements, the migrants have generally formed towns of greater human concentration; yet there are persons in the petroleum zones and along the banks of rivers who have adopted a dispersed pattern of settlement (IERAC 1976, MAG-ORSTOM 1978).

The waves of people arriving in the last decade tried to settle along the penetration roads originating in the sierra, along the roads opened for petroleum exploration, and along the Troncal de la Selva, a highway planned to connect the provincial capitals in Ecuadoran Amazonia. Numerous settlements arose spontaneously along the Loja-Gualaquiza, Cuenca-Macas, Ambato-Tena, and Quito-Coca roads.

In the petroleum zone there is no clear tendency for migrants of like origin to settle in the same place. What does appear to be a typical settlement pattern is concentration along the roads: "the first to arrive settle along the new highways, such that one farm is found every 250 meters on each side. . . . When both sides of the road are completely occupied, the new colonists form a line of settlement parallel to the first at a distance of 2000 meters (or 1600 in the Coca sector)" (MAG-ORSTOM 1978:8).

Colonization policies.—Up to this point we have shown that the occupation of the Ecuadoran Amazon, in gestation since colonial times, culminated after 1970. We have delineated the structural factors that occasioned this process and the official policies that reinforced it. In spite of the fact that the peopling of the Ec-

uadoran Amazon has for the most part been characterized by unplanned migration leading to spontaneous settlements, the state
has historically supported this occupation through diverse measures. The colonial administration sent expeditions and missionaries to take possession of the region, collect tributes, and cate-
chize the conquered villagers. During the Republican era the
government made contracts and agreements with the different religious orders, delegating to them so many functions that they came
to be lords of their jurisdictions. Among the principal responsibilities of the missions were colonizing the region and civilizing its
people: this entailed the opening of roads, the transport of colonists, the formation of populated centers, and even the forced imposition of new cultural patterns among the indigenous groups.
They began with the teaching of new religious beliefs and a new
language, Christianity and Spanish. The occupation of Amazonia
meant, from the beginning, the domination of colonists over natives and the acculturation of the latter.

With the passing of time, territorial disputes with other countries intensified: Ecuador lost extensive areas to Colombia, Brazil,
and Peru. This added a greater relevance to the idea of national
sovereignty (over territory, population, and all resources) and led
to the growth of military posts and the installation of civil authorities. In effect, the mission and military posts were the first
expressions of an official colonization policy in the Ecuadoran
Amazon.

Since the mid-twentieth century the Ecuadoran state has encouraged the spontaneous migration of inhabitants of the sierra
and costa and facilitated the realization of publicly controlled colonization projects. On occasion these policies were conditioned by
forces of expulsion such as the Toquilla straw hat crises, which
affected thousands of artisans in the provinces of Azuay, Cañar,
and Manabí, or the periodic droughts affecting the peasants of Loja
and Manabí. On other occasions colonization has been motivated
by the existence of forces of attraction such as the discovery and
exploitation of hydrocarbon resources in the Amazon region.

Since 1950, various public agencies have been created to implement colonization schemes at national and regional levels.
During the 1950s the government created the National Colonization Institute (now defunct) and the Center of Economic Recon-
version of Azuay, Cañar, and Morona Santiago (CREA). During the
sixties the Ecuadoran Institute of Agrarian Reform and Coloniza-

tion (IERAC) was established. The seventies saw the creation of the Regional Program of Development of the South (PREDESUR) and the National Institute of Colonization of the Ecuadoran Amazon Region (INCRAE).

The primary tendency of colonization policy has been to stimulate the spontaneous movement of people from the sierra and costa. During the 1960s, heavy emphasis was placed upon the execution of controlled colonization schemes. Initially this was due to a desire to attract colonists through a series of incentives offered by the directed and semidirected projects. Later, however, it was conceived as a measure to halt the disorderly occupation of the region. As we shall see, the policies of occupation themselves, and especially the indiscriminate taking of lands, have come into question. This is because, explicitly or tacitly, these policies have ignored the fact that the region has been inhabited for centuries by native groups and because the massive influx of migrants has provoked the systematic destruction of the Amazonian flora and fauna.

State policy concerning the Amazon is currently undergoing a transformation in its nature and form. The state is reassuming functions that in the past have been delegated to the religious missions. Colonization, health services, education, and other activities are now more in the hands of the official sector than in those of the religious missions. Likewise, there is a concentrated effort to rationalize Amazon policy in its formal aspects. That is, there is now a tendency toward the realization of detailed studies that will permit the long-range planning not only of colonization but also of integral development in the region. This constitutes an attempt to order what has hitherto functioned largely under its own dynamism, frequently causing irreparable damage to ecosystems and traditional ethnic groups (INCRAE 1979a).

Current Amazon policy revolves fundamentally around the issues of security and national development. From the national security point of view, it is necessary to secure the Amazon region though the presence of both military forces and a sufficient and permanent Ecuadoran population. This is generally described as the creation of live frontiers. Related to the issue of security is the question of integration, which implies that the Amazon region should be coupled with and form an integral part of the nation.

The dominant developmentalist tendency has emphasized the need to develop and integrate Amazonia economically so that it can contribute to the solution of structural problems at the national level, namely, unequal distribution of population and resources and insufficient agricultural production. It is frequently mentioned in official statements that there is a need for colonization in the Amazon in order to "widen the agricultural frontier" while "decongesting" the costa and sierra zones, regions which have a high population density and a "strong human pressure on the land"—a phenomenon that has provoked demands for radical change such as agrarian reform. Likewise, there is talk of the need for Amazonia to become integrated economically with the nation as a whole and to participate in prevailing patterns of production and consumption. Basically, it is hoped that the region will not only provide for the subsistence of human groups that have settled there, but will also produce a surplus in agriculture and cattle raising, which together with hydrocarbons will contribute to global growth in the economy (see MAG 1977; IERAC 1980; INCRAE 1979b, 1981; Whitten et al. 1981).

Intimately related to this developmentalist tendency is the fact that colonization greatly benefits large enterprises dedicated to the exploitation of Amazonian resources. Most visibly, population increase makes more local labor available, removing the need to import labor from other regions. For companies such as timber extractors, another significant advantage is that they can buy their raw product from the colonists. The tendency of the latter to cut down the forest and convert the land to pasture provides a major supply of timber. For the timber companies, this means lower costs of exploration and extraction. Finally, petroleum company exploration and development activities as well as colonization facilitate the establishment of businesses by installing the transport infrastructure and other services that large enterprises would otherwise have to provide for themselves.

The problems created by colonization, which in many cases have transferred defects of the traditional agrarian sector of the costa and sierra to Amazonia, have motivated legislation to regulate this activity. Hence, the Law of Fallow Lands, originally promulgated in 1875 and renovated in 1918, required that lands of which 20 percent had not been cultivated within ten years of their assignment be returned to the state. This measure was an attempt to control the accumulation of large tracts of land and to encourage agricultural production. Later laws, such as the Law of Fallow Lands of 1936 and Executive Decree no. 10 of February 24, 1954, established principles for the occupation, adjudication, and reversion of lands to the state. The Law of Fallow Lands and Colonization of 1964, currently in effect, combines precepts established under earlier legislation. But it is now considered insufficient and inadequate to regulate the intensive colonizing activity underway in the Ecuadoran Amazon (MAG 1977:23, 24). Consequently, in 1977 a new law was passed, the Law of Colonization of the Amazon Region of Ecuador. The aim of this legislation is to stimulate occupation of the region and to encourage the execution of controlled projects by an official institution created concomitantly, the National Institute of Colonization of the Amazon Region of Ecuador (INCRAE).

This law, presently in force, incorporates advanced and progressive principles. These include the provision that colonization should be realized in a planned fashion, the need for previous and adequate zoning to defend natural resources and to ensure the rational use of the distinct ecological zones, and the requirement that colonization respect the rights acquired by indigenous groups of the region (Registro Oficial No. 504, January 12, 1978; see especially Articles 1–8). The Law of Amazon Colonization also includes articles that some find disconcerting because, as we shall see later, they have engendered fears and mistrust between natives and colonists, especially among the inhabitants of spontaneous resettlements. Perhaps the two aspects that have brought the greatest opposition are the declaration that spontaneous colonization will be chanelled toward state controlled systems and the provisions that endow the Armed Forces with a preponderant role in the initial phase of putting the colonization process in order (see Articles 16–24). Given the predominance of individualistic spontaneous settlement in the region and the indigenous suspicion of state involvement, particularly in colonization, these measures are perceived as threats to the freedom of action and economic interests of these groups. Their rejection may impede even the aspects of the legislation considered to be positive.

Case study: the petroleum zone of the Nor-Oriente

The Nor-Oriente, embracing the river basins of the Napo and Aguarico, represents a laboratory for the study of colonization and spontaneous settlement since it has received the largest number of immigrants in the Amazon region of Ecuador. It has the greatest variety of ethnic groups, navigable rivers for smaller boats, and being the center of hydrocarbon production, a complete network of roads, pipelines, etc. The petroleum zone between the town of Lumbaqui to the west, kilometer 20 of the Tarapoa road to the east, the San Miguel River to the north, and the Napo River to the south, including the Shushufindi sector, has shown a rapid demographic increase. While in 1974 the population was reportedly 12,128, in 1976 it was 35,000, an increase of 193 percent (MAG-ORSTOM 1978:4). Conservative estimates gave the zone a population of 70,000 in 1982.

Directed colonization.—As already mentioned, the state's directed or controlled colonization programs began during the seventies. In some cases they were designed to generate the occupation of particular sectors and in others to orient the large volume of immigration into Amazonia and to promote the rational and orderly occupation of the region.

Controlled colonization is theoretically realized in two distinct forms: directed and semidirected. Directed colonization implies tight control of the process. It begins with planning of the project, selection of the most adequate locale, careful selection of colonist families, and orderly distribution of lots. Organizational support, close supervision of the colonists' activities, and technical and financial assistance to set the project in motion continue. The project moves ahead to the hypothetical date when the colonists will be capable of continuing on their own—that is, when it reaches a stage of self-management and self-financing.

Semidirected colonization consists in the partial control of the immigrants' pioneer activities. Through limited technical and financial assistance, the state attempts to stimulate settlement formation, land claims, and agricultural activity. In general, planning is limited; systematic qualification of colonists is not carried out, nor is there a major investment of fiscal resources.

In 1981, in all of the Ecuadoran Amazon, there were seven colonization projects, directed and semidirected: Shushufindi, Payamino, San Pedro de Rucullacta, and San Miguel de Putumayo, located in the province of Napo; Upano-Palora and San José de Morona in the province of Morona Santiago; and Nangaritza in Zamora Chinchipe.

Shushufindi, Payamino, and San Miguel are controlled projects, created with the intention of testing formulae of territorial occupation in order to establish future guidelines that would eliminate the problems caused by spontaneous settlement. They were initiated by IERAC in 1972 and taken over by INCRAE in 1979 in accordance with Article 39 of the Law of Amazon Colonization. The projects are located in the petroleum zone and represent different models. Their fundamental characteristics will be compared in order to arrive at a global evaluation.

These three directed colonization projects in the Nor-Oriente, significantly similar and different in their principal characteristics, together provide a basis for the evaluation of this type of settlement in Amazonia. The three projects have in common the general objective of occupying strategic areas in a zone of major petroleum production with people from densely populated areas of the Sierra and Costa regions. Each settlement has the established goal of expanding the agricultural frontier through cooperatively organized systems in which the greater portion of the lands are communal property and individual possession is restricted to ten hectares per colonist. All three projects receive official financial and technical support.

There are also important differences between Shushufindi, San Miguel, and Payamino. The execution time of the first (nine years) is greater than that of the remaining two (five and six years respectively). Planned goals also varied: in Shushufindi eighty families were to be settled on 3,400 hectares, in San Miguel three hundred sixty families on 18,000 hectares, and in Payamino four hundred families on 16,000 hectares. Of course, the actual number of families settled by the end of 1981 fell far short of the projected mark. In the first case there were approximately thirty, in the second forty, and in the last a mere fifteen.

Settlement patterns in the three settlements tend toward different models of nucleation, avoiding the dispersion characteristic of spontaneous settlements. In Shushufindi, the lots, which include the dwelling and individual cropping area, are placed along two intersecting roads. In San Miguel the lots, fifty hectares each, are distributed in a radial pattern. At the nucleus there is a service center around which are the colonists' dwellings, surrounded again by the individual lots and, finally, the communal lands. In Payamino, however, dwellings and individual lots are found along the principal road. Short distances between them allow a kind of population nucleus for which a service center is being built.

One final contrast lies in the level of development of each project. Shushufindi, where the soils are considered among the best in Amazonia, contains the most advanced physical infrastructure and services. In 1981 it had five hundred hectares in pasture and communal crops, approximately three hundred head of cattle, and an average "individual area in cultivation" of 1.7 hectares per colonist. In San Miguel, where soils are poor for agriculture and cattle raising, the construction of infrastructure has been limited. In 1981 the project had seventy-five hectares in communal production, fifteen head of cattle, and a mean "individual area in cultivation" of 2.5 hectares per colonist. Finally, Payamino, where soils are relatively poor, has practically no communal services (except for the facilities belonging to the administration located across the river and of little or no use). By 1981 it had seventy hectares in communal production, fifty head of cattle, and a mean "individual area in cultivation" of 3.3 hectares per colonist.

Determination of the success or failure of directed colonization in the Nor-Oriente is very complex. Nevertheless, certain preliminary conclusions can be offered. The success of directed colonization may be judged on the basis of two criteria: whether the projects have achieved their projected goals and whether colonists in directed projects live in better conditions than those in spontaneous settlements.

With respect to the first criterion, the state, through various agencies, has invested approximately 100 million sucres in the Shushufindi, San Miguel, and Payamino projects and has not reached projected goals. It was hoped that eight hundred families would be settled in the three projects, but the present total barely reaches one hundred. Timber has been exploited over large areas, but almost no reforestation programs have been applied. Cropping and cattle production are deficient: of approximately one thousand hectares in production, the largest part is planted in pasture—but in total there are only about four hundred head of cattle. In addition, the cooperative system has had unsatisfactory results due to weak organization. For example, the Unión Imbabureña cooperative in Payamino moved to dissolve itself in 1981, and the cooperatives in Shushufindi and San Miguel are surviving only with great difficulty. In general, members do not participate fully in the cooperative activities, especially in labor on the communal areas. They are more inclined to maintain an individualistic attitude, and their major ambition is to acquire their private lot of fifty hectares.

Comparison of the situation in the directed projects with areas of spontaneous settlement is difficult. Undoubtedly the colonists in the three directed projects have benefited from state investments, which have subsidized their efforts and contributed to their maintenance. This has meant that they can rely on certain basic services such as roads, water, electricity, and primary education. Nevertheless, the colonists themselves do not perceive that they are better off than their neighbors; they feel that the cooperatives have not produced effects sufficient to justify the efforts invested. They feel less free than persons in spontaneous settlements; furthermore, they feel that they have been discriminated against since they have received lots of only ten hectares for individual use whereas others have received parcels of from forty to fifty hectares.

In spite of the deficiencies of the Shushufindi, San Miguel, and Payamino projects, there is not enough evidence to indicate that the model is not applicable in Amazonia. A large part of the problem has to do with the project's poor administration, for the following reasons:

Autonomy and independent management have not been encouraged in the cooperatives. Economic assistance should have been withdrawn gradually and measures taken to avoid a paternalistic system in which the colonists express satisfaction when something is received but feel abandoned and protest when they are left on their own.

Technical assistance in agriculture, cattle raising, and forest exploitation has not been provided with continuity. Scarce technical personnel have occupied the greater part of their time in administrative work instead of work in the field.

Administration and policy have been characterized by discontinuity. Delays resulting from the transfer of control from IERAC to INCRAE paralyzed many activities and created dissatisfaction among the colonists.

Spontaneous settlements.—Spontaneous settlements may be found over most of the petroleum zone. The only exceptions constitute indigenous communal lands, directed projects, and a few enterprises. The spontaneous settlements arose simultaneously with petroleum exploitation. Since approximately 1968, as quickly as penetration roads were constructed into the Nor-Oriente, colonists began to settle along their margins. In general they established themselves on lots of forty or fifty hectares.

In spite of the fact that the Law of Amazon Colonization stipulates direct control of the occupation process, official policy also promotes noncontrolled spontaneous colonization. The fact that large portions of lands are considered "fallow" or have no owner other than the state (frequently ignoring prior rights of possession of indigenous inhabitants) has incited the unrestrained taking of lands by immigrants to the petroleum zone. In areas of highway construction (or projected construction), colonists take possession of the land and commence deforestation. Shortly thereafter they plant such crops as maize, bananas, and pasture.

The taking of land is generally carried out by groups of persons forming a "precooperative." Although the precooperative is not a juridically recognized organization, it is of significant use in gaining access to land. It permits its members to ask IERAC for recognition of their claims and to initiate the process for legal recognition of the cooperative and for the adjudication of occupied lands. Ironically, the destruction of the forest is one condition for the legal acquisition of land in Amazonia. This is required by IERAC for legal adjudication and by the Banco de Fomento for credit, as it must be shown that the land has been worked—demonstrating that the possessor intends to utilize the land for cropping or cattle production. If the lot is maintained with its natural vegetation, it is not considered to be worked. The process begun by the possession of lands and its official recognition continues with the delimitation of the lots and culminates with the concession of a title. The entire transaction goes on in the offices of IERAC.

It is important to point out that the taking of lands involves not only persons with a genuine interest in agricultural production but also persons who are not peasants and who, thanks to contacts and influence, acquire properties on which hired labor will be used for production or which they simply obtain for resale. Worse yet, the region has numerous groups involved in timber extraction and land speculation. Many of them, under the pretense of being colonists, take possession of the land, not with the intention of acquiring legal title and permanent settlement but with the objective of exploiting the more valuable trees and selling the worked lot or their supposed right of possession to a recent arrival, who will then presumably seek legal adjudication.

By 1976, the frontier of colonization had greatly expanded. In the province of Napo alone 12,500 units of agricultural production occupied 464,000 hectares and had a population of 74,000 persons—an average of thirty-seven hectares and six persons per agricultural unit. Nevertheless, only 148,000 hectares—less than one-third of the area occupied in 1976—were in production, an average of 11.8 hectares per agricultural unit (MAG-ORSTOM 1978:26, 27).

We should recall that the major part of this agricultural frontier expansion is due to the formation of spontaneous settlements. IERAC began legal adjudications of lands in 1972; by 1978, six years later, adjudications in the entire Napo province had reached a total of 266,120 hectares, involving 52,888 families, an average of fifty hectares per family. Since nationally figures for 1980 show that about 85 percent of adjudications correspond to spontaneous settlements, it may be estimated that approximately 226,200 hectares were ceded to spontaneous colonists in Napo, while the remainder went to directed projects and large enterprises (see IERAC 1980:3 and IERAC n.d.).

Soil management practices and the principal crops found in the areas of production demonstrate the inordinate eagerness of the colonists to exploit the timber resources of the tropical forest, and the general trend toward cattle raising. According to Wright (1977:14–15) agricultural practices are quite uniform in the region. The process generally begins with forest clearing and the felling of the larger trees, from which the more valuable are selected. When the deforested surface has decomposed, seasonal crops such as maize and beans, accompanied by plantain, papaya, yucca, and others, are planted. After yields have declined and it is no longer profitable to plant perennial crops, pasture is planted.

The principal crops of the petroleum zone (Table 1) are pasture (almost half of the total area in production), maize (17 percent of the area in Aguarico sector and 19 percent in Coca sector), and bananas (15 percent of the total area in production). Half of the average area in cultivation on each farm is dedicated to pastures, confirming the colonists' expressed desire to become ranchers. It is also significant that maize occupies almost 20 percent of the area in production. This not only reflects the dietary habits of a population primarily from the sierra but also represents the tendency to expand pastures "since the colonists are accustomed to planting maize on recently cleared land on which they will later plant pasture" (MAG-ORSTOM 1978:31).

The predominant settlement pattern in the petroleum zone is dispersion: that is, families tend to live on isolated farms and rarely form concentrated population nuclei. In 1976 it was calcu-

TABLE 1. Principal cultigens in production areas
of the petroleum zone of the Nor-Oriente

Cultigen	Percentage of area in production	
	Aguarico sector	Coca sector
Pasture	48.5	48.0
Maize	17.5	19.0
Bananas	14.0	15.0
Yucca	6.8	7.0
Cacao	5.6	5.0
Coffee	5.1	3.6
Rice	2.4	2.2

SOURCE: Adapted from MAG-ORSTOM 1978:34.

lated that 80 percent of the population resided on isolated farms;
there were only four agglomerated settlements with populations
between 1,000 and 5,000 inhabitants. The only two urban centers
of any importance were Lago Agrio and Coca, which together contained a population of about 5,000 inhabitants (MAG-ORSTOM 1978).

In 1982, the areas of spontaneous settlement revealed a clear
tendency toward concentration and the forming of towns. Many
farmers have acquired urban properties or rent dwellings in Lago
Agrio and Coca while maintaining farms at the same time. Research by the author in Lago Agrio reveals that the major reason
for this tendency is education of children. While Lago Agrio and
Coca have several schools, they are rare in rural areas and are run
by a single teacher. Consequently the populated centers of Amazonia are increasing in size as the combined effect of natural
growth and migration from surrounding rural areas. It has been estimated that in 1981 the populations of Lago Agrio and Coca to-
taled around 8,000 and 4,000, respectively. Other centers of rapid
increase in the petroleum zone are Joya de los Sachas and Shushufindi Central, each with over 1,000 inhabitants.

Conclusions

The colonization experience in Amazonia demonstrates that the
incentive of obtaining relatively extensive areas of land, on which
first the forest resources are exploited and finally selected crops
and pasture are planted, is sufficient to attract migrants from more
densely populated regions. Of course, population displacement is

greatest when there are access roads and opportunities for employment in nonagricultural activities. Such is the case in the petroleum zone of the Nor-Oriente, where relatively fertile lands have
been occupied. As the result of exploration for and exploitation of
hydrocarbons, an extensive network of roads has been established,
and a moderate quantity of local labor is employed.

Migrants or colonists generally seek state support, yet they do
not willingly accept state control over their activities or limitations on their individualistic ambitions. The pioneers' strong at-
tachment to private property in land and to the realization of
many activities within a context of independence has made spontaneous settlements more successful than the various schemes of
directed colonization.

From the point of view of national security and development—
translated as the occupation of lands in the Amazon by human
groups from other regions of the country and the expansion of the
agricultural frontier—the policies of colonization in Ecuador have
been successful. This is demonstrated by the rapid growth of spontaneous settlements, especially in the petroleum zone of the Nor-
Oriente. There remain other aspects of policy that must be considered in an analysis of the occupation process, including the impact
of colonization on native groups and the ecosystem and the consequences that present events may have for the long-range development of the region.

From the time of the Spanish rule until 1970, colonization
was concentrated in the high forest or sub-Andean region. At
times the colonists in this zone coexisted with indigenous groups
and frequently pushed them to the low forest zones of apparently
limited space. With the advent of petroleum exploration and exploitation, colonization took on massive proportions especially in
the Nor-Oriente, with grave consequences for the survival of ethnic groups—especially those of lesser numbers, which were therefore more easily injured.

Apparently a few benefits result from the presence of the state
and population groups from other regions. Among these are limited access to certain services such as education, health, and transportation, and contact with the outside world, which for many natives is a positive condition. Still, the disadvantages are more
numerous and sometimes have unpredictable consequences. In
many cases colonization has displaced indigenous peoples from
their traditional areas of settlement, has reduced the size of their

hunting and fishing areas, and has converted many persons into second-class citizens, who are frequently exploited. In summary, the avalanche of immigrants and enterprises of all kinds has directly threatened the capacity of indigenous peoples to develop their cultures normally. Furthermore, the effects of intense contact with "civilization" and national culture will have repercussions not easily anticipated but clearly negative.

Small native ethnic groups of the Nor-Oriente such as the Cofán, Siona-Secoya, and Huaorani are suffering substantial transformations. Although the majority have been granted communal territories (except the Huaorani) these are not considered sufficient to guarantee their survival as distinct cultures. It is, in the meantime, imperative that adequate extensions of land be adjudicated for their normal development, both physical and cultural. Fortunately, in the past few years the Ecuadoran state has taken significant steps in this direction and an important project for the delimitation of indigenous land is now underway (see Uquillas 1982).

Transformations of the environment occasioned by colonization are equally numerous and profound. It has been many years since the onset of deforestation in the mountain slopes and valleys of the sub-Andean region—the wildlife has fled and the landscape changed. Today the occupation of large areas of the Nor-Oriente is accompanied by destructive practices and by the mismanagement of natural resources. The creation of countless spontaneous settlements has led to massive deforestation in occupied areas due to the great demand for lumber in the country, to the misguided action of clearing land to make it appear "worked," to the inadequately managed and excessive cattle ranching activity, and to cropping practices based on the clearing of the land, which results in soil fertility decline. If to all this we add the almost total absence of compensatory actions such as reforestation and soil treatment, an Amazon characterized by eroded and lateritic soils may become a reality.

On the other hand, there are a few positive signs for the future. Until now most colonists have occupied areas of relatively fertile soils in exceptional areas such as the intermontane valleys and Shushufindi, which means a greater resistance capacity of the soils and more time to take corrective measures. Likewise, there is reason for hope that through hard and frequent failures colonists are learning techniques for maintaining soil fertility and sustained yields. Among these practices, which are becoming more wide-spread, are forest maintenance, crop rotation, preferential use of native vegetable species, and the application of a forest-pasture-cropping system.

Finally we should take into account the implications for long-term socioeconomic development. Setting aside from the present analysis the hydrocarbon resources, whose importance lies more at the national than the local level, and which will last only an estimated twenty years, it seems clear that if the poor utilization of resources in Amazonia continues, the possibility for sustained development will be eliminated. If reforestation is not practiced, timber, the principal income source for the colonists, will disappear. If adequate soil management is not practiced, production will continue to decline and the returns will no longer compensate for the efforts expended in agricultural labor. In 1982, the population of the Ecuadoran Amazon was incapable of supplying itself with sufficient agricultural products; it is doubtful that it will be able to do so in the future, especially if the population increases rapidly.

Another serious problem, and a difficult one to resolve, is the disadvantage that Amazonian products confront in commercial-ization at the national and international level. Production and transport costs, for example, are higher than in the Costa region, and agricultural surpluses therefore have a higher cost. The human potential in Amazonia is significant; the region has attracted many young and motivated people, free from oppressive social structures and with an open mentality amenable to change. Never-theless, the possibilities for future development in large part depend upon the reorientation of present tendencies. The region may achieve effective long-range development if resources are wisely used, especially if colonization is limited to areas suitable for agri-cultural activity and ample zones of forest are left as ecological re-serves of various types. These reserves could be used for tourism, and it might be possible to exploit certain resources selectively, taking the necessary precautions for their conservation.

References Cited

Gonzáles Suárez, Federico
    1970   *Historia General de la República del Ecuador.* Quito: Casa de la Cultura Ecuatoriana.

Harner, Michael J.
1973   *The Jívaro: People of the Sacred Waterfalls.* Garden City, N.Y.:
        Doubleday Anchor.
Instituto Ecuatoriano de Antropología y Geografía (IEAG)
1976   *Área del Río Bobonaza: Estudio Socio-Económico.* Quito: Uni-
        versidad Central.
Instituto Ecuatoriano de Reforma Agraria y Colonización (IERAC)
1980   Colonización. Quito.
n.d.   Cuadros Estadísticos. Quito.
Instituto Nacional de Colonización de la Región Amazónica Ecuatoriana
(INCRAE)
1979a   *La Problemática Socio-Cultural de la Amazonía Ecuatoriana.*
        Jorge Uquillas, ed. Quito.
1979b   *Seminario de Seguridad.* Victor Aulestia, ed. Quito.
1981   *Seminario Sobre la Problemática de Producción Agrope-
        cuaria.* Sixto Cadena, ed. Quito.
Junta Nacional de Planificación y Coordinación Económica (JNP)
1976   *Evaluación de la Colonización en la Provincia de Morona San-
        tiago.* Quito.
Ministerio de Agricultura y Ganadería (MAG)
1977   *La Colonización de la Región Amazónica Ecuatoriana: Obra
        Nacional.* Quito.
Ministerio de Agricultura y Ganadería—Instituto Nacional de Investiga-
ciones Agropecuarias (MAG-INIAP)
1977   *Breve Diagnóstico Agro-Socio-Económico de la Región Orien-
        tal para la Ubicación de un Centro Experimental Agrope-
        cuario.* Quito.
Ministerio de Agricultura y Ganadería–Office de la Recherche Scienti-
fique et Technique Outre Mer (France) (MAG-ORSTOM)
1978   *Informe sobre la Colonización en la Provincia del Napo y las
        Transformaciones en las Sociedades Indígenas.* Quito.
Munzel, Mark and Axel Kroeger
1981   *El Pueblo Shuar: de la Leyenda al Drama.* Quito: Mundo
        Shuar.
Naranjo, Marcelo F.
1977   Zonas de Refugio y Adaptación Étnica en el Oriente: Siglos
        XVI–XVII–XVIII. In *Temas sobre la Continuidad y Adaptación
        Cultural Ecuatoriana.* Marcelo F. Naranjo, José Pereira, and
        Norman Whitten, Jr., eds. Quito: Universidad Católica.
Registro Oficial
1978   Ley de Colonización de la Región Amazónica Ecuatoriana. No.
        504, January 12.
Uquillas, Jorge E., ed.
1982   *Informe para la Delimitación de Territorios Nativos Siona-
        Secoya, Cofán, y Huaorani.* Quito: INCRAE.

Vreugdenhil, Daniel
  1976 Inventario de las Áreas Silvestres Sobresalientes de la Cuenca Amazónica Ecuatoriana. Documento de Trabajo No. 29. Quito: UNDP/FAO/ECU /71/527.
Whitten, Norman E. Jr.
  1977 Etnocidio Ecuatoriano y Etnogénesis Indígena: Resurgencia Amazónica entre la Colonización Andina. In *Temas sobre la Continuidad y Adaptación Cultural Ecuatoriana.* Marcelo F. Naranjo, José Pereira, and Norman Whitten Jr. eds. Quito: Universidad Católica.
Whitten, Norman E., Jr., Dorothea Whitten, William Belzner, Ernesto Salazer, Anne Christine Taylor, Philippe Descola, and Theodore Macdonald, Jr.
  1981 *Amazonía Ecuatoriana: La Otra Cara del Progreso.* Quito: Mundo Shuar.
Wright, Charles S.
  1977 El Manejo de Suelos y Sus Problemas en Zonas de la Región Oriente del Ecuador en Vías de Colonización. [Report of the ad hoc group composed of FAO and various Ecuadoran public institutions.]

Colonization in the Transamazon and Rondônia

Emilio F. Moran

THE DECADE of the 1970s witnessed the large-scale intervention of the Brazilian government in the planning and implementation of Amazonian frontier colonization. In this paper my aim is to synthesize what we have learned from the process of colonization along the Transamazon Highway with a view to its possible relevance to the current colonization process in Rondônia, Brazil. When the 1970s began, interest in colonization as a research topic had been heavily focused on the Andean countries, where colonization had begun as early as the 1930s due to the penetration roads built to explore for oil east of the Andes in Ecuador and Peru (Moran 1982). On the Brazilian side, colonization had followed the major rivers, moving up their tributaries only to the obstacle posed by the rapids (Rocha Penteado 1978).

This pattern of colonization began to change in 1970 with the announcement by then President Médici that roads of national integration would be built across the Amazon basin and that land along these roads would be claimed by the state as a national security measure and redistributed to small farmers. The Médici administration reallocated funds from the Northeast Development Agency (SUDENE) and budgeted large sums for these new projects (Mahar 1979). When announced, the Program of National Integration and, in particular, the Transamazon Colonization project appeared to have all the makings of success (Moran 1975, Smith 1976, Fearnside 1978). Colonists were offered hundred-hectare plots on soils hailed as *terra roxa* "as good as those of Paraná." Recently arrived colonists received six months' minimum salary; credit at a 7 percent annual rate of interest for planting basic staple cereals; access to other inputs such as seeds, fertilizers, and pesticides; a ready-built house, either along the highway or in nucleated planned communities (*agrovilas*); roads linking farms to markets; schools and medical services; and a guarantee that the government would buy production (Kleinpenning 1975). As many as fifty-one government agencies were mobilized to serve the incoming population (Moran 1975).

The offices of the Colonization Agency (INCRA) were overrun with applicants during the first year, as the program became known through a national media blitz. The Transamazon was hailed as an effort equivalent to putting a man on the moon, given the little knowledge of the region at the outset and the scope of planning and investment that might be required. To many persons the project recalled the construction of Brasília, which required vast sums of money to accomplish the task within a short three- to five-year period. At the outset, some of the colonists were even flown by jumbo jet to the region, and young college students throughout the country proudly wore T-shirts with logos such as "Transamazonica: It Is Giant Brazil" and "Transamazonica: Integrate so as not to give it up." The mood was euphoric, and the willingness to accomplish the task was clearly there.

The social and demographic motives for colonization were given the most attention during 1971–72. The highway and its attendant colonization were hailed as solutions to underemployment and drought in Northeast Brazil and to inequities in access to land throughout Brazil. In short, the program was seen as a solution to the overpopulation of the Northeast and the underpopulation of Amazonia (Kleinpenning 1975, Ministério da Agricultura 1972).

Scholars meeting at a conference on the Amazon held at the University of Florida in 1973 pointed out that there seemed to be other motives present in this effort to integrate the Amazon by means of highways and colonization. Geopolitical motives noted by Tambs (1974) were confirmed by the trends in de facto occupation characterizing Brazilian westward expansion and in military writings by the intelligentsia of the War College (Couto e Silva 1957, Katzman 1977). Other scholars noted the hopes pinned on the discovery of natural resources that could help solve the severe negative balance of payments and foreign indebtedness of Brazil (Panagides and Magalhães 1974, Wagley 1974). Still others hoped that the Amazon might in due time become an important producer of livestock, forest products, and export staples (Condurú 1974).

Scholars at this conference were very concerned with potential problems, such as the impact of new highways on native peoples (Cardoso de Oliveira 1974, Meggers 1974, Wagley 1974), and the presence of numerous and possibly conflicting goals in this thrust to develop the Amazon. Still, there was considerable optimism that the recurrence of problems that acted as constraints to the development of small farmers in the Andean countries were being addressed in the Brazilian effort because of the systematic nature of project execution and the commitment of the state to it.

The Transamazon project

The Altamira Integrated Colonization Project (PIC Altamira) was selected early as the showcase for the execution of Transamazon highway colonization. There were several reasons for this. One was the apparent prevalence of terra roxa soils (i.e., alfisols in the U.S. 7th Classification) of medium to high fertility (IPEAN 1967, Falesi 1972). The area had been the site of some county-level colonization in the 1950s. Health conditions appeared to be better than in the area near Marabá, selected as another center for colonization (see Figure 1).

Despite the presence of a host of government bureaucracies geared at managing the colonization process in all of its aspects, by 1972 the colonization agency was already having trouble keeping up with the number of farmers being flown, trucked, or brought by river to Altamira (Moran, field notes 1972). As in many past colonization projects, the absence of feasibility studies preceding the decision to begin the road and colonization projects began to be felt by managers attempting to implement plans that lacked accurate details of what might be found on the ground. For example, the Bolivian Alto Beni and Yapacaní projects were undertaken without the benefit of such studies—only to discover that 60 percent of the areas occupied were unsuitable for settlement due to periodic flooding (Nelson 1973). INCRA managers showed some sensitivity to the heterogeneity that was noted in the soils of Altamira as farmers began to be settled. Some even contacted Amazonian caboclos (Moran 1974) and sought their advice on areas to

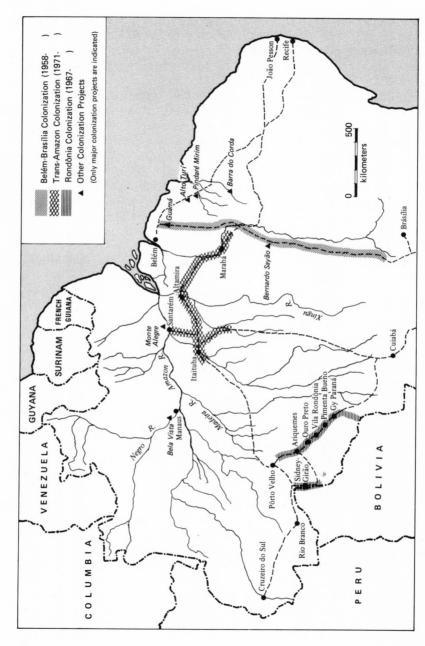

Fig. 1. Roads and colonization in the Brazilian Amazon.

avoid due to soil infertility (Moran 1975). However, the pressure to settle farmers arriving daily at the INCRA offices led to abandonment of local counsel and local criteria of soil quality. Instead, the farmers were permitted to choose any unoccupied plot. I have discussed elsewhere the inadequacy of the ethnoagronomic criteria for soil selection applied by many newcomers unfamiliar with the region but confident of their capacity to select soils (Moran 1981, 1977, 1976, 1975).

Contrary to indications by the media, which planners themselves had come to believe, the soils of Altamira were not homogeneously *terra roxa estruturada eutrófica* (Falesi 1972). They proved to be composed of a varied array of soils ranging from infertile podzolic sands through the common oxisols or latisols, with patches of terra roxa (Smith 1981, 1982). Farmers who chose the infertile areas found that the labor and capital inputs invested in food production gave scant results—and they grew increasingly indebted to the Bank of Brazil, which served as the lender to the farmers (Moran 1976, 1981).

Given that the project proceeded without the benefit of baseline studies at a scale appropriate for farm management, it was particularly important that colonists arriving have prior experience in commodity production. At first sight, it seemed that Transamazon colonization had addressed this traditional constraint to tropical land development (Nelson 1973). On closer examination, however, it became clear that farmers were not being selected for their proven performance as commodity producers but, rather, on the basis of gross indicators such as size of household and number of years working in agriculture (Kleinpenning 1975, Moran 1975). In fact, the government made it clear that they would give preference to Northeasterners, noting that they would make up 75 percent of the immigrant population. This strategy was appropriate for the social goal of giving land to the landless masses of Northeasterners. But, as Wagley (1974) noted, even if the goal of moving 100,000 families to the Transamazon were achieved, this relocation would not begin to make a dent in the demographic problems of the Northeast. Thus, the Transamazon suffered from the recurrence of the same problem as past colonization projects: giving preference to geographical areas and income groups rather than to proven commodity producers, but holding the immigrants to a standard of performance appropriate only to more experienced farm managers.

I have explored in other publications the inappropriateness of the criteria applied in colonist selection in the Transamazon (Moran 1975, 1979, 1981). Size of family and years of experience in agriculture were poor predictors of success. More accurate indicators proved to be previous ownership of land and stability of previous residence, together with liquid assets (or initial capital) and previous credit experience with banking institutions. The accuracy of these predictors was confirmed by Fearnside (1980) in another colonization area of Altamira, even though he used only two of the four criteria in selecting his sample.

Farmers associated with these backgrounds obtained impressive results by any standard: soils with a pH in excess of 6.0; twice the yield per hectare compared with farmers with characteristics selected for by INCRA; diversified cropping practices that brought a steady cash flow and high annual income; greater use of family labor in farm production processes; greater use of available technology; lower expenditures on consumption; and less dependence on wages to meet food needs, to name only the most marked differences (Moran 1979).

Scholars have long pointed out the constraint posed by the lack of all-weather roads on the development of the rural sector. Lack of good feeder roads leads to isolation, loss of production due to field molding, decreased health status, and reduced access to credit and other input facilities (Crist and Nissly 1973, Nelson 1973, Lewis 1954). Transamazon highway construction unfortunately fell prey to the same age-old constraint. Costs of highway construction proved to be three times the amount originally projected and budgeted for. As an economic measure, the decision was made to proceed with construction of the main trunk, while reducing the kilometers of feeder roads built. This decision virtually guaranteed that the small-farm sector would not develop and achieve the production goals that had been set for it. As much as 50 percent of farm output rotted in the fields, since farmers could not get the products to market and had no access to storage facilities. What production could be saved was mostly due to maverick entrepreneurs who braved the *piques* (hand-hewn forest openings) to buy sacks of rice and beans directly from the farmer.

Most studies view security of title as a relevant variable in farmer satisfaction and in choices of production strategies (Tavares et al. 1972, Wood and Schmink 1979, Tcheyan 1980, Moran 1981, Wesche 1982). For the Amazon, the problems faced by farmers in obtaining secure title seem particularly severe. There is a long-standing absence of cadastral surveys, personnel in cadastral offices are notoriously poorly paid and easily bribed, and laws that protect squatters' rights encourage land invasion and virtually assure access to land for those with the capacity to hire gunmen (Schmink 1982). Transamazon colonization appeared to be organized to avoid the recurrence of this crucial problem, but once again the lack of adequate management led to its reassertion. Most colonists on arrival were issued an "authorization of occupation," which gave them access only to short-term loans and prevented many from improving their farms to the degree they desired. The inefficient issuing of titles to land, even in a national security area wherein many past claims have been voided, suggests that there is both a structural and a behavioral resistance by state-level institutions to responding to the needs of agricultural development in the small-farm sector.

The Altamira Project had been hailed by Nelson (1973) as the acid test of the potential of tropical lands for settlement. Unfortunately, it demonstrated a serious and recurrent problem in the linkage between functional performance and the structural organization of development institutions. Planning, allegedly a rational process, proceeded in the absence of baseline data that would have allowed plans to be implemented with any degree of predictability. Colonist selection followed social goals, but the productivity of those selected was measured by strictly economic criteria based upon fairly high standards and expectations. Political goals received priority over agricultural development goals in the decision to complete the Transamazon highway but to reduce the completion rate of feeder roads. Farmers throughout the Altamira region were left saddled with heavy bank debts and no opportunity to sell much of their produce. Inefficient issuing of land titles reduced the effectiveness of credit arrangements and farm operations. In short, plans were overspecific despite the lack of data on which to base the projections, and managers at the level of implementation were unable to make adjustments to the differences between the plans and the empirical realities they faced.

The end result was that by 1974, incoming President Geisel announced that the development of the Amazon by means of small farmers had failed (cf. Brasil 1974). Seven thousand, rather than a hundred thousand, families had migrated in the first three years. Cereal production had been considerably below projections (Smith

1978). Soils between Itaituba and Rio Branco were extremely poor and inappropriate to commodity production (IPEAN 1974). It has been accurately pointed out that the reasons for the shift away from small-farmer colonization likely reflected political and economic pressure from interested parties wishing to receive priority in the flow of government subsidies for development (Wood and Schmink 1979, Schmink 1982, Pompermayer 1979, Foweraker 1981). In 1975 the Polamazônia Program was announced in which large-scale development was given regional priority.

The Transamazon colonization did not end in 1975. Many of the small farmers are still on their plots. While as many as 30 percent may have left, this is still a rather low rate of *desistentes* when compared with other projects such as the Bolivian Alto Beni (wherein as many as 95 percent left in the first two years). There has been considerable land consolidation, an unsurprising fact when one considers that farming operations cannot be programmed to a hundred-hectare grid, regardless of the choices made in farm operations, and of the variation in topography and soil quality from farm to farm. In fact, farm yields since 1975 have been steadily improving and have even surpassed the original projections of the planning documents. A restudy of the area researched a decade ago is currently underway to assess the social, cultural, and economic changes that have taken place among Altamira farmers (Santos n.d.)

Rondônia colonization: have we learned?

It would be naïve to suggest that Brazilian institutions have not learned a great deal about colonization management from the Transamazon experience. It is quite clear that the data base for Rondônia colonization is better today than was that for Altamira in 1971. Responsible agencies recognize the importance of all-weather roads, as witnessed by their request for World Bank funds to pave BR-364 between Cuiabá and Porto Velho (IBRD 1981). The wisdom of allowing colonists to self-select has been incorporated into the current emphasis on semidirected colonization (Valverde et al. 1979, IBRD 1981).

The Rondônia colonization areas are at a very different stage of development from the early colonization period discussed for the Transamazon highway. In fact, Rondônia has areas that have been colonized now for nearly a decade, while others are at the earliest stages of pioneering (see Nelson 1973, for terminological dis-

cussion of stages in settlement). My remarks will therefore focus
upon the older colonization areas on which there exist some data
that can be used to gauge the degree to which Rondônia may have
avoided the problems that plagued Altamira colonization, as they
had so many colonization areas before it.

Before 1970, Rondônia was sparsely settled because much of
the territory was inaccessible by river transportation. The BR-364
highway opened up the southern portion of Rondônia to settlement in the early 1970s, initiating a flow of population at a scale
unprecedented in the Amazon. During the 1970s the population of
Rondônia increased threefold. The first government-directed colonization project was modeled after the then ongoing Transamazon
Integrated Colonization Projects (PICS) and was located at Ouro
Preto (Muller 1980). The second project failed to attract and keep
colonists, since it was established at Sidney Girão on a relatively
isolated area away from the BR-364 and located on relatively poor
soils. After this failure, colonization policy shifted in 1974 in both
the Transamazon and Rondônia toward semidirected settlement.

The earliest semidirected projects were those of Gy-Paraná,
Padre Adolpho Rohl, and Paulo de Assis Ribeiro. INCRA's role centered on trying to regularize land occupation and to issue land
titles. By focusing on this central problem, authorities hoped to
avoid problems over land rights. This proved not to be the case. By
the end of 1976, around 80 percent of families in Rondônia were
awaiting clear titles within the projects and were, in the meantime, squatting on public or private lands (Muller 1980:149). In the
absence of clear land demarcations and given slow titling procedures, land conflicts between immigrants were common (Gall
1978).

INCRA shifted in 1977 to selling public lands in large tracts,
allegedly to ease the administrative burden by shifting responsibility to individual buyers or to private colonization firms. Some observers have noted that this shift was due to pressure from the private sector (Bourne 1978, Pompermayer 1979). As of 1977, only
35.2 percent of families in Rondônia colonization projects had
titles to the land they occupied.

Let us now proceed to examine if any of the other recurrent
constraints to small-farmer colonization have been effectively addressed in Rondônia. There seems to be little doubt that Rondônia
is gifted with many patches of fertile soils (Furley 1980). It would
be incorrect, however, to conclude that the existence of terra roxa

implies a high statistical frequency of such soil in Rondônia colonization areas. This was a mistake made in planning PIC Altamira settlement, and the current optimism about the extent of terra roxa in Rondônia is grounds for concern. Terra roxa is estimated to account for 10 percent of Rondônia's area as compared to 8 percent for Altamira. Although Rondônia is clearly larger than Altamira, and thus will have greater total acreage of terra roxa, from the farmer's point of view the question is whether he will be located on that 10 percent that occurs in patches rather than in vast homogeneous areas (Furley 1980). Patches of terra roxa often stand right next to oxisols and podzols (Moran 1981). Soil surveys remain considerably behind the rapid inflow of immigrants, and settler location is not determined by proven soil surveys at a scale of 1:10,000 but is left to the selection criteria of immigrants unfamiliar with the plant-soil associations of Rondônia.

Colonist selection as a government responsibility has been replaced by colonist self-selection. Government and international lending agencies alike hope that the immigrants to Rondônia have greater entrepreneurial capacity than did the immigrants to the Transamazon. The evidence for this difference is largely inferential. It is based on the historical experience that shows that spontaneous settlers tend to have better education and greater success within their lifetime than do those who stay behind or those who migrate through government subsidy. Also cited as relevant to the greater expectations of migrants to Rondônia is the fact that they come mostly from Paraná and the Minas Gerais–Mato Grosso area. I find both of these pieces of evidence an inadequate basis for realistic expectations. Peoples from southern and central Brazil do not have life histories consistently different from those of the Northeast. In fact, most people migrating from the south into the Central Plateau or the Amazon are themselves Northeasterners. In my study of PIC Altamira, region of origin failed to predict for effective farm management results (Moran 1979, 1981). Given that immigrants to Rondônia appear to have had an average of three previous migratory moves, I would predict that those immigrants with very high rates of previous residential mobility will have relatively low farm yields, lower incomes, and higher rates of *desistência* in Rondônia, than those with stable past residence (reflecting farm management capacity and land ownership). In short, management performance for Rondônia farmers should follow the same time-scale as that of the Transamazon, given the similarity

in farmer work experience before arrival. It takes more than three
to four years before any population knows how to effectively allo-
cate its labor and capital and to manage the new land resources.
Muller (1980:151) noted that the newly arrived colonists in Rondônia are already characterized in government reports as having
poor performance. This appears to be a recurrent problem and
shows a lack of understanding of the process of adaptation to new
environments and of the time required to bring about change in
farm management and behavior.

The recurrent constraints of poor feeder roads, poor marketing and credit facilities, and the lack of a site-specific agrarian
technology seem to plague Rondônia colonization as they did the
Transamazon (Muller 1980:151). Up to 1980 the feeder roads continued to be impassable for as much as six months in the year.
Wesche (1982) noted that poor roads were the most severe barrier
to farming success for the colonists in PIC Paulo de Assis Ribeiro.

The inefficiency of issuing land titles has restricted access to
bank credit to only that 35 percent of the colonist population fortunate enough to get permanent land titles. Muller (1980:151) also
noted that colonists to Rondônia work the land on the basis of
their past experience in other parts of Brazil—rather than according to appropriate land management systems for the humid tropics. The greater role being given to tree crops and perennials in the
development of Rondônia gives some ground for optimism (Furley
1980, Muller 1980, IBRD 1981). However, it is questionable whether
this agronomic practice, by itself, can overcome the recurrence of
so many other constraints. It is necessary that careful study be
made of the social consequences of the policy to promote tree
crops among small farmers. The small farmer throughout the
world is primarily a staple commodity producer, and his strategy
of farm management is most effective for crops in which intensification of labor makes a significant difference and in which the
quality of the product makes a major difference in price per unit.
The advantage of the small-farm sector over the larger operator
is in the former's ability to grow fresh produce and other high-
quality items for relatively accessible markets. In addition, proximity to urban areas provides an opportunity for the small farmer
to supplement his income by employing his surplus labor seasonally and during off times.

The paving of the BR-364 in the near future will enhance the
access of farmers to urban areas for employment, marketing, and

credit. However, I am not sure that the priority given to rubber, coffee, and cacao in Rondônia agricultural development provides the most competitive use of the small-farm sector in an otherwise large-scale oriented agriculture. I would predict that the small-farm sector in Rondônia will evolve toward medium and large operations because of the distance of colonization areas from markets and the fluctuations in the world price of export commodities—fluctuations that most small producers cannot bear with their limited savings.

Designing a viable small-farm sector

There is nothing in the design of Rondônia colonization that would suggest that the fundamental constraints to the success of small-farmer colonization have been addressed. The Transamazon Altamira PIC demonstrated the inability of institutions to correct the traditional constraints to colonization: lack of an adequate data base for planning; inadequate knowledge of soil quality at a scale appropriate for farm management decision making; colonist selection based on inappropriate criteria; seasonally impassable roads; insecurity of land title; lack of access to credit; and incorrect knowledge of soil-plant association characteristics. These problems remain in the current execution of Rondônia colonization in the areas studied.

Resource maps at a scale of 1:10,000 are not available for making specific cropping decisions, and farmers are relying on practices from regions of origin, areas characterized by very different environmental conditions. The population, although composed of spontaneous migrants, has a high rate of previous migration and comparably low rates of past bank credit experience and previous land ownership. Roads from farm to main trunk remain impassable during critical times of the year. Land titling has been improved, but it remains a constraint for significant portions of the population. Cropping practices remain based on aggregate priorities of the state rather than on comparative advantages offered by specific sites or by the structure of small-farm household labor. Priority is not being given to the fundamental needs of the small farmer: health, security of tenure, good roads, and education. These four areas continue to be neglected in service delivery systems. The concerns of policy still focus on aggregate yields and on institutional processes relevant at later stages in the development of colonization: provision of credit, export crop production, quality of administration, and maximum output from the sector.

There is very little in the development of Rondônia that would suggest an answer to the questions of the potential of the humid tropics for intensive agriculture or of the role of colonization in resolving the agrarian crisis in Latin America. Latin American institutions continue to treat the Amazonian frontier in ways that fail to respond to the special characteristics and goals of the small farm. Rarely do they recognize that the experimental nature of all present Amazonian agricultural activity requires caution and flexibility in development and colonization planning.

Given the experimental nature of the Amazonian adventure in development, I would propose a flexible and incremental approach that emphasizes the fundamental elements first, adding inputs over time as conditions and results justify. As in any attempt to specify what is a dynamic process, the model presented in Figure 2 should not be construed as a fixed design, but rather as the broad brushstrokes of a plan to improve the design of a viable small-farmer colonization sector in Brazil. The proposed timetable makes some allowances for the difficulty most governments face in carrying out preplanning feasibility studies of colonization areas. It also considers that capital resources are limited and that the best use of limited funds is to target them for what is most critical at various stages of the process. For heterogeneous areas like Rondônia, the timetable applies to specific sites and not to PICS or to regions. Each site has its own evolution, in which the exact length of any given stage will depend on the influence of neighboring colonization zones and the flow of ideas between them.

We have seen throughout this paper that all-weather roads, location near markets, secure title, and opportunity to experiment in the new area are fundamentals. Although health did not prove to be a major problem in Altamira, farmers consider this the most fundamental constraint to their ability to produce. Health services should be provided at the outset from mobile units rather than by construction of buildings. It is never clear what the best locations are for serving a population until a settlement has moved into a consolidation stage. After the first five years, for example, one can expect a portion of farmers to have abandoned any project. Clearer agronomic choices can then be made, and farmers' needs may be

FIGURE 2. Colonization: an incremental approach

Colonization plan requirements	Initial five years' priorities	Consolidation stage 5–10 years	Stabilization stage 10+ years
Locate near markets	1. All-weather trunk and feeder roads	1. Storage systems	1. Paving roads
	2. Mobile health services	2. Hospital services	2. Private sector
Allow local decision-making	3. Locate agronomic experiments on farmers' fields	3. Extension and experimental stations	3. Land capability maps, 1:10,000
Build road in stages	4. Secure title	4. Credit system	4. Cottage industries and processing
	5. Primary education	5. Secondary and technical education	5. Technical information on agricultural markets, etc.

more realistically known. Hospitals and banking facilities can be built in locations accessible to users without impeding their farm work. Educational services need to evolve gradually so that school location is optimized and the area can be made sufficiently attractive to prevent the loss of teachers due to inadequate living conditions—a phenomenon observed in Altamira and noted in other colonization areas.

By the end of the first decade it may be possible to aspire to land capability maps at a scale of 1:10,000; paved roads; secondary and technical schools; and sophisticated storage systems and co-operative marketing of produce. In most regions it takes at least that long to work out appropriate systems of farming in a given site, and the most appropriate forms to link institutions to the population. Forcing this process simply runs into constraints, and serves to drain limited resources from those for whom they are intended.

In short, the central problem of Amazonian development through colonization appears to be the same as that faced by development planning in general: a tendency to try to solve all problems at once rather than in a gradual and sequential manner that allows for adjustments and learning. In policy terms, this means that highways should be built in smaller stretches, making sure that adequate all-weather feeder roads are in place. This also serves to restrict access to areas whose agricultural potential is still unknown. Services should recognize what is most fundamental to the producer at each stage in the process. Colonization, like human adaptation to the habitat, is a timed process characterized first by the imposition of past routines, followed by experimentation (and both success and failure), and eventually by the emergence of an appropriate process of resource utilization (given economic and other external incentives). To force evaluation of a population before it has reached that final stage overlooks the nature of human adjustment and seriously misallocates national resources.

References Cited

Bourne, Richard
    1978   *Assault on the Amazon.* London: Gollancz.
Brasil, República Federativa do
    1974   *II Plano Nacional de Desenvolvimento (1975–79).* Brasília: Presidência da República.
Cardoso, Roberto de Oliveira
    1974   Indigenous Peoples and Sociocultural Change in the Amazon. In *Man in the Amazon,* C. Wagley, ed. Pp. 111–35. Gainesville: University of Florida Press.

Condurú, J.M.P.
  1974   Agriculture in the Brazilian Amazon. In *Man in the Amazon*. C. Wagley, ed. Pp. 230–42. Gainesville: University of Florida Press.
Couto e Silva, Golbery do
  1957   *Aspectos Geopolíticos do Brasil*. Rio de Janeiro: Biblioteca do Exército.
Crist, R. and C. Nissly
  1973   *East from the Andes*. Gainesville: University of Florida Press.
Falesi, Ítalo Cláudio
  1972   *Sólos da Rodovia Transamazônica*. Belém: IPEAN.
Fearnside, Philip
  1978   Estimation of Carrying Capacity for Human Populations in a Part of the Transamazon Highway Colonization Area of Brazil. Ph.D. dissertation. Department of Biological Sciences, University of Michigan.
  1980   Land Use Allocation of the Transamazonian Highway Colonists of Brazil and Its Relation to Human Carrying Capacity. In *Land, People, and Planning in Contemporary Amazonia*. F. Barbira-Scazzocchio, ed. Pp.114–38. Cambridge: University of Cambridge, Centre of Latin American Studies.
Foweraker, Joe
  1981   *The Struggle for Land: A Political Economy of the Pioneer Frontier in Brazil, 1930 to the Present*. London: Cambridge University Press.
Furley, Peter
  1980   Development Planning in Rondônia Based on Naturally Renewable Resource Surveys. In *Land, People and Planning in Contemporary Amazonia*. F. Barbira-Scazzocchio, ed. pp. 37–45. Cambridge: University of Cambridge, Centre of Latin American Studies.
Gall, Norman
  1978   *Letter from Rondônia*. American Universities Field Staff Reports No. 9–13: South America.
International Bank for Reconstruction and Development (IBRD)
  1981   *Brazil: Integrated Development of the Northwest Frontier*. Washington, D.C.: IBRD.
Instituto de Pesquisa Agropecuária do Norte (IPEAN)
  1967   Contribuição ao Estudo dos Solos de Altamira. Belém: IPEAN. Circular No. 10.
  1974   *Solos da Rodovia Transamazônica: Trecho Itaituba–Rio Branco*. Belém: IPEAN.
Katzman, M.
  1977   *Cities and Frontiers in Brazil*. Cambridge, Mass.: Harvard University Press.

Kleinpenning, J.M.G.
1975   *The Integration and Colonization of the Brazilian Portion of the Amazon Basin.* Nijmegen, Holland: Institute of Geography Planning.
Lewis, W. Arthur
1954   Thoughts on Land Settlement. *Journal of Agricultural Economics* 11(1):3–11.
Mahar, Dennis
1979   *Frontier Development Policy in Brazil: A Study of Amazonia.* New York: Praeger.
Meggers, Betty
1974   Environment and Culture in Amazonia. In *Man in the Amazon.* C. Wagley, ed. Pp. 91–110. Gainesville: University of Florida Press.
Ministério da Agricultura
1972   *Altamira 1.* Brasília: INCRA/MA.
Moran, Emilio F.
1974   The Adaptive System of the Amazonian Caboclo. In *Man in the Amazon.* C. Wagley, ed. Pp. 136–59. Gainesville: University of Florida Press.
1975   Pioneer Farmers of the Transamazon Highway. Ph.D. dissertation. Department of Anthropology, University of Florida.
1976   *Agricultural Development in the Transamazon Highway.* Bloomington: Indiana University, Latin American Studies Program, Working Papers Series.
1977   Estratégias de Sobrevivência: O Uso de Recursos ao Longo da Rodovia Transamazônica. *Acta Amazônica* 7(3):363–79.
1979   Criteria for Choosing Homesteaders in Brazil. *Research in Economic Anthropology* 2:339–59.
1981   *Developing the Amazon.* Bloomington: Indiana University Press.
Moran, Emilio F., ed.
1982   *The Dilemma of Amazonian Development.* Boulder: Westview Press.
Muller, Charles
1980   Frontier-based Agricultural Expansion: The Case of Rondônia. In *Land, People, and Planning in Contemporary Amazônia.* F. Barbira-Scazzocchio, ed. Pp. 141–53. Cambridge: University of Cambridge, Centre of Latin American Studies.
Nelson, M.
1973   *The Development of Tropical Lands.* Baltimore: Johns Hopkins University Press.
Panagides, Stahis and V.L. Magalhães
1974   Amazon Economic Policy and Prospects. In *Man in the Ama-*

zon. C. Wagley, ed. Pp. 243–61. Gainesville: University of Florida Press.

Pompermayer, Malori José
  1979   The State and the Frontier in Brazil: A Case Study of the Amazon. Ph.D. dissertation. Stanford University.

Rocha Penteado, Antônio
  1978   Condições Geo-ecológicas da Amazônia Brasileira. *Revista do Museu Paulista* 21:1–17.

Santos, Barbara
  n.d.   Cultural Ecological Change Along the Transamazon Highway. MS in preparation. Department of Anthropology, Indiana University.

Schmink, Marianne
  1982   Land Conflicts in Amazonia. *American Ethnologist* 9:341–57.

Smith, Nigel
  1976   Transamazon Highway: A Cultural Ecological Analysis of Settlement in the Lowland Tropics. Ph.D. dissertation. Department of Geography, University of California at Berkeley.
  1978   Agricultural Productivity along Brazil's Transamazon Highway. *Agro-ecosystems* 4:415-32.
  1981   Colonization Lessons from a Tropical Forest. *Science* 214: 755–61.
  1982   *Rainforest Corridors: The Transamazon Colonization Scheme.* Berkeley: University of California Press.

Tambs, Lewis
  1974   Geopolitics of the Amazon. In *Man in the Amazon.* C. Wagley, ed. Pp. 45–87. Gainesville: University of Florida Press.

Tavares, V.P., Claudio M. Considera and Maria Theresa L.L. de Castro e Silva
  1972   *Colonização Dirigida no Brasil.* Rio de Janeiro: IPEA No. 8.
  1980   *A Comparative Study of the Administration of Two Amazon Colonization Projects: Alto Turi and Ouro Preto.* Washington, D.C.: Center of Brazilian Studies, Johns Hopkins University School for Advanced International Studies. Occasional Paper Series, No. 10.

Valverde, Orlando et al.
  1979   *A Organização do Espaço na Faixa da Transamazônica.* Vol. 1: *Rondônia.* Rio de Janeiro: IBGE.

Wagley, Charles, ed.
  1974   Introduction. In *Man in the Amazon.* C. Wagley, ed. Pp. 3–20. Gainesville: University of Florida Press.

Wesche, Rolfe
  1982   Transportation, Spatial Organization, and Colonization Success in the Brazilian Amazon. Paper presented at the Conference on

Frontier Expansion in Amazonia, February 3–8, 1982. Center for Latin American Studies, University of Florida.
Wood, Charles H. and Marianne Schmink
1979   Blaming the Victim: Small Farmer Production in an Amazonian Colonization Project. *Studies in Third World Societies* 7:77–93.

Ecology and Development Potential

PART 3

FLYING OVER AMAZONIA at jet plane cruising altitude or traveling along one of the many rivers that form the region's complex fluvial network, one easily concludes that the terrain is monotonously flat. In the literature on the Amazon, as Nigel Smith (1982:31) notes, the region is often referred to as a plain. Consistent with this assumption is the commonly held notion that the climate and soils are homogeneous. Apart from recognizing the major ecological zones of forest, savanna, and river, one comes away only with the impression of a vast territory with indistinguishable seasons, whose rich vegetation springs from undifferentiated soils.

Following the rapid expansion of the agricultural frontier into Amazonia, scientific research coming out of the region provides a very different view. The presumption of environmental uniformity has been replaced by a growing awareness of many distinguishing localized and specific environmental characteristics. The heterogeneity of the region has sometimes been learned the hard way as development schemes have foundered on unexpected environmental variations. The colonization projects in Brazil are an example. Whereas relatively flat plateaus and terraces are occasionally encountered along the Transamazon, much of the land along the highway is a sequence of hills. In some areas the extremes of elevation within half a kilometer attain 40 meters from trough to crest (Smith 1982:31). Fine-scale variation in soil quality has also been found. Research findings by Moran (1981), Fearnside (1978), and Smith (1976) depict the colonization sites as a patchwork of soil types, with radical differences occurring within relatively short distances. The insensitivity of centralized planning bureaucracies to this microenvironmental diversity has been cited as one reason for the poor performance of the colonization projects in Brazil (see Moran in this volume).

The rational use of Amazonian resources will depend in part on a more thorough understanding of the region's environmental heterogeneity. William Denevan, drawing on his experience in the western Amazon region of Peru, focuses on the floodplain habitat.

The concept of ecological zonation, which traditionally refers to altitudinal changes in the topography, is applied horizontally to describe the zonation of biotopes where there is little or no change in elevation. As his study of the Shipibo Indian village demonstrates, the considerable ecological diversity along the floodplain provides ample opportunity for varied forms of agricultural production, conceivably including large-scale commercial ventures. These findings are significant given the productive potential of the underutilized alluvial soils, which total more than 30 million hectares in Brazil alone, and in light of the relatively little systematic research that has been devoted to the study of floodplain agriculture. His study is an important illustration of the valuable lessons to be learned from indigenous systems of management of diverse ecosystems.

Humid tropical environments represent an underexploited resource base that is sure to be increasingly tapped in the years to come. Because of population pressure and the sociopolitical factors that make the occupation of frontier areas attractive to national governments (see part II of this volume), the conversion of these ecosystems to new uses will intensify during the remainder of this century. Shifting cultivation, where soil remains fallow for a longer period of time than when it is cropped, a method traditionally used by small farmers, under certain conditions is well-adapted to the region. On the contemporary frontier, however, this shifting cultivation poses new difficulties. The opening of new roads, coupled with increases in population pressure, has led to the shortening of the forest fallow period and consequently of the soil fertility regeneration process. This implies, in effect, the conversion of an ecologically sound cropping system into one that is unstable, unproductive, and, in the long term, ecologically destructive. These trends have often led planners to conclude that small-farmer agriculture should be discouraged in the region. Yet as the foregoing papers in part II demonstrate, migration to the region continues.

If there is to be any chance for small farmers to achieve stability of production and at the same time preserve the ecological integrity of the Amazon forest, new systems of land use must be devised. Few such models have been systematically explored from a long-term perspective. The results of more than a decade of research in Yurimaguas, Peru, described by Nicholaides et al., are therefore particularly important. The project has tested a scale-neutral technology developed to permit continuous cropping on the basin's acid, generally infertile soils, which are most often subjected to shifting cultivation. Improved agronomic practices, including moderate applications of fertilizers, provide small farmers with an alternate cropping system thought to be both ecologically attractive and economically feasible. The test of the viability of these and other promising models of small-farmer agriculture awaits a more widespread application to the diverse social, technical, and ecological conditions in the region.

A realistic approach to Amazonia's agricultural potential requires analyses of the productive use of lowland floodplains and the development of appropriate technology to allow shifting cultivation to be converted to systems of continuous cropping. Also of concern are the ecological implications of the transformation of vast areas from forest to pasture, generally by large business enterprises. As Susanna Hecht notes, most of the deforestation that has recently occurred in Colombia and Brazil is directly attributable to the expansion of livestock production, a process whose long-term environmental consequences are hotly debated. In her analysis of selected regions of the Brazilian Amazon, Hecht concludes that soil changes after conversion to pasture are neither as catastrophic nor as beneficial as the divergent literature in the field suggests. Declines in productivity, although related to soil fertility, are also due to rapid weed invasion and to rising maintenance costs.

Despite these problems, cattle ranching continues to eclipse other forms of agriculture, both in land area and in capital investment. This is explained in part by the political and institutional structure of development policy in Amazonia. Pompermayer's study, presented in the final section of this volume, provides a detailed analysis of the way private interest groups in Brazil influenced the formulation of public policy so as to favor livestock production. Attractive credit lines, low capital gains taxes, and the growing importance of land in corporate portfolios combined to stimulate a land rush of unprecedented magnitude. As Hecht notes, the enormous speculative gains irrespective of productivity provided little incentive for the development of careful management techniques and served only to exacerbate the instability of existing pastures. Although government policies in recent years have deemphasized cattle ranching in the Amazon basin, further expansion continues through private initiatives.

In an ideal world, the occupation of Amazonia would be preceded by careful research sufficient to provide a sound basis for the rational planning and control of land use in the region. The extreme heterogeneity and complexity of Amazon ecology and the rapidity with which the region is already being occupied preclude this possibility. Learning about appropriate land uses will have to come not only from continuing and expanded research endeavors but also from the assessment of the conditions of land-use patterns already in existence. Lessons from indigenous resource management, from small-farmer colonization, and from ranching and other activities carried out by large enterprises must be carefully evaluated from ecological, economic, and social points of view. The understanding that emerges from research and evaluation must, in turn, be channeled into the process of policymaking in the various Amazonian nations. As the papers in this volume demonstrate, environmental concerns, however valid on their own terms, must ultimately be considered in the context of the larger social, economic and political systems of which they are a part.

References Cited

Fearnside, Philip
   1978   Estimation of Carrying Capacity for Human Populations in a
          Part of the Transamazon Highway Colonization Area of Brazil.
          Ph.D. dissertation, University of Michigan.
Moran, Emilio
   1981   *Developing the Amazon.* Bloomington: Indiana University
          Press.
Smith, Nigel
   1976   Transamazon Highway: A Cultural Ecological Analysis of Set-
          tlement in the Lowland Tropics. Ph.D. dissertation, University
          of California, Berkeley.
   1982   *Rainforest Corridors: The Transamazon Colonization Scheme.*
          Berkeley: University of California Press.

Ecological Heterogeneity and Horizontal Zonation of Agriculture in the Amazon Floodplain

William M. Denevan

> One does not farm the Amazon Plain, but [rather] hundreds of thousands of particular tracts of ground, each endowed with . . . a specific local climate and many other equally localized and specific environmental components. (Sternberg 1964:323)

THE CONCEPT of ecological zonation as a guiding principle of traditional land-use management in Latin America has been primarily considered in terms of altitudinal variation, or verticality, in the Central Andes (Murra 1975, Brush 1977). Different altitudinal zones are utilized in order to spread risk, to diversify crops, to spread demands on labor, and to utilize land that is close at hand. A related concept, environmental gradient, refers to how close biotopes are to one another (Porter 1965). A biotope is a microenvironment with relatively uniform landform, climate, soil, and biota. It is with such units of nature that individual humans inter-

NOTE: I am grateful for ideas and information from Roland Bergman, who introduced me to the Shipibo of Panaillo, and from Judith Gunn, who in 1982–83 held a Fulbright Fellowship to study agricultural scheduling on the Ilha dos Purus in the Amazon above Manaus, for which she is collaborating with the INPA in Manaus.

act, not with a polymorphous "tropical forest." On a mountain slope, farmers have easy access to a variety of biotopes. We say that the environmental gradient of a mountain slope is steep because of its spatially rapid changes in temperature, associated moisture, vegetation, and soils.

The concept of zonation, however, with a steep environmental gradient and the exploitation of multiple biotopes, need not be limited to mountain slopes. Zonation may likewise occur in aquatic situations and elsewhere. A good example is provided by Nietschmann (1973:98) for the Miskito Indian habitat on the Caribbean coast of Nicaragua. A wide variety of biotopes exist along a sea-to-shore-to-inland transect and are recognized and utilized. Denevan and Schwerin (1978:14) combined a cross section of biotopes with types of agriculture in the llanos altos of Venezuela. It seems appropriate, then, to speak of horizontal zonation where there is a marked environmental gradient but little or no change in elevation except at a micro scale.

Whereas the Amazon Basin (Figure 1) in the past has been thought to be ecologically uniform, with recognition mainly of forest, savanna, and river, Amazonian scholars are increasingly aware of its considerable heterogeneity. Frequently, this heterogeneity exhibits regularity or zonation, which is perceived and utilized by local people in their gathering, hunting, fishing, and agricultural activities.

Six major subdivisions of the Amazonian biome can be identified: humid forest, seasonal forest, montane forest, dry savanna, wet savanna, and floodplain. Each consists of a number of distinct biotopes. To describe each, their spatial patterns, and their potential or actual utilization would be a major undertaking. The floodplain habitat, which probably has the greatest heterogeneity, is examined here, with emphasis on the zonation of biotopes and agriculture.

Floodplains occupy only a small portion of the Amazon Basin, about 2 percent of the total area,[1] but nevertheless total some 64,000 square kilometers along the main Amazon channel in Brazil (Camargo 1958:17)[2] and possibly 141,000 square kilometers in the entire basin.[3] It is in the floodplains, however, that most of the population, settlement and economic activity are located; it is here that underutilized alluvial soils offer the greatest opportunity for expanding intensive agriculture. This paper will briefly demon-

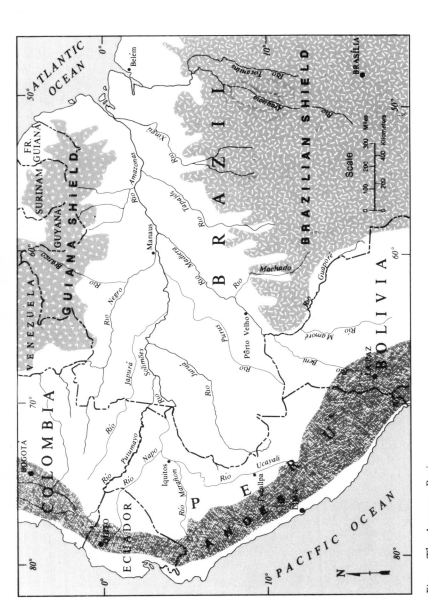

Fig. 1. The Amazon Basin

strate the zonation of biotopes and of agriculture in the Amazon floodplains.

At issue is the potential of the Amazon Basin for the production of food and other products on a sustained yield basis. For production to be effective, environmental heterogeneity must be recognized, utilized, and preserved. Resource surveys are essential to delimit environmental patterns. As for utilization of variable resources, much can be learned from traditional practices in specific habitats. I will draw on my own experience with Amazonian biogeography and native agriculture, which has involved the Mojo in the Bolivian savannas, the Campa in the Andean foothills of Peru, and briefly the Karinya in the Orinoco llanos and the Shipibo and Bora in the Peruvian Amazon.

Factors of floodplain variability

A transect across the floodplain of the Amazon River or one of its tributaries will intersect various biotopes in a regular and predictable sequence. Some portions of the sequence may be repeated several or even many times along the transect. By floodplain (*várzea* in the Brazilian Amazon)[4] we refer to the entire area between the rimming valley walls in which a river swings back and forth across recent alluvium. The width of the floodplain for the main Amazon is mostly between fifteen and fifty kilometers. The biotopes within the floodplain are created by or influenced by a number of micro and macro factors, which are summarized below.

Geomorphology.—The floodplain biotopes are best defined in terms of landforms that are constantly being created and destroyed by the annual floods and by the lateral movement of the river channel. The floodplain landscape features can be characterized as being erosional, drowned, or depositional (Sioli 1975a). The principal landforms include: (1) the river channel; (2) islands within the river channel, which may only be exposed during low water; (3) natural levees (*restingas*) of the river channel, and former levees or remnants of levees, which may be straight or curving; (4) side channels (*paranás*); (5) backswamps (*tehuampas*, or *igapós*), which may contain forest or grassland or lakes, either permanent or seasonal; (6) cut-off lakes, or oxbows, which are remnants of former meanders; (7) mouth bays, which are enormous floodplain lakes at the mouths of some rivers; (8) point bars, which are parallel ridges formed within the expanding loops of meanders; and (9)*playas* (*praias*), which are sand or mud beaches appearing at low water adjacent to levees, islands, point bars, or low terraces.

The features formed by the major channels are referred to as first-order topography; those formed by lesser channels and tributaries are referred to as second-order topography (Sternberg 1975:21). The result is a complex pattern of major and minor land and water features, often intergrading, whose dimensions are constantly changing as water levels rise and fall and channels shift. The origins and variations of these features have been well treated elsewhere (e.g., Sternberg 1956, 1957, 1960, 1975; Tricart 1977).

River morphology.—The presence and patterns of floodplain landforms vary with river morphology, of which there are three basic types (Goulding 1980:17–21). The main Amazon channel is braided, with minimal meandering, the river dividing and subdividing to create large lenticular islands (Sternberg 1975:20). The Río Ucayali, Río Purus, and many others, in contrast, are strongly meandering, with numerous cut-off lakes (Figure 2). The Madeira, Tocantins, Xingu, and Tapajós are all relatively channelized rivers, with reduced floodplains and comparatively straight courses (Goulding 1980:20). Landforms within floodplains are least stable where there is strong meandering.

Floodplain width.—The size, number, and variety of landforms present in a floodplain are affected by the width of the floodplain, which of course tends to become progressively larger moving downstream.

Hydrochemistry.—Amazon rivers can be further categorized by variations in water chemistry, which are largely determined by geology (Sioli 1968, 1975a, 1975b). The classical distinction is in terms of optical properties: white water, clear water, and black water (mapped in McIntyre 1972:460–61). These differences affect patterns of vegetation, fish and other aquatic life, insects, and soils. White-water rivers, such as the Amazon itself, carry large amounts of fine sediment from the Andes, have low transparencies, carry floating vegetation, have high phytoplankton production, and produce silty soil. Clear-water rivers (Tocantins, Xingu, Tapajós) arise in the Brazilian and Guiana highlands where there are resistant granitic and metamorphic rocks; they carry low amounts of fine sediment, have high transparencies and low nutrient levels, and produce sandy soils. The black-water rivers, such as the Negro, arise mainly in the Tertiary lowland *tierra* (*terra*)

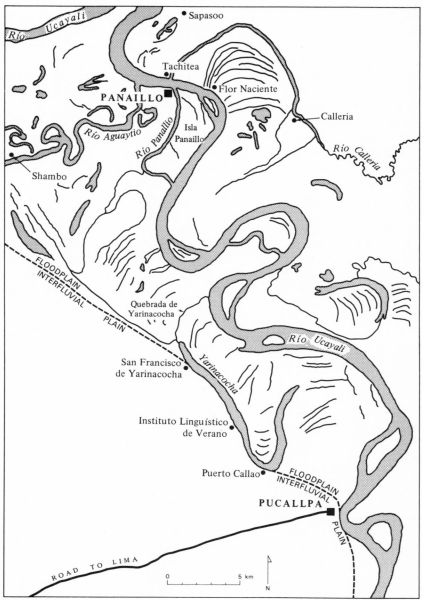

Fig. 2. The main Amazon channel.

firme, or interfluve surfaces; they are clear or black stained, contain dissolved and colloidal acid compounds (which may be toxic to many organisms), and form acidic, sandy podsols. Transitions exist between these categories, and mixing occurs where different types meet.

Geology.—Not only is water chemistry influenced by geology, but so are soils and structural characteristics such as channel location, size, and orientation. The basic geological formations are the Andean foothills, the Guiana highlands, the Brazilian highlands, and the Tertiary and Quaternary Amazon plain; these are shown for Brazil in Sioli (1975b:280).

Climate.—For Amazonia, the significant macroclimatic factors are total rainfall and length of the dry season. For the floodplains, however, both are secondary in importance to the rise and fall of rivers, which are controlled by climatic events external to the floodplains themselves. For a discussion of Amazonian climates, see Galvão (1959) and Ratisbona (1976). Annual rainfall is shown in Prance and Elias (1977:197).

Biogeography.—Patterns of flora and fauna within the Amazon floodplains vary with the above factors plus the rise and fall of water levels. Regional patterns of tropical forest phytogeography (Prance 1977:209) are reflected in variations in the floodplain forests, although probably to a lesser degree than in tierra firme forests.

Prance distinguishes seven types of Amazon forest subject to inundation:

(1) *seasonal várzea*—forest flooded by regular annual cycles of white-water rivers;

(2) *seasonal igapó*—forest flooded by regular annual cycles of black- and clear-water rivers;

(3) *mangrove*—forests flooded twice daily by salt-water tides;

(4) *tidal várzea*—forest flooded twice daily by fresh water backed up from tides;

(5) *floodplain forest*—on low-lying ground flooded by irregular rainfall, generally in upper reaches of rivers;

(6) *permanent white-water swamp forest;*

(7) *permanent igapó*—black-water forest (Prance 1979:26).

In addition, a variety of forests on the high ground of the natural levees are only occasionally and briefly inundated by high floods. Due to periodic destruction by floods, these forests generally are not as high, diverse, or old as the tierra firme or upland forests. Finally, some backswamps subject to seasonal flooding and dessication contain sections of grassland (*campos*), particularly along the Amazon below the Japura. The playas are barren of vegetation when first exposed, but may be rapidly invaded by wild canes and other herbaceous plants.

    Faunal patterns are also highly variable within the floodplains, varying both with type and size of landform or waterform and with the rise and fall of water levels. For recent studies of Amazonian fish and fishing, see Goulding (1980, 1981) and Smith (1981).

    Soils.—It must be emphasized that floodplain soils are not uniform. First of all, soils vary from floodplain to floodplain depending on the type and amount of sediment carried by a river, which are determined by source area and river dynamics. Second, larger rivers with greater internal velocities tend to carry coarser sediments than do smaller rivers. Third, when a river overflows its bank and water velocity is reduced significantly, the coarser sediments are dropped first and the finer sediments farther away. Thus, more sandy soils occur in levees and finer soils in the backswamps. Locations distant from a river may have heavy clay soils of relatively low fertility. Finally, there may be considerable microvariation in soil texture reflecting changes over time in water behavior or slight variations in water behavior across a landform. Higbee (1945:410), for example, diagrammed a playa near Iquitos, which was primarily sand, but with patches of clay loam and sandy clay loam. Farmers, very aware of these micro differences, planted rice on the clay loam and beans on the sandy clay loam, but they did not plant the less productive sand. For another description of microvariation in soils, see Momsen (1964). For a recent review of várzea soils in relation to agriculture, see Roosevelt (1980:112–19).

    Seasonality of river rise and fall.—"Each year there is a flood. All life has adjusted to accommodate it. It comes not as a disaster, but as a season. Day by day the river rises a few centimeters at a time, dropping a bit, then rising higher, not unlike the temperature changes of autumn that prepare the way for a northern winter" (Bergman 1974:73, 76).

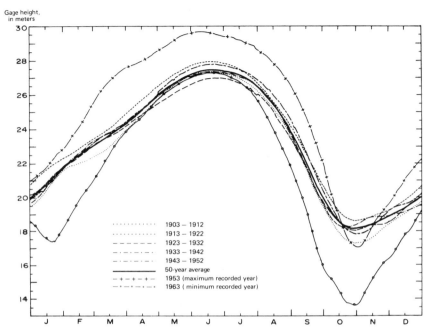

Fig. 3. River stages at Manaus, 1903–63. Source: Sternberg 1975:22.

At Manaus, the fifty-year average for high water is 27 meters above sea level and that for low water is 18 meters; the range between the maximum (30 meters) and the minimum (14 meters) is 16 meters (Figure 3). There is a fairly marked regularity in the annual fluctuation owing to the enormous size of the basin, the gentle gradient, and the great temporary storage capacity of the floodplain and estuaries, which combine to minimize the impact of short-term events from place to place in the basin. Upstream and in the tributaries, however, these influences are less and consequently there is less regularity in the seasonal rise and fall of waters and in their average and extreme ranges. The high-flow to low-flow ratio at Manaus is only about five to one, which is much less than that of most large rivers. Along the main river the water level changes progressively daily, with little variation in the cycle up or in the cycle down. On the tributaries, in contrast, a single big storm in the headwaters can cause a sudden rise in level followed by a sudden fall; playa agriculture, as a result, is more hazardous, even though at low water vast areas are exposed for long periods.

The annual range between high-water and low-water levels along the main channel of the Amazon varies considerably. At Porto Velho it averages 12.4 meters, at Iquitos 6–7 meters, at Manaus 9 meters, at Santarém 6–7 meters, at the mouth of the Xingu 4 meters, and at Belém only 0.5 meters (Goulding 1981:10, Gentry and López-Parodi 1980:1354, Parker 1981:69). Thus there is little variation in the estuarine area in contrast to extreme variation in the Middle and Upper Amazon.

At Manaus, highest water occurs in June and lowest water in October. The high-water (above 24 meters) period lasts six months, from mid February to late August. The lowest low-water period (below 20 meters) only lasts three months, from mid September to mid December, which may not be long enough to get a crop on the lowest ground. The duration of exposure of agricultural land at low water is of course relative to the relief of the land as well as to the rise and fall of the river. Of all the land exposed during lowest water, possibly as little as 10 percent will be exposed during highest water. For the amounts of land above water at different times of the year at specific locations along different rivers, almost no data are available.

Variations in water level have many ecological implications. Those for the dispersal and distribution of flora and fauna have been summarized by Sternberg (1975:23–24); also see Huber (1909) on the dispersal of várzea trees; Junk (1970) on floating meadows; and Goulding (1980) on fish. The variation of water level is of significance to people in almost all activities: transportation, location of settlement, harvesting of flora and fauna, utilization of labor, and agriculture. As water levels change, so too do these activities change in location and extent. Accurate prediction of water level changes is essential for success in economic endeavors, and while there is regularity in seasonal rise and fall of the water, adaptation is complicated by the instability of the land itself as the river swings back and forth across its floodplain, destroying land in one place, creating it in another (Sternberg 1975:17–18). A farm or village may disappear over night as banks cave in. A large playa fronting a village during low water one year may not reappear a year later. (The land ownership problems resulting merit study.)

For the farmer, annual flooding means the annual deposition of fertile sediment, which makes annual cropping possible. While floodplain soils are far superior to most tierra firme soils, considerable variation in soil texture and fertility create options for different crops, as previously mentioned. A second benefit of annual flooding, at least for the lowest land, is the destruction of pests and vegetation. Little or no land clearing is necessary, and crop losses to pests are minimal. The floods themselves are the main hazard. On the higher, forested ground of the levees the reverse is true, and short-fallow shifting cultivation is practiced, not so much because of deficient soil fertility as because of weed invasion and pest problems. There is little data on river levee cultivation cycles. On the Río Alto Pachitea of eastern Peru, Campa Indian swiddens average one to three years of fallow and three to four years of cropping for manioc and up to twenty years for bananas (Allen and Tizon 1973).

Agricultural patterns, including labor scheduling, amount of land cropped, and type of crop, are all linked to water level variation. Short growing season crops, such as maize, beans, peanuts, and rice, are grown on the lowest lying ground. The fine tuning of planting is best exemplified by rice, which is characteristically planted (or transplanted) in progressive steps as the river level drops. Manioc, bananas, and plantains dominate the levees. Permanent tree crops are located only on the highest ground where there is seldom or only brief flooding. Livestock is also raised in the floodplains, on backswamp grasslands and cleared swamp forest and by utilizing floating meadows for forage (Sternberg 1956).

Thus, there are numerous environmental variables creating ecological heterogeneity or biotope diversity in the Amazon floodplains. These combine to create both regional variations, including significant differences along the course of the same river, and local variations, which occur in regular patterns that generally are linear and parallel to the main channel. Associated with this regularity is a horizontal zonation of agriculture, which is a major concern here. The várzea could also be viewed as an archipelago, consisting of isolated units with different possibilities for aquatic and terrestrial wildlife and for human utilization. Another relevant spatial concept is that of "edges." Settlements tend to be located on the edges of certain types of biotopes adjacent to certain other types so that both can be readily exploited.

Cross-sectional models of the basic Amazon floodplain landforms or biotopes have been presented in several studies. One of the earliest is a simple diagram by Higbee (1945:408). More recent

322 Ecology and Development Potential

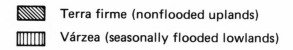

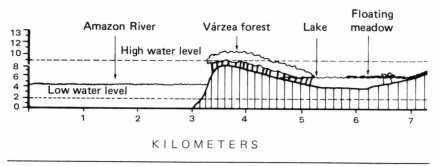

KILOMETERS

Fig. 4. Map of the floodplain at the Río Ucayali, eastern Peru, between Pucallpa

examples include Sioli (1975b:283), Smith (1981:6) (Figure 4), and
Baker (1978:226,227), but they are also oversimplified. Better
representation of existing diversity and complexity may require
maps or air photos (e.g., Sternberg 1975:20, 21; Bergman 1974:19;
1980:13).

Várzea sectors east-west along the main Amazon channel.—
It is incorrect to consider the Amazon várzea relatively homogeneous in fluvial dynamics from the western basin to the delta (Parker 1981:65–99). Rather than an undifferentiated várzea, there is
considerable variation and hence corresponding variation in agricultural possibilities.

Sombroek (1966:38) and Parker (1981:59–60) give the caboclo
classification as follows: *várzea do río,* along the river channel,
variations in water level due to differences in river discharge, good
soil, Middle Amazon; *várzea da chava,* away from the river channel, variations in water level due to differences in rainfall, poor
soil, eastern Marajó Island; *várzea do maré,* variation in water
level due to fresh-water tides, poor soils, delta area; *várzea do mar,*
variation in water level due to brackish-water tides, poor saline
soils, small fringe along the Atlantic Ocean.

Parker (1981:58–59, 65) differentiates three main sectors of

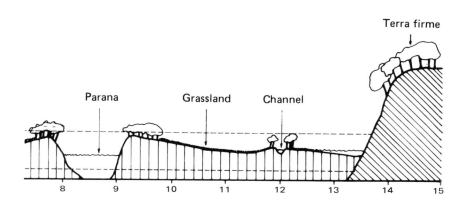

and Panaillo. Source: Bergman 1974:19.

várzea. The first, or upper, sector is located above the Japurá, extending into Peru. This is a very dynamic zone with extreme fluctuations of river level, considerable meandering, and constantly changing shores and channels due to alternating erosion and sedimentation. As a result, agriculture is considered difficult and risky. Also, forest extends to the river edge, and the large campos useful for livestock in the second sector are usually lacking.

The second, or middle, sector extends from the Japurá to the Xingu. Here there is much greater channel stability and flood regularity, with good alluvial soil. This várzea best conforms to the classic várzea image. Sombroek (1966:225) and Parker (1981:58), however, indicate that the classic várzea is best developed only between the Xingu and the Madeira (Parantins).

The third, or lower, sector is the estuarine várzea, located between the Xingu and the Atlantic Coast. Here there is almost no seasonal fluctuation in river level exposing large areas of playa for long periods. Instead there are twice daily tidal fluctuations, which alternately flood and expose the land. Higher, less flooded land only amounts to 12 percent or less of the várzea (Lima 1956:36). Furthermore, not much sediment reaches most of the flooded land. The soils are poor-humic gleys, poorly drained, heavy clay

textured, and very acid. Thus, because of the daily tidal floods and
poor soil, the agricultural possibilities are limited mainly to the
restricted high várzeas of the natural levees. However, reclamation
may be possible with the use of dikes and canals to control flooding and to manage irrigation, as attempted by Camargo (1958) and
by the wet rice project at Jari (Parker 1981:98–99).

Camargo (1958:17) estimates that 20,000 square kilometers, a
large portion of the Brazilian várzea, is estuarine (Lima 1956:39
gives 25,000 square kilometers). For the middle sector, extending
from the Xingu to the Jurua just above the Japurá, Camargo gives a
várzea area of 36,400 square kilometers, with another 8,000 square
kilometers in the upper sector from the Jurua to the Peruvian
border. This converts to about 31 percent estuarine, 57 percent
middle sector, and 12 percent upper sector.

Parker only considers the middle sector, particularly from the
Xingu to the Madeira (about 30 percent), as having significant possibilities for agricultural expansion. I would disagree. Despite the
greater river instability and hence greater risk in the upper sector
in western Brazil and eastern Peru, there was considerable pre-
Columbian aboriginal agricultural settlement (Denevan 1966);
there is considerable playa agriculture today; and there is considerable unused land that could be developed. Crops are lost from
floods and bank collapse, but there is sufficient stability and regularity to justify the taking of risk.[5] In any event, research is needed
on river dynamics in relation to agriculture in this sector. To date
there has been little in Peru, and in Brazil research on várzea agriculture seems to have been focused on the middle and lower
sectors.

Floodplain agricultural zonation

Considering the actual or potential importance of the nonestu-
arine Amazon floodplain for agriculture, it is remarkable that
there is little specific information published on traditional cultivation practices.[6] Sixteenth-century Indian populations within the
floodplain were relatively dense and were supported by floodplain
agriculture (Denevan 1976, Meggers 1971:121–49, Lathrap 1970,
Roosevelt 1980). Within two hundred years, however, the main
river tribes and their subsistence systems were destroyed. In the
Upper Amazon a few true floodplain tribes such as the Shipibo
still survive, and we have some information on their playa, levee,
and backswamp agriculture. Until very recently, várzea cultivation

was largely ignored by the Amazon caboclo peasantry, as was noted in 1953 by Charles Wagley (1976:72, 272). The reasons are not clear, but they probably involve an extractive economy orientation and a preference for manioc, which can only be grown on well-drained tierra firme and the higher levees (Ross 1978). In the process of his Amazon soils research during World War II, Edward Higbee (1945) wrote a general essay on playa cultivation, appropriately titled "The River Is the Plow," but it provides little detail and is long forgotten. There hasn't been much since on specific playa farming practices. Denevan and Schwerin (1978:19–23, 36–37) briefly describe playa cultivation along the Orinoco. Sternberg (1956) provides some information for the island of Careiro near Manaus, but his main focus is on cattle raising. Given this lack of attention, it is impossible to estimate even roughly how important playa agriculture is. Certainly one can motor along the Amazon for many hours, as I did in the summer of 1981 below Iquitos, and observe nearly continuous cultivation of rice and other crops during low water. Still, it is estimated that less than 1 percent of the full Amazon várzea is cultivated (Petrick 1978:33). Alvim (1977:350) estimates that one million hectares of várzea land in the Brazilian Amazon could be planted in rice, and that at 3,900 kilograms per hectare per year this would equal total current rice production in Brazil.

Not only is playa agriculture unstudied, but there is very little writing on levee cultivation. There seems to be an assumption that it is similar to tierra firme swidden practices, but it clearly is distinctive. Bergman (1974, 1980) gives some attention to playa and levee cultivation, but his best information is on backswamp farming. Thus, while there has been considerable research on traditional agriculture in Amazonia, most of it has been on tierra firme forest and savanna cultivation, with very little on the floodplains.

A Brazilian agronomist who has long and consistently argued for greater attention to the agricultural possibilities of the várzea is Felisberto Camargo (1950, 1958). He carried out experiments with simple water and soil management techniques, including siltation channels and drains. In his famous cross section of the Guama River, he showed different crops growing at different levels of the backswamp side of a natural levee (Camargo 1958:12). More recently, many ecologists and planners have called for greater attention to várzea agriculture (Barrow 1982, Cochrane and Sanchez 1982:149, Eden 1978:461, Goodland 1980:17–18, Katzman 1976:458, Meggers 1971:30, Schubert and Salati 1982:231, Smith 1982:184–85). However, Petrick (1978:43) believes that várzea cultivation in Brazil will remain secondary to terra firme agriculture.

As indicated above, ecological zonation within the várzea is clearly recognized in the literature. There is a general awareness of an associated agricultural zonation, as suggested by Camargo and by a map of Careiro Island by Sternberg (1975:25). However, a concept of land use zonation comparable to that of vertical zonation in the Andes has not been developed. The only clear diagrammatic attempt that I know of to correlate an ecological zonation with an agricultural zonation in the Amazon floodplain is that by Bergman (1980:60, 93) for the Shipibo of eastern Peru.[7]

A uniform pattern of crop zonation is difficult to define because of microvariation in soils and other factors. However, a typical sequence from river to levee to backswamp would be: rice and beans on the playas; maize, sugar cane, and jute on the foreslope of the levees; bananas, manioc, and orchard gardens on the tops of the levees; jute and sugarcane on the back slopes of the levees; and beans in the backswamps, along with pasture. Variation from region to region is considerable, but there tends to be local consistency in agricultural zonation. To illustrate this, the floodplain agriculture of Panaillo is examined.

The Shipibo village of Panaillo, Río Ucayali

Panaillo is a Shipibo Indian village of about a hundred people located at the juncture of the Río Panaillo and the Río Ucayali, one of the major tributaries of the western Amazon in Peru. The Shipibo here have regular contact with the river port city of Pucallpa, speak Spanish, and have a resident Peruvian school teacher. Their subsistence system remains largely traditional, being based on banana cultivation and fishing. The cultural ecology of the village was studied in 1971–72 by a research team led by Roland Bergman, and I spent a brief period with them in July 1971. The data here are mainly drawn from Bergman (1974, 1980).

The Panaillo resource area lies entirely within the floodplain of the Río Ucayali (Figure 4). Typical of Amazonian meander-type rivers, the Ucayali here forms a floodplain that is some thirty kilometers wide, an unstable network of natural levees, side channels, backswamps, sand bars and mud bars (barriales), islands, and lakes

(Lathrap 1968). During low water, extensive playas, which may be wider than the river itself, are exposed. Tributary streams, such as the Panaillo and the Aguaytia, add their own levees and backswamps to the complex floodplain landscape. The village of Panaillo is located along the top of the levee (*restinga*) of the Río Panaillo. Facing the river the levee breaks sharply down to the water. On the other side the levee grades down more gently into a large backswamp (*tehuampa*), which is bounded by a former levee of the Río Aguaytia, and behind that there is a permanent lake (*cocha*). Continuing westward, the area to the Aguaytia consists of lakes, backswamps, levee remnants, and playas. To the north lie the large playas and levees of the Ucayali.

The Shipibo farmer is thus faced with a varied environment, but with repetitive sequences of biotopes (zonation) and an annual sequence of rise and fall of water level (ten meter range in 1971). However, the size of individual biotopes and distances between biotopes vary considerably. Major advantages are diversity and good soil. The major disadvantages are early or unusually high floods. (The January 1971 high-water level overflowed the levee and destroyed a large portion of the banana trees.) Success in subsistence is dependent on knowledge of changing river levels and the related availability of biotopes for different lengths of time and hence for different specific crops. Bergman (1980:60, 90, 93) has mapped and diagrammed the land use of Panaillo, recording villages, individual fields, and crops and thus establishing the crops associated with the principal biotopes, as follows:

1. *Mud bar*—In the Río Panaillo; flooded annually, silt loam; short growing season crops, including maize, beans, rice, peanuts, sweet potato, watermelon; potentially farmed every year, but only small portions are above water long enough to be cropped.

2. *Levee foreslope*—Silt loam soil; sugar cane.

3. *Levee top, river side*—Sandy soil; orchard and garden crops, including star apple, guava, mango, cotton, lemon, shapaja palm, grapefruit, mammee, sugar cane, tangerine, soursop, and hog plum.

4. *Levee top, center*—Houses; dooryard plants, similar to biotope no. 3 but only a few scattered items.

5. *Levee top, backswamp side*—Dominated by permanent bananas; a few short-fallow swiddens with maize

and manioc; scattered guava, zapote, star apple, genipa, cacao, pejibaye, breadfruit, shapaja palm, tangerine; some commercial jute.

    6. *Levee backslope*—Silt loam; sugar cane.

    7. *Higher backswamp, lower levee*—Silt loam soils; swamp forest; maize, beans, watermelon, manioc, rice; potentially farmed every year.

    8. *Lower backswamp*—Swamp forest; no cropping.

    9. *Playas of the Río Ucayali*—Enormous sand and mud bars; exposed as long as six months; flooded annually; beans, maize, rice, and peanuts.

Thus, the Panaillo Shipibo make use of nine biotopes for several distinctive forms of agriculture—permanent, annual, and short fallow—each with different crops. If the village were located near the edge of the floodplain or on the adjacent bluff, as many Shipibo villages are (Lathrap 1968:74), the poor weathered oxisols of the tierra firme above the floodplain might also be used for long-fallow shifting cultivation emphasizing manioc.

Bananas (including plantains) are the principal crop, with manioc, maize, beans, and rice all secondary. These are supplemented by a variety of orchard and garden crops. Fish is the main source of protein except during the highest water (February–March), when fishing is poor. At that time, game, which tends to be trapped and concentrated on the levees, is important. In areas cultivated, there are 10.5 hectares of bananas, all on the levee. The low-water crops of maize (5.32 hectares), beans (1.13 hectares), and peanuts (0.11 hectares) total only 6.56 hectares, even though there is considerable unused backswamp land available. The low-water crops, however, cannot provide year-round food, as can levee crops— hence the traditional underutilization of the low-water biotopes despite their potential for high levels of annual production. The Panaillo Shipibo do not have much mud-bar land on the playas of the Río Panaillo that is exposed long enough to plant rice for commercial production. Most of the large nearby playas of the Ucayali, where there is good rice land, are controlled by mestizos.

There is also an ecological zonation of fish and game resources, based on types of water body, vegetation, and seasonality. The patterns of actual catches reflect the ecological zonation in combination with distance from the village. These patterns are mapped and described by Bergman (1980:135–66).

Biotope agricultural patterning at Panaillo is representative of the kind of zonation that occurs throughout the floodplains of the Amazon Basin. However, it is not necessarily typical, given the wide variation in the factors discussed earlier and in crop orientation, in accessibility to land or in land ownership, in population pressure, and in availability of commercial outlets.

Ecological zonation in other Amazon habitats

Ecological heterogeneity and agricultural zonation are most obvious in Amazonia in floodplains and hence have been emphasized here. Both, however, are also characteristic of other habitats to varying degrees. The humid and seasonal tierra firme forests of the interfluves grow not on level surfaces but rather on rolling terrain with relief of as much as ten meters or more. Accordingly, physical conditions vary in a fairly regular pattern from slope bottom to top, a sequence referred to in the soils literature as a catena. Topsoils are thicker and moisture greater at the bottom (often with swamp in the depressions) and are thinner and dryer at the top. Forest size and composition vary accordingly. While soils may be superior on lower slopes, insolation may be greater higher up. Also, rodents and other pests may be more of a problem on the lower slopes.

Montane subtropical forest occurs primarily on the eastern Andean slopes and extends from about 700 meters to 2,000 meters (ONERN 1976:95). Temperatures progressively decrease with elevation along with forest height and diversity of flora. Thus, vertical zonation is present, but there is also great horizontal zonation in rainfall, soil, and exposure.

Savannas can be divided into wet savannas, which are subject to seasonal inundation (Llanos de Mojos in Bolivia, the Pantanal of western Mato Grosso, the llanos bajos of Venezuela and Colombia), and dry, upland savannas, which do not normally flood and which have extremely impoverished soils (the *campo cerrado* of central Brazil, the llanos altos of Venezuela). The wet savannas are somewhat similar to floodplains in that vegetation and soils vary along gentle gradients, which are inundated for progressively different lengths of time. They are also interspersed with bodies of higher ground (levees, remnants of levees, dunes, and other features) having significantly different soils and vegetation (Sarmiento, Monastério, and Silva 1971). These grassy terrains can be and have been cultivated, as in the Bolivian and Venezuelan llanos

(Denevan 1966, Zucchi and Denevan 1979). The dry savannas, mostly on level plateau surfaces, exhibit less variation locally except where they are dissected by streams (Eiten 1972).

Thus, heterogeneity exists in all Amazon habitats, both on a local scale, as briefly described above, and on a regional scale as a result of macrovariations in climate, biogeography, geology, and geomorphology.

Conclusions

1. There is considerable ecological heterogeneity in the Amazon Basin, both local and regional.

2. Local heterogeneity often occurs in regular patterns, or as zonation, which can be anticipated when one has knowledge of local terrain conditions and seasonality.

3. Where the environmental gradient is steep (transitions from one biotope to another occurring within a short distance), opportunities for varied forms of agriculture are the greatest, thus minimizing subsistence risk by maximizing crop variability.

4. The greatest localized heterogeneity and best articulated zonation occur in the floodplains.

5. The floodplains offer the best opportunities in the Amazon Basin for annual cultivation. Despite the problems from flooding, which have led to negative perceptions regarding floodplain development (Falesi 1974:227), the floodplain is relatively densely settled and systematically farmed compared to the tierra firme. Much floodplain land isn't used now but could be cultivated given the careful attention to water level and microvariation in landscape and change that has long been characteristic of resident Indian and caboclo farmers.

6. It might be thought that large-scale commercial agriculture is not feasible on the várzea because of small, often ephemeral, fragmented units of farm land, problems of land ownership, and the difficulty of using machinery. This is not necessarily so. Some playas are very large, extending unbroken along the rivers. Machinery can be used under some conditions of accessibility, but may not be feasible for other reasons.

7. Floodplain agriculture, despite its importance and the recognition of this importance, has received very little descriptive or analytical study. Research opportunities for anthropologists, geographers, agronomists, and others therefore are nearly unlimited.

Notes

1. The usual proportion given is 2 percent. Sombroek (1966:18) and Sternberg (1975:17), however, give 1–2 percent.

2. For the area of várzea in the entire Brazilian Amazon, Pires (1974) gives a total of 70,000 square kilometers, including 55,000 in periodically flooded várzea and 15,000 in permanently flooded *igapó*.

3. This is based on the 2 percent figure and a total basin size of 7,050,000 square kilometers, which is the figure in the *Encyclopedia Britannica* (1974 1:653). Totals for the entire basin vary considerably, recent ones ranging from 5.9 million square kilometers (Sternberg 1975:15) to 7.8 million square kilometers (Goodland 1980:10). Goodland (1980:17) indicates the uncertainty as to the amount of várzea land by giving a range of from 50,000 to 300,000 square kilometers (5–30 million hectares) for all of Amazonia.

4. In common usage in Brazil, *várzea* refers to the entire floodplain, or to portions subject to annual flooding, with igapó used for portions permanently flooded. Prance (1979), however, uses várzea for white-water floodplains and igapó for black-water and clear-water floodplains. Brazilians also distinguish between high várzea (mainly natural levees) and low várzea subject to lengthy and deep flooding (Parker 1981:55,57).

5. In 1982 the flood level was the worst in many decades. In Peru this resulted in the loss of much of the rice crop and in the migration of many riverine families to Iquitos (Mário Hiroaka, pers. com.). Whether they will return is uncertain.

6. A dissertation has recently been completed on a Brazilian Amazon caboclo agricultural community by Parker (1981). For a discussion of and references to Brazilian government research on commercial várzea cultivation, see Barrow (1982) and Petrick (1978).

7. An excellent map of crop patterns for an Isconahua Indian village on the Río Callaria, a tributary of the Ucayali in Peru, is presented by Momsen (1964), but correlation with ecological variation is not clear.

References Cited

Allen, William L. and Judy H. de Tizon
    1973   Land Use Patterns Among the Campa of the Alto Pachitea, Peru. In *Variation in Anthropology*. D.L. Lathrap and J. Douglas, eds. Pp. 137–53. Urbana: Illinois Archaeological Survey.

Alvim, Paulo de T.
    1977   The Balance Between Conservation and Utilization in the

Humid Tropics with Special Reference to Amazonian Brazil. In *Extinction Is Forever*. Ghillean T. Prance and Thomas S. Elias, eds. Pp. 347–52. New York: New York Botanical Garden.

Baker, Victor R.
1978   Adjustment of Fluvial Systems to Climate and Source Terrain in Tropical and Subtropical Environments. In *Fluvial Sedimentology*. A.D. Miall, ed. Pp. 211–30. Calgary: Canadian Society of Petroleum Geologists, Memoirs No. 5.

Barrow, C.J.
1982   The Development of the Várzeas (Floodlands) of Brazilian Amazonia. Paper presented at the 44th International Congress of Americanists, Manchester, September, 1982.

Bergman, Roland W.
1974   Shipibo Subsistence in the Upper Amazon Rainforest. Ph.D. dissertation, University of Wisconsin, Madison.
1980   *Amazon Economics: The Simplicity of Shipibo Indian Wealth*. Dellplain Latin American Studies, No. 6. Ann Arbor: University Microfilms.

Brush, Stephen B.
1977   *Mountain, Field, and Family: The Economy and Human Ecology of an Andean Valley*. Philadelphia: University of Pennsylvania Press.

Camargo, Felisberto C.
1950   Reclamation of the Amazonia Flood-Lands Near Belém. In *Proceedings of the United Nations Scientific Conference on the Conservation and Utilization of Resources, 1949*. Pp. 598–602. New York: United Nations.
1958   Report on the Amazon Region. *Problems of Humid Tropical Regions*. Pp. 11–24. Paris: UNESCO.

Cochrane, Thomas T., and Pedro A. Sanchez
1982   Land Resources, Soils and Their Management in the Amazon Region: A State of Knowledge Report. In *Amazonia: Agriculture and Land Use Research*. Susanna B. Hecht, ed. Pp. 137–209. Cali, Colombia: Centro Internacional de Agricultura Tropical.

Denevan, William M.
1966   *The Aboriginal Cultural Geography of the Llanos de Mojos of Bolivia*. Berkeley: University of California Press, Ibero Americana, No. 48.
1971   Campa Subsistence in the Gran Pajonal, Eastern Peru. *Geographical Review* 61:496–518.
1976   The Aboriginal Population of Amazonia. In *The Native Population of the Americas in 1492*. W.M. Denevan, ed. Pp. 205–34. Madison: University of Wisconsin Press.

Denevan, William M. and Karl H. Schwerin
1978   Adaptive Strategies in Karinya Subsistence, Venezuelan Llanos. *Antropológica* 50:3–91.
Eden, Michael J.
1978   Ecology and Land Development: The Case of Amazonian Rainforests. *Transactions of the Institute of British Geographers.* New series 3(7):444–63.
Eiten, George
1972   The Cerrado Vegetation of Brazil. *Botanical Review* 38: 201–341.
Encyclopedia Britannica
1974   S.v. "Amazon." Chicago: Encyclopedia Britannica, Inc.
Falesi, Ítalo Cláudio
1974   Soils of the Brazilian Amazon. In *Man in the Amazon.* Charles Wagley, ed. Pp. 201–29. Gainesville: University Presses of Florida.
Galvão, Marillia Velloso
1959   Clima de Amazônia. In *Geografia do Brasil*, vol. 1, *Grande Região Norte.* Antonio Teixeira Guerra, ed. Pp. 61–111. Rio de Janeiro: IBGE.
Gentry, A.H. and J. López-Parodi
1980   Deforestation and Increased Flooding of the Upper Amazon. *Science* 210:1354–56.
Goodland, Robert J.A.
1980   Environmental Ranking of Amazonian Development Projects in Brazil. *Environmental Conservation* 7:9–26.
Goulding, Michael
1980   *The Fishes and the Forest: Explorations in Amazon Natural History.* Berkeley: University of California Press.
1981   *Man and Fisheries on an Amazon Frontier.* The Hague: Dr. W. Junk Publishers.
Higbee, E.C.
1945   The River Is the Plow. *Scientific Monthly* 60:405–16.
Huber, J.
1909   Mattas e Madeiras Amazônicas. *Bol. Mus. Para. E. Goeldi Hist. Nat. Ethnogr.* 6:91–225.
Junk, W.
1970   Investigations on the Ecology and Production Biology of the Floating Meadows (*Paspalo-Echinochloetum*) on the Middle Amazon. *Amazoniana* 2:449–95.
Katzman, Martin T.
1976   Paradoxes of Amazonian Development in a Resource-Starved World. *Journal of Developing Areas* 10:445–59.
Lathrap, Donald W.
1968   Aboriginal Occupation and Changes in River Channel on the

Central Ucayali, Peru. *American Antiquity* 33:62–79.
1970   *The Upper Amazon.* New York: Praeger.
Lima, R.R.
1956   A Agricultura nas Várzeas do Estuário do Amazonas. *Boletim Técnico do Instituto Agronómico do Norte* (Belém) 33: 1–164.
McIntyre, Loren
1972   The Amazon. *National Geographic* 142:445–95.
Meggers, Betty
1971   *Amazonia: Man and Culture in a Counterfeit Paradise.* Chicago: Aldine.
Momsen, Richard P., Jr.
1964   The Isconahua Indians: A Study of Change and Diversity in the Peruvian Amazon. *Revista Geográfica* 60:59–82.
Murra, John V.
1975   El Control Vertical de un Máximo de Pisos Ecológicos en la Economía de las Sociedades Andinas. In *Formaciones Económicas y Políticas del Mundo Andino.* John V. Murra, ed. Pp. 59–115. Lima: Instituto de Estudios Peruanos.
Nietschmann, Bernard
1973   *Between Land and Water: The Subsistence Ecology of the Miskito Indians, Eastern Nicaragua.* New York: Seminar Press.
Oficina Nacional de Evaluación de Recursos Naturales (ONERN)
1976   Mapa Ecológico del Perú: Guia Explicativa. Lima.
Parker, Eugene P.
1981   Cultural Ecology and Change: A Caboclo Várzea Community in the Brazilian Amazon. Ph.D. dissertation, University of Colorado, Boulder.
Petrick, Carsten
1978   The Complementary Function of Floodlands for Agricultural Utilization: The Várzea of the Brazilian Amazon Region. *Applied Sciences and Development* 12:24–46.
Pires, João M.
1974   Tipos de Vegetação da Amazônia. *Brasil Florestal* 5(17): 48–58.
Porter, Philip W.
1965   Environmental Potentials and Economic Opportunities: A Background for Cultural Adaptation. *American Anthropologist* 67:409–420.
Prance, Ghillian T.
1977   The Phytogeographic Subdivisions of Amazonia and Their Influence on the Selection of Biological Reserves. In *Extinction is Forever.* G. T. Prance and T. S. Elias, eds. Pp. 195–213. Bronx, New York: New York Botanical Garden.
1979   Notes on the Vegetation of Amazonia III: The Terminology of

Amazonian Forest Types Subject to Inundation. *Brittonia* 31:26–38.

Prance, Ghillian T. and Thomas S. Elias, eds.
  1977   *Extinction Is Forever.* New York: New York Botanical Garden.

Ratisbona, L.R.
  1976   The Climate of Brazil. In *Climates of Central and South America.* Vol. 12, Werner Schwerdtferger, ed. Pp. 219–93. New York: Elsevier.

Roosevelt, Anna C.
  1980   *Parmana: Prehistoric Maize and Manioc Subsistence along the Amazon and Orinoco.* New York: Academic Press.

Ross, Eric B.
  1978   The Evolution of the Amazon Peasantry. *Journal of Latin American Studies* 10:193–218.

Sarmiento, Guillermo, Maximina Monasterio, and Juan Silva
  1971   Reconocimiento Ecológico de los Llanos Occidentales. *Acta Científica Venezolana* 22:52–71, 153–69.

Schubert, Herbert O.R. and Eneas Salati
  1982   Natural Resources for Land Use in the Amazon Region: The Natural Systems. In *Amazonia: Agriculture and Land Use Research.* Susanna B. Hecht. ed. Pp. 211–39. Cali, Colombia: Centro Internacional de Agricultura Tropical.

Sioli, Harold
  1968   Principal Biotopes of Primary Production in the Waters of Amazonia. In *Proceedings of the Symposium on Recent Advances in Tropical Ecology,* Vol. 2. A. Misra and B. Gopal, eds. Pp. 591–600.
  1975a Amazon Tributaries and Drainage Basins. In *Coupling of Land and Water Systems.* Arthur D. Hasler, ed. Pp. 199–213. New York: Springer-Verlag.
  1975b Tropical Rivers as Expressions of Their Terrestrial Environments. In *Tropical Ecological Systems: Trends in Terrestrial and Aquatic Research.* Frank B. Golley and Ernesto Medina, eds. Pp. 275–88. New York: Springer-Verlag.

Smith, Nigel J. H.
  1981   *Man, Fishes, and the Amazon.* New York: Columbia University Press.
  1982   *Rainforest Corridors: The Transamazon Colonization Scheme.* Berkeley: University of California Press.

Sombroek, W.G.
  1966   *Amazon Soils.* Wageningen: Centre for Agricultural Publications and Documentation.

Sternberg, Hilgard O.
  1956   *A Água e o Homem na Várzea do Careiro.* Rio de Janeiro.
  1957   A Proposito de Meandros. *Revista Brasileira de Geografia*

19:477—99.

1964 Land and Man in the Tropics. In *Proceedings of the Academy of Political Science*, 27:319—29.

1960 Radiocarbon Dating as Applied to a Problem of Amazon Morphology. In *Comptes Rendus du XVIII Congres International de Geographie*, Vol. 2. Pp. 399—424. Rio de Janeiro: International Geographical Union.

1975 The Amazon River of Brasil. *Geographische Zeitschrift* 40 (Weisbaden).

Tricart, Jean L.F.

1977 Tipos de Planícies Aluviais e de Leitos Fluviais na Amazônia Brasileira. *Revista Brasileira de Geografia* 39:3—39.

Wagley, Charles

1976 *Amazon Town: A Study of Man in the Tropics.* New York: Oxford University Press.

Zucchi, Alberta and William M. Denevan

1979 *Campos Elevados e Historia Cultural Prehispánica en los Llanos Occidentales de Venezuela.* Caracas: Universidad Católica Andres Bello. (Also, Montalban, 9:565—736, Caracas).

Continuous Cropping Potential in the Upper Amazon Basin

J. J. Nicholaides, III, D. E. Bandy,
P. A. Sanchez, J. H. Villachica, A. J. Coutu,
and C. S. Valverde

TECHNOLOGY for continuous production of annual crops has been developed for some of the Amazon Basin's acid, infertile soils, which are normally subjected to shifting cultivation. Use of this scale-neutral technology could lead to increased food production and perhaps a consequent reduction in deforestation in the Amazon Basin.

The Amazon Basin contains approximately one-third of the world's 1,489 million hectares of humid tropics ecosystems. As in other areas of the humid tropics, its agricultural potential is made paradoxical by the possible ecological consequences of its deforestation. The U.S. National Research Council (1982) concluded in a recent study that "humid tropical ecosystems, especially lowland forests, . . . represent a very important underexploited resource for tropical countries" and that, as population pressures increase in these countries, "rapid and extensive development will and must take place if even the currently inadequate standard of living in most countries is to be maintained."

NOTE: This work was supported in part by Contract ta/C-1236 of the United States Agency for International Development.

337

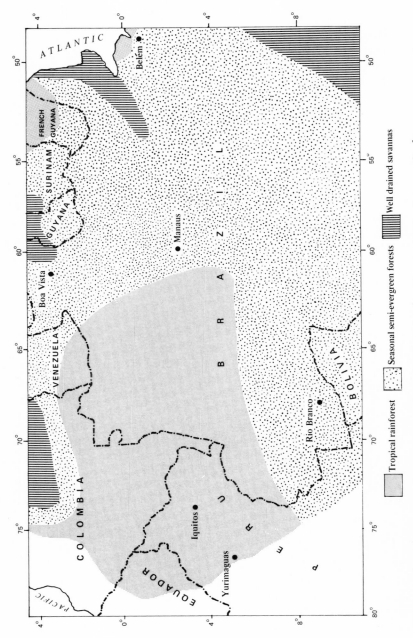

Fig. 1. The three major climatic-vegetative subregions in the Amazon Basin. Source: Cochrane and Sanchez 1982.

Shifting cultivators are responsible for much of the clearing of the tropical rain forests of the western or upper portion of the Amazon Basin (Figure 1); attempts to develop pastures are the primary goals for clearing of the seasonal semievergreen forests in most of the Brazilian portions (Myers 1980; Hecht and Fearnside, personal communication, 1982). What is needed, therefore, in the areas of the basin subjected to shifting cultivation, is the establishment and development of continuous cropping systems that provide "permanent field cultivation without first going through a sequence of increasingly shorter fallowing and associated environmental deterioration" (Denevan 1977).

Since 1971, the Tropical Soils Research Program of North Carolina State University (NCSU), under U.S. Agency for International Development (USAID) funding and in collaboration with the Peruvian Ministry of Agriculture's National Agricultural Research and Promotion Institute (INIPA), has been developing at Yurimaguas, Peru, continuous cropping systems for the acid, infertile soils of the Amazon Basin and other similar agroecological areas. The results of these research efforts offer attractive alternatives for the Amazon Basin's shifting cultivators.

Environment

A detailed description of climatic conditions and soil resources of the Amazon Basin is found in other publications (Cochrane and Sanchez 1982, Nicholaides et al. 1982). Pertinent to the present discussion is the fact that nearly 75 percent of the Amazon Basin is occupied by acid, infertile soils classed as oxisols and ultisols (Table 1). These soils are deep, usually well-drained, of red or yellow color, with generally favorable physical properties, but very acid and deficient in most nutrients. Recent soil mapping expeditions and the soil management research presented herein have substantiated Marbut and Manifold's (1926) observations that the soils of the Amazon Basin are strikingly similar to the main soils of the southeastern United States.

The major soil constraints to crop production in the Amazon Basin are chemical (Table 2). The seriousness of these chemical deficiencies depends on the crops grown. For instance, legumes need no nitrogen amendments if the correct *Rhizobia* are present or added; also, some crop species are capable of producing reasonable yields on acid and/or low-phosphorus soils. The chemical constraints to crop production in the Amazon Basin can be over-

TABLE I. General topographical distribution of major soils in the Amazon Basin (in millions of hectares)

Soil grouping	Poorly drained, level	Well-drained slopes			Totals	
		0–8%	8–30%	>30%	Area	%
Acid, infertile soils (oxisols and ultisols)	43	207	88	23	361	75
Poorly drained alluvial soils (aquepts, aquents)	56	13	1	–	70	14
Moderately fertile, well-drained soils (alfisols, mollisols, vertisols, tropepts, fluvents)	0	17	13	7	37	8
Very infertile, sandy soils (spodosols, psamments)	10	5	1	–	16	3
	109	242	103	30	484	100

SOURCE: Sanchez et al. 1982.

come through proper management practices, just as they have been alleviated in the southeastern United States.

Although only 8 percent of the Amazon Basin soils have been estimated to have a high or severe erosion hazard (Table 2), one notes from data of Sanchez et al. (1982) that 27 percent of the soils of the basin have slopes exceeding 8 percent. Certainly many of the oxisols and some ultisols in the basin have favorable structures that permit rapid water infiltration, thereby reducing runoff. Even those soils, however, and even on slopes less steep than 8 percent, can be susceptible to erosion if mismanaged. (To make accurate predictions concerning soil erosion susceptibility, a better inventory of soil topography must be made, perhaps partitioning the 0–8 percent category into 0–4 and 4–8 percent slopes.) Nicholaides estimates from his visits to various parts of the basin that perhaps as much as 40 to 50 percent of its soils have a moderate

TABLE 2. Gross estimates of major constraints to crop production in Amazon Basin soils

Soil constraint	Millions of hectares	Percentage of Amazon
Nitrogen deficiency	437	90
Phosphorus deficiency	436	90
Aluminum toxicity	383	79
Potassium deficiency	378	78
Calcium deficiency	302	62
Sulfur deficiency	280	58
Magnesium deficiency	279	58
Zinc deficiency	234	48
Poor drainage and flooding hazard	116	24
Copper deficiency	113	23
High phosphorus fixation	77	16
Low cation exchange capacity	71	15
High erosion hazard	39	8
Steep slopes (>30%)	30	6
Laterite hazard if subsoil exposed	21	4
Shallow soils (<50 cm deep)	3	<1

SOURCE: Adapted from Sanchez and Cochrane 1980, Cochrane and Sanchez 1982, and Sanchez et al. 1982.

NOTE: Nutritional deficiencies of boron and molybdenum, noted in some Amazon Basin soils, are not quantitatively estimable due to paucity of data.

erosion hazard. Proper management practices will be the key to controlling erosion in the cropped areas of the basin.

Another point deserving mention is the fact that the old laterization myth, that the Amazon Basin soils will turn to brick when cleared (McNeil 1964, Goodland and Irwin 1975, Friedman 1977, Irion 1978, Posey 1982), is just that—a myth. Only 4 percent of the Amazon Basin soils possess a laterization hazard (Table 2) and this is only when the subsoil is exposed. In the southeastern United States the percentage of similar soils is 7 percent (Sanchez and Buol 1975); many of these soils have been farmed continuously for the past 150–200 years without problems. The key is to prevent the soft plinthite in the subsoil from being exposed by erosion of the topsoil. It is only then that irreversible hardening takes place. Since most of these plinthite soils occur only on flat, poorly drained landscapes in the basin, the erosion necessary for plinthite hardening is unlikely to occur (Sanchez et al. 1982). Government leaders in several countries in the basin would like to find more plinthite because it is an excellent, low-cost material for roadbeds. The laterization hazard is therefore not a constant constraint to crop production; rather, its small quantities limit road building in most of the basin (Sanchez et al. 1982).

Only about 6 percent of the Amazon Basin soils have no major deficits for crop production (Sanchez et al. 1982). Agricultural efforts logically should be and are concentrating first on these soils. However, their limited extent, their susceptibility to flooding in many cases, the ensuing population pressures in the basin, and the fact that shifting cultivation is the primary production system for food crops in the predominant soils of the basin underscore the need for a technology of continuous cropping for the acid, infertile soils of the Amazon Basin.

Current cropping system—shifting cultivation

The term "shifting cultivation" is applied to many cropping practices around the world, including any system under which the soil alternately remains fallow longer than it is cropped. Shifting cultivation has been discussed in numerous publications (Moran 1981, Nicholaides 1979, Sanchez 1977a, Ruthenberg 1976, Sanchez 1973, 1976, Grigg 1974, Manshard 1974, National Academy of Sciences 1972, Nye and Greenland 1960).

Clearing.—Most shifting cultivators in the Amazon Basin employ the slash-and-burn technique in which the larger trees and shrubs are cut by ax and machete or chain saws during the period of low rainfall, allowed to dry at least 10–14 days, and burned either in place or in piles of smaller trees and shrubs. Others, such as those in very high rainfall areas of Ecuador's Amazon Basin, practice slash-and-mulch by broadcasting crop seeds in the forest, cutting the undergrowth, and using that vegetation as a mulch instead of burning it. Another variation of shifting cultivation is by the Kayapo Indians in the Xingu River Valley in the center of Brazil's Amazon Basin. These Indians plant root crops in the cleared forest prior to burning (Posey 1982). The root crops lose their greenery with the burn but not the vitality of their underground root systems, which absorb nutrients from the ash when the rains begin.

Not all land clearing in the Amazon Basin, however, is by the shifting cultivators. Large-scale ranchers and farmers with access to capital employ bulldozers, tree crushers, and D8 tractors with large chains between them to clear their lands. The increasing prominence of such mechanized clearing in portions of Brazil's Amazon Basin (Susanna Hecht 1981, personal communication) is not, however, necessarily equated with increased crop yields.

Cropping and fallow.—The most common cropping system practiced by the basin's shifting cultivators involves planting some combination of rice, beans, maize, cassava, sweet potato, and plantain among the ashed debris using a *tacarpo,* or stick, to make a hole into which seed or vegetative portions of the crops are placed. Moran (1981) reports that cassava and banana are often planted before rice and that cassava is planted to 90 percent of the basin's cultivated fields. In the Yurimaguas region of Peru, small farmers usually plant rice in monoculture following slash-and-burn clearing. Then an intercrop of maize, cassava, plantain, and sometimes pineapple is grown (Bandy and Sanchez 1981a). The common intercropping practice reduces, but does not eliminate, the need for manually weeding the crops.

However, after only one or two harvests, especially on the acid, infertile soils, crop yields decline drastically due to soil fertility depletion and consequent greater weed invasion. The land is therefore abandoned to forest fallow for 17–20 years, during which time soil fertility is regenerated by nutrient cycling of the forest growth and litter. The land is then cleared once again, cropped for one or two harvests, and again returned to fallow.

Although this traditional form of shifting cultivation is ecologically sound (Nye and Greenland 1960, Moran 1981) and functional, it has been described as guaranteeing perennial poverty for those who practice it (Alvim 1978). In some parts of the Amazon Basin in recent years, the opening of the Transamazon Highway and other roads (Moran 1981) has brought an increase in population pressure leading to shortening of the forest fallow period and concomitantly of the process of soil fertility regeneration; thus an ecologically sound cropping system has been converted into an unstable, unproductive one, which causes ecological damage (Sanchez et al. 1982). The adverse effect of fallow-period shortening is especially pronounced on the more infertile soils of the basin. Since these soils comprise 75 percent of the basin, the aggregate damage is severe. If there is to be any chance of producing more food in the Amazon Basin while at the same time preserving the

ecological integrity of the undisturbed Amazon rain forest, acceptable alternative cropping systems must be made available to the
shifting cultivators of the region's infertile soils.

Improved cropping systems—continuous cultivation

Certainly included among these alternative cropping systems for
the Amazon Basin's acid, infertile soils must be those developed
since NCSU's 1971 Tropical Soils Research Program in cooperation
with Peru's INIPA in Yurimaguas, Peru. These continuous cropping
systems were developed as NCSU and INIPA addressed the question
of whether continuous cropping of basic food crops would be agronomically possible and economically feasible on the basin's acid,
infertile soils.

Yurimaguas is the westernmost large fluvial port of the Amazon headwaters (5°45' S, 76°05' W, 184 m above sea level) and is
representative in both climate and soil properties of much of
the basin's rain forest subregion. Its mean annual temperature is
26°C; its well-distributed mean annual rainfall exceeds 2100 mm,
with three months averaging about 100 mm each and the rest
around 200 mm. The properties of the level, well-drained ultisol at
the Yurimaguas Agricultural Station reflect a sandy loam surface
over a clayey loam subsoil, both of which have a low cation exchange capacity, are very acid, contain toxic levels of aluminum,
and are deficient in most nutrients.

Land clearing.—The choice of the land clearing method is
the first step, and certainly one of the most important, affecting
cropping productivity of the basin's infertile soils. As shown in
Table 3, crop yields were found to be superior on soil cleared by
the traditional slash-and-burn method to yields on the same soils
cleared by bulldozer (Seubert, Sanchez, and Valverde 1977)—for
the reasons that ash has fertilizer value and the slash-and-burn
method avoids compaction and topsoil displacement caused by
bulldozing.

The traditional slash-and-burn clearing system was concluded
to be best for most farmers of the basin's acid, infertile soils, unless they can add additional fertilizer, lime, and tillage operations
to compensate for low soil fertility and compaction disadvantages
(Alegre, Cassel, and Bandy 1981) of bulldozer clearing. The crucial
question for the NCSU/INIPA Yurimaguas Program then became
how to keep these slash-and-burn clearings continually productive.

TABLE 3. Effect of land clearing method on crop yield at Yurimaguas, Peru

CROP Number of harvests	Fertility treatment[a]	Crop yield (tons per hectare) by cropping method		Ratio, bull- dozed ÷ slash- and- burn (percent)
		Slash and burn	Bulldozer	
Rice, upland	None	1.33	0.70	53
3	N, P, K	3.00	1.47	49
	N, P, K + lime	2.90	2.33	80
Maize	None	0.10	0.00	0
1	N, P, K	0.44	0.04	10
	N, P, K + lime	3.11	2.36	76
Soybean	None	0.70	0.15	24
2	N, P, K	0.95	0.30	34
	N, P, K + lime	2.65	1.80	67
Cassava	None	15.40	6.40	42
2	N, P, K	18.90	14.90	78
	N, P, K + lime	25.60	24.80	97
Mean relative	None			30
yields	N, P, K			43
	N, P, K + lime			80

SOURCE: Seubert, Sanchez, and Valverde 1977.

a. Applied were N, P, and K at 50, 172, and 42 kg per hectare, respectively, and Ca(OH)$_2$ at 4 tons of CaCo$_2$ equivalent per hectare.

Continuous cropping.—Components of the continuous cropping research included determining the most important crops, their best cropping sequences, their nutritional needs, and changes in soil properties with length of cultivation. Details of results are reported in various publications, including North Carolina State University 1972–1981; Bandy and Benites 1977; Sanchez 1977a, b, c; Villachica 1978; Wade 1978; Valverde et al. 1979; Nicholaides 1979; Bandy and Sanchez 1981a; Sanchez et al. 1982; Nicholaides et al. 1983. Various rotations and combinations of rice, maize, cassava, peanut, cowpea, soybean, sweet potato, and plantain were grown.

The climate and rainfall pattern of the Yurimaguas area per-

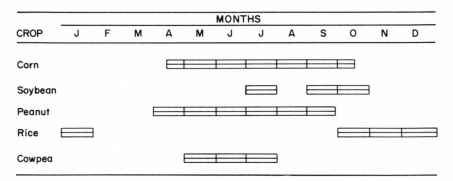

Fig. 2. Recommended planting dates in Yurimaguas, Peru. Source: NCSU 1978–79.

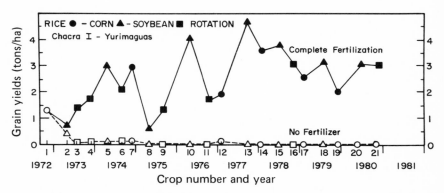

Fig. 3. Yield record of a continuous cultivated rotation of rice-corn-soybean in an ultisol of Yurimaguas, Peru, with and without complete fertilization and lime. Source: Nicholaides et al. 1982.

mit the production of three crops per year without any overlapping relay cropping. Recommended planting dates for the main annual crops in Yurimaguas are shown in Figure 2. Five crops per year were possible with intercropped combinations (Wade 1978). The farmers of the area are turning instead to rotational monoculture, and the most promising rotations, such as upland rice-maize-soybean, will be described here. Monocultures without rotations did not produce sustained high yields because of a buildup of diseases and insects.

    Twenty-one consecutive crops of the upland rice-maize-soybean rotation were harvested from the same field after it was cleared by the slash-and-burn method in October 1972. Without fertilization and lime, yields declined to zero with the third consecutive crop (Figure 3). With complete fertilization treatment, the average long-term yield of this rotation, replicated over three fields, was 7.8 tons of grain per hectare per year. Twenty-one consecutive crops of the upland rice-peanut-soybean rotation have also been harvested with equally high yields. In fact, peanut may be more appropriate for the area than maize due to the climatic constraints on maize. These results indicate that with adequate fertilization (Table 4), moderately high yields of these annual crops under continuous production can be achieved and sustained on some of the most infertile soils of the Amazon Basin.

These systems are as economically feasible as they are agro-

TABLE 4. Lime and fertilizer requirements for continuous cropping of a three-crop-per-year rotation of rice-maize-soybean or rice-peanut-soybean on an ultisol of Yurimaguas, Peru

Fertilizer input	Amount per hectare	Frequency
Lime	3 tons CaCO$_2$ equivalent	Once per three years
Nitrogen	80–100 kg	Rice and maize only
Phosphorus	25 kg	Each crop
Potassium	160 kg	Each crop, split applied
Magnesium	25 kg	Each crop, unless dolomitic lime is used
Copper	1 kg	Once per year or per two years
Zinc	1 kg	Once per year or per two years
Boron	1 kg	Once per year
Molybdenum	20 g	Mixed with legume seed during inoculation

SOURCE: Sanchez et al. 1982 and recent increase in potassium fertilization.

NOTE: Calcium and sulfur requirements are satisfied by lime, simple superphosphate, and Mg, Cu, and Zn carriers.

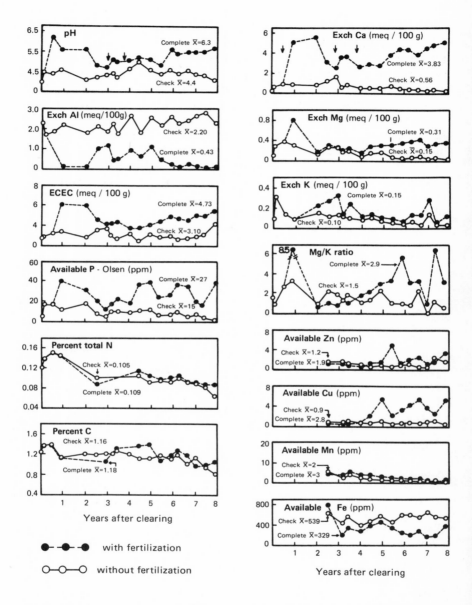

Fig. 4. Soil fertility of an ultisol of Yurimaguas, Peru, after converting a forest fallow to continuous crop production with and without complete fertilization and lime. Source: Bandy and Sanchez 1981.

nomically productive. A net return of U.S. $2.91 per $1.00 invested in fertilizer and lime at 1977 Yurimaguas prices, including transportation, was realized for the rice-peanut-soybean rotation (Bandy 1977).

Soil fertility dynamics: the key factor.—The understanding of soil fertility dynamics was the key to the development of the successful Yurimaguas technology. As with crop production anywhere, the nutritional needs and the consequent lime and fertilizer recommendations for crops in the upper Amazon Basin could be determined only by continual soil and plant sampling and testing.

Soil fertility dynamics were monitored by sampling soils after each harvest and analyzing them for the chemical indexes shown in Figure 4. Treatments of special interest are the "check" soil, which never received fertilizer or lime, and the "complete" soil, which received the best fertilization and liming practices according to soil and plant analyses and the accumulating experience of the program.

Time of appearance of fertility limitations and their intensities varied among clearings even though they had proximate locations, were on the same soil mapping unit, and had the same vegetation before being cleared. Burn intensity was considered a factor contributing to this variability.

A temporary increase in soil fertility produced by ash from the burn was reflected by increases in pH, total nitrogen, available phosphorus, exchangeable potassium, calcium, magnesium, and some micronutrients, with a concomitant decrease in exchangeable aluminum to less than toxic levels. Consequently, upland rice, the first crop planted in Yurimaguas, did not suffer from fertility limitations. However, by eight months after clearing, the nitrogen and potassium levels were reduced such that their deficiency symptoms appeared along with occasional deficiencies of sulfur, copper, and boron. Organic matter contents, as reflected by organic carbon in the topsoil, decreased sharply during the first year at an annual decomposition rate of 25 percent but reached a new equilibrium level beginning with the second year. The rapid organic matter decomposition released many H^+ ions that acidified the soil and increased exchangeable aluminum to toxic levels, thereby negating the liming effect of the ash (Sanchez et al. 1982).

During the second year, phosphorus and magnesium became deficient. Calcium became deficient within the first thirty months and zinc during the fourth year. Manganese deficiency was suspected after the eighth year. Deficiencies of molybdenum were detected occasionally in grain legumes. Thus, after eight years of continuous cultivation, crops grown on this ultisol have exhibited deficiencies of every essential soil nutrient except iron and chlorine.

Fertilizers and lime were added according to soil test recommendations in the complete treatment. However, during the third year yields declined rapidly in those treatments (Figure 3). Soil analysis identified the two factors responsible for this decline: a shorter than expected residual effect of the lime applied and a triggering of magnesium deficiency induced by potassium applications and a consequent potassium/magnesium imbalance (Villachica 1978). Crop yields stabilized (Figure 3) after correction of these factors. Monitoring of the soil fertility dynamics during the soil's transition from forest to cropland provided the key for continuous cultivation of these Amazon Basin soils.

The fertilizer needed for intensive continuous cropping on these soils (Table 4) is not greater than that required for crop production in ultisols in other parts of the world. In fact, fertilizer rates for continuous production of maize, soybean, and peanut on ultisols in the upper Amazon Basin were found not to differ substantially from those for these crops grown on ultisols of the southeastern United States. Total annual amounts are higher in the basin because three crops a year instead of one are grown. After the first crop, which does not normally require fertilization, chemical inputs (whether inorganic or organic) are required to produce and sustain moderately high yields.

These fertilizer recommendations, as with any sound ones, are site specific and thus only applicable to the soils and cropping systems in question. Table 4, developed after eight years of continuous cropping, gives an indication of the inputs required for continuous crop production on ultisols of the upper Amazon Basin.

Effects on soil properties.—A common concern in the literature is that soil degradation increases with cultivation in the humid tropics (McNeil 1964, Goodland and Irwin 1975, Friedman 1977, Irion 1978, Sioli 1980). Our results, however, indicate that soil properties improved with intensively managed, appropriately fertilized, and continuously cropped rotational systems (Table 5).

After seven years of properly liming and fertilizing twenty consecutive crops, the topsoil pH had increased from a very acid

TABLE 5. Changes in topsoil (0–15 cm) chemical properties after seven years of continuous production of twenty crops of upland rice, corn, and soybean with complete fertilization in Yurimaguas, Peru

Chemical property	Before clearing	Ninety months after clearing
pH	4.0	5.7
Organic matter (%)	2.13	1.55
Exchangeable Al (meg/100 cc)	2.27	0.06
Exchangeable Ca (meg/100 cc)	0.26	4.98
Exchangeable Mg (meg/100 cc)	0.15	0.35
Exchangeable K (meg/100 cc)	0.10	0.11
Eff. CEC (meg/100 cc)	2.78	5.51
Al saturation (%)	82	1
Available P (ppm)	5	39
Available Zn (ppm)	1.5[a]	3.5
Available Cu (ppm)	0.9[a]	5.2
Available Mn (ppm)	5.3[a]	1.5
Available Fe (ppm)	650[a]	389

SOURCE: North Carolina State University 1978–79.

a. Thirty months after clearing.

4.0 before clearing to a favorable level of 5.7. Organic matter contents decreased by 27 percent, mostly during the first year. The percent of aluminum saturation was decreased by liming—from a toxic 82 percent to a negligible 1 percent. Exchangeable calcium levels increased nearly twentyfold as a consequence of liming. Exchangeable magnesium levels doubled, although this figure fluctuated over time. Exchangeable potassium levels did not increase in spite of large quantities of potassium fertilizer applied, suggesting rapid utilization by crops and perhaps leaching to the subsoil. Effective cation exchange capacity CEC, a measure of the soil's capability to retain cations against leaching, doubled with time (a significantly important increase), probably as a consequence of the pH-dependent charge characteristics of the kaolinite clay and iron oxides. Fertilization also increased available phosphorus levels from below the critical level of 12 ppm phosphorus to substantially above it. The same trend occurred with zinc and copper, as both elements were applied as fertilizers. However, as no manganese fertilizer was applied, available manganese levels decreased to less than the critical level of 5 ppm, suggesting manganese deficiency. Available iron levels remained considerably above the critical level of 20 ppm. On the whole, these soil fertility changes are indicative of improvement in the topsoil chemical properties.

No unfavorable changes in soil physical properties have been detected thus far (North Carolina State University 1978–79) because of the protection that three well-fertilized crops per year provide against the impact of rain on the soil. Although crop residues are left in the field until the experimental plots are tilled in preparation for the next planting, the soil is exposed for up to thirty days until the crop canopy is established. Occasionally, before the crop canopy is completely developed, heavy rains have produced runoff losses on sloping land. In the continuously cultivated plots that received no fertilization, surface soil compaction was severe because crops never developed a complete canopy. In contrast, healthy fertilized crops produce a good or complete canopy, thereby having less surface soil compaction and less potential runoff.

The acid subsoils frequently act as chemical barriers to root development in the basin's oxisols and ultisols. Crop roots are unable to enter a subsoil with high aluminum saturation and low exchangeable calcium (Bandy 1976, Gonzalez et al. 1979, Ritchey et al. 1980). The consequent shallow root systems often result in drought stressed plants during rainless periods even while the subsoil has available water. Deep lime placement compared with normal or shallow lime placement resulted in maize roots being able to grow into the subsoil and consequently to use the subsoil moisture to reduce plant water stress (North Carolina State University 1978–79).

Deep lime placement is not necessary, however, if calcium movement into the subsoil occurs. The acid subsoil constraints have been alleviated over time following shallow lime and fertilizer placements in Yurimaguas. Downward calcium and magnesium movement producing increases in calcium, magnesium, and effective CEC and a decrease in aluminum saturation were found in subsoil layers at Yurimaguas after several shallow lime incorporations during ninety-two months of continuous cultivation (Sanchez et al. 1982). This resulted in an environment more favorable to root development than before clearing. Appropriate fertilization and continuous cultivation, therefore, improved rather than degraded this ultisol of the upper Amazon Basin.

Farmer acceptance

The true test of any improved technology for continuous cropping in the basin is its acceptance and utilization by the target group, the shifting cultivators. Thus, in 1978, the NCSU and INIPA team felt that research results had sufficient practical application to warrant testing at the farm level. Demonstration plots were established on selected shifting cultivators' slashed-and-burned fields within an eighty-km radius of Yurimaguas.

The small farmers themselves, with NCSU and INIPA support, planted and managed several technological systems using several three-crop annual rotations (Mesia, Bandy, and Nicholaides 1979). The systems were (1) the farmers' traditional system, (2) improved agronomic practices without lime and fertilizer, and (3) improved agronomic practices with moderate rates of lime (one ton calcium carbonate–equivalent per hectare per year) and fertilizer (60 kg nitrogen per hectare for rice and maize only, 35 kg phosphorus per hectare per crop, 66 kg potassium per hectare per crop, and 22 kg magnesium per hectare per crop). System 3 was the improved Yurimaguas technology and was considered equivalent to the complete treatments developed at the Yurimaguas Agricultural Experiment Station. The three-crop annual rotational systems were planted on 1- to 10-year forest fallow slashed-and-burned clearings in soils similar to typic and aquic paleudults and tropudults and more fertile than typic tropudults and vertic eutropepts of the Yurimaguas Agricultural Experiment Station.

The annual cumulative grain yields produced by System 3 ranged from 7.5 to 11.4 tons per hectare, while those from the traditional System 1 were 3.5 to 5.3 tons of grain per hectare (Table 6). These yields are similar to those obtained at the Yurimaguas Experiment Station and are much better than the traditional yields of 1 to 1.5 tons of grain per hectare usually produced on the shifting cultivators' farms in the basin (Smith 1981).

Soil analysis revealed soil fertility depletion in System 1 due to crop removal and loss of ash-liming effect after three consecutive crops. In System 1 at all farm locations, the soils had become deficient in phosphorus and more acidic, with exchangeable aluminum increasing and calcium and magnesium decreasing; organic carbon also decreased. This soil fertility depletion was reflected in declining yields of maize and soybean in the respective maize-peanut-maize and soybean-rice-soybean rotation (Table 6). As soil fertility depletion became more severe in the second year

TABLE 6. Average yields of eleven small-farmer-managed continuous cropping demonstration trials (in tons per
hectare)[a]

Production method	Crop rotation			
	Corn -	Peanut -	Corn	Total
I. Traditional	2.44	1.10	1.77	5.31
II. Improved, no lime or fertilizer	3.81	1.36	2.73	7.90
III. Improved, with lime and fertilizer	5.12	1.62	4.66	11.40
	Peanut -	Rice[b] -	Soybean	Total
I. Traditional	0.97	1.91	1.34	4.22
II. Improved, no lime or fertilizer	1.22	3.56	1.98	6.76
III. Improved, with lime and fertilizer	1.49	4.53	2.75	8.77
	Soybean -	Rice[c] -	Soybean	Total
I. Traditional	1.43	1.91	1.15	4.49
II. Improved, no lime or fertilizer	2.09	2.25	1.89	6.23
III. Improved, with lime and fertilizer	2.73	2.53	2.22	7.48

SOURCE: North Carolina State University 1978–79.

a. From July 1978 to June 1979 in an 80-km radius from Yurimaguas,
Peru.
b. Rice in system I is the traditional Carolino variety, in systems II and
III the improved IR 4-2 variety.
c. Rice in all systems is the traditional Carolino variety.

of the trials, yields declined even further in the traditional system.

Using an economic analysis that limited capital, labor, and
even work output by the nutritional intake of a model seven-
member small-farmer family, the System 3 maize-peanut-maize
rotation was revealed to give the highest net revenue per hectare
and the highest marginal rate of return, exceeding 600 percent
(North Carolina State University, 1978–79). The same system—
on a 1.45 hectare farm using U.S. $90 as owned capital, another
U.S. $90 as borrowed capital (at 64 percent APR), and the farm fam-
ily as the sole labor pool—could realize a net farm income of U.S.

$2,797 at the current rate of exchange (North Carolina State University, 1978–79). This net income is considerably greater than the current net farm income in the Yurimaguas area of U.S. $750, and the $1,500 annual net income of the top 25 percent of the families in Lima's slums (Hernandez and Coutu 1981).

Thus the small farmers in the region have a continuous cropping alternative enabling them to economically and permanently farm their infertile lands, normally subjected to shifting cultivation. After the first year, all eleven initial farmers in the project adopted the improved seed and insecticides, ten adopted the improved plant spacing techniques, six adopted weeding at critical time, five adopted fertilizer use, and none adopted lime use. As many of the farmers' plots were on a higher base-status soils, the need for lime was not exhibited as rapidly as it would have been on the more acid soils. Since the eleven farmers selected to participate in the initial demonstration project are respected community leaders, their neighbors are now learning from them.

Although plans called for only three consecutive crops on the initial eleven farmers' land, three farmers wanted to continue and did so for a second year and one continued into the third year, stopping only after he had grown seven consecutive crops on soil that could not have produced more than two under the traditional system. Those initial eleven farmers are true believers in and salespeople for the workability of the Yurimaguas technology on small farms. Several small farmers in the area are now pioneering the continuous cropping technology on fields larger than one hectare. In the 1979–80 and 1980–81 growing seasons, five and nineteen more small farmers, respectively, entered into the same demonstration arrangement as had the initial eleven.

A pilot project with twenty-seven rural schools in the Yurimaguas region was initiated also in the 1980–81 period in order to reach more small farmers and their families. This collaborative IN-IPA/Ministry of Education/NCSU project set up the same type of demonstration systems, but this time with rural school students, their families, and teachers planting and managing the trials. After only one year, over 50 percent of the 626 small-farm families involved in the project were interested enough to want to use at least some of the Yurimaguas technology on their own lands (Benites 1981). The local availability of fertilizer and credit has increased, and marketing facilities have improved in Yurimaguas due to favorable Peruvian government response to the Yurimaguas technology. Clearly, this is only a beginning, but it is a solid one on which the region can build.

Continued and new research

As important as are the findings that agronomically productive and economically feasible continuous cropping systems are available to some small farmers on the acid, infertile soils of the upper Amazon Basin, not all the answers have been obtained for changing the region's predominant agricultural practice from shifting to permanent cultivation. Several complementary options for sustained agriculture in the upper basin are being investigated by the NCSU/INIPA team and others. These include the following research thrusts.

Alternative land clearing methods.—Research in Yurimaguas is determining which of several combinations of traditional slash-and-burn clearing with small- or large-scale mechanization might be advantageous for the region's farmers. One of the most promising involves a bulldozer KG shear blade cutting the trees at soil surface, thereby minimizing topsoil removal, and removing the larger trees prior to burning the vegetation for fertilizer value of the ash (Cassel and Alegre 1982). Longer term research is needed in this area.

Lower-input systems.—Special emphasis is given to developing alternative systems with lower inputs for the region's small farmers.

1. One approach is evaluation of crop varieties for tolerance to soil aluminum. As soil acidity is a main limiting factor to crop production on soils in this region, determining tolerant varieties would result in lessening the costly, yet still economical, lime inputs. Evaluation of rice, peanut, cowpea, soybean, and sweet potato varieties for aluminum tolerance has identified promising varieties of rice and cowpea (Piha and Nicholaides 1981). These efforts are continuing.

2. Increasing efficiencies of nitrogen and potassium fertilizer and collaborative evaluation, with the International Fertilizer Development Center and the International Center for Tropical Agricultural (CIAT), of the use of rock phosphate compared with the more costly, yet still economical, phosphate fertilizers on these acid soils, are other promising components, which will require more research.

3. Use of organic inputs to replace or supplement the costly,

though economical, inorganic inputs has included mulching crops with residues from previous crops or *Panicum maximum.* Nonconclusive findings have shown generally detrimental results for upland rice, some yield increases in maize, and little effect on soybean and peanut after twenty experiments (Valverde and Bandy 1982).

4. Use of kudzu (*Pueraria phaseoloides*) as a green manure has provided positive results, often attaining crop yields similar to complete fertilization (Wade 1978). The labor involved in hand-harvesting, transporting, and incorporating kudzu into the soil has made this alternative unattractive to the small farmers.

5. Utilizing compost from crop residues appears to have some promise. For the first four consecutive crops, replacing complete fertilization with compost produced from various crop residues resulted in only a 20 percent yield reduction (Bandy and Nicholaides 1979). To maintain those yields on later crops, however, it was necessary to apply potassium fertilizer with the compost. The potential of this practice also may be restricted by its high labor requirements (Bandy and Nicholaides 1982).

6. Managed kudzu fallows are being investigated as an intermediate stage between shifting and continuous cultivation. Kudzu is easily established on the acid, infertile soils and rapidly develops a lush green canopy with an abundance of nitrogen-fixing nodules on its roots. After one or two years of fallow, it is easily killed by slash-and-burn. Reasonable crop yields have been obtained by rotating two crops with one to two years of kudzu fallow (Bandy and Sanchez 1981b). During the second rotation, however, potassium was needed to obtain moderate crop yields.

Low-input legume-grass pastures.—Because there is a demand for beef products in the Amazon Basin countries, much clearing there is for pasture development (Myers 1980); but many attempts to establish pastures fail, with adverse ecological consequences. Therefore, appropriate pasture production technologies must be developed for this region. Low-input legume-grass pasture production technologies are being developed by the NCSU/INIPA Yurimaguas Program. These are primarily for acid, infertile soils on slopes and use acid-tolerant legume and grass species selected by CIAT's Tropical Pastures Program (Toledo and Serrão 1982). Promising germ plasm has been tested for adaptation to an ultisol of pH 4.0 and 80 percent aluminum saturation with only eleven kg phosphorus per hectare applied as simple superphosphate. The legumes *Desmodium ovalifolium, Pueraria phaseoloides*, and *Centrosema pubescens* and the grasses *Andropogon gayanus, Brachiaria humidicola*, and *B. decumbens* were found to be well adapted to the soil, climate, pest, and disease constraints of the region. Legume-grass pastures are now being tested under grazing pressure (Ara et al. 1981); it is too early for conclusive results.

Agroforestry.—Also considered vital to development efforts in the Amazon Basin is the use of indigenous and imported tree species. Agroforestry is consequently an important new research component at Yurimaguas. Being initiated is collaborative research with the International Council for Research on Agroforestry to combine crop production systems at various input levels with promising tree species that can produce food, oil, or pulpwood. Species being tested include the peach palm (*Guilielma gasipaes*), oil palm (*Elaeis guianensis*), and pulp producing *Gmelina arborea* and *Pinus caribea.*

Other innovative agroforestry systems for similar soils are being developed by UEPAE/EMBRAPA near Manaus (UEPAE/ EMBRAPA, 1978–80).

Fertile, alluvial soils.—The Amazon Basin's relatively fertile alluvial soils not subject to flooding have great food production potential. The inherent native fertility and proximity to natural transportation systems stresses the importance of these soils. Farmers' use of improved rice varieties and spacing (Sanchez and Nurena 1972) doubled rice yields without eliminating shifting cultivation. Research at Yurimaguas is developing the most suitable paddy rice production technologies with river irrigation. Maize, soybean, and cowpea rotations are utilized when the soils are not flooded.

Implications

The increasing demand for more food production, both within and outside the countries sharing the common heritage of the Amazon Basin, will continue to motivate the clearing of the region's forests, through both spontaneous and government-directed colonization, in spite of the objections of concerned individuals and organizations. Development, extension, and use of agronomically and economically sound continuous cropping technologies, such as the Yurimaguas technology, provide alternatives heretofore unavailable to the small, shifting cultivators of the upper basin and to the rest of us concerned about the region's ecology.

The small farmers of the upper basin now have available and are beginning to use some of the Yurimaguas technology to increase crop production on the acid, infertile soils and to better their lots in life. In continuously cropping their lands, the small farmers could play a positive and viable role in increasing food production in the region and in preserving much of the upper basin's ecological integrity.

Rational decisions, however, must be made by the indigenous peoples, settlers, and especially governments of the Amazon Basin countries for this increased agricultural production to have no adverse ecological consequences. The Yurimaguas technology provides a means by which some of these decisions can be made.

Attempts to produce food crops and pastures without the correct technologies for the acid, infertile soils are likely to fail and could cause widespread ecological damage. The key to preventing that scenario is the development, extension, and use of appropriate technologies for these soils so that sustained, continuous cropping or pasture production can occur on smaller quantities of cleared lands, with a consequent preservation of the ecological integrity of the as yet uncleared portions of the Amazon Basin.

The NCSU/INIPA Yurimaguas Program has developed some of these technologies for continuously cropping the relatively level ultisols of the upper basin. Many necessary components of these systems are yet to be determined and the research must continue. The value of long-term field research cannot be overemphasized. Second-, third-, fourth-, and fifth-generation problems do not appear in the first years of continuous cultivation. Had the research been deemed a success and ended after one or two or even five or eight years, some of the techniques for longer-term continuous cultivation of annual crops on these soils would not now be available to the farmers.

Likewise, technologies for continuously cropping the basin's relatively level oxisols must also be found. These are being researched by several organizations, including a cooperative NCSU/EMBRAPA program located at UEPAE/Manaus in Brazil (Smith, Sanchez, and Bandy 1982). Several years of research will be required before any systems developed are judged adequate to extend to that area's farmers.

Lower input technologies, improved pasture production, and agroforestry systems must also be developed for the various regions of the basin to provide a range of alternatives for the indigenous peoples, settlers, and governments involved. The successful Yurimaguas technology is only one of many components necessary for increasing food production and minimizing ecological alteration in the basin.

Limitations.—It would be incorrect to infer that continuous production technologies described herein are directly applicable to all ultisols and oxisols in the Amazon Basin. The NCSU/INIPA research has concentrated on nearly level soils, thereby avoiding the erosion hazards of cultivating the undulating lands. Adaptation and modification of the Yurimaguas technology to sloping lands would be needed, perhaps terracing as practiced in areas of humid tropical Asia, perhaps mulching crop residues, perhaps alternating annual crops with pastures. Other options for the cleared undulating lands could be continual legume-grass pastures or agroforestry. Better yet would be to leave pristine the forests on sloping soils, and to concentrate food production on the level, well-drained 17 million hectares of fertile soils and on the level, well-drained 207 million hectares of acid, infertile soils.

Socioeconomic conditions also limit the widespread adaptation of the Yurimaguas technology. Though not a privileged region of the basin, the Yurimaguas area has an unpaved road to Lima and several rivers that link it with the rest of Peru and other countries, and therefore to markets. The present Yurimaguas socioeconomic conditions clearly indicate the economic feasibility of the Yurimaguas technology. But different cost-price ratios, an inelastic demand for products, changes in government policies, and many other time- and location-specific factors could make the same technology economically unattractive. Necessary for any region considering adopting the Yurimaguas technology are site-specific economic interpretations based on local and national factors.

Agronomic conditions also could differ within and among regions. Therefore, prior to widespread implementation attempts, the Yurimaguas technology must be tested through adaptive research trials to local situations. Modifications could include different fertilizer rates, planting dates, and crop species, varieties, and rotations. Vital to these adaptive research trials will be some type of soil fertility evaluation and improvement service to assist farmers changing from shifting to continuous cultivation.

Potential.—Once the limitations are realized and addressed successfully, the potential of the Yurimaguas technology is that settlers and governments in the Amazon Basin will have available the means to increase food production while sparing many hectares of forest. Farmers do not clear the basin's forests because they enjoy it. Slash-and-burn clearing is excruciatingly hard work. Farmers clear the rainforest because they need to produce food. If they can produce more food more economically with less work, as those involved with the NCSU/INIPA project are doing, they will do so without hesitation. If they cannot, then the Amazon Basin forest will continue to fall under the shifting cultivators' axes. For certain areas of the upper Amazon Basin, the Yurimaguas technology offers one agronomically, economically, and ecologically attractive alternative to that gloomy scenario.

References Cited

Alegre, J.C., D.K. Cassel, and D.E. Bandy
    1981   Effects of Tillage Practices on Reclaiming a Severely Compacted Ultisol in Yurimaguas, Peru. In *Agron. Abstrs.* Amer. Soc. Agron. 1981 Ann. Mtgs. P. 38. Madison, Wisconsin.

Alvim, P.T.
    1978   Perspectivas de Produção Agrícola na Região Amazônica. *Interciencia* 3(4):243–51.

Ara, M., P.A. Sanchez, D.E. Bandy, and J.M. Toledo
    1981   Adaptation of Acid-Tolerant Grass and Legume Pasture Ecotypes in the Upper Amazon Basin. In *Agron. Abstrs.* Amer. Soc. Agron. 1981 Ann. Mtgs. P. 38. Madison, Wisconsin.

Bandy, D.E.
    1976   Soil-Plant-Water Relationships as Influenced by Various Soil and Plant Management Practices on Campo Cerrado Soils in the Central Plateau of Brazil. Ph.D. dissertation. Ithaca, N.Y.: Cornell University.

    1977   Manejo de Suelos y Cultivos en Sistemas de Agricultura Permanente en la Selva Amazónica del Perú. Presented at the FAO Reunión-Taller Sobre Manejo y Conservación de Suelos en América Latina. October 3–14, 1977. Lima, Peru.

Bandy, D.E. and J. Benites
    1977   *Proyecto Internacional de Suelos Tropicales, Yurimaguas.* Ministerio de Alimentación. Lima, Peru.

Bandy, D.E. and J.J. Nicholaides, III.
    1979   Use of Composts for Crop Production on Ultisols of the Amazon Jungle. In *Agron. Abstrs.* Amer. Soc. Agron. 1979 Ann. Mtgs. P. 42. Madison, Wisconsin.

1982   Compost Residue Management in Yurimaguas, Peru. In *Agron. Abstr.* Amer. Soc. Agron, 1982 Ann. Mtgs. P. 42. Madison, WI.

Bandy, D.E. and P.A. Sanchez

1981a   Continuous Crop Cultivation in Acid Soils of the Amazon Basin of Peru. Presented at the Workshop on the Management of Low Fertility Acid Soils of the American Humid Tropics held at the University of Surinam, Faculty of Natural Resources, Paramaribo, Surinam, and sponsored by IICA. November 23–26, 1981.

1981b   Managed Kudzu Fallow as an Alternative to Shifting Cultivation in Yurimaguas, Peru. In *Agron Abstrs.* Amer. Soc. Agron. 1981 Ann. Mtgs. P. 40. Madison, Wisconsin.

Benites, J.R.

1981   Proposal and Recommendations for the Review of the Yurimaguas Small Farmer Extrapolation Program. Lima, Peru.

Cassel, D.K. and J.C. Alegre

1982   Unpublished data. North Carolina State University.

Cochrane, T.T. and P.A. Sanchez

1982   Land Resources, Soils, and Their Management in the Amazon Region: A State of Knowledge Report. In *Amazonia: Agriculture and Land Use Research.* S.B. Hecht, ed. Pp. 137–209. Cali, Colombia: CIAT.

Denevan, W.M.

1977   The Causes and Consequences of Shifting Cultivation in Relation to Tropical Forest Survival. Presented at the Congreso Internacional de Geógrafos Latinoamericanistas. August 3–9, 1977. Paipa, Colombia.

Friedman, I.

1977   The Amazon Basin, Another Sahel? *Sci.* 197:7.

Gonzalez, E., E.J. Kamprath, G.C. Naderman, and W.V. Soares

1979   Effect of Depth of Lime Incorporation on the Growth of Corn on an Oxisol of Central Brazil. *Soil Sci. Soc. Amer. J.* 43:1155–58.

Goodland, R.J.A. and H.S. Irwin

1975   *Amazon Jungle: Green Hell to Red Desert?* Amsterdam: Elsevier.

Grigg, D.B.

1974   *The Agricultural Systems of the World: An Evolutionary Approach.* London: Cambridge University Press.

Hernandez, D. and A.J. Coutu

1981   Economic Evaluation of Slash/Burn Cultivation Options in Yurimaguas, Peru. In *Agron. Abstrs.* Amer. Soc. Agron. 1981 Ann. Mtgs. P. 42. Madison, Wisconsin.

Irion, G.
   1978   Soil Infertility in the Amazon Rainforest. *Naturwissenchaften* 65:515–19.
McNeil, M.
   1964   Lateritic Soils. *Sci. Amer.* 211(5):96–102.
Manshard, W.
   1974   *Tropical Agriculture: A Geographical Introduction and Appraisal.* London: Longman Group Ltd.
Marbut, C.F. and C.B. Manifold
   1926   The Soils of the Amazon Basin in Relation to Agricultural Possibilities. *Geogr. Rev.* 16:414–42.
Mesia, R., D.E. Bandy and J.J. Nicholaides
   1979   Transfer of Agronomic Practices to the Small Farmer of the Amazon Jungle. In *Agron. Abstrs.* Amer. Soc. of Agron. 1979 Ann. Mtgs. P. 46. Madison, Wisconsin.
Moran, E.F.
   1981   *Developing the Amazon.* Bloomington, Indiana: Indiana University Press.
Myers, N.
   1980   *Conversion of Tropical Moist Forests.* Washington, D.C.: National Research Council/National Academy of Sciences.
National Academy of Sciences
   1972   *Soils of the Humid Tropics.* Washington, D.C.: National Research Council of National Academy of Sciences.
National Research Council
   1982   *Ecological Aspects of Development in the Humid Tropics.* Washington, D.C.: National Academy Press.
Nicholaides, J.J., III
   1979   Crop Production Systems on Acid Soils in Humid Tropical America. In *Soil, Water, and Crop Production.* D.W. Thorne and M.D. Thorne, eds. Pp. 243–77. Westport, Conn: AVI Publ. Co.
Nicholaides, J.J., III, P.A. Sanchez, D.E. Bandy, J.H. Villachica, A.J. Coutu, and C.S. Valverde.
   1983   Crop Production Systems in the Amazon Basin. In *The Dilemma of Amazonian Development.* E. Moran, ed. Chapter 5. Boulder, Colorado: Westview Press.
North Carolina State University
   1972, 1973, 1974, 1975, 1976–77, 1978–79, 1980–81
           Tropical Soils Research Program Annual Reports. Raleigh, N.C.
Nye, P.H. and D.J. Greenland
   1960   The Soil Under Shifting Cultivation. Comm. Agr. Bur. Tech. Comm. 51. Harpenden, U.K.

Piha, M. and J.J. Nicholaides, III
    1981   Field Evaluation of Legume, Sweet Potato, and Rice Varieties for Tolerance to Soil Acidity. In *Agron. Abstrs.* Amer. Soc. Agron. 1981 Ann. Mtgs. P. 45. Madison, Wisconsin.
Posey, D.
    1982   The Keepers of the Forests. *Garden* 6(1):18–24.
Ritchey, K.D., M.G. Souza, E. Lobato, and O. Correa
    1980   Calcium Leaching to Increase Rooting Depth in a Brazilian Savannah Oxisol. *Agron. J.* 72:40–44.
Ruthenberg, H.
    1976   *Farming Systems in the Tropics.* Oxford: Clarendon Press.
Sanchez, P.A.
    1973   A Review of Soils Research in Tropical Latin America. Bull. 219. Soil Sci. Dept. Raleigh, N.C.: North Carolina State University.
    1976   *Properties and Management of Soils in the Tropics.* New York: John Wiley and Sons, Publishers.
    1977a   Advances in the Management of Oxisols and Ultisols in Tropical South America. In *Proceedings of International Seminar on Soil Environment and Fertility Management in Intensive Agriculture.* Pp. 535–66. Soc. Soil Sci. and Manure. Tokyo, Japan.
    1977b   Manejo de Suelos Tropicales en la Amazonía Sur-América. *Suelos Ecuatoriales* 8:1–11.
    1977c   Manejo de Solos de Amazônia para Produção Agropecuária Intensiva. *Bol. Inf. Soc. Bras. Ciência Solo* 2(3):60–63.
Sanchez, P.A. and S.W. Buol
    1975   Soils of the Tropics and the World Food Crises. *Sci.* 180: 598–603.
Sanchez, P.A. and T.T. Cochrane
    1980   Soil Constraints in Relation to Major Farming Systems of Tropical America. In IRRI/Cornell Priorities for Alleviative Soil-Related Constraints to Food Production in the Tropics. Pp. 101–39. IRRI: Los Baños, Laguna, Philippines.
Sanchez, P.A. and M.A. Nurena
    1972   Upland Rice Improvement Under Shifting Cultivation in the Amazon Basin of Peru. North Carol. Agr. Exp. Sta. Tech. Bull. 210.
Sanchez, D.E. Bandy, J.H. Villachica, and J.J. Nicholaides
    1982   Amazon Basin Soils: Management for Continuous Crop Production. *Sci.* 216:821–27.
Seubert, C.E., P.A. Sanchez, and C. Valverde
    1977   Effects of Land Clearing Methods on Soil Properties of an Ultisol and Crop Performance in the Amazon Jungle of Peru. *Trop. Agric.* 54:307–21.

Sioli, H.
1980   Foreseeable Consequences of Actual Development Schemes
        and Alternative Ideas. In *Land, People, and Planning in Con-
        temporary Amazonia*. F. Barbira-Scazzocchio, ed. Pp. 256–
        68. Cambridge: Cambridge University Press.
Smith, N.J.H.
1981   Colonization Lessons from a Tropical Forest. *Sci.* 214:
        755–61.
Smyth, T.J., P.A. Sanchez and D.E. Bandy
1982   Nutrient Additions to the Soil by Slash and Burn Clearing of
        Tropical Rainforests in the Amazon of Peru and Brazil. In
        Agron. Abstrs. Amer. Soc. Agron. 1982 Ann. Mtgs. Madison,
        Wisconsin.
Toledo, J.M. and E.A.S. Serrão
1982   Pastures and Animal Production in Amazonia. In *Amazonia:
        Agriculture and Land Use Research*. S.B. Hecht, ed. Pp. 281–
        309. Cali, Colombia: CIAT.
UEPAE / EMBRAPA
1978, 1979, 1980
        Relatório Técnico Anual 1978, 1979, 1980. Manaus, Ama-
        zonas, Brazil.
Valverde, C.S. and D.E. Bandy
1982   Production of Annual Food Crops in the Amazon. In *Ama-
        zonia: Agriculture and Land Use Research*. S.B. Hecht, ed.
        Pp. 243–80. Cali, Colombia: CIAT.
Valverde, C.S., D.E. Bandy, P.A. Sanchez, and J.J. Nicholaides
1979   *Algunos Resultados del Proyecto Yurimaguas en la Zona
        Amazónica*. Lima, Peru: INIA.
Villachica, J.H.
1978   Maintenance of Soil Fertility Under Continuous Cropping in
        an Ultisol of the Amazon Jungle of Peru. Ph.D. dissertation.
        North Carolina State University, Raleigh, N.C.
Wade, M.K.
1978   Soil Management Practices for Increasing Crop Production
        for Small Farmers in the Amazon Jungle of Peru. Ph.D. dis-
        sertation. North Carolina State University, Raleigh, N.C.

Cattle Ranching in Amazonia: Political and Ecological Considerations

Susanna B. Hecht

THE AMAZON Basin has increasingly become the focus of international attention. As the largest area of remaining tropical rain forest biome, it has a relatively unexplored resource potential and is regarded as one of the last agricultural frontiers. Recent decades have witnessed the rapid conversion of Amazonian forest to agricultural landscapes (primarily pasture), a process stimulated by a combination of infrastructure development, fiscal incentives, and colonization programs. Estimates indicate that about one million hectares are deforested each year. Unfortunately, much of the area converted to pasture is only ephemerally productive, and a few years after conversion the productivity of these lands shows a pronounced decline. Estimates of the area of degraded pasture vary from about 20 percent (Serrão et al. 1979, Toledo and Serrão 1982) to those based on LANDSAT data indicating deteriorated pasture levels at closer to 50 percent of lands cleared (Tardin et al. 1977, Hecht 1982).

The conversion of substantial areas of tropical rain forest in Amazonia has been a source of considerable controversy. Biological scientists voice concern about species extinction (Myers 1980, Gomez-Pompa, Vasques-Yanes, and Guevara 1972, Pires and Prance 1977), changes in hydrologic regimes (Gentry and López-Parodi

NOTE: Funds for field research and lab analysis were provided by the Ford Foundation, the National Science Foundation, and AID.

1980), local and global climate modification (Salati et al. 1979; Molion 1975) and soil resources degradation (Goodland and Irwin 1975, Goodland 1980). Social scientists have pointed to the intense land conflicts (Schmink 1982, Martins in this volume), increasing peasant marginalization (Wood and Schmink 1979, Sawyer 1979, Santos 1979), extinction of indigenous groups (Davis 1977) and increased rural to urban migration (Martine 1982, Aragon 1978, Wood and Wilson, this volume) that have accompanied the process of land development through livestock expansion into the Amazon region.

In contrast to the concerns of biologists and social scientists noted above, Amazonian regional integration has been described as necessary to ensure that millions of Brazilians are not condemned to lives of abject poverty (Alvim 1978). What I will discuss in this paper is the political economy of Amazonian ranching development and how the processes of land degradation and capital accumulation are linked in the Amazonian context.

Theoretical models of environmental degradation

The models used for understanding environmental degradation in the humid tropical context are not well developed. By far the most prevalent thesis about land degradation is the Malthusian idea that increasing population pressure on tropical lands leads to a shortening of fallow times by shifting agriculturalists. While shifting agriculture is ecologically sound at low population densities (Sanchez 1976), demographic pressures or immigration cause fallow intervals to be reduced, leading to intensified use that results in depletion of soil nutrients and erosion. The generally low population densities of Amazonia weaken the ability of this argument to explain the observed degradation in the region. While unused land is still abundant in the Amazon region, access, control, and title are nevertheless at issue in some areas.

Another explanation of environmental degradation in the tropics blames export cropping for generating ecological difficulties. It is argued that the often highly mechanized nature of production for export produces local and secondary environmental problems. The effects associated with the overuse of pesticides are a classic example of this analysis.

Another widely cited model for explaining agricultural failures and their associated environmental deterioration is what Michael Todaro calls the "False Paradigm Model," or the "Inappropriate Technology Model" (Todaro 1977). In this view, planners or agencies apply land use technologies that, due to local environmental or cultural conditions, are not well adapted to the area and therefore cause undesirable ecological effects. The problems generated by inappropriate land use are seen as primarily technological in character, with improved technology as the solution.

I will argue that environmental degradation in Amazonia is not adequately explained by any of these models. Rather than analyzing regional ecological problems in Amazonia as strictly endogenous due to population increase or to the use of inappropriate technologies, one needs to examine the role that Amazonian development (especially the development of cattle ranching) played in Brazil, particularly after the military coup in 1964. In both substantive and ideological ways, the development of Amazonia addressed the strong national as well as international pressures that confronted the new military government. These pressures led policymakers to choose cattle ranching, the latifundio land use par excellence, over all alternative land uses, as the defining strategy of Amazonian occupation (see Pompermayer in this volume).

The military coup of 1964 and the question of legitimacy

In 1964, Brazil experienced a military coup of the type Barrington Moore (1968) would call a "revolution from above." Diverse political factions were supporters of the coup (Stepan 1968), but its outcome was particularly favorable to certain groups: the agroindustrial and industrial entrepreneurial elite. The coup inaugurated a variety of changes, if not in kind certainly in emphasis, in the Brazilian economic scene. These transformations were reflected in increased international investment, the strengthening of entrepreneurial capital, and significant modifications in the role of the Brazilian state in national and Amazonian planning.

When the military seized power, several basic political issues had to be addressed. First, the regime had to legitimate its right to govern. Second, it had to resolve many of the pressing economic constraints that had hampered capital accumulation by national elites (including wage demands, high inflation, import substitution industrialization policies, and lack of investment outlets). Third, it was necessary to solve, or at least foster the appearance of contending with, the social and political problems of rural areas as

reflected in stagnant agricultural production, low rates of investment, and rural out-migration (Knight 1971, Wood and Wilson, in
this volume).

Increased economic output was seen as a solution to the questions of legitimation and economic reorganization. The economic
growth policies chosen by the new regime relied on increased international borrowing, a profound wage squeeze, augmented transnational participation in the economy, repression, and conventional expansionist monetary and fiscal policies (Fishlow 1973,
Taylor et al. 1980, Belassa 1979). While the contribution of these
policies to the "Brazilian miracle" is open to question (Fishlow
1973, Belassa 1979, Malan and Bonelli 1977), the regime certainly
took credit for the rapid growth of the Brazilian economy during
the 1964–74 period. It was this unusual economic performance
that aided in the institutionalization of the various military regimes that followed the 1964 coup.

Agricultural and agrarian questions required a profound shift
in policy as well. Except for a few exports, the Brazilian agricultural sector in the late 1950s and early 1960s suffered from a lack
of credit and investment capital, import tariffs that made the cost
of inputs such as machinery and agricultural chemical stocks very
expensive, export taxes, and marked regional disparities in investment. Overvalued cruzeiros made Brazilian agricultural products
relatively costly on the international market, while national policies emphasized exports only as a vent for surplus production
(Knight 1971). Structural change and mechanization in Brazilian
agriculture began to erode access to land for tenant farmers and
sharecroppers, while the southern frontiers of Paraná and Rio
Grande do Sul further reduced agricultural options for the rural
poor (Foweraker 1981).

Attempts to confront the situation in the countryside took
the form of increased availability of funds for agriculture. Policy
mechanisms for agricultural change included subsidized interest
rates for rural modernization and mechanization (especially in the
Northeast and Amazonia), export incentives and revaluation of
the cruzeiro. The greater availability of financing for investments
in the agricultural sector was intended to modify the production
processes on the farm and in specific regions. Subsidized rural
elites, agroindustrialists, as well as urban entrepreneurs were attracted to agriculture in order to diversify their investment port-

folios and to take advantage of tax credits. These initiatives would ostensibly promote efficiency and rational economic behavior that would transform agricultural production in Brazil.

The agrarian question, whose outward symptoms were rural-to-urban migration and peasant activism, was addressed under the new regime by repression and the opening up of a new agricultural frontier, Amazonia. Amazonian development obviated the need for land reform and provided the appearance of a national will to include the rural poor in the government's development strategy.

The idea of occupying Amazonia resonated closely with other themes in the government programs. Most important was the military ideology of National Security. The large size of Amazonia (more than 50 percent of the Brazilian national territory), with its sparse population and unpatrolled borders shared with eight other countries, and with a history of annexation and border conflict between them, fueled a certain disquiet about the area. The geopolitical importance of Amazonia, reflected in the slogan "Integrar para não entregar," is present throughout the planning documents and propaganda statements regarding the region.

The military language characteristic of the development rhetoric also contributed to the sense of Amazonian occupation as the moral equivalent of war. Ideologically, such a military focus unifies national factions around a common national goal and justifies current sacrifices in welfare for a larger (future) good. Thus, General Castello-Branco stated in 1964 that "Amazonian occupation would proceed as though it were a strategically conducted war." The first post-coup body of legislation concerning the Amazon goes by the appropriately military title of "Operation Amazonia." Not only would Amazonian occupation function like a war in the ideological sense, but it would also stimulate the economy through construction and heavy industries linked to infrastructure development.

The concept of national security is closely allied to that of national integration, another common policy theme. The latter, in turn, can be seen as a version of Manifest Destiny, an idea consistent with the orthodox economic approach to the region. It implied greater economic linkage of the hinterland to urban centers, facilitated by the development of infrastructure and the creation of investment credits. The attack on regional disparities held out the image of the developed Center South as the achievable future of Brazil's backlands. Further, through regional occupation, the riches of Amazonia, rightfully Brazilian, could be realized, and contribute to the overall welfare of Brazil.

Through these various channels the new agricultural frontier in the Amazon was to provide a solution to vital economic and ideological questions, and thus served important political and legitimizing functions to the new regime. The role that cattle ranching was to play in this process can only be understood through an appreciation of the internal and international pressures that influenced the new government.

Internal pressures underlying policy

Significant internal pressures came to bear upon the new military regime (Stepan 1968, 1973). Urban unrest required police coercion, and the wage squeeze on workers characteristic on the post-1964 regime (Bacha 1977, Fishlow 1973, Malan and Bonelli 1977) exacerbated dissatisfaction (Stepan 1973, O'Donnell 1979). Since few other concessions were granted to labor by the regime, cheap food policies (especially for beef) were important priorities (Leff 1967, Bergsman 1970). The beef industry, however, was at a cyclic production low with price ceilings making cattle production uneconomic for producers, while urban and international demand soared.

The capacity of traditional landed elites to respond to this crisis was perceived as dubious, while the technological orientation of agribusiness and the entrepreneurial spirit of parts of the industrial sector, coupled with the new Australian pasture technologies, seemed a reasonable solution. The apparent viability of this avenue was contingent on the extent to which long-term credit could be made available and antiquated production bottlenecks could be circumvented. These credit and production constraints could be addressed through increased agricultural lending and horizontal expansion of land use through the sale of state properties to agroentrepreneurs.

The expansion of cattle production had other attractions, since it was consistent with the desire to expand exports of "nontraditional" Brazilian products, a fundamental feature of the new regime's economic policy. Little was known about Amazonian ecologies, but the three-hundred-year history of ranching on the island of Marajó and the existence of upland natural grass lands made it appear that only technical insufficiency limited the productivity of livestock in the region. Further, compared with the other agricultural options in the region, such as pepper, cacau, and rubber

plantations, ranching seemed relatively easy to implant and maintain and had low labor requirements. Cowboys for ranching, a
semiskilled labor pool, existed in and were easily available from
Goiás, Mato Grosso, and the Northeast. Moreover, periodic
droughts in the Northeast assured a supply of unskilled workers
that could be recruited by labor contractors (*empreiteiros*) to clear
land for pasture. The flexibility of animal marketing, and the fact
that animals could be walked to market if bridges collapsed or
roads became impassable, was also attractive. Finally, the use of
corporate entities was viewed favorably because these would have
the administrative capability to resolve certain infrastructural
problems (e.g. of public health, communications, food supply) that
otherwise would be the costly responsibility of the government.
Except for financing and major infrastructural development, the
actual involvement and responsibility of the government would be
minimal. The larger economic and political concerns of the government, as well as the practical considerations of the actual
physical occupation of the region, made ranching seem an attractive solution to these problems.

The expansion of ranching into the Amazon was also conditioned by high inflation periods of the 1960s and 1970s that increased the frequency of land in corporate, as well as private, portfolios. As the latter parts of this chapter will show, the fiscal
incentives and land concessions provided by the government in
Amazonia facilitated land acquisition and contributed to the extreme increase in the value of land in the region. Those who invested through SUDAM and other cattle projects could make enormous capital gains simply through the increased valorization of
land.

International factors affecting policy

International factors implicitly or explicitly played an important
role in the evolution of ranching as the main development strategy
for the Amazon, primarily through the expanded global demand
for beef during the mid-1960s. Feder (1979) has pointed out that
changes in the U.S. beef production system were important in the
expanded global beef demand, and in the increased lending for the
livestock sector by international agencies. In the 1950s the U.S.
embarked on a program to increase the production of high-quality
beef using the feedlot system. Grain-fattening of cattle was also a
means of disposing of surplus wheat and corn, a serious problem

in the late 1950s and early 1960s. Feedlots were capable of generating large tonnages of high-quality beef, but the success of this production system was not without some difficulties. In particular, demand for lower quality, utility beef used in fast foods, sausages, etc. began to soar. Utility, or cutter beef, is expensive to produce by the feedlot system, and suppliers turned to international sources for it. The rise in U.S. demand for international beef occurred at the same time that consumption and demand increased in Europe, the Eastern Bloc, and Japan. Since South American (as opposed to Central American) beef has traditionally been oriented to European markets, the expanded purchasing power of these countries in the mid-1960s was a major stimulus to demand.

The general international perspective for the expansion of Brazilian beef is summarized by FAO/ECLA's (1964) study called *Livestock in Latin America*. The FAO document indicated that while Brazil's existing productive capacity was rather low, it had great potential for expansion through the incorporation of new land and the rationalization of production. FAO argued that overcoming certain bottlenecks, primarily related to credit, was essential if Brazil were to capture a sizable market share. This document concluded that global beef markets were buoyant and would continue to expand as national and international demand increased, a tendency that was particularly strong in the early 1960s.

Finally, Brazil was seen as an appropriate area for the transference of the Australian pasture technologies. If the conditions of long-term credit and better grass varieties were met, FAO pointed out that Brazil could become one of the premier beef exporters. This influential document frequently underlay the great push toward ranching throughout Latin America in the 1960s (see, for example, Parsons 1976), the precise period when policy for the Amazon was being developed. Various international agencies such as the World Bank, which made up the "cattle mafia," were able to argue that with the proper technology and better credit lines, livestock represented an excellent investment for development. As a consequence, during the mid to late 1960s, financial resources poured into livestock projects.

For many years, World Bank loans had supported livestock development projects on a relatively small scale. From 1948 to 1960, 4 percent, and from 1960 to 1965, 7 percent of all loans went into the livestock sector. Between 1966 and 1970 this allocation jumped to 21 percent. In the years 1959 to 1973, a total of sixty-three loan projects were approved involving 839.2 million dollars, plus 1,004 million in counterpart funds. For the period of 1974 to 1980, the World Bank planned on seventy loan projects involving some 1.4 billion dollars of which 63 percent was to go to Latin America. Thus, the World Bank was to lend in seven years more than it had spent during the previous fifteen years on beef production.

The InterAmerican Development Bank statistics reveal the same general trends as those of the World Bank. The amount of livestock loans authorized during 1971 to 1976 increased in the aggregate by 120 percent, while for agriculture as a whole they increased by only 38 percent (IADB Annual Reports).

The total direct livestock support given by the World Bank and the IADB in the late 1960s and the 1970s, not including general infrastructure loans, was about 1.3 billion dollars. Indirect and counterpart funds provided an additional five to seven billion dollars. To estimate private foreign and domestic investments in the beef cattle system is virtually impossible, but at least a billion dollars has been invested in the SUDAM Amazon projects alone. Feder (1979) suggests that public and private investment in cattle ranching development is minimally fifteen billion dollars. This does not include operating capital.

The international investment picture coincided very well with Brazil's own development ambitions and dovetailed with Brazil's geopolitical and balance-of-payments concerns. It was against the backdrop of these internal and international pressures that, after several trips to the Amazon, General Castello Branco laid the groundwork for a program of legislation that was to become known as "Operation Amazonia."

Operation Amazonia

In late 1965 General Castello Branco began what he described as a new era in planning that would set the tone of regional development in Amazonia. He emphasized that planning would take place in an ambience where technical considerations would take precedence over cliental interests that had dominated the previous planning agency, SPVEA. He stressed greater efficiency in planning and emphasized the enhanced role of private enterprise in regional development. The government would provide infrastructure and general funding for development, while the actual task of regional occupation would be carried out by the entrepreneurs.

The fundamental legislation for Operation Amazonia was law

5.1744 (October 1966), which provided fiscal incentives by stipulating that 50 percent of a corporation's tax liability could be invested in Amazonian development projects, essentially permitting taxes to become venture capital. The projects could be either new ones or expansions of existing enterprises. Since several southern Brazilian land magnates already had substantial land investments in the Amazon, this was an attractive means for valorizing existing holdings.

To enterprises already established in 1966, the law provided exemptions of 50 percent of the taxes owed for twelve years; for projects implanted prior to 1972, it provided for exemptions of up to 100 percent. Qualifying firms were permitted to import machinery and equipment duty free and were exempted from export duties for regional products (for example, timber). The states of the region provided their own incentives and inducements (usually land concessions), while international lending institutions such as the InterAmerican Development Bank made special agricultural development credit available for Amazonia (Pompermayer 1979). These incentives differed from previous development funds in the magnitude of resources but more importantly in that land acquisition could be stipulated as part of the development costs.

Also encouraging to the private sector was FIDAM (Fundo para Desenvolvimento da Amazônia), which was to receive one percent of federal tax revenues, proceeds of BASA securities, and fiscal incentive funds not applied to specific projects (Mahar 1979). These would be invested by BASA in research and various private firms. Through such incentives, the federal government would supply 75 percent of the investment capital needed for the enterprises.

The new incentive provisions also raised the debt ceiling from 50 to 75 percent of capital costs and made grace periods more generous. Foreign corporations were, for the first time, made eligible for loans and tax concessions. (Although foreign investment in Amazonia is often discussed [Kohlhepp 1978, Davis 1977, Ianni 1978], the magnitude of foreign investment in Amazonia is comparatively low compared to Brazilian national investment. Evans [1979] has aptly pointed out that the foreign investor is a poor candidate for the entrepreneurial role when information is low. Further, foreign investment in Brazil was characterized during the 1964–78 period by its involvement in the industrial sector rather than agriculture.)

The combination of fiscal incentives and other credit lines re-

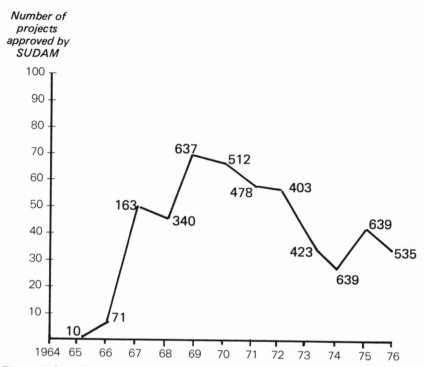

Fig. 1. Value of fiscal incentives to livestock investments, 1965–76 (in millions of 1976 cruzeiros).

sulted in an explosion of ranching in Amazonia. The number of SUDAM projects approved after 1964 and the level of SUDAM investments is presented in Figure 1. The peak investment period was 1967–72 as investors began to implant projects prior to the 1972 cutoff date for the twelve-year tax holiday. During these five years SUDAM approved some 368 new projects. By 1978, 503 cattle projects had been approved; of these, 335 were new and 168 were reorganizations (*reformulações*) or expansions (*ampliações*) of existing SUDAM projects. By 1978 about one billion dollars of SUDAM funds had been invested in these ranches, or on the order of 2.7 million dollars per ranch in direct investment. Other loans made to these ranches represented another subsidy that is almost impossible to assess.

Throughout the 1960s, livestock production was publicized as the most promising investment to be made in the region. As the president of BASA, de Lamartine-Nogueira (1969), put it: "Ranching . . . is an activity that has all the necessary conditions to be transformed into a dynamic sector of the northern economy . . . the fiscal incentives and road construction have generated a remarkable preference for livestock, and for this reason, a new era in the sector is opened."

Not only was there a marked preference for ranching, but also a bias toward certain regions: northern Mato Grosso, southern Pará, and northern Goiás. The extraordinary fiscal incentives and the (seemingly) relatively low risk associated with ranching created an unparalleled opportunity for gaining control of land. As Mahar (1979) has shown, investment in crop production in the Northeast (where incentives were also available) was comparatively risky, as is most crop production in the north. But if land values increase, then the desire for investment becomes understandable because land tends to hold value in inflationary economies. This was certainly the case in Brazil throughout the 1960s and 1970s. Infrastructural development in an area like the Amazon also increases the value of land. Incentives that allowed the acquisition of land as part of the development costs created a situation in which, as Mahar (1979) has noted, the value of Amazonian land increased at 100 percent per year in real terms (see Figure 2). Speculation was driven in part by the hope of future production returns or the future value of resources. But land, and its modification by ranching, became the primary vehicle for capturing enormous state subsidies.

The nature of land in the Amazonian economy began to change in a fundamental way. Land itself, not its product, became a commodity, since even lands whose productivity was declining were increasing in value because of this speculation. What became crucial at this juncture was the emphasis on the exchange rather than the use value of lands.

In the late 1960s, criticism of the expansion of corporate livestock operations was mounting, both for ecological and social reasons. Partly because the laws were so obviously biased in favor of large holders, and partly because of the pronounced drought in the Brazilian northeast, President Médici in 1970 adopted a new direction for Amazon policy.

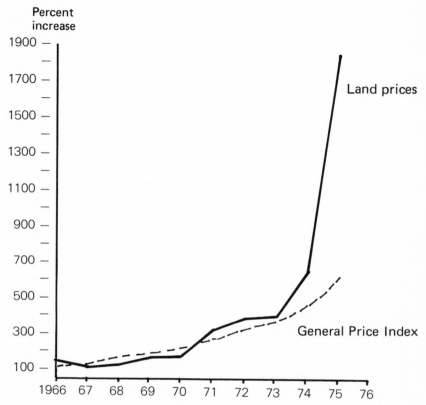

Fig. 2. Average prices of Amazonian pastureland, 1966–76.

National integration program 1970–74

Possible motives for changing the policy's emphasis from large- to small-scale holders are discussed in other sources (e.g., Pompermayer 1979, Mahar 1979, Wood and Schmink 1979, Bunker 1979, Smith 1976). The New Integration Program (PIN) shifted the focus of Amazonian occupation from the purely economic to a social perspective. Instead of "Amazonia is your best business," it was to be "O Homen é a meta" ("Man is the goal"). From the misery of the drought-wracked Northeast, men without lands would be linked via the Transamazon Highway and other infrastructural programs to the lands without men in Amazonia. A more cynical

version of the new programs saw the Transamazon Highway linking poverty and misery. The new policies expressed in PND I (the
first National Development Plan) reiterated the themes of the agricultural frontiers as escape valves for surplus population, the
importance of national security, and the necessity of national
integration.

The goals of the entrepreneurs, and of advocates of small-scale
Amazonian occupation, came into sharp conflict. Inter-ministerial
rivalry between SUDAM (which had not retreated from its position
that corporate development was the best means of Amazonian occupation) and INCRA and the Ministry of the Interior became quite
severe, as Pompermayer (1979) has documented (see also Martins
in this volume). During the 1970–74 period, INCRA, due to its contradictory roles, pressures from a variety of interest groups, inter-
agency rivalry, and its advocacy of social occupation, came under
sharp attack (Bunker 1979, Pompermayer 1979). By 1974, as the
ecological and production problems of the Transamazon became
acute (Smith 1976, Moran 1981), the Association of Amazonian
Entrepreneurs was able to reassert in policy its position that large-
scale occupation was the only rational means of occupying the region (see Pompermayer in this volume). The crises within INCRA
and in Amazonian policy were constantly linked to the ideas and
ideologies of social versus economic occupation. Brazil's worsen-
ing economic situation, it was argued, made social concerns a lux-
ury. The tensions became so extreme that it became necessary to
sell ten areas of public land (under INCRA control) of 50,000 hectares so that SUDAM could designate a new group of entrepreneurs
for ranching development. Reis Velloso, the minister of the Interior, traveled along the Transamazon with twenty entrepreneurs
to whom he offered land that had been reserved for colonization
and agrarian reform (Pompermayer 1979).

The program for Amazonian development,
1975–79

In August of 1973 after his junket to the Transamazon, Velloso addressed a meeting in SUDAM and articulated the policy shift that
would be formalized in PDAM I (the Amazon Development Plan):
"Until now, the Transamazon has emphasized colonization, but
the necessity of avoiding predatory occupation with consequent
deforestation and of promoting ecological equilibrium leads us to
invite large enterprises to assume the tasks of developing the re-

gion." In the same document, Velloso offered up another 2.5 million hectares of colonization lands for private investment.

SUDAM and MINTER followed these pronouncements with a series of documents criticizing the functioning of INCRA and the idea of solving the problems of the Northeast by transferring them to the Amazon. Further, the colonization programs had generated a great deal of spontaneous migration (Aragon 1978). The migrants were viewed as agriculturally ignorant: "[They] carry out the only and dangerous activity they can undertake: deforestation and the exhaustion of soil for subsistence agriculture" (SUDAM 1974), a charge that could just as easily have been made against ranching enterprises. These ideas were translated into policy with the publication of PDAM I.

This document, and the PDN II (the second National Development Program), prefaced the Amazonian sections by pointing out that cattle had acquired special importance in the region during the preceding decade as a function of the expansion of global markets for beef, although at the time of this pronouncement global beef markets were quite depressed. The reports also indicated that sixty million hectares of Amazonia were apt for ranching at stocking rates of about one agricultural unit per hectare. It was further argued that Amazonia's meat production had to be oriented to external markets, whose demand would rapidly surpass the global supply (MINTER 1975).

With the caveat that ranching would be best developed in the mata fina of southern Pará and Mato Grosso and in some cerrado regions, areas where large-scale ranches already predominated, ranching was reinstated as the main development trajectory. The re-emphasis on cattle was associated with the perception that cattle actually improved soil nutrients and represented an environmentally sound alternative to other agricultural enterprises. The question of the environmental effects of converting forest to pasture, particularly in reference to soil resources, is discussed in the next section.

Conversion of forest to pasture: development or destruction

Opinions have differed substantially among scientists who have investigated the effects on soils in the Latin American tropics of the conversion of forests to grassland and the subsequent performance of those pastures. Goodland (1980) has argued that ranching represents the worst of all conceivable land-use alternatives for Amazonian development since it causes high ecosystem losses and creates only short-term profits and low employment potential. Myers (1980), Fearnside (1978), and others have argued, for a variety of reasons, that ranching is a relatively unstable and unproductive land use for the region. Others, notably Serrão et al. (1979), Alvim (1980), and Falesi (1976) disagree. Central to the forest-to-pasture conversion controversy is a widely cited study by EMBRAPA (Empresa Brasiliera de Pesquisa Agropecuária, the research arm of the Ministry of Agriculture).

The EMBRAPA study (Falesi 1976) maintains that conversion of forest to pasture improves soil properties, particularly calcium, magnesium, and pH. While it found increases in phosphorus to be transitory, pasture response to phosphorus applications was quite positive even if economically questionable. These results were frequently used by the Ministry of the Interior in policy conflicts to help undermine the credibility of small-scale agricultural holdings. Peasant agriculturalists were perceived as ecologically damaging, while large-scale ranchers were portrayed as environmentally rational.

Based on the EMBRAPA results, it was suggested that "the formation of pastures on low fertility soils is a rational and economic means by which to rationalize and increase the value of extensive areas" (Falesi 1976). Serrão et al. (1979) argued that "the subsequent substitution of pasture with perennial crops would require only a small amount of phosphorus fertilizer for development . . . due to the favorable conditions of the majority of soils components after a long period under pasture." In the international development literature, Cochrane and Sanchez (1982) indicated that "the data suggest a remarkable degree of nutrient cycling and maintenance of soil fertility under pasture. . . . These data are encouraging because they indicate a very high beef production potential with minimum inputs."

In spite of such optimism, the roughly ten million hectares of land converted from forest to pasture do not appear to be particularly stable. Estimates of the area of severely degraded pasture range from 15 percent (Toledo and Serrão 1982) to 50 percent (Tardin et al. 1977, Hecht 1982). The major factors involved in pasture land degradation include soil nutrient changes, compaction, and weed invasion.

In the next section, I present data on soil changes in the major cattle areas in eastern Amazonia, comparing more recent research with the EMBRAPA study. Methodological issues and the differences between the studies are presented in more detail elsewhere (Hecht 1982). The most important difference, however, is that of sample size. The EMBRAPA study was based on five samples per age class, while this study involves eighty samples per age class of pasture.

Results of conversion studies

Effect on soil pH.—When forests are felled and burned, an increase in pH occurs as the bases held in the biomass are transferred to soils, regardless of the land use (Nye and Greenland 1960, Sanchez 1976). As Figure 3 shows, there are substantial increases in the soil pH for the sites examined in the EMBRAPA study. By contrast the clay loam oxisol showed a rise of only one pH unit. While the ranges of pH in the clay loam included some values as high as those of the other sites, the pH increases become less dramatic as the number of samples increases. This result is corroborated in other data (presented in Sanchez 1976) analyzing soil changes before and after deforestation on sixty sites. These samples were analyzed at the EMBRAPA laboratories. An interesting aspect of the pH data is that the liming effect is maintained through time. Cochrane and Sanchez (1982) and Toledo and Serrão (1982) believe that efficient nutrient cycling on the part of the grasses is responsible for the persistence of the pH improvement. While Tietzel and Bruce (1972) have shown in Australia that *Panicum maximum* (the most widely planted grass species in the Amazon) is a reasonably effective cycler of calcium, magnesium, and potassium, an alternative interpretation also merits consideration. When forests are cut and burned to form pasture, only about 20 percent of the slash actually combusts. Since 80 percent of the total ecosystem calcium, magnesium, and potassium are stored in tree boles, their gradual decay after cutting could supply these elements at a rate that could maintain the pH. Since the maintenance of pH is recorded for other agricultural systems after forest conversion (Bandy and Sanchez 1981), it may be that cycling is less important than decay of the slash. This hypothesis, of course, does not exclude the possibility of nutrient cycling by the grasses.

Soil calcium and magnesium.—Closely associated with the increase in pH are additions of calcium and magnesium to soil. The rise in these elements (and their variability) is most pro-

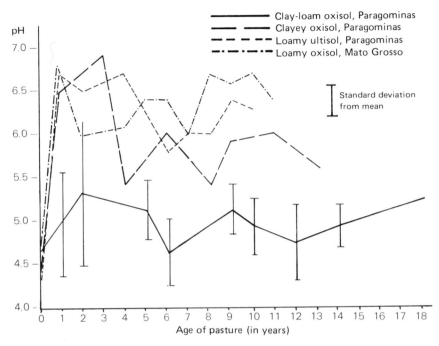

Fig. 3. Changes in pH after conversion from forest to pasture.

nounced in the years immediately following clearing. Since rain forests store over one ton each of calcium and magnesium per hectare (Klinge, Brunig, and Fittkau 1975) and the ash additions after burning supply immediately at least 100 kg of calcium (Seubert, Sanchez, and Valverde 1977), the rise in calcium and magnesium after conversion is not surprising.

The EMBRAPA data indicate major increases in calcium and magnesium in the clayey oxisol (see Figure 4), but these decline after five years and oscillate around 2 meq/100 gms. The other sites show modest gains and the tendency to equilibrate around a fairly low value. The clay loam oxisol shows less substantial increases and a decline to about one meq/100 gm and a relative stabilization at this value. It is worth pointing out that these calcium and magnesium values for all soils are very low, placing them at the lowest range for South American soils (Cochrane and Sanchez 1982). While soils may be improved in terms of calcium and magnesium contents, in fact the overall level of these elements is be-

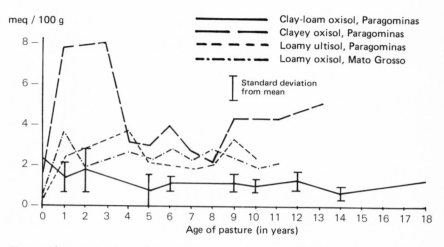

Fig. 4. Changes in Ca and Mg after conversion from forest to pasture.

low the level critical for pasture production (Coordenadoria de Assistência Técnica Integral 1974).

Soil potassium.—Potassium is a monovalent cation that is stored mainly in vegetation in tropical ecosystems; it cycles quickly, and is quite vulnerable to leaching. In general more than one ton of potassium per hectare is stored in the forest biomass. Due to the mobility of this element, potassium values are quite erratic throughout the pasture sequence (see Figure 5) reflecting periodic burning, weed invasion, and other management activities. The coefficient of variation of this element is so high however, that there is no statistical significance between the potassium values of forest and pasture (Hecht 1982). Soil improvement of potassium after conversion is thus open to question. Deficiencies of this element have been documented for pastures in Paragominas, Brazil (Koster, Khan, and Bossert 1977).

The high value for potassium in the Mato Grosso oxisol probably reflects an initially high potassium level as well as a greater frequency of palms, both in the native vegetation and in the pasture weed invaders. Palms have a relatively high level of potassium in their leaves (Silva 1978).

Phosphorous levels in soil.—The most crucial element for pasture production in Amazonia is phosphorus (Toledo and Serrão 1982), and ten ppm is usually considered the minimum value for

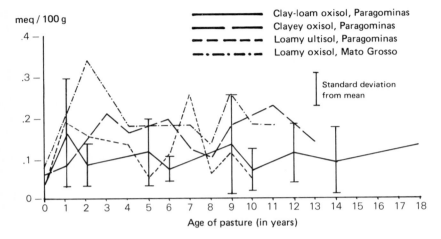

Fig. 5. Changes in K after conversion from forest to pasture.

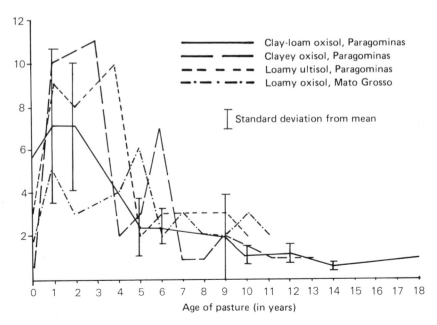

Fig. 6. Changes in P after conversion from forest to pasture.

sustained production of pastures. After forest conversion, phosphorus values increase dramatically (see Figure 6), but after the fifth year they tend to decline continuously to a level of about one ppm.

The decline of phosphorus has been identified by some researchers as the main reason for pasture instability in Amazonia (Serrão et al. 1979). Drastic drops in pasture productivity, which often result in pasture abandonment, have been attributed to the high demand of *Panicum* for phosphorus coupled with losses due to (1) erosion and animal export and (2) the competition from weeds adapted to low phosphorus levels. Although the grass responds well to fertilization (Serrão et al. 1979), the high transportation, application, and opportunity costs as well as the erratic availability of phosphorus make widespread fertilization uneconomical at this time.

Soil nitrogen.—Soil nitrogen values reflect both nitrogen accumulating activities like nitrogen fixation and additions from the atmosphere and from organic matter decay as well as nitrogen decreasing activities like volatization, denitrification, leaching, erosion, and plant uptake. Many of these processes are mediated by the biota, and the rates of loss and addition are affected by environmental factors (pH, temperature, soil moisture). Nitrogen is an element that can vary strongly from site to site. As Figure 7 suggests, the Paragominas ultisol shows a slight initial increase and a subsequent equilibration, indicating that differences between forest and pasture nitrogen soil storage are insignificant. In the clay loam oxisol, soil nitrogen decreases, but when analyzed through multiple range tests, pasture soils are not significantly different from forest soils except in the oldest pastures and during the first year after clearing (Hecht 1982).

The heavy clay oxisols from Paragominas and Mato Grosso both show nitrogen declines although the Paragominas samples are decidedly more erratic. The high nitrogen values in year thirteen in the Paragominas heavy clay soil may reflect nitrogen fixing by native weedy legumes. On the other hand, the Mato Grosso site nitrogen levels decline by 50 percent after conversion.

Organic carbon in soil.—Soil carbon levels often drop with burning, but they can increase if there is an addition of fine charcoal, which probably occurred in clay loam and loamy oxisols, and the loamy ultisol (Figure 8). Levels of carbon can increase due to slash decomposition, organic matter additions from the grass, and

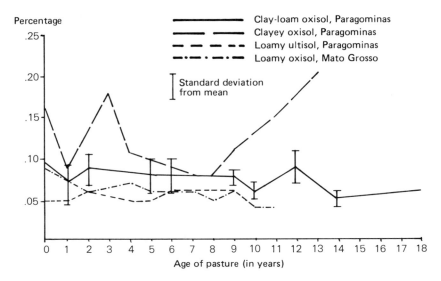

Fig. 7. Changes in N after conversion from forest to pasture.

heavy weed invasion, but such gains can be short-lived. In the
Mato Grosso oxisol and Paragominas ultisol, carbon declined after
clearing. In the Mato Grosso site the value dropped to 50 percent
of the forest level.

Summary of soil findings.—The effect of conversion of forest
to pasture on soil chemical properties can be described as relatively neutral for nitrogen and potassium, negative for phosphorus
and carbon, and mildly positive for calcium, magnesium, and pH,
particularly in the first years after clearing. The widely cited dramatic increases in these elements after conversion seem to be
moderated when larger sample sizes are used. In any case, the absolute levels of calcium and magnesium are low to marginal for
pasture production. Soil nutrients during the first five years are adequate for animal stocking rates of one animal unit per hectare but
drop to .25 a.u. per hectare after five or six years. This is due not
only to soil chemical changes but also soil compaction and weed
invasion.

Other factors affecting pasture productivity.—Soil physical
changes also affect productivity. For example, soil bulk densities
that double with increasing pasture age reduce infiltration that influences sheet and other types of erosion.

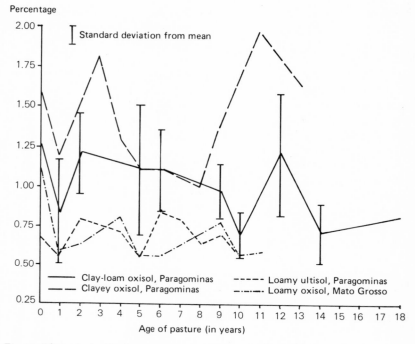

Fig. 8. Changes in C after conversion from forest to pasture.

Amazonian pastures are rapidly invaded by shrubby weeds that reduce pasture productivity by competing with forage grasses for nutrients and water. Although many weed species are in fact browsed by animals, weed control is expensive and absorbs about 20 percent of a ranch's operating cost. Ranches that did not receive fiscal incentives are squeezed between declining productivity and escalating weed and infrastructure repair costs. Not surprisingly, when livestock operations pass the five-year mark, they are often repossessed or sold. By 1978, about 85 percent of the ranches in Paragominas had failed, according to the director of the Pará state cattlemen's cooperative.

Conclusions: accumulation and environmental decay

Even as pasture productivity declined, for the reasons mentioned, the value of pasture land increased due to the infrastructure development, mineral resource potential, and the generous fiscal incentives and sweetheart loans made available to investors. The creation of a land market in Amazonia, where previously none had existed, generated an extraordinary speculative boom that held sway throughout the 1960s and 1970s. What is essential here is that the exchange value of the land itself was far higher in this speculative context than was the exchange value of any commodities it could produce. Entrepreneurs depended for profits not on the annual productivity of the land but on the rate of return to investment.

Whether ranching achieved many of its hoped-for results is quite dubious and requires a more extensive analysis than can be presented here (see Mahar 1979, Pompermayer 1979, Hecht 1982). However, pastureland created from forests is expensive to implant and to maintain, and the value of the animal product does not recompense its production costs even with large subsidies (Hecht 1982).

Declining pasture productivity was not the only consequence of converting forest to pasture. Ranching expansion played a key role in marginalizing small landholders as land increasingly came under the control of large estates. Areas where ranching dominated, such as the south of Pará and the north of Mato Grosso, were characterized by land distributions where 6.7 percent of the landholders controlled fully 85 percent of the private sector lands, while almost 70 percent of the remaining farms owned merely 6 percent of the area. Along the Belém-Brasília highway, one of the earliest upland cattle ranching areas, Gini coefficients for landowning increased from 0.66 to 0.77 in the years between 1967 and 1975 (Santos 1979), indicating extreme concentration. Such marginalization produced a great deal of land conflict, as other authors in this volume have discussed (see Martins).

I would like to return now to the issues raised in earlier sections of this article where I discussed the main models used to explain land degradation in the humid tropics. I will describe why each of these models does not adequately explain the dynamics of environmental deterioration in the eastern Amazon.

The Malthusian perspective, as it has been applied to Amazonia, generally asserts that shifting cultivation, while it may be ecologically sound at low human population densities, becomes environmentally destructive when population increases reduce the land area per person ratios, leading to shortening of fallow times so that land cannot recover its production potential after cropping. Soil fertility declines from overuse, weeds hamper crop production, and erosion results.

There is no question that much of the shifting cultivation observable in eastern Amazonia along roads and in colonization areas follows such a pattern of land deterioration, but this phenomenon is unrelated to human population numbers or physical availability of land. Roughly ten million people live in the Brazilian Amazon, a region that encompasses about 60 percent of the Brazilian national territory. The situation is instead due to the extraordinary maldistribution of land, as the figures cited in earlier paragraphs show. The problems of agricultural land use in eastern Amazonia that are caused by shortened fallow times must be understood as essentially distributional rather than demographic. There is no shortage of arable land in Amazonia.

Other theories used to explain environmental degradation in tropical agriculture center on the role of export crop production. There are two main approaches, one based on analysis of the production process, the other focused on the role of the state. These models of export crop production leading to environmental decay can certainly inform an understanding of the dynamics of resource degradation in Amazonia even though they do not constitute a complete analysis. It is important to recognize that Amazonian beef is not an export product in the usual sense of the term. Although Amazonian development policy stated that "beef [from] Amazonia should be oriented fundamentally toward export markets" (MINTER 1975), in fact cattle were only occasionally exported to Surinam (via boats from Marajó) and walked or trucked in small numbers across the Venezuelan border. Indeed, the federation of exporters of the state of Pará reported that, in the first years of their records, beef generated only $44,000 compared to the $33,000,000 of export revenues from Brazil nuts (FIP 1977). Amazonia itself remains a net meat importer. Roughly 40 percent of the animals slaughtered in the Pará abattoirs in the late 1970s were trucked from Goiás. Thus, strictly speaking, Amazonian beef cannot be considered an export commodity in spite of hopes to the contrary. The first export-oriented explanatory model argues that development takes place under the discipline of international commodity prices, which demand that exports be produced as intensively and efficiently as possible. Therefore, agronomic technologies with high productivities are employed; they are generally mechanized, and imply the use of large amounts of fertilizers, pesticides and herbicides, and thus are very capital intensive. These methods can generate direct environmental effects such as compaction and indirect effects such as water contamination and poisoning of fauna.

If the relationship of capital investment to employment and output is analyzed for eastern Amazonia, cattle ranching is more capital intensive than is industry per job created or per unit of output (Mahar 1979, Hecht 1982). Given the high levels of capital investment, the first export paradigm—a highly technified production process—might appear to apply to the eastern Amazon area, particularly since the use of mechanical clearing is fairly widespread and becoming more so. Forest conversion to agriculture and pasture with machinery in the humid tropics has been shown to undermine the productivity of soil resources and to reduce yields (Seubert et al. 1977). Mechanical deforestation is also substantially more expensive than is manual (Toledo and Serrão 1982). I have argued elsewhere (Hecht 1982) that mechanical clearing on large ranches is related to the desire to minimize the use of labor on ranches for a variety of reasons, including public health, fear of squatters and of violence, and the difficulty of controlling huge work teams. The capital intensiveness of eastern Amazonian cattle operations is not reflected in the actual process of animal production, since the technologies are quite primitive, and require few laborers and the land is less costly than pasture land in, for example, São Paulo. What makes cattle ranching in Amazonia capital intensive are the very high entry barriers and infrastructure costs, not expenditures on production technology per se.

The second model of the role of export production concludes that state subsidies (such as tax credits) and high international commodity prices make it possible for landowners to make profits in spite of inefficient production organization and unsound land practices. This model has been applied to Central American livestock (Nations 1980). Pasture productivity in Central America declined because of poor management and ecological reasons, but not so much that land was put completely out of production. Animals can still be stocked in very low numbers while farmers expand grasslands into new areas to produce for the international demand.

This explanatory model contains some persuasive arguments, since the role of tax incentives and the patterns of land distribution in Amazonia and Central America are similar. But several differences nevertheless make the two areas incommensurable. First, as noted, Amazonian beef is not an export commodity. Moreover, the price of beef is controlled in Brazil, making livestock profitability marginal even under the best of circumstances (Lattimore and Schuh 1979). Livestock production in the Amazon is far more expensive than in other areas of the country (*O Globo*, January 5, 1980) and is usually not profitable on improved pastures even with extensive subsidies. Finally, Amazonian pastures generally go completely out of production within ten years, a crucial difference between the Amazonian and Central American situations.

A third model I discussed, the "inappropriate technology" model, argues that environmental problems result when well-intentioned planners mistakenly recommend technologies that for cultural or ecological reasons generate resource degradation. The difficulties that occur are perceived as simple technological problems that can be resolved with a "technological fix." Such a point of view has some historical validity in eastern Amazonia: the pasture species initially used there were not well adapted to the low soil fertility levels, and subsequently introduced species, though more tolerant of the soil conditions, have been bothered by insect attack. But the problem may defy solution by the implantation of better cultivars since the dynamics of the pasture ecosystem may be inappropriate to the region. The central policy question is why certain land uses and technologies are promoted over alternative ones. Ranching, as I have demonstrated, served important political and ideological functions—and these functions, not the availability of suitable varieties of *Panicum*, are what motivate the promotion of pasture ecosystems for Amazonia despite their instability.

The environmental degradation associated with pasture development in eastern Amazonia is best understood as a consequence of the role of land in inflationary economies, the traditional function of land as a means of acquiring large areas cheaply, the stimulating effect of the physical opening of the agricultural frontiers on certain industrial sectors of the economy, and the role of large government subsidies in the creation of land markets and speculation in the Brazilian Amazon. The expansion of ranching through tax breaks, fiscal incentives, and road development generated enormous untaxed capital gains for certain groups. Acquisition of land was the vehicle for capturing direct and indirect state subsidies. The productivity of the land became secondary because the land itself was the commodity (see Sawyer in this volume). Due to the peculiarities of state subsidies, a radical disjuncture between the value of land for production, and its value for exchange was created. If the productivity of the land itself is of low importance, cautious land management becomes irrelevant and environmental degradation is the inevitable result.

References Cited

Alvim, P.T.
  1978   Perspectivas de Produção Agrícola na Região Amazônica. *Interciencia* 3:243–51.
  1980   Agricultural Production Potential of the Amazon Region. In *Land, People and Planning in Contemporary Amazonia*. F. Barbira-Scazzocchio, ed. Cambridge: Center for Latin American Studies, Cambridge University Press.
Aragón, L.
  1978   Migration to Northern Goiás. Ph.D. dissertation, Michigan State University.
Bacha, E.L.
  1977   Issues and Evidence on Recent Brazilian Economic Growth. *World Development* 5(2):47–67.
Bandy, D. and P.A. Sanchez
  1981   Continuous Crop Production on Acid Soils in the Peruvian Amazon. Paper presented at Workshop Management of Low Fertility Acid Soils, University of Surinam, Paramaribo, Surinam.
Belassa, B.
  1979   Incentive Policies in Brazil. *World Development* 7(2): 1023–42.
Bergsman, J.
  1970   *Brazil's Industrialization and Trade Policy*. New York: Oxford University Press.
Bunker, S.
  1979   Power Structures and Exchange Between Government Agencies in the Expansion of the Agricultural Sector in Pará. *Studies in Comparative and International Development* 14(1): 56–76.
Cochrane, T. and Sanchez, P.A.
  1982   Land Resources of the Amazon Basin. In *Amazonia: Agriculture and Land Use Research*. S.B. Hecht, ed. Pp. 137–211. Cali, Colombia: CIAT.

Coordenadoria de Assistência Técnica Integral
1974   Normas Para Manejo de Pastagens. Boletim Técnico 81, Belém, Brazil.
Davis, S.
1977   *Victims of the Miracle.* Cambridge: Cambridge University Press.
Evans, Peter
1979   *Dependent Development: The Alliance of Multinationals, the State, and Local Capital in Brazil.* Princeton: Princeton University Press.
Falesi, I.
1976   Ecosistema de Pastagem Cultivada na Amazônia Brasileira. Boletim Técnico 1. CPATU. Belém, Pará: EMBRAPA.
FAO/ECLA (United Nations Food and Agricultural Organization/Economic Commission on Latin America)
1964   *Livestock in Latin America.* Rome:FAO.
Fearnside, P.
1978   Estimation of Carrying Capacity for Human Populations in a Part of the Transamazon Highway Colonization Area of Brazil. Ph.D. dissertation, University of Michigan.
Feder, E.
1979   Lean Cows, Fat Ranchers, a Study of the Mexican Beef Industry. Manuscript. Berlin.
FIP (Federação de Indústrias do Pará)
1977   Pará Exportação. Belém: FIP.
Fishlow, A.
1973   Brazilian Size Distribution of Income. *American Economic Review* 62(2):391–402.
Foweraker, J.
1981   *The Struggle for Land: A Political Economy of the Pioneer Frontier in Brazil, 1930 to the Present.* London: Cambridge University Press.
Gentry, A. and J. López-Parodi
1980   Deforestation and Increased Flooding in the Upper Amazon. *Science* 210:1354–56.
O Globo
1980   January 5.
Gomez-Pompa, A., Vasques-Yanes, C. and Guevara, S.
1972   The Tropical Rain Forest: A Non-renewable Resource. *Science* 177:762–65.
Goodland, R.
1980   Environmental Ranking of Development Projects in Brazil. *Environmental Conservation* (7)1:9–25.
Goodland, R. and Irwin, H.

1975   *Amazon Jungle: Green Hell to Red Desert?* Amsterdam: Elsevier.

Hecht, S.B.
1982   Cattle Ranching in the Brazilian Amazon: Evaluation of a Development Strategy. Ph.D. dissertation, University of California, Berkeley.

Ianni, O.
1978   A Luta Pela Terra. Petrópolis: Vozes.

InterAmerican Development Bank (IADB)
1971–1976   Annual Reports. Washington, D.C.:IADB.

Klinge, H. Rodrigues, E. Brunig and E.J. Fittkau
1975   Biomass and Structure in a Central Amazonian Rainforest. In *Tropical Ecological Systems*. F. Golley and E. Medina, eds. Pp. 115–22. New York: Springer Verlag.

Knight, P.T.
1971   *Brazilian Agriculture, Technology, and Trade*. New York: Praeger.

Kohlhepp, G.
1978   Erschliessung und Wirtschaftliche Inwertsetzung Amazoniens. Entwicklungsstrategien Braślianischer Planungsfrolitik und Privater Unfernehmen. *Geografische Rundschau* 30(1):2–13.

Koster, H., E.J. Kahn, and R. Bossert
1977   Programa e Resultados Preliminários dos Estudos de Pastagems na Região de Paragominas Pará, e o Nordeste de Mato Grosso. Belém: SUDAM/IRI.

Lamartine-Nogueira, F. de
1969   A Agropecuária e o Processo de Desenvolvimento da Amazônia. Belém: BASA/MINTER.

Lattimore, R.G. and G.E. Schuh
1979   Endogenous Policy Determination: The Case of the Brazilian Beef Sector. *Canadian Journal of Ag. Econ.* 27(2): 1–16.

Leff, N.H.
1967   Export Stagnation and Autarkic Development in Brazil. *Quart. Jour. Econ.* May:286–301.

Mahar, D.J.
1979   *Frontier Development Policy in Brazil: A Study of Amazonia*. New York: Praeger.

Malan, P.S., and R. Bonelli
1977   The Brazilian Economy in the 70's: Old and New Development. *World Development* 5(1/2):19–37.

Martine, G.
1982   Expansão e Retração de Emprego na Fronteira Agrícola. In

Expansão de Fronteira Agrícola. N. Gligo and C. Mueller, eds. Brasília: Univ. de Brasília.

MINTER (Brazil, Ministério do Interior)
1975   *Programa Nacional de Desenvolvimento.* Brasília: MINTER.

Molion, L.C.
1975   A Climatic Study of the Energy and Moisture Fluxes of the Amazonas Basin With Considerations of Deforestation Effects. Ph.D. dissertation, University of Wisconsin.

Moore, B.
1968   *The Social Origins of Dictatorship and Democracy.* Boston: Beacon Press.

Moran, E.
1981   *Developing the Amazon.* Bloomington: Indiana University Press.

Myers, N.
1980   *Conversion of Moist Tropical Forests.* Washington, D.C.: National Academy of Sciences.

Nations, J.M.
1980   Deforestation in Central America. Report to the Tinker Foundation.

Nye, P. and D. Greenland
1960   *The Soil Under Shifting Cultivation.* Farnham Royal, Bucks, England: Commonwealth Agricultural Bureau.

O'Donnell, G.
1979   *Modernization and Bureaucratic Authoritarianism.* Berkeley: University of California Press.

Parsons, J.J.
1976   Forest to Pasture: Development or Destruction? *Revista de Biologia Tropical* 24(1):121–38.

Pires, J.M. and G.T. Prance
1977   The Amazon Forest: A Natural Heritage to be Preserved. In *Extinction Is Forever.* G.T. Prance and T. Elias, eds. Bronx: New York Botanical Garden.

Pompermayer, M.J.
1979   The State and Frontier in Brazil. Ph.D. dissertation. Stanford University.

Salati, E., A. Dall' Olio, E. Matsui, and S.R. Gat
1979   Recycling of Water in the Amazon Basin: An Isotope Study. *Water Resources Research* 15(5):1250–58.

Sanchez, P.A.
1976   *Properties and Management of Tropical Soils.* New York: Wiley Interscience.

Santos, R.
1979   Sistema de Propriedade e Relações de Trabalho no Meio Rural Paraense. In *Amazônia: Desenvolvimento e Oc-*

cupação. Monteiro de Costa, ed. Rio de Janeiro: IPEA/
INPES.

Sawyer, D.
1979   Peasants and Capitalism on the Amazonian Frontier.
            Ph.D. dissertation. Harvard University.
Schmink, M.
1982   Land Conflicts in Amazonia. *American Ethnologist* 9:2
            (May): 341–57.
Serrão, A., I. Falesi, J.B. Vega, and J.F. Teixeira
1979   Productivity of Cultivated Pastures on Low Fertility Soils
            of the Brazilian Amazon. In *Pasture Production in Acid
            Soils of the Tropics*. P.A. Sanchez and L.E. Tergas, eds.
            Cali, Colombia: CIAT.
Seubert, C.E., P.A. Sanchez, and C. Valverde
1977   Effects of Land Clearing Methods on the Soil Properties
            and Crop Performances on an Ultisol of the Amazon
            Jungle of Peru. *Tropical Agriculture* 54:307–21.
Silva, L.F.
1978   *Influência do Manejo de un Ecosistema nas Proprie-
            dades Edáficas dos Oxisolos de Tabuleiro*. Itabuna, Bahia:
            CEPLAC.
Smith, N.J.
1976   The Transamazon Highway: A Cultural and Ecological
            Analysis of Settlement in the Humid Tropics. Ph.D. dis-
            sertation, University of California, Berkeley.
Stepan, A.
1968   *The Military in Power*. Princeton: Princeton University
            Press.
1973   *Authoritarian Brazil*. Princeton: Princeton University
            Press.
Superintendência de Desenvolvimento da Amazônia (SUDAM)
1974   *O Problema da Ocupação Econômica da Terra*. Belém:
            SUDAM.
Tardin, A.T., A. dos Santos, E.M. Morães-Novo, and F.L. Toledo
1977   Relatório dos Atividades do Projeto SUDAM/INPE No.
            1034 NTE. São José dos Campos, Brazil: INPE.
Tardin, A.T., et al
1979   Levantamento de Áreas de Desmatamento na Amazônia
            Legal Através de Imagens do Satélite LANDSAT. INPE Re-
            port No. 411-NTE/142. São José dos Campos, Brazil: INPE.
Taylor, L., E. Bacha, E. Cardoso, F. Lysy
1980   *Models of Growth and Distribution for Brazil*. New
            York: Oxford University Press.
Tietzel, J. and R. Bruce
1972   Fertility of Pasture Soils in the Wet Tropical Coast of

Queensland. *Australian Journal of Experimental Agriculture and Animal Husbandry* 12:49–54.

Todaro, M.

1977   *Economic Development in the Third World.* London: Longman.

Toledo, J. and A. Serrão

1982   Pasture and Animal Production in Amazonia. In *Amazonia: Agriculture and Land Use Research.* S.B. Hecht, ed. Pp. 281–309. Cali, Colombia: CIAT.

Wood, Charles and Marianne Schmink

1979   Blaming the Victim: Small Farmer Production in an Amazon Colonization Project. *Studies in Third World Societies* 7:77–93.

State and Private Capital

PART 4

THE FOLLOWING FOUR PAPERS share a common approach to the study of frontier expansion in Amazonia; they adopt a holistic perspective to explain events on the frontier, relying on historical investigation of the overall socioeconomic and political forces that affect the nation-state. Analyses of concrete events in Amazonia are used to substantiate the authors' conceptual and theoretical contributions. The central problem they address is how the economy and polity interact in a relationship of reciprocal causation to determine the distribution of social goods. The authors examine either the economic origins of development policies and the mechanisms by which these are affected by actions of dominant economic interests or, alternatively, the role of state intervention in shaping the economy. Whichever causal direction may be assumed at a given point, these institutional realms are understood to be interrelated.

Applied to the study of the frontier, this perspective calls special attention to the role of the state as it affects, and is affected by, the conflict of interests between social classes employed in different forms of production. Observation of the most casual sort is sufficient to identify the importance of public policy in shaping the pace and the character of frontier expansion. But the concern here transcends the mere documentation of official plans promulgated by governments and goes well beyond studies that center on tracing the consequences of particular development schemes. Rather than taking the action of public institutions as given, these four studies seek to identify the pressures and counterpressures that come to bear on the mechanisms of policy formulation and administration, especially as these relate to the structure of the economy and to the interests of the ruling class. The point of departure for such analysis is a broad definition of the state and a distinct conceptualization of its character and function.

According to liberal political theory, the state is arbiter of the interests of the community in general. It is the arena of legitimate authority embodied in the rules of the political process, supported by some combination of normative consensus and the preferences of the majority of the members of society. In practical terms, research in this tradition tends to treat politics as isolated from its articulation with economic forces and narrows the scope of analysis to the government per se.

Such an approach contrasts with the philosophical outlook of the following papers, that of political economy. Political economy extends the definition of the state to include the army, the police, the judiciary, and the administrative bureaucracy. Rather than a neutral arbiter, the state is seen as a class-based apparatus that acts primarily in the interest of dominant economic groups. At the same time, the state exercises a certain degree of power that is independent of the will of the capitalist class, which is itself internally divided. This relative autonomy notwithstanding, the state is conceptualized as an entity that assures through various mechanisms (which are themselves the objects of research) the continued accumulation of private capital and which fosters the conditions necessary for the reproduction of the class structure and the asymmetry of class rule. In his study of Colombia, Camilo Domínguez reminds us that events on the frontier are not solely a function of domestic issues. The country's economy and the very actions of the state itself vis-à-vis private capital do not exist in isolation of the larger world system. The theoretical underpinnings of his analysis draw insights from the dependency school of international development. In contrast to the neoclassical economic perspective and the modernization paradigm, the nation-state is conceptualized as part of an international organization, linked by trade and capital flows, that operates to the advantage of some countries (the core, or metropoles) and to the disadvantage of others (the periphery, or satellites). In this way, his conclusions as to the role and the fate of peasant producers on the frontier in Colombia (which are consistent with many of the studies presented earlier in this volume) are interpreted in the context of the fundamental changes that have recently taken place in the Colombian economy, which, in turn, are affected by the evolution of the country's place in the international system.

At the level of the nation-state, the centralization of power under an authoritarian regime has profound consequences for the form of the interrelationships that emerge between the state and private capital. Under these circumstances the military and the administrative bureaucracy assume a degree of importance far exceeding that found in the United States and in other liberal democracies. Dominant economic groups respond by seeking direct access to the executive and to the administrative branches of government. Malori Pompermayer's detailed study of the Association of Amazonian Entrepreneurs provides clear evidence of the way in which this tendency has affected the pattern of land use in the Brazilian Amazon. By virtue of its internal organization and its access to key decisionmakers within the regime, this organization has successfully influenced public policy so as to favor cattle ranching by providing credit and fiscal incentives for this economic activity. But, as Pompermayer notes, the expansion of cattle into Amazonia cannot be attributed solely to such development policies. Other factors internal to the economy itself are also important. It is this type of analysis which gives concrete meaning to such abstract conclusions as the statement that the role of the state affects, and is affected by, the economy.

Roberto Santos offers a panoramic view of the historical changes in land tenure in Brazilian Amazonia and the forms of economic activities that have characterized the region. His particular concern is the way in which these transformations are reflected in the legal superstructure that governs legitimate access to land. While favoring the small farmer in some instances, which is itself explained by the exigencies of particular economic circumstances, the force of law has typically sided with the powerful landed oligarchy. Indeed, the very structure of the judiciary (broadly defined to include lawyers, land officers, and other auxiliary agencies and personnel) is viewed as an institution that systematically works to the disadvantage of the small farmer, although Santos sees room in the contemporary Brazilian context for the emergence of a form of social advocacy whose goal is to improve the lot of the subordinate classes in the countryside.

A similar theme is pursued by José de Souza Martins. In his analysis of agrarian reform in Brazil, he notes that the original proposals espoused by the leftist Goulart regime, which in part led to the overthrow of the civilian government in 1964, were in large measure the same initiatives subsequently undertaken by the military government that took over from him. Recognizing the need for reform measures, the military thus found itself in the ironic situation of carrying out an agrarian policy that was contrary to the very social groups that had brought it to power. As his detailed study shows, the regime is nonetheless adept in attending to the interests of the dominant economic groups. Reform policies are selectively applied to defuse increasing conflicts over land. In isolated instances such measures thus operate in favor of the small farmers, although the overall impact is to foster the conditions that permit the continued expansion of large landholdings. This process, according to Martins, is accompanied by the depoliticization of civil organizations in the countryside and the increasing militarization and centralization of authority in Amazonia and, indeed, in the country as a whole. Unions, peasant leagues, and other forms of political expression are silenced as the state assumes a more direct role in managing the land conflicts generated by the concentration of land ownership and the expansion of capitalist social relations of production in rural areas.

Collectively these studies focus on the complex interrelationships between the state and private capital as these interactions condition events on the frontier. They offer theoretical explanations for the recurring theme of this volume that what occurs on the frontier is neither unique nor idiosyncratic, but rather is integrally part of socioeconomic and political trends at the national and international level. Second, the empirical analyses presented here demonstrate the class bias of the state, which operates primarily (although not exclusively) in the interests of capital.

From this standpoint, the failure of small-farmer colonization schemes and the tendency to reproduce on the frontier the same patterns of land concentration that characterize long-settled areas are not viewed as the outcome of purely ecological factors or as the result of the bureaucratic inefficiency of administrative agencies. The trends, rather, are seen as consistent with the function of the state apparatus in a society where capitalism is the dominant mode of production. The approach similarly clarifies the underlying reasons for the failure of Amazonian countries to effectively safeguard indigenous rights to valued resources. If, as suggested in part I of this volume, it is the responsibility of social scientists to examine and question the ideological bases of development trends and policies, then studies such as these are an important contribution. A more adequate understanding of the powerful structural forces that influence the outcome of policy decisions is a necessary basis for identifying the possible ways by which future Amazon development may be guided toward rational and humane goals.

National Expansion and Development Policies in the Colombian Amazon

Camilo A. Domínguez

F OR THOSE who believed in the possibility of giving land to the dispossessed in Latin American through the colonization of the Amazon Basin without also changing the relations of production at the national and international level, the end of the 1970s brought a rude awakening. By then it had become apparent that old slogans, such as "Land without people for people without land" or "New lands for new men," were only so many empty words. Recent data confirmed the occurrence in colonized areas of the same trends observed in established agricultural ones: the decomposition of the peasantry and the concentration of landholdings. The peasant colonist does not migrate alone. Nor does migration take place in a social vacuum. Rather, colonists who move into new areas reproduce the peasant social relations of production on the frontier. In effect, the colonist does not create a new free space on the frontier; he simply enlarges the geographic context in which peasants are dominated.

Within Amazonia, the failure of colonization by and for the small peasant is most clearly seen in Brazil. The opening of communication and transportation routes and the existence of fiscal incentives to promote land appropriation by capital have heightened and accelerated class conflicts, promoting a massive expropriation of land and a growing proletarianization of the peasantry (Hébette and Acevedo 1979, Martins 1980, Ianni 1979). The government has come to accept and further promote these trends. Regional policies have been adopted to benefit large agricultural enterprises, particularly those oriented to export production. This position was made official in 1974 with the *Polamazônia* program. Government policies that fostered the transformation of land into a commodity resulted in the appropriation of land by large capital. The effect was to close the possibility of free settlement for the colonist and open the door for an escalation of social conflicts in the countryside (Martins 1980, Schmink 1981, Becker 1981).

Although the degree of frontier expansion in the other Amazon countries (Bolivia, Peru, Ecuador, Chile, and Venezuela) has not reached the same level as in Brazil, it has been shown in some of these countries that colonization has not brought significant change in the structure of land use and land tenure. In Bolivia in 1980, despite the limited development colonization in the west, Hiroaka concluded that "The major beneficiaries of internal migration have been the large property owners. At the very least, for lack of marketable goods, the new inhabitants provide cheap labor to the landowners engaged in commercial production, especially producers of cotton and sugar. The result has been to strengthen the position of the large landholders, who have expanded spatially and economically at the expense of the small farmers" (Hiroaka 1980:43). In the Ecuadoran Amazon, Hiroaka and Yamamoto observed a similar concentration of land in the hands of the commercial ranchers. "A reasonable cash offer is sufficient to convince the original owners to sell their land. The alternative for those who sell land is to move to colonization areas on the frontier, to go to the emerging urban centers, to become wage laborers employed by the new enterprises, or to keep a small piece of land for subsistence agriculture. The result is the creation of the same patterns of *latifúndio-minifúndio* that characterize the Ecuadoran highlands. Land concentration is concurrent with the polarization of wealth" (Hiroaka and Yamamoto 1980:443–44). In Peru, as well as in Venezuela, a similar process seems to be underway, although less information is available on these issues. In the Colombian Amazon, as the following analysis will show, the phenomena of concentration and expansion of capital follow the same general trends outlined above.

Colombia: national expansion as growing dependency

Like the other nations of Latin America, Colombia is part of a hegemonic multinational block, whose centers of power lie outside of its national territory. The ruling classes in Colombia have adapted the management of the country as a dependent state to the needs of transnational capital, which they have historically served. The so-called railroad fever of the nineteenth century, for example, meant enormous profits for England. This, in turn, defined the political economy of the country for over a hundred years (Arrubla 1979). Through loans, contracts, advising, and outright blackmail, the country's transportation system and its economy were suited almost exclusively to meet the demand for raw materials in the metropolis.

Since the 1920s, Colombia has experienced industrial growth. The so-called import substitution phase, which occurred when international capitalism was weak, allowed the national bourgeoisie an unusual degree of autonomy (Furtado 1969). In the last ten years, however, a rapid change has been observed in terms of the concentration of the most profitable industries and businesses in the hands of foreign capital and transnational entities. In 1970, 48 percent of foreign investment recorded in Colombia was concentrated in six industrial sectors: chemicals, paper, rubber, electrical appliances, pharmaceuticals, and food products (Matter 1977:146). Two years later, the automotive industry expanded as Renault and Chrysler began auto production. With the local bourgeoisie as associates or as mere administrators, these transformations have brought about the internationalization of the Colombian economy (Kalmanovitz 1980).

The evidence of this process is visible in the marketplace. National products are rapidly replaced by international brand names and new products are introduced. These trends reflect the growing homogenization of products with respect to North America and Europe. Coca-Cola, General Electric Appliances, Bayer fungicides, Nestle products, and Renault cars are examples of Colombian-made commodities that are the consequence of the physical expansion of international capital. It follows that any analysis of Colombia or of one of its regions must necessarily take into account the conditions of international dependency.

Through its association with transnational capital, the bourgeoisie that has arisen in Colombia has lost much of its nationalism. Its interests coincide with those of its foreign associates, except when contradictions arise that are especially difficult to override. The latter explain certain short-lived and ineffectual eruptions of nationalism, such as the nominal nationalization of the banking system decreed by the López government in 1975, a step that, in the end, led to stronger ties between national and foreign capital. Accumulation on the part of the Colombian bourgeoisie, which grew slowly during the 1960s, confronting continual crises, experienced accelerated growth beginning in 1968, especially during the five-year period from 1970 to 1974.

Just as international capital took advantage of a favorable situation to garner markets and cheap labor, so too did the local bourgeoisie take advantage of the opportunity to acquire technology and financial capital and to make inroads into monopolized international markets. This combination of forces enlarged the market for industry as well as agriculture. Manufactured exports increased by 560.9 percent from 1970 to 1974, equivalent to an annual growth rate of 41.2 percent (Kalmanovitz 1980:145). Agricultural exports increased by 100 percent between 1970 and 1975, rising from U.S. $550 million to U.S. $1,000 million in the five-year period. The country went from the almost exclusive export of coffee to the export of a wide variety of new products, especially meat, rice, sugar, and cotton. Due to the higher prices in the international sphere, these products are sold abroad rather than in the expanding domestic market (Kalmanovitz 1980:152).

The entry of agriculture into the marketplace in such a broad way has caused a profound transformation in the Colombian countryside. The introduction of capitalism into agriculture has revolutionized the modes of production, altering land use and land tenure. Since the early 1960s the tenants and sharecroppers have been expelled from the large landholdings located on the best soils. This land has been rented to the agricultural bourgeoisie, who plant commercial crops, especially sugar cane, cotton, soy, and sorghum (Kalmanovitz 1980). It is often the large landlord himself who transforms his holdings into a capitalist enterprise.

The introduction of tractors and mechanized harvesters has drastically reduced the need for laborers, thus forcing the peasants to migrate to the cities or to the colonization areas in search of work or land. The poor peasant settled on small plots in the mountainous eroded soils has also entered into the proletarianization process. Pressured by the state through taxation, he is obliged to enter a marketplace where he is exploited. He sells his produce at a low price and buys industrial inputs at relatively high prices. Because of a deterioration in these terms of trade, he is forced to sell his labor temporarily on the large plantations or to migrate with all or part of his family to the city or to colonization areas in search of better opportunities (Moncayo and Rojas 1979, Sanz de Santamaría et al. 1981).

These transformations of the rural economy and the decomposition of the peasantry form part of the same process of capitalist expansion throughout the country. The proletarianized peasant, deprived of his means of production, is thus assimilated into the production and reproduction of capital. Unable to produce his food or household goods for his own use, he must sell his labor in order to purchase his survival needs. He thus enters into the circulation of capital both as buyer and seller, whether as a factory worker or as a rural fieldworker. Even when unemployed or underemployed (street vendors, shoe shiners, etc.), the individual must purchase or illegally acquire enough goods to reproduce his labor power, the only commodity he has left to sell. By the same token, the small landowning peasant who survives on his land or the peasant-colonist who opens up a new plot is linked to capital. To withstand the pressure from commercial agriculture and the usury that overexploits their labor, peasants become obligatory consumers of manufactured products and of services (Sanz de Santamaría et al. 1981).

The expansion of capital on the frontier

For the average Colombian, colonization connotes an act of valor by a pioneer, who seeks freedom and economic independence. After confronting the test of the jungle and its dangers, the colonist, it is widely believed, becomes the owner of his own land and builds a future for himself and his family. Opinions to the contrary are rarely heard. This impression is largely based on the case of the early settlement of western Colombia (Parsons 1949), considered to have been the epitome of successful colonization, in spite of the serious doubts that exist today about that historical experience. By analyzing the way in which colonization has developed, we can identify the ideologies that obfuscate the process of exploitation to which its main actors are subjected.

In an earlier paper on colonization policy in Colombia (Domínguez 1973), I described the basic process followed by the first or "founding" colonizer as follows: The agricultural products grown by the colonist produce only a precarious living. Although they generate a small economic surplus, this is insufficient to lead to upward economic mobility. Later, there is the additional problem of rapid soil depletion. In most of these regions the land cannot withstand intensive cultivation for more than three years. At the end of this period, it must be left fallow for five to ten years in order to recover part of its former agricultural potential, or the plot is converted to pasture.

Although cattle raising is more productive and has a better market than food crops, the purchase of the animals and the construction of fences and corrals requires a high initial investment. Since the colonist does not have this capital, he resorts to the sale of cleared land. The land is purchased, in most cases, by wealthy businessmen located in the major towns. These individuals have accumulated capital primarily through dealings with the colonists. Thus in colonization sites the typical businessman rancher emerges as the only actor with the potential for economic prosperity in newly settled areas. This process is further bolstered by the fact that his relatively strong economic position also provides him political power.

The true colonist, meanwhile, is dislodged from his land. Usually new areas are cleared on the edge of the colonization frontier. Each move takes him further from the market centers to places that are less profitable because of increased transportation costs. Others are pushed out of the colonization areas altogether and must migrate to cities in search of new sources of income (Domínguez 1973:227). More recent studies of the area confirm these findings (INCORA 1974, Carrizosa 1981).

An analysis of the three principal colonization areas in the Colombian Amazon based on a socioeconomic questionnaire survey carried out in 1972 by the Colombian Agrarian Reform Institute (INCORA 1974), shows a direct relationship between the age of the colony and the number of lots acquired by purchase. The more time that has passed, the greater the number of founding colonists who have sold their land. We arrive at this conclusion by combining the information contained in the previously cited INCORA publication (1974:84, 187) (see Tables 1 and 2).

El Retorno was an area that began to be colonized in 1968 as a special project. For this reason the great majority of the colonists were recent arrivals in 1972, the year of the survey. In spite of this it is worth noting that, in the short span of only four years, 21.9 percent of the plots had already been sold. This indicates how rapidly the phenomenon of expropriation of colonists is taking place.

El Putumayo, although it has been populated by migrants since

TABLE 1. Duration of occupancy of plots (percentage of respondents surveyed in 1972)

	Years of occupancy		
	0–4	4–10	Over 10
El Retorno	66.7	33.3	0.0
Putumayo	37.3	37.6	25.1
Caquetá	16.6	40.1	43.3

SOURCE: INCORA 1974:84.

TABLE 2. Means by which land was acquired, 1972 (in percentages)

	Forms of acquisition			
	Clearing	Purchase	Mixed	Other
El Retorno	64.4	21.9	13.7	0.0
Putumayo	43.4	34.4	16.7	6.1
Caquetá	23.9	50.5	19.2	6.4

SOURCE: INCORA 1974:187.

the colonial era, only began to receive large contingents of colonizers in 1957. At that time roads were constructed and oil deposits were discovered and exploited. This created a market for agricultural produce. With a longer period of settlement, the data on this population indicate that 34 percent of the plots were acquired by purchase. Another 16.1 percent were classified as mixed (partly purchased and later expanded with clearing done by the buyer). A total of 50.5 percent of the plots had been sold by their original owners.

An established and dynamic colonized area, Caquetá was first colonized thirty years ago. Significant growth has occurred since 1950. According to the census, there were 40,950 cleared hectares in 1951. This increased to 103,718 hectares in 1964 and reached 186,850 hectares by 1972. In this area, 83.4 percent of the sampled population had been there for over four years. The majority of the plots were acquired through full or partial purchase. Only 23.9 percent of the plots cleared by the founding colonists remain in the hands of the original owners. These figures indicate that, over a long period, only one in four founding colonists has managed to keep the land they directly colonized. If we assume that among the mixed acquisitions, half of the owners are successful founding colonists who succeeded in enlarging their original plots, the results suggest that about one in three founding colonists continued as owners of their land in Caquetá in 1972.

Given that two of every three founding colonists in Caquetá were pushed off their lands, we can take a closer look at the conditions of those who managed to stay on their land. A point of departure for the analysis is to examine the way land was divided and to analyze the current situation of the various strata that have emerged. For this purpose we consider the information in Table 3.

The data from the Caquetá property survey clearly reveal a high concentration of land ownership. Well over half (58.5 percent) of the plots under fifty hectares cover only 13.3 percent of the land, while the 11 percent of the plots over one thousand hectares account for 33.3 percent of the land area. This pattern suggests that, in a short period of time, the land tenure situation which has long existed in the Andean areas (where 10 percent of the farms cover 80 percent of the land) has been reproduced and perhaps even surpassed in newly settled regions (Fals Borda 1979:125).

It is important to note that, because of the poor quality of the soil in Amazonia, one needs a minimum of fifty to a hundred hectares in order to carry out a profitable system of production. INCORA itself has classified farms of less than fifty hectares as minifundios (INCORA 1974:470). Poor peasants, who have no other resources but their own labor and that of their families, are thus unable to exploit their small plots of land beyond subsistence level. They have, once again, become *minifundistas*. From that point on their fate is well known: they produce low-priced food that provisions urban centers, and they sell their labor on a seasonal basis to large property owners. In the case of a future expansion of capital, their expropriation will become definitive, obliging them to turn to a new colonization area, to become a rural wage laborer, or to migrate to the city to join the ranks of the reserve army of the unemployed.

Taking the process as a whole, we can see that the result in no way differs from the conditions the smallholder faces in traditional settlement areas. While the social classes are the same, on the frontier they confront one another in new areas that are brought under the domination of capital, a process in part fueled by the exploitation of the colonists' labor. Colonized territories are simul-

Table 3. Distribution of farms by size of plot and area cleared,
Caquetá, 1974

Size of plots (hectares)	Number of plots	Percent of total number	Total area (hectares)	Percent of total area
1–5	998	10.4	1,376.9	0.2
5–50	4,558	48.1	110,060.0	13.1
50–200	3,293	34.7	290,664.0	34.5
200–1,000	540	5.1	158,688.0	18.9
Over 1,000	107	1.1	280,826.0	33.3
Total	9,496	99.4	841,614.9	100.0

Source: Cadastral data taken by Carrizosa Leytra and Mantilla (Carrizosa 1981:55, table 6).

taneously subordinated to the national economy governed by a native bourgeoisie, and to the hegemony of transnational capital.

The Indian

Modes of production that do not participate, directly or indirectly, in the supply and demand of commodities in the marketplace are incompatible with the expansion of capitalist production. For this reason any mode of production other than the capitalist mode is destroyed or is adapted to the interests of capital. What has always been presented as a moral, religious, and political struggle has actually been a struggle to obtain markets and labor. Through an ideology appropriate to each case, the profit motive is couched in the name of civilization and progress. The final result is the settlement of capital on the ruins of an entire people (Ribeiro 1971).

This fact largely explains the open hostility of the mestizo bourgeoisie toward the few Indian populations that still exist in the country. An indigenous community is self-sufficient through its own agriculture, its artisans, and its utilization of natural resources. What little it cannot do for itself it obtains through simple exchange with similar communities. It produces use values rather than commodities that enter the marketplace. In addition, since the lands occupied by the Indian produce neither rent nor commercial agriculture, they always tend to be considered vacant lands, which can be occupied without implying an invasion of private property.

The colonist, hungry for land, and the small businessman,

hungry for profits on the frontier settlements, enthusiastically en-
dorse the image of the savage Indian. As an ideology it justifies the
expropriation, proletarianization, and extermination of indigenous
groups. The colonists steadily invade Indian lands, forcing native
groups to retreat. Meanwhile the Indian becomes progressively indebted to the businessman, who finally puts him to work. Employment usually consists of extracting the natural products from the
Indian's own land or laboring on lands the businessman has bought
(often from Indians).

In the three main colonization areas of the Colombian
Amazon in 1973 (El Retorno, Caquetá, and Putumayo), INCORA
(1974:180) located approximately 2,380 Indians belonging to the
Huitoto, Coreguaje, Macaguaje, Siona, Ingano, Cofán, Guayabero,
and Carijona, along with some members of the Desano, Tariano,
and Tucano groups. Numerous communities belonging to these
and other groups had already disappeared. The rest were in grave
danger of disappearance, according to this document. INCORA admits that it is incapable of containing the destructive process of
"civilization" advancing upon the "barbarians." Since we are not
dealing with a confrontation between local groups played out in an
individual battle, the process will undoubtedly continue. The process entails the imposition of one mode of production over another. As such it implies a fundamental change in the region under
new social relations of production. With the emerging dominance
of wage relations the Indian community is obsolete. Under capitalism the Indian is of value only as an individual producer and
consumer and is thus "incorporated" into the lowest stratum of
the social structure.

State policy in the Colombian Amazon

For the Colombian state, the Amazon has traditionally been a hypothetical reserve of natural resources and a refuge for the relative
surplus population generated by the deplorable distribution of
land in the interior. It is only recently (since 1960) that an increasingly significant policy has developed to incorporate Amazonia
into the rest of the national economy.

The process began with Agrarian Reform Law 135 of 1961,
passed during the administration of Alberto Lleras Camargo. This
legislation, which created the Colombian Institute of Agrarian Reform (INCORA), was imposed on Colombia as well as on other Latin
American countries by the Punte del Este meeting of the O.A.S in

1960. Though intended to bring about a more equitable distribution of land, in the end it stimulated the colonization of new territories. The large landholding class in power could not accept the erosion of their privileges in spite of the imminent danger they faced. Following the Cuban revolution, there had been an enormous welling up of sentiment in Latin America against social inequality. Systematically opposing the redistribution of land, the landowning class succeeded in directing the funds and efforts of INCORA toward the colonization of the country's empty lands, achieving what Ianni has called an agrarian counterreform (Ianni 1979). According to a study carried out by the Center for Development Research (CID), "The judicial decisions involving national or empty lands account for 96.5 percent of the lands distributed and 92 percent of the titles awarded through mid-1969" (Tamayo 1970:14).

In Amazonia the "Caquetá II" and "Putumayo I" colonization projects were initiated, complemented later by the El Retorno colonization area, belonging to the Meta 1 project and located in the Guaviare Reservation. The Caquetá project in particular showed such a high rate of growth that it stimulated INCORA to concentrate most of its resources in this region, using it as an example of agrarian reform. By the end of 1973, the colonists had appropriated 966,000 hectares in Caquetá, and the area continued to expand rapidly. As a result, it accounted for 28.4 percent of the 3,400,000 hectares of colonized land in the country (INCORA 1974:206).

If, as we have seen, colonization is merely a form of disintegration of the peasantry, it is clear that the landholding class has triumphed. It successfully avoided the expropriation of its lands and rechannelled the resources slated for agrarian reform to stimulate the opening of new territories, which in the end would come under their power. During the 1970s, the apparent failure of agrarian reform in the country (as in the rest of Latin America) and the development of industrial and agricultural export under the leadership of the dependent bourgeoisie, linked to large international capital, produced a strong reversal in state policy. In the rural areas attention was focused on large mechanized property, producing for industry or export. The large landholding became an agribusiness and was once again supported by the state. As a guarantee of this support, the Chicoral Agreement was signed in 1972. Discarding any remaining vestige of agrarian reform, the state pledged its support for the industrialization of large landholdings (Kalmanovitz 1980:151).

Since this new policy emphasis implies an even greater entrenchment of existing social inequalities, now more important for capitalist expansion, the solution is to increase the repressive power of the armed forces. The so-called Security Statute allows for the adoption of a form of government which, in practice, means a presidency shared between the Constitutional President and the Minister of Defense, whose power has been arbitrarily broadened.

As is apparent in Caquetá, the Amazonian colonization areas are helping to create ranching estates whose production is destined for the international market and the national industrial centers. The region already had 81,450 head of cattle in 1972 (INCORA 1974:224), part of which was exported to Peru or went to meet the demand in other provinces. Credit and other forms of state aid are being channeled to this type of production, now that INCORA is in the process of disintegration, and the banks require proof of economic solvency and impose conditions on the use of inputs that only the richest landowners can afford. The colonization frontiers and the recently established small plots (minifundios) continue to fulfill another objective. Aside from opening up the land and providing their labor to capital, they produce the food required by the ranches and the new urban centers that have emerged. This production is indispensable to capital, since it cuts production costs by decreasing the costs of reproduction of the labor force, which determines the workers' base salary.

Summary

By acts of commission or of omission, the Colombian state has created a situation which today demonstrates the following characteristics in the colonization areas of Amazonia:

Large and middle-sized properties, established through the purchase of lands cleared by the founding colonists, have been converted to pasture for cattle raising.

The frontier continues to advance into open territories and into Indian lands. The planting of food crops (maize, rice, cassava, and plantains) for subsistence and for the local market, increases the value of lands which seldom stay in the hands of the founding colonists.

The small plots belonging to the original colonists continue to exist alongside the large ranches. The colonists are placed under conditions of tenant farming and small plot subsistence (minifundio), growing food products for the local market, and selling their labor to cattle ranches.

There is a growing free labor force, which lives solely by the sale of its labor in the countryside or by subsistence activities in the towns. It is composed of former colonists and Indians pushed off the lands and proletarianized by the advance of capital.

The cities, large and small, continue to grow, as local centers of power and as entrepots for the merchandise that enters and leaves the Amazon.

The growth of mechanized, high-technology agriculture and the increasing destruction of self-sufficiency among the Indians and the colonists enlarge the market for the commodities produced by transnationals, which are linked to the national bourgeoisie. The region thus conforms to the national and international conditions that serve the expansion of capital.

References Cited

Arrubla, Mario
  1979   *Estudios sobre el Subdesarrollo Colombiano.* 2d ed. Bogotá: La Carreta.

Becker, Bertha
  1981   *A Atuação do Estado na Expansão da Fronteira: Uma Contribuição Geo-política ao Estudo da Região Araguaia-Tocantins.* Brasília: Seminário Regional Expansão da Fronteira Agrícola e Meio Ambiente na América Latina.

Carrizosa, Julio
  1981   *La Ampliación de la Frontera Agrícola en el Caquetá (Amazonía Colombiana).* Brasília: Seminário Regional sobre Expansão da Fronteira Agropecuária e Meio Ambiente na América Latina.

Domínguez, Camilo
  1973   La Política Colonizadora en Colombia. In *Estudios Colombianos.* Bogotá: CID.

Fals Borda, Orlando
  1979   *Historia de la Cuestión Agraria en Colombia.* Bogotá: Punta de Lanza.

Furtado, Celso
  1969   *Formação Econômica da América Latina.* Rio de Janeiro: Fundo de Cultura.

Hébette, Jean and Rosa Acevedo
  1979   *Colonização para Quem?*. Belém: NAEA.
Hiroaka, Mario
  1980   Agricultural Colonization in the Bolivian Upper Amazon. In
          Annual Report No. 2, *Special Research Project on Latin
          America.* Japan: University of Isukuba.
Hiroaka, Mario and Shozo Yamamoto
  1980   Agricultural Development in the Upper Amazon of Ecuador.
          Geographical Review 70(4):423–45.
Ianni, Octávio
  1979   *Colonização e Contra-Reforma Agrária na Amazônia.* Petró-
          polis: Vozes.
Instituto Colombiano de Reforma Agraria (INCORA)
  1974   *La Colonización en Colombia: Una Evaluación del Proceso.*
          Bogotá: INCORA.
Kalmanovitz, Salomo
  1980   *Ensayos sobre el Desarrollo del Capitalismo Dependiente.*
          Bogotá: La Oveja Negra.
Martins, José de Souza
  1980   *Expropriação e Violência: a Questão Política no Campo.* São
          Paulo: Hucitec.
Matter, Konrad
  1977   *Inversiones Estranjeras en la Economía Colombiana.* Medel-
          lín: Ediciones Hombre Nuevo.
Moncayo, Victor and Fernando Rojas
  1979   *Producción Campesina y Capitalismo.* Bogotá: CINEP.
Parsons, James
  1949   *La Colonización Antioqueña del Occidente de Colombia.*
          Bogotá: Banco de la República.
Ribeiro, Darcy
  1971   *Fronteras Indígenas de la Civilización.* Mexico: Siglo XXI.
Sanz de Santamaría, Alejandro et al.
  1981   Las Migraciones Laborales en Regiones de Economía Cam-
          pesina: Una Propuesta Metodológica para su Estudio Em-
          pírico. *Economía y Sociedad* 5:(December).
Schmink, Marianne
  1981   *A Case Study of the Closing Frontier in Brazil.* Amazon Re-
          search Paper Series, No. 1. Gainesville: University of Florida.
Tamayo, Hector
  1970   *La Reforma Agraria en Colombia: Una Base Para su Evalua-
          ción.* Bogotá: CID.

Strategies of Private Capital in the Brazilian Amazon

Malori José Pompermayer

SINCE THE mid-1960s, an important aspect of the occupation of the Amazon frontier has been the manner in which interest groups from southern Brazil, most notably from São Paulo, have responded to the invitations of various governments to invest in the region. To benefit from government incentives, private capital has pressured public institutions to favor investment in cattle ranching. To this end a civil society was formed in 1968 called the Association of Amazonian Entrepreneurs, or AEA.[1] The society, registered in Belém, is headquartered in São Paulo. This organization has played a role in shifting state policy with regard to the Amazon in favor of a model of frontier occupation that would better serve the interests of its members. Through intense interactions between the association and various state institutions responsible for public policy in the region, the AEA has influenced fundamental decisions related to the occupation and exploitation of Amazonia.

This paper focuses on some aspects of the political practices of private interest groups as they operate through the AEA.[2] Of special concern are the mechanisms by which the interests of private capital are represented within the state in the context of changes in the structure of political domination that have taken place since 1964. Also important is the relationship between these entrepreneurial groups and the recent transformations of social classes in Brazilian agriculture (see Pompermayer 1979). Although the various public policies enacted since 1964 should not be viewed as the sole or even the most important determining aspect of the dynamics of the recent agricultural frontier in the Brazilian Amazon, it should be recognized, nonetheless, that the state-sponsored initiatives, when articulated with the strategies adopted by private capital, impart a character to Amazonia that is distinct from that of Brazil's traditional agricultural frontier.

History of the AEA

To understand the AEA and its political activity, it is important to trace its origins. Even before 1964, when the major policies concerning the region were first adopted, certain economic groups from the south had already taken an interest in Amazonia. Indeed, the form of the relationship between the state and capitalist groups that took place after the initiation of fiscal incentives in 1966 was conditioned, to some extent, by the fact that these original groups had already invested in the region. This is so because private investors, who had been operating in Amazonia prior to 1966, constituted the basic nucleus of the AEA. Thus the subsequent actions of this organization, together with those of various federal agencies, influenced the model of development formulated for the occupation of the new frontier.

Long before 1964, at least three large Paulista business groups had already diversified their investments into ranching in southern Pará, northern Mato Grosso, and Goiás. After opening a cattle ranch in the north of Goiás, João Lanari del Val moved on to the south of Pará in 1957, acquiring 400,000 hectares of land in the municipality of Conceição do Araguaia. Shortly thereafter, he was followed by Nicolau Lunardelli, who purchased more than 700,000 hectares. As owners of agricultural and industrial enterprises in the south, these two businessmen used their own capital to initiate ranching enterprises in the Amazon. In 1961, the Ometto group, together with an associate Ariosto da Riva, opened the 600,000 hectare Suia-Missu ranch in northern Mato Grosso. Ometto, an industrialist from São Paulo involved primarily in sugar production, decided to invest in ranching in Amazonia after considering other alternatives in Paraná and in southern Mato Grosso. With their own resources, and through their administrators and managers, these investors initiated the construction of roads and the clearing of land for pastures.

Lanari and Lunardelli found that the land they acquired in the south of Pará had long been inhabited by squatters (*posseiros*), as

well as a few Indian families. Similarly, Ometto, in Barra do Garças, had to deal with Xavante Indians. Through strategies designed
to gain the confidence of the Indians and, later, through the help of
the Indian Protection Service (predecessor of FUNAI) and missionaries, these tribes were eventually removed from the area.

Other businessmen from São Paulo began to invest in Amazonia in the late 1950s and early 1960s. They moved into the region, not in isolation but together with other traditional ranchers
and peasant families, who headed to the new frontier as construction proceeded on the Belém-Brasília highway (Valverde 1967,
Hébette 1977, CEDEPLAR 1977). An important distinction should
be made, however, between the "Paulista" groups of the type mentioned above and those referred to here as traditional ranchers.

The latter are generally individual proprietors linked to agriculture, commercial capital, and earlier forms of exploitation of
the rural labor force. They represent the classical type of agricultural producers and merchants who, in response to a deterioration
of land and labor at the place of origin and because of the availability of new areas, strive to take advantage of the opportunity to
acquire new lands. With their families in tow, they move to the
agricultural frontier, often with insufficient capital to start a new
business. For this reason they resort to various means, including
violence, to acquire the areas worked by posseiros, hiring dispossessed small farmers and other workers to clear the forest and
prepare the land for pasture. Although not always the case, it is primarily among the traditional ranchers that we find the persons commonly called "*grileiros,*" or landgrabbers, who attempt
through fraudulent means to gain title to the lands they have
appropriated.

The Paulista groups can be distinguished from these traditional ranchers in the Amazon region. The large investors from
southern Brazil represent segments of modern industrial and agroindustrial capital that have emerged from capitalist accumulation
in Brazil's more developed Center-South. This occurred in the context of the growing articulation between large state capital and private national and multinational groups, a process that had already
begun in the 1950s. Indeed, it was the growth of agricultural production in the second half of the 1950s that made possible the expansion of what has come to be called the agroindustrial complex.
Increased agricultural output generated a market for industrial
products, a fundamental change that more closely linked agricul-

ture to industry and to commercial and financial capital. In this way the agricultural sector was transformed into an arena for the realization of surplus value by the industrial sector. At the same time, new social classes emerged in the countryside and the peasantry became increasingly integrated into agroindustry (see Sorj 1980).

The consolidation of the agroindustrial complex in Brazil and its particular characteristics associated with the opening of the country to monopoly capital acquired full force within the context of the agricultural policies adopted in the post-1964 period of authoritarian rule. Yet the policies of the military government should not be isolated as the single determining factor. The creation and expansion of the agroindustrial complex, rather, are more closely tied to the history of Brazilian economic development itself. Of particular importance was the rise in demand for machinery and other industrialized inputs that converted the agricultural sector into a primary source of profits for industrial capital. It is in the context of this structural transformation in the Brazilian economy that the role of public policy can be understood. If, as we have seen above, economic groups already linked to modern agroindustrial capital in southern Brazil branched out into Amazonia independently of state action after 1964, it was nevertheless the major policy initiatives adopted by the government (especially fiscal incentives, which were themselves influenced by pressure from the private sector) that subsequently set the pace and character of capital expansion into the region.

As capital moved into Amazonia, ranching was the logical form of investment, at least in the initial stages. In the 1950s and 1960s transportation and other services were poorly developed, yet land was readily available. Cattle ranching, moreover, does not require so extensive an infrastructure as do other types of agricultural production. In the second and third phases of frontier expansion, however, agroindustry in the north region was able to begin its expansion into activities better suited to Amazonia. One element that encouraged diversification was the corporatist strategy used by capital groups.

Forms of representation

Considering the corporatist form of representation of private interests within the state, it is important to emphasize the role played by entrepreneurs that were interested in Amazonia before, and independently of, the new development policies enacted after 1966. As the first to benefit from fiscal incentives, these businessmen were also the same groups that encouraged similar investments by others located in São Paulo. These entrepreneurs formed the initial membership of the Association of Amazonian Entrepreneurs, created in 1968. The first president of the AEA was Hermínio Ometto, a well-known businessman who later sold his Suia-Missu ranch in the Amazon to a multinational firm. His first official act as head of the organization was to invite "all state ministers associated with the area, along with the superintendent of SUDAM," to visit the region on an inspection tour. As one of the directors of the AEA explained years later, the association was created because it was realized that the common interests of this segment of agroindustrial capital needed to be defended in the centers of national decision making. "The creation of SUDAM to organize the disbursement of fiscal incentives," he noted, "awakened the southern businessman's interest in investing in the Amazon, especially in cattle ranching." However, "general ignorance of [SUDAM] . . . and the clear tendency to copy the SUDENE model were obstacles that could not be easily circumvented in isolation, and from this emerged the need for an association capable of bringing together the entrepreneurial class to defend its common interests and to launch the development of the Amazon" (*Revista Amazônia* 1977, 24:23–25).

That segments of modern capital recognized their mutual interests in a specific area of the national territory and that they were able to express these interests within the state apparatus through the AEA had an important result. As the director of the AEA noted in 1975, it led to "the interweaving of official agencies with the business community, to repeated changes in regulations, to the realization of projects, and a whole range of services that made possible the establishment of a large number of investments" (*Revista Amazônia* 1977, 24:23–25).

With regard to the new frontier, modern capital represented by the AEA pursued strategies different from those adopted by traditional ranchers. Unlike the large corporate entities from the south, the traditional ranchers failed to develop a collective political representation capable of influencing public policy. They relied instead on isolated initiatives that were limited in character, and that operated via local police and other authorities. One organization that could have represented their interests was the Union of

Rural Landowners (Sindicato de Proprietários Rurais) associated
with the National Federation of Agriculture (CNA). However, because these organizations were formally linked to the state and
since they represented a wide range of heterogeneous interests, it
was impossible for the institutions to adopt a consistent and effective stand in order to lobby the government. With regard to the
Amazon, for example, the CNA has done little more than emphasize general objectives without proposing concrete policies. The
CNA, for its part, favors releasing public land for private colonization projects and has denounced Marxist infiltration in the area as
well as the initiatives of the Catholic Church in Amazonia. At the
national level, the organization has taken a very traditional view.
The president of the CNA, for example, has considered credit for
agriculture machinery to be a matter of secondary importance,
while at the same time deploring the government's tendency to
favor industry over agriculture (Sorj 1980:78).

Unlike traditional landowners and commercial capital in the
Amazon, modern agroindustrial groups are characterized by coordinated and focused attempts to influence various governmental
agencies. In addition to defending their immediate interests, they
have developed a long-term strategy that serves to coordinate specific tactics. This approach is manifest in such statements as the
need to "define a model for the occupation of the new frontier."
Thus, in 1976, the new president of the AEA set forth as his principal aims "first, to participate in the resolution of problems that
affect enterprises in Legal Amazonia, and second, to contribute
. . . to the formulation of development policies for the socioeconomic occupation of Amazonia." Another priority was the
need "to continue to make the Amazon present in public and private decision centers in other areas of the country in order to seek
the support for the development of the north region" (Revista Amazônia 1977, 25:8). As late as 1981, when the association included
more than two hundred fifty members, its objectives remained essentially the same (AEA 1981a).

In effect, the AEA has become one of the principal forums for
debate on Amazon issues. This applies to the debate among members of the association as well as to public discussion and the influence of opinions through access to the media.[3] As is the case for
other interest groups in the country at large, the presence of the
AEA, and its capacity to mobilize economic and political power
with regard to Amazon related issues provides the government and

other public agencies with the ability to anticipate potential conflicts of interest that might arise as a result of particular policies.
This process is greatly facilitated by the fact that the ideology of
modern, technical efficiency, which is endorsed by the association,
expresses the values shared by the state planning agencies (see AEA
1977b).

The emphasis on sophisticated technology and the aggressive
pioneering spirit of modern capital distinguishes these enterprises
from the traditional rural landholders. Moreover, the self-image of
corporate entrepreneurs closely coincides with the character of the
technocratic state bureaucracy and the model of multinational development based on the concentration and centralization of capital, a pattern that emerged in the 1950s and later became dominant
in the country in the 1960s. In the agricultural sector this trend
was associated with increased technology and rationality in the
production process. The self-proclaimed superiority of the large
enterprise often implied little more than speculation on the frontier. This attitude was nonetheless instrumental in the lobbying
efforts of private capital, for it resonated closely with the ideas
held by planners and bureaucrats.

The Association of the Amazon Entrepreneurs emerged at a
very specific time in Brazil. The transformations in the state apparatus that took place after 1964 and the new forces that crystalized
as a result of these changes disrupted the traditional channels
through which different interest groups operated (see Martins,
in this volume). New mechanisms were created whereby multinational capital and investors associated with domestic groups
could lobby for their interests. These "class-based" associations
had already begun to emerge prior to 1964. In the earlier period,
however, they operated parallel to the traditional mechanisms that
characterized the populist state. After 1964, in contrast, these new
associations took on greater importance. As they gained direct and
immediate access to the state apparatus, they were able to circumvent the more traditional forms of "state corporatism" (Boschi
1979; Dreifuss 1981; Sorj, Pompermayer, and Coradini 1982).
While these segments of modern capital were able to achieve direct
access to the decision-making process within the state, the reverse
was true for labor. In the specific case of the rural sector, peasant
groups were systematically excluded.

Strategies and consequences

It was in the context of the institutional and political reorganization that took place after 1964 that the Association of the Amazon Entrepreneurs was created in 1968. Originally it was closely linked to SUDAM, the agency in charge of fiscal incentives, and to the Ministry of the Interior, which housed the superintendency. Initially, this relationship (Operação Amazônia 1966–70) significantly facilitated the influence of the AEA over SUDAM. The AEA was able to channel fiscal incentives into cattle ranching, the economic activity favored by southern investors, thus making it possible for private capital to acquire large tracts of land and realize profitable investments at low risk.

In the second phase of frontier expansion, the government established public colonization projects for small farmers and much of the region came under the control of INCRA. During this period, tensions mounted between SUDAM and the Ministry of the Interior on the one hand, and INCRA and the Ministry of Agriculture on the other. The dispute, at this point, centered on the distribution of public lands by INCRA, a policy incompatible with the interests of private investors. Support for public colonization projects, moreover, hindered private initiatives in this area. Working through the Ministry of the Interior and SUDAM, the AEA pressured for a policy that would institutionalize the process of private colonization and the acquisition of land by private investors. Simultaneously, the organization lobbied against regulations that prevented INCRA from selling land in the public domain in lots exceeding three thousand hectares.

In large measure most of these policy modifications were carried out during the 1975–77 period. Since then the AEA has taken a special interest in their practical implementation. Aside from its opposition to other policies (such the small farmer colonization schemes and more general land-use policies for the region), the AEA gave increasing priority to large-scale private colonization efforts and to the diversification of economic activities among the association's members. Begun under Geisel,this strategy was consolidated under the Figueiredo regime.

Fiscal incentives, together with successful efforts to channel resources into cattle ranching and, later on, policies in favor of private colonization projects had a profound impact on the frontier, especially in areas along the periphery of the Amazon. With the help of the incentives program, the expansion of cattle ranches led to an unprecedented land rush. These lands were acquired under conditions that were advantageous to the investor. In many cases the size of the areas acquired far exceeded what was needed. This excess land, in turn, has been the basis for most of the private colonization projects established in the region, especially since IN-CRA restricted access to public land for this purpose. By 1982, for example, twelve members of the AEA, including the ex-president of the association (José Carlos de Souza Meirelles), had established colonization projects in areas surrounding cattle ranches.

These examples testify to the past and present importance to the AEA of the so-called Integrated Colonization Projects. These projects generally involve large- and medium-sized enterprises as well as colonists who formerly owned small, family farms in southern Brazil. Thus, the original emphasis given by the AEA to large-scale cattle ranches can be seen as the first step in a more long-term strategy. Once the creation of cattle ranches served to establish the minimum services and infrastructure, the second phase envisioned private colonization projects that would sell plots to small farmers engaged in agricultural production in the integrated projects.

In early 1979, José Carlos de Souza Meirelles, then president of the AEA, evaluated events in the region. Reaffirming the same model that the AEA had always advocated, he declared: "In the first instance the occupation of frontier areas foresaw the presence of medium- and large-size holdings since these alone would have the means to establish large unassisted projects in virgin regions. But, in the last few years, this phase of the occupation process (at least in peripheral areas of the Amazon) has been consolidated, and today the small holder is a better option for the new phase of economic development in the region" (*Revista Amazônia* 1979:46). In the current phase, according to Meirelles, "economic occupation should concentrate on areas that possess appropriate infrastructure, so as to avoid additional expenditures in new areas. This occupation should be carried out by large, integrated projects, which, analyzing soil and vegetation conditions, should give priority to family farms" (*Revista Amazônia* 1979:46). The regions classified as having adequate infrastructure can be understood to refer to those areas where cattle ranches have already been established. This assured that ranching would remain a viable option.

The tension and misunderstandings that characterized the

earlier period have disappeared. By 1982 a perfect accord evolved between the AEA and the agencies that once opposed private colonization projects. Before the current president of INCRA assumed his post in 1979, the AEA invited him to visit colonization projects in northern Mato Grosso. The future president of INCRA agreed that colonization should be carried forth by private initiatives, and that INCRA should restrict its mandate to resolving problems of land conflicts in certain areas. In July, 1980, even the president of Brazil was taken on a tour of several projects by the AEA, accompanied by ministers and the entire directorate of the association. In October 1981, after long debate in the headquarters of the AEA, the association's directors forwarded to the Brazilian president a document stressing, among other things, the need for greater participation by private enterprise based on their "experience in the Amazon." In a press release, the head of the AEA said that the Association "could offer a solid base for the creation of a plan that would multiply the number of landholders, principally those that are small and medium in size, throughout the region" (*Boletim Informativo* 1981:36).

The nature of investments

As outlined above, southern investors linked to modern industrial capital moved into the Amazon region in part as a result of attractive fiscal incentives. The low interest rates on government loans and the inflation in land prices were among the primary causes of speculation in cattle ranches on the frontier. Privately financed colonization projects, in turn, commercialized surplus land that had been previously acquired. The negative consequences of the exploitation of native and migrant populations and the devastating ecological impact of ranching activities will not be evaluated here. We shall focus, instead, on the behavior of capitalist groups in Amazonia, analyzed in the context of the social forces that impinge upon them.

The establishment of a viable agroindustry in the region signaled a second watershed in the process of frontier expansion in the Amazon. Agroindustry was established as a result of the strategies pursued by private capital as well as the initiatives undertaken by the state (if such a distinction can still be made). With regard to cattle ranching, for example, once the intense land-grabbing phase was over, a selection process began to weed out those who were in Amazonian investments for purely speculative reasons. In 1979,

SUDAM cancelled its support for sixty projects of this type. When they no longer received fiscal incentives, many were absorbed by other, presumably larger and more capable firms. In another category were the projects that were cancelled altogether. Because they were not viable economic ventures to begin with, they were taken over by SUDAM. In this sense the "boom" created by the fiscal incentives, which permitted the easy creation of cattle ranches, is now over. In its stead, there has been a process whereby the firms that fail to adopt a rational and technically appropriate production process are beginning to be selected out. The success of some cattle ranches linked to other colonization projects in the Amazon has stimulated the emergence of meat packing plants established by national and multinational firms. Examples include Sudanisa in Barra dos Garça, Sadia Oeste in Cuiabá and the Atlas plant, located in Conceição do Araguaia (owned by Volkswagen). Projects owned by Swift-Armour as well as Liquifarm and Borden are also significant in this regard.

Although less salient, agroindustrial food processing has made important advances. In 1979, for example, the AEA suggested that "as a complement to the integrated projects, a prominent role be given to the establishment of agroindustry in areas producing primary products. This would generate greater investment opportunities, would absorb labor in shortage areas, lead to a greater decentralization of the economy, and avoid the irrational and unnecessary transportation costs to bring raw materials from the producing to the processing areas" (AEA 1979). In a meeting that included the Ministry of the Interior, SUDAM and SUDECO, as well as about a hundred businessmen, the tendency toward greater diversification and the development of complementarity of activities became clear. As the Superintendent of SUDAM put it, "in other words, (production) will not be limited to cattle ranching, but will include agriculture, agroindustry, and colonization, which are activities that are labor intensive." On the other hand the decentralization of SUDAM and the transferring of public lands to the states carried out under Figueiredo's regime implied that these administrative agencies had a freer hand to distribute resources. As a result, industries that relied on regionally produced raw materials were the primary beneficiaries (Revista Amazônia 1976).

Related to the diversification of business activities in the Amazon has been a gradual diversification of the AEA membership. Until 1976 the ranks of the association included only the enterprises involved in cattle ranching. Later on the organization "included also business associated with agroindustry and industries that produced inputs for the agricultural sector" (AEA 1981b). In 1982 the AEA thus represented the interests of entrepreneurs in all sectors of the economy.

Concrete examples already exist of the articulation between colonization enterprises and industries in the transformative sector. This relationship has come about through a slow process of experimentation by the colonization companies. Colonists have been advised to produce certain perennial crops, especially those that have a comparative advantage in Amazonia (guaraná, cacao, rubber, black pepper, coffee, Brazil nuts, and palm oils), as well as to exploit regional hardwoods. For example, in 1977 Indeco, a large colonization company owned by Ariesto da Riva, an influential member of the AEA, planned for the colonists in the project to plant six million coffee trees, four hundred thousand stands of cacao and a hundred thousand guaraná trees, in addition to papaya and rubber plants. One objective was to process much of the output in the colonization area itself. At present the company has established a plant to process papain, an enzyme obtained from the unripe papaya fruit that is used as a meat tenderizer (AEA 1977a, Isto É, 1981).

In 1981 the largest private colonization project in northern Mato Grosso (Sinop) inaugurated the Agro-Chemical Sinop plant. With a billion cruzeiros obtained from the national Proálcool Project, the plant produces alcohol from the manioc roots grown by colonists. To assure a supply of raw materials the company organized a cooperative of manioc producers. The colonists in the cooperative numbered 2,600 in 1977. Projected membership is expected to reach 3,800 colonists, with about 107,000 hectares of land devoted to manioc. In addition to the crops already planted by the colonists, Sinop establishes quotas for manioc, which is grown with the technical assistance of the cooperative. This arrangement serves to integrate the agricultural sector with the chemical industry. A five-year projection made in 1977 anticipates an annual production of about one million liters of alcohol per day.

In a manner similar to the production of alcohol through the Proálcool Project, other programs have served to finance specific products. Proborracha and Ceplac stimulate the production of rubber and cacao, respectively. Sinop itself, with the help of Proborracha and Ceplac, is directing its colonists to plant 700 hectares of rubber trees and 2,000 hectares of cacao. In addition, 810,000 hectares are planned for pepper plants and 60,000 hectares for guaraná. The shift toward these perennial crops by Sinop was the result of the poor results of the initial attempt to have colonists plant coffee, an experiment that, like cattle ranching, was unsuccessful (*Revista Amazônia* 1976, *Isto É* 1981, *Boletim Informativo* 1981:11).

Despite their importance to colonists (in terms of time expended and the volume of the production), traditional crops such as rice, beans, and maize are, from the standpoint of the capitalist firm, seen as secondary products. As a result, these crops suffer from numerous problems, including inadequate storage facilities and difficulties in commercialization. The colonist finds himself at the mercy of merchant capital or federal agencies (the Commission for Financing Production).

Other colonization firms that have recently branched out from cattle production foresee the creation of food processing industries. At present, however, they are waiting to see if the raw materials produced by colonists will permit the establishment of a viable production system. One of the factors that stimulated the move toward processing food products locally is the high transportation costs resulting from the large distances separating the Amazon from large markets. The processing of regional products is most advanced in the area of wood products, since sawmills are often part of the operations carried out by cattle ranchers. In addition to Sinop and Indeco, the Jurena firm (owned by a person who was president of the AEA for six years) has five mills producing wood laminates. In this sense the association's opposition to the proposed subsidies and concessions designed to expand timber mills is consistent with its contention that further investments should be limited to the areas that already have established infrastructure. According to Meirelles, the ex-president of the association, the increase in supply that would result from such concessions would drive prices down. It is preferable, he argued, to promote "rational use of wood in the areas that already produce cattle and agricultural products, since this would be good for the internal market and for exports" (*Revista Amazônia* 1979:46).

The expansion of agroindustry and capitalist firms into Amazonia does not provide optimistic prospects for a solution to the social problems that confront the majority of the people in the region. As numerous studies indicate, the problems faced by migrant

colonists, squatters, wage laborers, or small farmers will not be resolved by capitalist production, especially under the continuation
of authoritarian capitalism.

The idea we wish to emphasize here is that the recent expansion of the frontier in Amazonia has a fundamentally different relation to the national economy compared to earlier historical periods. In the case of traditional frontier occupation in the past,
which was carried out under the aegis of merchant capital, the output of small farmers played a central role in supplying the internal
market. In the contemporary situation, in contrast, production is
vertically integrated. It is closely linked to the industrial sector
not only as a supplier of raw materials but also as a purchaser of
industrialized products. In this context the traditional peasant
farmer is destined to play an increasingly marginal role as a supplier of foodstuffs for the domestic market.

This should not be taken to imply that the new character of
the frontier has completely supplanted older forms of horizontal
expansion. On the contrary, the continuous opening up of new
lands still provides the incentive for merchant capital to move
into frontier areas in order to appropriate and market the surplus
produced by small farmers. These processes also create the conditions that permit the expansion (through violence or other means)
of traditional latifundios (see Foweraker 1981, Oliveira 1971).

In contemporary Amazonia, however, the alliance between
the state and large capitalist investors leads to a situation in which
large firms take the lead in frontier expansion. At the same time,
this does not exclude small farmers nor does it prevent merchant
capital from also moving into these areas. Indeed, merchant capital is still the primary mechanism by which the surpluses
produced by small farmers are commercialized. Corporate investors, on the other hand, are more interested in establishing conditions appropriate for production of the commodities best adapted
to the large, agroindustrial firm.

Peasant differentiation and forms of representation

The modernization and expansion of agroindustry, especially in
southern Brazil, has led to a differentiation among small producers.
This has occurred not only because peasants are subordinated to
capital but also because of the way that the small farmer ensures
his own reproduction. When agroindustry is not vertically integrated and does not have a high degree of fixed capital (which leads

to the proletarianization of the labor force), peasant producers are nonetheless partially linked to capital through the marketplace or are directly linked through contractual arrangements (see Tavares 1978; Montali 1979; Coradini 1981; Sorj, Pompermayer, and Coradini 1982).

The complete or partial integration of the small producer with agroindustry implies a continual selection process whereby small farmers with insufficient socioeconomic resources are excluded. This process is widespread in southern Brazil, where many peasants who are unable to establish linkages with agroindustrial capital are recruited to participate in private colonization projects in the Amazon. In the final analysis, the fundamental question for family-based producers is not their subordination to industrial, financial, or traditional merchant capital but the ever-present threat of losing the minimal conditions for their existence, namely the loss of their land (their principal means of production) (Sorj, Pompermayer, and Coradini 1982, Coradini 1981).

In this context it is important to refer to the forms of class conflict and class representation that arise under different conditions. As noted in the case of southern Brazil, the small farmers that are linked at one level or another to industrial capital may not be much better off in levels of living than the rest of the family farmers. Nonetheless, they can count on certain guarantees to finance and market their produce. As a result, their demands are of an economic and administrative nature: higher prices, cheaper credit, and greater support for the commercialization of commodities. The mechanisms by which these demands are expressed include cooperatives, class associations of various kinds, and even rural labor unions. These forms of representation rarely call into question the broader issues at stake but focus, rather, on specific and immediate concerns, normally revolving around the degree of exploitation.

The traditional peasantry, on the other hand, which is marginalized from the more modern sector, does not translate its class interests into purely technical or administrative questions. On the contrary, its position is much more political since the demand is for land, the provision of which would require fundamental social and institutional reform. For issues of this specifically political nature there are few institutional channels through which peasants can express their demands. As a consequence, they are often represented by organizations that are clearly political and ideologi-

cal in character. These include political parties and certain sectors
of the church. The forms of conflict that emerge, such as land invasions, are therefore strictly controlled by the state. These forms of
political struggle are treated either as isolated instances to be dealt
with bureaucratically by relevant state agencies or, in some instances, as police matters.

The largest contingent of small farmers in Amazonia is comprised of traditional peasants from southern Brazil who have been
pushed off their land. Their conflicts over land are thus repeated in
frontier areas. Although agroindustry is present on the frontier, it
has not incorporated peasant producers widely. Those who are
hired on cattle ranches to clear away the forest cover to create pasture are only temporary wage laborers. When their labor is no
longer needed, their struggle for land resumes. As in other parts of
the country, this raises the question as to the means of political
representation for this mass of disspossessed farmers. In the contemporary Amazon, the church has taken the side of the peasants,
confronting the repressive role of the state.

Strategies of the large enterprise

The movement of private enterprises into the countryside does
not imply the mechanical or automatic imposition of the domination of capital over peasant producers. To the contrary, in their
struggle for survival and by their attempts to acquire or hold on to
land, small farmers often hamper the expansion of capital. In the
ensuing competition for land, the state has become the central reference point for economic groups that perceive their interests to
be threatened.

Since the late 1960s, we can identify three more or less distinct phases in frontier expansion, when the struggle for land by
peasants has interfered with the establishment of large capitalist
firms in the region. These instances can be inferred from the demands that the AEA has made of the state. Before migrants were
attracted to Amazonia by colonization and road projects, business
groups had an easier time acquiring land without entering into
disputes with other social groups. Squatters represented few obstacles, and the labor needed for land clearing was recruited by third
parties contracted for this purpose. During this phase, the AEA's demands focused primarily on the speedy approval of ranching
projects by SUDAM, the opening of new roads, and the containment
of Indian groups in limited reservation areas (Pompermayer
1979:chap. 5).

The second phase coincided with the construction of roads and the in-migration of people who had been pushed off their land in other parts of the country. The large enterprise confronted squatters and land speculators who were often the first to move into newly opened territories, a process that hindered the acquisition of land titles. The lobbying efforts of the association reflect these new conditions. Emphasis shifted from the "economic and physical" occupation of the area to a concern for the "legal and juridical" occupation of state lands by private investors. In effect, this meant the titling of land before the mass of migrants moved in. If this were not done, the AEA argued, it would "hinder not only the establishment of enterprises in the region, but would also discourage new investments" (Pompermayer 1979:chap. 6).

Traditional cattle ranchers and merchant capital had different interests. Since these groups had fewer resources to invest in the frontier to begin with, the value added to the land by the clearing carried out by squatters was more important to them. On the other hand, for modern, corporate investors who had greater resources and access to fiscal incentives, the prior clearing of land by squatters was relatively unimportant. For these groups, the priority was to obtain legal title to the land before it was occupied by small farmers, since their occupancy would create difficulties in the acquisition of large properties.

The recent period represents a third phase. For entrepreneurs in the AEA, the issue was not so much acquiring title to new lands as consolidating their investments in order to retain the large tracts of land they already controlled. These priorities emerged as a result of several factors. Many wage laborers who were once employed to clear the land for pasture have been fired, and they have joined the ranks of the growing surplus population that is in search of small agricultural plots in the region. These events, together with the church's leadership, have led to a situation where land invasions have become a constant threat, thereby jeopardizing the security of present and future investments in the region. The institutional protection of land rights has thus emerged as a priority concern for the AEA. More than during any other period in the past, AEA pressure for government action emphasizes the need not only to make land available but also to guarantee the security of private investment and to reduce the growing incidence of land conflict.

The mounting number of land invasions has made this strategic objective increasingly important. In addition to surplus labor, the discovery of mineral resources in the region on lands owned or appropriated by cattle ranchers has stimulated land invasions, notably by individuals seeking to establish placer mines to extract valuable stones and metals. According to businessmen, this "threatens the establishment of organized projects." The AEA has therefore fought for the exclusive rights of title holders to mineral deposits, not only for investment purposes but also as protection against the invasion of their land by miners. Where incursions do take place, the large firms expect to count on the enforcement of the law by the government.[4]

In recent years the state has responded to these demands and has taken a more active role. Emphasis has been given to formulating mechanisms that guarantee the security of threatened areas and to providing institutional means to make some concessions to small farmers searching for land. It is as yet too early to assess the outcomes of these measures.

Notes

1. The original name, Associação dos Empresários Agropecuários da Amazônia, translates literally as the Association of Agricultural and Cattle-Raising Entrepreneurs of the Amazon. After 1976, when the association began to admit members linked to food and animal agroindustries, the name was changed to the Association of Amazonian Entrepreneurs (AEA). For the sake of consistency, the association is referred to throughout this paper as the AEA.
2. Much of the information and analysis contained here was initially developed in Pompermayer 1979. Unless works are cited, information comes from that source.
3. In order to bring its views to the general public, the AEA published the *Revista Amazônia* until December 1980. For internal use by members, the biweekly *Boletim Informativo* contains information on association activities and its negotiations with the government. Besides routine AEA activities, biweekly meetings are held of the Diretoria Executiva and the Conselho Administrativo, either at the São Paulo headquarters or in one of the six regional offices in the Amazon (Barra do Garças, Belém, Conceição do Araguaia, Cuiabá, Rio Branco, and Goiânia). Members of the Administrative and Advisory Councils have always been elected from large national firms and from multinational corporations such as Volkswagen, Swift-Armour, Liquifarm, Drury's, and Borden. The vice-president elected in 1981 is a retired army general and director of four firms in the Amazon. His specific function is to maintain direct contacts with the government (see AEA, 1981b).

4. From interviews with AEA personnel in October 1981. The association
has maintained continual contact with the head of GETAT (Grupo Executivo de Terras do Araguaia-Tocantins), including a meeting in November,
1981 when forty businessmen presented their opinions and suggestions
for action (Boletim Informativo 1981:32; see also AEA 1981a and 1981c.

References Cited

Associação dos Empresários da Amazônia (AEA)
1977a   Indeco: A Riqueza Planejada. Revista Amazônia 26.
1977b   O Modelo de Ocupação Integrada da Amazônia. São Paulo:
         AEA.
1979   Elógios, Críticas e Esperanças dos Empresários. Revista Am-
         azônia 46 (February).
1981a   Amazônia—O Homem e a Terra. Unpublished internal
         document.
1981b   Associação: Metas para 1981. Revista Amazônia 55.
1981c   Mineração na Amazônia. Unpublished internal document.
1981d   Perfil da Associação dos Empresários da Amazônia. São
         Paulo: AEA.
Boletim Informativo
1981   No. 11 (July), No. 32 (October), No. 36 (October). São Paulo:
         AEA.
Boschi, Renato
1979   Elites, Industriais e Democracia. Rio: Graal.
CEDEPLAR
1977   Migrações Internas na Região Norte: Estudo de Campo na
         Região de Marabá. Belém: SUDAM.
Coradini, L.O.
1981   Classes Sociais, Estrutura de Poder e Cooperativismo Agrícola
         no Sul do Brasil. Belo Horizonte, Brazil: Cadernos DCP 6.
Dreifuss, René A.
1981   1964: A Conquista do Estado: Ação Política, Poder e Golpe
         de Classe. Petrópolis, Brazil: Vozes.
Foweraker, Joe
1981   The Struggle for Land: A Political Economy of the Pioneer
         Frontier in Brazil, 1930 to the Present. London: Cambridge.
Hébette, Jean
1977   Colonização Espontánea, Política Agrária e Grupos Sociais.
         Belém: University of Pará (mimeo).
Isto É
1981   No. 226 (April 22).

Montali, Lili
1979 Do Núcleo Colonial ao Capitalismo Monopolista: Produção de Fumo em Santa Cruz do Sul. São Paulo: USP (mimeo).
Oliveira, Francisco de
1971 A Economia Brasileira: Crítica à Razão Dualista. *Estudos* CEBRAP 2.
Pompermayer, Malori José
1979 The State and the Frontier in Brazil: A Case Study of Amazonia. Ph.D. dissertation, Stanford University.
Revista Amazônia
1976 No. 19 (September).
1977 No. 23 (January), No. 24 (February), No. 25 (March), No. 26 (April). São Paulo: AEA.
1978 No. 42 (October). São Paulo: AEA.
1979 No. 46 (February), No. 48 (April), No. 55 (November). São Paulo: AEA.
Sorj, Bernardo
1980 *Estado e Classes Sociais na Agricultura Basileira.* Rio: Zahar.
Sorj, Bernardo, M. Pompermayer, and L. Coradini
1982 *Camponeses e Agroindústria.* Rio: Zahar.
Tavares, José V.
1978 *Colonos do Vinho.* São Paulo: Hucitec.
Valverde, Orlando Picas
1967 *A Rodovia Belém-Brasília.* Rio: IBGE.

Law and Social Change: The Problem of Land in the Brazilian Amazon

Roberto Santos

THE PRACTICE of agrarian advocacy in the Brazilian Amazon has typically had as its objective the preservation of the legal order. More specifically, its goal has been to use the legal system to defend the precepts and arguments that are in the interest of attorneys' usual clients. These include large landholders involved in extractive industries (such as rubber and Brazil nuts), cattle ranchers, mining companies, road construction firms, lumber companies, and the like. In recent years, however, a new development has changed the picture. As in other parts of the country, there have emerged in Amazonia groups of attorneys committed to what might be called "social advocacy," the defense of peasants and rural workers. Where land conflicts have been intense (primarily in southern Pará, northern Goiás, and Acre), these lawyers have resorted to civil law, the Land Statute, and even human rights arguments in order to defend the interests of squatters (*posseiros*) and their families as well as rural unions. Some attorneys have organized regional and national meetings to exchange ideas and to formulate a common strategy. The first such national convention (called "the First Meeting of Lawyers for Rural Workers") was held in 1978. One objective was to propose the inclusion

NOTE: The author expresses his sincere thanks for the collaboration of Alex Nunes Athias in collecting basic information that was indispensable for this study.

439

in law school curricula of agrarian law courses taught "from the peasant's point of view." Precursors to this new group include Francisco Julião, who led the Peasant Leagues in the Northeast before the military coup in 1964, as well as nineteenth-century figures such as Castro Alves and Rui Barbosa.

My objective is to situate this group of attorneys in Amazonia in historical perspective in order to see if the emergence of "social advocacy" derives from distinctions that have occurred historically in the legislation (which will be examined later) and from intensification of social conflict in the regional countryside. To do so, it will be necessary to reconstruct the history of agrarian legislation in the region, paying particular attention to the basic trends, specifically the one in which social advocacy has evolved. (For a discussion of this method of inquiry, see Santos 1980a:326–27.)

The ascent of the latifundio: 1616–1824

For our purposes, the short history of Amazonia (365 years) can be divided into two periods. The first phase begins in 1616 and runs until about the time of independence, say 1824, when the system of *sesmarias* (royal land grants) came to an end in Pará. The second period includes the century and a half between 1824 and the present. In my view the predominant trend in the first phase was the emergence and the dominance of large landholdings that were based on individualistic interests. The second was characterized by two conflicting tendencies: on the one hand, the decline in the traditional latifundios and the emergence of small, family-run farms; on the other, the growth of large-scale capitalist enterprises.

In the first phase, legal changes, primarily in judicial interpretation of the law, increasingly served to advance the concept of private property, independent of its social use. Since this trend was underway in the rest of the country, it is unsurprising that it should also be manifest in Amazonia, even though Amazonia was administratively separate from Brazil until just before independence (see Reis 1966:98, Meireles 1960:187).

During the colonial period, the Crown ceded land in Amazonia (as in the rest of Brazil) in sesmarias. These large grants of the use of land were subject to certain conditions; if they were not met, the property would revert to the Crown (see Diégues Jr. 1959:39, Vianna 1904a:149). Thus the grantee held his land only provisionally. This provisional right to the use of land was fundamentally different from the concept of private property that appeared during the Roman Empire and that was restored centuries later by the bourgeois revolution. Because the size of the sesmaria was not explicitly limited, extravagantly large concessions were permitted. In the Northeast, some exceeded fifty leagues across (see Guimarães 1977:51, Sodero 1968:190).

The size of the sesmarias in Amazonia in the 1600s is not clearly documented. Land grants were recorded only in the last few years of the seventeenth century. The records that do remain document the grievances of the inhabitants of the colony requesting action by the Crown, and they suggest that the concessions during that period were vast. The complaints refer to the "inequality by which the state commonly makes large grants of the best lands to the powerful, leaving the poor with none" (Royal Decree of September 16, 1705). In 1697 the size of concessions was limited to an area of one by three leagues, a rule that also applied to Brazil (see Annães, 1902, vol. 1). The fact is that such a tract of land, equal to 13,068 hectares, already constituted a latifundio. Such an area could be exploited without risk of losing the land grant only by someone with substantial capital and a number of slaves. In view of the scarcity of Negro slaves and the resistance by the Indians to becoming slaves, the land grants were permanently under threat of expropriation. But to enforce the law would have meant the end of the colony. The alternative of colonization based on smallholders was beyond Portugal's ability since her population was already reduced by high rates of emigration to an empire that included several continents. This is the origin of the tensions between enforcing the law and tolerating its abuse, and prohibiting the enslavement of Indians and allowing it to occur under certain conditions.

Any productive activity that would contribute to the objectives of colonization invariably faced a labor shortage, which military personnel and colonists sought to overcome through enslavement of the Indians. This they managed to achieve to some degree, despite the opposition of missionaries, whose methods of subjugating the natives were more lenient. The history of Indian slavery reveals the impotence of royal rule in maintaining the freedom of native groups. Chicanery and blatant violation of the law made the capture of Indians the most lucrative business in the colony. At times even the law abandoned its protectionist stance in response to local pressures. The swings in Indian policy are notorious, particularly during periods when Jesuits lost favor with royal authority.

Extractive activities that produced export commodities contributed little to a dynamic economy. An internal market based on the circulation of money and the production of agricultural goods and urban services failed to develop (see Azevedo 1901:193). The amount of commerce with the metropolitan centers was not significant. These market restrictions and the availability of low-cost Indian labor fostered a complacency among the colonists. At the same time these conditions may have reduced the value of land, which remained largely unoccupied. Large landholdings and slavery were institutions that reinforced one another. Permitting sesmarias as large as three leagues, the law authorized the acquisition of land grants that could only be made economically viable through a large number of workers. While an object of the social conscience of the colonists, the enslavement of Indians seemed to be the best means of exploiting vast areas, although at a low level of productivity.

Until the middle of the eighteenth century, the method used by missionaries (especially the Jesuits) was somewhat different. Apparently there were two types of enterprises, each based on a different form of land use. There was the large establishment, owned and efficiently administered by the Order. It often produced tobacco, sugar, cacao, cotton, and manioc, or became involved in cattle ranching, salt mining, or the production of cured fish. The other form was the supervision of Indian villages, where land remained communal property or was distributed according to native traditions. Profits were reinvested in the villages in order to upgrade the community (Azevedo 1901:208–10). Neither the large establishment nor the village-based enterprise can be considered a capitalist venture.

Individuals who were recipients of royal land grants, ignoring their social responsibility, typically treated their concessions as a means to make money without working. They were often absentee landlords who rented portions of their holdings to third parties (see Annães 1902, 1:187). A century after Governor Negreiros received instructions to repossess land that had not been cultivated in order to distribute it among the needy, the directive remained a dead letter. Even the survey of the land grants, which was essential to establishing a minimum degree of order in the distribution of property among individuals, was rarely carried out. As a result, the boundaries were never clearly defined. They tended to follow the accidents of geography rather than a systematic process of land partition. These circumstances led to land invasions and to conflict over property lines.

The decree published on October 5, 1795, was the final attempt to systematize the rules regarding the sesmarias. It demanded that the grantees survey their concessions within a two-year period or else forfeit them automatically. Before the deadline, the interest groups affected by this decree were able to have it suspended. In the State of Grão-Pará, the rule apparently remained in effect yet was never enforced. The practice of not demarcating property lines and the continued existence of nonproductive landholding remained unchallenged (see Vianna 1904a:154).

At about this time the bourgeois revolution in Europe had completed its initial phase. This was accomplished by the evolution of the bourgeois notion of private property, sanctified by the Napoleonic Code. This concept contributed to the process of consolidating and ratifying the latifundio in Brazil.

A new problem had also begun to take shape in the countryside: increasingly, migrant families who had been pushed off lands granted to individuals by the Crown were appropriating land without legal title. As the geographic dispersion of small farmers created food shortages in the urban areas, awareness of the need for reform mounted (Sodero 1968:193). In this context, landholders could view the arrival in Brazil of João VI in 1808 as a threat, since it implied the enforcement of laws regarding sesmarias. Surely José Bonifácio's proposal put forth in 1821, which argued that uncultivated land should return to the national patrimony, ran counter to the irresponsible practices that had been in effect in the colony. It is not surprising, then, that a year later Dom Pedro I ended the sesmarias. But rather than taking Bonifácio's advice, his decree of July 17, 1822, deferred the concession of any future sesmarias until the Convocation of the General Constitutional Assembly, thereby leaving existing land grants untouched.

The effect of abandoning the idea of expropriation was to establish firmly the legal existence of colossal landholdings. The Constitution of 1824 endorsed the concept of private property. Article 179, Section 22, established the right to private ownership and made it clear that land could only be expropriated in special cases where the public interest was at stake and could be carried out only with prior compensation.

On August 15, 1823, Pará declared its independence from Portugal—which the rest of the country had done almost a year earlier on September 7, 1822. Technically the arrival of João VI in Brazil, which terminated the administrative distinction between Brazil and Pará, meant that no further sesmarias should have been granted after 1822. Nonetheless, the concessions continued in Amazonia until 1824. This was probably an attempt by the government to meet the requests for land that had been made prior to 1822.

In summary, the system of land tenure in Amazonia substantially changed over time. The system of granting public lands to individuals who were subject to clearly defined sanctions enforced by the state (especially with regard to surveying boundary lines and cultivating the land) gave way to unregulated private ownership of property. Noncompliance with the original conditions attached to the sesmarias, which at first was merely tolerated, later received formal recognition before the law. The recipients of royal land grants thus became owners of private property; their rights were guaranteed under the Constitution except in special cases where fully compensated expropriation was deemed necessary.

Small farmers versus the capitalist firm: 1824 to the present

Guimarães (1977:110) notes: "while in other continents . . . large landholdings emerged and developed on the ruins of small peasant producers, in our country, by contrast, it was the latifundio which was first established, and small farmers only came about much later when the rigid system of latifundios began to break down." As we have just seen in the previous section, Amazonia was characterized by large landholdings from the very beginning of its founding. The questions posed here are how small farmers came about in the region and how the legal system dealt with this new reality. From such a perspective we are better able to understand the subsequent resurgence of the latifundio, which came about in different forms in more recent years. Signs of this tension clearly appear in agrarian and related legislation.

Articles published in 1890 by Conselheiro Pães de Andrade provide some insight into the agrarian history of Pará. He confirms the fact that, for the most part, the sesmarias rarely met the conditions established by law. To this he adds a surprising point: "Before law 601, of September 18, 1850, the territory was mainly held by primary occupants." This suggests that the sesmarias, even though they evolved into a tenure system of private property, began to falter. Since the eighteenth century, this opened opportunities for small farmers to establish themselves on uncultivated lands (Andrade 1890). It was as if public authority, which had tolerated the abuses of the large sesmeiros, lost the ability and the will to control its own properties. Lying idle, these abandoned lands readily lent themselves to occupation by both small and large posseiros, or squatters. Because the region was immense and the number of latifundios relatively small, this type of settlement probably did not lead to social conflict. Clearly the agrarian history of the region would have been much different had the commodities produced by the latifundios been more economically viable. This might have led large landowners to tighten their hold on the land or to expand into the areas cultivated by small farmers.

The precise moment that marks the appearance of the small farmer is difficult to establish. There is some indication that this may have occurred as a result of a law passed on June 6, 1755, which emancipated the Indians, or of another law passed in 1798 (abolition of directories of Indian villages). This took place during Pombal's time, when his brother Mendonça Furtado served as governor of Amazonia. Although this legislation did not eliminate the abuses and the capture of Indians, it had greater impact than previous laws. It marked the beginning of the process that led to the freedom of those who managed to survive the various forms of destruction the Europeans had imposed on native groups. Recall, for example, the testimony of Baron de Guajará, who noted that, once the Indians were no longer subjugated, "they quickly dispersed and took refuge in the backlands" (Raiol 1902:158). Other evidence can be inferred from the decline in the demand for sesmarias, which occurred precisely during the period of economic growth brought about by the Companhia Geral do Grão-Pará e Maranhão between 1755 and 1784, as shown in Table 1.

A plausible explanation for this trend is the increased difficulty in obtaining Indian labor after the emancipation, when the Indians retreated into the interior. African slaves were much more expensive. As a result, only a small fraction of the dominant class, mainly those who had most benefited from the recently estab-

TABLE 1. Sesmarias granted in the Brazilian Amazon, 1725–1824

Period	Duration in years	Number of grants	Average number per year
1725–54	30	1,523	51
1755–84	30	303	10
1785–1814	30	232	8
1815–24	10	120	12
Totals/average:	100	2,178	21

SOURCE: Annães da Biblioteca e Archivo Público do Pará.

NOTE: Data before 1725 are incomplete. After 1824 and before 1836, only two sesmarias were granted.

lished monopolies, was able to expand through the acquisition of new sesmarias. The majority lost power and fully realized that further land acquisition would be of little value. Moreover, the Indian who migrated into the interior was stripped of tribal identity. As a result the only alternative available to him was a family-based subsistence agriculture combined with hunting and fishing activities.

The impoverished *caboclos* (offspring of a white man and an Indian woman) joined the people who appropriated lands granted to others but never cultivated or who squatted on public property. Later, freed Negro slaves and the descendants of the half-bloods of Negro ancestry also joined this group (see Spix and von Martius 1823, 3:21). It is quite possible that runaway slaves in the mid-nineteenth century may have organized peasantry experiments besides cooperative forms of production (see Salles 1971:220–36). And at about the beginning of the nineteenth century, families from the Northeast fled to Amazonia to escape the drought, thus increasing the region's peasant population.

The above history confirms Sawyer's (1979) periodization of the formation of a peasantry in Amazonia. This evolution, according to Sawyer, includes the following phases: (1) the period of 1616–1750 characterized by the almost total lack of a peasantry; (2) the formation of subsistence producers from 1750 to 1850 (which were, however, under pressure to become wage laborers for the export economy); (3) the period from 1850 to 1930, characterized by the expansion of small-scale commodity production; and

(4) the phase of "national integration," from 1930 to the present, when small farmers began to migrate to Amazonia, thereby expanding the peasant frontier in Brazil.

Imperial Law 601: 1850 to 1889

The gradual emergence of a peasantry, both in Brazil and in the Amazon, was to influence legislation. After the legal abolition of the sesmarias, the country was deprived of any kind of agrarian regulation. This disarray interested few people, least of all the dominant class.

It was in this context that Imperial Law 601 was promulgated on September 18, 1850. This law, for the first time in the history of Amazonia, provided the basis for modest upward mobility for small producers. The latter were allowed legal access to land at a moment when economic conditions were exceptionally favorable. The increase in the world price for rubber provided opportunities for family-based extractive activities. Large landholders, affected by the Cabanagem and the end of the slave trade, suffered from a severe shortage of manpower. Although they tried to attract subsistence farmers by offering salaries or sharecropping arrangements, such workers preferred to engage in rubber production in more distant areas. Barbara Weinstein (1980:chap. 2) provides a thorough description of this process and demonstrates the reasons why the elites in Amazonia, before the height of the rubber boom, consistently criticized extractive activities in favor of agriculture. The exalted view of agriculture even applied to small family producers, a position that would appear to be inconsistent for a dominant class that was coexistent with slavery. It is true that a portion of this new group became so involved in the *aviamento* system that, by the end of the century, they were little better off than the rubber gatherers who had migrated to Amazonia from the Northeast. At the same time there is some indication that another portion of the gatherers managed to legitimize their property and to preserve a degree of autonomy.

Cases such as these moved Messias Junqueira to say that Law 601 was "the most brilliant victory by the humble farmer over the proud sesmeiro." The law was passed by the same cabinet that, only days before, had proscribed the slave trade (Junqueira 1964:67). The objectives of Law 601 and the regulatory decree (1.318 of January 30, 1854) were relatively simple: (a) to respect the occupation of land, even if the occupant had no title, provided that the land was a place of "effective cultivation and habitual residence"; failure to meet either condition (by the small farmer or the sesmeiro) would result in the land being classified as unoccupied; (b) except under the conditions noted in (a) above, unoccupied land would no longer be distributed free of charge and the invasion of lands would be subject to penalty from that day forward; (c) a registry of all claimed land would be created; (d) property lines were to be established through obligatory land surveys.

Nonetheless, nearly forty years later, at the time of the proclamation of the Republic, land tenure in Pará was still in disarray. The land registry was never created, and only about a fourth of the landholdings were legalized. The simple occupation of land was the principal method of acquiring land by peasants and large landholders alike, both of which groups operated with impunity. In 1860 the provincial government tried to force all occupants to regularize their holdings by instituting the sale of land "on time." This system was elaborated by additional decrees (of June 3, 1874) stipulating that the cost of surveying the land would be paid at the time of the sale. But the high price demanded by surveyors, as well as the cost of the land itself, made it impossible for the small farmer to obtain legal title. As a result, most peasants continued the traditional practice of occupying land without formal title or documentation. This worked to the benefit of the large landholders who could afford the surveyor's fees. In many instances they appropriated their neighbor's lands without compensating them for any improvements that had been made.

At that time, the loss of land in one place did not imply an insoluble problem. Land was readily available in other places. Moreover, the high price received for rubber made things easier for the peasants, so they rarely resisted the expansion of the latifundios. Often they would become the large landholders' clients by taking certain consumer goods and tools in exchange for rubber at the end of the harvest. The rubber gatherer from the Northeast at the end of the nineteenth century had no land whatsoever and was little more than a wage earner for the *seringalista* (rubber gathering controller), who would exploit him unmercifully.

During this period from 1850 to 1889, a number of general and regional laws were passed to facilitate colonization by small farmers of foreign extraction. Most of the experiments were unsuccessful. The principal attempts were carried out by the Mauá firm, which settled families from Portugal and China near Manaus in

1854. Several North Americans came to Santarém in 1866–71. A so-called French colony in 1875 attracted French, Italian, and German immigrants (Muniz 1916, Santos 1980b:88–92, Guilhon 1979; see also Moura 1957).

In general this period exhibits two contrasting tendencies within the legal system. One was to favor small-scale, family-based production. The other was to preserve the integrity of the large landholdings. Whether properties were large or small, few property lines were ever firmly established since land claims boundaries followed rivers or other accidents of geography. These background elements would continue through the Republican period, although with certain changes.

State dominance in the administration of land tenure: 1889–1970

The republican Constitution of 1891 reaffirmed the right of private property, a principle bolstered by the stipulation that expropriation could only occur with prior compensation to the landowner. The most salient change was to transfer control over unoccupied land to the states (except in the case of frontier areas—see article 64). Subsequently, three juridical events dominated the history of agrarian legislation in Pará: Decree 410 of 1891, Decree 1.044 of 1933, and Law 57 of 1969.

Decree 410 outlined the major aspects of legislation regarding land. It set forth the rules for measuring property, for buying and selling land, for obtaining title, and for the recording of land claims. These rules recognized all landholdings on the date that the Republic was proclaimed, including small farmers' claims as well as the grants held by sesmeiros or their descendants. The old royal land grants were subject to "revalidation," and the land claims of squatters were to be legitimized. In both cases, the tests were whether the land was effectively cultivated and whether it was the claimant's place of habitual residence (see Lamarão 1977).

By this time, however, rubber gathering was no longer an activity carried out by small operators. The owners of rubber trees and the merchants involved in the rubber trade had joined the ranks of the elite (Weinstein 1980). The rubber areas, like natural pastures used for cattle raising, required no cultivation. Hence, Article 6 of Decree 410 defined the conservation of forest for "extractive industry" as a form of effective cultivation. As Benedito Monteiro (1980:22–23) noted, Article 6 provided the breakthrough for the retention and the expansion of the latifundio. But the rest of the legislation continued to serve the interests of the small producer, whether farmer or laborer.

At the same time, the decline of the agricultural latifundio was accelerated by the migration of farm labor to the rubber areas. Small farmers who remained were unable to meet the demand for foodstuffs in Belém, Manaus, and the other cities in the region. The problem of food supply led to the colonization by small farmers of the Zona Bragantina, in Pará. A railroad was constructed to bring Northeasterners into the region. This was undoubtedly the most important colonization effort carried out in Amazonia until that time (Penteado 1967). The descendants of these colonists later became an important electoral force, which led to the creation of various counties (*municípios*) as the population grew.

The end of the century was a propitious time for the administrative organization of land distribution. The end of slavery brought a wave of liberal thought to the region. The economy prospered, and there were few conflicts that revolved around questions of land tenure. Had an adequate survey of landholdings been carried out at that time, many twentieth-century problems would have been avoided. But negligence or incompetence prevented the needed surveying.

Ordinarily, unoccupied public lands could only be transferred through sale or by being set aside for special purposes (Indian reservations or colonization projects), as specified in Decree 410. The collapse of the rubber boom changed the situation. The emigration of labor from the region led Governor Enéas Martins (1914) to adopt an unusual incentive to keep small farmers there. A free concession would be granted to "any citizen who needed it, of plots of public lands in any municipality of the state, up to a hundred hectares in size" (Law 1.432 of 1914). Governor Lauro Sodré elaborated this system by instituting "provisional titles" to land. This amounted to a permit to cultivate public property, allowing the occupant to obtain a definitive title at the end of a two-year interval (Law 1.584). During this period, several colonies were established. Such measures, aimed at retaining labor and the development of small-scale agriculture, allowed the region to maintain, however modestly, a degree of employment in the face of a severe economic depression.

As rubber gathering declined, two other extractive industries expanded: Brazil nuts and lumber. Both were organized in a fashion similar to the rubber collection system. These activities, except for the ones undertaken by the cattle ranchers on the island of Marajó and the few large agricultural enterprises, were the primary factors that influenced agrarian policy up to 1930. These interest groups managed to establish long-term lease agreements (*emphyteusis*) that gave them control over tracts of land that were larger and cheaper to obtain than they could buy outright. This was one way of pitting the Civil Code (1917) against Decree 410. The leasing process transferred complete control of the Brazil nut groves to the leaseholders. In Pará, the cost of the lease amounted to about 2 percent of the cost of the land, a fact that ran counter to the intentions of Decree 410. On the same day that Governor Sodré enacted the perpetual lease law, he also permitted the acquisition of larger tracts of land by agroindustrial groups. In this way it became possible to justify enormous landholdings, sometimes exceeding one million hectares, a factor that caused great scandal during the administration of Governor Dionysio Bentes (Coimbra 1981:125–32).

Leaders of the Revolution of 1930 took note of these events. Their actions were not limited to mere reprimand. Among the first initiatives undertaken, Decree 11 (November 7, 1930) required the immediate return to the state of all Brazil nut groves (even those held with definitive title) until a commission could consider the issue. Magalhães Barata, in charge of enforcing this policy, declared that the leases were voided "because they were contrary to the Revolutionary Government's program and were an aberration of the principles of law." Barata appeared to be personally sensitive to the needs of the masses. In March 1931, he revoked the provision that required colonists to bear the cost of surveys and exempted them from taxes and other charges associated with obtaining title. He also entrusted local governments with the power to promote colonies for the "settlement of unemployed persons." This decree (184 of March 12, 1931) was in keeping with the objectives of the Revolution.

The law that governed access to land until 1966 (Decree 1.044 of August 19, 1933) was one of the best formulated by the state government. Consolidating previous legislation and fusing it with the initiatives of the revolution, the new regulation reflected the extent to which the new leadership perceived the financial difficulties of the state. Barata was forced to retract the total exemption for colonists since local governments, without a source of income, lacked the resources to survey land, a process more costly than the state could assume. Nonetheless, the actual concession of the plots remained free of charge. Other legal initiatives, both before and after the Estado Novo, also benefited the small farmer.

In the state of Amazonas the creation of a peasantry was also underway, beginning with the family-based rubber collector, who was often a client of rubber traders and creditors. A major step toward strengthening the small-farmer sector was the arrival in 1937 of fifty Japanese families, who intended to produce jute in the seasonal floodland areas (*várzeas*). Their success was emulated by Brazilians, who began similar activities in the Zona Bragantina of Pará (see Miyasaki and Ono 1958).

Until the mid-1950s, the peasant sector and the large landholdings were treated as separate entities. There was one set of laws for latifundios and another for agricultural colonies and small farmers. Different government agencies were in charge of each. Since there was little contact between the two sectors, conflicts were rare and highly localized. The gradual emergence of wage laborers did not result from dispossessions generated by capitalist expansion; rather, it was the consequence of underemployment together with the depletion of soils, inadequate education, and the general market and credit conditions that characterized the region (see SPVEA 1955).

Before long the two sectors would confront each other in Amazonia. In 1956, Law 2.975 committed the government to the construction of the Belém-Brasília Highway. While the area to the west attracted people to Rondônia in search of cassiterite, the area to the east was sought after by ranchers for fattening cattle for the market in Belém. Small farmers migrated to the region to obtain plots of the recently discovered fertile soils. The frontier zone attracted people from all over Brazil and from diverse social classes. The demand for public lands increased in the state of Pará. The land office, which had sold 35,000 hectares between 1949 and 1953, sold 61,000 between 1954 and 1958. This awakened the prospect of speculative profits from real estate, which intensified the demand for land. In 1962 the Brazilian economy entered a crisis that cut off other investment options. In addition, inflation rose at a rate that continually increased the cost of material goods. Transferring capital to Amazonia in order to maintain or increase its value was an excellent investment option at the time, especially for cattle ranchers (see Santos 1979a:chap. 3, 1979b:21). The rush for land in Amazonia during this period was intense. Between 1959 and 1963, the State of Pará sold over 5.6 million hectares of land, most of it to large capitalist enterprises or land speculators. Lamarão (1977 1:18) notes that "between the completion of the Belém-Brasília and the revolution in 1964, essentially in 1962 and 1963, land titling in Pará fell into an incredible state of disorder." False titles and fraud were common, multiple claims to the same land occurred, property was bought in the name of people who never existed or who had disappeared, and the boundaries that small farmers had established were disregarded.

The new state government tried to respond. All land sales were practically halted, and transport and communications support were extended to the small farmers. Law 3.641 of May 1, 1966, tried to bring some order to the chaos that characterized the administration of lands in Pará. But events led to a different outcome. After the military takeover in 1964 the federal government set out to dismantle the entire fragile apparatus of unions and associations that had begun to emerge among the peasantry and rural wage laborers. Leaders were imprisoned or threatened, thus quelling the legitimate means of representing the interests of this class. The rural labor movement in Pará, although less widespread than is currently the case, encompassed over twelve unions in 1964. These were organized around groups with headquarters in the capital, such as the Communist party and the Catholic church.

Before the coup, groups in the National Congress saw that a fiscal incentives program was one way to stimulate investment that was needed due to the country's economic crisis. Consequently, the federal program of incentives, first applied in the Northeast, was extended to Amazonia (Mahar 1978:107–11). From that point on, capital from southern Brazil and from foreign enterprises began to move into Amazonia, partly as a result of the subsidized credit programs. With the creation of SUDAM (which replaced SPVEA), the fiscal and credit incentives, formerly restricted to industry, were given to agricultural and cattle ventures. As a result, legal institutions came under pressure from powerful interest groups. The latter benefited because of their superior bureaucratic, technical, and political organization, and especially because they were able to mobilize large sums of money (a great part of which was acquired from public sources).

The federal takeover: 1970 to the present

At the state level, Law 57 (of August 22, 1969) was an attempt by the government to shield large landholders from the legal ambiguities that existed and to create mechanisms to resolve conflicts over land. The programs in support of small-farmer settlement fell by the wayside. But the state of Pará did not command sufficient resources to satisfy the large companies in their haste to make use of the federal incentives offered through SUDAM. Thus began a series of initiatives that restricted the state's control over its own land. Constitutional Amendment No. 1 (of October 17, 1969) facilitated this process since the military junta that took over the country once again made agrarian policy a matter of federal control.

In 1970 and 1971, the national government assumed control over all unoccupied land in Amazonia. With no compensation to the states, it turned over the land to INCRA. Large projects were started to improve the region's infrastructure so as to stimulate private investment. The Transamazon Highway was built and construction of the Cuiabá-Santarém Highway was begun. Port facilities, airports, and hydroelectric dams were constructed, and mineral surveys were carried out. The National Integration Program (PIN) set aside ten kilometers on either side of federal roads for colonization purposes (Law 1.106 in 1970). This was later extended to include a strip one hundred kilometers wide along the highways (Law 1.164 in 1971).

Economic growth was not long in coming. Between 1965 and 1975 regional income rose 4.5 times, increasing its proportion of total income in Brazil from 1.9 percent to 2.7 percent. From 1960 to 1978, per capita income rose from $Cr7,876 to $Cr25,052. In constant U.S. dollars, this implied a change from $304 to $968. These figures, however, do not speak to the question of the drastic concentration of landholdings and of income that took place during the period. Nor do the data reveal anything about the rapid increases in land conflicts that occurred in rural Amazonia, which had repercussions throughout the whole country. Small farmers found themselves in frontal confrontation over access to land with large landholders, speculators, timber companies, and other agents of capitalist expansion. Even the traditional Amazonian peasant, the *caboclo*, was affected by the spread of capitalist social relations of production and the rise in prices, both of which contributed to his dispossession. Similarly, Indian nations were affected by the advancing frontier. Indians suffered at the hands of small farmers in search of land as well as from the arrival of large enterprises and land speculators.

Failing to understand the larger historical context, the federal government increasingly centralized the political decision-making process. It became increasingly bureaucratically involved, without comprehending the situation, which only aggravated the turmoil that was occurring in areas of social conflict. Decree 71.615 (of December 22, 1972) called for "the colonization and concession of unoccupied lands through colonization projects, rural enterprises, and agroindustrial and cattle raising ventures initiated by public institutions or private or corporate groups." As will be noted below, this decree signaled a change in emphasis in the National Integration Program, which had favored the colonization of small farmers in 1970. The same law required the prior consent of the National Security Council (NSC) before INCRA could approve any project along the federal highway. The council reserved the right to "repeal any project or activity related to unoccupied land."

The NSC apparently became involved as a result of the guerilla movement that was discovered in southern Pará and northern Goiás in the early 1970s. Yet even after that time, the NSC continued to have considerable power. The effect of this intervention was to convert an administrative problem into a military one. The cloak of mystery and danger, which characterizes the military perspective, further complicated the matter. To administer the remaining land, Pará in 1975 created the state Land Institute (Law 4.584 of October 8, 1975). By this time, however, the state could not take any important steps without consulting the NSC. On the first of February, 1980, through Decree Law 1,767 (later altered by Law 1,799 of August 5, 1980) the federal government created an institution that was directly subordinated to the National Security Council. The Grupo Executivo das Terras do Araguaia-Tocantins (GETAT) was established with the explicit purpose of accelerating the titling process for small farmers. Similar institutions were created to control land in Baixo Amazonas. The proliferation of administrative agencies (IBDF, INCRA, FUNAI, ITERPA, GETAT, and so on), in conjunction with the rigid centralization of decision making, produced few positive results for the small farmer.

We conclude that a principal characteristic of this period in

Amazonia was the development of the large rural capitalist enterprise, as well as the continuance of the traditional latifundio. It
was also after 1964, however, that the idea of an agrarian reform gained new impetus. Through a constitutional amendment
(number 10 of November 9, 1964), the requirement of prior cash
compensation was done away with. The Land Statute (Law 4.504
of November 30, 1964) was approved, and the Brazilian Institute
for Agrarian Reform (IBRA) was created in order to carry it out. In
this way legal mechanisms were created to support the stability of
land occupation, which was recognized as valid so long as the plot
was worked during a certain amount of time (see Monteiro 1980:
149–55; Duque Corredor 1981). The effect was to legitimize the
direct acquisition of land so long as the claim remained uncon-
tested for a defined period of time. In the same spirit, state law
57/69 granted the right to turn over lots 100 hectares in size to
small farmers. Similarly, the initial intent of the National Integration Program was to create a colonization project based on small,
family held farms. In fact, two undertakings symbolize conflicting
tendencies within the legal system: the support of the enormous
multinational project on the Jari River, and the simultaneous creation of a small-farmer colonization program along the Transamazon Highway. Economic, ecological, and administrative problems plagued both. Although these issues will not be dealt with
here, it is important to note the role that the opening of the frontier played, independently of the intentions of the government. Its
purpose was to relieve social conflict in critical areas of the Northeast and in certain places in southern Brazil without directly attending to the social demands of the peasantry and of rural wage
laborers as a whole. Numerous studies have dealt with this issue
(see Guimarães 1977, Prado, Jr. 1966, Martins 1975 and 1980,
Velho 1972 and 1976, Singer 1977, Ianni 1978, Katzman 1977,
Sawyer 1979, Graziano da Silva 1980, Graziano da Silva et al.
1978, Bunker 1979, Dias 1978 and 1979, Araujo 1979, Schmink
1981, Foweraker 1981, Pinto 1977 and 1980, Santos 1979a and
1979b).
    With the help of certain groups, especially the Catholic
Church, peasants in Amazonia began to develop an attitude that
favored resistance. This resistance was usually passive; at times,
however, as a result of the actions by the large landholders and
their henchmen, peasants resorted to violent defense of their land.
As it happens, the Land Statute did little to regularize land titles,

nor did it create the legal mechanisms to defend property rights when these were threatened. Judges and lawyers therefore apply the old and now obsolete rules of the Civil Code. According to the Code, "the landholder has the right to maintain or reinstate his claim through his own force, provided that he does so immediately." Acts of redress or of defense could not "go beyond that which was necessary for the maintenance or restitution of the plot. . . . The landholder with just cause to suspect harassment may petition the judge to protect him from imminent violence by punishing anyone transgressing this injunction" (Article 499). However, it is almost impossible for a small farmer to defend himself "by his own force" when he is isolated and confronted by gunslingers or tractors. His only recourse is through the judge. But, in such a case, three sorts of problems become relevant.

The law and social advocacy

The first problem concerns the private character of the legal system in the interior. With the exception of judges and juries, all other actors within the legal structure function on the basis of remuneration from the individual or firm involved. Clerks, notaries, appraisers, and other functionaries directly or indirectly associated with the proceedings all operate on a pay-for-service basis. Thus they are not civil servants in the traditional sense of the word. An archive or a civil registry can be equated to any agency that provides a service but that also collects its own fees. There is a legislative provision for free legal services for the poor (Law 1,060 of February 5, 1950), but given the multitude of the poor who are potential clients, its correct application would quickly lead to the insolvency of the region's notaries. This demonstrates the incompatibility of this public service with its private and commercial character. In addition, the rules governing the behavior of these agencies are very vague. This permits them a great deal of leeway as they are almost never subject to supervision. This situation, aside from creating a breeding ground for graft and corruption, causes the cost of legal services to rise. The effect is to exclude the peasantry from the legal system.

A second problem relates to the legal requirement that litigants retain a lawyer. Most of the areas in Amazonia have no attorneys at all. In many cases the closest one available may be hundreds of kilometers away. The third problem is the attitude of the judges, which can be traced to their Romanist education. Even when small farmers are able to get together to hire a lawyer and meet all of the other requirements, judges tend to view poor peasants with suspicion, if not outright hostility.

Lawyers defending peasants confront these problems, which are aggravated by two others. The chronic inadequacy of the state judicial system in Amazonia is one. Another is the presumption that parties in a suit are equal before the law, an ideal that is rarely true. According to the law, the police must be an arm of the judiciary. In fact they are much more active than the judicial agencies, given the power at their disposal. Were they to act in favor of the just possession of land and under the strict command of the courts, the police could play a major role in solving social conflicts and establishing law and order. However, observations in the field in places of intense land disputes indicate the very opposite practice. The police generally connive with thugs, are prone to the excessive use of force, and nearly always work against peasants.

As a profession, legal advocacy also has its problems. Destitute clients are unable to pay the cost of professional advice or even to cover the expense involved in traveling the long distances that are involved in Amazonia. Transportation by bus is slow and unreliable, which means that lawyers, to take on cases in the rural area, must be away from their practice for long periods of time.

It follows that advocates of peasant rights must operate under extremely adverse conditions. A commitment to the cause requires professional training as well as a certain heroism and unselfishness, qualities that are rarely found together. Social advocacy in Amazonia has historical roots that can be traced back to 1824 when the sesmarias were abolished. In this sense, past legislation, by recognizing the rights of slaves and caboclos, to some degree was a precedent for this new form of advocacy. At the same time this contemporary activism, with its accumulated experience, can create the conditions for new and broader forms of peasant rights.

Still, the ability to change the law should not be exaggerated when it comes to the Brazilian Amazon. Law encompasses not only values but also a set of rules and institutions composed of courts, prisons, and police. Justice, inspired by a commitment to human rights, can only reach the peasantry via the transformation of rules and strategically located institutions. As we have seen, the likelihood of such change in the region is not encouraging.

Ultimately the rural workers in Brazil will demand the substitution of the traditional judiciary for a corps of specialized magistrates. Attempts in this direction have been made (see CONTAG 1979:166, Mendonça 1977 and 1981). The success of such an undertaking will depend in large part on the training such future magistrates will receive and on many other structural changes that are necessary. The need to clarify and to support these demands is among the challenges now faced by the new social advocacy.

References Cited

Andrade, Romualdo de Sousa Pães de (Conselheiro)
    1890   A Propriedade Territorial no Estado No Pará. A República. Series of articles beginning November 5.
Annães da Biblioteca e Archivo Público do Pará
    1902   Volume 1, reprinted by Biblioteca em Belém, 1968.
    1902   Volume 2, reprinted by Biblioteca em Belém, 1968.
    1904   Volume 3, reprinted by Biblioteca em Belém, 1968.
    1926   Volume 10, Belém.
Araujo, Braz José de (coord.)
    1979   Reflexões Sobre a Agricultura. Brasileira. Rio: Paz e Terra.
Azevedo, João Lúcio D'
    1901   Os Jesuítas no Grão-Pará. Lisbon: Tavares Cardosa & Irmão.
Bunker, Stephen
    1979   Power Structures and Exchanges between Government Agencies in the Expansion of the Agricultural Sector. Studies in Comparative International Development 14(1):56–76.
Coimbra, Creso
    1981   A Revolução de 30 no Pará; análise, crítica e interpretação da história. Belém: Conselho Estadual de Cultura.
CONTAG (Confederação Nacional dos Trabalhadores na Agricultura)
    1979   Anais. Brasília, D.F.: 3 Congresso Nacional dos Trabalhadores Rurais.
Dias, Guilherme Leite da Silva
    1978   Estrutura Agrária e Crescimento Extensivo. Tese de Livre-Docente da Univ. de São Paulo; xerocopy.
Dias, Guilherme Leite da Silva, ed.
    1979   Pobreza Rural no Brasil: Caracterização do Problema e Recomendações de Políticas, vol. 16. Brasília: Comissão de Financiamento da Produção do Min. da Agricultura, Coleção Análise e Pesquisa.
Diégues Jr., Manuel
    1959   População e propriedade da terra no Brasil. In 50 Textos de História do Brasil. Déa Ribeiro Fenelon (org.), União Pan-Americana, Washington, D.C. São Paulo: Hucitec. 1976.

Duque Corredor, Román J.
1981   La Posesión Civil y la Posesión Agrária. Conferência no. 1:
        Encontro Internacional de Jus-Agraristas. Belém, May.
        (mimeo)
Foweraker, J.
1981   The Struggle for Land: A Political Economy of the Pioneer
        Frontier in Brazil, 1930 to the Present. London: Cambridge
        University Press.
Graziano da Silva, J.F.
1980   O Que É a Questão Agrária. São Paulo: Brasiliense.
Graziano da Silva, J.F. et al.
1978   Estrutura Agrária e Produção de Subsistência na Agricul-
        tura Brasileira. São Paulo: Hucitec.
Guilhon, Norma
1979   Confederados em Santarém. Belém: Conselho Estadual de
        Cultura.
Guimarães, Alberto Passos
1977   Quatro Séculos de Latifúndio. 4th ed. Rio: Paz e Terra.
Ianni, Octávio
1978   A Luta Pela Terra. Petrópolis: Vozes.
Junqueira, Messias
1964   As Terras Devolutas na Reforma Agrária. São Paulo: Revista
        dos Tribunais.
Katzman, Martin T.
1977   Cities and Frontiers in Brazil: Regional Dimensions of Eco-
        nomic Development. London and Cambridge, Mass.: Har-
        vard University Press.
Lamarão, Paulo
n.d.   Comentários à Legislação de Terras do Estado e Outros En-
        saios. Belém: Grafisa.
1977   Legislação de Terras do Estado do Pará, 1890–1977. 2 vols.
        Belém: Grafisa.
Lorena, Carlos
1979   Alguns Aspectos da Posse e Uso da Terra nos Estados Unidos.
        Boletím da Associação Brasileira de Reforma Agrária, ano
        IX, no. 2, March/April.
Mahar, Dennis J.
1978   Desenvolvimento Econômico da Amazônia; Uma Análise
        das Políticas Governamentais. Rio: IPEA/INPES, Relat. de Pes-
        quisa, no. 39.
Martins, José de Souza
1975   Capitalismo e Tradicionalismo. São Paulo: Pioneira.
1980   Expropriação e Violência (A Questão Agrária no Campo).
        São Paulo: Hucitec.
Meireles, Mário M.
1960   História do Maranhão. Imprensa Nacional: DASP.

Mendonça, Otávio
1977   Justiça Agrária, Paz Social e Desenvolvimento Econômico. Conferência no. 2: Forum Nacional de Debates sobre Ciências Jurídicas, Brasília. In O Liberal, Belém, 14 August.
1981   O Direito Agrário e o Desenvolvimento da Amazônia. Palestra no. 1: Encontro Internacional de Jus-Agraristas, Belém, 25 May (xerocopy).
Miyasaki, Nobue, and Morio Ono
1958   O Aviamento na Amazônia. Sociologia 3–4. São Paulo: Escola de Sociologia e Política.
Monteiro, Benedito
1980   Direito Agrário e Processo Fundiário. Rio: PLG Comunicação.
Moura, Levi Hal de
1957   Esquema da Origem e da Evolução da Sociedade Paraense, 1616–1901. Belém: H. Barra.
Moura, Sílvio Hall de
1974   Elementos para a História da Magistratura Paraense. Belém: Universidade Federal do Pará.
Muniz, Palma
1916   Immigração e Colonização—História e Estatística, 1616–1916. Belém: Imprensa Oficial.
Penteado, Antônio Rocha
1967   Problemas de Colonização e Uso da Terra na Região Bragantina do Estado do Pará. 2 vols. Belém: Universidade Federal do Pará.
Pinto, Lúcio Flávio
1977   Amazônia: O Anteato da Destruição. Belém: Grafisa.
1980   Amazônia: No Rastro do Saque. São Paulo: Hucitec.
Prado, Jr., Caio
1966   A Revolução Brasileira. São Paulo: Brasiliense.
Raiol, Domingos Antônio (Barão de Guajará)
1883   Motins Políticos. 3 vols. Belém: Reeditado pela Universidade Federal do Pará, 1970.
1902   Catechese de Índios no Pará. Annães. 2.
Reis, Arthur Cézar Ferreira
1966   Aspectos da Experiência Portuguesa na Amazônia. Manaus: Edicões Governo do Estado do Amazônas.
Salles, Vicente
1971   O Negro no Pará. Fund. Getúlio Vargas. Rio: Universidade Federal do Pará.
Santos, Roberto
1979a   A Economia do Estado do Pará. Belém: Instituto do Desenvolvimento Econômico Social do Pará.
1979b   A 'Fronteira' Amazônica e a Reformulação da Política de Ter-

ras. *Boletím da Associação Brasileira de Reforma Agrária* 9:1 (January-February).

1980a Pessoa humana e tendências do Direito do Trabalho no Brasil. In *Tendências do Direito do Trabalho Contemporâneo*. 3 vols. Em homenagem ao Prof. Cesarino Jr. Ed. Cassio de Mesquita Barros Jr. São Paulo: Instituto dos Advogados de São Paulo.

1980b *História econômica da Amazônia, 1800–1920*. Thomas de Aquino de Queiroz, ed. São Paulo.

Sawyer, Donald Rolf
1979 Peasants and Capitalism on an Amazon Frontier. Ph.D. dissertation, Harvard University. Cambridge, MA.

Schmink, Marianne
1981 *A Case Study of the Closing Frontier in Brazil*. Gainesville: Amazon Research and Training Program, Center for Latin American Studies, University of Florida.

Singer, Paul, et al.
1977 *Capital e Trabalho no Campo*. São Paulo: Hucitec.

Sodero, Fernando Pereira
1968 *Direito Agrário e Reforma Agrária*. São Paulo: Livraria Legislação Brasileira.

Spix (von), J.B., and C.F.P von Martius
1823 *Viagem Pelo Brasil, 1818–1820*. 3 vols. 3d. ed. Translated (into Portuguese) by Lúcia Furquim Lahmeyer. Edicões Melhoramentos-IHGB-MFC; revised by Ernst Winkler, 1976.

SPVEA (Superintendência do Plano de Valorização Econômica da Amazônia)
1955 *Primeiro Plano Quinquenal*. 2 vols. Rio: Departamento de Imprensa Nacional.

Velho, Otávio Guilherme
1972 *Frentes de Expansão e Estrutura Agrária*. Rio: Zahar.
1976 *Capitalismo Autoritário e Campesinato*. São Paulo: Difel.

Veríssimo, José
1892 *A Amazônia (Aspectos Econômicos)*. Republished in José Veríssimo, *Estudos Amazônicos*. Belém: Universidade Federal do Pará, 1970.

Vianna, Arthur
1904a As Sesmarias. *Annães* 3.
1904b Catálogo Nominal dos Posseiros de Sesmarias. *Annães* 3.

Weinstein, Barbara Sue
1980 Prosperity without Development: The Paraense Elite and the Amazon Rubber Boom, 1850–1920. Ph.D. dissertation, Yale University.

The State and the Militarization of the Agrarian Question in Brazil

José de Souza Martins

O N SAINT Joseph's Day, 1964, women of good family, along with their husbands, children, and servants, took to the streets of São Paulo to carry out the March of the Family with God for Freedom. They asked for the intervention of the armed forces in the political process and for the fall of the constitutional government of President João Goulart. They were alarmed by the rising popular pressure in favor of basic reforms. One demand especially motivated their opposition: agrarian reform. The march was organized by the Brazilian Rural Society (Sociedade Rural Brasileira), a long-standing organization that brought together the large, traditional São Paulo coffee producers, who had been somewhat marginalized from the center of political power since the Revolution in 1930. The march was actually planned by members of the Institute of Research and Social Studies (Instituto de Pesquisas e Estudos Sociais: IPES). This organization was under the direction of a civil-military general staff that involved members of the Commercial Association, the Federation of Industries, the Federation of Rural Associations, and the Club of Store Directors (Dreifuss 1981:297–98).

The day before the event, the Diário Oficial da União published the decree that had been publicly signed by Goulart during the proreform street demonstration held Friday, March 13, in Rio de Janeiro. The presidential decree called for the expropriation of rural areas along federal roads and national railroads and of lands

463

improved by federal works if they were not being exploited or were being used in ways contrary to the social function of property (IN-CRA 1978:839–42). The decree, in fact, had little impact on large landholders. The persons primarily affected were landowners, both large and small, whose main interest was in real estate speculation.

More important than this decree, which is typically invoked to justify the military coup, were other presidential acts related to the land question. Two years before, in September of 1962, the National Congress had approved a law that defined the cases in which lands were subject to expropriation for social interests. This legislation implemented Article 147 of the 1946 Constitution and opened the way for agrarian reform (INCRA 1978:752–53). While the constitutional obstacles of a "prior and equitable cash compensation" remained, the door was partially opened for a change in agrarian structure. By April of 1963 the federal government had decreed the first expropriations in the State of Rio de Janeiro. Before the overthrow of the civilian government, similar action followed in Rio de Janeiro, Goiás, Minas Gerais, and the Northeast.

During its very first days, the new government revoked some, but not all, of these decrees. Meanwhile, many of those who commended the takeover as a means of defending rural property would have to wait only about seven months to see which direction the military government would take with regard to the agrarian question. At the opening of the National Security Council on October 18, President of the Republic Marshal Humberto de Alencar Castelo Branco ended his message to the National Congress by proposing a constitutional amendment. This action modified the terms for compensation so that property expropriated in the social interest could be indemnified through public bonds (Viana Filho 1975:273).[1] A few days later the Congress, in approving the amendment, also approved the Land Statute. Thus, even before the first year of military rule ended, the government had already established the legislation and the criteria that would serve as the instruments and institutions to effect an agrarian reform. Evidently Castelo Branco had been more persuasive than Goulart in the National Congress, which approved in just over a month's time what it had refused to approve during the preceding eighteen years.

The speed with which the agrarian reform proposal was formulated (an initiative actually carried out by the Minister of Planning Roberto de Oliveira Campos) was due to the fact that the proposal had been previously planned by IPES and actually finished before the military coup (Viana Filho 1975:274, 278; IPES 1964). Curiously, the principal objection to the government's project came, not from the PSD (Partido Social Democrático), a party that represented the older oligarchic interests of the rural sector, but from the UDN (União Democrática Nacional), a party backed by the large modern interest groups in the economy, who were often allied with foreign capital. Opposition to the agrarian reform measures was voiced by Deputy Bilac Pinto with the counsel of economist Antônio Delfim Neto and of entrepreneur Severo Gomes (Viana Filho 1975:280).

In the course of the dictatorship, the military regimes gave legal form to several of the demands that, prior to 1964, had been key political platforms of the left (Gomes da Silva 1971:137–38, Viana Filho 1975:283–84). For having defended these causes, many Brazilians would be persecuted, tortured, or killed. Aside from having overturned the constitutional requirement of cash compensation in cases of land expropriation, under the leadership of Marshal Arthur da Costa e Silva and through Institutional Act No. 9, the government in 1969 also did away with the notion of prior indemnification, a requirement that had survived in the Constitution of 1967. In addition, in 1971, General Emílio Garrastazu Médici placed under the control of the federal government and the National Security Council one hundred kilometers on each side of federal roads, both planned and constructed, to be used for colonization projects in Amazonia (INCRA 1978, 2:876ff; 5:2,036–37; 2,308–9). This far exceeded the mere ten kilometers that Goulart had attempted to set aside a few days before the military takeover.

These apparent contradictions, in my view, capture the spirit of the government's actions regarding the land question and the struggles for land. On the one hand, the military regime carried out, on the basis of legal and institutional changes, an agrarian policy that ran counter to the interests of the social groups that had brought it to power. On the other hand, in order to defend the interests of these same groups, the government appropriated and legalized the proposals and demands of the regime it had deposed, persecuting the persons who had supported the very policies that the military government now endorsed.[2]

In Message no. 33, which accompanied the government's proposal for changing Article 147 of the Constitution, Castelo Branco justified the appropriation of the policies of the deposed regime on the grounds that under Goulart "governmental action only led to an exacerbation of tensions and to an aggravation of the contradictions of the Brazilian rural system, leading to disquiet on all sides" (CONTAG, 1975:6). The military government separated the social and economic problem of land concentration from the political questions raised by organizations such as unions, peasant leagues, parties, and political groups, which found legitimacy as mediators between the struggles of rural workers and peasants and the state, whose composition collided with these pressure groups. The military government understood, therefore, that the reform measures would be necessary but that the political organizations to make them a reality were both unnecessary and harmful. Instead of carrying out the reform from the bottom up, legitimized by popular participation, it would be done from the top down, conducted as a technical and military problem rather than a political one. The point was to execute the reform process without threatening property rights, particularly avoiding the confiscation of large landholdings.[3]

In spite of the variations in government policy related to the agrarian question, throughout eighteen years of military government one policy has remained unchanged: the depoliticization of the land question and the political exclusion of the peasantry from decisions that affect their interests. This stand has implied severe restrictions on the rights of rural workers. The government has carried out actions in addition to the ban on political activity in the countryside, especially the repression of popular and opposition groups that sided with peasants.

Recently the president of the National Institute of Colonization and Land Reform restated this notion in a newspaper article:

Union organizations and the most varied forms of associations are multiplying, with the intention of representing segments of the national rural sector. In this desirable development, there are momentary distortions until the authentic mechanisms of demonstration are consolidated and nationally recognized, purging the process of those groups alien to it that were created with other objectives (Yokota 1982:50).[4]

From the speeches of Castelo to those of Yokota, the military government takes a narrow view of peasant struggles and the agrarian question. In this context two processes occur: the expansion of the capitalist firm in the countryside and the depoliticization of the countryside. These processes clash to the extent that economic development, supported especially by the policies of fiscal incentives and tax exemptions for ranching activities, provokes the intensification of social tensions in the rural area, the proliferation of conflicts, and the broadening of the struggle for land.

The direction of the agrarian policy by the military dictatorship could not be separated from the question of economic development, especially of agricultural development, understood as the strengthening and expansion of the large capitalist firm. The government tried to adjust the land problem to its economic development objectives and, at the same time, to its national security objectives. Politically this meant impeding or deterring the political unfolding of the struggle for land.

The Land Statute itself was elaborated so as to favor the development and proliferation of the rural firm. The privileged beneficiary of the statute is not the peasant, the small farmer whose base is family labor. It is the businessman, the producer imbued with an entrepreneurial spirit, who organizes his economic activity according to the imperatives of capital accumulation.[5]

In the classification of rural properties—*minifúndio, empresa, latifúndio por exploração,* and *latifúndio por dimensão—* the penalty is different for the minifundio compared to the latifundio. The minifundio is targeted with measures that specifically refer to the size of the property, such as those impeding fragmentation through inheritance, and reducing the other pressures that lead to the division of property. The latifundio, by contrast, may even use subsidized credit to transform itself into a "firm" by IN-CRA's definition. It is thus able to avoid the effects of progressive taxation without facing any particular problems of property division. Furthermore, the firm is exempt from expropriation even in places where agrarian reform is designated by presidential decree.

For these reasons reform remained limited to cases of grave social tension. Land redistribution took place in priority areas when expropriation was considered to be in the social interest. It was also applied in other regions that involved the resettlement of minifundiarios, the victims of conflicts. In these cases, the regions of resettlement and colonization referred to pioneer areas, which at that point meant primarily Legal Amazonia. It is on the basis of this conception of agrarian reform, therefore, that Amazonia is incorporated into the structure of social, economic, and power relationships that constitute the contemporary basis of peasant struggles for land in Brazil. And it is in this sense that, in my view, the struggles for land in Amazonia are not correctly understood if they are analyzed separately from the land conflicts that occur in all regions of the country. While there are regional factors specific to the agricultural frontier and to peasant struggles in Amazonia, the struggles are not divorced from peasant struggles elsewhere in the country. The question of Amazonia is, in part, the regional manifestation of the broader agrarian question, which is itself a consequence of the expanded reproduction of capital and of the process of appropriation of ground rent by capital.

Between one and two years after the ratification of the Land Statute, the government approved two laws that, along with the statute, became pillars of the agrarian policy of the military regime. On December 1, 1965, Constitutional Amendment No. 18 extended to Amazonia the fiscal incentives and the favorable credit terms conceded to the Northeast, which resulted in the creation of SUDAM (Superintêndencia do Desenvolvimento da Amazônia) the following year. In September of 1966, fiscal incentives were instituted for forestry enterprises in all of Brazil (INCRA 1978, vol. 3:1,183; 1,513–14). The land conflicts that were already occurring in Paraná, in Rio de Janeiro, in São Paulo, in the Northeast, and in Minas Gerais, progressively extended into forest areas and into Amazonia.

These new economic policies stimulated massive pressure for the occupation of the land by large-scale capital. With the creation of SUDAM the government earmarked for the occupation by large economic concerns the same territory that, shortly before, had been set aside for the resettlement of small farmers. The latter had been dislodged by concentration of land ownership, by economic transformations in the structure of agricultural production, and by the surplus population created by these trends.

The policies that favor large firms in the countryside were and are premised on the expropriation of land from small farmers and the transfer of rural workers to the city as well as the concentration of landownership and the progressive increase of economic efficiency and of agricultural productivity. In contrast, the policy of resettling of colonists, even presuming the capitalist spirit of the small producer, also presumed to some extent the redistribution of land. The dual character of the government's policies through these years was, at the very least, ambiguous. This characterization applied not only to Amazonia but also to other regions of the country.

The combination of these different measures was what defined the place and the reach of the legal and administrative instruments that the government had available to carry out an agrarian reform. From the very outset the reform was subordinated to the process of capital accumulation and of the expanded reproduction of the large enterprise. In this way the true function of the statute can be seen. It is an instrument designed to control the social tensions and conflicts generated by the process of land expropriation and of the concentration of property and capital. It is an instrument by which to contain and deactivate conflicts so as to guarantee economic development based on the penetration of large-scale capital in agriculture. It is an escape valve that comes into play when social tensions reach the point where they might spill over into serious political tensions. Together with other measures to limit and to defuse social conflicts, the statute is thus central to the government's strategy in the countryside.

Consequences of an ambitious agrarian policy

The contradictory agrarian policy soon led to the multiplication rather than the reduction of land conflicts. Conflicts have particularly tended to increase in pioneer regions, precisely those areas that were to absorb small farmers driven out of other regions of the country (Table 1). Land conflicts did not disappear in the older regions of Brazil. The highest number of incidents still took place in

TABLE 1. Land conflicts in Brazil, 1971–76
(biennial percentages of national total)

Area	1971 −72	1973 −74	1975 −76	1971 −76
South-Southeast (N = 146)	27.4	35.6	37.0	100.0
Northeast (N = 67)	19.4	10.4	70.2	100.0
North–Center-West (N = 234)	17.1	18.4	64.5	100.0
All Brazil	20.8	22.8	56.4	100.0

SOURCES: Rodrigues and Silva 1975, 1977.

NOTE: The data from Maranhão, which include thirty-five conflicts, are excluded from the Northeast totals and included in the North–Center-West totals.

the South, Southeast, and Northeast until 1974, after which the
proportion diminished slightly for these regions. The numbers presented in Table 1 are underestimates: they were taken from newspapers, and correspond to only 5 percent of the conflicts registered
by the federations of rural workers in 1971 (see Rodrigues and Silva
1975:6). In 1979, the Comissão Pastoral da Terra (CPT) in Maranhão
registered 128 conflicts in the state, four of which involved more
than a thousand families. In the same year the local CPT in the
State of Rio de Janeiro listed ninety-four conflicts. Aside from these
states, Bahia, Paraiba, Paraná, Mato Grosso, Goiás, Acre, and the
Federal Territory of Rondônia (now a state), are also places where
rural violence is common. These observations provide some idea
of just how widespread land conflicts have become in Brazil.

Various factors have combined to multiply the number of land
conflicts in the Amazon. It is possible to identify two of these.
One is the reproduction in new pioneer regions of the same system
of land tenure as found in older regions (something that the Land
Statute was supposed to avoid).[6] The size distribution of the new
areas incorporated into agricultural establishments during the intercensal periods provides a clear indicator of what happened on
the frontier following the establishment of the military government (Table 2). A hundred-hectare plot, which is the size of the
module designated for Amazonia, serves as a reference point in
this table. It is important to note, however, that the largest establishments (over one thousand hectares), received 71 percent of the
new lands between 1970 and 1975.

While the large landowners appropriated immense territories
in the Amazon region and recreated the latifundio system on lands
that were, in principle, intended to absorb surplus population, the
factors of expulsion and conflict continued to operate in older areas
of the country. In Rio Grande do Sul and Paraná, the spread of soy
and wheat production led to the concentration of land ownership
and the expulsion of small farmers, many of whom headed for
Mato Grosso and Rondônia. In Espírito Santo and the neighboring
part of Minas Gerais, the eradication of coffee and the planting of
pastures sent huge contingents of migrants on the road in the direction of Rondônia. The populations evicted from the Northeast,
by drought or latifundio, further contributed to the migratory
streams into Eastern Amazonia, toward Maranhão, Goiás, Mato
Grosso, and Pará. Northeastern migrants, who less than twenty

TABLE 2. Allocations of new land during intercensal periods
(percentages of national totals)

	1950–60	1960–70	1970–75
To establishments under 100 hectares	84.6	35.3	0.2
To establishments over 100 hectares	15.4	64.7	99.8

SOURCES: IBGE 1950,1960; FIBGE 1970, 1975.

years earlier had settled in Goiás and Maranhão, also moved in this direction.

The latifundio is not the only factor in the expulsion of peasants from the older regions. In the South and Southeast the fragmentation of the minifundio and the impossibility or difficulty of sustaining family agriculture, have also been particularly important.

Between 1940 and 1975 the average size of Brazilian farming establishments between one and ten hectares in size fell by 13 percent. Those with more than a thousand hectares declined by only 3 percent. But the average size of the large agricultural and cattle raising establishments grew in this period by 28 percent. On the average, these figures imply that each large agricultural establishment in 1975 had an additional area corresponding to eighty-seven small agricultural establishments (which would not have occurred if the average size of large farms had decreased at the same rate as their smaller counterparts). This suggests that the relative advantage of large landholdings in 1975 blocked the creation of some 3,600,000 small farmholdings. Large farms incorporated an area equivalent to almost two times the total area occupied by small farms in that year.

As will be shown later in this study, even within the context of limited agrarian reform legislation, the reform primarily implied an economic policy of land expropriation and of expulsion of rural worker. The large migration flows into Amazonia, caused by population pressure, were offset by ever larger movements toward the cities and the urban market. In other words, the government developed a policy that implicitly led to the progressive destruction of small family agriculture. In my view, it is for this reason that the conflicts over land can be seen as a peasant struggle against the capitalist form of development underway in the countryside.

Another factor increasing the conflict for land in the regions of Amazonia is the frequent subordination of public authority to private interests in the more remote places in the interior, particularly in the newer pioneer regions (Almeida 1981:9, Martins 1980: 111). Police deputies, soldiers, and judges of Rondônia, Mato Grosso, Goiás, and Pará are frequently aligned with land grabbers, hired gunmen and large landholders and businessmen arriving from the South. They have engaged in illegal and violent acts of terror to clear the peasant population off the land. These actions are just as often directed against recently arrived farmers as against long-term residents, who assume they have acquired permanent rights to land by virtue of having worked it for many generations.[7] The subordination of the public authority to private interests, a common feature in the interior (Correia de Andrade 1973), was reinforced by the dismantling of the old power structures run by local bosses, a process that served to place public officials at the service of powerful new groups on the frontier.

A contradictory and explosive situation was thus created. The same government that appropriated the slogans of the left, that suppressed the obstacles to the agrarian reform, and that strengthened the legal apparatus that supposedly favored rural workers, at the same time encouraged the relocation of small farmers to regions where the laws are not generally complied with. This should not be treated as an accidental phenomenon. It is sufficient to note the events that took place as a result of Decree No. 70430, signed by Costa e Silva in 1972, enacted to deal specifically with the squatters and farm laborers on the Codeara farm owned by the National Credit Bank in Mato Grosso. The decree held that squatters could not be removed from their homes and land without a prior audience with the Ministry of Agriculture. This disposition was an attempt to circumvent action by hired gunmen, who had unleashed a veritable war against inhabitants in the Santa Terezinha region. Meanwhile, lawyers who advocated application of the decree were labeled communists by the National Security Council. If we recall the fact that torture and death were the regime's daily political weapons during that period, it is possible to appreciate the significance of these actions (Casaldáliga 1978, Santana 1981).

The situation was in no way accidental, for denunciation to the authorities has been and continues to be frequent. The relocation of population groups—sometimes as a result of official propaganda, sometimes by actions of governmental agencies—was intended to ease social pressures in the countryside (Santos 1979, Martins 1980, Ianni 1979), and, above all, to reduce the pressure for agrarian reform. It was only in this limited sense that the statute could be applied. At no time before or after the coup was there any intention of carrying out an agrarian reform on a scale sufficient to meet the needs of the landless rural workers or the land-poor small farmers. Governmental initiatives were always localized and accompanied by attempts to transfer farmers to the Transamazon or the Cuiabá-Santarém highways or to Mato Grosso.

Social pressure on the agrarian structure in the older regions and the ensuing struggle for land have resulted in the politicization of land conflicts. In contrast to their circumstances before 1964, rural workers today have the nation's largest union; it also has the highest membership rate, for about 52 percent of the economically active population in agriculture is unionized. (This compares to only some 28 percent for the economically active urban population.) Moreover, in the older areas, civic and grass-roots groups are much better organized. They remain in a condition of permanent readiness against violent practices carried out directly or indirectly by the state. It is sufficient to note that in past years sugar cane workers of the Northeast, who number close to 200,000, have annually struck and have taken their employers to work tribunals to air their demands for labor rights and to push for collective bargaining agreements. In a world where only forty years ago relations of personal dependence predominated and the only expression of individual rights was bound in mysticism, this fact represents a true revolution, a breaking of the chains that have traditionally bound the agricultural worker to his landlord.

The dispossessed and those who moved to the frontier are subjected to a kind of repression characterized by the permanent annulment of individual rights and the indirect distortion of the law and of public authority. In southern Pará, it has taken many years for workers to establish their own organizations. In the region of São Felix do Araguaia, a place of widespread and violent conflicts, it took almost ten years for rural workers to succeed in creating their union. In pioneer regions the political efficacy of popular demands is thus immensely attenuated and delayed. These difficulties undoubtedly work to the advantage of the government and business enterprises, by reducing or annulling the political need to reform the existing land tenure system.

A particularly critical period

The period from 1969 to 1973 was particularly important in defining the direction of agrarian issues and the role of the state. In that period, Costa e Silva was replaced by the military junta, which in turn passed the reigns of power to Médici. Political repression reached its height both in the city and in the countryside. It was during this time that three military campaigns were carried out against the guerilla forces in Araguaia. Key ministries changed hands—from individuals who advocated an agrarian reform to those who were opposed to it and were in favor of policies to expand large-scale firms in the countryside. These were among the changes that provoked the intensification of land conflicts after 1974.

During the Castelo Branco government, it was assumed that social problems, including land conflicts, the rural exodus, and need for greater agricultural output, could be solved through purely economic and financial policies without threatening property rights. At the outset of the Costa e Silva government, the land problem, particularly in Amazonia, became progressively transformed into a military issue. The Ministry of the Interior, headed by General Albuquerque Lima, a nationalist general identified with the Superior War College, gave high priority to the need to integrate Amazonia into the rest of the economy. Reducing the question to its simplest terms, it was assumed that the social and agricultural problems of the Northeast could be resolved in Amazonia through the occupation of "empty spaces" and through the creation of development poles, both of which were to be executed with the direct involvement of the armed forces (Camerman 1977:73).

At that point there were few agrarian problems in Amazonia compared to the Northeast, the South, and Southeast. In the second half of 1968, General Costa e Silva called for action by the Brazilian Institute of Agrarian Reform (IBRA), an institution created by the Land Statute and charged with the task of resolving the agrarian question. At about that time, an inquiry noted irregularities in the way in which lands were expropriated in Paraná. In September the Special Agrarian Reform Group (GERA) was created in order to identify the obstacles that stood in the way of the planning and execution of measures designed to change the structure of land tenure. When GERA concluded its work and presented its

suggestions in January of 1969, Albuquerque Lima was being replaced in the Ministry of the Interior by Colonel Costa Cavalcanti
(see INCRA 1978, vol. 5:2,036—37). A few months later in Porto
Alegre, Cavalcanti stated that the "agrarian reform will maintain
the current land tenure structure as the government's policy is
to be accomplished without partitioning land" (Magalhães et al.
1971:226). In effect, there would be no agrarian reform. Because
the three regional development agencies (SUDENE, SUDAM, SUDECO)
were under the Ministry of the Interior, Cavalcanti's appointment
undermined the likelihood of any significant reforms.

Even so, important institutional and legal measures were undertaken. By April of 1969, Costa e Silva signed Institutional Act
No. 9. As we have seen, this did away with the need to give compensation prior to expropriating land. This enabled the government to carry out expropriations in as little as seventy-two hours.
At the same time, General Carlos de Morais, president of IBRA, emphasized the need for agrarian reform, a position that was contrary
to the views of the new minister of the interior. Meanwhile, a list
prepared by GERA of the 198 municipalities in the entire country
with agrarian problems was already in the hands of the Ministry of
Agriculture. The first regions targeted for reform were the Zona da
Mata in Pernambuco, the northeastern region of Minas Gerais, and
Vale do Jaquaribe in Ceará. Speaking at the National Police Academy on June 10, 1969, the same minister, Ivo Arzua, denounced
those who sought to limit the agrarian reform: "In the play of economic and political forces that pressure the government for measures to support and stimulate particular activities, those that
emerge in the agricultural sector are generally minimized by the
power and aggressiveness of the landholding groups, bankers, and
industrialists" (Camerman 1977:79–80).

Little more than a month before this denunciation, the minister Costa Cavalcanti met with members of the Association of Amazon Entrepreuneurs and with the president of FUNAI (the National
Indian Foundation). At that meeting complaints were aired about
the bureaucratization of project approvals, budget restrictions by
SUDAM and by the Bank of the Amazon (BASA), the overcentraliza-
tion of decision making in Belém, and the lack of infrastructure,
especially for transportation. The Indian reservations were considered too large, and the attacks by native groups were condemned.
The entrepreneurs succeeded in rerouting the BR-080 highway
through the Xingu National Park, cutting off the territory of the

Txucarramãe Indians. Ten years later, after the road had already caused irreparable damage to these native peoples, the government recognized that the highway was useless and decided to deactivate the road (Magalhães et al. 1971:220–21, Casaldáliga 1971:39; Cardoso and Müller 1977:154).

When Médici took over the government in 1969 the agrarian reform issue remained under the aegis of the Ministry of Agriculture, headed by Cirne Lima. The minister was a southerner known to favor the policy of stimulating the spontaneous migration of people from areas of social tension into Amazonia (Camerman 1977:87). President Médici, meanwhile, promised a "revolution in the countryside, in agriculture, and in the supply of food." In this connection, Médici's spokesman on agricultural affairs was Reis Veloso in the Ministry of Planning rather than Cirne Lima. The difference was fundamental. Veloso saw the issue as a problem of output. For Cirne Lima "agrarian reform is the unbounded desire of all those sensitive to the Brazilian reality; for it incorporates the farmer who lives on the land into the consumer market. . . . We think of agrarian reform in terms of colonization and the partitioning of land" (Camerman 1977).

Médici's regime was characterized by the attempt to balance pomp with circumstance. The pomp was reflected by large and ambitious development projects, such as the National Integration Plan (PIN), announced in June of 1970, and PROTERRA, put forth the following year. The circumstance included the dramatic and politically volatile drought in 1970 and the hunger and need for land among workers in the Northeast. Public policy was supposedly designed to resolve these problems.

A month after launching the PIN, Médici created INCRA, the National Institute of Colonization and Agrarian Reform. This institution replaced other federal agencies involved in the land question, including IBRA. While the latter had answered directly to the president of the Republic, with a rank nearly equal to other ministries, INCRA was housed within the Ministry of Agriculture. As a consequence, the question of land tenure became a sectoral concern that was isolated from the other powerful federal agencies, such as the Ministries of Interior and Planning and the National Security Council (which has played an important role in the occupation of Amazonia since at least 1967).

The subordination of INCRA to the Ministry of Agriculture relegated the agrarian question to a secondary concern. The principal effect was to separate economic planning from any need to take into account the social issues related to landless workers. This change reflected a tendency that became quite pronounced in the next three years. Development projects were disengaged from the question of land tenure and greater weight was given to private interests. Government policy aimed to shift migration flows out of the countryside so as to permit the expansion of large enterprises, especially in frontier areas. In effect, these trends implied that the government reneged on its original plans for Amazonia and tacitly revoked the Land Statute. In this way Médici's regime appeared to act in favor of landless rural workers while, at the same time, it progressively undermined the institutional basis for an agrarian reform.

Positions favorable to an agrarian reform were finally silenced in May 1973. After a meeting with Médici, in which the Transamazon Highway was discussed, Cirne Lima announced his still controversial resignation as Minister of Agriculture (Camerman 1977:95). In addition to criticizing the favoritism shown to multinational corporations and denouncing the price policies whereby the agricultural sector subsidized foreign companies, Cirne Lima maintained that the colonization of the Transamazon should be carried out through spontaneous migration that would be merely disciplined by governmental actions. The adoption of bureaucratic and administrative criteria to settle new lands represented, in his view, a retreat from the original objective, which was to provide land to the landless people of the Brazilian Northeast.

While still President of INCRA, the new head of the Ministry of Agriculture (Moura Calvalcante) had offered "large tracts of land to the members of the Brasilian Association of Cattle Raisers, of São Paulo" (Pinto 1980:68). In this way Calvalcanti (together with the Ministers of Planning and of Interior) became part of the triumvirate required to push through policies in support of big businesses in Amazonia (see Pompermayer, in this volume). In the second half of 1973 the three ministers, accompanied by twenty of the most powerful entrepreneurs from southern Brazil, took a three-day trip through the Amazon. The tour led to new initiatives. One group of businessmen was interested in private colonization and another in ranching. Ten days later, they announced the purchase of two million hectares of land at the crossroads of the Transamazon and the Cuiabá-Santarém highways. The government decided to provide incentives to large concessions in Amazonia (with an average size of 100,000 hectares). In addition, the government announced that it would invest a billion dollars in the region during 1973–74 (Pinto 1980:63–68).

At the end of 1973, while cattle raising was being emphasized as the Amazon's "calling," newspapers began to publicize the idea that the region's lands were unsuitable for agricultural production. These accounts coincided with the withdrawal of support for the official colonization projects along the Transamazon. The appointment of Lourenço Vieira da Silva as head of INCRA culminated in the abandonment of the small-farmer settlement scheme. A new phase that emphasized regional development centers was thus inaugurated (Martine 1980, Camerman 1977:121).

It was at the beginning of Geisel's regime that the Amazon came to be seen as a resource frontier. There was much talk of agriculture, not just as a supplier of the internal market but also as a source of foreign exchange (Mahar 1979:44). With the creation of Polamazonia in 1974, the implications of this change became clear. Government policy was designed primarily "to guide public investment, principally to support and implement . . . productive activities under the responsibility of the *private sector*" (INCRA 1978:2:699, emphasis added).

The outcome of this trend appeared in 1976, when the National Security Council presented General Geisel with two statements of intent (Numbers 005 and 006). For a long time these were treated as more or less secret resolutions. The resolutions, in effect, represented a small, illegal coup against the powers of the federal senate. One of them (Number 005) established the basis for "solving the existing land disputes in Legal Amazonia, related to the private occupation of public lands, in the interest of fostering agricultural, ranching, forestry, and agroindustrial production capable of contributing to the region's economic and social development" (Santana 1981:44). The beneficiaries were clearly identified. "Because of failures on the part of the public authorities, this occupation often took place in an illegal manner. In many cases businessmen from other parts of the country rushed into the area and, using the practices to which they were accustomed, took little care to properly verify land rights. Some, it is worth noting, started projects that were approved by the federal government, and several investments were carried out with the help of fiscal incentives." These were situations that, *"even though constituted through devious, reprehensible practices, constituting a breach of law and order . . . redeem themselves to the extent they promote development of the region"* (Santana 1981:115, emphasis added). Basically, what the secretary of the National Security Council (General Hugo de Andrade Abreu), and the head of the Ministry of Agriculture (Alyson Paulinelli) successfully proposed to the president was that the government clear the titles to lands probably seized illegally, without going through the Senate, as required by law (Santana 1981:115).

Resolution 006 extended the scope of these measures to border areas and to other lands "indispensable to the national security and to national development." Included in this category was the strip two hundred kilometers wide along federal roads (either planned or operational) in Amazonia. This permitted the legal appropriation of public lands in tracts larger than one hundred hectares (Santana 1981:117), provided that the individual actually had worked and lived on the land for at least ten years. This effectively excluded squatters who came into the region after 1971 in response to the propaganda about the colonization projects (Pinto 1980:42).

Destruction of the institutional basis for agrarian reform

The destruction under Geisel's regime of the institutional basis for the agrarian reform (noted earlier in this study) as well as the increasing involvement of the government in the land question were not the outcome of an ambiguous or contradictory policy. The true meaning of this apparent duplicity lay not with the agrarian situation but with the question of national security.

This period of military rule meant a centralization of political power that took place in a number of realms, including the strengthening of the executive at the expense of the legislative branch of government and the strengthening of federal power to the detriment of regional and local interests. It also meant the bureaucratization of the political process, and the strengthening of the system of public administration. It is in this context that government land policies begin to make sense. It is impossible to understand these measures if we assume that the objective is to provide plots to peasants engaged in a struggle for land, since this is not the perspective used by the government. The Brazilian military is an inherently centralizing force and has traditionally acted to centralize political power. Historically this was evident during the Empire; under the Republican period; when the National Guard was disbanded; during the peasant uprisings in Canudos; during the *Contestado*; and also in the military's opposition to the power wielded by local political bosses (*coronelismo*). More recently, this attitude is reflected by the hostile response to new forms of political expression free from the traditional ties of personal dependence. From these examples we can surmise that the military as an institution is characterized by a corporatist perspective, which maintains that the greater the centralization, the greater the national security. These factors account for the military's concern over land conflicts, which has led to the government's increasing involvement. The culmination of this tendency is represented by the creation of GETAT (Grupo Executivo de Terras do Araguaia-Tocantins) in February of 1980.

From what can be inferred from General Golbery do Couto e Silva's lecture before the Superior War College, the military is engaged in the creation of a national entity. This necessarily presupposes national integration and the need to override oligarchic power bases at the regional level. It is also necessary to defuse social tensions and to reduce the risk of separationist movements (more or less latent in Amazonia) (Couto e Silva 1981).

But the political bases for greater centralization were already present before the military coup in 1964. Two events are of particular significance: the creation of SUDENE in 1959 under President Kubitschek and the establishment of GETSOP (Grupo Executivo para as Terras do Sudoeste do Paraná) in 1962 under Goulart's regime. The latter was designed to deal with land problems in Paraná, which had been pending ever since the peasant uprising in 1957. These measures reflect the interrelationships between the centralization of political power, economic development, and land conflicts. The new regional development agencies created by the military regimes (especially SUDAM) meant that the process of local economic development was brought under federal control.

The extension of federal power into the Amazon region also occurred as a result of the decision taken in 1970 to colonize the ten kilometers on either side of the new highways. Federal control was subsequently expanded in 1971 to include a two hundred kilometer strip along the roads. This land, under the aegis of the National Security Council, was effectively placed under military control (Pinto 1980:121–38). From that moment on, public land that had once belonged to the states became federal property. As a result, it has become practically impossible to separate the land question from the militarization of rural areas in Amazonia.

The federalization of land was a necessary condition for the geopolitical centralization of Amazonia. Without appropriating the principal power base (land) and taking over the mechanisms by which to distribute land, it would have been impossible for the federal government to superimpose its power over the oligarchies that controlled local areas. The federalization and militarization of land in Amazonia were the means by which development was taken out of the hands of merchants and traditional landowners. This opened the way for large capital, which in turn further contributed to the centralization of political power.

Until 1973, the social question of landless or land-poor workers had to be combined somewhat anomalously with the geopolitics of centralization. The federalization of land would have to shelter colonization projects in order to absorb traditional Northeastern farmers whose demand for land lay behind the rural tension in that region. However, the increase in spontaneous movement of migrants into the frontier regions began to accentuate confrontations with those economic interests favored by the military policy of centralization. The massive influx of migrants into Goiás, Maranhão, Pará, and Mato Grosso momentarily jeopardized the government's dual objective of achieving national security on the one hand, and development through large capitalist enterprises on the other.

From the moment the military became aware of a Communist guerilla force in southern Pará (around 1969 or 1970), certain actions were taken to prevent land conflicts from becoming explosive (Ianni 1979:34). The colonization of the Transamazon served as the principal mechanism to reduce social tensions. But even though the colonization policy appears to have been adopted partly in response to the threat posed by the guerillas, there was no significant change in government policy with regard to land tenure.

The onset of the guerilla movement in April 1972 showed how unprepared the military was to deal with the situation, a fact that led to defeat in the first campaign. Sectors of the military involved in national security were adept at political repression and torture, particularly in urban areas. But they had little experience with military action in the countryside. As a result it took nearly ten thousand soldiers about three years to defeat a guerilla force of about sixty combatants (Doria et al. n.d., Portela 1979, Pomar 1980).

The evidence appears to suggest that the guerilla movement in Araguaia was not a major factor in leading to public policies in favor of small farmers in Amazonia. To the contrary, there was a reduction in the number of land expropriations carried out at that time and, as noted earlier, an increase in the concessions given to large enterprises. Even the preference for clients in the colonization projects shifted away from northeasterners and toward small landholders from southern Brazil, who were in a position to sell their plots and buy new property in Amazonia. The beneficiaries of this change were private colonization companies, which profited from these transactions. From the government's standpoint, southern Brazil (rather than the Northeast) had become the area of priority concern (Ianni 1979:98, Martine 1980). This shift permitted the conciliation of security and development goals, the defusing of tension in politicized areas of minifundios, and at the same time, provided lucrative profits to private colonization companies.

After the armed conflict came to an end, the military adopted boldly antipeasant policies. The defeat of the guerillas had taught the military a few things. One was that there was a gap between peasant struggles and guerilla movements, a limit beyond which peasants will not engage in armed confrontation. Another was the value of the tactics used by the guerillas. By offering assistance to the population, the opposition gained the confidence and sympathy of the people (a factor that contributed to the defeat of the military forces early in the campaign). The military itself was able to achieve the same results by making similar concessions on a *local* basis. Following this policy, some assistance was given to urban towns and to villages in the rural area. Similarly, small farmers received land along the roads that had been built by the military during the conflict.

The military appears to have become convinced of the need to populate empty territories and to neutralize peasant unrest that could have political repercussions. From that point on, the tactic has been to defuse social tensions without seriously adopting a colonization policy or carrying through an agrarian reform. In other words, the attempt has been to localize land conflicts and to deal with them in such a way that peasant unrest was prevented from becoming a widespread social movement. By keeping peasant struggles fragmented, local, and focused on obtaining a plot of land, the military could avoid the growth of collective organizations and the emergence of political awareness. Following the defeat of the guerillas, the government abandoned the public colonization projects, and adopted other priorities to guide its policies in Amazonia.

The change in land policy

The change in land policy in 1973–74 represented a victory for persons who questioned whether agrarian reform could be a tool of economic and social planning. This point of view was held by UDN party-member Bilac Pinto, who relied on the advice of economist Delfim Neto. For Delfim Neto, "agriculture has five tasks in development: (1) to increase the food supply and reduce inflationary pressures; (2) to supply the industrial sector with raw materials; (3) to increase production and *release labor*; (4) to increase export commodities and (5) to underwrite development by transferring resources from the primary to the secondary sector" (Viana Filho 1975:279–80, emphasis added). In a signed news release in 1979, Delfim Neto reiterated this perspective as a solution for the current economic crisis (*Estado de São Paulo*, August 19, 1979). With regard to the question of land tenure, the government's position is no longer ambiguous. The proreform views cultivated by IPES and extolled by Roberto Campos have been abandoned. This change meant a shift in emphasis from a policy designed to contain the rural exodus and to redirect it toward frontier areas, to one that supported large enterprises in the countryside and that was solely concerned with the economic role of the modern agricultural sector.

This policy change, which was completed by Médici and further consolidated under Geisel's regime, is correlated with the intensification of land conflicts. For strategic military purposes (as opposed to a concern for social welfare), the government applied the legal and institutional instruments for agrarian reform in order to federalize and to militarize the newly occupied territories. By opting to side with private interests and to support capital accumulation by large firms, while, at the same time, having at its disposal the means to carry out a reform, the government's role became more complicated. The alliance between the state and private capital became much more clear, as did the opposition to initiatives favorable to small farmers.

The widespread land conflicts in the South, Southeast, and Northeast regions spread into Amazonia. This was particularly true after 1976, when the government legally recognized the right to lands that had been illegally obtained. In Brazil as a whole, 715 land conflicts were documented between January 1979 and July 1981. Most of these were of recent origin: 88.1 percent were started after 1973; only 11.9 percent were begun prior to that date. These figures confirm the results shown in Table 1, which are derived from a different source. Approximately a million and a half people are estimated to have been involved in the 913 documented land disputes. The South-Southeast accounted for 146; 207 occurred in the Northeast (excluding Maranhão); and 560 took place in the North–Center-West (including Maranhão) (Comissão Pastoral da Terra 1981).

The increase in land conflicts has forced the government to resort to the Land Statute to expropriate property. However, this has been done on a scale small in relation to the number of disputes. Most of the expropriations have taken place in the long-settled areas, although the number has also increased rapidly in frontier areas, especially in Mato Grosso and Acre (see Table 3). This indicates that agrarian reform measures have become necessary, not only in areas that have been occupied for a long time, but in the newly settled regions as well.

Apart from the economic trends, the proliferation of land conflicts can also be attributed to political factors. As noted earlier, the military understood the need for agrarian reform when it took power in 1964. But if it saw a reform as necessary, the government also understood that it was unnecessary to allow the emergence of grass roots political forces that came about in the struggle for land. From the standpoint of the military, the enactment of reform measures thus presupposed the depoliticization of the countryside. The political vacuum created in the rural area was a necessary condition for the survival of the military government and for the success of its development plans.

This void, however, has led to a continuous (and increasing) number of political problems. It is not simply a matter of preventing the emergence of a proreform political movement. Rather, the government's dilemma is related to its development and land policies, which have destroyed or weakened the traditional power bases. The police and local political bosses, which are a source of political support for the government, are the very ones whose

TABLE 3. Expropriations of lands (in percentages)

	1965–72	1973–80[a]
South-Southeast (N = 53)	41.5	58.5
Northeast (N = 33)	27.2	72.8
North–Center-West[b] (N = 24)	8.4	91.6
All Brazil (N = 110)	30.0	70.0

SOURCES: PRODASEN (Data Processing Center for the Federal Senate, Brazil).

a. In 1981, fourteen expropriation decrees were signed: five in the South-Southeast, three in the Northeast, and six in the North–Center-West.

b. Data on Maranhao were excluded from the Northeast and included in the North–Center-West region.

power is undermined by the development policies adopted by the government. Because the centralization of authority is incompatible with the fragmentation of the political power, the government has responded in several ways. One was to turn certain localities into national security areas. In this way local mayors became federal appointees. Another measure that extended federal control downward to the state level was the instituting of the indirect method of electing governors.

As we have seen, large capitalist enterprises that take advantage of fiscal incentives to expand into Amazonia with cattle raising projects are the economic agents of greater centralization. To some extent this has excluded the local bourgeoisie from the benefits generated by the occupation of new territories. This economic and political usurpation by southern interest groups probably explains the birth of regionalism in Rondonia, Pará, and Acre. The development policies applied to Amazonia not only impeded the emergence of a peasant-based political movement but also destroyed the traditional power structure in the region. In this sense the action of the federal government has created a political vacuum.

But the centralization and militarization of the countryside have led to a troublesome contradiction: on the one hand, centralized power is necessary to preserve the military dictatorship; on the other, the outcome of this attempt is problematic because the destruction of the local structure of authority potentially allows the creation of a popular movement in the rural area. Govern-

ment action must, as a result, continually strive to maintain or reproduce this political vacuum. The needs to replace local power
bases and to continue political repression in the countryside are
the factors that have forced the military to become increasingly involved in the agrarian question and in land disputes. This has included the repeated intervention in institutions created by the
military itself: in 1968 in IBRA, which was replaced in 1970 by
INCRA, itself partially replaced in 1980 by GETAT for the tense
Araguaia-Tocantins area. The creation of GETAT effectively transformed a government land agency into a military instrument: its
local sites are used as both administrative offices and jails.

Actions by the military government to guarantee its power
hegemony in the countryside are evident in the repression of union
activities, party politics, and the work of priests. Especially alarming is the failure of authorities to investigate murders of peasant
leaders, union leaders, rural workers' lawyers, and religious agents.
Between January 1979 and July 1981, fourteen rural union leaders
and three indigenous leaders were killed in Brazil, half of them in
Amazonia (Comissão Pastoral da Terra 1981:7–8).

Growing conflicts between the church and state are evident in
the imprisonment or deportation of pastoral workers, especially
in the most combative areas of Legal Amazonia (Fathers Jentel,
Maboni, Fontanela, Francisco, and Aristides). The detention and
interrogation of bishops Dom Estevão, Dom Alano, and Dom Pedro
Casaldáliga have been part of this confrontation, which is unprecedented in Brazilian history. Furthermore, defamatory daily broadcasts by two government firms (Empresa Brasileira de Notícias and
Rádio Nacional de Brasília) seek to undermine the work of the
Catholic Church in the region (see CEDI n.d., Couto e Silva 1981).

Conflict over land in Brazil, particularly in Amazonia, has
produced three distinct forms of violence. Physical violence by the
police and gunslingers against squatters or rural workers was the
first step in strengthening private over public authority. Second,
evictions carried out by gunmen and other private agents constitute a form of violence by the courts in favoring the interests of
private firms over personal rights. The consequences of these two
have led to a third type of violence: the direct intervention by the
executive branch in land questions, and the exclusion of other
public and private entities. In effect, the military must deal with
the political vacuum that it has created. The more the government
becomes immersed in defending the expansion of private enter-

prise in Amazonia, the more politicized land disputes become. In my view, the increasingly significant confrontation between capital and the state on one side, and peasants on the other, has led the military government to a political impasse. The full extent of this dilemma is something that the political parties themselves have yet to take the trouble to evaluate.

Notes

1. Actually, on April 25, Planning Minister Roberto de Oliveira Campos had already established the general guidelines for agrarian reform: (a) progressive taxation; (b) a special tax on land whose value had risen as a result of government works; (c) the creation of public colonization projects; (d) technical and financial assistance (see Camerman 1977:52).

2. Marshal Castelo Branco could see no way to postpone the agrarian reform. To counter the Communist exploitation of troublesome situations courageous action was necessary, even if these initiatives harmed certain interests (letter from Gilberto Freyre to Luis Viana Filho, December 29, 1971). In 1963, Castelo Branco (then commander of the IV Army) attended a conference on agrarian reform, organized by the Instituto Joaquim Nabuco, in Recife. Speakers included, among others, Miguel Arrães, Francisco Julião, Father Crespo and Father Melo (see Viana Filho 1975:275).

3. The confiscatory character of the agrarian reform carried out by the military is subject to question in light of government policy to apply monetary corrections to public debt incurred by land expropriations (see Viana Filho 1975:282).

4. The same argument appears in a recent document published by General Golbery de Couto e Silva (1981).

5. This point is made by Roberto Campos (1965), citing Max Weber, in the *Estado de São Paulo*.

6. According to Martine (1980) if there is anything "new" about the expanding demographic frontier, it has to do with the occupation of a geographic space, rather than a change in social structure (see also Martins 1975:45).

7. For more detail, see Santana (1975:9−12, 1980; 1981), Casaldáliga (1977), Carvalho (1980:15−19), and Kotscho (1981:39−60).

References Cited

Almeida, A. Wagner Berno de
1981 *Transformações Econômicas e Sociais no Campo Maranhense*. São Luís, Maranhão: Comissão Pastoral da Terra.
Camerman, Cristiano (ed.)
1977 *Pastoral da Terra: Posse e Conflitos*. São Paulo: Estudos CNBB, Edições Paulinas.
Campos, Roberto
1965 Agricultura Brasileira. *O Estado de São Paulo*, 20 June:3.
Cardoso, F.H. and Geraldo Müller
1977 *Amazônia: Expansão do Capitalismo*. São Paulo: Brasiliense.
Carvalho, Murilo
1980 *Sangue da Terra: A Luta Armada no Campo*. São Paulo: Brasil Debates.
Casaldáliga, D. Pedro
1971 Uma Igreja em Conflito com o Latifúndio e a Marginalização Social. In *Igreja e governo: Documentos Oficiais da* CNBB. Pp. 37–46. São Paulo: Edições Símbolo.
1977 Questão agrária, uma questão política. In *Sedoc*, 10(105, October-November):351–87.
1978 *Creio na Justiça e na Esperança*. Rio: Civilização Brasileira.
Centro Ecuménico de Documentação e Informação (CEDI)
n.d. *Repressão na Igreja no Brasil*. São Paulo: Comissão Arquidiocesana de de Pastoral dos Direitos Humanos e Marginalizados da Arquidiocese de São Paulo.
Comissão Pastoral da Terra
1981 Conflitos de Terras no Brasil. Goiânia, mimeo.
Confederação Nacional dos Trabalhadores na Agricultura (CONTAG)
1975 *Questões Agrárias*. Brasília: CONTAG.
Correia de Andrade, Manuel
1973 *Aceleração e Freios ao Desenvolvimento Brasileiro*. Petrópolis, Brazil: Vozes.
Couto e Silva, Golbery
1981 *Conjuntura Política Nacional: O Poder Executivo e Geopolítica do Brasil*. Rio de Janeiro: Livraria José Olympio.
Dória, Palmério, S. Buarque, V. Carelli, and J. Sautchuk
n.d. *A Guerrilha do Araguaia*. São Paulo: Alfa-Omega.
Dreifuss, René Armand
1981 *1964: A Conquista do Estado*. Petrópolis: Vozes.
Estado de São Paulo,
1979 August 19.
Fundação Instituto Brasileiro de Geografia e Estatística (FIBGE)
1970 *Censo Agropecuário*
1975 *Censo Agropecuário*

Gomes da Silva, José
1971 A Reforma Agrária no Brazil. Rio de Janeiro: Zahar.
Ianni, Octávio
1979 Colonização e Contra-reforma Agrária na Amazônia. Petrópolis: Vozes.
Instituto Brasileiro de Geografia e Estatiística (IBGE)
1950 Censo Agrícola
1960 Censo Agrícola
Instituto Nacional de Colonização e Reforma Agrária (INCRA)
1978 Vade-Mecum Agrário 2. Brasília: Centro Gráfico do Senado
Federal.
Instituto de Pesquisas e Estudos Sociais (IPES)
1964 A Reforma Agrária. São Paulo: IPES.
Kotscho, Ricardo
1981 O Massacre dos Posseiros. São Paulo: Brasiliense.
Magalhães, Irene Maria, Maria Aparecida Alves Hime, and Nancy Alessio
1971 Segundo e terceiro ano do governo Costa e Silva. Dados (8).
Mahar, Dennis J.
1979 Frontier Development Policy in Brazil: A Study of Amazonia.
New York: Praeger.
Martine, George
1980 Recent Colonization Experiences in Brazil: Expectations Ver-
sus Reality. In Land, People, and Planning in Contemporary
Amazonia. F. Barbira-Scazzocchio, ed. Pp. 80–94.Cambridge:
Centre for Latin American Studies.
Martins, José de Souza
1975 Capitalismo e Tradicionalismo. São Paulo: Livraria Pioneira.
1980 Expropriação e Violência: a Questão Política no Campo. São
Paulo: Hucitec.
Pinto, Lúcio Flávio
1980 Amazônia: No Rastro do Saque. São Paulo: Hucitec.
Pomar, W.
1980 Araguaia: o Partido e a Guerrilha. São Paulo: Brasil Debates.
Portela, F.
1979 Guerra de Guerrilhas no Brasil. São Paulo: Global.
Rodrigues, Vera L. G. da and José Gomes da Silva
1975 Conflitos de Terras no Brasil: Uma Introdução ao Estudo Em-
pírico da Violência no Campo-período 1971 a 1974. Reforma
Agrária, 3–4.
1977 Conflitos de Terras no Brasil. Reforma Agrária, 1 (Jan.-Feb.).
Santana, Jeronimo
1975 As Perseguições ao Povo de Espigão d'Oeste. Brasília: Cámara
de Deputados.
1980 Corrupção e Violência Policial em Rondônia. Brasília: Cámara de Deputados.

1981   *Combatendo a grilagem na Amazônia e Defendendo os Colonos e Posseiros de Rondônia.* Brasília: Cámara de Deputados.

Santos, Roberto
1979   Sistema de propriedade e relações de trabalho no meio rural paraense. In *Amazônia: Desenvolvimento e Ocupação.* José Marcelino Monteiro da Costa, ed. Rio: IPEA/INPES. Pp. 103–40.

Viana Filho, Luís
1975   *O Governo Castelo Branco.* Rio de Janeiro: Livraria José Olympio.

Yokota, Paulo
1982   A Questão Fundiária Brasileira. *O Estado de São Paulo,* 3 January:50.

Contributors

CARLOS EDUARDO ARAMBURÚ is professor of anthropology and demography in the Social Sciences Department of Peru's Catholic University. He received his Licenciatura in social anthropology from this university and a Master of Science degree in demography from the London School of Economics. He is currently involved in research on population issues in Amazonia; he has published a book and several articles on internal migration in Peru.

NELLY ARVELO-JIMENEZ is associate professor of anthropology at the Venezuelan Institute for Scientific Research in Caracas. In 1981–82 she took a sabbatical year at Harvard University's Anthropology Department and is associated with Cultural Survival in Cambridge, Massachusetts, and the Anthropology Resource Center in Boston. Her main line of research has been the sociocultural impact of development programs on the indigenous peoples of the Amazon Basin.

WILLIAM M. DENEVAN is professor of geography and chairman of the Department of Geography, University of Wisconsin, Madison. He received his Ph.D. from the University of California, Berkeley. His research has been on cultural ecology, particularly in tropical South America. His books and monographs include *The Aboriginal Cultural Geography of the Llanos de Mojos of Bolivia* (1966), *The Native Population of the Americas in 1492* (editor, 1976), *Adaptive Strategies in Karinya Subsistence, Venezuelan Llanos* (co-author, 1978), and *Campos Elevados e Historia Cultural Prehispánica en los Llanos Occidentales de Venezuela* (co-author, 1979).

CAMILO DOMÍNGUEZ is a Colombian sociologist and candidate for the Master's degree at the Núcleo de Altos Estudos Amazô-

nicos, Belém, Brasil. Since 1968, he has devoted his research to so-
ciogeographical problems in the Amazon region. He has published
several articles on colonization in the Colombian Amazon and a
book entitled *Amazonía Colombiana Bibliografía General* (1974).
He is now associate professor of human geography at the Universidad Nacional de Colombia, Bogotá.

SUSANNA B. HECHT is assistant professor in the Graduate School
of Architecture and Planning, University of California, Los An-
geles. She holds the Ph.D. in geography from Berkeley and writes
on social and biological aspects of the Latin American livestock
industry. She is the editor of *Agriculture and Land Use Research
in Amazonia* and is currently writing one book on the role of livestock in Latin American tropical land transformation and another
on South American tropical deforestation.

JAMES C. JONES is assistant research scientist in the Department of Anthropology, University of Florida, and is currently training coordinator for the Farming Systems Support Project, an AID-
funded project managed by the Office of International Programs of
the Institute of Food and Agricultural Sciences, University of Florida. He holds a Ph.D. in social anthropology and a master's degree
in agricultural economics, both from the University of Florida. He
is a native of Harlan, Kentucky.

JOSÉ DE SOUZA MARTINS is professor of sociology (sociology
of daily life and sociology of agrarian society) in the Department
of Social Sciences, University of São Paulo. He received his master's and doctoral degrees at the University of São Paulo. He was a
visiting scholar at the Center of Latin American Studies of Cambridge University and with the Amazon Research and Training
Program, University of Florida. Among other books, he has published *A Imigração e a Crise do Brasil Agrário* (1973), *Capitalismo e Tradicionalismo* (1975), *O Cativeiro da Terra* (1979), *Expropriação e Violência* (1980), *Os Camponeses e a Política no
Brasil* (1981).

DAVID MAYBURY-LEWIS is professor of anthropology at Harvard University, where he was for many years chairman of the department. He took his doctorate at Oxford before moving to the
United States, and his research has been particularly concerned

with South American Indians. He is the founder and president of Cultural Survival, an organization which works on behalf of tribal and minority peoples. He has recently edited and published *Dialectical Societies* (1979) summarizing the work he and his students carried out in Central Brazil and *The Prospects for Plural Societies* (1983).

EMÍLIO F. MORAN is associate professor of anthropology and chairman of the Department of Anthropology at Indiana University, Bloomington. His *Developing the Amazon* was the first book to analyze the social and ecological consequences of the Transamazon highway colonization scheme; it was based upon three field expeditions to the Amazon. He is the editor of the recently published volume *The Dilemma of Amazonian Development* (Westview Press 1982), and he has also published *Human Adaptability* (1979) and *The Ecosystem Concept in Anthropology* (1983).

J. J. NICHOLAIDES, III is coordinator of the Tropical Soils Research Program and associate professor of soil science, North Carolina State University. D. E. BANDY is the former on-site leader of the Yurimaguas project and currently associate director for research in the North Carolina State University Mission to Peru and assistant professor of soil science. P. A. SANCHEZ is coordinator of the Tropical Soils Program and professor of soil science, North Carolina State University. J. H. VILLACHICA is the former director of the Jungle Research Institute and professor of soil science, National Agrarian University, Peru. A. J. COUTU is professor of economics and business, North Carolina State University. C. S. VALVERDE is director of planning and international collaboration, National Institute for Agricultural Research and Promotion, Ministry of Agriculture, Peru, and in 1983 was senior research fellow, International Service for National Agricultural Research, The Hague, Netherlands.

SUTTI ORTIZ is associate professor of Anthropology at Boston University. She received her Ph.D. from the University of London and has taught at the London School of Economics, Case Western Reserve, and University of California, Berkeley. Her interests in Colombian Amazonia developed from an experience as a consultant to the World Bank. She has published *Uncertainties in Peasant Farming* and a number of articles on the impact of risk on resource allocation as well as marketing and other constraints affecting the performance and welfare of the peasant sector.

MALORI JOSÉ POMPERMAYER is professor of political science at the Federal University of Minas Gerais, Brazil. He received his Ph.D. degree in political science from Stanford University. He is the author of various articles dealing with Brazilian agriculture and with state policies in the Amazon. He co-authored with Bernardo Sorj and Luíz O. Coradini *Camponeses e Agroindústria* (1982).

ALCIDA R. RAMOS is a Brazilian anthropologist who teaches at the University of Brasília (Brazil). She received her Ph.D. from the University of Wisconsin, and has taught at the Museu Nacional (Rio de Janeiro) and at the Federal University of Santa Catarina (Brazil). Her most extensive research has been with the Sanuma, a subgroup of the Yanomami Indians in north Brazil. She has published on social organization and Indian policy, including *Hierarquia e Simbiose: Relações Intertribais no Brasil* (1980).

ROBERTO SANTOS has a law degree in the state of Pará and a Master's degree in economics from the University of São Paulo, and is a judge at the Labor Tribunal in Belém and professor at the Federal University of Pará. He is currently teaching in the undergraduate program in economics and the graduate program in law, and coordinates an interdisciplinary study on the relationship between urban criminality in Belém and the agrarian question in Brazil. Among his publications are *Leis Sociais e Custo de Mão-de-obra no Brasil* (1973) and *História Económica da Amazônia— 1800–1920* (1980).

DONALD R. SAWYER is professor and research coordinator at CEDEPLAR, Faculdade de Ciências Econômicas, Universidade Federal de Minas Gerais, Brazil. He received a Ph.D. in sociology from Harvard University. He began doing research on frontier settlement in the Amazon region of Brazil in 1968. Since 1977, he has taught and carried out research at CEDEPLAR in the Economic Demography program. In 1982, he was Mellon Visiting Professor in the Amazon Research and Training Program, Center for Latin American Studies, University of Florida.

MARIANNE SCHMINK is executive director of the Amazon Research and Training Program, Center for Latin American Studies, University of Florida. She received her Ph.D. in anthropology from the University of Texas, Austin. She has written on colonization and migration, on land conflicts, and on social change among placer miners in the Brazilian Amazon region. She has also worked extensively in urban areas of Latin America and is currently co-manager of a Population Council/USAID project entitled Women, Low Income Households and Urban Services in Latin America and the Caribbean.

ALLYN MACLEAN STEARMAN, assistant professor of anthropology at the University of Central Florida, received her Ph.D. in anthropology from the University of Florida in 1976. Her experience in lowland Bolivia dates from 1964 when she was sent to this region as a Peace Corps volunteer to work in colonization and community development. Since that time, she has continued to pursue her interests in the anthropology of the *Oriente* through additional field research and writing. Her most recent work involves a restudy of the Siriono Indians, first researched by Allan Holmberg in 1941 but not since revisited.

ANTHONY STOCKS is assistant professor of anthropology at Idaho State University, a position he chose because of his intense desire to be a native. He has a doctorate in anthropology from the University of Florida, where he specialized in the human ecology of the Amazon Basin. With his family, he has spent several years researching Tupian Indian peasants in eastern Peru and has survived with a sense of humor. He continues to maintain a strong interest in Amazon research.

JORGE E. UQUILLAS is a consultant to the Amazon Colonization Institute of Ecuador and has taught both at the University of Florida, Gainesville, and at the Catholic University of Quito. He holds a Ph.D. with a certificate in Latin American Demographic Studies from the University of Florida. During the last few years, he has oriented his research as well as applied work toward the study of human settlements in the humid tropics and the solution of land problems faced by indigenous peoples of Amazonia.

WILLIAM T. VICKERS is associate professor of anthropology and chairperson of the Department of Sociology and Anthropology at Florida International University (Miami). He is the author of a number of articles dealing with the subsistence ecology of Amazonian Indians and recently co-edited *Adaptive Responses of Native Amazonians* (with Raymond B. Hames). He has also worked with Cultural Survival, Inc. of Cambridge, Massachusetts and various Ecuadoran governmental agencies to assess and formulate policies concerning the land needs of the Siona-Secoya and Cofán Indians of northeastern Ecuador.

CHARLES H. WOOD is associate professor in the Department of Sociology and the Center for Latin American Studies at the University of Florida in Gainesville. He holds a Ph.D. from the University of Texas at Austin, where he specialized in population studies. His current research interests include the demographic causes and consequences of the style of recent development in Brazil, frontier expansion in Amazonia and the seasonal migration of Caribbean cane cutters into Florida. JOHN F. WILSON is presently at the University of Florida (Center for Latin American Studies) completing a Ph.D. in anthropology. He has undertaken research on the Brazilian frontiers in Eastern Paraguay and in the territory of Rondônia. His current research on the agricultural development of the frontier is being carried out in Ariquemes, Rondônia.

Index